# CHAPTER 5: BIOLOGICAL AND PSYCHOLOGICAL THEORIES

| THEORY | MAJOR THEORISTS | WHAT THE THEORY EXPLAINS | POLICY IMPLICATIONS | INFLUENTIAL ACTORS |
|---|---|---|---|---|
| **BIO-CRIMINOLOGY** | | Searches for the causes of antisocial behavior within the brain or body. | Head Start programs, youth programs that develop the brain and provide nutrition, drug and alcohol rehabilitation programs, parenting classes. | researchers, scientists, doctors, social workers, nutritionists, teachers |
| **Genes and behavior** | Adrian Raine, Guang Guo | The idea that both genes and environment are responsible for behavior. | | |
| **Evolution, aggression, and survival** | | Antisocial behavior influences human evolution. | | |
| **Neurological perspectives** | | Neurological conditions affect antisocial behavior. | | |
| **Environmental perspectives** | | The substances most commonly connected to antisocial behavior and criminal offending are drugs and alcohol. | | |
| **PSYCHO-LOGICAL AND PSYCHIATRIC PERSPECTIVES** | | | School and after-school programs, parenting classes, recreational programs, Head Start programs, psychological counseling. | researchers, scientists, doctors, social workers, nutritionists, teachers |
| **Behaviorism** | B. F. Skinner | Environment and learning mainly determine behavior. | | |
| **Social learning theory** | | People learn behavior from watching others, then develop their own thoughts and attitudes about that behavior. | | |
| **Cognitive theory** | Lawrence Kohlberg | Used to learn more about the mental processes that precede the decision to break the law. | | |
| **Language Impairment and IQ** | | IQ and language ability affect delinquency and adult offending. | | |
| **Antisocial personality disorder, psychopathy, and insanity** | Robert Hare | Mental disorders affect the propensity of individuals to break the law. | | |

# Think
# Criminology

## John Randolph Fuller
The University of West Georgia

Published by McGraw-Hill, an imprint of The McGraw-Hill Companies, Inc., 1221 Avenue of the Americas, New York, NY 10020. Copyright
© 2012. All rights reserved. No part of this publication may be reproduced or distributed in any form or by any means, or stored in a database or
retrieval system, without the prior written consent of The McGraw-Hill Companies, Inc., including, but not limited to, in any network or other
electronic storage or transmission, or broadcast for distance learning.

This book is printed on acid-free paper.

1 2 3 4 5 6 7 8 9 0 DOW/DOW 1 0

ISBN: 978-0-07-337998-2
MHID: 0-07-337998-0

Vice President, Editorial: *Michael Ryan*
Editorial Director: *Bill Glass*
Publisher: *Katie Stevens*
Senior Sponsoring Editor: *Bill Minick*
Director of Development: *Nancy Crochiere*
Developmental Editor: *Elisa Adams*
Executive Marketing Manager: *Leslie Oberhuber*
Editorial Coordinators: *Erika Lake, Amy Mittelman*
Editorial Intern: *Emily DiPietro*
Media Project Manager: *Jennifer Barrick*
Managing Editor: *Anne Fuzellier*
Art Editor: *Robin Mouat*
Design Manager: *Andrei Pasternak*
Cover Designer: *John Hamilton*
Interior Designer: *Amanda Kavanagh*
Photo Research Coordinator: *Nora Agbayani*
Photo Researcher: *Judy Mason*
Illustrators: *Patti Isaacs, Peter Willems*
Buyer II: *Louis Swaim*
Composition: *10.5/12.5 Adobe Garamond Regular by Thompson Type*
Printing: *45# Liberty Dull by RR Donnelley*

Cover image: Christopher Zacharow/Stock Illustration Source/Getty Images
The credits section for this book begins on page 386 and is considered an extension of the copyright page.

**Library of Congress Cataloging-in-Publication Data**
Fuller, John R.
    Think criminology / John Fuller. — 1st ed.
      p.  cm.
    Includes bibliographical references and index.
    ISBN-13: 978-0-07-337998-2 (alk. paper)
    ISBN-10: 0-07-337998-0 (alk. paper)
  1. Criminology. 2. Criminology—Study and teaching. I. Title.
    HV6025.F876 2011
    364—dc22

2010044521

The Internet addresses listed in the text were accurate at the time of publication. The inclusion of a website does not indicate an endorsement by the
authors or McGraw-Hill, and McGraw-Hill does not guarantee the accuracy of the information presented at these sites.

www.mhhe.com

This book is dedicated to my mother-in-law, Melanie, whose love and support I treasure.

## What if:

- You could engage your students in truly thinking critically about criminology?
- You could get your students interested in criminological theory?
- You could help them understand how criminology is relevant to everyday life?
- You could illustrate to your students that criminology is an ever-evolving field with new trends constantly emerging?

Sound impossible? It's not. *Think Criminology* was written in the 21st century for a 21st-century audience. It was designed specifically to address these issues that, according to our research, are the primary objectives and challenges of most instructors teaching the course.

*Think Criminology* is designed to engage students of this generation CRITICALLY and ACTIVELY in the classroom and in their world.

### Critically

Critical-thinking skills help students better understand criminological theory and how it applies to crime and will serve them well as law enforcement professionals, citizens, and consumers of the news. Students need critical-thinking skills to:

- break down complex theories into meaningful and useful parts
- identify the reasons why people break the criminal law
- interpret the role of victims within criminology and the criminal justice process
- evaluate how race, gender, and socioeconomic class affect how justice is dispensed
- recognize how power influences the creation of the criminal law
- analyze how terrorism has fundamentally changed the nature of criminology and our society

Both instructors and students are inspired when class discussion is elevated from the mere recitation of facts and theory to developing innovative responses to the problems of crime and delinquency. The critical-thinking approach encourages free-flowing class discussions that challenge the status quo, allow students to appreciate the issues of crime and justice, and envision how they can be improved.

### Actively

*Think Criminology* is written with today's generation of students in mind. Through exciting and clear graphics, presentation and reinforcement of learning objectives, review charts, and opportunities for students to "Think Back" and "Think About It," students become engaged in the process of learning and begin to think critically about criminology. In addition, cutting-edge content actively engages students who have grown up in a world where the intersection of terrorism, technology, and international crime makes the study of criminology unique to their generation. In contrast to many other books, *Think Criminology* was developed for today's generation; the up-to-the-minute content is not an add-on, it is an integrated part of the text narrative.

# So how are we able to accomplish all this?

## The Critical-Thinking Framework

The critical-thinking framework of this text is based on Bloom's Digital Taxonomy, which guides students from lower-order thinking skills (remembering, understanding) to higher-order skills (evaluating, creating), thereby enhancing their understanding. I've developed the following framework to guide students' thinking through each chapter:

- **Learning objectives** provide goals for the student requiring various levels of understanding.

- **Repetition of learning objectives** in the margins shows students where each concept is covered and reminds them what their learning outcome should be. It is especially important to remind students of the primary chapter objectives in a course in which, according to our research, they can easily become overwhelmed by criminological theories.

- **Think About It** interludes, which appear at key points in the chapter, allow students to analyze, apply, and evaluate the material, as well as create solutions for classroom discussion.

- **Thinking in Action** questions ask students to reflect on the content of a high-interest boxed feature such as *Theory to Practice* (see below) and consider its implications.

- **Think Back** definitions remind students of the meaning of important terms they learned earlier in the course.

- **An end-of-chapter summary,** based on learning objectives presented at the front of the chapter, allows students to review their understanding of the material covered.

## New Trends in Criminology

In a uniquely integrated manner, our book acknowledges the ways in which crime has changed in the 21st century and how this change challenges criminologists to develop new theories and perspectives.

I highlight new developments in criminology that fall into three broad categories.

- **Maturation and innovation in criminological theory.** I examine the most recent changes in criminological theory by focusing on advances in biological explanations of crime; emphasizing life-course and integrated theories; and covering critical theories that emphasize the political and social influences of variables such as gender, social class, and race. Discussion of new research and innovative concepts concerning the motivations for crime helps students and instructors gain insight into the theoretical understanding of criminology and develop an appreciation of criminological theory.

- **A blurring of domestic and international crime control** makes the structure and mandate of U.S. criminal justice agencies a moving target. An expanded global vision of criminal activity has introduced new political and structural changes in how the United States responds to crime. This text emphasizes how what happens in other parts of the world influences the perception and reality of safety in the United States. Similarly, it demonstrates how U.S. crime-control policy has consequences for our relationship with other countries and how it affects the way crime crosses borders and frustrates interagency and international cooperative agreements.

- **The introduction of new types of crime.** New technologies have resulted in many new types of criminal offenses and allowed lawbreakers to become more sophisticated in committing offenses that cause more damage and are more challenging to detect. I examine how the discipline of criminology is struggling to develop theories and responses to new forms of criminal activity like insider trading; identity theft; and the threat of biological, chemical, and nuclear terrorism.

## Special Features

The text includes several types of feature boxes that reinforce our emphasis on new trends, critical thinking, and student engagement. Questions at the end of these features are written so there is no single "correct" answer, and students and instructors can discuss an appropriate resolution.

- **So What's New?** presents the latest information on various criminological topics. This feature focuses on cutting-edge issues and practices within the study of criminology and the criminal justice system that demonstrate changes in policies, practices, and ideologies.

- **Doubletake** explores the history behind the policies, programs, and philosophies considered to be prevailing wisdom in criminology and discusses the ways in which this conventional wisdom has been circumvented or supplanted. I also discuss the motivations of tradition, prejudice, or self-interest that lie behind much of criminal justice theory and practice.

- **Theory to Practice** provides examples of how specific theories have been translated into real-life policies that drive the criminal justice system and other institutions concerned with social control.

- **Theory Flowcharts** visually represent some of the more popular and difficult criminological theories in order to help students better understand their complexities.

*Think Criminology* strives to spark students' interest in the fascinating and rapidly changing field of criminology. Instructors and students might not agree with every point made in this text, but disagreements are welcome. Well-reasoned and defended differences of opinion stimulate thinking and encourage all of us to discover what else is new in the field of criminology.

John Randolph Fuller
*University of West Georgia*

# The features of
# Think Criminology

**Think Criminology** challenges students to think critically about the evolving field of criminology:

## Think about it

### Remember

Which ethnic groups are traditionally associated with organized crime?

### Understand

In what ways did the prohibition of alcohol in the United States contribute to the rise of organized crime?

### Apply

Explain how the Racketeering Influenced and Corrupt Organizations Act (RICO) allows prosecutors to target organized crime.

### Analyze

How has the media distorted our understanding of organized crime?

### Evaluate

How serious is organized crime in terms of financial losses for the nation and personal violence between offenders and victims?

### Create

What types of actions can the government take to control organized crime?

**Think About It** provides critical-thinking questions at the end of major sections in every chapter. Based on Bloom's taxonomy, the questions encourage students not just to memorize, but to analyze, apply, and evaluate the material as well.

**Repetition of learning objectives** in the margins shows students where each concept is covered and reminds them what their learning outcome should be.

## LO1:

**Explain** why the supernatural perspective dominated social control for centuries.

## doubletake

doubletake

**The Chicago Area Project's Detached Worker Program**

Critics of the Chicago Area Project (CAP) question how effective it is in reducing gang activity, specifically calling into question its detached worker program. That program, which CAP started in the late 1940s, has community residents work with gang members; advocate for them in court; and help them to find jobs, health care, and educational assistance. The purpose is to transform gangs from antisocial to pro-social groups. Several other programs adopted this approach in the 1960s, including the Group Guidance Program and Ladino Hills Project of Los Angeles. However, the Ladino Hills Project found that instead of decreasing gang activity, the program actually encouraged tighter relationships among gang members and encouraged others to join gangs, which led to even more gang-related crime. As of the 1990s, evaluations of detached worker programs have reported no decrease in gang membership or activity.[1]

[1]Finn-Aage Esbensen, "Preventing Adolescent Gang Involvement," US Department of Justice, Office of Juvenile Justice and Delinquency Prevention, Juvenile Justice Bulletin, September 2000, 6–7, http://www.ncjrs.gov/pdffiles1/ojjdp/182210.pdf.

**Doubletake** invites students to explore how what is considered to be prevailing wisdom in criminology has often been circumvented or supplanted.

### THINKING
### *in* ACTION

Can you think of other ways that gangs might be transformed into pro-social groups?

# Think Criminology encourages students to *actively* engage with the material:

**Theory to Practice** provides examples of how specific theories have been translated into real-life policies. At the end of all boxed features, **Thinking in Action** questions ask students to reflect on the ideas presented and consider their implications.

## theory to **practice**

### Who Owns a Crime?

Crime victims often feel left out of the criminal justice system. Although victims are the ones who suffer, the state, working through the prosecutor, can "take the crime away" from the victim. The prosecutor must make several decisions based upon the strength of the case, the workload of the office, and the court system's punishment philosophy. The prosecutor changes the nature of the case to one in which society is the victim, and society decides what will happen to the suspect. However, criminologist Nils Christie has argued that victims should be brought back into the system because they are part owners of the conflict that resulted in their victimization.

▲ Restorative justice programs teach participants about coming to terms with their offenses and convictions.

This perspective, practiced by the restorative justice movement, seeks to allow victims and offenders to work out their differences in a less formal arena than court. According to Christie, this personalized encounter with the offender has been taken away from victims:

> The victim is so totally out of the case that he has no chance, ever, to come to know the offender. We leave them outside, angry, maybe humiliated through a cross-examination in court, without any contact with the offender. He will need all the classical stereotypes around 'the criminal' to get a grasp on the whole thing. Of course, he will go away more frightened than ever, more in need than ever of an explanation of criminals as non-human.[1]

The idea of a conflict as something that victims partly own returns the victim to the justice equation. The case is no longer the offender versus the state but rather the offender versus the victim, the state, and the community. When all parties are included in the resolution, it is more likely that not only will everyone be satisfied, but also that the underlying causes of the conflict can be addressed and harm repaired.

[1]Nils Christie, "Conflicts as Property," *The British Journal of Criminology* 17, no. 1 (1977): 8.

### THINKING *in* ACTION

1. What do we mean by the idea of conflict as property?
2. How does the traditional criminal justice process leave the victim out?

## so**what'snew**?

### Dogfighting, Gambling, and Crime

Gambling on animals is a centuries-old form of entertainment. Some of these sports, such as racing, have become mainstream and have regulatory bodies that ensure the animals' health and safety. Other forms, such as dogfighting, continue in the shadows of society.

According to The Humane Society of the United States, dogfighting is a competition in which dogs are bred, conditioned, and trained to fight each other. Two dogs are placed in a small, enclosed area called a "pit," where they fight each other until one can no longer continue. Fights usually last about an hour but can last as long as two hours. To get the dogs to fight, a weak "prey" animal, such as a cat, rabbit, or injured dog, is thrown between the two dogs. Spectators typically place bets on which dog will win. Dogs that win three times are "champions" and might be retired to stud, while losing dogs are often left to die.[1]

Dogfighting, which has been popular in the rural South for decades, has recently increased in popularity throughout the United States, especially in North Carolina and Virginia.[2] The betting pool at some fights can grow to $10,000 or more. A Baltimore animal rescue expert calls dogfighting "big sport, big-money betting."[3] Ohio Attorney General Marc Dann, who observed a southwest Ohio raid, said the warehouse that housed the activity resembled a casino.[4]

▲ Although dogfighting is a felony in every state, people continue to raise animals specifically for fighting.

Aside from animal cruelty, a major reason that dogfights concern law enforcement is that they attract a criminal subculture that also tends to be involved in drug-dealing, illegal gun sales, and illegal gambling. A 2001–2004 Chicago Police Department study found that in 382 dogfighting cases, 59 percent of the owners were gang members, and 86 percent had been arrested at least twice. A local police official in Ohio—who said that in all his department's dogfighting search warrants, drugs were found in every case but one—explained that dogfighting is an expensive activity that requires the kind of disposable income that drug-selling provides.[5]

Currently, dogfighting is a felony in every state. The Animal Fighting Prohibition Enforcement Act of 2007 amended existing federal law to impose a fine and/or prison sentence of up to three years for "(1) sponsoring or exhibiting an animal in an animal fighting venture; (2) buying, selling, transporting, delivering, or receiving for purposes of transportation, in interstate or foreign commerce, any dog or other animal for participation in an animal fighting venture; and (3) using the mails or other instrumentality of interstate commerce to promote or further an animal fighting venture."

[1]Childs Walker, "Dogfight 'Culture' Reaches to Baltimore," *Baltimore Sun*, June 1, 2007, 1A.
[2]Bill Burke, "Once Limited to the Rural South, Dogfighting Sees a Cultural Shift," *Virginian-Pilot*, June 17, 2007.
[3]Walker, "Dogfight 'Culture' Reaches to Baltimore," 1A.
[4]James Hannah, "Dogfighting Bust Shows How Crime Is Becoming More of a Focus," Associated Press, April 4, 2007.
[5]John Futty, "Dogfight Raids Not Just About Animals: Crackdown Turns Up Many Other Crimes," *Columbus Dispatch*, April 2, 2007.

### THINKING *in* ACTION

Discuss the reasons why dogfighting is a felony in all states. What is your opinion of the criminalization of dogfighting?

**So What's New?** focuses on cutting-edge issues and practices within the study of criminology and the criminal justice system that are meaningful to today's post-9-11 generation of students.

>< **THINKBACK**
antisocial—Following standards of behavior intended to harm society and individuals.

**Think Back** definitions encourage students to recall important terms they learned earlier in the course.

# About the Author

**John Randolph Fuller** is the current coordinator for the criminology program at the University of West Georgia, where he has taught for more than 29 years. He also has been named as the Faculty Ombudsman where he uses his many years of experience and expertise to assist faculty, staff, and students in resolving their conflicts. Dr. Fuller brings both an academic and applied background to his scholarship in criminology at the University of West Georgia, where he has been recognized as an outstanding teacher and scholar. Previously, Dr. Fuller worked in the criminal justice field as both a probation and parole officer as well as a criminal justice planner. As a probation and parole officer in Florida, he managed a caseload of more than 100 felons. As a criminal justice planner, he worked with every type of criminal justice agency in a three-county area in addition to writing grants for the Law Enforcement Assistance Administration that were designed to reduce crime and improve the criminal justice system. This applied perspective allows him to identify the types of practical concerns and issues that students will face once they start working in the criminal justice system.

Dr. Fuller is the author or co-author of more than 40 publications including six books. His texts *Criminal Justice: Mainstream and Cross Currents* and *Juvenile Delinquency: Mainstream and Cross Currents* are used in universities across the nation. Dr. Fuller has been designated as a Governor's Teaching Fellow and was awarded a Fulbright-Hayes Fellowship for study in China. In addition, he has been named the University of West Georgia's College of Arts and Sciences Distinguished Scholar.

On a personal level, Dr. Fuller enjoys painting and playing golf. He is an avid reader, particularly of biographies, and hopes one day to develop writing projects on major criminological theorists. Students and professors are encouraged to correspond with Dr. Fuller on all things pertaining to the study of criminology. He can be reached at jfuller@westga.edu.

I would like to thank the following reviewers, focus group participants, and symposium attendees, all of whom provided helpful comments to guide the development of this text:

Margaret Austin, Central Piedmont Community College

Robert Barnes, Westchester Community College

Katie Bass, Eastern Illinois University

Ashley Blackburn, University of North Texas

Sonya Brown, Tarrant County College

Alan Bruce, Quinnipiac University

Kevin Buckler, University of Texas-Brownsville

Bryan Byers, Ball State University

Steven Christiansen, Joliet Junior College

Kenneth Christopher, Park University-Parkville

Gregory Clark, McNeese State University

Ellen Cohn, Florida International University

Lucy Craig, Motlow State College

Mary Dodge, University of Colorado at Denver

Joy Feria, University of North Florida

Harold Frossard, Moraine Valley Community College

Carly Hilinski, Grand Valley State University

Jennifer Huck, Indiana University of Pennsylvania-Indiana

Suman Kakar, Florida International University

F. E. Knowles Jr., Valdosta State University

Charles Kocher, Cumberland County College

Lisa Konczal, Barry University

Lisa Landis, University of South Florida-Tampa

Anthony Larose, University of Tampa

Anna Leggett, Miami-Dade College

Samantha Lewis Carlo, Miami-Dade College

Larry Linville, Nova Community College-Annandale

Miriam Lorenzo, Miami-Dade College

Joel Maatman, Lansing Community College

Sean Maddan, University of Tampa

Christine Martin, University of Illinois-Chicago

J. Mitchell Miller, University of Texas at San Antonio

Matt Nobles, Sam Houston State University

James Nolan, West Virginia University-Morgantown

Angela Ondrus, Owens Community College

Janice Panella, Arkansas State University-Heber Springs

Michael Paquette, Middlesex County College

Michael Pittaro, Lehigh Valley College

Jesenia Pizarro, Michigan State University-East Lansing

Peter Puleo, William Rainey Harper College

Joanne Savage, American University

Jennifer Schulenberg, Sam Houston State University

Richard Steinhaus, New Mexico Junior College

Carl Taylor, Michigan State University-East Lansing

Bethany Teeter, Park University-Parkville

Prabha Unnithan, Colorado State University

David Wedlick, Westchester Community College

Bradley Wright, University of Connecticut-Storrs

Jeffrey Zack, Fayetteville Tech Community College

I wish to further acknowledge the wonderful people at McGraw-Hill who had the vision and faith to see this project through to the end. Specifically, I wish to credit Katie Stevens for her wise counsel and vision. Bill Minick also deserves acknowledgment for his work on this book as does my director of development, Nancy Crochiere. Finally, Leslie Oberhuber has great marketing skills and has assisted in shaping this book into something students will appreciate.

At the University of West Georgia, I have been lucky to have supportive colleagues in the Department of Sociology and Criminology, including N. Jane McCandless, David Jenks, Catherine Jenks, Mike Johnson, Richard Lemke, Neema Noori, Todd Matthews, and Paul Luken. They have provided an intellectually stimulating environment. My graduate student Heather Kelley was valuable in providing much of the background research. Finally, Amy Hembree was instrumental in the completion of this project. She is my first editor, fiercest critic, and best friend.

*Think Criminology* has an **Online Learning Center** that offers the following tools for students and instructors:

## For Students

- **Practice Quizzes** that test them on their understanding of each chapter's content.
- **YouTubedia**—Links to relevant YouTube videos and critical-thinking questions about the significance of the video.
- **Flashcards** that help students practice their mastery of key terms.

## For Instructors

- A **test bank** containing 40 multiple-choice questions and 5 essay questions for each chapter, along with page references for the multiple-choice questions, question type (basic, moderate, difficult) and the level of critical thinking (according to Bloom's taxonomy) that each question tests: knowledge, comprehension, analysis, application.
- A **computerized test bank.** McGraw-Hill's EZ Test is a flexible, easy-to-use electronic test-building program. It accommodates a wide range of question types, and instructors may add their own questions. Any test can be exported for use with a course management system, and the program is compatible with Windows and Macintosh operating systems.
- An **Instructor's Manual** that includes for each chapter: a brief summary, lecture outline, complementary lecture topics, class discussion topics, suggested readings.
- **PowerPoints** for the entire text that include illustrations from the text.
- **NBC video clips.** More than an hour's worth of video clips (each between 3 and 8 minutes long) from NBC news add realism to criminological issues and generate discussion. A set of critical-thinking questions is provided for each clip to engage students in critical conversation.

### Blackboard

What does this mean for you?

- **Your life simplified.** Now you and your students can access McGraw-Hill Connect and Create right from within your Blackboard course—all with one single sign-on. No more logging in to multiple applications.
- **Deep integration of content and tools.** In addition to single sign-on, you get deep integration of McGraw-Hill content and content engines right in Blackboard. Whether you're choosing a book for your course or building Connect assignments, all the tools you need are right there: inside Blackboard.
- **Seamless gradebooks.** Tired of keeping multiple gradebooks and manually synchronizing grades into Blackboard? When a student completes an integrated Connect assignment, the grade for that assignment automatically (and instantly) feeds your Blackboard grade center.
- **A solution for everyone.** Whether your institution is already using Blackboard or you just want to try it on your own, we have a solution for you. McGraw-Hill and Blackboard can now offer you easy access to industry-leading technology and content, whether your campus hosts it or we do. Be sure to ask your local McGraw-Hill representative for details.

### Create

Craft your teaching resources to match the way you teach! With McGraw-Hill Create, www.mcgrawhillcreate.com, you can easily rearrange chapters, combine material from other content sources, and quickly upload content you have written like your course syllabus or teaching notes. Find the content you need in Create by searching through thousands of leading McGraw-Hill textbooks. Arrange your book to fit your teaching style. Create even allows you to personalize your book's appearance by selecting the cover and adding your name, school, and course information. Order a Create book and you'll receive a complimentary print review copy in 3-5 business days or a complimentary electronic review copy (eComp) via email in about one hour. Go to www.mcgrawhillcreate.com today and register. Experience how McGraw-Hill Create empowers you to teach your students your way.

## CourseSmart eTextbook

This text is available as an eTextbook at www.Course Smart.com. At CourseSmart your students can take advantage of significant savings off the cost of a print textbook, reduce their impact on the environment, and gain access to powerful Web tools for learning. CourseSmart eTextbooks can be viewed online or downloaded to a computer. The eTextbooks allow students to do full text searches, add highlighting and notes, and share notes with classmates. CourseSmart has the largest selection of eTextbooks available anywhere. Visit www.CourseSmart .com to learn more and to try a sample chapter.

## Tegrity

Tegrity Campus is a service that makes class time available all the time by automatically capturing every lecture in a searchable format for students to review when they study and complete assignments. With a simple one-click start-and-stop process, you capture all computer screens and corresponding audio. Students replay any part of any class with easy-to-use browser-based viewing on a PC or Mac.

Educators know that the more students can see, hear, and experience class resources, the better they learn. With Tegrity Campus, students quickly recall key moments by using Tegrity Campus's unique search feature. This search helps students efficiently find what they need, when they need it across an entire semester of class recordings. Help turn all your students' study time into learning moments immediately supported by your lecture.

# 1

# Thinking Critically About

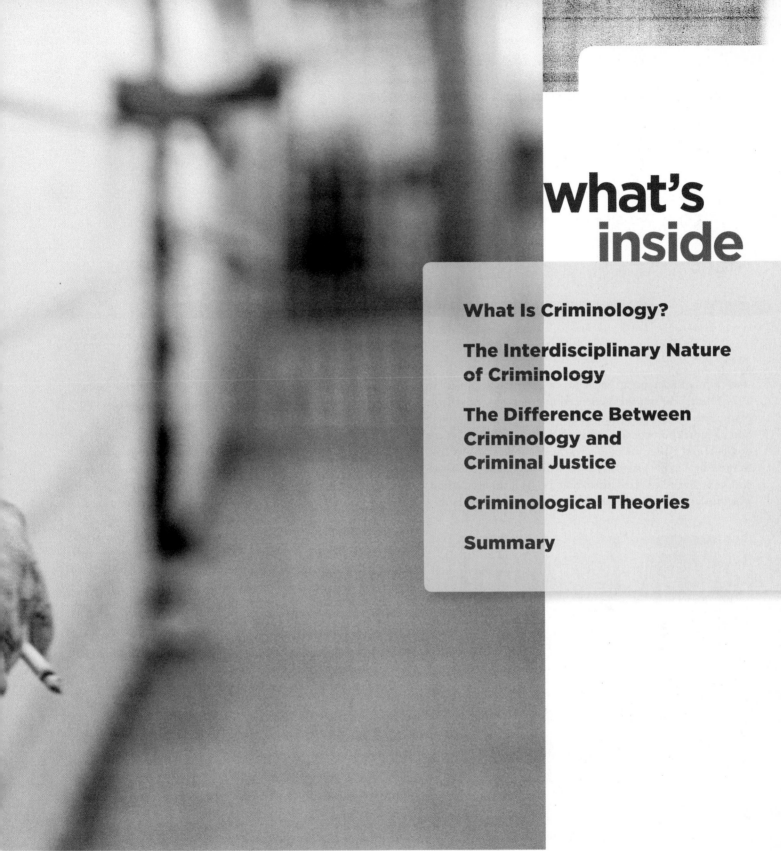

# what's inside

# Crime

**As you read, keep in mind these learning objectives:**

**LO1:**    State Sutherland's definition of criminology.

**LO2:**    Demonstrate how political science, economics, psychology, law, biology, and sociology contribute to criminology.

**LO3:**    Differentiate between criminology and criminal justice.

**LO4:**    Describe the role criminological theory plays in shaping our understanding of antisocial behavior, improving criminal justice response, shaping policies for offender rehabilitation and medical and psychological treatments, and rendering victim assistance.

Dennis Rader began what he called his first project in 1974. Nearly 30 but inexperienced and nervous, he cut the phone lines of a house he had been watching, then he waited. Soon a small boy opened the back door, possibly to let the dog out, and Rader forced his way inside where he was confronted by Joseph Otero, Sr., his wife Julie, and their two children. Rader realized then that he had made a serious miscalculation: Joseph Otero was not supposed to be home.

Wielding a pistol, Rader made up a story about being wanted by police and needing food and a car. Then he had the family lie down in the living room. After deciding this was a bad idea, he forced the family to a back bedroom and tied them up. Joseph Otero told Rader that he was uncomfortable because he had a cracked rib from a car accident, so Rader put a pillow under his head. Rader then began to strangle the Oteros, but they kept regaining consciousness. After several botched tries involving ropes and bags put over the family members' heads, Rader managed to kill everyone except 11-year-old Josephine Otero. He took Josephine to the basement and hanged her, then engaged in what he called "some sexual fantasies." After straightening up the house, he left.

Between 1974 and 1991, Dennis Rader, who called himself "BTK" for "bind, torture, kill," murdered six more people. During those years, he earned a bachelor's degree, fathered two children, embarked on a career in security, and became a city code enforcement officer and a church council president.[1] At the time of his arrest in 2005, he was planning another project.[2]

## What Is Criminology?

The classic definition of **criminology** was hammered out by sociologist Edwin Sutherland, who stated that, "Criminology is the study of the making of laws, breaking of laws, and society's reaction to the breaking of laws." To understand the purpose of criminology, let's break this definition down using the opening scenario.[3]

**LO1:**

State Sutherland's definition of criminology.

▲ Serial murderer Dennis Rader committed his first murders in 1974 and continued to kill until 1991. Police finally captured Rader in 2005.

**criminology** The study of the making of laws, the breaking of laws, and the social reaction to the breaking of laws.

**Table 1.1    The Major Differences Between Criminal Law and Civil Law**

| | Criminal Law | Civil Law |
|---|---|---|
| **What it does ...** | The criminal law enforces the laws that keep society safe. It is composed of the rules that define criminal offenses and how these offenses are prosecuted by the state. | The civil law is for the settlement of disputes between private citizens and other entities, such as businesses. |
| **An offense is called ...** | A "crime" or "criminal offense" | A "tort" |
| **Examples** | Murder, robbery, rape, burglary | Contested divorces, property ownership disputes, contract disputes |
| **Who brings the action ...** | The state prosecutes criminal offenses in the name of the state (not the victim), which also has the only right of enforcement. | An individual or group |
| **A case is won when ...** | The guilt of accused defendants is proven beyond a reasonable doubt | A preponderance of evidence favors one party over another |
| **Possible punishments ...** | Restitution, probation, incarceration, death | The party who loses the case must pay a specified amount of money |

## The Making of Laws

Laws are written by legislatures to ensure that society runs in an orderly fashion. Legislatures are composed of elected individuals who may spend a great deal of money campaigning and building their influence. Once elected, they work with other legislators to create law. This is an extremely simplified explanation, but it is basically how lawmaking in the United States works.

We divide law into **criminal law,** which guides the definition and prosecution of crime, and **civil law,** which governs private rights and disputes between citizens (see Table 1.1 for more on the difference between the two). In this text, we are concerned with criminal law from a criminological perspective.

The criminal law is perhaps most important to ensuring that society is orderly. For a society to be orderly, its citizens must feel safe. Most of the offenses defined as crime are those that threaten other people in some way: murder, rape, assault, robbery, and so on. The offenses perpetrated by Dennis Rader are those society deems most heinous, so many laws have been created to specify exactly what actions constitute these and similar offenses, how the criminal justice system will deal with them, and what will be done with the perpetrators. In this text, we will encounter some theories that critique the criminal law and how it is written and applied. From a broad perspective, however, the basic social rules that

criminal law Legal statutes that guide the prosecution and definition of crime.

civil law Law that is related to private rights and disputes between citizens.

specify offenses such as Dennis Rader's are required for people to feel safe enough to go about the business of making a society work. Law, then, is what makes a society a society rather than just a collection of people, many of whom are violent, doing what they please.

## The Breaking of Laws

Why laws are made is pretty obvious. The mystery begins with why they are broken. Some say laws are made to be broken. Laws are not *made* to be broken, but they are *certain* to be broken. Human beings are not perfect, and neither is society. The reasons people give for breaking the law are many, the most common ones being necessity, choice, mental or physical defect, or to somehow make up for their own victimization by an individual or society. Often, the offender just does not know.

Much of criminological theory—perhaps the bulk of it—is devoted to understanding *why* people break the law so we can control the amount of offending. Basic criminal laws are similar across most industrialized nations, but societies have different rates of offending. For example, Japan's crime rate is quite low compared with the crime rate in the United States, although both nations have similar criminal laws. A murder in Japan is just as illegal as it is in the United States. A serial murderer—an offender who murders a sequence of victims—such as Dennis Rader provokes the same amount of fear and official concern in both nations.[4] So why does the crime rate differ so widely between the two societies?[5] The answer lies in how and why people break the criminal law. The reasons differ not only among individuals, but also among neighborhoods, towns, cities, and whole societies.

However, if we can understand the causes of crime and address them, then we can better control crime. These are the answers criminology seeks.

## Society's Reaction to the Breaking of Laws

This issue is not as clear as you may think. Society's reaction to the breaking of laws includes fear, anger, and even disgust. However, this is not always the case. Society's reaction to the breaking of laws may be as varied as the reasons people break them, and these reactions vary among individuals, regions, and societies.

One common reaction you may not expect is fascination. The breaking of laws is fascinating. This is probably why you are reading this text right now. Maybe you or someone you know has been a crime victim, and you are angry or at least determined to study criminology and perhaps even become a criminologist or criminal justice professional so you can go out and do something about it. It is more likely, however, that you have never been a victim of serious crime, and you may not even know anyone who has. Given the proliferation of crime-related media—true-crime books, novels, serial-killer biographies, television dramas, talk shows, films, and websites—it is clear that the more gory and outrageous the offense, the more people want to know about it. Specific aspects of crime come into vogue. Murder mysteries have always been popular. Your parents or grandparents probably watched television shows about private eyes and tough police investigators. As a child, you may have watched "cop shows" replete with car chases. A few years ago, serial murderers were all the rage. Now everyone seems to be interested in forensic investigation.

Society's reaction to crime, then, is complex. When we learn of especially heinous offenses, we are outraged. When crime hits close to home, we are aggrieved and incensed. If it hits too close to home, we are devastated or perhaps even the victim. When it happens to a stranger, we are often interested.

It has been said that a single death is a tragedy, but a million deaths are a statistic.[6] This holds true for crime. The media will often spend a lot of airtime on the disappearance or murder of an attractive or interesting person. However, few people beyond criminologists and criminal justice professionals are interested in crime statistics. Many people believe that crime is always rising (it isn't), and we were safer in the "good old days" (not necessarily).[7] The funding for much criminological research, which comes from public coffers as well as programs directed at rehabilitation and criminal justice reform, is endangered, and the public often seems

▲ Entertainment about solving crimes has always been popular. This scene is from the current CBS drama, *The Mentalist.*

little concerned except to demand tougher laws and more prisons.[8] Few people know what the crime rate is in their city, state, or region. Even fewer know any criminological theories. Society's reaction to the breaking of laws from a statistical and theoretical perspective—that is, a *criminological* perspective—is poorly informed. Crime *stories,* however, get the public's attention, which is evidenced by the large number of crime-related dramas and talk shows.[9] The story of a serial murderer is always welcome (see *Doubletake*).

Many incarcerated serial murderers get fan mail. In the mid-1990s, Charles Manson—who still gets quite a bit

▲ The media often sensationalizes serial murder cases, especially if the defendants are particularly charismatic. In his trial, serial murderer Ted Bundy, who confessed to about 30 murders, acted as his own defense attorney.

of mail—had a website administered by a devotee.[10] John Wayne Gacy, convicted of the murders of 33 young men and boys, sold enough of his paintings in prison to leave $100,000 to his heirs.[11] Many people are repulsed by a murderer making millions from a book or film. On the other hand, many people pay to read such books and see the films. There is even a bustling trade in so-called "murderabilia" in which anything belonging to an offender, from writings to mementoes to nail and hair clippings, is sold over the Internet.[12]

As we can see, the public's reaction to crime is a multifaceted mixture of fear, disgust, and fascination. We expect the first two reactions, especially from anyone who has ever been or known a crime victim. Many people who have never been victims of crime are afraid of becoming victims—even if the chances are unlikely—and take extra precautions such as installing home security alarms and extra locks. The last reaction, fascination, is one many people have but may not admit to. However, a degree of fascination with crime is not only natural—after all, crime is social in nature, and we are social creatures—but desirable. A healthy interest in crime is at the root of criminology.

# Think about it

## Analyze

Explain the three components of Sutherland's definition of criminology.

## Evaluate

Critique the public's perception of the frequency of serial murder.

**serial murder** The killing of a sequence of victims committed in three or more separate events over an extended period of time.

# doubletake
doubletake

### Serial Murder and the Media

We began this chapter with an example of a particularly infamous serial murder case because it illustrates some important criminological issues. However, when we think critically about crime, we must recognize that **serial murders**—the killing of a sequence of victims committed in three or more separate events over an extended period of time—are actually rare. They have become part of the national conversation because of intense media scrutiny that creates a distorted picture of the danger posed by serial murderers, their prevalence, and the amount of attention law enforcement gives to them. This bias occurs for three main reasons:

- *All crimes are local.* Because of the availability of a variety of communication devices, especially television and the Internet, events that occur thousands of miles away now seem local. When a serial killer strikes in a distant state, it becomes news on our local and cable television stations. This gives the impression that the killer is right around the corner, and we must protect our loved ones. In actuality, the chances of being harmed by a serial killer are extremely small.
- *Serial killings are sensational.* Crime news must compete with other news and other media to get attention, so the most sensational cases get the most coverage. Although a gruesome murder may make news for a short period of time, a series of murders that appear linked can generate coverage for weeks or months. Many people become fascinated by these unsolved murders and speculation about the predators as well as anxious about the possibility of future victims.
- *Our culture fosters the creation of celebrity.* Media attention makes instant celebrities of both the perpetrators and the victims. Covering these sensational cases has also made celebrities of some television hosts, who specialize in nothing but picking apart the minutest details of such offenses and making entertainment of them.

Most criminal offenses do not get the level of attention that serial murder attracts. This does not mean serial murder is not serious or does not do great physical and psychological harm. However, it does mean that criminology students must be vigilant about the media's effect on our understanding of crime. We must remember that crime is not entertainment but rather a serious social problem that requires not only critical thinking, but also mature judgment and compassion for all involved.

## THINKING *in* ACTION

1. Explain why the media are so interested in serial murder and other sensational offenses.
2. Show how innovations in communications have allowed sensational crime from other states and countries to become treated as local crime.

# The Interdisciplinary Nature of Criminology

In 1990, Tyrone Brown and Lewis Bivins, both 17, pleaded guilty to a small-time street robbery that netted them $2. No one was injured, and the judge sentenced each of the young men—considered adults in Texas—to ten years of probation. Brown and Bivins both got into trouble again while on probation. Bivins stole a car, and Brown tested positive for marijuana. The judge sent Bivins to boot-camp detention, then let him return to probation. Brown was sent to prison for life.[13] Eventually, a newspaper pointed out that the judge who sentenced Brown to life for smoking marijuana had given probation to John Alexander Wood, a politically well-connected man who pleaded guilty to murder after shooting an unarmed man in the back. Seventeen years into his incarceration, Brown was released.[14]

As a relatively new field of study, criminology is interdisciplinary. This means that it draws upon other academic disciplines, including political science, economics, psychology, law, biology, and sociology (see Figure 1.1). Understanding the problems of crime and criminal justice requires knowledge of many areas of study, and experts from all these fields contribute knowledge and research. Using the case of Tyrone Brown, let's see how this works.

## LO2:

**Demonstrate** how political science, economics, psychology, law, biology, and sociology contribute to criminology.

## Political Science

As we will see later, political forces control how crime is defined and how criminal law works, so some political scientists contribute to criminology by studying the role of political power in social control. The Tyrone Brown case is rife with politics. First, the criminalization of marijuana began as a political issue rather than an effort to protect public health. The drug had been introduced into the United States via Mexico, but apparently it was not considered a problem until whites began using it in the 1930s.[15] We can also observe racial politics in the sentencing of Tyrone Brown, an impoverished black man, compared to the sentencing of the white man who pleaded guilty to murder.

## Economics

Economic principles are at the heart of many of the transactions defined as crime. For instance, some economists have

## Figure 1.1   Criminology

**Several disciplines contribute knowledge and ideas to the relatively new discipline of criminology.**

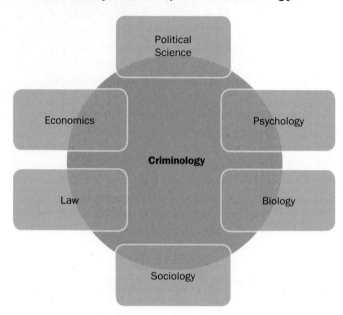

mathematically modeled the cost-benefit analysis some offenders use. From this perspective, Tyrone Brown and Lewis Bivins weighed the chance that a street robbery would net them a substantial amount of money against the chance it would bring little money and/or they would get caught. They decided the robbery was worth the risk. You may consider what happened—the men walked away with $2 and got arrested—and conclude their risk assessment was faulty. However, it is also possible they had committed many similar robberies before and had been far more successful. Or they may have calculated that even if they were caught, the penalty would not be too severe—and they were right up to a point. Brown's life sentence for his probation violation was a surprise to nearly everyone involved in the case.

## Psychology

Criminologists rely on many psychological perspectives. Psychologists often treat inmates to determine why they have broken the law as well as to provide rehabilitation to help prevent further **antisocial** behavior, that is, behavior intended to harm society and individuals. For example, a psychologist would look into the reasons Brown and Bivins committed the robbery and then continued to break the law while on probation. Criminal psychologists, however, would also be interested in society's reaction to the breaking of laws—in this case why Bivins and Wood, who committed auto theft and murder, respectively, received far lighter sentences than Brown, who smoked some marijuana.

**antisocial** Following standards of behavior intended to harm society and individuals.

## Law

The study of law is integral to criminology. Laws specify actions that society decides should be punished and how justice is dispensed. Because laws are made by people to control other people, criminologists are interested in how laws are made, what activities they control, and, in turn, who they control. For example, the war on drugs has continued for several decades, generating scores of laws written to specify how that war is to be waged. Many critics assert that these laws are harshly out of proportion to the activities they were created to control. In the case of Tyrone Brown, a judge used the criminal law to specify a harsher sentence against a marijuana user than either a car thief or a confessed murderer.

## Biology

Many criminologists and biologists are looking for the roots of antisocial behavior within the human body. Is there a biological reason that Brown and Bivins committed robberies for money instead of earning money by legal means? Why did both continue to break the law even after being sanctioned? Why did the men's behavior so often clash with what society expected of them? Why do other young men in impoverished social settings similar to that of Brown and Bivins follow a path that is **pro-social,** or supportive of society and individuals? A criminologist working from a biological perspective may look for answers in the men's brain chemistry, hormones, or other physical factors that affect mood or personality.

## Sociology

Of all the academic disciplines, sociology has contributed the most to the field of criminology. The United States has a long history of applying sociological analysis to the study of crime, and sociologists did much of the pioneering work in criminology. As a result, several sociological theories can offer reasonable explanations for the actions of Tyrone Brown and other offenders like him as well as critiques of his treatment by the criminal justice system.

As we can see, criminology borrows from many different academic disciplines to give us a fuller and more comprehensive view of crime. This will become apparent in future chapters as we see how these various academic perspectives are used to construct criminological theories.

# Think about it
## Analyze

Choose two of the disciplines that criminology draws on and compare and contrast how they approach the Tyrone Brown case.

pro-social Following standards of behavior that are supportive of society and individuals.

# The Difference Between Criminology and Criminal Justice

When Troy Erik Isaac was 12, he got into a fight with some other kids and was sent to a California juvenile corrections facility. Small and thin for his age, Isaac says that although he did not know his sexual orientation, he knew he was different. Almost immediately other boys at the facility, many of whom were larger, older delinquents, began harassing Isaac. Eventually, one boy who was a gang member forced him to have oral sex. He told Isaac, "Your name is gonna be Baby Romeo and I'm Big Romeo" and said he would protect Isaac from the other boys. The older boy did not keep his promise, and Isaac was raped again by another boy. Isaac decided that the best way to protect himself was to convince the staff to isolate him, so he began cutting his wrists. In a statement prepared for a Senate subcommittee looking into the safety of juveniles in custody, Isaac said the trauma of being raped repeatedly while facility staff looked the other way sent him into a "cycle of imprisonment." First sent to detention in the mid-1980s, Isaac was in and out of juvenile facilities and prison, where he continued to be assaulted, until 2008.[16]

What is the difference between criminology and criminal justice? Criminology emerged from sociology because social scientists wanted to understand a major social problem: crime. Criminal justice, in turn, emerged from criminology because practitioners wanted to understand the social mechanisms for dealing with crime.

## LO3:
**Differentiate** between criminology and criminal justice.

To better understand the differences between criminology and criminal justice, let's consider the case of Troy Erik Isaac. One of the priorities of both juvenile and adult detention facilities is inmate safety, and one of the issues of greatest concern to criminal justice practitioners—which includes police officers, parole and probation officers, judges, correctional officers and administrators, as well as social workers, lawyers, and counselors—is inmate rape. Rape, assault, torture, and death at the hands of other inmates or staff are never part of any criminal sentence. Although the public may consider such suffering an informal part of the punishment for convicted offenders—an attitude best defined by the adage "If you can't do the time, don't do the crime"—it should not be. Part of the correctional process is treatment and rehabilitation—though

# theory
## to **practice**

### Recidivism and Criminological Theory

Recidivism, or repeat offending, is frustrating to both criminologists and criminal justice practitioners. Many offenders tend to repeat their offenses or commit entirely new ones and get arrested again. The so-called "revolving door" of the criminal justice system speaks to the failure of society to positively change offenders. Depending upon how we measure recidivism—by rate of re-arrest, reconviction, or re-incarceration—more than half of offenders recidivate.[1] Several criminological theories can guide policies for reducing recidivism. Let's look at three theories that feature policies aimed at reducing the numbers of recidivists. We will discuss each of these in detail in later chapters, but here they are useful to illustrate how theory can guide the formulation of laws, rehabilitation efforts, and criminal justice policies.

- *Deterrence theory.* Deterrence theory suggests that if the consequences of breaking the law are unattractive enough, individuals will not do it anymore. Policies derived from deterrence theory involved hiring more police officers, specifying severe and harsh punishments, and developing special initiatives to discourage certain types of offending. Examples include increasing penalties for driving while under the influence of alcohol, the war on drugs, and "three-strikes"

▲ Deterrence theory suggests that people won't break the law if they know the consequences will be harsh. Here, a driver takes a field sobriety test. If he is found to be driving under the influence of alcohol, the penalties could be serious.

penalties that prescribe harsh sentences for those convicted of a third offense, even minor ones. The idea is that potential recidivists will think twice about breaking the law again because they understand that the benefits of doing so do not outweigh the consequences if they are caught.

- *Labeling theory.* Criminal offenders may be identified as felons, swindlers, convicts, sex offenders, and so on according to their offense. These labels can damage an ex-offender's prospects for employment, educational funding, and emotional relationships. Some criminal justice policies attempt to mitigate the negative effects of the "criminal" label, such as programs in which defendants who successfully complete treatment have their criminal record expunged. Just as important, these "first-offender policies" may prevent the offender from internalizing the label and making it a self-fulfilling prophecy.

- *Social disorganization theory.* Social disorganization theory suggests that neighborhoods with transient, low-skilled, and alienated residents tend to have more crime. Policies aimed at increasing these communities' social support could significantly reduce the crime rate. Social disorganization theory suggests that residents who have sufficient schools, good jobs, and strong community networks are likely to be more invested in their communities and to behave in a pro-social manner.

These are just three theories with the potential to reduce recidivism. Each focuses on a different aspect of why people break the law, and each suggests different policy alternatives. The lesson here is that there is no single solution to the problems of crime, and we can apply a variety of theories to different types of factors that may be responsible for the development of crime.

[1]US Department of Justice, Office of Justice Programs, "Recidivism," http://www.ojp.usdoj.gov/nij/topics/corrections/recidivism/welcome.htm.

## THINKING
### *in* ACTION

1. Summarize the arguments that two of the three theories would use to explain recidivism.
2. In your opinion, what is the most accurate measure of recidivism: re-arrest, re-conviction, or re-incarceration?

these goals have not always been met in recent decades—and it is difficult to convince an inmate of the justness of the justice system and the benefits of pro-social behavior if he or she lives in fear of other inmates or staff.

Other aspects of this case that would interest criminal justice experts are the system that sent Isaac to juvenile detention; the conditions of his detention, especially the process that placed a 12-year-old first-time delinquent with larger, older repeat delinquents; the professionalism of the staff that allowed him to be abused; and the failure of the system to rehabilitate Isaac and ensure that he did not recidivate, or commit more offenses. (See *Theory to Practice* for more on **recidivism,** or repeat offending).

A criminologist, on the other hand, will be more interested in how and why Isaac began to engage in antisocial behavior. As we will see later in this text, many criminological theories are actually theories of delinquency. The reason is that adult antisocial behavior is considered to begin in childhood. Therefore, Isaac's case is particularly interesting because his criminal career began so early in his life. Another outstanding criminological issue is Isaac's repeated rape. A criminologist would be interested in the prevalence of rape in incarceration facilities and what leads heterosexual males and females to engage in situational homosexual activity while incarcerated, even while retaining heterosexual identities. Also of interest are the attitudes of staff members who allowed or were unable to control such predatory behavior. Finally, criminological theory would address the role Isaac's experiences in the juvenile detention facility played in his adult criminal career.

As we can see, there is a lot of overlap between criminology and criminal justice. Although criminology explores a number of criminal justice areas, our focus in this text will be limited to theories of crime causation, types of crime, victimization, and special topics such as terrorism and individual rights.

# Think about it

## Understand

Describe the reasons you are interested in either criminology or criminal justice.

## Analyze

Compare and contrast criminology and criminal justice.

## Criminological Theories

Thomas F. Quinn has been in trouble with the law since 1966. Now 72, he began racking up injunctions and federal criminal convictions when he was 28. Federal authorities say he has stolen about $500 million during his criminal career, and a federal judge once called Quinn an "incorrigible" recidivist. Prosecutors in Quinn's current case call him a "serious flight risk." Yet in the 44 years that authorities in the United States and France have been after him, Quinn has spent only six years in prison. Why would such an unrepentant lawbreaker spend so little time locked up?

The answer is that Quinn's convictions and alleged offenses are all for **white-collar crimes**—criminal offenses committed by an individual employee of a business during the course of legitimate business that take advantage of the business or its customers and benefit the employee. Elusive and uncooperative with authorities, Quinn is alleged to have helped orchestrate a $500 million insurance fraud and to have participated in a $50 million telecommunications fraud and a $26 million stock fraud.

Until recently, white-collar crime has not been considered as serious as violent crime. For example, in 1970 Quinn served only six months for his first securities-fraud conviction. In his 1993 conviction, he served no time in the United States beyond the six years he had already served in Europe. Federal law enforcement caught up with Quinn once more in November 2009 as he got off a plane in New York City. Charged with telecommunications fraud, Quinn now faces more than 20 years in prison.[17]

## LO4:

Describe the role criminological theory plays in shaping our understanding of antisocial behavior, improving criminal justice response, shaping policies for offender rehabilitation and medical and psychological treatments, and rendering victim assistance.

A major criminological finding is that most offenders in the United States are young white males. Although they typically start breaking the law early in life, usually during childhood, most stop in young adulthood and go on to lead responsible, pro-social lives. However, some offenders, such as Dennis Rader and Thomas F. Quinn, continue to engage in antisocial behavior well into adulthood. The reasons for this and other criminological phenomena are not clear, which is why criminologists construct theories to help explain why some offenders behave as they do. Remember, although theory is complicated, it is not just academic hot air. By better understanding antisocial behavior, we can improve criminal justice response, offender rehabilitation, medical and psychological treatments, and victim assistance (see *So What's New?*).

To better illustrate the importance of criminological theory, let's take a look at how three specific theories can be applied to the case of Thomas F. Quinn. We will address these theories in detail later in the text. For now, just use these examples to get a feel for how theory is used.

**recidivism** Repeat offending. *Also* recidivate.

**white-collar crime** A criminal offense committed by an individual employee of a business during the course of legitimate business that takes advantage of the business or its customers and benefits the employee.

# so what's new?

## The New Challenge for Criminology

Science has little effect on much of our public policy because the making of laws is largely a political process. Science and evidence often do not translate into how or why laws are made. Public crime endeavors such as the war on drugs, the war on terrorism, and three-strikes laws tend to be based on appeals to voters' emotions. However, complicated public problems such as crime require solutions based on what actually works rather than on what the public wants to work.

In his presidential address to the American Society of Criminology, Todd Clear (see photo below) out-lined criminologists' opportunities to encourage policymakers to develop responses to crime based on evidence rather than ideology. Clear cautioned criminologists to ensure their research is not only informed by science, but also aimed at giving legislators and policymakers tangible, realistic evidence upon which to base criminal justice policy. To be effective, criminologists must present their findings so they can be shaped into laws that address the problems of crime and delinquency.

*Source:* Todd R. Clear, "Policy and Evidence: The Challenge to the American Society of Criminology: 2009 Presidential Address to the American Society of Criminology," *Criminology* 48, no. 1 (2010): 1–25.

## THINKING *in* ACTION

1. Why is it important that criminologists provide scientific evidence to criminal justice policymakers?
2. Explain why criminal justice policy is often influenced by politics.

## Life-course Theory

As mentioned earlier, most offenders begin breaking the law during childhood but desist as adults. This finding is an aspect of life-course theory, which examines offenders at different points in their lives (we will learn more about life-course theory in Chapter 7). According to theorist Terrie Moffitt, there are two types of offenders. "Adolescent limited" means the offender stops serious breaking of criminal law in adolescence or early adulthood. "Life-course-persistent" means the offender continues breaking the law from childhood throughout adulthood. Under life-course theory, then, Thomas F. Quinn is considered a life-course-persistent offender. At age 72, he is still being pursued by law enforcement.

So how does life-course theory explain a life-course persistent offender like Quinn? According to Moffitt, some youths—for biological and social reasons not fully understood—never completely integrate into society. They are always at the edges. For example, a friend of Quinn's says that as a teenager Quinn stole beer by posing as a market deliveryman, and that he once scammed a street vendor by

◀ Most offenders in the United States are young white males.

flashing a fragment of a torn $10 bill to buy hotdogs for all the kids in his neighborhood.[18]

The application of life-course theory to policy is complex: It requires paying close attention to juvenile delinquents until adulthood to ascertain their patterns of offending. This is often a challenge because offenders may break the law in different jurisdictions and states, and, as of this date, it is difficult to collate these records into a coherent portrait of an offender. Many delinquents such as Quinn are never caught, or they are caught and dealt with informally and have no juvenile records. Quinn's first brush with the law came at age 28. It is possible that if his propensity for cons and scams had received legal attention earlier in his life, he may have followed a different course.

## Merton's Strain Theory

Strain theory is a broad concept that has a few different versions. In general, criminologist Robert Merton's strain theory proposes that Americans value material wealth and success and have several ways of reaching that goal. Strain is much like stress; being unable to reach the goal of wealth and success creates strain with social mores, personal strain, strain with family members, and so on. Merton's version of strain theory—which we will cover in detail in Chapter 6—states that people deal with strain using one of five methods. The method Thomas F. Quinn uses is called "innovation." Quinn accepts that the cultural goal of attaining wealth and success is valid, but he has rejected the legal, pro-social means of reaching that goal. Twice he has been convicted of using an illegal, shortcut method of amassing wealth, and recently he has been charged with using such methods again.

Merton's strain theory may be more useful as a critique of society and as a way of recognizing the social reasons some people behave as they do. According to Merton, attaining wealth is such an overarching goal in American society that it is possible some crime can be traced to the fact that many people feel worthless if they cannot meet this goal and believe they must break the law in order to do so.

## Conflict Theory

According to conflict theory, which we will cover in detail in Chapter 8, crime stems mainly from social-economic imbalance rather than from individuals. Conflict theorists consider most crime to be rooted in impoverishment and that the powerful perpetuate the social imbalances leading to impoverishment and crime. One view is that the law is created by those who have power to favor themselves and their peers. A conflict perspective of Quinn's case, then, would focus not on his individual behavior, but on his treatment by the criminal justice system.

The law deals most harshly with **street crime**—materially destructive or violent criminal offenses that are often interpersonal and represent those for which the police are most often called—which consists of violent offenses and common property-related offenses such as theft, vandalism, and arson. In fact, the work of local police revolves around street crime: They investigate offenses, make arrests, detain suspects, defuse violent situations, and generally enforce the laws against rape, murder, assault, robbery, and so on. Street crime is mainly the realm of the lower and middle classes, from the impoverished to the moderately well-off. White-collar crime, however, tends to be the realm of the wealthy.

Traditionally, the criminal justice system, from legislators

▲ A major concern of law enforcement is street crime, which consists of violent offenses and common property-related offenses such as theft and vandalism.

**street crime** Materially destructive or violent criminal offenses that are often interpersonal and represent those for which the police are most often called.

to the courts, has treated white-collar crime much more gingerly than street crime. For example, a white-collar offender—if incarcerated at all—may be sent to a medium- or low-security institution and serve a few years. A street-crime offender, depending on how violent, is typically sent to a high-security institution. The stated reason is that white-collar offenders are rarely, if ever, violent. In fact, there are no violent white-collar offenses: They are all related to fraud and finance. The street-crime category contains all the violent offenses. A conflict theorist sees the situation differently, however.

A street offender may be more violent than a white-collar offender, but this is not always the case. Many street offenders are thieves, shoplifters, burglars, prostitutes, con artists, and drug sellers who are not violent. The prisons, in fact, are full of inmates who are not violent. Violence, the conflict theorist would say, is not the defining difference between the treatment of street offenders and white-collar offenders. Rather, the lifestyle and social class of white-collar offenders, especially the successful ones, match that of legislators, judges, prosecutors, attorneys, and law enforcement administrators. Some of those individuals may even aspire to the white-collar offender's lifestyle (without the crime). On the other hand, how often does a police officer admire an impoverished murder suspect she is arresting and want to imitate his lifestyle?

According to conflict theory, then, the white-collar offender is more likely to receive lenient treatment than the street offender. When a powerful, wealthy person crosses the law, other powerful, wealthy people "circle the wagons," so to speak, to protect that person because their basic interests reflect one another and may even overlap. For example, when the infamous swindler Bernard Madoff went to prison in 2009 for fraud, many wondered why he was not caught sooner (we will cover this case in depth in Chapter 3). Several times, federal regulators did not appear to do their job investigating Madoff's wrongdoing. Critics point out that the regulators were young, inexperienced government employees with relatively low earnings who aspired to work at a prestigious firm. Madoff awed and intimidated the very regulators who were supposed to be investigating him.[19] Thomas F. Quinn may have benefited from the same attitude. Both times he was convicted, he did not receive grave sentences because his offenses were probably not considered serious, and his wealthy, globe-trotting lifestyle may have inspired envy in those who were supposed to punish his actions.

The practical aspects of the conflict perspective have only recently begun to make themselves felt. In recent years, the economic recession, the apparent irresponsibility of financial and corporate professionals, and the revelation that several white-collar offenders became wealthy by victimizing others for decades have finally led to harsher penalties for white-collar offenses.

With these examples, we can see how criminologists use theory to explore criminal behavior in a systematic way. Without clearly stated and testable theories, criminology would be reduced to competing opinions based on biases, political agendas, stereotypes, and unexplored assumptions. Criminological theory is a work in progress, and the popularity of various theories waxes and wanes as new evidence is presented, new social conditions appear, and scholars improve their research. In her biography of Nobel Prize winner Barbara McClintock, author Evelyn Fox Keller explained how competing theories never quite go away.

One of the characteristics of scientific development that most plagues historians is the enormous diversity of viewpoints that continue to persist long after it appears that a consensus has been reached. The difficulty arises not only because consensus is never total, but also because of the fact that consensus always means consensus of a particular community. Scientists make up many communities, and communities vary by subject, by methodology, by place, and by degree of influence. Science itself is a polyphonic chorus. The voices in that chorus are never equal, but what one hears as a dominant motif depends very much on where one stands. At times, some motifs appear dominant from any standpoint.

▼ The lifestyle and social class of successful white-collar offenders is much like that of legislators, judges, prosecutors, attorneys, and law enforcement administrators. Television personality Martha Stewart was sentenced to five months in prison and two years of probation for lying to investigators about a stock sale.

But there are always corners from which one can hear minor motifs continuing to sound.[20]

As we think critically about criminological theory, we will see that criminology has offered many different explanations of why people break the criminal law and ideas about how society should respond. Like the varied voices in a chorus, these theories present a number of motifs that go in and out of style. The challenge for criminology students and scholars is to appreciate the subtle differences between these theories, examine the evidence supporting each, and apply the theories to real-life problems of crime.

# Think about it

## Remember

List and describe three criminological theories that can be applied to real-life examples of crime.

## Evaluate

Explain how criminological theory can resemble a chorus.

# Summary

**LO1:** **State Sutherland's definition of criminology.**
- Sutherland created the classic definition of criminology. It states: "Criminology is the study of the making of laws, breaking of laws, and society's reaction to the breaking of laws."

**LO2:** **Demonstrate how political science, economics, psychology, law, biology, and sociology contribute to criminology.**
- Criminology is interdisciplinary, meaning that it draws upon other academic disciplines. Understanding the problems of crime and criminal justice requires knowledge of many areas of study.

**LO3:** **Differentiate between criminology and criminal justice.**
- Criminology and criminal justice are not interchangeable. Criminology emerged from sociology to focus on the social issue of crime. Criminal justice emerged from criminology to focus on the social mechanisms for dealing with crime.

**LO4:** **Describe the role criminological theory plays in shaping our understanding of antisocial behavior, improving criminal justice response, shaping policies for offender rehabilitation and medical and psychological treatments, and rendering victim assistance.**
- Criminologists use theory to explore criminal behavior in a systematic way and to help explain why some offenders behave as they do. Theory is important because by better understanding antisocial behavior, criminal justice response, offender rehabilitation, medical and psychological treatments, and victim assistance can be improved.
- The popularity of various theories comes and goes as new evidence is presented, new social conditions appear, and scholars develop better research techniques.

# Questions

1. What is Sutherland's classic definition of criminology?
2. What is the difference between criminal law and civil law?
3. Does criminology focus on why people break the law or on what society does about it?
4. In what ways is criminology interdisciplinary?
5. What academic discipline does criminology draw from the most?
6. What are the major distinctions between criminal justice and criminology?
7. Describe how life-course theory, strain theory, and conflict theory might offer different explanations of the same offense.
8. Do you think criminologists have created all possible theories of crime causation? Why or why not?

# 2

# Measuring
# Crime

# what's inside

**As you read, keep in mind these learning objectives:**

**LO1:** Identify and explain the differences between the three major ways of measuring crime.

**LO2:** Summarize the advantages and limitations of the Uniform Crime Reports.

**LO3:** Identify police motivations for under- or over-reporting crime.

**LO4:** Compare and contrast the National Incident-Based Reporting System and the Uniform Crime Reports.

**LO5:** Discuss the reasons for the creation of the National Crime Victimization Survey.

**LO6:** Discuss why the Uniform Crime Reports and the National Crime Victimization Survey have recently begun to show similar statistics.

**LO7:** Outline the advantages and disadvantages of self-report studies as tools to measure crime.

**LO8:** Explain how the reporting and measuring of crime can affect the development of criminological theory and public policy.

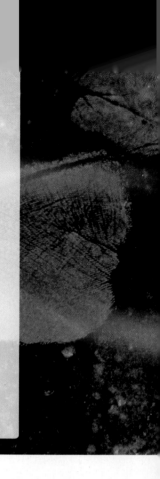

It is difficult to study the breaking of criminal law and develop theories to explain it without knowing which laws are being broken, who is breaking them, why, and how often. Although measuring crime might seem a relatively straightforward activity in which criminologists record the type and frequency of criminal offenses across jurisdictions, in reality it is an extremely complex task.

This chapter covers the four major sources of crime statistics—the Federal Bureau of Investigation's Uniform Crime Reports, the National Incident-Based Reporting System, the National Crime Victimization Survey, and self-report studies—illustrates their strengths and shortcomings, and discusses the political dimension of crime measurement. Crime statistics affect law enforcement agencies and communities, so criminal justice officials and administrators sometimes attempt to control the collection and dissemination of crime data. These examples illustrate why.

- A criminal justice official may wish to acquire more police officers and other resources, such as weapons, vehicles, or communication equipment. By showing a rising crime rate and an agency ill-equipped to deal with new challenges, law enforcement officials may try to convince local government that more resources are needed.

- A criminal justice official may be criticized because of a high crime rate and fear that he or she could be fired or lose an election.

- A jurisdiction may be in competition for federal anti-crime funds and need to show a significant crime problem. By emphasizing a significant problem with illegal

drugs or gangs, the community may become eligible for funds it can use for a variety of purposes.

- A jurisdiction that derives substantial income from the tourism and convention industries must project itself as safe. A sharp increase in crime statistics is bad for business. Other jurisdictions trying to attract business and residents may see their efforts rendered useless by a high crime rate or even the public perception that the area is not as safe as others.

These examples illustrate the concerns of law enforcement officials and city administrators about how crime statistics portray their jurisdiction. Although measuring crime is a serious business fraught with political and economic concerns, substantial efforts have been made to do it in an accurate, scientific manner. Although each method of crime measurement has its strengths and weaknesses, together they provide different perspectives on crime.

Another point about the measurement of crime—and one that may surprise you—is that all of the methods are flawed. The statistics of the Uniform Crime Reports, the National Incident-Based Reporting System, and the National Victimization Survey are not exact counts of how many offenses have occurred. Because of the problems of reporting and recording criminal offenses, the crime data we are all familiar with and that are reported by the government and trumpeted by the media are only a vague representation of the actual amount of crime. Furthermore, counting the actual number of criminal offenses is impossible.

▲ Law enforcement officials and city administrators are concerned about how crime statistics portray their jurisdictions.

Finally, we will look at how these methods of measuring crime affect criminology itself. In addition to conducting their own studies, criminological researchers use statistics to build theories and hypotheses as well as suggest and help implement public programs. Because researchers are using the same flawed statistics as everyone else as well as conducting their own flawed surveys, we will learn how they try to work around these imperfections to get closer to the true amount of crime. First, we must comprehend the most significant obstacle to achieving an accurate count: the dark figure of crime.

## The Dark Figure of Crime

Much more crime occurs than we know. The offenses recorded in government statistics are only a representation of the true amount of crime. The unknown amount is called the **dark figure of crime.** Two types of offenses feed the dark figure of crime: the vast number that are not reported and those that are reported but not recorded (see Figure 2.1).

For offenses to enter the measures of crime, they must be both reported to the proper authorities who define it as a criminal offense and recorded in the appropriate category. This presents two decision points critical to accurate reporting: whether to bring the activity to the attention of the official record-keeper (in most cases the police) and whether to identify the activity as a criminal offense. Between these two decisions, a large amount of crime goes unreported and unrecorded. We will get into reasons that offenses go unrecorded

**dark figure of crime** A term that describes criminal offenses that are unreported to law enforcement officials and never recorded.

### Figure **2.1**  The Dark Figure of Crime

The Uniform Crime Reports, the National Crime Victimization Survey, and self-report studies shed some light on the dark figure of crime. Although it is possible that crime reported in one measure may have been reported in one or both of the other measures, we cannot know this for certain.

*This includes the unreported and unrecorded crimes that do not find their way into any of the three crime reporting systems.

later in the chapter. First, let's look at reporting. A criminal offense may not be reported for a number of reasons.

- *It is not recognized as an offense.* An offense may occur, and witnesses and/or victims may not actually deem it a criminal offense. For instance, someone passes counterfeit money at a bank, and the bank teller does not recognize that the bills are not legal tender. If a $20 bill is exchanged hundreds of times before it is recognized as bogus, it will be recorded as a criminal offense only the final time it is exchanged.

- *Fear of retaliation.* A victim or witness may fear the possible consequences of reporting an offense. This is especially true in cases of domestic assault in which a spouse or children are routinely beaten. Neighborhood residents may also hesitate to report drug sales because they are afraid of the dealers.

- *Fear of legal consequences.* The victim of a crime may not be totally blameless. A person cheated in a transaction of illegal drugs is not likely to report it to the police.

- *Lack of faith in the system.* Individuals may not believe that police are able to make an arrest or that judges will impose a significant sentence. On occasion, a victim may attempt to seek justice in his or her own way by engaging in vigilante activities. In neighborhoods where the police are not trusted, victims may not report offenses because they do not want to "snitch" or cooperate with police.

▲ A victim, such as an abused spouse or child, may fear the possible consequences of reporting an offense.

■ *Lack of insurance.* Victims often go to the trouble of reporting an offense in the hope that an insurance company will reimburse them. Victims who do not have insurance cannot be compensated for the theft of their property, so they may see no reason to report the offense.

These are but a few of the reasons that people may not report a criminal offense. This can be observed by comparing the statistics in the Uniform Crime Reports and those in the National Crime Victimization Survey, which asks participants if they have been crime victims (we will discuss both these measures in detail later). The number of reported offenses, especially violent ones, is traditionally higher in the National Crime Victimization Survey than in the Uniform Crime Reports. A comparison of the 1995 versions of both reports found that the Uniform Crime Reports recorded 12.2 million property offenses and 1.9 million violent offenses, whereas the National Crime Victimization Survey recorded 32 million property offenses and nearly 11 million violent offenses.[1] Clearly more criminal offenses are occurring than are being reported to police.

The non-reporting of crime is also closely related to social class, sex, and race. One example is related to the reputation of the police in unstable neighborhoods or among minorities. The police may not be trusted, or victims of earlier offenses may have had what they considered to be unjust experiences with the criminal justice system. These victims may feel safer dealing with their victimization in some other way, such as vigilantism, than in calling the police. None of the criminal offenses committed in these common examples would be reported to the police, and they would remain unrecorded. If the level of non-reporting in these cases is as high as many researchers believe, then much of recorded crime is the product of reports by victims who are relatively affluent, white, male, residing in stable neighborhoods, or all these. This bias distorts the picture of crime and can lead policymakers to misallocate crime-control resources to protect those who already have privileged status in society.

Although a lot of crime goes unreported, the major sources of crime data still generally agree with one another. Even if these sources cannot be matched number for number, scholars point out that they show similar broad patterns and distributions of crime. The crime statistics recorded by the Uniform Crime Reports tend to agree in *pattern,* if not in *volume,* with those recorded by the National Crime Victimization Survey. Until the recent convergence of these surveys—which we will discuss later—researchers considered these two measures of crime to complement rather than contradict each other. The same goes for self-report studies, which show some agreement—again, in patterns of offending if not in number of offenses reported—with both the Uniform Crime Reports and the National Crime Victimization Survey. For example, in juvenile self-report studies, the groups of juveniles whom the justice system most often designates as "delinquent"—that is, boys, minorities, poor students, and youths with delinquent peers and family issues—self-report more delinquent activities than groups of juveniles who have no records of delinquency and do not fall into those categories.[2] That juvenile delinquents admit to committing more delinquent acts seems to be a common-sense observation, but it is relevant when it confirms other independent surveys.

Perhaps most important for criminologists and criminology students to understand is that no crime-measurement technique is perfect. All have their flaws and drawbacks, and pulling something useful out of them is more difficult than the media would have us believe. Although headlines shouting that crime trends are headed up or down are indeed based on government statistics, with quotes from criminologists to boot, the reality is far less clear-cut. For example, according to the Uniform Crime Reports, the violent crime rate increased sharply between 1960 and 1990, then began to decline in the mid-1990s. However, victimization surveys showed stable violent victimization rates between the 1970s and mid-1990s, then a decline similar to that described by the Uniform Crime Reports.[3] How could the Uniform Crime Reports show a steady increase in violent crime for 30 years while victimization surveys showed a flat rate? It is irregularities such as these that keep researchers looking for the source of the discrepancies, and there are several. Before we get to that, however, let's first learn a bit more about these sources of statistics.

## Think about it

### Remember
List the reasons why someone might not report a criminal offense.

### Understand
Show how the major methods of measuring crime attempt to shed light on the dark figure of crime.

### Evaluate
Identify the four reasons individuals and criminal justice officials may alter crime statistics.

## Government Statistical Efforts

The three major government efforts to measure crime in the United States come from the Federal Bureau of Investigation (FBI). They are the **Uniform Crime Reports** (UCR), its offshoot the **National Incident-Based Reporting System** (NIBRS), and the **National Crime Victimiza-**tion Survey (NCVS). The UCR has been around the longest and is the workhorse of crime statistical reports. Its purpose is to provide statistics for the administration of the criminal justice system. Without the UCR, we would have little idea of the actual incidence of crime. Its numbers are freely available, and anyone from researchers to criminal justice professionals to the general public can use them to study crime. The NIBRS is like the UCR in that it follows many of the same rules for collecting statistics, scoring items, and reporting data; however, it is far more detailed. Finally, the purpose of the NCVS is to provide information about victims, offenders, and unreported crime. Let's look at the UCR first.

### The Uniform Crime Reports

The FBI collects and publishes data from more than 17,000 jurisdictions with the objective of providing reliable statistics to assist law enforcement in operations and management.[4] The federal government makes participation in the UCR program voluntary, but about 38 states require police departments to send data either to a state program or directly to the FBI.[5] This makes the UCR the most comprehensive crime data collection effort in the nation. Since the UCR has continued for 80 years, some of the **methodology**—the rules and principles that govern how research is performed—that makes reporting crime such a difficult endeavor has been worked out. Currently, the UCR represents one of the most reliable measures of certain types of violent and property offenses.

**LO2:**
**Summarize** the advantages and limitations of the Uniform Crime Reports.

Getting every agency to use standard definitions of crime and record offenses in consistent ways is an ongoing challenge for the UCR program. Before 1929, when the International Association of Chiefs of Police began to standardize crime reporting, crime statistics were not systematically collected. Although some large cities recorded arrests and offenses, the definitions of offenses and standards for recording them varied widely. For instance, the attitude of the police and the public toward lynching, abortion, domestic violence, drug and alcohol use, and dueling depended on the jurisdiction. Some jurisdictions abhorred some of these

**LO1:**
**Identify and explain** the differences between the three major ways of measuring crime.

**Uniform Crime Reports (UCR)** An FBI program that collects law enforcement statistics from voluntarily participating agencies throughout the United States.

**National Incident-Based Reporting System (NIBRS)** The FBI's incident-based reporting system in which data are collected on every single offense.

**National Crime Victimization Survey (NCVS)** A survey of a nationally representative sample of residences that collects information about crime from victims.

**methodology** The rules and principles that govern how research is performed.

activities and made them offenses, while tolerating others. A jurisdiction that supported dueling was less likely to define a resulting death as a homicide; until recent decades, chances were good that assaulting a spouse, domestic partner, or children would not be recorded as an offense.[6]

Developing crime statistics is difficult because U.S. law enforcement is decentralized; each state and municipality has its own police force. In nations like England, where the police force is highly centralized, it is much easier to consistently define and record offenses. In the UCR's early years, some jurisdictions were dropped because the numbers they reported diverged so widely from those of other jurisdictions of the same size and demographic composition. The Department of Justice could not guarantee the accuracy of crime statistics from many jurisdictions and cautioned readers about making comparative judgments. The 1930 Wickersham Commission offered the following caveat: "It takes but little experience of such criminal statistics as we have in order to convince that a serious abuse exists in compiling them as a basis for requesting appropriations or for justifying the existence of or urging expanded powers and equipment for the agencies in question."[7]

The early UCR measured seven offenses that, in 1960, became the Crime Index: murder and non-negligent manslaughter, rape, robbery, aggravated assault, burglary, larceny, and motor vehicle theft. These offenses were selected for five reasons.

- They were the most likely to be reported to police.
- Police could easily establish that an offense had occurred.
- The offenses occurred in all geographic areas of the United States.
- They occurred with sufficient frequency to provide an adequate basis for comparison between jurisdictions.
- They were serious in nature and volume.[8]

Although the FBI tinkered somewhat with the definitions and types of offenses included in the Crime Index—

▼ The UCR counts four types of violent offenses and four types of property offenses, including robbery.

## Figure 2.2 Number of Recorded Violent and Property Offenses in the United States, 2005–2008

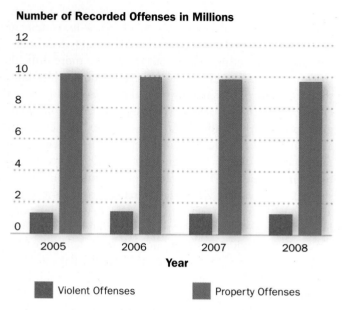

**Number of Recorded Offenses in Millions**

Violent Offenses        Property Offenses

*Source:* Federal Bureau of Investigation, Uniform Crime Reports, *Crime in the United States, 2005–2008,* http://www.fbi.gov/ucr/ucr.htm.

arson was added in 1979 to create the Modified Crime Index—it remained substantially unchanged until 2004 when the Crime Index and Modified Crime Index were discontinued in favor of a simple violent crime total and property crime total. (See Figure 2.2 for the levels of violent and property crime in the United States from 2005 to 2008.) The Crime Index and Modified Crime Index were determined to inaccurately represent the degree of crime because they were inflated by the most-committed offense, which is usually larceny-theft. Therefore, a jurisdiction that appeared to be dangerous because of a high crime index may simply have had a large number of larceny-thefts and not necessarily a large number of more serious offenses.

Today, the UCR counts four types of violent offenses and four types of property offenses (see Table 2.1).[9] Violent offenses use force or threat of force. The property offenses—burglary, larceny-theft, and motor vehicle theft—include the taking of money or property, but victims suffer no force or threat of force. Although arson victims may experience force, arson is a property offense because property is destroyed.

Currently, the UCR comprises seven data collections: Offenses Known to the Police, Arrests, Law Enforcement Officers Killed or Assaulted, Police Employment, Arson Reports, the Supplementary Homicide Reports, and the Hate Crime Supplement. All data are based on records that state and local police agencies submit to the FBI either directly or through state UCR programs. Offenses Known to the Police, Arrests, Police Employment, Arson Reports,

## Table **2.1** Uniform Crime Reports Violent and Property Offenses

**The Uniform Crime Reporting program records information about four violent offenses and four property offenses.**

| Violent Offenses | Property Offenses |
|---|---|
| Murder | Burglary |
| Forcible Rape | Larceny-Theft |
| Robbery | Motor Vehicle Theft |
| Aggravated Assault | Arson |

*Source:* Federal Bureau of Investigation, Uniform Crime Reports, *Crime in the United States,* 2008, http://www.fbi.gov/ucr/cius2008/index.html.

and Supplementary Homicide Reports make up the annual FBI publication *Crime in the United States,* which is the publication used most when describing the extent of crime in the United States.[10] The FBI defines each collection as follows.

■ *Offenses Known to the Police.* The UCR collects data on violent and property offenses known to law enforcement, as well as data regarding **clearances,** the closure of an offense by either arrest or "exceptional means." Exceptional means refer to situations beyond the police agency's control that prevent it from arresting and formally charging a suspect, such as the death of the suspect. (For the reporting system, the UCR does not distinguish between offenses cleared by arrest and those cleared by exceptional means.)[11] The FBI also collects supplementary data about offenses, such as time of day. Expanded offense data includes trends in crime volume and crime rate.[12]

■ *Arrests.* Arrest data are collected for 29 offenses. The UCR counts one arrest for each separate instance in which a person is arrested, cited, or summoned for an offense. Because the same person may be arrested several times during a year, the data do not reflect the number of individuals arrested, just the number of arrests.[13]

■ *Law Enforcement Officers Killed or Assaulted.* This collection provides data about officers who were feloniously or accidentally killed or assaulted during their duties.[14]

■ *Police Employment.* The UCR defines "law enforcement officers" as individuals who carry a firearm and a badge, have full arrest powers, and are paid from government funds allotted specifically for sworn law enforcement representatives. The data provide a count of existing staff levels of law enforcement officers, including totals for patrol officers, officers assigned to administrative and investigative positions, and officers assigned to special teams.[15]

■ *Arson Reports.* This report includes only fires that have been determined to have been willfully set, not fires labeled as suspicious or of unknown origin.[16]

■ *Supplementary Homicide Reports.* These data include information about the age, sex, and race of murder victims and offenders; the types of weapon used; the relationship of victims to offenders; and the circumstances. Information is also collected on justifiable homicides, or "certain willful killings" that are limited to (1) "the killing of a felon by a peace officer in the line of duty," and (2) "the killing of a felon, during the commission of a felony, by a private citizen."[17]

■ *Hate Crime Supplement.* The 1990 Hate Crime Statistics Act required the collection of data "about crimes that manifest evidence of prejudice based on race, religion, sexual orientation, or ethnicity." The report includes the type of offense, type of location, bias motivation, type of victim (individual, business, institution, or society), number of individual victims, number arrested, and their race.[18]

One of the UCR's most controversial reporting techniques is the **hierarchy rule,** which states that in any incident involving more than one offense, the most serious offense is the only one officially recorded. For instance, if your house is broken into (burglary) and you are beaten (aggravated assault), if your spouse is killed (murder) and your car stolen (motor vehicle theft), only the most serious of these offenses, murder, is recorded in the UCR. The exception is arson, which is always reported regardless of what other offenses have occurred. The hierarchy rule means the actual number of offenses is under-reported by design. (A more elaborate discussion of this rule appears in Chapter 9.)

The UCR includes not only the total numbers of specific offenses, but also the **crime rate.** The crime rate is not the actual number of offenses but a rate of occurrence calculated by dividing the number of offenses in a given jurisdiction by its population and multiplying by 100,000. For instance, the total number of offenses in a large city such as New York or Los Angeles will be far greater than in a smaller city, but it is possible for the smaller city to have the higher crime rate, that is, more offenses per 100,000 people (see Figure 2.3). By compensating for population size, the crime rate makes it easy to compare crime across jurisdictions.

This ease of comparing crime rates has led to what many criminologists believe is a misuse of the UCR: The media and other organizations that rank "best places to live" often

**clearance** The closure of an offense by either arrest or other means.

**hierarchy rule** The FBI's practice of recording in the Uniform Crime Reports only the most serious offense in a set of offenses.

**crime rate** The number of offenses divided by the population, usually expressed as a rate of offenses per 100,000 people.

## Figure 2.3 Calculating Crime Rates

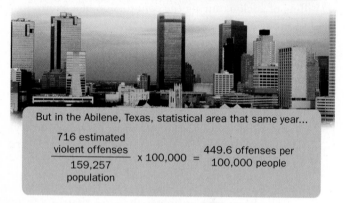

$$\frac{\text{Number of offenses}}{\text{population}} \times \text{per number of people}$$

For example, in the New York City statistical* area in 2008...

$$\frac{75{,}772 \text{ estimated violent offenses}}{19{,}004{,}225 \text{ population}} \times 100{,}000 = \begin{array}{c} 398.7 \text{ offenses per} \\ 100{,}000 \text{ people} \end{array}$$

But in the Abilene, Texas, statistical area that same year...

$$\frac{716 \text{ estimated violent offenses}}{159{,}257 \text{ population}} \times 100{,}000 = \begin{array}{c} 449.6 \text{ offenses per} \\ 100{,}000 \text{ people} \end{array}$$

Abilene, Texas had a higher violent crime rate than New York City in 2008.

*Statistical areas may include several surrounding jurisdictions.

*Source:* Federal Bureau of Investigation, Uniform Crime Reports, *Crime in the United States, 2008,* Table 6, http://www.fbi.gov/ucr/cius2008/data/table_06.html.

use the figures to compare the safety of jurisdictions. The UCR strongly cautions against making such comparisons:

> Figures used in this *Report* are submitted voluntarily by law enforcement agencies throughout the country. Individuals using these tabulations are cautioned against drawing conclusions by making direct comparisons between cities. Comparisons lead to simplistic and/or incomplete analyses that often create misleading perceptions adversely affecting communities and their residents.[19]

That the UCR can be misused this way points to one of its major shortcomings: Its statistics give a vague, simplistic picture that shows the outlines of the crime problem but not the details.

## Problems with the UCR

Because of the concentrated effort to train personnel and law enforcement agencies to define and record offenses in a consistent manner, the UCR provides valuable data for policymakers and law enforcement

## LO3:

Identify police motivations for under- or over-reporting crime.

administrators. However, along with the hierarchy rule, the UCR has three other significant limitations.

- It records only offenses that are reported to the police.
- It is focused on **street crime.**
- Its data are incomplete.

Let's explore these limitations a bit further.

A criminal offense must be reported to the police to be included in the UCR. As you will recall from the discussion about the dark figure of crime, many offenses are not reported. This means the UCR is a reliable measure of what law enforcement agencies do but an unreliable measure of the actual amount of crime.

><THINKBACK

street crime (ch. 1)— Usually materially destructive or violent criminal offenses that are often interpersonal and represent those for which the police are most often called.

The UCR also has a significant and often overlooked bias: It is focused on street crime, the offenses that typically represent those for which the police are most often called. The UCR does not provide a good picture of white-collar, corporate, organized, or environmental crime because these offenses are far more difficult to capture and measure. Remember, the UCR was designed by the FBI, a federal law enforcement agency, to measure what the police do and help them do it better. Police departments are concerned with curtailing street crime, so those are the statistics recorded in the UCR. A complicated, major corporate financial offense investigated by the Securities and Exchange Commission will not be recorded in the UCR although such an offense may involve more money and even be more damaging to the public than a series of robberies or burglaries. Much of criminological theory is focused on street crime. If white-collar, corporate, environmental, and organized offenses were counted in the same manner as street crime, perhaps more criminological theories would be developed to explain them, and they would draw more public and media attention.[20]

Despite the improvement in developing consistent definitions of criminal offenses, police departments, as we saw in the introduction, have political motivations to provide data that support their agency agenda (see *So What's New?*). A law enforcement agency may under-report offenses to present a better crime rate and improve the picture of the work it does. An agency may over-report crime to procure more funding or resources. Finally, an agency may report no crime data at all. In fact, a significant amount of data is missing from Offenses Known to the Police, and more is apparently going missing every year.[21]

Recall that UCR participation is voluntary; agencies are not required by federal law to participate. Some agencies will report offenses in a time or place other than when or where they occurred, report the year's offenses in December rather than when they became known to the police, or not report anything. Although more than 17,000 agencies participate in the UCR, some send reports for only one month.

# so what's new?

## Bad Numbers

The misreporting of crime statistics by police is a serious problem in the collection of crime statistics. Regardless of the reasons for misreporting—under-reporting to make a jurisdiction appear safer than it really is, for example, or over-reporting to attract more funding—the results mean that criminologists, the media, criminal justice officials, and the public cannot make accurate assumptions about crime.

But how much misreporting is actually occurring? Is it the result of the occasional "bad apple" police chief, or does it happen in many, if not most, police departments? Like the dark figure of crime, the true amount of crime misreporting can never be known. Often it is only when police officers come forward and admit to fudging the statistics that misreporting comes to light.

1. In 2010, former New York Police Department (NYPD) officer Adrian Schoolcraft accused officers at his Brooklyn precinct of downgrading and not reporting offenses to make the precinct appear safer. According to Schoolcraft's accusations, some victims were talked or intimidated out of reporting offenses, some offenses were downgraded, and some were not investigated.[1] Retired NYPD captain Ernie Naspretto says that in his Bensonhurst precinct, he "delayed" reporting offenses that occurred on the last night of 1997 until the first day of 1998. Naspretto says all the offenses were recorded, just not when they occurred. Although the delay was only a few hours, it appeared as if crime was down in the precinct for the entire year of 1997 because two offenses that actually occurred in 1997 were not recorded until 1998. Naspretto claims police officials are under such intense pressure to show a consistent drop in crime that it is leading to "paranoia," which, he says, is worse than a slight increase in crime.[2]

2. A self-report study of retired NYPD officials conducted by criminologists Eli B. Silverman and John A. Eterno, also a retired NYPD captain, appears to confirm widespread misreporting to show lower crime rates. Officers would check the Internet for low prices on items reported stolen so they could downgrade thefts from felony grand larcenies to misdemeanor thefts. Sometimes they were sent to crime scenes to talk victims out of filing charges or talk them into changing their reports so the offenses could be downgraded.[3]

3. The police forces at colleges and universities are also under pressure to show safe campuses because perceived safety can affect enrollment rates. In 2004, Yale University was accused of under-reporting campus sexual assaults. However, FBI statistics are not the only issue. Under the Clery Act—named for a student murdered at Lehigh University in 1986—schools must report certain offense statistics to the U.S. Department of Education. In 2006, evidence surfaced that several schools were recording burglaries—which must be reported to the Education Department—as larcenies, which do not have to be reported.[4]

[1]Rocco Parascandola, "Brooklyn's 81st Precinct Probed by NYPD for Fudging Stats; Felonies Allegedly Marked as Misdemeanors," *New York Daily News,* February 2, 2010, http://www.nydailynews.com/news/ny_crime/2010/02/02/2010-02-02_precinct_probed_for_fudging_stats_li_say_bklyns_81st_wanted_to_improve_its_crime.html.

[2]Ernie Naspretto, "Former NYPD Captain Didn't Fudge Crime Statistics in Past—He 'Delayed' in Reporting Them," *New York Daily News,* February 7, 2010, http://www.nydailynews.com/ny_local/2010/02/07/2010-02-07_why_i_bent_crime_stats_excop_tells_of_pressure_from_brass.html.

[3]William K. Rashbaum, "Retired Officers Raise Questions on Crime Data," *New York Times,* February 7, 2010, late edition, A1.

[4]Zachary M. Seward, "FBI Stats Show Many Colleges Understate Campus Crime," *Wall Street Journal,* October 23, 2006, B1.

## THINKING *in* ACTION

1. What is harmful about the misreporting of crime statistics?
2. Think of ways to find out how much crime is misreported.
3. Should police departments that are caught misreporting crime be penalized?

Three states—Indiana, Mississippi, and New Mexico—do not have state crime-reporting programs, so data from these states are submitted by individual participating agencies.[22] Although that may not sound problematic, nearly three-quarters of law enforcement agencies in states with statewide UCR programs submit complete reports, but in states without UCR programs, just over half do so.[23]

This means the UCR does not include data from every police department in the nation, and some sets of data have substantial gaps.[24] For instance, although the FBI notes in its UCR publication *Crime in the United States, 2008* that the 17,799 law enforcement agencies participating in the UCR provided reports representing 95 percent of the total U.S. population, not all submitted complete data. Some contributed as little as three months' worth. In 2003, for instance, only 65.5 percent of agencies, which accounts for about 87.9 percent of the U.S. population, sent data for all 12 months.[25]

Although data are considered missing when law enforcement agencies do not properly report offenses or arrests, most of the missing data can be attributed to agencies that do not report at all. If this missing data were randomly distributed across the nation, its absence might not be so troubling. However, it appears that data are missing in chunks from specific places, which can compromise the UCR's effectiveness. Imagine a fishing net with a few holes scattered evenly throughout it. If the holes are far enough apart, the net will still be strong enough to haul in fish. But what about a net with gaping holes in the corners? This net may be missing as many links at the first net, but it is weaker because the holes are grouped in specific places where fish slip through, so fewer are caught. According to a 2008 study, the missing data in the UCR are much like the missing links in the second, more compromised net; agencies that do not submit data tend to be grouped into specific types and geographic areas:

- small agencies
- from rural and suburban counties
- from the New England and South Atlantic regions
- in states without UCR programs[26]

Because the missing data is so concentrated, the UCR cannot afford to ignore it. The holes must be accounted for somehow.

The FBI has two ways to estimate missing data in order to compute annual state and national crime rates. First, for an agency that has reported at least three months of crime data, the FBI will apply the crime rate for those months to the entire year. Second, for an agency that has submitted two or fewer reports, the FBI will throw out the data and instead use the crime rate from a similar agency and jurisdiction. These methods are adequate for providing large-scale estimates of crime but not for estimating county-level crime rates or seasonal crime-rate variations.[27]

This inadequacy is not a big problem when looking at only one year, but it is often noticeable when comparing years. For example, the estimate of the volume of Index crimes in the 1992 UCR is 13,858,202 offenses without estimating the missing data and 14,660,364 when the missing data are estimated, a difference of only 5.7 percent. However, the picture changes when we compare years to determine whether crime is headed up or down and by how much. Uncorrected data show a 4.7 percent decrease in crime from 1992 to 1993, but corrected data show the decrease to be only 1.91 percent. Both sets of data show a decrease, but the raw data show the greater decrease.[28] What this means is that the UCR contains a large, unknown amount of error, and researchers are still uncertain how this error affects our understanding of the actual amount of crime. We can therefore draw three conclusions.

- The UCR records most offenses known to law enforcement.
- The UCR does not record every single offense known to law enforcement.
- The exact error rate is unknown.

So, the UCR, although the most reliable method of measuring crime in the United States, does not give a complete, reliable picture of crime. That is why researchers and criminal justice administrators try to complete the picture with two other measures: the FBI's National Incident-Based Reporting System and the Bureau of Justice Statistics' National Crime Victimization Survey.[29]

## The National Incident-Based Reporting System

Designed as an improvement upon the UCR, the National Incident-Based Reporting System (NIBRS) is run much the same way as the UCR, but it includes more information about offenses reported to police. The NIBRS collects data on each single incident and arrest within 46 specific offenses, which are called Group A offenses. There are also 11 Group B offenses for which only arrest data are reported (see Table 2.2). Compare this to the UCR, which collects extensive data on four violent offenses and four property offenses and arrest data on 29 offenses. In addition to collecting more detailed data about crime, the NIBRS is considered a more accurate reflection of crime because it does not use the hierarchy rule. In a multi-offense incident, each offense is recorded. This increases statistical accuracy and better reflects the overall level of crime. For this reason, NIBRS and UCR statistics are not comparable.

**LO4:**

**Compare and contrast** the National Incident-Based Reporting System and the Uniform Crime Reports.

## Table **2.2**  National Incident-Based Reporting System Offenses

**Extensive crime data are collected for the 22 Group A offenses. Only arrest data are reported for the 11 Group B offenses.**

| Group A Offenses | Group B Offenses |
|---|---|
| Arson | Bad checks |
| Aggravated assault, simple assault, intimidation | Curfew, loitering, and vagrancy violations |
| Bribery | Disorderly conduct |
| Burglary, breaking and entering | Driving under the influence |
| Counterfeiting or forgery | Drunkenness |
| Destruction, damage, vandalism of property | Non-violent family offenses |
| Drug/narcotic offenses, drug equipment violations | Liquor law violations |
| Embezzlement | Peeping tom |
| Extortion/blackmail | Runaway |
| Fraud, false pretenses, swindle, confidence game, credit card/automatic teller machine fraud, impersonation, welfare fraud, wire fraud | Trespass of real property |
| Gambling, betting/wagering, operating/promoting/assisting gambling, gambling equipment violations, sports tampering | All other offenses |
| Murder and non-negligent manslaughter, negligent manslaughter, justifiable homicide | |
| Kidnapping, abduction | |
| Larceny/theft, pocket-picking, purse-snatching, shoplifting, theft from building, theft from coin-operated machines or devices, theft from motor vehicle, theft of motor vehicle parts or accessories, all other larceny | |
| Motor vehicle theft | |
| Pornography, obscene material | |
| Prostitution, assisting or promoting prostitution | |
| Robbery | |
| Forcible rape, forcible sodomy, sexual assault with an object, forcible fondling | |
| Incest, statutory rape | |
| Stolen property | |
| Weapon violations | |

*Source:* Federal Bureau of Investigation, National Incident-Based Reporting System (NIBRS), http://www.fbi.gov/ucr/faqs.htm.

Administered by the FBI, the NIBRS began collecting data in the late 1980s and has been under development since. As of 2008, 31 states were certified to report NIBRS data; nine state UCR programs were testing the system, and six state agencies were working on system planning and development.[30] Approximately 25 percent of the U.S. population is covered by the NIBRS, which represents 26 percent of the nation's reported crime. Authorities hoped that many more agencies and jurisdictions would be participating in the NIBRS by now, but due to funding limitations and political considerations, its use is not as widespread as planned. Currently, the NIBRS remains ill-funded and underdeveloped.

The system also has a few other drawbacks.

- *The complexity of the coding schemes, the number of categories, and other definitional issues.* The increased complexity of the NIBRS over the UCR makes the system cumbersome for law enforcement officials.

- *Lack of incentives for agency participation.* Although the NIBRS provides good data collection, it requires time that some police agencies view as better spent responding to the public.

- *Fear of the perception of an increase in crime.* By eliminating the hierarchy rule, the NIBRS may show an artificial increase in a jurisdiction's crime rate. Given that police agencies are often evaluated on their ability to keep crime low, police agencies may be threatened by the change in reporting systems.[31]

## The Politics of Crime Measurement

Despite the best efforts of law enforcement to collect accurate crime data, the dark figure of crime remains large and significant. We've discussed many reasons people do not report crime, but some issues remain that affect the level of reporting. One has to do with public confidence in the police. In some neighborhoods or jurisdictions, the police have a rapport with citizens that encourages the reporting of crime. In others, the police are viewed as ineffective or, even worse, as working against citizens. For instance, in some minority communities, the police are considered to be an invading army or even a rival street gang. Although the police may be only doing their job, their presence and paramilitary demeanor discourage some citizens from cooperating.

Scholars have suggested that race and social-class biases are inherent in policing. This has been a consistent criticism of law enforcement for many years; even with racial and gender integration of law enforcement agencies, the perception remains that laws are disproportionately enforced against the impoverished and people of color. Criminologist John Irwin argues that the criminal justice system disproportionately incarcerates impoverished individuals as a method of managing the underclass. He refers to these individuals as the "rabble" who find themselves detained and arrested with little provocation. Instead of concentrating on controlling crime, the police are performing a sort of public-order maintenance that results in the over-representation of impoverished people in criminal justice statistics.[32]

Another problem with these reporting systems is methodological—that is, how the crime rate is calculated. The crime rate may be reasonably accurate in years recent to the last census. But by the time eight or nine years have passed, the population may have grown significantly larger or even shrunk. Some jurisdictions in the Southeast and Southwest grew tremendously in population in a few short years. Crime significantly increased. But because of the outdated population estimate, it appeared to be a less serious problem than it actually was.[33]

## The National Crime Victimization Survey

Conducted annually by the Bureau of Justice Statistics (BJS), the National Crime Victimization Survey (NCVS) is the primary source of criminal victimization data in the United

▼ Census Bureau interviewers use a supplement survey during regular Census data collection to obtain information for the National Crime Victimization Survey, the primary source of criminal victimization data in the United States.

▶ The NCVS gathers information about offenses regardless of whether they are reported to the police.

States. Census Bureau interviewers working with the BJS collect information from individuals age 12 and older in about 38,000 households about the frequency, characteristics, and consequences of crime.[34] This information allows researchers to estimate the likelihood of rape, sexual assault, robbery, assault, theft, household burglary, and motor vehicle theft for the entire U.S. population, as well as for groups such as women, the elderly, minorities, and urban residents.[35] Over the past decade, the NCVS has also begun to record details about hate crimes and identity theft as well as respondent disabilities in order to estimate the amount of victimization of the developmentally disabled.[36] Because it depends on self-reporting, the NCVS, unlike the UCR, excludes homicide, arson, commercial criminal offenses, and offenses against children under age 12 because victims cannot report or reliably report their experiences.[37]

**LO5:**

Discuss the reasons for the creation of the National Crime Victimization Survey.

The value of the NCVS is that it gathers information about offenses regardless of whether they are reported to the police and thus captures valuable information about the dark figure of crime. In questioning a respondent about an incident, the interviewer does not ask whether the respondent was a victim of a specific offense. Instead, the interviewer asks about the details of the offense. Only later are these details analyzed and coded as a specific offense, such as "assault."[38] NCVS researchers do not want respondents to speculate about offenders' motives, only to report the incident as accurately as possible. This means the NCVS defines some offenses slightly differently from the UCR. For example, the UCR defines burglary as the unlawful entry of a structure to commit a felony or theft, but the NCVS defines it as the entry or attempted entry of a residence by a person who had no right to be there. The UCR's definition would require the respondent to assume the offender was there to commit a felony or theft.[39]

The purpose of the NCVS has changed since 1967 when President Lyndon Johnson's Commission on Crime and the Administration of Justice declared a need for a national victimization survey. At a time beset with demonstrations, riots, and civil unrest, the nation had also suffered an explosion in street crime. To many, criminals seemed to be running rampant, victimizing innocent citizens at will. The first victimization survey, called the National Crime Survey, was designed to inform the public about the nature and extent of crime victimization as well as to check the efficacy of the UCR. Today, after several major revisions, the NCVS still performs this task, but crime and the public response to it have changed. For example, although people still fear offenses committed by strangers, we now know **intimate-partner violence** (IPV)—abuse that occurs between two people in a spousal, domestic, or romantic relationship—and offenses perpetrated by acquaintances or relatives comprise a significant amount of crime. Also, financial and information-related offenses have become more visible, especially identity theft, which did not exist in any significant fashion in the late 1960s.[40]

## Problems with the NCVS

As useful as the NCVS is, it has a persistent problem that has to do with time. Respondents are asked to report only on incidents that occurred within the last six months. So respondents must not only recall the incidents and many of the details, but also place the event within the last six months. This is more difficult than it sounds. Respondents may erroneously include incidents that did not happen within the last six months and omit incidents that did. They may completely forget important details or entire incidents, especially victimizations they deem trivial. They may also lie out of embarrassment, the desire to give what they believe

intimate-partner violence (IPV) Abuse that occurs between two people in a spousal, domestic, or romantic relationship.

is a socially acceptable response, distrust of the interviewer, a desire to protect the perpetrator, or lack of interest in answering questions.[41]

Most of the problems are related to under-reporting of victimization; however, some respondents may over-report victimization. Interviewers can discover under-reporting fairly easily by questioning respondents who have reported offenses to the police. Therefore, if the respondent is on record with the police for having reported an incident but does not report that incident to the victimization survey, researchers can safely assume that the respondent is under-reporting victimization. Over-reporting is a different matter, however. If a respondent tells the NCVS interviewer about victimizations that have not been reported to the police, the interviewer cannot know whether the respondent is lying. An Oregon study found that only 48 percent of the offenses respondents claimed to have reported to police were actually listed in police records.[42]

Some NCVS observers point to another issue: "series incidents." Crime occurs more often in some places than others, and some people are victimized more often than others, often repeatedly. If an NCVS respondent reports six or more similar victimizations in a six-month period without providing details about each incident, NCVS interviewers record this as a "series incident" and collect information on only the most recent incident. Sorting out and recording details for what might be dozens of intermittent victimizations can be difficult for the respondent and interviewer. Unfortunately, the NCVS is designed to record separate victimizations, such as a one-time burglary, for example, and not intermittent victimizations that continue for months and years. Therefore, series incidents are excluded from the BJS published annual victimization rates. According to some researchers, this is problematic for two reasons.

1. The national crime tally is severely underestimated. In 1993, for example, about three of every five violent victimizations were excluded from published figures. Integration of these series incidents into the 1993 count would have raised victimization estimates by more than 30 percent.

2. Some groups are more likely to experience series victimization than others. If females are more likely to report series incidents, perhaps such as those related to intimate-partner violence, the level of crime among this population will be underestimated because not all the victimizations will be counted. Routinized victimizations that are often related to sex, age, or impoverishment are omitted from the crime tally and compose a large portion of the dark figure of crime.[43]

A significant amount of research shows that relatively few people experience much of the crime that occurs. The 1993 British Crime Survey reported that 44 percent of the crime happened to only 4 percent of the population, a figure that points to repeat victimizations. Therefore, it is possible that a considerable amount of crime could be addressed if policies or programs helped these groups of repeat victims early in their victimizations.[44]

## Divergence and Convergence: The UCR and the NCVS

The UCR and NCVS do not produce matching crime statistics. As we have discussed, victims have always reported far more offenses in the NCVS than police recorded in the UCR. Criminologists grudgingly accepted this phenomenon and attributed the divergence largely to differences in procedures, definitions, counting rules, and population. For example, the UCR represents a flat count of offenses reported to the police; it is not a sample, so the error is supposedly slight. However, NCVS statistics are based on a sample of offenses reported by a set of randomly selected households from the last six months. Sampling errors, then, are inherent in the NCVS method.[45]

**LO6:**

Discuss why the Uniform Crime Reports and the National Crime Victimization Survey have recently begun to show similar statistics.

Despite the fact that the NCVS has sampling errors and the UCR has none, the surveys' findings began to converge in 1992. In other words, the number of offenses police recorded in the UCR began to more closely match the number of offenses victims reported to the NCVS. This convergence has continued, although some researchers say the surveys are now beginning to diverge again. The phenomena of convergence and divergence puzzle many criminologists, who are of three opinions about the situation.

- *Divergence is to be expected, and it is good.* The UCR and NCVS complement one another. They are conducted in different ways and define crime differently. They take different pictures of crime as would two photographers standing in different places to take pictures of an elephant. The photographs would be different, but both would represent the animal correctly.

- *Divergence is to be expected, and it is bad.* The UCR and NCVS compete. They measure the same thing—the amount of crime in the United States—and it should be possible for both to do so objectively. If the UCR records 101 burglaries in Wabasha, Minnesota, but the NCVS reports 945, then one (or both) of the surveys is flawed and must be corrected. The surveys cannot diverge by that much and both be correct. Some criminologists believe that consistency among the UCR, victimization studies, and self-report studies (discussed below) means social phenomena have been successfully measured, and too much divergence is a sign of something wrong.[46]

- *Convergence is interesting, but why is it occurring now?* That the UCR and the NCVS are showing more similar sta-

▲ Intimate-partner violence offenses such as fights, arguments, and threats with firearms are now often recorded as aggravated assault.

tistics makes a bit more sense—citizens, the media, and policymakers certainly prefer it—but why did convergence begin when it did in the 1990s? Is it an artifact of changes in the surveys? Does this mean the surveys no longer complement each other or that they never did?[47]

Shannan M. Catalano, a U.S. Department of Justice statistician, has attributed much of the convergence to changes in police reporting and in the social perception of crime, especially aggravated assault. The police and the courts, driven by public opinion, are treating aggravated assault far more seriously than in previous decades by upgrading some offenses to aggravated assault and recording others as aggravated assault that, before the 1990s, were not recorded at all.[48] Although victim reporting of aggravated assault to the NCVS has increased 5 percent since 1973, for instance, police recording of the offense in the UCR increased 116 percent from 1973 to 1995.

According to Catalano, one of the main reasons for increased UCR reporting is intimate-partner violence legislation. What the public once considered a private matter between a husband and wife is today a criminal matter of assault

# doubletake
doubletake

## The Assault on Measures of Crime

In the United States, it is easy to take public services for granted, and criminologists are no exception. The UCR, the NIBRS, and the NCVS are public services that cost money to produce and are paid for with public funds like other public venues and structures such as libraries, roads, and bridges. Because these statistical efforts are so critical to our understanding of crime and therefore to public safety, it is easy to assume their budget is safe. However, this is not always the case.

The recent economic recession, combined with the need to allot funds for other public aims such as healthcare reform and defense, has forced the government to cut the budget for many things, including criminological surveys that have been around as long as the 80-year-old UCR and 40-year-old NCVS. In fact, the budget for the 2006 NCVS was cut so deeply and suddenly that it created statistical anomalies the BJS could not reconcile. The report was released with a warning that "national-level estimates were not comparable to estimates based on NCVS data from previous years."[1]

This was the first time in the survey's history that such a setback had occurred. At one point, the federal subcommittee responsible for allotting funds to science

agencies recommended the budget of the BJS be cut by more than two-thirds, which could have caused the NCVS as well as other data-collection efforts to be suspended permanently. After a concerted effort by criminologists and other researchers who explained the importance of the NCVS to subcommittee members, the BJS budget was saved. However, the incident shows how vulnerable science and research budgets are in times of economic uncertainty, and how dispensable their results are considered by the same legislative authorities elected on "get-tough-on-crime" platforms.[2]

[1]Michael Rand and Shannan Catalano, *Criminal Victimization, 2006* (Washington, DC: US Department of Justice, 2007).

[2]Janet L. Lauritsen, "Safeguarding and Improving the Nation's Statistics on Crime and Justice," *The Criminologist* 34, no. 5 (September/October 2009): 1–5).

## THINKING *in* ACTION

1. Which public or government projects do you think are more important than crime surveys and why?

2. What happened to the 2006 NCVS? Why was this event problematic?

or aggravated assault, and the definition of "intimate partner" has broadened to include unmarried and same-sex couples. It is probable that the police are now acting on and recording IPV incidents that they used to handle informally or not at all.[49] Other offenses are also likely contributing to increased recording of aggravated assault through simple "upgrade." Offenses such as fights, arguments, and threats with firearms that once may have been recorded as simple assault are now often recorded as aggravated assault. This increased response to both IPV and other street violence is indicative of changes in the way the police operate and, therefore, in what they record.

Catalano goes on to caution that convergence between the UCR and NCVS has occurred at the same time as a general drop in crime and thus may be an artifact of that drop. The number of offenses reported to police fell a little, whereas the number of offenses not reported to police (as evidenced by NCVS data) fell a lot. It is possible that if, or when, crime begins to rise again, the UCR and NCVS will once again diverge.[50]

### The Future of the UCR and the NCVS

Many criminologists and researchers consider the future of the UCR and the NCVS, as well as other government crime statistical efforts, to be grim. The shift to the NIBRS and the gain and loss of some state programs have brought about troubling gaps in the quality and quantity of UCR data. The NCVS budget has been cut considerably and today conducts a smaller survey than it did a decade ago. Some experts consider both surveys unstable and in need of money to continue producing quality crime data.[51] Unfortunately, the drop in street crime and the advent of other pressing problems, namely terrorism and economic instability, have drawn the attention of citizens, policymakers, and the media away from the problems of crime.[52] Certainly, people are still worried about street crime and complain that their neighborhoods are not as safe as they used to be, although statistically they are much safer. But good news about the crime rate does not grab headlines the way news about a rising crime rate did. See *Doubletake* for more on the problems of underfunding.

Criminologists warn that this halcyon period in the history of crime in the United States will not last. Regardless of whether the UCR and the NCVS diverge or continue to converge, the crime rate is bound to rise again. And when it does, it is possible that the statistical surveys critical to our understanding of crime in the United States will have been crippled beyond repair.[53]

## Think about it

### Remember

Who is responsible for gathering and disseminating the UCR?

### Understand
Explain the rationale for the selection of offenses the UCR measures.

### Apply
State some of the reasons the future of the NCVS may be in peril.

### Analyze
Compare and contrast the strengths and weaknesses of the UCR and the NIBRS.

### Evaluate
Defend the FBI's caution against using the UCR to compare the level of seriousness of crime across jurisdictions.

Assess why NCVS respondents may underreport a victimization.

### Create
Develop a plan for reducing the UCR's limitations.

Formulate reasons that the convergence between the UCR and the NCVS is either desirable or undesirable.

## Self-Report Studies

**Self-report studies**—research based on data that is offered by respondents about themselves—have evolved into a useful alternative to government crime reports, though they have their own limitations and do not give us a comprehensive and clear picture of crime. However, in conjunction with other measures, they play a meaningful role in helping us understand the frequency and seriousness of crime.

**LO7:**
**Outline** the advantages and disadvantages of self-report studies as tools to measure crime.

Self-report studies ask individuals about any illegal activities (from a list) they have committed within a given time period, typically the past six months, year, or two years. The three primary goals are (1) to establish the prevalence and incidence of crime and delinquency within specific populations that better represent the actual incidence of crime and delinquency than government measures, (2) to find out what activities or attitudes correlate with lawbreaking, and (3) to test theories about the causes of crime.[54] One of the reasons criminologists developed self-report studies was to provide an alternative look at the crime picture and reduce reliance

**self-report study** Research based on data that is offered by respondents about themselves.

on government statistics. Researchers decided that reliance on government statistics would limit what they could learn about crime and its causes.

Self-report studies are considered to be better, more adaptable tools for researchers to discover exactly what they need to know, especially if the government data skirt a particular issue. For example, self-report data are considered to be better than police or victimization data for gathering information about so-called victimless crimes such as substance abuse.[55] Self-report studies have greatly contributed to our understanding of what makes people break the law, such as versatility (committing different types of offenses), intermittency (starting and stopping criminal activity), escalation (committing increasingly serious offenses), and age of onset.[56] Self-report studies provide a better picture than the UCR and the NCVS of the demographics and personal characteristics of offenders, which makes self-report studies suitable for testing and developing criminological theory. In particular, Hirschi's social bond theory (which we meet in Chapter 6) was developed on the basis of self-report data.[57]

The first problem to tackle when conducting a self-report study is deciding whom to include. On one hand, it makes sense that those who have been incarcerated would be good sources for self-report studies. On the other hand, if we surveyed only the incarcerated, we would miss collecting data from those who broke the law without detection. Researchers survey several different types of populations to ascertain self-reported criminality. Asking questions of each has its own concerns and issues. But taken together, self-report studies are an extremely useful tool in developing an accurate picture of crime. In criminology, many if not most

self-report studies are carried out with youths, very young adults, and juvenile delinquents. The first reason for this is that it is easier to find groups of young people than groups of adults. Once adults enter the workforce, it is difficult to find groups of them to test. Most non-delinquent youths are in school, and delinquent youths can be found in training schools, group homes, or other youth correctional facilities. The second reason is that youths are more likely to tell the truth about themselves on self-report studies than adults. Adults are more concerned about their social standing, more aware of how they appear to the interviewers, and more cautious about admitting to serious criminal offenses.[58] However, self-reports are still used to estimate the prevalence and frequency of offending among groups such as incarcerated adults.[59]

Self-report studies have been used in criminology since the middle of the 20th century. The first published results appeared in the 1940s, when Austin Porterfield isolated 55 offenses committed by a group of juvenile delinquents and administered a self-report study to a group of college students asking whether they had committed any of the offenses. Porterfield's study uncovered what became a recurring theme in self-report studies on juvenile delinquency: the relationship between social class and delinquency. The college students had committed all of the 55 offenses the delinquents had but not as frequently, and few had come into contact with law enforcement.[60] In the 1950s, James Short and F. Ivan Nye produced another set of landmark self-report studies that also focused on delinquency. Short and Nye's studies were distinguished by their sophistication and, like Porterfield's, examined the relationship between social class and delinquency. Both Porterfield's and Short and Nye's studies, along with many that came later, challenged prevailing criminological theory that assumed a relationship between low social class and delinquency.[61] From a practical standpoint, their studies suggested that the juvenile justice system tended to make determinations of delinquency based partly on class.[62]

Although criminologists expect some level of convergence between self-report studies and government statistics—for example, the demographic characteristics recorded in self-report

◄ Many criminological self-report studies are carried out with youths, very young adults, and juvenile delinquents.

studies are consistent with the UCR measures, as are the rank order of offenses committed by youths—they also expect absolute estimates of crime to be much higher in self-report studies than in government measures. Like government measures, self-report studies also show more commission of property offenses. Finally, they have been known to predict government measures to some extent. In one particular instance, self-report studies reported an increase in juvenile violence before it was recorded in police data, which means that juveniles were self-reporting violent offending before their activities were reflected by increased arrests.[63]

## Problems with Self-Report Studies

Self-report studies are designed and executed by academics for research purposes; for the most part, researchers seem satisfied with their performance. However, like government crime measures, self-report studies have some inherent weaknesses that prevent complete accuracy. The first and perhaps most glaring is that like the NCVS, self-report studies rely on samples and not on exact counts. A delinquency self-report study will not include every youth in the United States. Researchers sample a group of youths, then extrapolate data from that sample. Whenever a sample is used, sampling errors are likely.

Two properties important to all research studies are reliability and validity. Briefly, **reliability** is the consistency of a study, or how successfully it can be repeated and still provide similar results. For example, a self-report study that gets similar answers from several similar groups of youths about the amount of vandalism they have perpetrated in the last six months is considered reliable. **Validity** describes whether a study is measuring what it is designed to measure. If most of the youths decide to lie about how often they commit vandalism, then the study is not very valid. Criminologists have decided that although the reliability of self-report studies is generally acceptable, validity is more difficult to ascertain because there is nothing to measure respondents' answers against. As in victimization studies, researchers must trust that participants are telling the truth.[64]

Self-report studies are also problematic when quantifying some types of offending and offenders. The studies have been criticized for excluding or under-representing repeat offenders and youths who tend to commit serious delinquency as well as for measuring little more than non-serious delinquency and property offending.[65] Trivial and frequent offending tends to be over-reported—imagine the teen who wants to appear tough to the interviewers—but very serious offending, such as homicide, is under-reported, presumably due to respondents' fear of being caught.[66]

The methodology of, or procedures of researching, self-report studies has grown increasingly sophisticated. Now, we will review three of the more developed studies that have the state-of-the-art resources necessary to assess the frequency and seriousness of crime as reported by those who commit it.

## The National Youth Survey Family Study

Initiated in 1976, the National Youth Survey was one of the first and most impressive self-report studies to assess delinquency. Between 1977 and 1981, researchers interviewed 1,725 adolescents from ages 11 to 17 and one parent in their homes on an annual basis and between 1981 and 1995 on a two- or three-year basis. The study continues to this day; although some of the participants have become unavailable for various reasons, more than 90 percent remain in the sample.

The National Youth Survey has evolved into a more comprehensive data-collection effort called the National Youth Survey Family Study. One of its more interesting aspects is the addition of a genetic component. In addition to asking questions about delinquent and criminal involvement, researchers collected the participants' DNA to see whether there was any interaction of genes, the environment, and antisocial behavior. Specifically, they were looking for a connection between the MAOA gene (see Chapter 5 for details about this gene) and aggressive behavior, which had previously been shown in both mice and humans. In this study, the MAOA gene did not show a correlation with aggressive behavior, but researchers continue to use this expansive database to look for other measures of a genetic influence on behavior.

A number of other studies using the National Youth Survey database have provided a wealth of information about the conditions under which delinquency occurs. Researchers have looked at the relationships between crime and gender, race, and social class as well as the influence of drug use on antisocial behavior.[67] The strengths of this study are twofold. First, because it used a scientific and systematic sampling procedure, it allows for generalization to the entire nation based upon interviews with only 1,725 respondents. Second, the study is a **longitudinal** research effort—that is, it has followed the respondents throughout their adult lives or a significant proportion of their lives. This allows researchers to ascertain the stability of their respondents' antisocial behavior in ways not possible when looking at interview data based on only one year.

## Monitoring the Future

The Monitoring the Future study is an ambitious effort to assess the values, attitudes, and behaviors of youths. Each year, researchers survey approximately 50,000 students in 8th, 10th, and 12th grade and follow up on a sample of those who were studied in previous years. The results are useful to government policymakers—for example, to monitor progress to-

---

**reliability** Refers to how successfully research can be repeated and provide similar results.

**validity** A statistical property that describes how well a study is measuring what it is designed to measure.

**longitudinal** A type of survey that follows respondents throughout their lives or a significant proportion of their lives.

▲ A successful shift from high school to college or work can affect a young person's likelihood of breaking the law.

ward national health goals and assess trends in substance use and abuse among adolescents and young adults—and are used routinely in the White House Strategy on Drug Abuse.[68]

The study has a number of advantages over previous self-report studies in that it is both longitudinal and repeated each year with new respondents. This feature allows researchers to assess trends in two ways. First, as the youths move through 12th grade and beyond, it is reasonable to expect that their delinquent and criminal behavior patterns will change. By doing follow-up studies on those previously surveyed, researchers are able to track such changes. Second, the survey's methodology allows researchers to see whether new **cohorts**—groups of people who share statistical or demographic characteristics—of youngsters are reporting different levels of delinquency and crime than previous cohorts. In this way the study is able to look at four levels of change:

- *Changes in particular years reflected across all age groups.* Changes in the economy, such as a recession, could affect all young people across the nation regardless of what grade they are in. When jobs are scarce, parents are unemployed, and recreational programs are denied funding, youngsters feel the economic effects regardless of their age or location.

**cohort** A group of people who share statistical or demographic characteristics.

- *Developmental changes that show up consistently for all panels.* Moving through the life course can affect delinquency and crime. Although these developmental changes may not be identical for each age group, a longitudinal study can reveal the pressures to commit or desist from crime.

- *Consistent differences among class cohorts through the life cycle.* One of the reasons for selecting youngsters of different ages for this type of research is to reveal how self-reported delinquency can differ by age cohort. For instance, in any particular year when 12th-graders are graduating from high school, they may have a better chance of getting a job if unemployment is low. Contrasting this opportunity with years when the unemployment rate is high helps correct for the economic environments into which adolescents graduate, which can affect their rate of delinquency and later criminal offending.

- *Changes linked to different types of environments (high school, college, employment) or role transitions (leaving home, marriage, parenthood).* Making the transition from high school to college or the work environment can affect the propensity for breaking the law. By tracking the youths as they move through their high school years, researchers can discern how changes in their status as well as in their age are reflected in their self-reported delinquency.[69]

The Monitoring the Future study has continued for more than 30 years, adding questions that reflect changes in both society and delinquency. Questions about crack cocaine were added in 1986, about crystal methamphetamine in 1990, and about ecstasy in 1996. Perhaps the most important and significant feature of the Monitoring the Future surveys is the way researchers have refined their questionnaires to make self-reported delinquency a more robust and valid way of measuring crime.

## The National Survey on Drug Use and Health

Conducted since 1971, the National Survey on Drug Use and Health conducts annual interviews with more than 70,000 randomly selected individuals age 12 and older.[70] Some might legitimately question the expense of doing so many interviews each year. This survey is an example of how technology has allowed researchers to focus on a large sample scattered throughout the United States. It uses a combination of computer-assisted personal interviewing in which interviewers ask questions face-to-face in respondents' homes and audio computer-assisted self-interviewing for confidential questions regarding admitted drug use. It is believed this latter technique draws more honest answers about drug use because there is no personal interaction.

The National Survey on Drug Use and Health is a **cross-sectional survey**—research in which different individuals are studied during each research period—as opposed to a longitudinal survey. This means it surveys different individuals each year and makes no effort to track specific individuals from year to year. The cross-sectional method allows the survey of a larger number of individuals, though without being able to track changes in their behavior.

# Think about it

## Understand

Explain why self-report studies that use longitudinal data can answer different questions than cross-sectional studies.

## Apply

Illustrate how researchers use self-report studies to develop criminological theories.

## Analyze

Critique the methodology of self-report studies in terms of reliability and validity.

## Evaluate

Review the development of self-report studies.

## Create

Hypothesize about why some individuals are included in self-report studies while others are not.

# Putting It All Together

Criminological theory is not developed in a vacuum. Theorists do not just come up with ideas from their armchairs and send them out into the world for other criminologists to think about and students to memorize. To be useful, theories must accurately describe some aspect of how and why the law is constructed and broken, or who is breaking it, or how society reacts to these activities. The development of sound criminological theory depends on the accurate reporting and measurement of crime. Just as good crime data help criminal justice administrators plan budgets and programs, they also help criminologists develop and test hypotheses and theories. This is important because many programs are based on criminological theories and are implemented to utilize and test their ideas. However, if the crime data are not accurate, then everything based on the data—hypotheses, theories, programs, and criminal justice administrative efforts—is weakened as well.

**LO8:** Explain how the reporting and measuring of crime can affect the development of criminological theory and public policy.

In *The Mismeasure of Crime,* authors Clayton J. Mosher, Terance D. Miethe, and Dretha M. Phillips consider several criminological theories (which we will study in detail later in this text) and point out how their accuracy depends on the accuracy of crime data. Without delving too deeply into the particular theories at this point, here are three examples.

- *Opportunity theories of victimization.* According to opportunity theories, the chances of victimization are related to an individual's lifestyle, amount of routine exposure to offenders, attractiveness as a crime target, and availability of those who can protect the individual from victimization. The correct assessment of these attributes and their frequency depends on accurate data from demographic and victimization surveys. However, if the victimization surveys are inaccurate—which can be caused by anything from respondents' faulty memories to the survey's rules for counting victimizations—then the validity of opportunity theories of victimization must be questioned.

- *Biological theories of sex differences in violent crime.* Some theories of crime seek biological reasons to explain why most crime, especially most violent crime, is committed by males. However, for this search to be valid, sex differences in the commission of violent and antisocial behavior must be consistent across time, culture, and geography. In other words, to assert that males are more violent and commit the most crime, similar statistics showing this must be collected from different years, places, and cultures. Although some nations have highly developed sta-

**cross-sectional survey** Research in which different individuals are studied during each research period.

tistical collection efforts, others do not, so wide-ranging, accurate numbers on sex differences in violent offending are not available.

- *Social disorganization theories.* These theories consider crime as the product of neighborhoods or jurisdictions that are impoverished and have transient populations, poor social and physical infrastructure, and lack of economic opportunity. Data that show more arrests of people of low socioeconomic status could certainly be explained by social disorganization theories, but what if the police are simply biased toward the arrest of impoverished, disadvantaged people? If people from higher socioeconomic classes are arrested less often because of police bias, even if they commit the same amount of crime, then it is faulty to blame disadvantaged neighborhoods for a high crime rate. For the sake of argument, if crime-data collection focused on white-collar or corporate offenses, then advantaged neighborhoods could just as well be considered a major source of crime. Thus, the focus of crime-data collection on street crime is a major problem for sociological theories that depend heavily on police data sources.[71]

So, how do researchers deal with flaws they know are likely to occur in their data? In some cases, researchers just do not use the data. One researcher suggested that county-level UCR data, which tend to be weak and inaccurate, are so small and difficult to work with, they do not produce a quality study, even though statistical techniques could correct some disadvantages.[72]

In a self-report study, gang members were answering questions about their recent drug use. This study posed two major validity issues: First, were the self-selected "gang members" actually members of gangs, and second, were they telling the truth about their drug use? The second issue was easy to check with urinalysis tests. The first item, however, was impossible to confirm. There is no scientific test to prove an individual's gang membership. So what did the researchers do? They used the educated guess. One-fourth of the juvenile arrestees self-reported past or current gang membership, a number the researchers decided was too high to be entirely inaccurate. Certainly, some of the respondents would lie about being in a gang in order to seem tough but not as many as one-fourth. The researchers also found that two other studies reported 18 percent and 28 percent of respondents admitting to gang membership. So, although they allowed for the likelihood of error in their survey, on the whole it appeared to draw a fairly accurate picture of the amount of drug usage in gangs.[73]

In yet another study using self-reports, this time on the effect of abusive families on delinquency, nearly half the youths who had been arrested during the interview period did not report any arrests, and nearly one-quarter who had no arrest records reported being arrested. How could this data, so much of which was poorly recalled and falsely

▼ Social disorganization theories consider crime as the product of neighborhoods that are impoverished and have transient populations, poor social and physical infrastructure, and lack of economic opportunity.

reported, be useful? The researchers admitted that if the survey set out to learn about delinquent patterns *within* individuals, the data would have been problematic because so many individuals were incorrectly reporting their arrests or lack of arrests. However, the researchers were looking for information about delinquent patterns among a group of individuals. In this case, the data confirmed that abusive families in impoverished neighborhoods produce more juvenile arrestees.[74]

The four major sources of crime data discussed in this chapter—the UCR, the NIBRS, the NCVS, and self-report studies—provide a complementary picture of crime. Each data collection effort offers a particular view of crime. Taken together, they provide a more coherent view of the nature and extent of crime. The UCR and the NIBRS represent police records of offenses and arrests; the NCVS utilizes victims' experiences; and researchers' self-report studies look closely at the offending patterns of individuals and groups by asking them to describe their personal experiences in committing crime.

# Think about it

## Understand

Describe how researchers deal with flaws that occur in their data.

## Analyze

Analyze how criminological theory depends upon the accurate measurement of crime.

# Summary

**LO1:** **Identify and explain the differences between the three major ways of measuring crime.**
- The measurement of crime is important and challenging. Government statistics are only a representation of the true amount of crime. The unknown amount, the dark figure of crime, includes the vast number of offenses that are not reported and those that are reported and not recorded
- At least three issues affect the level of crime recording: the level of public confidence in the police; the possible and/or perceived disproportionate enforcement of laws against the impoverished and people of color; and methodological difficulties, such as the way the crime rate is calculated.
- The three major government efforts to measure crime in the United States are the FBI's Uniform Crime Reports (UCR), the National Incident-Based Reporting System (NIBRS), and the National Crime Victimization Survey (NCVS).
- The development of sound criminological theory depends on the accurate reporting and measurement of crime. If the crime data are not accurate, then everything based on the data—hypotheses, theories, programs, and criminal justice administrative efforts—is also weakened.

**LO2:** **Summarize the advantages and limitations of the Uniform Crime Reports.**
- The UCR collects data from more than 17,000 jurisdictions to provide statistics for the administration of the criminal justice system. The most comprehensive crime data collection effort in the nation, it has four significant limitations: It applies the hierarchy rule (reporting only the most serious offense if more than one is committed); it records only offenses reported to the police; it focuses on street crime; and its data are incomplete.

**LO3:** **Identify police motivations for under- or over-reporting crime.**
- A law enforcement agency may under-report offenses to present a better crime rate and improve the picture of the work it does. An agency may over-report crime to procure more funding or resources.

**LO4:** **Compare and contrast the National Incident-Based Reporting System and the Uniform Crime Reports.**
- The NIBRS was designed as an improvement upon the UCR and follows many of the same rules but is far more detailed. The NIBRS collects data on each single incident and arrest for 46 specific offenses.

**LO5:** Discuss the reasons for the creation of the National Crime Victimization Survey.

- The NCVS is conducted annually by the BJS and provides information about victims, offenders, and otherwise unreported crime within the past six months. Its shortcomings are related to respondent reporting. Respondents may erroneously include incidents that did not happen, omit incidents that did, forget incidents or important details, or lie.

**LO6:** Discuss why the Uniform Crime Reports and the National Crime Victimization Survey have recently begun to show similar statistics.

- The UCR and NCVS do not produce matching crime statistics and, until recently, produced divergent ones. Their findings began to converge from 1992 until very recently, although some researchers say they are beginning to diverge again.

**LO7:** Outline the advantages and disadvantages of self-report studies as tools to measure crime.

- Self-report studies are designed and executed by academics for research purposes. Their goals are to (1) establish the prevalence and incidence of crime and delinquency within specific populations, (2) find out what correlates with lawbreaking, and (3) test theories about the causation of crime.

- Self-report studies do not use absolute counts, which makes sampling errors likely. Two properties that are important when discussing self-report studies are "reliability" and "validity." Three highly developed self-report studies are the National Youth Survey Family Study, Monitoring the Future, and the National Survey on Drug Use and Health.

**LO8:** Explain how the reporting and measuring of crime can affect the development of criminological theory and public policy.

- Many criminologists and researchers consider the future of government crime statistics to be problematic. The shift to the NIBRS and the gain and loss of some state programs have caused gaps in the quality and quantity of UCR data. The NCVS has sustained deep budget cuts and reduced the size of its survey pool.

# Questions

1. What are the three major methods of measuring crime?
2. Why would an individual not report a criminal offense?
3. What are the strengths and limitations of the UCR?
4. Why does the FBI caution against using the UCR to compare the frequency of crime between jurisdictions?
5. How is the NIBRS an improvement over the UCR?
6. How does the NCVS differ from the UCR?
7. What are the methodological limitations of the NCVS?
8. Is it reasonable to expect individuals to accurately report the offenses they have committed?
9. How have self-report studies been improved to get a more accurate picture of crime?
10. What are the differences between longitudinal surveys and cross-sectional surveys?

# 3

# Victims
# of Crime

# what's inside

**As you read, keep in mind these learning objectives:**

**LO1:** Define victimology.

**LO2:** Understand macro-victimization and micro-victimization.

**LO3:** Discuss the problems of victimization.

**LO4:** Describe the special victimization problems of children, the elderly, and the disabled.

**LO5:** Identify the reasons for rendering better assistance to victims.

**LO6:** Analyze the ways in which the criminal justice system tries to satisfy victims' need for justice.

The origin of the word "victim" is the Latin *victima,* which means an animal destined for sacrifice. This ancient definition perhaps puts the plight of crime victims in sharpest perspective. The picture of a **victim**—a person who suffers a criminal offense—as an innocent with no control over his or her past, present, or future and whose fate is destined, has best matched the criminological and criminal justice treatment of victims, at least until very recently.

Until the Middle Ages, victims (or their families) were expected to deal with their victimizers themselves. The philosophy of *lex talionis,* or an eye for an eye, is a legacy of this practice. Gradually, however, as Western systems of criminal justice matured, the state became the aggrieved party; the victim, cut out of the justice process, became merely an element of the criminal act, much like evidence or witnesses.[1] In the United States, the role of the victim in crime was ignored for decades until the 1940s. Then criminologists, seeking to understand what early researcher Hans von Hentig called the "criminal–victim dyad," began looking to victims as much as to offenders to fathom crime.

## The Study of Victimology

**Victimology,** the study of the various types of harm people suffer as a result of crime, began when researchers realized fully half of the victim–offender dyad was being overlooked. Victimology research began with the study of rape victims, those who contributed to their victimization, the socially weak such as the very young or old, recent immigrants, and the mentally ill. As the crime rate rose throughout the 1960s, the President's Commission on Law Enforcement and the

**victim** In criminology, a person who suffers a criminal offense.

**victimology** The study of the effects of crime on victims.

Administration of Justice asked criminologists to study victimization more thoroughly to help law enforcement catch offenders and prevent offenses. Since then, other goals have come to include reducing victims' suffering, improving the criminal justice system's responses, and restoring victims' mental and physical health and financial resources. Some criminologists assert that offenders themselves are often victims of class and economic differences. However, victimology has lately concentrated on direct victims of crime who through little or no fault of their own have been targeted by an offender.[2]

**LO1:**

Define victimology.

Victimologists study the effects of crime on victims. They do not directly assist victims, which is the task of legal and criminal justice professionals as well as physical and mental health professionals. Instead, victimologists research:

- victims' plight
- the effects of physical and psychological injuries and financial losses
- public reaction to victims
- the way criminal justice professionals deal with victims[3]

The study of victimization has its critics. Some scholars point to a growing culture of victimhood in which everyone is a victim of everything: themselves, others, and society. Sociologist Joel Best identified a "victim industry" in which a rapidly expanding mental health field continues to identify classes of victims and pointed out that society responds to this because identifying victims is an easy way to deal with broad social injustices.[4] The merits and criticisms of this search for victims are subject to debate. However, in this chapter, we will adhere to the basic motivations of victimology: to understand the effects of crime on its immediate victims.

◀ The infamous 19th-century feud between the Hatfield and McCoy families of Appalachia produced many offenders and victims.

interviewed 42,093 households and 77,852 individuals twice that year.[5]

Violent and property crime rates remained low for 2008, and victim characteristics were unchanged. Males, blacks, and people age 24 and younger tend to be victimized in violent offenses at higher rates than females, whites, and people over 25.[6]

## Think about it

### Understand

What is victimology?

### Evaluate

Assess the argument that there is a "victim industry."

## The Extent of Victimization

One of the first things we must know in the study of victims is who the victims are, how they are victimized, who victimizes them, and what they lose. The Uniform Crime Reports from the Federal Bureau of Investigation (FBI) records information about criminal offenses, arrestees, and clearances, but it records less about the victims besides what is reflected in the offense statistics. We will not find statistics describing victims' families, the physical and psychological effects of victimization, or how the criminal justice system processes the cases. The National Crime Victimization Survey (NCVS) produced by the Bureau of Justice Statistics (BJS) and the Centers for Disease Control and Prevention (CDC) capture deeper victimization statistics.

**LO2:**

Understand macro-victimization and micro-victimization.

The NCVS collects statistics on non-fatal violent and property victimizations against people age 12 and older and measures rape, sexual assault, robbery, aggravated assault, simple assault, household burglary, motor vehicle theft, and personal theft. Unlike the UCR, the NCVS records offenses that are both reported and not reported to police and looks at only a sample of the U.S. population. In 2007, the NCVS

- *Sex.* Men are victims of violent offenses, robbery, and aggravated and simple assault at higher rates than women, whereas women are more likely than men to be victims of rape or sexual assault. Women are most often victimized by someone they know; slightly more than half of males are victimized by strangers except in cases of simple assault. Women are about eight times more likely than men to be victims of intimate partner violence.[7] (We discuss violent offenses in detail later in this chapter.)

- *Race.* Blacks are more likely than people of other races to be victims of robbery and aggravated and simple assault. In 2007, survey respondents reporting to be of two or more races were victims of violence at higher rates than people reporting to be of one race. As of 2007, no significant differences were reported in the overall violent victimization rates of Hispanics and non-Hispanics.

- *Age.* As you can see in Figure 3.1, the age of violent victimization drops steadily throughout adulthood. Although the elderly are perhaps the most fearful of victimization, statistically they are the least likely to be victimized, as opposed to the very young, who tend to be the least afraid but are the most likely to be victimized.

- *Property offenses.* Property offense rates were higher for low-income than for higher-income households. Households earning less than $7,500 per year experienced property crime rates about 1.5 times higher than households earning $75,000 or more per year.[8]

- *Firearms.* In 2008, 7 percent of all violent offenses were committed with a firearm. Offenders used firearms in 5 percent of assaults and 24 percent of robberies.[9]

- *Reporting to the police.* Violent offenses are more likely to be reported to police than property offenses. In 2008, nearly half of all violent victimizations were reported as opposed to 40 percent of property offenses. Robbery was reported more often than rape, sexual assault, and simple assault; violent offenses against black women were more likely to be

## Figure **3.1**  Rate of Violent Victimization in the United States by Age, 2008

Note that after age 24, the rate of violent victimization drops steadily.

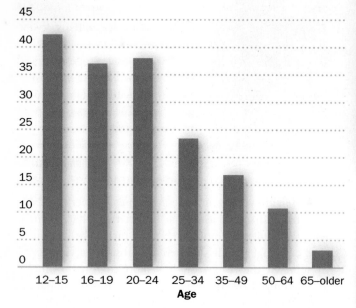

**Rate of Violent Crime**

*Source:* Michael R. Rand, *Criminal Victimization, 2008* (Washington, DC: U.S. Department of Justice Office of Justice Programs Bureau of Justice Statistics, 2008), 4, http://bjs.ojp .usdoj.gov/content/pub/pdf/cv08.pdf.

▲ The National Violent Death Reporting System seeks to identify risk factors for multiple homicides and to get a better picture of victim-perpetrator relationships.

reported than those against women of other races. Motor vehicle theft was the most reported property offense.[10]

■ *Economics.* In 2008, the average robbery victim lost $1,315, whereas individual larceny-theft victims lost about $925.[11] About $2,079 worth of goods and cash was taken per burglary, and arson victims lost about $16,015 per offense.[12] In 2007, consumers reported a total loss of $1.2 billion to the Federal Trade Commission, and victim compensation programs allocated $453 million.[13]

Reporting on victim characteristics will likely improve. In 2002, the CDC established the National Violent Death Reporting System, which collects data on violent deaths from sources including death certificates, police reports, medical examiner and coroner reports, and crime laboratories. This system seeks to identify risk factors for multiple homicides or homicides-suicides by linking records from different sources and to get a better picture of victim-perpetrator relationships.[14]

## Macro-Victimization

When we think of crime victims, we tend to think of individuals. **Macro-victimization,** on the other hand, considers

**macro-victimization** The harm caused to masses of people by large-scale criminal offenses.

very large masses of people as victims of large-scale criminal offenses. We can divide this new field into three broad categories: terrorism, large-scale corporate and environmental crime, and crimes against humanity.

Macro-victimization is different from street-crime victimization. Two of the categories, crimes against humanity and terrorism, are related to war. The other, corporate and environmental victimization, represents offenses so large and complicated that they are difficult to imagine as crime in the traditional sense. It is easy to imagine a robber pointing a gun at another person as victimization. It is not easy to read hundreds of pages of financial documents or ferret out who on the board of directors knew what and when so we can understand who was victimized and how. However, the size and complexity of a destructive event does not make it any less of a criminal offense. Sometimes it is not useful to imagine a victim as a single person victimized by a street crime as defined by the FBI. Victims comprise groups of unrelated people, children, the elderly, the disabled, civilians living with the horrors of war, and their families.

## Terrorism Victimization

Author William Gibson wrote, "Terrorism as we ordinarily understand it is innately media-related."[15] Because terrorists seek to produce panic and gain media notice for their cause, their victims are typically civilians and occupy an especially critical position in the offender–victim dyad. Early on, adult victims of terrorism and political violence suffer shock, anxiety, confusion, sorrow, grief, survivors' guilt, and other forms of psychological distress. Later, they suffer increased anxiety, depression, phobias, reduced sense of safety, post-traumatic stress, and increased tobacco, alcohol, and drug usage.[16] Experts are still studying how best to help them, although trauma counseling seems no more therapeutic than simply talking to friends and family, according to researchers.[17] Some governments have set up legal means for victims to recover financially, even if all their psychological wounds cannot be addressed.

**Victimization in the United States**    The United States is new to providing for victims of domestic and international terrorism primarily because such attacks are relatively recent. U.S. government agencies have set up special offices and victims' funds.

- *Justice Department's Office for Victims of Crime Terrorism and International Victims Unit.* This agency, among other activities, administers the International Terrorism Victims Compensation Program, which allows U.S. citizens who are victims of international terrorism to apply to a single federal office for compensation.[18]

- *FBI's Office for Victim Assistance, Terrorism Victim Assistance Unit.* This office provides emergency assistance to injured victims and families of victims killed in domestic and international attacks.

- *September 11th Victim Compensation Fund.* Although now closed, this special fund represented an unprecedented attempt to financially assist U.S. victims of terrorism and their families. (In comparison, victims of the 1995 bombing of the Murrah Federal Building in Oklahoma City received only a few thousand dollars each from the federal government.[19]) Victims of the September 11 attacks received payments in exchange for an agreement not to sue the airlines and other defendants. The fund handled 97 percent of its claims within 33 months and paid $7 billion to survivors and the families of the deceased. Perhaps the biggest criticism of the fund was that individual payouts were based on the amount the victim would have made if his or her life had continued. Therefore, high wage-earners received more money than low wage-earners.[20]

**Victimization in Other Nations**    Almost 50,000 people worldwide were killed or injured in terrorist attacks in

▼ The September 11th Victim Compensation Fund rendered financial assistance to American victims of terrorism and their families.

## Figure **3.2**  Deaths by Category of Victim, 2008

**There were 15,765 deaths worldwide due to terrorism in 2008. Children were counted twice as both children and civilians.**

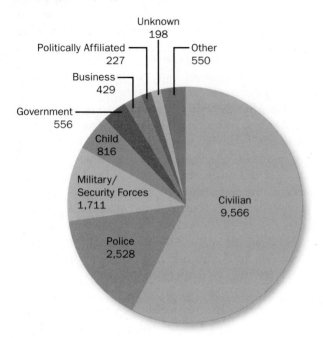

*Source:* National Counterterrorism Center, *2008 Report on Terrorism,* April 30, 2009, 23, http://wits-classic.nctc.gov/Reports.do?f=crt2008nctcannexfinal.pdf.

2008.[21] Some countries have been politically unstable for so long that few of their citizens can remember a stable government, and terrorism has become a fact of life. In this section, we will briefly consider how victimization occurs, characteristics of the victims, and forms of victim assistance, if any. Outside the United States, children and civilians are disproportionately terrorism victims (see Figure 3.2). In 2008, despite a decline in the overall number of terrorism victims, the number of child victims rose by 10 percent.[22]

A typology offered by Jelena Jauković, who studied the 1990s Balkan wars in the former Yugoslavia, described the types of groups that victimized civilians during that conflict. This typology is applicable to civil wars and some domestic terrorism, especially that which occurs in developing countries.

- *Organized armies.* Armies force massive, often unexpected, movements of civilians, who must abandon all, including food, clean water, and sanitation.
- *Paramilitary forces.* These often makeshift forces act on their own accord and terrorize others with robbery, murder, rape, kidnapping, blackmail, and threats. Sometimes these forces act in the name of politically, racially, or culturally similar citizens who do not wish to participate but are later victimized or punished for the paramilitaries' activities.

- *Criminal groups.* These groups might have little or no interest in the conflict but take advantage of it to traffic in weapons, narcotics, human beings, or anything that offers profit or material advantage.[23]

The 2005 Council of Europe guidelines for the treatment of terrorism victims basically held that European states should ensure that victims and their families receive emergency assistance; medical, psychological, social, and material assistance; access to the law; fair, appropriate, and timely compensation; protection of privacy and family life; and protection of dignity and security. Finally, the granting of services should not depend on whether the terrorists are identified, captured, or convicted.[24]

The reality of assistance to terrorism victims in other nations is not as systematic or fair. Depending on the nation, terrorism victims may receive anything from good assistance to no assistance. Victims in Western nations may receive money from public and private organizations as well as counseling and other assistance. Unfortunately, in nations where terrorism occurs almost daily, international organizations such as the Red Cross may offer counseling, but financial reparations or legal redress is unlikely.

## Corporate and Environmental Victimization

The true number and characteristics of victims of corporate and environmental offenses cannot be known because some of the offenses are so wide-ranging in terms of geography and time that they may affect whole nations, or even continents or hemispheres, for decades. A particularly serious oil spill affects not only the health of the local people, animals, and plants, but also whole industries such as fishing, tourism, and anything else that depends on a healthy environment. To generate an accurate picture of this type of victimization, we will look at four modern examples of corporate and environmental offenses: the Exxon Valdez disaster, Amazon rainforest deforestation, the Enron scandal, and the Bernard Madoff Ponzi scheme.

**The Exxon Valdez Disaster**  Just after midnight March 24, 1989, the oil tanker Exxon Valdez struck Bligh Reef in Prince William Sound, Alaska, and spilled more than 11 million gallons of crude oil. The spill not only disrupted the region's commercial fishing industry, but also endangered 10 million birds and hundreds of sea otters, harbor porpoises, sea lions, and whales.[25] Permanently affecting what were some of the richest fishing waters in the United States, the spill covered 11,000 square miles of ocean, damaged 1,300 miles of coastline, and killed half a million seabirds almost immediately as well as thousands of mammals. Billions of salmon and herring eggs, the lifeblood of the fishing industry, were destroyed.[26]

Exxon, which was indicted for felony and misdemeanor violations of federal law, pled guilty to misdemeanor charges under the federal Migratory Bird Act, the Clean Water Act, and the Refuse Act; it paid a criminal fine of $125 million and $900 million in civil damages.[27] CEO Lawrence Rawl admitted that ship captain Joseph Hazelwood had been drunk. Although the company had ordered Hazelwood into rehab, management had allowed him back at work despite numerous reports of relapse.[28]

Research has revealed that the oil has remained toxic and that complete dispersal will require more than a century.[29] In 2007, the National Oceanic and Atmospheric Administration estimated that 26,000 gallons of oil remain on the coastline.[30] Prior to the disaster, herring had been commercial fishers' main catch; however, the herring fishery was so damaged that as of 2009 the season had been called off for 16 of the last 18 years.[31]

Although Exxon was ordered to pay $5 billion in punitive damages in 1994, that amount was halved in 2006; two years later the U.S. Supreme Court cut it to $500 million, which is roughly four days' worth of Exxon Mobil Corporation's quarterly profits.[32] That payout, which was to be shared by the 32,000 commercial fishers, food processors, and Alaskan natives whose livelihoods were directly affected

by the spill, lowered the average individual punitive damages award from $75,000 to $15,000. In cutting the punitive damages in 2008, the Supreme Court ruled that the spill was an accident.[33]

**Amazon Rainforest Deforestation**   A complicated issue, the logging and clearing of land in South America's Amazon rainforest may be one of the most destructive artificial environmental events in history. The rainforest is home to one-fifth of the world's plant and animal species, absorbs nearly 2 billion metric tons of carbon dioxide a year, and is responsible for 20 percent of the world's flow of fresh water.[34] Each year, an area of forest larger than the state of Massachusetts is cut down. The countries within the Amazon ecosystem are aware of the value of the rainforest to themselves and the world as well as the consequences of its destruction to indigenous tribes. Some of these countries, with help from the international community, have sought to make unlicensed deforestation a criminal offense.

With more than half of the Amazon within Brazil, that nation has probably struggled the most with the treatment of deforestation as a criminal offense.[35] Although the Brazilian government appears to be taking the criminalization of deforestation seriously, local politicians often ignore the problem to gain votes from wealthy, powerful soy and cattle farmers.[36] Armed land squatters, who illegally clear land to plant crops to sell to international companies, often use impoverished and illiterate slave labor to clear the land. Lured from rural areas, the laborers are transported to remote areas, then told they owe a debt. When their work is done, the laborers are sent to another plantation where the cycle begins again. Sometimes, their captors simply kill them.[37]

The scope of victimization for environmental offenses committed within the Amazon rainforest is quite broad. It ranges from indigenous peoples who are forced from their lands or enslaved for work, to the rainforest nations, which are slowly losing their most valuable natural resource, to the world, which is losing a key actor in the global environmental balance.

**The Enron Scandal**   In Chapter 11, we detail the offenses committed by the officers of the energy company Enron. But what about the victims? The criminal offenses of the company's officers led to the firing of 20,000 employees, many of whom worked for businesses Enron had purchased.[38] All of those who worked directly for the company lost not only their jobs, but also thousands of dollars in pensions. Even employees of companies that Enron did not own suffered: 28,000 people lost their jobs at Arthur Andersen, Enron's audit firm that was also indicted in the scandal.[39]

In cases of corporate and white-collar offending, the criminal justice system can send individuals to prison—as it

◀ An area of forest larger than the state of Massachusetts is cut down each year in the Amazon.

did in the case of Enron's corporate officers—and force businesses to make financial restitution. For example, the Securities and Exchange Commission's settlement with two banks close to Enron's wrongdoing—Citigroup and J.P. Morgan Chase—included a payment of $255 million into an Enron victims' fund.[40] Enron's former chief executive officer, Jeffrey Skilling, was ordered to pay $45 million in restitution.[41] Victims were also allowed to speak at Skilling's initial sentencing and resentencing in 2009.[42] Unfortunately, restitution money probably will not cover the years' worth of pensions that some employees built up: At least $1 billion in employee retirement funds were decimated.[43] In sentencing Skilling, U.S. District Court Judge Sim Lake said, "His crimes have imposed on hundreds if not thousands of people a life sentence of poverty."[44]

**The Bernard Madoff Scheme**    In March 2009, hedge fund manager and NASDAQ stock exchange executive Bernard Madoff pleaded guilty to a complicated **Ponzi scheme** in which he defrauded about 5,000 clients of at least $65 billion. Many people lost their life savings as a result of a scheme in which Madoff took money from new investors to pay regular, high returns to earlier investors. In June 2009, the 71-year-old Madoff was sentenced to 150 years in prison and restitution payments of about $171 billion.[45]

Currently, investigators are still trying to work out exactly when he began the scheme (possibly as early as the 1970s), exactly how much was taken (at least $65 billion), and who was in on it.[46] Investigators are still trying to seize as much of Madoff's assets as possible and split the proceeds of their sale among the victims, which number about 7,000 individuals and institutions.[47] However, investigators so far have located only about $1 billion.[48] To help Ponzi scheme victims, the Internal Revenue Service announced that victims could deduct up to 95 percent of their losses.[49]

Madoff's scheme sheds new light on the effects of financial crime, which typically does not get the media attention that street crime does because the process of committing a financial offense is often difficult to understand and complicated to explain. A street crime, in contrast, is visceral and dramatic. Investigating a financial offense can be a tedious struggle. Although corporate crime and street crime are considered differently by both the public and the criminal justice system, the rash of corporate offenses in recent years may change that. A robbery victim may lose some cash and a sense of safety, but financial crime victims may lose all of their money. Forensic psychologist J. Reid Meloy said that offenders like Madoff share psychopathic qualities with serial killers such as Ted Bundy, taking fi-

> **Ponzi scheme**  A financial offense in which the offender accepts money for investments from clients but uses it to pay returns to earlier investors instead of investing the money.

▲ It is possible that extreme white-collar offenders like Bernard Madoff share psychopathic qualities with serial killers.

nancial lives instead of committing physical murder and showing little remorse.[50]

## Victims of Crimes Against Humanity

A look at any ancient text will confirm that human beings can justify any cruelty for political, religious, or social gain. However, it was only in the 20th century during the Nuremberg Trials of Nazi officers that the term *crimes against humanity* was coined to describe such activities. Crimes against humanity include "murder, extermination, enslavement, deportation, imprisonment, torture, rape, or other inhumane acts committed against any civilian population."[51] This definition was revised in 2002 by the Rome Statute of the International Criminal Court to include "enforced prostitution, forced pregnancy, enforced sterilization, other comparably severe forms of sexual violence of comparable gravity, the enforced disappearance of persons, apartheid and other inhumane acts intentionally causing great suffering or serious injury, when such acts are knowingly committed as part of a widespread or systematic attack directed against any civilian population, with knowledge of the attack."[52]

Crimes against humanity are typically state sponsored, that is, they are committed by some form of government against a civilian population. Modern criminal court jurisdiction is firmly established not only by the Nuremberg Trials, but also by several more recent international statutes including the Geneva Convention, the Universal Declaration of Human Rights, and the International Criminal Court.[53]

Given growing populations, declining resources, unstable world and national politics, and advanced weaponry that simplifies the control and extermination of large numbers of people, a crime against humanity probably occurs somewhere in the world every day and probably always has. With better and increased communications, however, including media coverage, these offenses are now better and more frequently known. We will now turn to some examples of crimes against humanity in an effort to better understand the issues.

**Nazi War Atrocities** The isolation, imprisonment, sterilization, torture, and murder of 6 million European Jews and at least 11 million political and religious dissenters, Polish, Soviet, and Romani civilians, and German homosexual and handicapped individuals first helped define the term *crimes against humanity*.[54] From 1945 to 1946, Allied prosecutors tried the 22 German officials deemed most responsible for Nazi atrocities, including party leaders, military officers, and government bureaucrats. Most were found guilty and hanged, although some were sentenced to prison; three were acquitted; Hermann Goering, Hitler's second-in-command, committed suicide.[55]

Helping the victims has been a monumental task that has continued since World War II ended. The offenses included not only imprisonment, torture, and murder, but also the theft of untold amounts of wealth, much of which was never returned. It was not until the end the 20th century that Swiss banks, which handled much of the wealth that the Nazis took, agreed to a financial settlement with some survivors of Nazi atrocities.[56]

As we will explore in the next two sections, one of the problems of assisting victims of crimes against humanity is the scale of the offense. Often, there are too many victims for each individual to be helped effectively. Even after Allied soldiers liberated the Nazi concentration camps, thousands of sick, weak survivors still died despite efforts to help them. In some cases, the vast number of corpses made pestilence and disease such a serious threat that bulldozers were used to push heaps of bodies into the mass graves.[57] Whole families who perished in the camps were buried this way. Even the most valiant efforts to assist victims shrivel in the wake of this kind of offense.

**The Balkan Wars** This complicated series of wars followed the breakup of the former Yugoslavia and its three main ethnic groups: Bosnians, Serbs, and Croats. In March 1992, shortly after Bosnia voted to secede from Yugoslavia, Serb soldiers and militia began systematically beating and killing Muslims and Croats.[58] The wars eventually left 250,000 people dead and 2.5 million homeless.[59] The conflict was particularly hard on Bosnians: About 200,000 were killed between 1992 and 1995.[60] In a 1996 attack, Serbians killed 3,000 Albanian Muslims and forced 300,000 from their homes.[61]

The wheels of international justice have turned slowly in the capture and trial of suspected war criminals in this conflict. Serbian leader Slobodan Milosevic became the first head of state ever to stand trial for crimes against humanity, war crimes, and genocide.[62] Milosevic went to trial in 2002 but died four years later in his cell as the trial dragged on without a verdict.[63] Still, the International Criminal Tribunal for the former Yugoslavia has dealt with 158 of its 161 indicted suspects.[64]

As with other criminal offenses, one of the first steps toward helping victims is dealing with the offenders. However, as stated in the prior section on Nazi war atrocities, one of the problems peculiar to crimes against humanity is the range of the damage. The ethnic makeup of whole towns in the former Yugoslavia was changed, probably forever. Rape was used pervasively as a weapon against men, women, and children.[65] Prior to the war, the town of Foča was 51 percent Muslim. In 1992, Serb forces began systematically killing all the males and repeatedly raping the females. Today, Foča is almost completely Serbian. Although some individual war crime offenders were convicted, the objective of making the town Serbian was achieved.[66]

Relief organizations and others involved in assisting Balkan war victims still struggle with the task. Part of the difficulty is that the focus on individual healing probably does little good on its own. Political and social justice must also take place. Recalling the offenses in Foča, sociologist Judith Pintar states, "Rape counseling for a Bosnian woman does not comfort her parents in their grieving for her, does not prevent her children's nightmares, cannot stop her husband from beating her, and, most importantly, it does not get the man who raped her arrested so that she and her neighbors can return to their village without fear."[67]

**Darfur** The civil war in Darfur, Sudan, a desert African region about the size of France, is an ongoing conflict. Darfur has two ethnic groups: nomadic tribal Arab-Africans and non–Arab-Africans. Arabs have historically ruled the country. In 2003, rebels who believed the government oppressed non-Arabs began attacking government targets. The government is accused of using an Arab militia group to rape, murder, and forcibly relocate non-Arab civilians. Nearly 3 million civilians are in refugee camps, and the United Nations states that up to 300,000 people have died from war, famine, and disease.[68]

In March 2009, the International Criminal Court (ICC) charged Sudan's President Omar al-Bashir with five counts of crimes against humanity, the first time the court has pressed charges against a sitting head of state. However, the ICC has

▲ The civil war in Darfur, Sudan, is an ongoing conflict. Here, members of a rebel group are on the move.

no jurisdiction to extract al-Bashir from Sudan, so he probably will not be prosecuted. In retaliation, al-Bashir expelled international aid groups that provided critical help for many victims. In this case, international attempts to help victims of crimes against humanity may actually hurt them more.[69]

## Micro-Victimization

**Micro-victimization** describes the type of victimization that we are most familiar with: individual street-crime victimization, that is, the harm caused to small groups of people or individuals by small-scale criminal offenses. It is easier to measure than macro-victimization, and victims probably receive more productive assistance as well. It is simply a matter of numbers. An individual robbery victim in a politically stable country can get faster, better help than the families of a thousand genocide victims in a civil war.

The federal government has tried to recognize the plight of crime victims and better integrate them within the criminal justice process. The Justice for All Act of 2004 establishes and enforces the rights of crime victims in federal criminal proceedings by allowing victims to be heard at public proceedings about offender release, pleas, or sentencing. The U.S. Department of Justice Office of Community Oriented Policing Services suggests several factors to note in creating a more satisfactory criminal justice response to victims.

- Victims are key participants in the immediate response to an offense, the investigation of the incident, and efforts to prevent further crime.

- Victim service organizations have unique knowledge and capabilities that may enhance efforts to investigate and control crime.

- Better communication between police and victims leads to more productive investigations and crime-control efforts.

- An effective response to crime reduces the risk of repeat victimization. The police should develop community partnerships to improve their response to victims. Vic-

**murder**  Willful homicide.

**felony**  A serious offense usually punishable by a prison sentence of more than one year or sometimes by life imprisonment or death.

**micro-victimization**  The harm caused to small groups of people or individuals by small-scale criminal offenses.

tim service organizations should also help victims who are at risk of further victimization to better plan for their safety.[70]

Now let's look at the victims of the major types of crime in the United States. The four major violent victimizations as typified by the FBI—murder, rape, robbery, and assault—are discussed individually because they are so serious. The four major property victimizations—burglary, larceny-theft, motor vehicle theft, and arson—are discussed as a unit.

## Murder Victims

**Murder** is willful homicide, that is, the killing of another person on purpose with forethought. Accidental homicides, even those committed because of recklessness or assault, are not usually considered first-degree murder; instead, they are typically labeled as manslaughter or a lesser degree of murder (discussed in Chapter 10). Because the legal definition of murder requires purposeful action and motive on the offender's part, the offender–victim relationship is important. Usually, they know each other.[71]

**The Extent of Murder** In 2008, the FBI recorded 16,272 murders in the United States, a slight decline from 2007.[72] The most frequent companion **felony**— a serious offense usually punishable by a prison sentence of more than one year or sometimes by life imprisonment or death—to murder was robbery. There were 924 murder/robberies in 2008 (see Figure 3.3 for statistics on companion felonies); most murder weapons were handguns (6,755) and knives (1,897).[73] The number of white and black victims was close (6,838 and 6,782, respectively), but male victims (11,059) far outnumbered female victims (3,078).[74] Most victims were over the age of 18. Black offenders typically murdered black victims, and white offenders typically murdered white victims (see Figure 3.4).[75] When victims' race and sex were combined, black males were the most likely murder victims, followed by white males, white females, and then black females.[76]

According to the UCR, the three victim–offender relationships with the most murders in 2008 were "acquaintance" (3,068 murders), "stranger" (1,742 murders), and "wife" (577 murders). (See Figure 3.5.)

The largest category, in which the relationship between victim and offender is unknown, had 6,268 murders.[77] This category has become

## Figure 3.3 Felonies that Occur with Murder, 2008

In 2008, the four felonies that most often occurred with murder were robbery, drug trafficking, burglary, and rape. In the "other" category, the offense was unspecified.

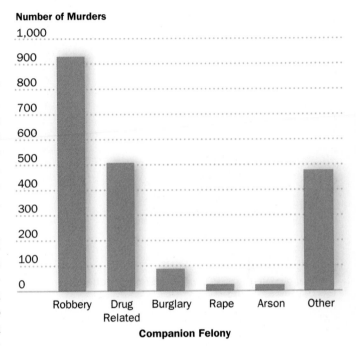

*Source:* Federal Bureau of Investigation, *Crime in the United States, 2008,* "Expanded Homicide Data Table 12," http://www.fbi.gov/ucr/cius2008/offenses/expanded_information/data/shrtable_12.html.

## Figure 3.4 Races of Murder Victims and Offenders in the United States, 2008

In 2008, white offenders killed 230 black victims and 3,036 white victims. Black offenders killed 504 white victims and 2,722 black victims.

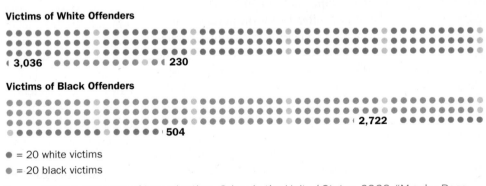

*Source:* Federal Bureau of Investigation, *Crime in the United States, 2008,* "Murder Race and Sex of Victim by Race and Sex of Offender, 2008, Expanded Homicide Data Table 6," http://www.fbi.gov/ucr/cius2008/offenses/expanded_information/data/shrtable_06.html.

## Figure **3.5**  Murder Victim/Offender Relationships, United States, 2008

This figure shows the four relationship categories in which murders occurred most in 2008.

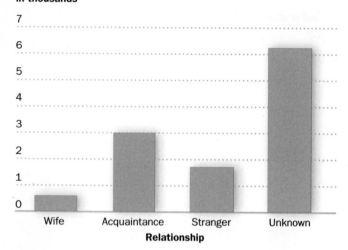

**Number of murders committed, in thousands**

*Source:* Federal Bureau of Investigation, *Crime in the United States: 2007*, "Expanded Homicide Data Table 9," http://www.fbi.gov/ucr/cius2007/offenses/expanded_information/data/shrtable_09.html.

▲ Victim precipitation occurs when the victim initiates the murder. Here, Amber Cummings leaves court after being charged with murdering her husband, whom she says was abusive and planning to sexually abuse their 9-year-old daughter. Although Cummings pleaded guilty, a judge suspended her eight-year prison sentence.

problematic in the last few decades. The percentage of unknown offenders jumped from 6 percent in 1963 to nearly 50 percent in 2008.[78] One study concluded that although unknown cases probably contain incidents from all categories of victim–offender relationship, they are likely to be stranger-murders.[79] Stranger-murders do not necessarily preclude hostile motivations or make instrumental motivations more likely, but they do make the issue more difficult to study.

**Victim Precipitation** Victim precipitation occurs when the victim plays an active role in initiating or escalating the offense. Precipitation is different from provocation, a legal concept used to focus on the offender for the purposes of establishing guilt and deciding sentencing.[80] Victim precipitation is concerned with the victim's behavior for the purpose of analysis and not to establish fault. It is important to clarify this concept because it is often mistaken for "blaming the victim." Victim precipitation merely considers the victim's actions and the role he or she played in a violent event.[81]

Consider two groups of inebriated people walking home from a bar. A man in Group I makes a disparaging comment about a woman in Group II, and the men in

Group II demand a fight. Group II loses badly after a short brawl, and one member dies. From a criminal justice perspective, the key questions are who threw the first punch and who was fighting in self-defense. The Group I men might be charged with some lesser degree of murder. The victim precipitation perspective, however, would study the actions of Group II and its members' role in the incident. Some criminology scholars now consider long-term victim precipitations, such as when a woman kills an abusive husband. In this case, the victim's actions that contributed to his murder took place over a number of years and not just in an isolated incident.

Related to victim precipitation is criminologist David Luckenbill's concept of murder as a **situated transaction,** or the idea that a scenario is the result of agreed-upon norms, interactions, and roles played by those involved. In Luckenbill's study of 70 cases, a pattern emerged.

---

**victim precipitation**  An offense in which the victim plays an active role in initiating or escalating the offense.

**situated transaction**  The idea that a scenario is the result of agreed-upon norms, interactions, and roles played by those involved.

1. The victim made a move the offender thought offensive.

2. The offender retaliated with a verbal or physical challenge.

3. The victim's response typically cemented an "agreement" to use violence to settle the situation.

4. The victim lay dead or dying after a fight.

5. The offender ended the scene in a manner related to the relationship with the victim and any observers. If the victim was a family member or other intimate, the offender would usually remain on the scene and notify the police; if the offender and victim were acquaintances, the offender would try to destroy evidence, dispose of the body, then flee. If observers were present, their relationship to the offender would determine the offender's actions: Victim-supportive observers would direct the offender to remain; victim-hostile observers would encourage the offender to flee; neutral observers would do nothing, leaving the offender to act.[82]

The idea of situated transactions has helped clarify criminologists' understanding of both intimate-partner violence and some neighborhood street violence since both develop between parties familiar with one another and can include some concept of saving face or honor.[83]

### Rape Victims

Historically, rape is the only violent offense in which the victim was also a suspect. Feminists, scholars, researchers, and criminal justice professionals have worked for decades to ensure that rape victims were treated as victims and not as willing participants or, at best, parties in some vague physical altercation.

**Forcible rape** is sexual intercourse performed without the victim's consent through force, threat of violence, or intimidation. In 2008, the NCVS recorded 203,830 rapes and sexual assaults. Of the 164,240 female victims, 63 percent knew their attackers. Of these non-stranger rapes, 18 percent were committed by intimate partners and 42 percent by friends or acquaintances. Of the 39,590 male victims, all knew their attackers, who were nearly all friends or acquaintances. The survey also found that weapons were not used in 80 percent of the cases.[84]

**History and Prejudice in Rape Victimization**  Because women play a vital role in family lineages, female sexuality has historically been tightly controlled. In many ancient cultures, a woman's value was directly related to her ability to produce healthy children for a male who was sure that the children were his. A man whose wife was raped could not be sure that the child she bore, if any, was his. A victimized

girl lost her value for the same reason and would remain a burden to her father, who could not marry her off. For these reasons, although the traditional object of rape has been women, the traditional victims were men, and the women merely property. This is one source of the paradox in which women were never considered true victims of rape yet were the focus of rape laws.

Rape exists in some form in all societies, but some condone it more than others, and some use it for social control.[85] In some hunter–gatherer societies, rape is less about controlling women for their reproductive value than it is about simply controlling them. In *Against Our Will*, feminist author Susan Brownmiller discusses gang rape as a means of social control among several South American tribes. Females who did not "toe the line" were gang raped to keep all females under control.

> Institutionalized gang rape . . . had been personally observed by [anthropologist] Charles Wagley . . . among the Tapirapé Indians of Brazil in the case of an independent young woman who refused to join the other females in manioc processing. The woman in this case was unmarried and she was turned over to the village men for punishment by her brother. The action of the Tapirapé brother suggests that the deviation of a female constitutes a crisis that requires direct and immediate action regardless of bonds of kinship.[86]

The ancient laws that led to English common law—which is the basis of U.S. law—were likewise concerned with control of females. Because males are not controlled in this way, it was long considered that they cannot be raped. Despite advances in our understanding of rape, an echo of these ancient prejudices can be seen in the FBI's definition of forcible rape today: "the carnal knowledge of a female forcibly and against her will." This definition does not specify the rape of men. According to the FBI, "Sexual attacks on males are counted as aggravated assaults or sex offenses, depending on the circumstances and the extent of any injuries."[87]

Historical prejudices concerning rape have wronged male victims as much as female victims. Presumably because male–male rape did not present reproductive issues, the assault was deemed (a) not important, (b) a loss of honor, (c) the spoils of war, (d) just punishment for a crime, or (e) merely homosexual play. Although most rape victims are female, and most offenders are male (see Figure 3.6), male victimization remains an important issue.[88] The stigmatization of homosexuality has added a dimension to the plight of male victims. The idea that a heterosexual male can be raped by another heterosexual male (outside prison) is still alien. Too often, a male who does not fight off his attacker is considered to have consented to the rape. For this and other reasons, males often wait years to report an attack, and many never do.[89]

---

**forcible rape** Sexual intercourse performed without the victim's consent through force, threat of violence, or intimidation.

## Figure **3.6**  Gender of Rape Offenders and Victims in the United States, 2007

Of all rape victims in 2007, about 95 percent were female (see first figure). Of all rape offenders, nearly 95 percent were male.

Males                                    Females

**Gender of
Rape Victims**                      **Gender of
Rape Offenders**

*Source:* U.S. Department of Justice Office of Justice Programs Bureau of Justice Statistics, *Criminal Victimization in the United States, 2007 Statistical Tables,* "Table 38: Percent Distribution of Single-Offender Victimizations, by Type of Crime and Perceived Gender of Offender," and "Table 2: Number of Victimizations and Victimization Rates for Persons Age 12 and Over, by Type of Crime and Gender of Victims," February 2010, http://bjs.ojp.usdoj.gov/index.cfm?ty=pbdetail&iid=2173.

## Figure **3.7**  Age Distribution of Sexual Assault Victims

According to the National Incident-Based Reporting System, the rate of sexual assaults, which does not include forcible rapes, generally peaks at age 14 for both male and female victims and then drops steadily. Most assaults of males occur at about age 5, and most assaults of females at about age 14. Both male and female peaks appear on the chart below.

**Rate per 1,000 Victims**

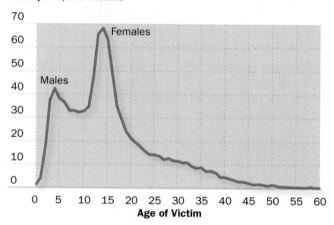

**Age of Victim**

*Source:* Howard N. Snyder, *Sexual Assault of Young Children as Reported to Law Enforcement: Victim, Incident, and Offender Characteristics* (Washington, DC: Bureau of Justice Statistics, 2000), 2.

**Child Rape and Sexual Abuse**  Although child rape and sexual abuse are among the most highly publicized serious offenses, it is difficult to estimate how often they occur. One reason is that they simply go unreported. The victim is often too young to understand what happened or is afraid or unable to tell anyone. According to the American Academy of Child and Adolescent Psychiatry (AACAP), children age 5 or older may feel trapped between love or affection for their abusers, who may be relatives or adult friends of the family, and the feeling that the sexual activities are wrong. Children who try to end the abuse may be threatened with violence or loss of their abusers' love. Federal statistics, then, probably underestimate the actual occurrence of child rape and sexual abuse. In 2008, AACAP reported that child sexual abuse is reported almost 80,000 times a year.[90]

The UCR does not differentiate sexual assaults against juveniles from those against adults. However, National Incident-Based Reporting System data indicate that in 2000 and 2001, about 52 percent of all violent-crime victims under 18 were victims of sexual assaults. Most female victims were about 14, and most males about 5.[91] The age 14 group had the greatest proportion of reported sexual assault victims (see Figure 3.7).

**History and the Law**  The proscription on sex with children, specifically pre-pubescent children, is recent in the West. It is possible that modern laws and social attitudes have made child sexual abuse and rape less prevalent now than in prior centuries. In ancient Greece and Rome, sex between men and boys was common. Throughout the Middle Ages in Europe, sexual activity between adults and children was almost a social norm. What we now call "statutory" rape—sex with a person under a specific age, usually 18—was not prosecuted at all, and prostitution of girls under age 15 was common. Not until the 19th century did France and England adopt modern attitudes and laws toward child–adult sex.[92]

In June 2008, the U.S. Supreme Court ruled the death penalty unconstitutional for the rape of a child. In a controversial 5–4 decision, the Court overturned laws in Louisiana and five other states, but it did not overturn federal military law, which Congress amended in 2006 to allow capital punishment in child-rape cases.[93]

## Robbery and Assault Victims

**Robbery** is the taking or attempting to take anything from another person or persons by violence or the threat

**robbery** The taking or attempting to take anything from another person or persons by violence or the threat of violence.

▲ Offenses concerning sex with children are becoming more visible.

of violence. More males are robbery victims than females, and most perpetrators are strangers to the victim.[94] More than 120,000 robbery suspects were arrested in 2008, with 18-year-old males posting the highest number of arrests.[95] A study by criminologists Richard T. Wright and Scott H. Decker found that robbers' main motivation is to get cash or valuable items, but their secondary motivation is control over their victims and the excitement of the offense. The robbers in the study did not plan their offenses and committed robbery so casually that they could not keep up with how many people they had robbed.[96] Robbery without a weapon is often called "strong-arm robbery," a method used in nearly half of 2008 robberies.[97] Strong-arm robbery is more likely to harm the victim, possibly because victims are more confident they can defend themselves. An armed robber is more likely to be confident and organized and less likely to beat the victim, who is usually frightened enough by the weapon not to resist.[98]

Wright and Decker found that robbers preferred white victims because they were less likely to fight back than blacks. White victims usually carried only credit cards and checkbooks, though, if they had cash, the amount was substantial. The robbers also preferred drug dealers or drug buyers as targets, although drug dealers were more likely to be armed and connected with others who could take revenge. Preferred victims were white drug users who entered the robbers' neighborhood to buy drugs. Such victims were likely to carry large amounts of cash and unlikely to call the police.[99]

**Assault Victims**    **Assault** is the criminal offense of attempting to inflict immediate bodily harm or making another person fear that such harm is imminent. According to the NCVS, more females are victims of aggravated and simple assault than males.[100] Blacks were also more likely than other races to be victims of aggravated and simple assault.[101] Male aggravated assault victims were more likely to be attacked by strangers. In simple assaults, however, they were more likely to be victimized by someone they knew, as were females.[102] Age is also a factor; assault is the most common violent offense juveniles commit.[103]

**Victims of Intimate-Partner Violence**    Females are more likely than males to suffer nonfatal **intimate-partner violence** (IPV), which occurs between two people in a spousal, domestic, or romantic relationship. Between 2001 and 2005, non-fatal victimizations represented 22 percent of those against females 12 or older but only 4 percent of those against males 12 or older. Intimate partners committed 30 percent of female homicides and 5 percent of male homicides. Women 20 to 49 were at a greater risk of non-fatal IPV than older females; women 20 to 24 were at greatest risk. Between 2001 and 2005, both women and men who were separated or divorced had the greatest risk of non-fatal IPV, whereas married or widowed adults reported the lowest risk. Spouses committed most IPV homicides.[104]

><THINKBACK
intimate-partner violence (IPV) (ch. 2)—Abuse that occurs between two people in a spousal, domestic, or romantic relationship.

Intimate-partner violence has a particularly strong connection to economic hardship. On average, women living in households with lower annual incomes suffered the highest rates of non-fatal IPV. Victims risk losing their jobs because they miss work while finding new housing, separating from their victimizers, and getting medical attention, and because employers fear the perpetrator may cause problems at the workplace. A third to one-half of employed domestic violence victims lose their jobs. As a result, several states and jurisdictions have passed legislation prohibiting employers from firing employees for problems related to domestic abuse.[105]

## Property Offense Victims

The UCR records four property offenses:

- **burglary**—the unlawful entry of a structure with the intent to commit a felony or theft

**assault** The criminal offense of attempting to inflict immediate bodily harm or making another person fear that such harm is imminent.

**burglary** The unlawful entry of a structure with intent to commit a felony or theft.

- **larceny-theft** —the unlawful taking of money or property from another person
- motor-vehicle theft
- **arson**—the deliberate setting of fires

With larceny-theft, there is no force or threat of force against victims (as with the crime of shoplifting). The other three offenses may include physical harm to victims, threat of harm, or intent to inflict harm. In 2008, larceny-theft offenses accounted for 67.5 percent of all property offenses.[106]

About 9,767,915 property offenses occurred in the United States in 2008. In addition:[107]

- Burglary victims lost an estimated $4.6 billion worth of property, with the average loss per offense totaling $2,079.
- Larceny-theft victims lost an estimated $6.1 billion.
- About $6.4 billion worth of motor vehicles was stolen at an average of about $6,751 per vehicle.
- Arson victims lost about $16,015 per offense.[108]

For all types of property crime, households of six or more were victimized more than smaller households, and lower-income households were also more likely to be victimized.[109]

One effort to help victims that presents an alternative to the traditional criminal justice process is victim–offender mediation. Because property offenses are less serious than violent offenses, victim–offender meetings are a realistic scenario. The object is to allow the victim to confront the offender in a safe, structured setting and to help develop a satisfactory restitution plan for the victim. Victim–offender mediation emphasizes dialogue, victim healing, offender accountability, and restoration of losses.[110] We will discuss this in more detail later in the chapter.

## Transnational Victimization

Although nations define and handle crime differently, most define the same behaviors as criminal offenses: murder, rape, assault, theft, robbery, and so on. The major differences are in the details of how the offenses are handled. The same goes for victim assistance. Some nations offer little or no help for victims, whereas others have special laws and networks of government and private agencies. Most nations probably fall between these two extremes.

In this section, we focus on micro-victimization that is especially relevant to the new criminology: crime that involves victims and offenders in more than one nation. The 21st century's instant communications, global economy, and ability to move large amounts of goods vast distances cheaply, although convenient, is a growing problem. Not only is it easier than ever to break the laws of several nations at once, it is increasingly profitable. But what happens to the victims of these offenses? To understand this, we will look at transnational crime and how it affects individual victims.

**Transnational crime** involves offenses that originate in one nation, cross one or several national borders (or oceans), and find victims in still other nations. Credit card theft is an example: People in one nation access an online database, steal the credit card numbers of people in another nation, and either sell the numbers or use them to purchase items. Transnational crime often depends on exploiting the differences and distances between national borders. Because doing this successfully requires a certain amount of resources and sophistication, criminal organizations often perpetrate transnational crime. Common transnational offenses are trafficking in some banned material such as intellectual property, wildlife, drugs, body parts, human beings, stolen goods, oil, food, precious metals and stones, and medicine. Corruption, bribery, money laundering, environmental offenses, and some forms of terrorism and sea piracy may also be perpetrated transnationally.

A common form of transnational **human trafficking,** the buying and selling of human beings, is prostitution. Women from nations in Africa, Asia, and some Eastern European countries are taken to nations with booming tourist economies where their captors confiscate their documents, passports, and other means of communication with their families and force them to work as prostitutes. Other forms

▼ Human trafficking for the purpose of prostitution is a common form of transnational crime.

POWERLESS...
HELPLESS...
CHOICELES...
DEBT BOND...
INTIMIDATED...
THREATENED...
ENSLAVED...
RAPED...
ABUSED...
EXPLOITED...

IS SHE
VICTIM OR ACCUSED

SEX TRAFFICKING
DESTROYS A PERSON

of human trafficking involve taking shiploads of people to work in foreign sweatshops (including some in the United States), kidnapping for ransom, and even harvesting vital organs from unwilling donors.[111]

Often, transnational crime resembles domestic organized crime. For example, automobile thieves often steal cars in the United States to sell overseas. The cars are shipped across the world to nations where they can bring handsome black-market profits. For the victim, the only difference between international and domestic theft is that the victim has no chance of getting the car back if it has gone overseas.[112]

Finally, transnational crime can include environmental offenses, such as illegal logging and timber smuggling, wildlife smuggling, illegal dumping of hazardous waste, and illegal trade in environmentally harmful chemicals. Without the assistance of the host country (which may be profiting from some offenses), these offenses are difficult to control. Victims can include individuals, groups, nations, or, in the case of wildlife smuggling, other species.[113] Unfortunately, unstable global politics and shaky economies can make obtaining justice dangerous, which leads governments to consider the issue not worth pursuing.

# Think about it

## Remember
Show how corporate and environmental victimization are difficult to measure.

## Analyze
Distinguish between micro-victimization and macro-victimization.

## Evaluate
Justify the argument that victims precipitate their own victimization.

## The Problems of Victimization

Criminal victimization, especially violent victimization, involves far more than a brief event for the victim. After the offense, the victim and often his or her family and friends try

**larceny-theft** The unlawful taking of money or property from another person.

**arson** The deliberate setting of fires.

**transnational crime** Criminal offenses that originate in one nation, cross one or several national borders, and find victims in other nations.

**human trafficking** The buying and selling of human beings.

to resolve a series of physical, psychological, financial, and legal problems. Even the simplest questions may seem monumental: Do I call the police? Seek medical care? Get counseling?[114] The experiences of victimized children can affect their adult lives, and elderly victims tend to be more vulnerable to physical injury.

**LO3:** Discuss the problems of victimization.

Generally, crime victims' problems are physical, emotional, family related, economic, or caused by the criminal justice system itself. It is indicative of victimization that police officers are instructed to understand the "three major needs" of crime victims: the need to feel safe; the

**LO4:** Describe the special victimization problems of children, the elderly, and the disabled.

need to express emotions; and the need to know what comes next in terms of the criminal justice system, the victim's worries for his or her family, and economic costs of the offense.[115] In this section, we will consider each of these problems.

### Physical Trauma

Physical injury, usually the first type of trauma we associate with being a crime victim, is more obvious than psychological or financial injury. Physical injury is easier than psychological injury for police, judges, and juries to empathize with, and for doctors to treat or at least define. Generally, injury rates are higher among the young, the impoverished, those who live in cities, blacks, Hispanics, and American Indians. Injury rates tend to be lower among the elderly, the wealthy, the educated, and people who are married or widowed. Victims of IPV are more likely to be injured than people victimized by acquaintances or strangers.[116] In 2007, nearly half of the victims of violent offenses went to the hospital.[117] Those in the age group 20 to 34 were the most likely to go (6.8 percent), whereas those 50 to 64 and over were least likely (3.6 percent).[118]

Victims may sustain physical injury from abuse inflicted by the offender or from resisting the offense. Some research has shown that resistance reduces both the chance and severity of injury, with forceful tactics being the most successful.[119] Relatively few victims fight off their attackers with a weapon. In 2006, only 1.2 percent of victims who took self-protective measures counter-attacked with a weapon. Most simply resisted or somehow captured the offender (22.9 percent), talked the offender out of the attack (13 percent), or ran away or hid (14.8 percent).[120]

### Psychological Trauma

It is normal for victims, especially those of violent offenses, to experience psychological and emotional problems after the offense. The four indicators of psychological issues are depression, post-traumatic stress disorder, anger, and anxiety; violent crime victims typically experience higher levels of these symptoms. Such trauma is usually increased by subsequent victimizations.[121] Victims of even minor offenses can experience psychological trauma. One study of identity theft victims, especially those whose cases were unresolved, showed that they experienced increased psychological and even physical distress. The longer the case went unresolved, the more stress the victim experienced.[122]

## Family Trauma

Victims' families may be distressed about the event and the victim's feelings, or about his or her being unable to work, being injured, or suffering post-traumatic stress or depression. Distress may also arise from significant loss of possessions or money through, for example, arson or fraud. The ultimate trauma occurs when a family member is murdered.

In the last 30 years, more than 500,000 people have been murdered in the United States, which makes the number of affected families and friends quite a bit larger than half a million. One recent study reports that 9.3 percent of adult respondents had friends or relatives who had been murdered; the Virginia Mason Medical Center estimates that between 120,000 and 240,000 people annually lose friends or family to murder. It is difficult, if not impossible, to completely move on after such an event. Two-thirds of survivors still felt significant distress five years later and were more likely than the direct victims of less serious offenses to exhibit post-traumatic stress symptoms for the rest of their lives.

Survivors typically describe their grief as "intense, persistent, and inescapable," which increases with the perceived intentionality and viciousness of the murder. They are more anxious about their own safety and that of relatives and friends.[123] Appetite and sleep problems, gastrointestinal and cardiovascular disorders, and poor immune response are all symptomatic of survivors' distress. It is not uncommon for very close relatives to die within a few years of the murder: Men tend to suffer heart disease and early death, and women become anxious and depressed.[124] Ethnically or socially marginal families, or those engaged in antisocial activities themselves, receive little or no support from their communities, which may feel the victim "deserved it" and the families should "get over it."[125]

## Economic Trauma

Victimization can be expensive. Aside from economic losses stemming directly from the offense, such as in a robbery or burglary, the victim may also have to pay for medical care, mental health care, property repair, and some types of legal proceedings. Medical bills, even with insurance, can be crushing, and some injuries are permanent and can result in job loss.

Property and money are often unrecoverable. Many, if not most, of the victims of Bernard Madoff (discussed earlier) will never see any significant portion of their life's savings returned.[126] Identity theft victims not only are victims, but may also be mistaken for offenders. One identity thief wrote checks on a bank account opened in the victim's name. The victim was arrested when the checks bounced and had to pay $1,500 bail and $5,000 for a lawyer.[127]

Generally, the less money a victim has, the more likely it is that he or she will be victimized and the more difficult it is to recover economically. Crime can also wreak indirect economic damage by affecting property values in neighborhoods where crime rates are highest. Although we can ask which came first—the impoverished neighborhood or the crime—the result is the same. Everyone who can afford to leave a crime-affected neighborhood does, and property values plummet for those who remain.[128]

## Legal Trauma

The legal proceedings that sometimes follow victimization, such as a suspect's trial, have often been described as "secondary victimization" because of stress the victim (or victim's family) endures during the process. The most common victim reaction to secondary victimization is bewilderment and frustration. Some study participants said the legal proceedings harmed them more than the offense itself.[129] The mere expectation of secondary victimization keeps many victims from reporting offenses because the legal proceedings are not "worth it." Other research has found that innovations like victim-impact statements, compensation, and counseling have not improved victims' satisfaction with the criminal justice process.[130]

Secondary victimization is perhaps most associated with rape trials. Before the passage of rape shield laws (statutes that limit the introduction of evidence about a victim's sexual conduct), victims were often subjected to intense and humiliating personal inquiries by the defense. Sometimes, victims suffered insensitive treatment by the criminal justice system. In one case, a sexual assault victim was waiting in a large, crowded room in a courthouse to give testimony. As the bailiff retrieved witnesses, the woman realized that her suspected assailant was sitting next to her.[131]

The police have turned out to be an especially important element in the prevention of secondary victimization. A study of rape victims found that when police were courteous and showed interest, victims were less likely to be traumatized by further criminal justice proceedings.[132] Still, statistics indicate that only about half of violent offenses and a little less than half of property offenses are reported. This is unfortunate because some research shows that participation in the criminal justice process helps some victims by encouraging their sense of "justice being done."[133]

Many victims feel the criminal justice system will not deal with the offenders harshly enough. After the stress of a trial, many victims find out that the rapist sentenced to 10 years was out in 7, the robber sentenced to 8 years was released in 4, and the murderer sentenced to 16 years got out in 8.[134] Murder cases present especially heartbreaking problems for victims. A registered nurse writing about helping homicide survivors details the problem eloquently:

> Where sufficient evidence permits charges to be filed against the alleged killer, family members find that the 'state' is the victim, not their loved one; in fact, their loved one's name is rarely used during the proceedings. Family members often are excluded from the courtroom, either on the pretext they may be called as witnesses or because of the fear their emotional reactions might somehow influence the jury. In cases where there is insufficient evidence for the jury to find the defendant guilty, the family may feel even more anguish, helplessness, and rage that their loved one's killer was not brought to justice. Plea bargaining may bring additional frustration to family members. Even if the perpetrator is found guilty, surviving family members may find the sentence wasn't long enough or that the sentence given was not the sentence actually served.[135]

## Special Victims: Children, the Elderly, and the Disabled

Children, the elderly, and the disabled are typically mentally and physically dependent and provide easy targets for abuse and financial exploitation by caregivers as well as strangers. Because they may have limited communication skills and ability to travel, they may be cut off from anyone who can intervene, report the victimization, or get help.

### Children

The risk of violent victimization is greatest during youth, especially from late adolescence to early adulthood.[136] Routine or extreme victimization can interfere with the maturation process, damaging the child's socialization and psychological development, eventually producing an adult who is paranoid, anxious, and unable to cope. Violent victimization in particular undermines the child's confidence, educational and future socioeconomic achievement, and perceptions of how society is supposed to work. It also increases the child's risk of later involvement in crime and antisocial activities.[137]

Much of the literature on child victimization addresses child abuse, which is defined as victimization or neglect by adults. However, because of the increase in fatal school violence since the 1990s, the subject of bullying—the victimization of children by other children—has received more attention. Still, most child victimizations, whether abuse or bullying, are not reported to police, and many are not reported to any authority, including parents. There are several basic reasons for this.

▲ Most child victimizations are not reported to law enforcement because the child may not want to involve parents or school officials, or the parents may not want to involve police.

1. The child or parent may not define the offense as serious or as a criminal offense.
2. The child may not want to involve parents or school officials, or the parent may not want to involve police.
3. The child may not want his or her autonomy infringed.
4. The child or parent may have emotional issues or antisocial attitudes.
5. The parent may not want to spend time or money dealing with the issue.[138]

Finally, it is difficult to prosecute cases in which children are victims or witnesses. Sometimes adults have difficulty testifying and facing an alleged victimizer; the task is that much more difficult for children, who may suffer lasting effects. Courts can help by shielding children behind screens, having them testify via closed-circuit television or videotape, or excluding from the courtroom anyone without a direct interest in the case.[139]

## The Elderly

Of all age groups, the elderly are the least likely to be victimized by street crime, although they fear it the most. However, it is possible that because the elderly probably take greater precautions against it, they are the least victimized. When it does happen, victimization is much more serious than for younger people. An elderly person who is assaulted and robbed is much more likely to need medical care, end up in a nursing home or other institutionalized care, or even die.[140] Unfortunately, the elderly may have the most to fear from their own families and caretakers.

In the past 20 years, the number of reported cases of domestic elder abuse has greatly increased. Physical victimization most commonly occurs at the hands of an adult child, spouse, or sibling. The typical victim is a woman over 70 and in poor health. Abusive sons are more likely to commit assault and financial victimization; abusive daughters are more likely to commit neglect or emotional abuse.[141] Home health aides or nursing home staff may also be abusive.

Financial victimization often goes uninvestigated because no one reports it. Victims may not know or understand what is happening, or they may fear the perpetrator, who is often someone they know.[142] Elders exploited by a stranger may not report it because they do not want close family members to find out for fear of losing financial independence. Finally, elderly victims may think nothing can be done and thus may be willing to let the offense go.[143]

## The Disabled

Like the elderly and children, disabled people are often under the care of others who may be family or staff in an institution, and the abuse can take many forms. In one 2006 incident, a woman who was responsible for the care of her developmentally disabled sister, including receiving her sister's Social Security checks, forced her sister into prostitution. The perpetrator solicited customers online and told her sister that if she did not cooperate, she would be returned to a group home. The victimization was revealed only when the perpetrator called police to complain about harassment by neighbors who complained about the prostitution.[144]

This example is typical of the victimization the developmentally disabled face: They may fear their caretakers, who threaten them with institutionalization; they may be exploited financially and physically; and they may be unable or afraid to report the abuse. The victimizer may be the victim's sole caretaker, so if the victimizer is incarcerated, the victim's situation may worsen with transfer to an institution or group home. An Australian study found that although all disabled adults were as likely as nondisabled adults to report victimization, intellectually disabled adults often reported victimization to a caregiver who did not report it to police.[145]

Like the elderly, the developmentally disabled are in more danger from relatives and caretakers than from strangers. Victimization may occur at any age and via any type of offense. However, there is somewhat less risk of property offenses, possibly because the developmentally disabled own so little property.[146] Disabled children were more likely than typical children to suffer physical abuse resulting in injury, as well as severe sexual abuse, with the risks of sexual abuse increasing with higher levels of disability.[147] One study of developmentally disabled murder victims found that of those who could be identified by age and gender, the typical victim was a boy less than four years of age, with more than half being age 14 or younger. Generally, such murders were carried out by simple neglect, followed by burning, beating, shooting, or asphyxia.[148]

# Think about it

## Remember

List the five types of trauma that crime victims may experience.

## Evaluate

Evaluate how special victims of crimes such as children, the elderly, and the disabled are differently affected by victimization.

# Getting Help for Victims

The benefits to society of assisting crime victims are as great as they are for rehabilitating offenders. Unfortunately, both initiatives tend to be neglected in favor of prosecuting and punishing offenders. Victimology seeks to focus attention on an overlooked but important element of the crime equation: rendering better assistance to victims. There are several practical reasons for this.

**LO5:**

Identify the reasons for rendering better assistance to victims.

- *Recovery is costly and time-consuming.* Violent-crime victims have an increased risk for physical and mental health problems. Receiving help soon after an offense reduces this risk and the intensity of any problems that do develop. With better help, victims can continue to provide for their families and be active in society.

- *The criminal justice system needs victims' help.* Victims often have valuable information that can help police catch suspects, help courts deal with defendants, and help the corrections system control convicted offenders. It is difficult, sometimes impossible, for prosecutors to prepare cases without victim cooperation. Parole boards also need

**LO6:**

Analyze the ways in which the criminal justice system tries to satisfy victims' need for justice.

information from victims to decide which offenders may be released.

- *Helping victims increases public confidence in the criminal justice system.* Victims who return to their communities with "horror stories" about the criminal justice system make other victims less likely to report offenses and follow through with prosecutions. Poor treatment of victims can even breed contempt for the law if the community believes the system does not care.[149]

## Victims' Rights

The Crime Victims' Rights Act of 2004 states that the federal government will try to accord victims of federal offenses the following rights:

- the right to be reasonably protected from the accused
- the right to reasonable, accurate, and timely notice of any public court or parole proceeding about the offense or any release or escape of the accused
- the right not to be excluded from any such public court proceeding, unless the court, after receiving clear and convincing evidence, determines that victim testimony would be materially altered if the victim heard other testimony
- the right to be reasonably heard at any public proceeding in the district court concerning release, plea, or sentencing, or any parole proceeding
- the reasonable right to confer with the attorney for the government in the case
- the right to full and timely restitution as provided by law
- the right to proceedings free of unreasonable delay
- the right to be treated with fairness and respect for the victim's dignity and privacy[150]

All states provide victims some variation of these rights, although they differ in who is eligible and what rights are provided. All states provide for compensation rights, notification of court appearances, and submission of a presentencing **victim-impact statement** (VIS), a communication to the court by those directly affected by an offense that states the personal effects of the offense. About 40 percent of the states extend these, and sometimes other, rights to all victims; some states extend these and other rights only to victims of violent offenses. Most states provide the right to restitution, to attend sentencing hearings, and to consult with officials before offers of pleas or release of defendants.[151]

To educate criminal justice agencies and the public, victims' rights compliance programs in more than a dozen states conduct training seminars, take calls from victims, provide information and referrals to other victim services,

and take complaints from victims who believe their rights have been violated.[152]

All states have a crime victim compensation program. Programs that accept federal funding must follow federal guidelines. This makes victim compensation programs uniform from state to state. According to the National Center for Victims of Crime, violent offense victims who report in a timely fashion and cooperate with investigation and prosecution may have some offense-related expenses paid, such as uninsured medical and counseling expenses, some lost wages, and funeral costs.[153]

## Offender Punishment, Restorative Justice, and Victim-Impact Statements

Punishment, restorative justice, and victim-impact statements are three ways in which the criminal justice system attempts to satisfy victims' need for justice. One motive for punishing offenders is to satisfy victims' and society's urge for **retribution,** or "just deserts"—the idea that any punishment proportional to the offense is just. **Restorative justice,** a fairly new practice, seeks to resolve some types of offenses through cooperation of the victim, offender, and justice system. Finally, as discussed above, victim-impact statements are declarations of how an offense has affected the victim.

### Offender Punishment

One motive for punishment is **deterrence,** the idea that punishment will prevent offenders and others from further lawbreaking. Victims often want to see their victimizers incarcerated or, if the offense is particularly violent, executed "so they can't do this to anyone else." According to legal scholar Gerard V. Bradley, however, retribution is not about deterrence or revenge but instead stands as the only moral justification for punishment and is required to restore social balance.[154]

A new trend in punishment is the payment of **restitution** to victims to compensate for loss or injury. Before the advent of criminal justice systems, the offender was often under social pressure to repay his or her offense to the victim. As such systems developed, victims were excluded in part to ensure they did not overly influence punishments. Economic penalties, such as fines, then became payable to the state and not the victim.[155] Modern restitution has been criticized for not being severe enough for the wealthy, who can usually easily afford it, and too severe on the impoverished, who typically

**retribution** The idea that any punishment proportional to the offense is just.

**restorative justice** A form of resolving offenses that emphasizes repairing the harm done by crime through cooperation of the victim, offender, and justice system.

**deterrence** The idea that punishment for an offense will prevent that offender and others from further breaking the law.

**restitution** Money paid to compensate for loss or injury.

**victim-impact statement (VIS)** A communication to the court by those directly affected by an offense that states the personal effects of the offense.

# theory
## to **practice**

### Who Owns a Crime?

Crime victims often feel left out of the criminal justice system. Although victims are the ones who suffer, the state, working through the prosecutor, can "take the crime away" from the victim. The prosecutor must make several decisions based upon the strength of the case, the workload of the office, and the court system's punishment philosophy. The prosecutor changes the nature of the case to one in which society is the victim, and society decides what will happen to the suspect. However, criminologist Nils Christie has argued that victims should be brought back into the system because they are part owners of the conflict that resulted in their victimization.

This perspective, practiced by the restorative justice movement, seeks to allow victims and offenders to work out their differences in a less formal arena than court. According to Christie, this personalized encounter with the offender has been taken away from victims:

> The victim is so totally out of the case that he has no chance, ever, to come to know the offender. We leave them outside, angry, maybe humiliated through a cross-examination in court, without any contact with the offender. He will need all the classical stereotypes around 'the criminal' to get a grasp on the whole thing. Of course, he will go away more frightened than ever, more in need than ever of an explanation of criminals as non-human.[1]

The idea of a conflict as something that victims partly own returns the victim to the justice equation. The case is no longer the offender versus the state but rather the offender versus the victim, the state, and the community. When all parties are included in the resolution, it is more likely that not only will everyone be satisfied, but also that the underlying causes of the conflict can be addressed and harm repaired.

[1]Nils Christie, "Conflicts as Property," *The British Journal of Criminology* 17, no. 1 (1977): 8.

▲ Restorative justice programs teach participants about coming to terms with their offenses and convictions.

## THINKING *in* ACTION

1. What do we mean by the idea of conflict as property?
2. How does the traditional criminal justice process leave the victim out?

---

cannot pay. Regardless, courts sometimes use economic sanctions because they are quantifiable. Restitution in general is becoming more popular for three reasons.

- *Justice is expensive.* Law enforcement, incarceration, and the legal process are becoming so expensive that offenders are now expected to bear some costs in the form of fines and fees.

- *Concern for victims is increasing.* When restitution is paid, victims at least get some material relief for their suffering.

- *Restitution is an alternative to incarceration.* High costs and space shortages are making it impractical to impose long periods of incarceration, especially for non-violent offenders.[156]

Finally, some victims may never collect. The court can order restitution, but it is difficult for an offender serving years in prison to earn the hundreds or thousands of dollars he or she is often ordered to pay. Many victims are satisfied, however, if the offender was at least held accountable in this way.

At the other end of the punishment spectrum is execution. Most victims are happy to see offenders go to prison. In the case of murder, however, some families want the offenders and their families to suffer as much as they have. There is wide debate about whether witnessing an offender's execution can help families deal with the loss of a relative. At least 13 states allow victims' families to observe an offender's execution, and, in Texas, at least, the number who do so has increased each year. One study found that no families who witnessed the execution of their loved ones' killers regretted it.[157]

### Restorative Justice

Restorative justice was developed in New Zealand and Canada in an effort to deal with the overwhelming number of indigenous youths in the criminal justice system. The idea was that the youths might respond better to their families and tribal leaders than to the legal system. Having the youths directly face their victims and the consequences of their offenses has meant that fewer went to prison as adults.[158]

Good results led to restorative justice practices spreading to other legal systems around the world, and victims have benefited (see *Theory to Practice*). A study in the Czech Republic found that compensation, acknowledgment, punishment, and forgiveness tend to ameliorate victims' desire for retribution.[159] Research has shown that offenders are more likely to admit their wrongs, apologize, and reaffirm their moral obligations to the community.[160] Other evidence suggests offenders often want to apologize, and victims want to hear that apology. The apology directly addresses the offense, which may reduce recidivism and help victims feel empowered in the criminal justice process.[161]

### Victim-Impact Statements

Commonly heard at sentencing, the victim-impact statement is a way for victims to participate in the criminal justice process. If the victim is unable to make the statement,

# doubletake

doubletake

### Being Heard: The Voices of Victims

A difficult aspect of being the victim of a large-scale financial crime is that few people feel sorry for you. A common misconception was that all Bernard Madoff's victims were wealthy. This was not true, however. Many were elderly, middle-class wage-earners who had saved for retirement. Other clients were charities, some of which had to close due to the scandal. Other clients had never heard of Madoff: They invested in funds that invested in Madoff's funds without disclosing this information.

Another misconception is that Madoff victims expected abnormally large returns. Actually, Madoff Securities provided lower but steady returns that appeared to be conservative. A final misconception was that the investors "should have known" that Madoff was crooked. However, even many financial experts did not see the scam. Madoff's reputation was impeccable. He was chairman of the NASDAQ stock exchange; his decades-old firm had operated with an excellent record, and the U.S. Securities and Exchange Commission gave the firm a clean bill of health.

Investigators will be on the case for years since it involves more than what Madoff took. Investors are pressing the Internal Revenue Service for refunds of taxes they paid on investment gains that never existed, and, given many investors' advanced age, some will likely die in poverty. Here are typical extracts from the victim-impact statements submitted before Madoff's sentencing.[1]

- I am 86 years old, I have a broken knee, I have lung cancer and thanks to Madoff, I am now bankrupt. I served in the army during the second world war, then worked my way through college. I held various jobs and eventually went into my own business. [I] had $2,300,000 in my family account. . . . Two weeks later, I was bankrupt. [I] am trying to survive on my social security income of $900 per month.

- My husband was a school teacher and I worked as a school secretary in the New York City School System until I retired at 63. We put all of our hard earned savings and IRAs into Madoff. I have been wiped out—I cannot get a job—who would hire me at my age? Bernard Madoff should pay a very heavy price for what he has done to so many.

- In August of 2008 I asked that my account be closed and all of my money be returned. I did this because of concerns with the economy falling and knowing that my two grown children would need help. I was assured that my money was safe and that I should hold back from taking such action by one of the investment accountants in the Madoff firm.

[1]All portions of victim statements were acquired from a June 12, 2009, U.S. Department of Justice document reprinted by *The New York Times*. This document is available online at http://graphics8.nytimes.com/images/blogs/dealbook/madoff_victims_impact.PDF.

## THINKING *in* ACTION

1. Bernard Madoff, in his 70s when arrested, received a prison sentence of 150 years. Was this fair? Why or why not?

2. Some experts have compared Madoff's behavior to that of a serial killer. Which aspects of this offense are similar to serial murder? Which are not?

the victim's survivors, the parent or guardian of a juvenile victim, or the guardian of an incompetent, incapacitated, or disabled victim may do so. Every state and federal court allows VISs at sentencing, and most require the information to be included in the presentence report. (See *Doubletake* for examples of what Bernard Madoff's victims had to say in their VISs.)

VISs typically detail the effects of the offense on the victim and the victim's family, descriptions of the treatments the victim has required to recover, and the need for restitution. Some states list what information a VIS must include, and some allow the victim to state what sentence he or she believes is appropriate for the offender. Most states also allow defendants to contest the veracity of the VIS information, and a few states allow cross-examination of victims.[162] Some states allow VISs in capital cases, which are typically introduced in the sentence phase. Although critics argue that the emotional content of VISs in this context leads to harsher sentencing (capital punishment versus life in prison), at least one study found that the VIS did not affect the court's acceptance of aggravating or mitigating factors.[163]

# Think about it

## Understand

Describe how VISs give crime victims a voice in criminal justice proceedings.

## Apply

Show how restorative justice is an alternative to the usual criminal justice process.

## Analyze

Discuss the provisions of the Crime Victims' Rights Act of 2004.

## Create

Construct a list of reasons why restitution is a popular remedy for crime victims.

# Summary

**LO1: Define victimology.**

- Victimology is the study of the harm that people suffer as a result of crime.
- Victimologists study the effects of crime on victims.
- The goals of victimology include reducing victim suffering, improving the responses of the criminal justice system, and restoring victims' mental and physical health and financial resources.
- Victimologists study the plight of victims; the effects of physical and psychological injuries, including financial losses; the public reaction to the plight of victims; and how criminal justice professionals deal with victims.
- Major victimization statistics are captured by the Uniform Crime Reports, the Bureau of Justice Statistics National Crime Victimization Survey, and the Centers for Disease Control and Prevention.

**LO2: Understand macro-victimization and micro-victimization.**

- Macro-victimization is the consideration of very large masses of people as a victim of singular, large-scale criminal offenses.

- The types of groups responsible for civilian victimization during civil wars and some types of domestic terrorism can be classified as organized armies, paramilitary forces, and criminal groups.
- Corporate and environmental offenses can be wide ranging in terms of geography and time, and some offenses may affect whole nations, or even continents or hemispheres, for decades.
- Crimes against humanity typically stem from some form of government against a civilian population.
- Micro-victimization best describes individual street-crime victimization.
- Victims of street and small-scale crime in other nations are subject to the criminal justice systems and laws of their individual nations.

**LO3: Discuss the problems of victimization.**

- The problems of crime victims can be typified as physical, emotional, family related, economic, or caused by the criminal justice system.

**LO4:** **Describe the special victimization problems of children, the elderly, and the disabled.**

- Children, the elderly, and the disabled are especially vulnerable to victimization because they are typically mentally and physically dependent and thus provide easy targets for abuse and financial exploitation by caregivers and strangers.

**LO5:** **Identify the reasons for rendering better assistance to victims.**

- Reasons for rendering better assistance to victims include improved victim recovery, the need for victims' help in addressing crime, and increased public confidence in the criminal justice system.

**LO6:** **Analyze the ways in which the criminal justice system tries to satisfy victims' need for justice.**

- A victim-impact statement is written or oral declaration of the effect of an offense on the victim and is a way for victims to participate in the criminal justice process.
- Part of the motive for punishing offenders is to satisfy the retributive urges of victims and society and to effect general deterrence. A new trend is the payment of restitution to victims.

# Questions

1. What is victimology?
2. What is the offender–victim dyad?
3. What is macro-victimization? Micro-victimization?
4. What is important about the relationship between murder victims and offenders?
5. Give several reasons that adult rape victims of both sexes have had difficulty being considered as victims.
6. What is transnational victimization? Give an example.
7. Describe some of the problems of victimization.
8. What kinds of decisions must victims (or their families) face after an offense?
9. Why are children, the elderly, and the disabled especially vulnerable to victimization?
10. What rights does the government try to accord to victims of federal offenses?

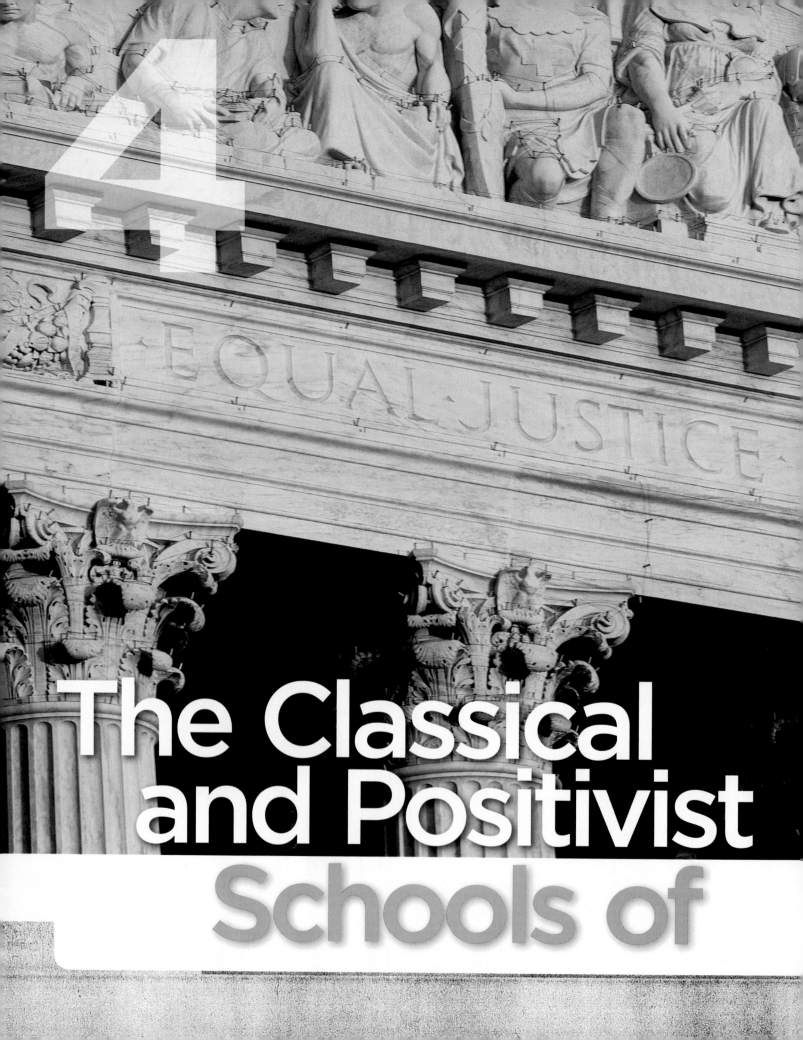

# 4

EQUAL JUSTICE

# The Classical and Positivist Schools of

UNDER LAW

# Criminology

**As you read, keep in mind the learning objectives:**

**LO1:** Explain why the supernatural perspective dominated social control for centuries.

**LO2:** Summarize why contemporary criminologists do not consider the concept of evil an explanation of crime.

**LO3:** Analyze the classical school of criminology's focus on the offense as opposed to the offender by emphasizing the concept of free will.

**LO4:** Discuss the Enlightenment's contribution of the social contract to criminology.

**LO5:** Compare and contrast the ideas of Cesare Beccaria and Jeremy Bentham as the primary architects of the classical school of criminology.

**LO6:** Analyze the positivist school of criminology's assertion that individuals are influenced by external forces.

**LO7:** Show how neoclassical criminology recalls the principles of classical criminology, including deterrence and rational choice.

To appreciate criminology, we must understand how certain behaviors became defined as criminal offenses and why people engage in **antisocial** behavior. The goal of this chapter is to trace the development of explanations of the reasons for crime and the role of law from the earliest times to the present day. To accomplish this, we will focus on the two main schools of criminology: the classical/neoclassical school and the positivist school. Before we explore these, however, we will consider how the causes of crime were perceived in ancient times.

> **>\<THINKBACK**
> antisocial (ch. 1)—
> Following standards of behavior intended to harm society and individuals.

As long as humans have collected into societies, members of those societies have broken the rules. As the centuries wore on and societies matured, thinkers and philosophers sought to understand why some people broke the rules in spite of dire punishments that included humiliation, shame, exile, disfigurement, torture, and death. Sometimes, the reason for an offense seemed good enough, such as a man stealing bread to feed his hungry family. But why risk getting caught if the punishment was the amputation of a hand? The thief's motivation was clearly his family. But what factor moved him or her to risk the consequences? Some men with equally starving families would not steal the bread; they would find some way to deal with the situation that was within the law. What is the difference between two people in similar situations, then, one of whom obeys the law and the other who breaks it? Was the lawbreaker influenced by a demon and the

obedient man by a benevolent spirit? After considering the risks and rewards, did both freely choose their paths under no influence at all but their own? Or did the lawbreaker experience different mental, physical, genetic, or societal influences than the one who obeyed the law?

These questions describe the three explanations of crime we will cover: supernatural, the classical/neoclassical school, and the positivist school. Supernatural explanations—which have not been entirely discarded in modern times—look to explanations for crime that lie beyond the physical world. The classical/neoclassical school looks for explanations within rational thinking. The positivist school looks for external explanations that affect rational thinking. We begin our exploration with supernatural explanations.

## Supernatural Explanations of Crime

To ensure their survival, early societies structured approved behavior patterns that also supported meaningful communities. Societies developed a range of rules to govern the most basic interactions, such as obligations between husband and wife; the discipline of children; and the setting of group standards for sexual activity, control of property,

**LO1:**
Explain why the supernatural perspective dominated social control for centuries.

and conflict resolution.[1] As societies became more complex, these rules grew into laws and sanctions that defined what individuals were prohibited or encouraged to do. Before the Enlightenment in the 17th and 18th centuries, societies based their standards of behavior upon religious doctrine. Religious matters were ingrained not only in the way societies conceived and worshiped their god(s), but also in the laws by which they governed themselves. For example, prior to the Enlightenment, kings were invested with the authority to determine what God intended for the group. This "divine right of kings" specified the king as the sole arbiter of God's law and applied that law to the king's subjects.[2]

## Demonology

In some societies, it was difficult to tell the difference between religious and secular authority. Church officials and government officials were often the same people. This meant religious doctrine was often the law of the land, and those who engaged in deviant religious behaviors, such as blasphemy, were punished.[3] It was assumed that crime was motivated by impure thoughts and poor religious instruction, which meant the church was primarily responsible for

▼ According to the demonic perspective, deviance signifies a loss in the supernatural battle between good and evil.

the correction of all types of inappropriate behavior. This pre-Enlightenment model for dealing with crime is called **demonology**—a perspective of crime that considers antisocial behavior as caused by an evil entity who lives inside an individual and overtakes his or her personality. The struggle to control antisocial behavior in this model is continually waged between those who are in control and those who are defined as outsiders. Those in control believe the outsiders constitute a threat to the healthy functioning of society and therefore they must be defined and sanctioned as criminal. Steven Pfohl argues that controlling social life is much like a battle:

> The story of deviance and social control is a battle story. It is the story of the battle to control the ways people think, feel, and behave. It is a story of winners and losers and of the strategies people use in struggles with one another. Winners in the battle to control "deviant acts" are crowned with a halo of goodness, acceptability, normality. Losers are viewed as living outside the boundaries of social life as it ought to be, outside the "common sense" of society itself. They may be seen by others as evil, sleazy, dirty, dangerous, sick, immoral, crazy, or just plain deviant. They may even come to see themselves in such negative imagery, to see themselves as *deviants*.[4]

Deviance was therefore equated with sin. According to the demonic perspective, deviance is a transgression of the will of the gods that signifies a loss in the supernatural battle between good and evil. According to Pfohl, demonic influence can be manifested in one of two ways.

- *Temptation.* Properly socialized individuals are able to tell the difference between good and evil and make the appropriate choice. However, they will sometimes knowingly make the wrong choice and choose evil not because they do not know better, but because they are tempted by the seductions of deviance. A good example is in the biblical story of Adam and Eve in which Eve succumbs to the temptation of Satan and eats the forbidden fruit. According to the demonic perspective, humankind inherited this weakness for temptation and must continually battle the forces of Satan to make righteous choices.

- *Possession.* Individuals may be possessed by the devil. In this instance, they do not succumb to temptation of their own free will but rather are subject to antisocial behavior at the instigation of demonic forces. An example of the concept can be seen in occasional news reports in which parents claim their children are possessed by demons and seek exorcism or attempt to exorcise the demons themselves

**demonology** An ancient perspective of crime that considers antisocial behavior as caused by an evil entity who lives inside an individual and overtakes his or her personality.

(situations that, unfortunately, can lead to abuse and sometimes the child's death).[5] Modern criminal justice does not generally accept the demonic explanation of possession.[6]

It is difficult to overestimate the influence religion has had on explanations for antisocial behavior in the past. Religion is a powerful social force that informs the thinking of many people.[7] Many religions exert equally powerful influences on the control of social behavior. We can best understand the demonic perspective by observing how it responded to crime. When the devil was determined to have possessed an individual's body, the response was often to attack that body to drive the demon out. Consequently, a variety of physical punishments were used to exorcise the devil.[8] These punishments had two purposes. First, pain was considered to purge the demon. Second, the public administration of these punishments was believed to restore the community as people witnessed how God, acting through his human agents (the king and the church), maintained social control.

Physical punishment thus had a symbolic aspect that encouraged intense, brutal, and painful rituals, such as burning at the stake, that evoked an image of hell. Steven Pfohl discusses physical punishment:

> Another symbolic aspect of religious punishment was found in the principle of *lex talionis,* or an 'eye for an eye, a tooth for a tooth, stroke for stroke, burning for burning.' This principle was used to justify the mutilation of sinners. Thus, the thief had a hand cut off, while the penis of a rapist, the tongue of a liar, or the heart of a traitor might be ritually excised. Such punishments underscored the subordination of natural bodies to supernatural struggles between good and evil.[9]

All sorts of physical punishments were invented to enable the church to battle the devil by punishing the sinner's body. For instance, the particularly brutal "breaking on the wheel" broke the sinner's bones. It was believed evil spirits would then have a more difficult time living in the body because the bones were its most enduring part. Similar logic underscored the requirement that the bodies of people who had been hanged had to remain hanging. It was believed their bodies were full of demons who would endanger the earth's fertility if the bodies were buried. Consequently, until relatively recently, hanged bodies were allowed to dangle from trees until they decomposed.[10]

To the modern mind, the demonic perspective leaves much to be desired. As an explanation for the causes of crime, its emphasis on religion placed too much power in the hands of clergy and kings. Its response to crime focused on purging demons from the body, thus justifying gruesome tortures that elicited confessions and often destroyed the body to such an extent there was little left to bury and little closure for surviving family members.[11]

The demonic perspective gradually gave way to the ideas of the Enlightenment, but we still see its influence in the

▲ In centuries past, the church sought to battle the devil by punishing the sinner's body.

criminal justice system today. Many mainstream religions have codes such as the biblical Ten Commandments that prescribe religious and social behavior that have made their way into various legal systems. Without a religious basis for social control, many commentators suggest that crime and antisocial behavior are natural outcomes.[12] For the most part, however, contemporary criminologists do not advocate a demonic perspective for the explanation of crime for two reasons. First, from a scientific perspective, it would require the demonstration and measurement of an omniscient "good" pro-human force and a partially omniscient "bad" anti-human force, and evidence that those forces can inhabit human bodies and affect human behavior. Second, the demonic perspective's policies of torture and mutilation are no longer permissible in Western countries.

## Evil and Immorality

In recent decades, some social science scholars have proposed to define and study evil. Although not strictly considered demonology, evil is a concept that fits well into the idea of demonology. As a concept, it resists measurement and often definition, but it is one of those concepts that people "know when they see it."

Like a demon, evil is considered to inhabit some people and not others. Some religious people believe it can be exorcised. Modern criminology has no "theory of evil," but the idea that some criminal offenders, murderous political leaders, and terrorists are affected by something terrible but inconceivable still fascinates some scholars. A brief 1999 study that consisted of interviews with forensic psychiatric nurses found they categorized as "evil" offenders who had committed extreme criminal behavior that seemed deliberate and planned, such as the murder of a child. In this case, then, the nurses defined evil as some component of free will. They did not consider "evil" those offenders who were clearly extremely mentally ill, such as those exhibiting schizophrenia.[13] This agrees with Pfohl's idea of demonic temptation: The patients that seemed healthy were presented with an evil choice and took it.

## LO2:

Summarize why contemporary criminologists do not consider the concept of evil as an explanation of crime.

Other scholars have sought to typify evil from a biological standpoint. A study on the "neurobiology" of evil distinguished between the ideas of banal evil and sadistic evil: "Whereas banal evil may involve a dissociation of corticostriatal processing from limbic input (reason without passion), sadistic evil may involve a dissociation of limbic processing from frontal controls (passion without reason)." To translate: Banal evil is represented by the bureaucrat who does his or her job regardless of its horrendous effects—for example, the Nazi clerks who calmly sent millions to their deaths in concentration camps. Sadistic evil is best represented by the serial killer who appears to have little control over the urge to kill and mutilate.[14] Again, this follows Pfohl's demonic typology: Banal evil results from the choice to give in to temptation, and sadistic evil represents demonic possession. Academic debate about the study of evil is alive and well, but this is perhaps the nearest that scholarly discussion ventures to supernatural explanations of crime.

Some scholars argue that the cause of crime is a lack of religious-based morality.[15] It may be somewhat of a stretch to attribute the perspective of scholars William Bennett, John DiIulio, and John Walters to supernatural ideas, but their theory of moral poverty and crime echoes some very impor-

tant aspects of this perspective. Specifically, Bennett and his colleagues decry the permissiveness of contemporary American culture and advocate a return to a period when self-control, good manners, responsibility, and accountability were taught in the family, schools, and church. Bennett and his colleagues adopt a conservative view of society that considers the family and the church the primary agents of socialization; they view crime as the failure of these institutions to instill healthy values in children. They see abuse, neglect, and lack of control of children as the reasons for a diminishing of the moral character of American youth. The culprits, in their view, are the moral relativism of modern American life (the belief that standards of right and wrong are not absolute but vary among individuals); a lax criminal justice system; the values clarification perspective (a technique for encouraging students to relate their thoughts and feelings) that is taught in public schools; gratuitous acts of violence; and the media's portrayal of promiscuity, adultery, and homosexuality. To counteract these negative features of contemporary society, Bennett and his colleagues suggest:

> The flip side of moral poverty is moral health. Being born healthy to or raised by loving biological or adoptive parents or guardians of whatever race, creed, color, social economic status, or demographic description is perhaps the luckiest state that can befall a human being. To be born into or raised by such a family and to grow up surrounded by loving, caring, responsible—parents or guardians, neighbors, teachers, coaches, clergy—is to be raised in moral wealth.[16]

This perspective on moral poverty is an extension of the notion of evil as a cause of crime and antisocial behavior. The

▶ Some scholars argue that a lack of religious-based morality is the source of crime.

notions of moral poverty and evil are both vague, difficult to define, and impossible to measure, but they both look to the poor status of individual souls as a cause of problems in society.

# Think about it

## Understand

> Describe the two ways the devil was thought to influence people to break the law.

## Apply

> Show how physical punishment was justified as an appropriate way to dispense justice.

## Evaluate

> Defend Pfohl's argument that the pre-Enlightenment struggle to control antisocial behavior was cast as a battle between good and evil.

# The Classical School of Criminology

The **classical school of criminology** is a set of ideas that focuses on deterrence and considers crime to be the result of offenders' free will. It represents the most important era in Western legal reform and a major step toward a more humanitarian way of thinking about crime.[17] The classical school is an important

**LO3:**

> **Analyze** the classical school of criminology's focus on the offense as opposed to the offender by emphasizing the concept of free will.

prerequisite to the modern criminal justice system, and it would be a mistake to consider it as ancient history because it underlies contemporary justice policies.

Two basic tenets of classical thought are that criminal offenders freely choose to break the law and that punishment should be only as serious as the offense. Before the classical school, no one thought about what motivated offenders beyond supernatural forces. Although classical thinkers aimed to bring humanitarian reform to the legal system, they sought change, not to make life easier for criminal offenders, but to protect society from the harm done by those offenders. From a classical standpoint, overly harsh, arbitrary, and inconsistent punishments harmed society and actually encouraged lawbreaking.

## The Enlightenment

In the 17th and 18th centuries, Western societies developed a new understanding of science and the relationship of human beings to the world. During this period, the **Enlightenment,** great strides in philosophy and science were made. The Enlightenment fostered a new "age of reason" that sought to replace religious dogma with intellectual reasoning.[18] The Enlightenment broadened many aspects of learning, including geography, geology, biology, and politics. It changed

**LO4:**

> **Discuss** the Enlightenment's contribution of the social contract to criminology.

not only what was known about the world, but also who had the expertise and authority to claim that knowledge. This shift saw the power of the clergy and royalty diminish as the influence of merchants, scientists, and even regular people increased.[19]

Inspired by Enlightenment philosophy, classical school thinkers such as Cesare Beccaria and Jeremy Bentham observed how the legal systems of their nations approached crime and lawbreakers. They did not participate in research studies or interview offenders, victims, and law enforcement. Because the basis of classical thought is not only philosophical, but also centuries old, scientific testing of classical ideas has been carried out only in recent decades.[20] Still, many people today find the idea that offenders freely choose their actions to be simple common sense, especially in a nation like the United States where individuals have a wide range of choices about how to live. Why would someone choose the risky offense of robbing a convenience store when he could just get a job? The answer is easy: The robber is too lazy to work, wants fast money, and is sure of getting away with the crime. The robber has chosen the route of robbery. Although this line of thinking seems obvious to us now, it took centuries to develop. However, to understand how the classical school of criminology took shape, we must first understand the philosophical groundwork that was laid during the Enlightenment.

The Reformation's religious upheaval had already stimulated the development of a number of Protestant sects that challenged the authority of the Roman Catholic Church, and the earlier invention of the printing press made it possible for commoners to acquire knowledge and education and ultimately challenge the status quo.[21] Along with the Enlightenment, these developments set the stage for a new concept of the relationship between human beings and the state, and stimulated thinkers such as Thomas Hobbes, Jean-Jacques Rousseau, and John Locke to question the supremacy of the aristocrats.

---

**classical school of criminology** A set of ideas that focuses on deterrence and considers crime to be the result of offenders' free will.

**the Enlightenment** A period during the 17th and 18th centuries in Europe in which great strides in philosophy and science were made.

This new philosophy profoundly influenced the development of criminological thinking. The supernatural perspective was replaced by a view that emphasized the "natural" rights of human beings, that is, rights that were universal and did not depend on a legal authority for their existence. The key to this new perspective was the idea that individuals were motivated by calculated consideration and the need for rational dealings with others. We find an example of this view at the beginning of one of the foremost products of Enlightenment thinking, the U.S. Declaration of Independence (1776):

> We hold these truths to be self-evident, that all men are created equal, that they are endowed by their Creator with certain unalienable Rights, that among these are Life, Liberty and the pursuit of Happiness. — That to secure these rights, Governments are instituted among Men, deriving their just powers from the consent of the governed. . . .

These few lines contain the ideas that some rights are natural; that they entitle humans to life, liberty, and the pursuit of happiness; and that they are secured by some sort of social contract. Let's now explore the relationship between these obligations and classical criminology.

## The Social Contract

According to Enlightenment thinkers, the **social contract**—the idea that individuals in a society are bound by reciprocal obligations—formed the basis for meaningful communities. Instead of envisioning members of society bound by some supernatural spirit, philosophers saw the relationships as being bound by reciprocal obligations based on the idea that each person had to give up some rights and liberties in order to achieve cooperation and safety for all. This social contract also required that individuals respect others' rights and properties in order to receive the same consideration.

Thomas Hobbes (1588–1679) had a pessimistic view of governments based on an even more negative view of human nature. According to Hobbes, individuals concede to the sovereign the right to make the rules of society and to enforce them. By giving up their liberties and freedoms, they are assured safety and uniform enactment and enforcement of laws. Hobbes, who is famous for his argument that "life is nasty, brutish, and short," viewed the sovereign as having almost universal and complete power over his subjects. Although today this view seems negative and extreme, according to Hobbes, it is necessary in order to control the competing desires and demands of members of society.[22]

At first blush, Hobbes's idea of the social contract may not seem drastically different from the supernatural perspective in that the sovereign or the church has complete power. However, it is significant for distinguishing between the divine right of the sovereign and the willing surrender of liberties by subjects who fear chaos and disorder. In the 21st century, the surrender of liberties can be witnessed by Americans' reaction to the terrorist acts of September 11, 2001. Congress rushed to pass the USA PATRIOT Act apparently without considering how it would affect American rights and freedoms or the conventions of international law, including the Geneva Convention, which specifies how prisoners of war are to be treated.[23]

John Locke (1632–1704) further advanced the idea of a social contract. Like Hobbes, Locke believed individuals give up rights and liberties in order to live under a sovereign who provides security. However, Locke had a more positive view of this relationship and framed it in a more reciprocal fashion. The power of the sovereign, according to Locke, is not absolute. To receive obedience, the sovereign must respect the rights of the governed; if the sovereign violated the social contract, subjects had a right to rebel.[24] This is a major departure from previous political philosophies that envisioned the sovereign's power as ordained by God and not freely given by society. In Locke's view (also reflected in the Declaration of Independence), the subjects could demand a change in sovereign based upon the sovereign's failure to live up to the social contract.

You may notice that Locke's political philosophy, although a departure from the past, falls far short of the expectations we have of the relationship between state and individuals today. Locke, like his contemporaries, was a product of his time and believed individuals fit into social upper and lower classes that determined their rights and opportunities. In his capacity as commissioner of trade and plantations, he wrote in one report:

> If the causes of this evil be well looked into, we humbly conceive it will be found to have proceeded neither from scarcity of provisions nor from want of employment for the poor, since the goodness of God has blessed these times with plenty no less than the former, and a long peace during those reigns gave us as plentiful a trade as ever. The growth of the poor must therefore have some other cause, and it can be nothing else but the relaxation of discipline and corruption of manners; virtue and industry being as constant companions on the one side as vice and idleness are on the other. The first step, therefore, towards the setting of the poor on work, we humbly conceive, ought to be a restraint of their debauchery by a strict execution of the laws provided against it, more particularly by the suppression of superfluous brandy shops and unnecessary ale houses, especially in country parishes not lying upon great roads.[25]

John Locke was very much the aristocrat who, although liberal in his time, would today be considered an elitist.

**social contract** The idea that individuals in a society are bound by reciprocal obligations.

However, we credit him with advancing the social contract by arguing that the sovereign was responsible for the governed.

Jean-Jacques Rousseau (1712–1778) took the idea of the social contract a few steps further. In his book, *The Social Contract* (1762), he formed the idea of extending the opportunity to participate in public affairs to as many people as possible. Furthermore, Rousseau stated that the majority is more often right than wrong. His complex philosophy considers the state as having a personality, which is not simply a mechanism for satisfying human wants but also has a morality that can fulfill the will of the community.[26]

One of the primary benefits of reading Rousseau is to grasp his distinction between natural law and man-made law. Natural law, the idea promoted by many philosophers including Thomas Aquinas, Thomas Paine, and Thomas Jefferson, postulates that there are inalienable natural rights granted to humanity because they are inherent in the social contract. With common sense and rationality, we can ascertain that these rights are necessary to the formation of meaningful communities. In contrast, human-made law is a product of individuals deciding among themselves how their affairs ought to be governed. For instance, a major distinction between capitalism and communism is the crucial issue of ownership of property. Under capitalism, the individual ownership of property provides incentives for people to work hard and increase their estates. Conversely, communism specifies that societies function most efficiently and fairly when everyone owns property as a collective.[27] These distinctions are a result of political decisions rather than something we can rationally define from natural law.

Human-made law, according to the Enlightenment thinkers, should be a logical extension of natural law. That is, human laws should take advantage of rationality and provide incentives for cooperative behavior that encourages individuals to look beyond their own personal circumstances and consider the welfare of the community. By passing laws based on the utilitarian notion of the greatest good for the greatest number of people, these philosophers sought to find a basis of government that everyone could embrace. This period of the Enlightenment greatly affected the origins of classical criminology. As we study the development of classical criminology, with special emphasis on Cesare Beccaria and Jeremy Bentham, we will trace the history not only of this perspective, but also of those related to contemporary issues of crime and justice.

## Cesare Beccaria

Cesare Beccaria (1738–1794), an Italian thinker appalled by the medieval conditions of Italy's prison system, sought to provide the rationale for a more fair and humane system of social control. His 1764 treatise, *On Crimes and Punishments,* presents 41 short chapters that range from how to prevent crime to the origins of punishment and the right

*Marchese Cesare Beccaria*

▲ Italian thinker Cesare Beccaria sought to provide the rationale for a more fair and humane system of social control.

to punish. Uncertain political conditions made his harshly critical book an immediate success, but they also meant that initially Beccaria had to remain anonymous as its author. The only book of note Beccaria produced, the volume had a lasting effect on the development of Western law. Thomas Jefferson and John Adams used it partly as the basis for constructing the new government of the United States. Pfohl explains the book's popularity:

> The book appealed almost instantaneously to a curious mix of conservatives, who defended the continuance of monarchy, and radicals . . . who were setting in motion the forces that would topple it. . . . Both abhorred the continuation of antiquated demonic control policies, viewing them as

### LO5:

**Compare and contrast** the ideas of Cesare Beccaria and Jeremy Bentham as the primary architects of the classical school of criminology.

harsh and arbitrary reminders of the previous days of Inquisition in holy terror. Beccaria's book represented a masterful stroke of timing, an opportunity to bring dark, meaty evil penal practice into the age of Enlightenment.[28]

The heart of Beccaria's argument is that punishment should be not "an act of violence," but "essentially public, prompt, necessary, the least possible in the given circumstances, proportionate to the crimes, dictated by the laws."[29] We can distill the most important aspects of Beccaria's ideas into six principles.

- *Rational punishment is necessary to preserve the social contract.* Orderly societies would not be possible if each of us were free to punish in our own individualistic and emotional ways. One of the cornerstones of the social contract is that governments are vested with the responsibility for maintaining social order. Citizens cede to the government the authority and ability to respond to transgressions of the law. Rather than lynching a horse thief or castrating a rapist ourselves, we have created courts to rationally determine guilt and correctional systems to induce punishment. By insisting on a system of rational punishment, society prevents chaos.

- *The legislature makes law, and a judge determines guilt.* In order to have a rational system of justice, laws must be written by the legislature and guilt determined by judges. Before the Enlightenment, the despot could make the law up and use torture to coerce a confession from a suspect. Mere charges were considered evidence, and secret accusations and torture were accepted as part of the justice process. Beccaria argued that a rational system of justice invested the legislature with determining both law and punishment and the judge with determining the suspect's guilt. Today, legal codes specify punishments according to the severity of the offense; juries determine guilt, and judges typically determine the sentence. The important advancement of Beccaria's argument is that the law should be transparent, which means not only that it is written but that evidence is made available to the defense, which has the opportunity to refute it.

- *Individuals act to maximize pleasure and minimize pain.* According to classical criminology, individuals perform a moral calculus when deciding whether to break a law. They weigh the rewards of successfully completing an offense against the likelihood of capture and punishment. Government can thus discourage crime by ensuring that antisocial individuals are likely to be discovered, quickly captured, and severely punished.

- *Rationally calculated punishment is a form of social control.* If individuals decide to break the law based upon rational calculation, it is advisable for the government to set its punishments according to a manageable scale that can inform reasonable people. For instance, a rational person

may choose not to commit a capital offense because the death penalty is possible. Instead, this individual might choose to commit a lesser offense in which the penalty is not so severe. By exactly specifying the level of punishment available for each offense, the government can ensure that punishments are sufficiently severe to deter most potential offenders.

- *Deterrence is the object of social control.* **Deterrence** is a very important feature of modern-day criminal justice systems because it prevents a great deal of harm and damage. For deterrence to be effective, justice must be swift, certain, and sufficiently severe. In today's criminal justice system these principles are sometimes hard to achieve. For instance, justice is not always swift. Because of a lengthy appeals system, it is often many years before death sentences are carried out. Similarly, justice is not always certain. Many criminal offenders succeed in avoiding detection and capture. In many ways, prisons are full of the unlucky and foolish, while the talented, well-connected, and inventive escape detection and punishment.

> **>< THINKBACK**
> deterrence (ch. 3)—The idea that punishment for an offense will prevent that offender and others from further breaking the law.

- *The law should focus on the acts and not the actors.* This important principle of classical criminology assumes that all offenders exercise their free will in deciding whether to break the law. Classical criminology does not consider whether a person is impoverished, uneducated, hungry, desperate, or of low intelligence; it does not consider the offender's motivation. By focusing on the act rather than the offender, classical criminology treats similar offenses in a similar way. It ignores offenders' rationalizations and excuses and instead punishes them for their behavior. Consequently, the law considers what has been done rather than who did it.[30]

Beccaria's ideas represented a major departure from the way governments responded to crime. We can readily trace many of the principles of the contemporary criminal justice system to his reforms.[31] In time, other theorists and philosophers, such as Jeremy Bentham, expanded these principles of classical criminology.

## Jeremy Bentham

An English philosopher and political radical, Jeremy Bentham (1748–1832) sought to reform the archaic British legal system. Like Beccaria, he advocated a new way of dealing with crime based upon the concept of **utilitarianism.** According to utilitarianism, individuals should behave according to the principle of "the greatest good for the greatest number of people." This simple idea has far-reaching consequences for

**utilitarianism** The idea of seeking the greatest good for the most people.

▲ English philosopher and political radical Jeremy Bentham advocated a new way of dealing with crime based upon the concept of utilitarianism.

determining how individuals ought to behave ethically. For example, the most direct way of acquiring material wealth is to steal it.[32] However, if everyone pursued this line of reasoning, it would become a "dog eat dog" world. Some people would profit from stealing, but others would be harmed, and disorder would prevail. Utilitarian principles argue that ethical behavior allows the greatest number of people to benefit, and society is in much better shape when all benefit than when each individual looks out only for his or her interests.[33]

What is the motivation to engage in this type of utilitarian behavior? According to Bentham, a criminal offender does a **hedonistic calculus** in which he or she calculates the

worth of breaking the law by estimating the positive consequences versus the possible negative consequences. In effect, the offender weighs the benefits of a criminal offense against not only the prospect of being caught and punished, but also against the effect it may have on society. For example, many inmates in correctional institutions rationalize or excuse their own behavior yet believe most of their fellow inmates deserve punishment. Because inmates have family members outside the institution, they support the incarceration of murderers and rapists who might prey on their loved ones.

In 1789, Bentham laid out his extensive philosophy in his book, *An Introduction to the Principles of Morals and Legislation*.[34] A major contribution was the suggestion that if potential offenders actually do measure the projected pleasure of breaking the law against the pain of getting caught, then the legislature should take this into consideration and set penalties for each offense at a level designed to deter the unlawful behavior. This is the idea of **proportionality.** It states that the most serious offenses should have the most severe penalties, thus producing a hierarchy of punishments. (See *Theory to Practice* for details about proportionality in modern sentencing.)

Bentham's goal in producing a hierarchy of punishments was to deter crime. He believed that potential offenders freely make complex and what they believe are rational choices in deciding not only what type of offenses to commit, but also the severity. To deter these offenses, the legislature must clearly specify the range of penalties. A potential offender cannot do the hedonistic calculus without knowing all the variables. For example, more harm is done to individuals and society in an armed robbery with a gun than in one with a club or a knife. Today, then, many jurisdictions define armed robbery with a firearm as a more egregious offense than robbery without a firearm and allocate a more severe range of punishments for the former.

Bentham was a pragmatist who advocated policies he believed would be most effective in deterring crime. One of his ideas was to require citizens to have their names tattooed on their wrists so they could be identified by police. We would see this as intrusive today, but there have been serious proposals to require all U.S. citizens to carry identification cards. Legal and moral concerns surround this type of policy. But from Bentham's pragmatic perspective, many conservative individuals believe it is necessary to alleviate problems inherent in current U.S. immigration policies.[35]

Bentham's ideas for social control have had far-reaching implications. One for which he is still known is his design for a prison based upon surveillance. The Panopticon was a circular prison with the cells on the outside and the control station in the middle. This would allow prison staff line-of-sight surveillance of all inmates at all times. The model was not without controversy. Michel Foucault, who saw the

**hedonistic calculus** A method proposed by Jeremy Bentham in which criminal offenders calculate the worth of breaking the law by estimating the positive consequences versus the possible negative consequences.

**proportionality** The idea that the most serious criminal offenses should have the most severe penalties.

# theory to practice

### Let the Penalty Fit the Crime

One of the principles of deterrence theory is that the most serious offenses should have the most serious penalties in order to provide justice and discourage people from breaking the law. Therefore, the federal and state criminal justice systems have created sentencing schedules that specify the type and amount of penalty for each offense level.

Sentencing schedules are designed for two purposes. First, more serious offenses incur more drastic penalties to discourage people from committing them. This is a relative innovation in the criminal law. There was a time when the death penalty was meted out for many offenses that today we would consider relatively minor. The second purpose of the schedules is to enhance uniformity in sentencing. Offenders who commit similar offenses should receive similar penalties. When judges are permitted to be arbitrary and provide draconian sentences for minor offenses or light penalties for major offenses, the public will quickly lose faith in the fairness of the criminal justice system.

The classical school advocates introducing proportionality and reason into the sentencing process so gross injustices are avoided. This philosophy is still deeply embedded in the U.S. criminal justice system where offenders are held accountable for their offenses with little regard for their personal attributes.

## THINKING in ACTION

1. Does requiring the severity of penalties to be commensurate with the severity of offenses deter potential offenders? Why or why not?
2. Should judges be allowed to sentence offenders as they see fit without using sentencing schedules?

---

Panopticon model as a significant problem because it did not allow inmates privacy or dignity, believed the idea of the Panopticon applied to all of society because individuals are subject to the discipline and surveillance of the state.[36] George Orwell's novel *1984* in which "Big Brother" constantly watches citizens is a fictional but logical extension of the Panopticon. Regardless of privacy and dignity issues, this architectural model has found currency elsewhere such as in hospital intensive-care wards where nurses can watch over all the patients from their central station.

We can trace to the classical school many of the principles that guide the way social control is exercised over offenders in the criminal justice system today. These principles include a view of human nature based upon *hedonism,* in which individuals are assumed to seek pleasure and avoid pain, as well as the idea of free will, in which individuals are viewed as making rational decisions about whether to break the law, thus allowing governments to set proportional penalties. A third principle is the concept that government is obligated to respect citizens' rights to the degree that is consistent with public safety. This principle of individual rights is always in contention in a democratic society, especially in an age of terrorism in which many are willing to forgo some rights in order to feel safe.[37] Finally, classical criminology emphasizes due-process procedures in the criminal justice system as well as the presumption of innocence and the state's obligation to prove guilt before punishment.

## Think about it

### Understand

Explain how deterrence is one of the foundations of the classical school.

### Analyze

Summarize why Cesare Beccaria's work appealed to both the conservatives and radicals of the 18th century.

### Evaluate

Assess how the societal contract changed the way that people relate to society.

### Create

Devise a modern sentencing scheme that incorporates the concept of proportionality into today's moral and political environment.

## The Positivist School of Criminology

The 19th century was an exciting time for science. Great strides were made in many fields, and amateur scientists made significant contributions to our understanding of how the world works. For instance, before he went on his historic voyage around the world on the HMS *Beagle,* the young Charles Darwin collected insects.[38] His later books, especially *Origin of Species,* laid the groundwork for his theory of natural selection; *Descent of Man* extended his ideas to human evolution. Darwin's theory of natural selection is a testament to the practice of making deductions based upon observation.[39] His work is widely recognized as fundamental to the development of the **scientific method**—a process of investigation in which phenomena are observed, ideas are tested, and conclusions are drawn—which underlies positivist criminology.

Rather than relying on armchair theorizing about offenders' motivations, as practiced by the classical school of criminology, early contributors to the **positivist school of criminology** instead looked at offenders' behavior and attempted to link their explanations of it to external, observable forces that can be measured, such as offenders' biological, psychological, and sociological traits.[40] This significant departure from the classical school relies on a new set of assumptions.

- *Determinism outweighs free will.* The classical school assumes that offenders make rational choices in deciding to break the law. The positivists instead believe that individuals' actions are influenced ("determined") by myriad forces that may be beyond their control and even their consciousness. For instance, for reasons that may be embedded in the biological, psychological, or cultural differences between males and females, each potential offender is affected by his or her sex. This influence can be conscious or unconscious and can be intertwined with other factors such as race or social class. Positivists thus do not consider people to have the broad range of free will that the classical school assumes. The policy implications of these differing assumptions are profound. Whereas the classical school relies on deterrence to alter the moral calculus potential offenders do, the positivist school is more concerned with affecting the conditions assumed to cause crime and providing treatment for offenders so they may avoid **recidivism**.[41]

><THINKBACK
recidivism (ch. 1)—Repeat offending.

- *The offender matters more than the offense.* Deterrence in the classical school focuses on the penalties for committing the offense, increasing the chances of getting caught, and ensuring timely punishment. In contrast, the positivist school focuses on identifying the social forces that influence offenders and developing treatments to alleviate the underlying problems assumed to cause crime. As we will see in subsequent chapters dealing with biological, psychological, and sociological theories of crime, positivists view offenders as possessing qualities or traits that differ from those of law-abiding people and that are subject to remediation. This difference between focusing on the offense and focusing on the offender has important implications for assigning the responsibility for deviant behavior. For instance, when positivists attribute chronic poverty to fostering conditions conducive to crime, policy suggests reducing the disparity between rich and poor. Classical theorists would suggest making penalties more severe so impoverished people would decide not to risk breaking the law.

- *Science trumps philosophy.* The positivist school attempts to find what *is* rather than what *ought to be.* Positivists use science to attempt to understand why offenders break the law and prescribe remedies so they do not continue to do so.

- *Indeterminate sentencing is more effective than determinate sentencing.* One of the more striking policy implications of the contrast of classical and positivist criminology is the role of punishment and rehabilitation in sentencing. The classical school, with its concentration on the crime, advocates that all offenders receive the same sentence for the same offense. In contrast, the positivist school employs the indeterminate sentence in which the length of incarceration is determined not by the judge but rather by correctional experts, primarily the parole board. The reasoning is that only these experts can ascertain when an offender has been successfully rehabilitated and can be returned to the free world.

This difference in sentencing policy illustrates the competing goals of the criminal justice system. Classical criminology is concerned with deterrence and punishment, whereas positivist criminology is more concerned with the causes of crime and the rehabilitation of offenders. The criminal justice system has aspects of both positivist and classical criminology in its policies, and these philosophies are continually being debated.[42]

In the next four chapters, we will see how the positivist school has contributed the majority of theories of contemporary criminology. The development of positivist theory shows how scientific knowledge and cultural pressures affect how societies respond to crime. The science has not always been good, however, and gross injustices have been visited upon alleged offenders due to misguided assumptions about the nature of human beings.

For instance, in the 19th century, young orphans were taken from the major cities on the East Coast and sent to the developing Midwestern and Western states as part of a

**LO6:**

**Analyze** the positivist school of criminology's assertion that individuals are influenced by external forces.

---

**scientific method** A process of investigation in which phenomena are observed; ideas are tested, and conclusions are drawn.

**positivist school of criminology** A set of ideas that considers crime to be the result of external, observable forces that can be measured.

▲ The positivist school focuses on developing treatments to alleviate the underlying problems assumed to cause crime, such as poverty and neighborhood disorganization.

plan to rescue them from the problems of urbanization. It was believed that matching these youths with farmers who needed their labor would teach them marketable skills and allow them to grow up in a healthier environment. Many of the young people sent west on these "orphan trains" were placed in situations in which their labor was exploited, and they were subject to physical, psychological, or sexual abuse. The decision-makers were well meaning, but the actual practice had consequences that were often disastrous.[43] In future chapters, we will detail numerous similar examples of how faulty science and the inept implementation of programs based upon the positivist rehabilitation ideas backfired. The positivist school has greatly increased our understanding of crime and response to unlawful behavior, but it has some issues that require consideration.

1. *Positivism accepts the legitimacy of the criminal justice system and its place in the social system.* We will see later that critical theories of criminology disapprove of the wholesale acceptance of inequities based on race, gender, and social class. For instance, for decades the only treatment available in women's penal institutions supported traditionally female social roles. Women were not encouraged to challenge the patriarchy, the family, the workplace, or the criminal justice system. Male offenders were trained in automotive technology, carpentry, or other trades in which they might make a living, but women offenders were encouraged to learn to cook, sew, style hair, or pur-

sue other traditionally female occupations. In many ways, then, positivism locked offenders into social inequities.

2. *Positivism encourages people to look at the external and internal forces that influence their behavior and seek ways of alleviating their antisocial propensities.* Positivism fails to consider the classical school's concept of free will, so it is sometimes viewed as overly deterministic. According to those who subscribe to classical criminology, positivism's focusing of blame outside the offender prevents offenders from taking responsibility for their own behavior.

3. *The positivist school envisions offenders as different from law-abiding people and in need of intervention to reform.* Positivism has attempted to demonstrate how offenders' biological, psychological, and sociological conditions vary from the norm. Offenders are viewed as "sick or damaged" and in need of drug therapy, psychological counseling, "tough love," or other programs designed to make them healthy and productive citizens. By contrast, the classical school envisions offenders as people who have made bad choices and who can be encouraged, through deterrence and punishment, to make better choices in the future.

This brief introduction to positivism only hints at the contributions this perspective makes to criminology. In subsequent chapters, we will explore several theories that hinge on positivist assumptions. Since criminal justice system reforms come from both the positivist and classical schools of criminology, however, we should not look for which school is right or correct, but rather we should appreciate how the development of criminology has benefited from many perspectives and how much theoretical work remains. We will now turn to the resurgence of some of the ideas of classical criminology in neoclassical criminology, which also uses some positivist concepts to define its perspective.

# Think about it

## Apply

Illustrate some of the major criticisms of the positivist school.

## Analyze

Compare and contrast the major ideas of the classical school with the positivist school.

## Neoclassical Criminology

Developed over the past 40 years, **neoclassical criminology** is a theoretical resurgence in classical criminology that emphasizes free will and deterrence and acknowledges some of the effects of positivism on decision making. It revives some of the principles of classical criminology and combines them with ideas from economic game theory, which argues that people choose their behaviors based upon perceived outcomes with the goal of maximizing their gain while minimizing the resources and output necessary to achieve their goals. This perspective is very useful in determining consumers' buying patterns. For instance, a person wanting to buy a new high-definition television will shop around for the best price as well as financing options, installation costs, and warranties. The goal is to make the best purchase for the lowest possible cost. Neoclassical criminologists use this model to explain crime. Just as someone buying a television would investigate all the options and select the best price within the context of other features, neoclassical theory presumes a potential offender will make a choice about what type of offense to commit and when to commit it.

Neoclassical criminology has developed a number of theories, which include rational choice theory and routine activities theory, that employ the classical concept of deter-

**LO7:**

**Show** how neoclassical criminology recalls the principles of classical criminology, including deterrence and rational choice.

rence. Furthermore, neoclassical criminology emphasizes the offender's character and argues that the choice to break the law is contingent upon both opportunity and personal integrity. If opportunities are limited by deterrence, individuals who are wavering in their decision to break the law may decide the costs are too high. This deterrent works best for first-time and minor offenders and may not be sufficient for career offenders or those with mental disorders who cannot adequately evaluate the costs and benefits of crime.

The neoclassical perspective has been embraced by conservative observers who desire more severe punishments for offenders. It marks a return to emphasis on the offense rather than the offender; however, it recognizes that offenders make choices and that society can influence those choices by limiting opportunities and imposing stiff sanctions. Neoclassical criminology has also been influenced by more recent perspectives, especially positivism. Recall that the positivist school takes issue with the concept of free will and views individuals as influenced by a number of factors that limit their choices. For instance, a young man growing up in a community with substandard schools, prevalent drugs and violence, few jobs, and urban blight does not have the same opportunities for living a lawful life as someone in different circumstances might have.[44]

With this in mind, neoclassical criminology asserts that an element of free will exists even for those in the most difficult social circumstances. It emphasizes individual character and the principle that each of us is responsible for our actions.[45] Rather than considering the behavior of individuals to be determined by economic conditions, socialization, and genetics as the positivist school does, neoclassical criminology argues that deficiencies in these areas can be overcome by rational choices made by individuals who take responsibility for their actions. Therefore, instead of envisioning a choice between hard determinism and free will, neoclassical criminology inserts between them a **soft determinism**—the idea that free will is affected by outside influences. (See Figure 4.1.)

The concept of soft determinism allows neoclassical criminology to downplay the social forces that affect individual behavior and reassert some classical ideas. Specifically, neoclassical criminology challenges the positivist emphasis on rehabilitation.[46] More important, the neoclassical school still holds to the concept that free will significantly influences the reasons that people break the law and should be considered when making law.[47] However, positivism has contributed three limiting factors to the neoclassical idea of free will.

■ *Premeditation.* **Premeditation** in reference to crime is the planning of a criminal act. It is considered more important for a first-time offender than for a repeat offender

**neoclassical criminology** A theoretical resurgence in classical criminology that emphasizes free will and deterrence and acknowledges some of the effects of positivism on decision making.

**soft determinism** The idea that free will is affected by outside influences.

**premeditation** In reference to crime, the planning of a criminal act.

## Figure 4.1   The Classical and Positivist Schools of Criminology

The major differences between the classical and positivist schools of criminology begin with their differing views of the role of free will in the commission of crime. Note that neoclassical criminology is in the middle of the spectrum.

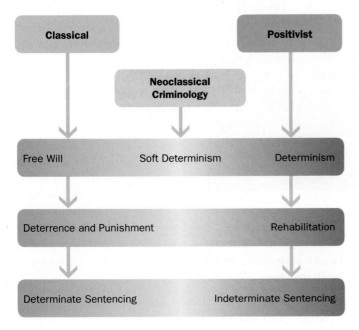

**Classical and Positivist Schools of Criminology**

because breaking the law has not yet become a habit. Therefore, say neoclassical criminologists, by considering the factors present when first-time offenders decide to break the law, it should be possible to alter their decision-making through deterrence. For the repeat offender, however, laws and punishments are less likely to alter the decision to break the law.[48]

- *Mitigating circumstances.* Several circumstances, such as stress, poverty, social pressure, and even the weather, may inhibit the individual's exercise of free choice. By allowing for such mitigating factors, neoclassical criminology moves closer to the idea of determination. However, it does not go as far as positivist criminology and still leaves room for the idea that the decision to break the law is determined not solely by outside forces, but also by the individual.

- *Insanity.* This third modification of the neoclassical perspective considers how free will may be perverted by mental illness. In the landmark case of Daniel McNaughton, which underlies the insanity defense, the neoclassical school recognizes that McNaughton did not have the mental capacity to fully understand the consequences of his actions. McNaughton believed he had direct communication with God, who informed him that Satan had a

plan to establish a reign on earth using the Tory party (Britain's conservative political party) as his instruments. McNaughton attempted to kill the leader of the Tory party, Sir Robert Peel, but killed his secretary by mistake. According to the courts, McNaughton did not and could not have full control of his mental facilities because he believed he was doing God's will. Therefore, this case did not meet the standard of accountability necessary for a murder conviction. McNaughton was declared not guilty by reason of insanity.[49]

Although the classical school may seem as outmoded as the supernatural perspective, many of its principles have been modified by the neoclassical school, and these principles can be seen in contemporary theories that inform public policy. Let's consider a classic study by Marvin Wolfgang and colleagues that shows how public policy may be considered in the sentencing of juvenile delinquents.

Wolfgang's study showed that most juvenile delinquents dropped out of a life of crime after one or two offenses. The study concluded that crime tends to be an episodic and situational phase for most young males and that eventually the vast majority desist. In fact, most delinquents in the study stopped breaking the law by their second offense regardless of how they were treated. The study recommended, therefore, that the full brunt of the law not be brought upon delinquents until their third offense. A small percentage—only 647 of nearly 10,000 individuals—committed five or more offenses, and these youths were responsible for more than half the total number of offenses committed by this cohort. Wolfgang's suggestion was to impose a swift and certain but mild punishment for first and second offenders and to reserve severe punishments for those who continued to break the law. This would accomplish two things. First, most youths would not be subject to the debilitating effects of severe punishment and could get on with their lives. Second, resources would be reserved for the more serious delinquents who required incarceration.[50]

Wolfgang and his colleagues can be considered neoclassical scholars because they suggest reserving severe sanctions for the most serious offenders and because their work laid the foundation for a return to the classical concept of deterrence as a criminal justice goal. Wolfgang's study had a profound effect on criminology; it appealed to both liberal and conservative thinkers. Treating first- and second-time offenders leniently appeals to liberals' sense that young people should be given the benefit of the doubt because most will not offend again. For conservative thinkers, the policy implications suggest that resources are better spent on chronic offenders, who may be incarcerated for long periods to enhance public safety. Although Wolfgang and his colleagues cannot be placed easily in either the conservative or the liberal camp, and their ideas straddle the philosophies of the classical and the positivist schools, their viewpoints demonstrate that the neoclassical school has practical implications

◄ Wolfgang's study concluded that crime tends to be a phase for most young males and that most eventually stop committing serious offenses.

decides not to commit similar behavior. General deterrence is thought to be the most important of the two concepts because it affects all of us and not just those who have already broken the law.

Some modern criminologists, however, no longer adhere to the sharp division between these two types of deterrence. Mark Strafford and Mark Warr argue that most people are likely to have a mixture of direct and indirect experience with punishment and punishment avoidance. They contend that in order to fully appreciate the deterrent effect, researchers should examine four factors individuals may consider when deciding whether to break the law:

for modern criminal justice. We now consider neoclassical theories based on rational choice.

## Deterrence Theory Reconsidered

Long a mainstay of classical criminology, **deterrence theory** is the concept that punishment prevents more crime from occurring. That is, people will not break the law if the benefits of doing so fall short of the consequences if they are caught. (For a look at the relationship between deterrence and capital punishment, see *Doubletake*.) When considering breaking the law, individuals consider the likelihood that they will succeed and get caught (certainty), the time frame between possibly getting caught and punished (swiftness), and the possible consequences (severity). Historically, deterrence has been envisioned as one of two types: specific and general. **Specific deterrence** is the idea that punishing one person for an offense, usually by incarceration or execution, will prevent that person from committing another offense. It occurs when an offender is caught and punished and decides not to break the law anymore. **General deterrence** is the idea that punishing one person for an offense will provide an example to others not to engage in crime. It occurs when the rest of society sees what has happened to the offender and

1. Has the individual already been punished for any offenses? This question examines his or her direct experience with punishment.

2. Is the individual aware of others who have been punished? This question examines the individual's indirect experience with punishment.

3. Has the individual avoided punishment? This question examines the individual's direct experience with punishment avoidance.

4. Is the individual aware of others who have avoided punishment for criminal offenses? This question examines the individual's indirect experience with punishment avoidance.[51]

Looking at both direct and indirect experiences with punishment and avoidance of punishment allows researchers to untangle the theoretical distinctions between specific and general deterrence. For instance, if a juvenile is arrested and sent to a training school, he or she not only experiences direct punishment, but also interacts with other delinquents and appreciates what happens to them. This indirect experience with punishment influences the delinquent's behavior over and above his or her direct experience. Strafford and Warr argue that this expanded view of deterrence theory is most evident when we look at people who commit a variety of offenses. Someone who commits a burglary and is caught and punished for it may be specifically deterred from committing burglary again

**deterrence theory** The concept that punishment prevents more crime from occurring.

**specific deterrence** The idea that punishing one person for an offense, usually by incarceration or execution, will prevent that person from committing another offense.

**general deterrence** The idea that punishing one person for an offense will provide an example to others not to engage in crime.

but, in addition, may be generally deterred from committing other types of offenses.

This advancement in deterrence theory calls for research that will likely be complicated. For instance, when we attempt to determine an individual's evaluation of the certainty of being caught and convicted, other theories may come into play. Specifically, self-control and learning ability greatly influence an individual's determination of the certainty of getting caught, so theories that seek to explain self-control and learning (which we will cover in later chapters) would have to be considered.[52]

Strafford and Warr's extension of deterrence theory demonstrates how neoclassical scholars have adapted classical criminology to contemporary crime and justice issues.

# doubletake

### Deterrence and the Death Penalty

The deterrence debate focuses on a number of issues, but perhaps the one studied most is capital punishment. According to deterrence theory, the execution of offenders who commit capital offenses will prevent others from committing capital offenses. However, the evidence for the deterrence effect of capital punishment is controversial and has been subject to debate for 40 years.

In 1975, economist Isaac Ehrlich published an influential study in which he claimed that each execution prevented eight murders. Over the years, several other studies found evidence of a deterrent effect for capital punishment; however, the methodological sophistication of these studies has been questioned. In 2005, Jeffrey Fagan, a professor of law and public health at Columbia University, testified before committees of the New York State Assembly that studies supporting the deterrent effect of capital punishment have significant shortcomings that make their findings suspect. Fagan cited the following:

■ *The studies treated all murders alike.* Not all murderers are equally deterred. Domestic murders in which passion is involved are less likely to be deterred than other types of murder. It is questionable whether people are rational during crimes of passion.

■ *Results have been inconsistent.* Many studies have shown that capital punishment has little deterrent effect or even a "brutalization" effect that increases the rate of homicides following executions for murder.

■ *The studies ignored missing data.* There were two periods in which data from Florida were not included in the studies, which, according to Fagan, could have biased the results.

■ *The studies did not directly test deterrence.* There is no way of knowing whether murderers are actually aware of the status of capital punishment in their state.

▲ According to deterrence theory, the execution of capital offenders will prevent others from committing capital offenses. However, the evidence for the deterrence effect of capital punishment has been questioned.

■ *Most of the deterrent effect is attributable to one state.* If the Texas data is removed from the statistical models, the effect vanishes.[1]

Fagan testified about other methodological issues that question the effectiveness of research claiming capital punishment can reduce the number of murders. Although common sense leads many people to believe people would think twice about murder if they themselves would be killed for it, there is little evidence to support this.

[1] Jeffrey Fagan, *Deterrence and the Death Penalty: A Critical Review of New Evidence,* Testimony to the New York State Assembly Standing Committee on Codes, Assembly Standing Committee on Judiciary and Assembly Standing Committee on Correction, January 21, 2005, http://www.deathpenaltyinfo.org/FaganTestimony.pdf.

## THINKING *in* ACTION

1. In your opinion, is capital punishment an effective general deterrent?
2. Does the deterrent effect of capital punishment merit more study? Why or why not?

However, it is not the only theory that employs the rich heritage of classical criminology to explain current criminal justice issues. We turn next to rational choice theory.

## Rational Choice Theory

**Rational choice theory** is the concept that offenders calculate the advantages and disadvantages not only of breaking the law, but also of what type of offenses to commit. It has practical implications for criminal justice policies.[53] It is directly linked to classical criminology because it assumes individuals freely choose whether to break the law. On the other hand, it is neoclassical in that it considers ways in which these choices are bound or limited by circumstance or the offenders' ability. For instance, not every offender has the opportunity to commit certain offenses, such as embezzlement, nor does every offender have the information to make informed choices. Nevertheless, rational choice theory as espoused by neoclassical thinkers assumes that offenders make choices based upon their desire to acquire pleasure while avoiding pain.

Derek Cornish and Ronald Clarke developed rational choice theory to capture some of the reasoning behind the decision to break the law. For instance, when considering the costs of breaking the law, the offender looks not just at the expected formal punishment, but also at informal costs such as shame, parental or family disapproval, and feelings of guilt.[54] Cornish and Clarke also consider the difference between criminal involvement and criminal events. Offenders must make two decisions: first, whether to commit an offense (involvement) and, second, what type of offense to commit (event). This is an important distinction. Presumably a motivated potential offender could be deterred from committing one type of offense after calculating the odds of getting away with it and the expected gains. However, having decided to commit an offense, he or she will likely commit a different one if the first looks too dangerous given the expected payoff.[55]

What are the policy implications of rational choice theory? By studying offenders' thinking processes, law enforcement officials and security experts can take steps to discourage criminal activity. Let's turn now to a perspective derived from rational choice theory called situational crime prevention.

### Situational Crime Prevention

**Situational crime prevention** is an extension of rational choice theory. Developed by Ronald Clarke as a way of explaining the choices offenders make, situational crime prevention looks at situational factors that can be modified to discourage crime. According to Clarke, the first modification is a reduction in physical opportunities to break the law. This "target hardening" includes using padlocks, security cameras, and increased lighting to protect property. However, the problem of "crime displacement" is always a consideration. When one target appears protected, the potential offender may simply search for a more vulnerable one. Nevertheless, target hardening is a way of affecting the choices potential offenders make in selecting when and where to break the law.[56]

A second situational modification Clarke advocates is to increase the risks of apprehension. Stepped-up police presence is an obvious policy implication. For instance, retail employees can provide a surveillance function in addition to their service and sales functions. By regularly approaching potential shoplifters with offers to help them in their selection of items, employees can reduce the likelihood that they will steal anything. Similarly, research has shown that buildings with doormen have less vandalism and burglary than similar buildings without doormen. The message here is that potential offenders are less likely to strike when an adequate number of employees and security officials are visibly responsible for the establishment.[57]

Further policy implications of situational crime prevention range from reducing the number of guns available to

▶ Security cameras in retail establishments and banks are a good example of situational crime prevention.

improving the technology designed to prevent drunk driving. For example, some jurisdictions may require cars of motorists with a history of driving under the influence to be fitted with a device that the driver must blow into to test his or her sobriety. If the driver's blood alcohol level is above a preset level, the device will prevent the car from being started. Situational crime prevention is also at work in airport baggage and passenger screening in which travelers must present photo identification to board the plane. This is not far from Bentham's idea that people should have their names tattooed on their wrist so they could be readily identified. Classical criminology is constantly being updated by the neoclassical thinkers, who believe it is desirable to focus on crime and its prevention rather than exerting resources on offender rehabilitation or attacking the causes of crime.

## Routine Activities Theory

Developed by Lawrence Cohen and Marcus Felson, **routine activities theory** is a neoclassical concept based upon the premise that crime occurs when three elements converge: motivated offenders, attractive targets, and the absence of capable guardians.[58] Opportunities for crime are highest, then, when an attractive target has no capable guardians. For example, a bank may be an attractive target for robbers, but if it is protected by security devices and guards and monitored by the FBI as well as local police, it has an abundance of capable guardians that make it less attractive.[59] Routine activities theory is neoclassical because it focuses on the offense rather than the offender. The offenders, merely one aspect in the theoretical triangle, freely decide to commit the offense because the other two points in the triangle—attractive targets and the absence of capable guardians—are present.

According to Cohen and Felson, motivated offenders represent a constant in the routine activities theory equation. This means we can always assume potential offenders are motivated to break the law, but the theory tells us little about their *level* of motivation. More important in this theory are the other two conditions: attractive targets and the absence of capable guardians. It is relatively simple to make a target less attractive to would-be thieves. For instance, FedEx has stenciled on its trucks that there is no cash on board, and some convenience stores have "drop safes" that clerks can deposit cash in but only the manager can open.

**rational choice theory** The concept that offenders calculate the advantages and disadvantages not only of breaking the law, but also of what type of offense to commit.

**situational crime prevention** An extension of rational choice theory that considers situational factors that can be modified to discourage crime.

**routine activities theory** The concept that crime occurs when three elements converge: motivated offenders, attractive targets, and the absence of capable guardians.

The third component of routine activities theory is the absence of capable guardians, another easy condition to alter in order to discourage crime. Capable guardians include security cameras, private security guards, increased lighting, alarm systems, and guard dogs (see *So What's New?* to learn more about how some parents use technology to act as a capable guardian of children). Guarding property is a multibillion-dollar business whose products range from steering wheel locks on automobiles to gated communities. When targets are made less attractive and attractive targets are closely watched, routine activities theory postulates that potential offenders will be deterred. This emphasis on deterrence is another hallmark of neoclassical theory.

The fact that Cohen and Felson do not emphasize the first component of their theory, motivated offenders, is both a weakness and a strength. By placing limited importance on motivated offenders, they avoid the difficult task of identifying and measuring motivation, which is not easily discernible. To measure offender motivation, one would have to talk to offenders and attempt to understand why they do what they do. This type of research has substantial obstacles. Access to offenders is problematic because those who are incarcerated have little to gain by exposing their motivations

▲ Rehabilitation programs can help alter the way offenders think about crime.

# so what's new?

### Spying on Your Kids

One of the core principles of routine activities theory is that capable guardians deter offenses. A good example is modern technology that lets parents keep tabs on their children in surreptitious ways. A wide variety of surveillance technology is available to parents via companies like Spy Parent.[1] Spy Parent, according to its website, provides "high quality safety and monitoring equipment . . . and vital information for parents, daycare providers, foster parents, and other service providers of youth." Anyone who wishes to conduct surveillance may purchase equipment that appears sophisticated enough for law enforcement authorities or intelligence operatives. Available devices include:

- *Video recording devices.* Parents can buy a system that employs up to four cameras to provide live pictures of what is happening on their property. The systems can be linked to the Internet so parents can monitor their children's activities via computer from anywhere in the world.
- *Internet monitoring.* A number of devices allow parents to determine what Internet sites their children visit and monitor their children's computers from their own computer in real time without the children's knowledge. If the child is visiting a pornography website, corresponding with undesirable friends, or placing inappropriate material on social networking sites, parents can immediately intervene. Other devices allow parents to record all the websites a child visits and all keystrokes, as well as passwords, without the child's knowledge.
- *GPS tracking devices.* Using geographic positioning systems technology, parents can keep track of their children's whereabouts. These devices can be placed in the family automobile, and parents can view their child's travel through a variety of websites. This allows parents to see where their children have the automobile at any time as well as monitor their speed.

Whereas this technology may make some parents feel better about their child's safety, privacy is at issue. This technology allows parents to substitute their presence and enables children a greater range of freedom in some respects while also being under constant surveillance. Perhaps the greatest privacy concern is that parents may use this type of technology without the child's knowledge.

The potential for preventing crime with these technologies, however, is significant. When potential offenders understand that their movements and activities can be monitored from remote locations, they may be less likely to break the law. It seems likely, however, that offenders may also keep pace with law enforcement in blocking such technology or using it for their own ends.

[1]http://www.spyparent.net/index.php.

## THINKING *in* ACTION

1. Should sales of sophisticated surveillance technology be restricted to law enforcement agencies? Why or why not?
2. How did your parents keep up with your computer usage? Did they monitor you?

to researchers, and those who have not been caught are difficult to identify. It is easier for researchers to measure the attractiveness of targets and the presence of capable guardians than it is to determine offender motivation. Thus, treating motivation as a given lets us assume that every offender is motivated by financial gain; therefore, researchers can concentrate on the other two components of rational choice theory.[60]

Ignoring offender motivation is also a weakness of routine activities theory. Even though the theory can explain why targets may be deemed attractive and why guardianship may look inadequate, motivation is difficult

# theory to practice

## Criminological Perspectives in Film

The three schools of criminological thought are often portrayed in films about crime. A useful and entertaining exercise for film buffs and crime scholars is to try to pick out which perspective appears in which film. Often, criminological theory is key to the plot as the filmmakers seek to provide a reason for the lawbreakers' behavior. For practice, let's look at five popular films and the criminological perspectives they employ.

The Supernatural Perspective

- *The Exorcist* (1973). In this classic film, a young girl is possessed by the devil and commits one murder, several assaults, and quite a bit of household vandalism. This film is one of the best examples of the use of the devil working through human beings to break the law as a major plot device and explanation for crime.

The Classical School

- *Oceans 11* (2001). In this humorous film, a group of thieves rationally decide to rob a casino. The main characters, one of whom lies to his parole officer about his whereabouts, devise an elaborate plan and methodically recruit others to assist. One character is even aware that he will return to prison, but he decides robbing the casino is worth it. *Oceans 11* is a good example of how offenders may carefully weigh the risk of getting caught against the potential rewards of successfully completing their offenses.

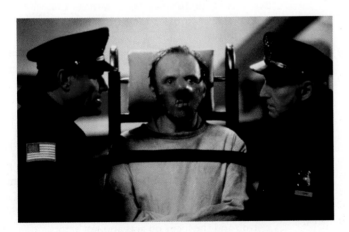

▲ The crimes of serial killer Hannibal Lecter in the films *The Silence of the Lambs* and *Hannibal* can be viewed through a positivist perspective—his antisocial behavior is the result of mental illness.

- *No Country for Old Men* (2007). This film is a sobering look at offenders who rationally decide to pursue their criminal offenses, not only for wealth, but also for personal principles. All the offenders in the film are coldly rational, and some are convinced that a large amount of money is worth committing multiple murders for as well as risking their own lives. One character's moral calculus, which is based on satisfying his personal principles, requires him to break the law even when nothing is at stake. *No Country for Old Men* is an excellent portrayal of the moral calculus as applied to crime.

The Neoclassical Perspective

- *A Clockwork Orange* (1971). Possibly the best film about criminological theory, *A Clockwork Orange* is director Stanley Kubrick's film adaptation of Anthony Burgess's novel about a young hoodlum, Alex, who is rehabilitated. Alex's antisocial behavior, which appears to be freely chosen, is modified by external forces through rehabilitation.

The Positivist School

- *The Silence of the Lambs* (1991). In this popular thriller, an FBI agent pursues one serial killer with the help of another, the incarcerated Hannibal Lecter. Although the film's portrayal of the two serial killers may be exaggerated, it is clear that the source of their antisocial behavior is mental illness, not rational choice.
- *Malcolm X* (1992). This biographical film portrays the life of the social activist Malcolm X, who, as a youth, was driven by racism, violence, and poverty to a life of crime. Sent to prison in 1945 for burglary, Malcolm X converted to Islam and renounced the criminal lifestyle. His life meshes neatly with many positivist ideas, especially that antisocial behavior can be brought about by a destructive environment and that offenders can be rehabilitated.

## THINKING *in* ACTION

1. Are any of these films among your favorites? Do you agree with the explanations of the criminological perspectives given above? Do you see other criminological perspectives in these films?
2. Watch some of your favorite crime films again, and see if you can determine the criminological perspectives they take.

to measure. Understanding offender motivation may help in developing crime-prevention techniques. For instance, when dealing with motor vehicle theft, it can make a big difference whether the thief is a teenager intent on joyriding or a professional who plans to dismantle the car and sell its parts.

Finally, understanding offender motivation may provide an opportunity to alter their thinking by providing them with legitimate means of obtaining resources like job training, education, drug treatment, and other rehabilitative programs. This approach, however, is very different from attempting to affect the attractiveness of targets or providing more capable guardianship. By changing offenders' life conditions, we are moving away from classical school principles and toward those of the positivist school and its concern with understanding and altering the offender's behavior. As a final exercise to anchor your understanding of the three families of theories, take a look at *Theory to Practice* to see how criminological perspective is used in film.

# Think about it

## Remember
List the policy implications of Clarke's theory of situational crime prevention.

## Understand
Describe the reasons that the neoclassical perspective may appeal to modern political conservatives.

## Analyze
Distinguish between specific and general deterrence.

## Evaluate
Compare the reasons that individuals choose to commit a specific offense according to routine activities theory.

# Summary

**LO1:** **Explain why the supernatural perspective dominated social control for centuries.**
- Before the Enlightenment, societies based their standards of behavior upon religious doctrine, and crime was conceived of as demonic influence.

**LO2:** **Summarize why contemporary criminologists do not consider the concept of evil as an explanation of crime.**
- Modern criminological perspectives do not accept supernatural reasons for antisocial behavior. However, the concept of evil is still studied by some scholars.

**LO3:** **Analyze the classical school of criminology's focus on the offense as opposed to the offender by emphasizing the concept of free will.**
- The two main schools of criminology are the classical/neoclassical school and the positivist school.
- The classical school of criminology represents the most important era in Western legal reform. The basic tenet of classical thought is that criminal offenders freely choose to break the law.

**LO4:** **Discuss the Enlightenment's contribution of the social contract to criminology.**
- The Enlightenment idea of the social contract requires that individuals respect the rights and properties of others in order to expect that others show them the same consideration.

**LO5:** **Compare and contrast the ideas of Cesare Beccaria and Jeremy Bentham as the primary architects of the classical school of criminology.**
- Italian thinker Cesare Beccaria sought to provide the rationale for a more fair and humane system of social control in his 1764 treatise *On Crimes and Punishments*.
- The most important aspects of Beccaria's ideas are rational punishment is necessary to preserve the social contract; legislative determination of law; judicial determination of guilt; the hedonistic psychology of deviance: maximizing pleasure and minimizing pain; social control as rationally calculated punishment; deterrence as the object of social control; and the focus on acts and not actors.

- English philosopher Jeremy Bentham advocated a new way of dealing with criminal behavior based upon the concept of utilitarianism, which states that individuals should behave according to the principle of "the greatest good for the greatest number of people."

**LO6: Analyze the positivist school of criminology's assertion that individuals are influenced by external forces.**

- The focuses of the positivist school of criminology include determinism versus free will; the offense versus the offender; science versus philosophy; and determinate versus indeterminate sentencing.
- The shortcomings of the positivist school are that positivism accepts the legitimacy of the criminal justice system and its place in the social system; it encourages people to look at the external and internal forces that influence their behavior and seek ways of alleviating their antisocial propensities; and it envisions offenders as being different from law-abiding people and in need of intervention to reform.

**LO7: Show how neoclassical criminology recalls the principles of classical criminology, including deterrence and rational choice.**

- Neoclassical criminology is based on the principles of classical criminology but also asserts that free will is influenced by positivism in three ways: premeditation, mitigating circumstances, and insanity.
- Deterrence theory states that people will not break the law if the benefits for doing so are less than the consequences if they are arrested. Some criminologists argue that most people are likely to have both direct and indirect experience with punishment and punishment avoidance.
- Rational choice theory assumes that individuals freely choose whether or not to break the law (classical theory) and considers ways in which these choices are bound or limited by outside influences (neoclassical theory).
- Situational crime prevention theory is an extension of rational choice theory. It looks at situational factors that can be modified to discourage crime.
- Routine activities theory is based upon the premise that crime occurs when three elements converge: motivated offenders, attractive targets, and the absence of capable guardians.

# Questions

1. In early Western culture, why was the church primarily responsible for the correction of all types of inappropriate behavior?
2. How did Pfohl believe demonic influence could be manifested?
3. What are two of the basic tenets of the classical school of criminology?
4. What were the implications of the Enlightenment for criminological thought?
5. Who were Cesare Beccaria and Jeremy Bentham? What were their contributions to the classical school of criminology?
6. What is the Panopticon? How is it related to crime control, and what evidence of it can we see in today's society?
7. The classical school emphasized reason. What is the corresponding basis of the positivist school of criminology?
8. The positivist school focuses on the offender rather than on the offense. How does this affect the criminal justice system?
9. Identify the two types of deterrence. How are they different? Which one is more important?
10. What distinguishes the neoclassical perspective from the classical perspective?
11. What are the three elements of routine activities theory? Which one do its theorists consider least important?

# 5

# Biological and Psychological

# Theories

The introduction of science revolutionized the development of criminological theory. The Enlightenment in the 18th century transformed the way we understand the physical world and began the search for external causes of crime. Rather than relying on religion or philosophy to tell us why and how people break the law, several thinkers cast a scientific eye on a broader range of ideas and possibilities.

This chapter highlights the history of the scientific perspective and illustrates some of the limitations and abuses of science that have plagued the criminal justice system. As the quality of science improves, biological and psychological explanations hold great promise for advancing our understanding of crime. By understanding the history of these explanations, we can not only better appreciate their potential for explaining crime and delinquency, but also avoid their possible abuse.

## Early Biological Approaches

Early biological theories of criminology were limited by the technology and scientific knowledge of their times. They emerged largely from 19th-century Europe, spurred by the publication of Italian physician Cesare Lombroso's work, *L'Uomo delinquente* (1876).[1] The text, which debuted to great criticism and some awe from the scientific community, offered few, if any, new criminological ideas. Instead, it presented some old-fashioned ideas in a **positivist** light and placed them in charts and tables, along with a striking collection of ancient representations of "criminal types" and photographs of modern criminal offenders com-

**LO1:**

**Tell** why early biological theories of criminology advance our understanding of criminology.

>≺THINKBACK
positivist (ch. 4)—The emphasis on observable facts.

plete with their tattoos, handwriting, and graffiti. It was not Lombroso's content that caught the imaginations of scientists and the public, but his presentation of it in an orderly and documented fashion. It seemed Lombroso had learned how to measure a soul.[2]

Meanwhile, the United States was experiencing increased industrialization, heavy immigration, urban growth, and the aftermath of a devastating civil war. The first three factors, which intensified until after World War II, contributed to a general increase in the crime rate. At the same time, **physiognomy,** the practice of determining a person's character by facial characteristics, and **phrenology,** the practice of determining a person's character and mental faculties by measuring bumps and other features of an individual's skull, were both becoming popular. Together with positivism, they provided an attractive way to try to probe criminality. If the nature of a plant or animal was related to its physical appearance, wouldn't the same hold true for human beings?

The problem with this idea is that our perception of human appearance is greatly affected by our culture and social expectations. As we now understand, what one culture finds beautiful and desirable another finds ugly and undesirable. A face that a 19th-century European would have defined as "criminal" may not have appeared remarkable at all in another part of the world. In fact, recent research has discovered that even some facial expressions, such as fear and disgust, are not universal as was once thought and that people from various cultures interpret some expressions differently.[3] Not understanding this, proponents of physiognomy and phrenology continued to measure noses and eyes and bumps

**physiognomy** The practice of determining a person's character by facial characteristics.

**phrenology** The practice of determining a person's character and mental faculties by measuring bumps and other features of an individual's skull.

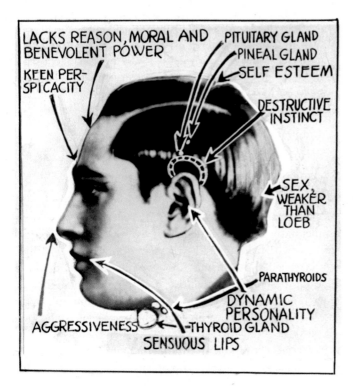

LACKS REASON, MORAL AND BENEVOLENT POWER

KEEN PERSPICACITY

PITUITARY GLAND

PINEAL GLAND

SELF ESTEEM

DESTRUCTIVE INSTINCT

SEX, WEAKER THAN LOEB

PARATHYROIDS

DYNAMIC PERSONALITY

AGGRESSIVENESS

THYROID GLAND

SENSUOUS LIPS

▲ Although developed at the turn of the 19th century, phrenology still has adherents.

on the head well into the 20th century. These forays into measurement are significant, however, because they represented a first attempt in the new pursuit of criminology (it was not yet a science) to measure **antisocial** behavior.

><**THINKBACK**

antisocial (ch. 1)—Following standards of behavior intended to harm society and individuals.

## Physiognomy and Phrenology

Physiognomy has been practiced for centuries and likely represents one of the first formalized searches for character and personality within the human body. After all, human emotion shows mainly on the face, so why not look for clues to character there?

Some of the first written references to physiognomy appear in ancient Greek texts. One ancient writer tells of Socrates recognizing Plato's philosophic abilities upon first studying his face. Aristotle wrote extensively about physiognomy, including how to recognize a variety of character dispositions in facial features. An 1836 magazine article that reports this history of physiognomy asserts the practice was out of style and remained popular only among the "low born, those given to belief in old saws, superstitions, and the marvelous, and as a parlour game. . . ."[4] In fact, physiognomy gained in popularity as positivism took root in the late 19th and early 20th centuries, and its criminological adherents were serious about using it to recognize and predict criminality.

Phrenology, developed sometime at the turn of the 19th century by Franz Josef Gall, has hung on for a long time, even until the present day. Its official website states that "Phrenology is a true science, which is there to benefit humanity," and is a "powerful instrument" for, among other things, law enforcement.[5] An 1849 article describing its merits listed the "fundamental principles" of phrenology as:

1. The brain is the organ of the mind.
2. The mental powers of man can be analyzed into a definite number of independent faculties.
3. These faculties are innate and each has its seat in a definite region of the brain.
4. The size of each of these regions is the measure of the power manifesting the faculty associated with it.[6]

Phrenology seems to have been more popular than physiognomy both as a parlor game and as a criminological tool. Criminology was never the main concern of phrenology: People visited phrenologists for all sorts of advice about daily living and revelations about their personalities. Some criminologists, however, did try to use it to divine criminality. As with Lombroso's work, the importance of phrenology lies not in any theory it offered, but in the way it approached the study of people. Franz Joseph Gall, a medical doctor, practiced in Vienna where he also pursued phrenological research by studying people—alive and dead—in prisons, insane asylums, and royal courts. The Austrian emperor demanded that Gall stop because his efforts located the mind in the physical brain and not in the immortal soul. This radical concept undermined religious teachings, threatened royal authority, and inspired the idea that an individual's actions spring from an organ that can be measured and understood as a product of this world and no other.[7]

## Body Types

A 2008 study of Arkansas prison inmates found that an unusually large percentage of those incarcerated for violent offenses were physically fit. The study's authors cautioned that an athletic build does not predict criminality but rather may be tangentially related to it. For example, the drive to stay in shape may be related to aggression, or athletic people may end up in violent situations more often because they feel they can "handle it."[8]

This study is an example of **body-type theory,** a school of thought that developed in criminology in the first half of the 20th century. Although this idea's main thrust—that the shape of the body directly predicts criminality—has fallen out of favor, it is important because it tried to find some logical basis for criminality and a way to measure it. Popular in the mid-20th century, body-type theory is associated with several well-known criminologists who used aspects of it in

**body-type theory** The idea that the shape of the body directly predicts the propensity for criminal offending.

their work or were inspired by it. Unfortunately, as we will see when we turn to genetic theories of criminology, early body-type theory influenced and was influenced by racism, fascism, and the idea that breeding could be used to "cleanse" humanity of "impure" types. We now look briefly at the three pioneers of body-type theory: Earnest Hooton, an originator of the theory; William Sheldon, whose ideas are still referenced today; and Sheldon and Eleanor Glueck, whose groundbreaking study of juvenile delinquents utilized some aspects of Sheldon's work.

## Earnest Hooton and the Criminals Study

Earnest Hooton, an anthropologist at Harvard University from 1913 to 1954, spent much of his career trying to prove Lombroso's assertion that the body displayed evidence of criminality. In the late 1920s, Hooton embarked on an ambitious, thorough study, gathering data on 17,000 prison inmates from ten states as well as hundreds of militiamen, hospital patients, and firemen that he used as control groups.

Hooton determined that each offender type exhibited specific characteristics he deemed "inferior." First-degree murderers tended to be older, heavier, and taller than other offenders. Hooton also determined that offenders exhibited state-based differences. In his book *Crime and the Man,* Hooton illustrated the differences between the narrow forehead, short ears, and thick lips of a Kentucky offender and the wavy hair, heavy beard, and long earlobes of a Texas inmate.[9] In the end, Hooton came up with so many different types based on such a variety of criteria, such as race, state, offense, and country of birth, that his conclusions were useless.

Although Hooton's work saw some popular success, fellow academics and scientists heavily criticized it. The development of sociological theories of crime (which we will cover in Chapter 6) was in full bloom, but Hooton was having none of it. As late as 1939, he insisted that "environment is the universal alibi of human failure," and he continued to pursue the idea that body shape was both source and sign of criminality.[10] His insistence that criminal offenders were "inherently inferior" beings who could not be reformed, should be sent to live on reservations, and should not be allowed to breed marked him as a vocal proponent of **eugenics,** the concept that human beings can degenerate or improve through breeding.

## William Sheldon and Somatotypes

William Sheldon was an itinerant scholar who made the study of body shapes and personality his life's work. Although he never earned a permanent appointment at any university and alienated many of his supporters, including Hooton, Sheldon's work is perhaps most associated with body-type theory. His system of **somatotypes,** the practice of determining a person's character by the shape of the body, is based on studies done in the 1920s by German psychiatrist Ernst Kretschmer. It still crops up today in descriptions of various body shapes. Sheldon proposed three basic somatotypes.

1. endomorphs—soft and round, often obese
2. mesomorphs—athletic, muscular, compact
3. ectomorphs—thin, fragile, intelligent

Sheldon's somatotype system was more complicated than simply identifying one of three body types, however. For example, individual physiques displayed some measure of each type, which Sheldon rated on a scale from 1 to 7. An athlete would rate 1-6-3—that is, low on endomorphic qualities, high on mesomorphic qualities, and somewhat less than average on ectomorphic qualities. An obese endomorph would rate 7-1-1. According to Sheldon, the perfect physique rated 4.5-4.5-4.5.

In a later study of juvenile delinquents, Sheldon found that, relative to a control group of college students, the delinquents tended to be mesomorphs. This particular study was based on only 16 cases, however, and even Sheldon suspected that many non-criminal active types, such as athletes, generals, and businessmen, were also mesomorphs. Later criminologists found this result interesting. Recall that in the 2008 Arkansas study above, researchers found most of the prison inmates physically fit and even used Sheldon's terminology, classifying the inmates as mesomorphs.

Sheldon's critics pointed out that most people did not precisely fit his categories and were more complex than the categories allowed. Although Hooton and Sheldon pursued similar ideas, they arrived at different conclusions. Hooton thought his data proved offenders to be physically inferior. Sheldon's data showed them to be fine physical specimens. Regardless, both thought humanity needed to be saved from its own biology, and the way to do this was through what Sheldon called "discriminate breeding" or Hooton's outright eugenics.[11]

## The Gluecks and Juvenile Delinquency

The most comprehensive study of juvenile delinquents, *Unraveling Juvenile Delinquency,* was conducted by researchers Sheldon and Eleanor Glueck in the 1950s. The Gluecks gathered detailed and wide-ranging data on 500 delinquent boys and 500 non-delinquent boys, including statistics on their families, personal characteristics, intelligence, school performance, friends, church attendance, health, and body type. Although the Gluecks used somatotyping and were inspired and assisted by Hooton and Sheldon, they were careful researchers who gathered valuable data.

---

**eugenics** The concept that human beings can degenerate or improve through breeding.

**somatotype** The practice of determining a person's character by the shape of the body.

▲ Sheldon's three basic somatotypes are endomorphs, who are soft, round, and often obese; mesomorphs, who are supposedly athletic, muscular, and compact; and thin, fragile, and intelligent ectomorphs.

Their **longitudinal** study was so thorough that in the 1990s criminologists Robert J. Sampson and John H. Laub resurrected it and followed up with many of the subjects.[12]

>◀THINKBACK
longitudinal (ch. 2)—A type of survey that follows respondents throughout their lives or a significant proportion of their lives.

The Gluecks reported that their study's delinquents tended toward mesomorphic physiques and seemed more virile than the boys from the control group. Does this mean male delinquents and criminal offenders are more athletic and virile than law-abiding males? Probably not. Somatotyping represented only a single aspect of the Gluecks' study, and they were careful to assert that antisocial behavior did not stem from biology alone and that body shape in no way determined propensity for criminality. Like the Arkansas researchers, the Gluecks sought to explain their findings by proposing that people who are more energetic and athletic (especially boys) are more likely to act out because they can. Decades later, Sampson and Laub found that although the Gluecks' delinquents were often mesomorphs, this quality did not affect their likelihood of adult offending. Sampson and Laub proposed that 1950s judges reacted more harshly to athletic boys than to weaker-looking boys; as a result, more mesomorphs were found delinquent than endomorphs or ectomorphs.[13]

## Early Biocriminology

Modern biological theories of criminology, or **biocriminology,** represent research that considers the brain and body as a source of antisocial behavior. Since antisocial behavior is an aspect of criminal offending, it is important to stress that biocriminologists look for behaviors, not offenses. No one can look at DNA or a brain scan and tell if that person is a shoplifter, a murderer, or a law-abiding person. Biocriminologists look at physical and mental processes, typically in combination with environmental factors, to understand how they may influence behaviors that influence a person to act contrary to what the law prescribes. Biocriminological factors may be genetic, neurological, hormonal, nutritional, or evolutionary.

The search for the causes of crime and hypotheses about the heritability of behavior has been volatile. Theories about society, culture, environment, and free will have always constituted the basis of criminology, and it is not unusual for theories about the heritability of antisocial tendencies to be dismissed outright. As criminologist Simon A. Cole observed, modern biocriminology is basically ignored by mainstream criminologists, and the work of biocriminologists is "almost never cited by anyone other than the authors themselves."[14] There is good reason for this: The history of biocriminology is not pretty. It involves Nazis, eugenics, racism, classism, misogyny, and the classification as "feebleminded" (a favorite term of eugenicists) whole families whom experts recommended should be prevented from reproducing.

Even as Lombroso was writing his work describing the physical manifestations of the "criminal type," Augustinian monk and father of genetics Gregor Mendel was wrapping

**biocriminology** The search for the causes of antisocial behavior within the brain or body.

up his groundbreaking studies of **heredity,** the biological process in which genetic characteristics are inherited by one generation from the last, and Charles Darwin's *The Origin of Species* (1859) had just been published, demonstrating in the **theory of evolution** that biological forms change over time through genetic inheritance. Neither Darwin nor Mendel directly addressed crime: Mendel studied pea plants almost exclusively, and Darwin was partial to marine invertebrates and insects. However, many social thinkers were eager to apply Darwin's and Mendel's ideas to human behavior—often with malicious results. The resulting pseudoscience of eugenics (discussed in more detail in the next section) was inspired by ideas about heredity and some early evolutionary theory. Given a mid-18th-century rise in crime, immigration, and general social unrest, eugenics was an explosive philosophy. At its worst, it led to forced sterilization and the Nazis' murder of millions in World War II.

## Perspectives on Heredity, Human Evolution, and Crime

The concepts of heredity and the theory of evolution greatly affected criminological thinking in the late 19th and early 20th centuries. Some scholars shifted away from the classical concept that offenders were like anyone else except that they decided to break the law to the positivist idea that lawbreakers were physically or mentally different from law-abiding people. Although they did so with the best intentions, some chilling social attitudes resulted.

Although Darwin's theory of evolution does not specifically address antisocial behavior or crime, this did not stop some thinkers from trying to apply it to criminology. Early criminological thinkers incorrectly interpreted Darwin's theory to mean that lawbreakers were less evolved than the law-abiding. Actually, Darwin's view of evolution was that organisms do not necessarily evolve into something better and that no "arrow" of evolution directs organisms from crude to perfect. Early social thinkers placed lawbreakers at a point on an imaginary line closer to beasts than to human beings.[15]

Darwin did produce some social commentary. His ideas on social and moral evolution in *The Descent of Man* (1871) helped inspire the concept of **social Darwinism,** or the idea that public welfare of any sort only helped the unfit survive to weaken society. Herbert Spencer, the English philosopher who originated social Darwinism, believed society is literally

an organism and crime a disease that had to be "cured." Like germs, lawbreakers had to be eliminated if society were to thrive.[16] At the individual level, German morphologist Ernst Haeckel's concept of **atavism** stated that some people were born before they progressed through all the evolutionary stages to become fully human and were "throwbacks" to an earlier stage of evolution. Although atavism was eventually discredited, it had a profound effect on criminology as did the idea of devolution, or "backward" evolution.[17]

A related concept was "degeneracy," which was considered to be heredity gone wrong. Instead of conferring physical and mental health and intelligence, heredity burdened degenerates with such harmful traits as criminality, mental and physical illness, and impoverishment (typically called "pauperism"). It was not unusual for social theorists to assign a single cause, such as degeneracy, to a host of mental, physical, and social problems and then to decree that the cause was the product of a similar host of social ills. For example, the champion of the degeneracy concept, French physician Bénédict Auguste Morel, determined degeneracy to be caused by moral turpitude; the failure of individuals to educate themselves; wet, marshy environments; alcohol and opium abuse; and poverty, disease, and crowded urban living. Degeneracy could be inherited or acquired, but subsequent generations were susceptible to inheriting it.[18]

In 1877, Richard Dugdale, an employee of the New York State Prison Association, published a landmark eugenics study, *The Jukes: A Study in Crime, Pauperism, Disease and Heredity.* The Jukes were a set of 42 families from upstate New York who boasted an unusual number of criminal offenders, vagrants, ne'er-do-wells, and "feebleminded" persons. After collecting a large amount of data, Dugdale concluded that the Jukes were costing taxpayers a great deal in welfare, incarceration, and social services. However, he did not claim the Jukes' problems were biological. Not only did he point to the families' impoverished circumstances and environment as the root of their behavior, he also called attention to the fact that criminality ran in wealthy and successful families. This part of his work went ignored, however, and *The Jukes* was cited as proof that criminal forebears produced criminal descendants.[19]

Ideas about inheritance, heredity, and degeneracy were thus typically applied only to those who were considered to be weak: immigrants, nonwhites, the mentally ill, and the impoverished. The Victorian era was ending, and people accustomed to its strict social mores were aghast at the new century's rising squalor, chaos, social confusion, and crime. It was easy to point to petty lawbreakers and large, impoverished immigrant families and proclaim they must be closer to beast than human. Apparently, it was not so

---

**heredity** The biological process in which genetic characteristics are inherited by one generation from the last.

**theory of evolution** The idea that biological forms change over time through genetic inheritance.

**social Darwinism** The idea that public welfare of any sort only helped the unfit survive to weaken society.

**atavism** The idea that some people are born before progressing through all the evolutionary stages to become fully human.

easy to observe the era's robber barons, men responsible for vast financial and criminal offenses, and decry them as degenerates or devolved. As we will see, the eugenicists' prescriptions for social health never applied to the wealthy and upper class. Indeed, they were considered the "breeding stock" that would save American society through "good" marriages.

# doubletake

## The Undesirables

Although we associate forced sterilization with totalitarian governments and war crimes, the idea of sterilizing certain people was once openly discussed in the United States. In 1911, a panel of the American Breeders Committee, composed of several of the country's top medical and government professionals, created a list of ten "antisocial classes" to be eliminated through sterilization. When all the "defectives" were totaled—including institutionalized and noninstitutionalized people, those deemed of "inferior blood," and their apparently normal relatives—the number of people to be sterilized was about 11 million, or what was then 10 percent of the population. The plan was never implemented.

Ten classes were targeted for sterilization:

1. The feebleminded—This blanket term presumably included anyone of low intelligence, the intellectually disabled, and the mildly mentally ill.
2. The pauper class—Impoverished people.
3. The inebriate class—Alcoholics.
4. Criminals—This included everyone from serious offenders to those jailed for offenses like nonpayment of fines.
5. Epileptics.
6. The insane.
7. The constitutionally weak—This presumably refers to people who were unhealthy for unspecified reasons.
8. Those predisposed to specific diseases.
9. The deformed.
10. Those whose could not see, hear, or speak.[1]

[1]Edwin Black, *War Against the Weak* (New York: Four Walls Eight Windows, 2003), 58.

## THINKING *in* ACTION

1. What gave rise to proposals for forced sterilization?
2. Are you or is anyone you know on the list of "undesirables"?

## Eugenics

Charles Darwin's cousin, British scholar Francis Galton, defined eugenics as "the study of the agencies under social control, that may improve or impair the racial qualities of future generations, either physically or mentally."[20] As we discussed earlier, this refers to the selective breeding of people to include desirable qualities and exclude undesirable qualities. In the early 20th century, Galton's work helped replace vague ideas about inheritance with more solid theories about heredity and inspire the search for genetic predispositions to antisocial behavior in individuals.

The eugenics movement grew in popularity from about the turn of the 20th century to World War II. It mainly focused on improving human breeding in the United States partially by sterilizing social undesirables such as the impoverished, the "feebleminded," epileptics, the mentally ill, and so on (see *Doubletake*). Criminality was one of the undesirable qualities that eugenicists believed children could inherit. "Criminal," in this case, referred to anyone from shoplifters to murderers, and many criminologists believed frequent offenders should be sterilized. In the 1924 edition of his text *Criminology*, eminent criminologist Edwin H. Sutherland wrote: "In so far as it can be determined that criminality is connected with an inherited abnormal trait, it is clearly desirable to stop the reproduction of people who have that trait."[21]

Forced sterilizations, which were particularly easy to carry out on incarcerated offenders and other institutionalized people, continued until the early 1970s. In 1907, Indiana became the first state to legalize the mandatory sterilization of incarcerated offenders as well as those living in poorhouses and mental institutions; as of 1909, Washington and California had ratified their own versions of sterilization laws, followed later by Nevada, Iowa, New Jersey, and New York. In all, 29 states had some sort of mandatory sterilization legislation, with the sterilization of offenders figuring prominently.[22]

Thanks to constitutional restrictions on cruel and unusual punishment, criminal offenders did not suffer the brunt of sterilization laws; instead, this was the sad burden of the intellectually disabled, mentally ill, and "feebleminded." However, some states did manage to sterilize many offenders. The practice was largely ended in 1942 with the U.S. Supreme Court's decision in *Skinner v.*

▶ The Nazis sought to use eugenics to create a so-called "master race."

*Oklahoma.* In this case, a three-time recidivist successfully challenged Oklahoma's 1935 Habitual Criminal Sterilization Act, which declared that "habitual criminals"—anyone convicted of three offenses of "moral turpitude"—should be sterilized. The case turned on the Constitution's equal protection clause—the sterilization requirement did not apply to violators of the "prohibitory laws, revenue acts, embezzlement, or political offenses"—rather than on the morality of forced sterilization. It effectively halted the states' push to sterilize criminal offenders.[23]

# Think about it

## Remember

List the legal objections to the eugenics movement.

## Analyze

Analyze how early biological approaches to explaining crime may have been unfair and harmful.

## Evaluate

Differentiate between body types and somatotypes.

## Modern Biological Perspectives

With advances in medicine and genetic science, criminology has returned to the search for a biological component to antisocial behavior. Instead of looking for indistinct markers of criminality and seeking sterilization for recidivists and the

**LO2:**

**Describe** how genes, neurotransmitters, hormones, and the brain may interact with the environment to produce antisocial behavior in human beings.

mentally ill, however, researchers are now able to look directly at the brain, DNA, and other biological factors that may affect individual antisocial behavior. Many, if not most, researchers theorize that the interplay between biology and environment, often referred to as "nature and nurture," affects antisocial behavior and not one or the other exclusively. Still, academic criminology has not fully accepted biocriminology. Social theories of criminology—which we turn to in Chapter 6—have largely held sway since the 1930s. However, work on finding a link between biology and antisocial behavior continues.

### Genetic and Evolutionary Perspectives

Research into the possible effects of genes and evolutionary influences on behavior has surged in recent decades, spurred by the discovery of genes for various ailments and psychological conditions and the use of DNA in investigating criminal offenses and wrongful convictions. Although researchers still arrive at dead ends, such as XYY syndrome (see the next section), other lines of inquiry show promise, including the search for which genes (if any) affect behavior, twin and adoption studies, and hypotheses about the evolution of human behavior.

### XYY Syndrome

Human beings have 23 pairs of chromosomes. Females have two X chromosomes (XX), and males have one X and one Y (XY). **XYY syndrome** occurs when males receive an extra

**XYY syndrome** Syndrome that occurs when males receive an extra copy of the Y chromosome.

copy of the Y chromosome. They may be taller than average but typically have no other unusual physical features. However, they are usually at increased risk of learning disabilities and delayed speech and language development, delayed motor skills development, weak muscle tone, and sometimes behavioral and emotional issues. Most XYY cases are not inherited.[24]

In 1965, British researchers studying a group of 197 Scottish inmates discovered that seven of them had an extra Y chromosome and calculated that XYY males represented about 3.5 percent of the male prison population. These "supermales" were said to be potentially more violent than normal males.[25] Since then, studies of the possible relationship between XYY syndrome and antisocial behavior have been inconclusive. According to a roundup in 2000 of current hypotheses, scholars are trying to discourage the notion that XYY males are more likely to break the law, and studies showing high rates of XYY males in prison populations have been challenged. There have been few, if any, rigorous criminological studies on XYY and criminality in the past 20 years; with the consensus that "most XYY carriers lead normal, productive lives," this hypothesis appears to be dormant.[26]

## Genes and Behavior

The suggestion of a straightforward relationship between genes and behavior is perhaps one of the most controversial in biocriminology. As mentioned earlier, biological researchers, including biocriminologists, believe both genes and environment are responsible for behavior rather than genes alone.[27] Criminologist Adrian Raine corrects several other misconceptions about the influence of genes on crime.

- *One gene is not responsible for antisocial behavior.* There is no "crime gene." A likely scenario for any connection between genes and crime is that a set of genes is responsible for biological processes that make an individual somewhat more likely to break the law.

- *Genetics cannot explain antisocial behavior in individuals.* Heritability applies to populations, not individuals. It is impossible to pinpoint in a criminal offender how much of his or her behavior is genetic, how much is environmental, and how much is free choice.

- *Genetically determined antisocial behavior can be changed.* Environmental factors have such a strong effect on behavior, it is impossible to state that any genetic predisposition to antisocial behavior cannot be altered by such things as therapy, rehabilitation, or punishment.

- *Genetic study reveals information about more than genetic influences.* Genetic study can, in fact, provide much information about the effects of environment. For example, twin and adoption studies (discussed in detail later) provide particularly important data about environmental factors such as home life; nutrition; and sibling, parent, and peer relationships.

- *Genes may predict a propensity for antisocial behavior.* A common criticism of biocriminology is that the concept of crime exists only as a social construct, so criminality cannot be genetically determined. However, the symptoms of some mental disorders that may lead to antisocial behavior are socially defined. Raine gives the example of schizophrenia. Although the symptoms and effects of this mental illness are socially defined, it has a strong genetic component and has been found to run in families.[28]

So how are researchers studying the genetic aspects of antisocial behavior? It is a challenging task because, as sociologist Guang Guo explains, environmental influences are so pervasive and complex, it is not uncommon for genetic studies to produce inconsistent findings. Samples that appear similar may produce different results simply because they were subjected to different environments. Guo points out that some theories consider people who are more likely to break the law to lack impulse control and empathy and to be more likely to take risks and resort to violence. Guo and other biocriminologists believe it is possible that these broad propensities are biological in origin.[29] Some studies claim to have found clear evidence of a genetic basis for personality traits such as novelty-seeking, aggressiveness, and **impulsivity,** or action taken on a whim without consideration of the consequences—all of which are considered related to antisocial behavior.[30]

Here are three examples of the types of studies researchers are pursuing.

- Research on children has found genetic propensities not only for aggressive behavior related to bullying, but also for introverted behavior related to being bullied. That is, both bullies and victims show hereditary personality traits related to their social positions as either bully or victim or both. One heritable personality trait found to be particularly related to this complex of behavior is "emotional dysregulation," a condition characterized by mood and personality swings. Found in both bullies and victims, it is particularly strong in children who are both.[31]

- An especially important criminological subject is juvenile delinquency. It is rare for a person to go through childhood and adolescence with perfect behavior and then begin serious offending as an adult. One study claims to have pinpointed not only three genetic variants for serious and violent delinquency, but also ways the environment affects these variants. One variant is affected by family meals, social services, and the presence of two biological parents; another is affected by school attachment and repeating a grade; another is affected by a friend's delinquency. Researchers found that strong family, school, and social networks dampen the delinquency effects of the genetic

**impulsivity** Action on a whim without consideration of the consequences.

◄ Some research has found genetic propensities not only for aggression related to bullying, but also for behavior related to being bullied.

studies have played the most important role in revealing the influence of genes on behavior.[35]

**Twin Studies** Produced by the division of a single fertilized egg, identical twins have the same set of genes and thus offer researchers a unique opportunity to study similarities or differences in their reactions to their environments. Using adoption studies, researchers can observe the effects of a familial environment on someone who does not share that family's DNA. Both types of study can separate the effects of genes and environment somewhat.[36] A study of 1,133 twin pairs in Sweden explored the effects of socioeconomic environments on adolescent delinquency. The twins self-reported their antisocial behavior, and their families' socioeconomic status was determined by education and occupation. Researchers assessed neighborhood socioeconomic conditions through ethnic diversity, educational level, unemployment level, purchasing power, and crime rate. They found genetic influences on antisocial behavior were more apparent in adolescents in wealthier socioeconomic environments, whereas they had diminished influence on the antisocial behavior of adolescents in less-wealthy socioeconomic environments. In other words, a delinquent teen in a wealthy neighborhood is more likely to be influenced by genes, but a delinquent teen in less advantaged surroundings needed less genetic prompting to break the law and was more likely to be influenced by environment.[37]

variants, and weak networks increase them. This, the study explains, is why chaotic environments produce delinquency in some children (who possess the genetic variants) but not in others (who do not possess the variants).[32]

■ A controversial line of inquiry is "epigenetics," the study of the biochemical signals that turn genes on or off. When applied to the study of behavior, epigenetics takes the genetic/environment relationship to a new level. For example, an article from the environment, say a nutritional factor, affects a parent's genes, which then passes that effect to the parents' offspring. An example of this was found in a study on agouti mice. Under normal circumstances, the fat, yellow agouti mice, which are prone to cancer and diabetes, have offspring just like them. However, if researchers fed the female mice a special diet while they were conceiving their litters, most of the offspring were slim, brown, and healthy. So, although the mothers passed along the agouti gene to their litters, a chemical in their food negated its effects.[33] The application of epigenetic effects to the study of inheritance in human behavior is infinitely more complicated. However, discoveries suggest the environment of a child's parents or even grandparents may determine aspects of the child's behavior as well as health.[34]

## Twin and Adoption Studies

Studies of identical twins and people raised by non-biological parents are a particularly useful form of research on the effects of genes and environment on behavior. According to researchers Michael Rutter, Terrie E. Moffitt, and Avshalom Caspi, although twin studies have revealed important genetic influences on most types of psychopathology, adoption

**Adoption Studies** Research on adopted subjects must use studies in which the subjects' biological parents are known. One database that provides this information is the Danish Adoption Cohort Registry. A 1983 study using this registry concluded that the antisocial tendencies of biological parents were more indicative of an adopted subject's likelihood to break the law than those of the adoptive parents. For example, males whose biological fathers and adoptive parents were criminal offenders were most frequently convicted of breaking the law themselves. Males whose biological fathers were offenders but whose adoptive parents were not were the next most frequent lawbreakers. Females showed these same relationships although in lower numbers. All the subjects' convictions were for property offenses, not violent offenses, and the researchers found no relationship between parental offending and violent offenses.[38]

## Evolution, Aggression, and Survival

According to some perspectives, antisocial behavior influences human evolution. Behavior considered inappropriate and destructive in our society may once have played a useful role in the development of human beings, and possibly it still does. Hypotheses typically address aggression as related to mate selection, reproduction, survival, and status. Let's look at a few examples of these ideas.

- *Rape.* Some researchers propose that rather than being a particularly egregious example of antisocial behavior, rape is an adaptation that helps some males better distribute their genes. Biological scholars Randy Thornhill and Craig T. Palmer hypothesize that women are traditionally more physically invested in child-bearing than men due to their role in pregnancy, nursing, and caring for infants. Therefore, women are choosier than men about the quality of their mates. Men, who have little investment in individual children, but more interest in increasing the number of offspring who carry their genes, are more interested in quantity of mates. Rape allows them to increase the number of mates and, therefore, the number of possible offspring.[39] A criticism of this hypothesis is that it assumes rape is purely a biological process involving no psychological, cultural, or social processes, such as belief systems or customs and their effects on individual decision-making.[40]

- *Aggressive behavior.* This perspective views both aggression and aggression-control as having evolutionary advantages. Aggression, in this case, includes a range of behaviors such as self-defense, hunting, athletic competition, occupational competition, children's play behaviors, as well as what we now consider criminal behavior. From an evolutionary standpoint, being aggressive enough to fight off intruders and win competitions but not so aggressive that clan members are constantly fighting each other is advantageous.[41]

- *Status-striving.* According to evolutionary neuroandrogenic theory, females have evolved to prefer males who strive for status; in response, males spend more time and energy than females trying to attain status. The act of "status-striving" is actually a type of aggressive behavior that exists on a continuum from competitive to victimizing. At the competitive end of the continuum, status-striving activities are typically sophisticated and rewarded by society (for example, by attaining a high-paying job or being good at sports). Status-striving behaviors at the victimizing end are those society punishes (for example, bullying, fighting, crime). Males begin to display this behavior at puberty when they start to compete for mates. Those with better learning abilities quickly move from victimizing status-striving to competitive status-striving behavior. Males with poor learning abilities move slowly or not at all.[42]

## Neurological Perspectives

Some criminologists and behavioral scholars think neurological conditions affect antisocial behavior. These conditions are related to genetic and evolutionary criminological perspectives because, except in the case of injury or some illnesses, they are likely affected to some degree by heredity and adaptation, which affect brain functioning. As in the genetic and evolutionary perspectives, most scholars stress that antisocial behavior is not a product of physical attributes alone but is most likely a function of the interplay between biology and environment. Biological behavioral research is just beginning to understand the relationship between the functioning of the human body and the social environment, so the theory is still developing. With that in mind, we will take a look at three promising areas of research: neurotransmitters, hormones, and the brain itself. This research does not look for direct links to crime but for antisocial behaviors that may lead to crime.

### Neurotransmitters

Neurotransmitters are chemicals that transmit messages between nerve cells in the brain. The amount of neurotransmitters in an individual's brain is determined by genes, which is why genetics is important to the study of neurotransmitters and behavior. The amount of *active* neurotransmitters is controlled by the brain enzyme monoamine oxidase A (MAOA). Located on the X chromosome, MAOA breaks down neurotransmitters and makes them inactive. Studies have shown that people with low MAOA are more aggressive and react more strongly to stress than those with high MAOA. The neurotransmitters most important to the study of behavior are serotonin, norepinephrine, and dopamine, which control mood and feelings such as aggression and pleasure.

A longitudinal study of 442 males from New Zealand followed the male subjects from birth to age 26 and recorded their individual levels of MAOA activity and whether they were abused as children. The researchers were looking for evidence of a relationship between genes and environment—in this case, how an individual's MAOA gene equipped him to react to his environment.[43]

The study found that 36 percent of the men had suffered frequent changes in primary caregivers, rejection by their mothers, or physical or sexual abuse from ages 3 to 11. Men who were abused as children and had the low-activity MAOA gene were nine times as likely as the rest of the **cohort** to fight, bully, lie, steal, and disobey during adolescence. This small subgroup of antisocial males, 12 percent of the cohort, accounted for

>< THINKBACK
cohort (ch. 2)—A group of people who share statistical or demographic characteristics.

44 percent of the group's violent offense convictions. The more serious the childhood abuse, the more violent the low-MAOA males became. The other three subgroups—males with the high-MAOA gene who had been abused, those with the low-MAOA gene who had not been abused, and, of course, those with the high-MAOA gene who had not been abused—were all equally unlikely to engage in antisocial behavior.[44]

An interesting aspect of this study is that experts estimate about a third of males carry the low-MAOA gene, which means it probably has a purpose, although no one knows what it is. Finally, this research also offers an explanation of why women are less prone to violent antisocial behavior. The MAOA gene is carried only on the X chromosome, so men, who have one X and one Y chromosome, get only one copy of it. Women, with two X chromosomes, get two MAOA copies, which makes them more likely to receive a high-activity version of MAOA and therefore, some researchers say, makes them more likely to be buffered against a bad environment.[45]

## Hormones

Hormones are chemicals produced by the body that control the activity of cells and organs. The hormones discussed in this section affect the brain and behavior, specifically aggression and fear. Nervous, chemical, and perceptual signals stimulate hormone production, which may regulate short-term activities such as a quick response to an external threat or long-term processes such as sex differentiation, maturation, and reproduction.[46]

Hormones can both affect and indicate how the brain functions. The study of hormones has practical applications in the criminal justice system because they are easy to measure and target for treatment. In this section, we will look at the hormones testosterone and cortisol, prime candidates for biocriminological research because they have been associated with antisocial behavior and with some characteristics of psychopathy, such as lessened reactions to stress, fearlessness, aggression, and stimulation seeking.[47]

**Testosterone**   Testosterone, which stimulates the development of male sex characteristics, is produced in significant amounts by the testicles and in small amounts by the ovaries. It is popularly associated with "macho," aggressive behavior, but the relationship is not as simple as "more testosterone equals more machismo." Rather, testosterone is only one factor in a complex of physiological, psychological, and social influences.[48]

However, evidence suggests the aggressive, risk-taking behavior that testosterone appears to affect can become antisocial behavior. Men with higher testosterone levels are more likely to be arrested, traffic in stolen property, sustain bad debts, and use a weapon in fights.[49] Testosterone levels also peak in young adult males, which coincides with the fact that most criminal offenses are committed by young adult males.

Evolutionary neuroandrogenic theory, discussed above, states that male sex hormones affect the brain to increase the probability of violent criminal offending.[50] A study found positive correlations between self-reported criminal offending and physical characteristics associated with androgens (the class of male sex hormones that includes testosterone). Self-reported violent offending was correlated with "masculine body appearance, physical strength, strength of sex drive, low–deep voice, upper body strength, lower body strength, and amount of body hair. Among males, even penis size was found to be positively correlated with criminality."[51] According to evolutionary neuroandrogenic theory, testosterone and other androgens are responsible for helping the male brain learn what researchers call "competitive/victimizing behavior." Although males are born with competitive/victimizing tendencies, the rush of testosterone at the onset of puberty further pushes them into this behavior. Young males may manifest these changes with rule-breaking and boundary-testing, including increased aggression and juvenile delinquency.[52]

**Cortisol**   Cortisol is a hormone released during stress that activates a fear response to mobilize the body's resources and provide energy. It is also believed to help generate sensitivity to punishment and induce individuals to withdraw from difficult situations. High cortisol levels make reaction to stress more likely; low cortisol levels make them less likely. Apparent at an early age, low cortisol might be involved in the development of antisocial behavior. Associated with weak fear reactions in young children and increased sensation-seeking in adult males, low cortisol may decrease sensitivity to punishment and increase dependency on rewards. Several studies have shown low cortisol levels in psychopathic offenders,

▶ Testosterone, which stimulates the development of male sex characteristics, is popularly associated with aggressive behavior.

# theory
## to practice

### A Picture of Insanity?

When scientific theory or hypotheses is put into practice in the courtroom, the results are not always predictable. It is common to hear of forensic evidence assisting in the acquittal or conviction of a defendant, but sometimes the judgment is not what the public believes is just or even conceivable, even if it is scientifically possible.

One of the first trials to admit brain images as evidence was that of John Hinckley, Jr., who was accused of attempting to assassinate President Ronald Reagan in 1981. The defense argued successfully that Hinckley's brain image appeared similar to those of schizophrenia patients, and Hinckley was found not guilty by reason of insanity. The verdict left many Americans in shock and disbelief and ultimately led to the rewriting of many states' insanity defense laws, as well as federal law (see Table 5.3 on page 113).[1] Today, brain imaging is sometimes used in trials to demonstrate abnormal brain functioning in defendants.[2]

[1]William F. Buckley, Jr., "The Hinckley Mess," *National Review* 34, no. 14 (July 23, 1982): 916.

[2]Yaling Yang, Andrea L. Glenn, and Adrian Raine, "Brain Abnormalities in Antisocial Individuals: Implications for the Law," *Behavioral Sciences & the Law* 26, no. 1 (2008): 65–83.

### THINKING *in* ACTION

Do you think we know enough about the brain to determine whether someone was insane at the time the person committed a crime?

---

aggressive children, adolescents with conduct disorder, and violent adults.[53] Finally, research has found that individuals who are the most violent have high levels of testosterone and low levels of cortisol.[54]

## The Brain

Some researchers believe antisocial behavior may be affected by structures within the brain, injury to those structures, or the nature of the brain itself. (See *Theory to Practice* to learn more about one of the first uses of brain imaging in court.) Two brain regions that researchers think particularly affect behavior are the amygdala and prefrontal cortex, which both control mood and decision-making. A good example of how the brain's condition may affect behavior occurs in the juvenile brain. Many scientists now assert that before the age of 20 and possibly even 25, the brain does not function like the brain of a fully mature adult and that adolescents and children may perform poorly when challenged with situations requiring foresight, judgment, and wise decision-making.[55]

**The Amygdala**    Located in the middle of the brain, the amygdala is an almond-shaped structure that plays a role in initiating emotional memories, rage, fear, aggression, and sexual feelings. It may also influence our awareness of important events and help us separate the significant from the common. Damage to this important structure may cause increased feelings of aggression and fear.[56] One researcher has even stated that diminished amygdala response to emotional stimuli is typical of psychopathic brain activity. That is, people with healthy amygdalas respond to the distress of others with increased amygdala activation; those with low-responding amygdalas show little emotional response to others' distress (or to their own) and therefore have trouble caring about others, which is an important aspect of moral decision-making.[57]

The most infamous example of possible amygdala disruption is the 1966 case of Charles Whitman. After killing his wife and mother, he barricaded himself in a tower at the University of Texas and fatally shot 14 people and wounded 31 others before being killed by police. Whitman, who had been an Eagle Scout, Marine, and university student, had also come from an extremely abusive family. As a young adult, he began having intense headaches and described disturbing thoughts, including the desire to "take a deer rifle and start shooting people." After his behavior began to deteriorate in 1961, he was court-martialed, lost his scholarship, began beating his wife, and in 1964 had his father—the man who beat him as a child—help him procure an honorable discharge from the military. As a University of Texas student, he told a school psychologist that he feared something was wrong with him. Before embarking on the killings, Whitman left notes expressing how much he loved his wife and mother and wondering why he killed them, as well as a note requesting an examination of his brain upon his death.

Although an autopsy revealed a walnut-sized tumor compressing his amygdala, experts still do not agree whether this caused his behavior given his meticulous planning and preparation for the shootings. Still, some researchers point to the disruption of Whitman's amygdala as a likely causative element within a group of factors that included childhood abuse; school, family, and work stress; and the use of pharmaceutical stimulants.[58]

**The Prefrontal Cortex** The prefrontal cortex is a frontal lobe structure highly developed in human beings and responsible for problem-solving, emotion, and complex thought. Damage to this structure has been reported to impair emotional and social abilities such as empathy, insight, and recognizing emotions in others. Several types of mental illness, such as schizophrenia, bipolar disorder, and attention deficit hyperactivity disorder, show abnormal patterns in the prefrontal cortex.[59] Brain imaging studies have found that low prefrontal cortex volume, as well as abnormal activity and reduced interconnections from the frontal lobes to the rest of the brain, are common in people who are depressed, under constant stress, incarcerated or sociopathic, or who have committed suicide.[60] Because the prefrontal cortex integrates information from other parts of the brain to help produce choices and decisions, a severely damaged structure may translate into actions the type of thoughts the thinker, who knows the actions to be wrong or unwise, would typically repress.[61]

In one case, part of the prefrontal cortex of a 35-year-old man was removed due to cancer. Although the surgery did not affect the man's intelligence and memory, it did compromise his ability to act appropriately and morally. Formerly extremely moral and loved by his friends and family, he began to make poor financial decisions that eventually cost him his family and his job, and he later married and quickly divorced a prostitute. Although he could apply moral judgment to ethically problematic situations, he could not act upon this judgment. Despite knowing the best choice, he consistently chose immediate gratification although he knew it would lead to a bad outcome for himself and others.[62]

Frontal lobe abnormalities in general seem to be closely associated with violent and criminally offensive behavior. Studies have found that adults with damage in certain frontal lobe areas tend to exhibit impulsive, aggressive behavior; in other studies, subjects with antisocial personality disorder displayed a significantly reduced prefrontal area and diminished prefrontal activity. In short, researchers are finding the frontal cortex regions essential to behavioral inhibition, as well as the anticipation of punishment and reward, neurological activities critical to successful social function.[63]

**The Juvenile Brain** Although it has been acknowledged for decades that children's decision-making abilities are less developed than those of adults, no one was sure why. Now, brain imaging allows us to see exactly how young brains differ from adult brains and to understand how this difference affects information-processing, perception, and moral reasoning. Neuroscience is beginning to play an important role in the legal treatment of juveniles.

A brief submitted by the American Medical Association in *Roper v. Simmons* (2005) in which the U.S. Supreme Court considered the constitutionality of the death penalty for offenders who had committed capital offenses before age 18 stated that the incomplete prefrontal development of adolescent brains means adolescents are less able to control their

▲ Children's decision-making abilities are less developed than those of adults. Lee Boyd Malvo (in photo) and John Allen Muhammad shot 13 people, killing 10, during a three-month spree in the Washington, DC area. Malvo's defense team claimed Muhammad brainwashed Malvo, who was a juvenile at the time of the shootings.

impulses and cannot be held fully accountable for their actions.[64] In the end, the Court held that the execution of such offenders was unconstitutional

Exactly what is different about the young brain? Neuroscientists believe the frontal lobe—which, as we discussed, helps restrain impulsive behavior—does not begin to mature until age 17. That means the part of the brain the legal system is most concerned with—the part that controls rational decision-making—is not even fully active until late adolescence. Some neuroscientists believe full maturation does not occur until age 25. So although adults and juveniles have the same basic brain structures, adults process information in a more complex fashion than juveniles. One study found that in decision-making tasks, youths relied mainly on the prefrontal cortex, whereas adults used other parts of the brain as well. Studies that focus on the amygdala, which processes emotional and risk responses, indicate that adolescents act more erratically than adults. Although this should not surprise anyone who has raised teenagers, it is remarkable to find evidence for it within the brain.

In the study, researchers had adolescents and adults identify facial displays of emotions in a series of photographs. Brain scans of both young and mature brains showed the amygdala firing upon perceiving a face that showed fear; however, the prefrontal cortex, which became markedly active in adults, showed little response in adolescents. Researchers interpreted this to mean that adolescent brains do not process emotional responses like adult brains do. This dimmer response could also indicate that the adolescents often misidentified fearful faces as angry. Brain researchers agree adolescents also have trouble with the neurological activity that allows predicting the consequences of risky actions, which means they are likely to take more risks.[65]

## Environmental Perspectives: Drugs and Alcohol

Some environmental elements, including nutrition and harmful substances such as lead, are considered to affect antisocial behavior.[66] Two studies of young adults who grew up in impoverished urban neighborhoods linked childhood lead exposure to a significant loss of brain tissue in the areas responsible for impulse control, emotional regulation, judgment, and anticipation of consequences. The study found that the higher the concentration of lead in the subjects' blood during childhood, the more likely they were to be arrested during adulthood, particularly for violent offenses.[67] Still, the substances most commonly connected to antisocial behavior and criminal offending are drugs, including illegal substances and pharmaceuticals, and alcohol. Whereas statistics on the antisocial effects of nutrition and common chemicals must be gathered through research, the federal government keeps a tally of the effects of drugs and alcohol on crime, which makes them much easier to observe.

Drugs and alcohol are closely associated with crime. According to a 2002 Bureau of Justice Statistics study, 53 percent of jail inmates were habitual drug users, compared to 47 percent who were habitual alcohol users.[68] Inmates who were substance dependent or substance abusers were more likely than other inmates to have a prior criminal record.[69] Despite the U.S. "war on drugs," alcohol abuse appears to be a bigger problem than drug use. During one five-week study, about 25 percent of incidents in which the police were called involved alcohol, whereas only 3 percent involved drugs.[70]

Alcohol is implicated in more than 50 percent of violent offenses; the cost of alcohol-related crime is estimated at about $205 billion.[71] Violence between intimates is especially likely to include alcohol abuse.[72] About four in ten offenders, including those on probation, in jail, and in state prison, report using alcohol at the time of their offense.[73]

### Alcohol

Alcohol is related to antisocial behavior and crime, though its exact role is unclear. However, criminologists question whether inebriation *causes* antisocial behavior or crime. Clearly, not everyone who gets drunk breaks the law; indeed, most people who become drunk manage to avoid doing so. Therefore, criminologists seek to understand the relationship between alcohol and crime more fully rather than simply pointing to alcohol as causing crime. A better understanding of the inebriation/crime relationship would help lighten the burden on the criminal justice system by improving preventive, therapeutic, and rehabilitative measures for people who commit alcohol-involved offenses or who are at risk of doing so. Researchers seek to understand the effects of alcohol, the characteristics of drinkers, the situations in which alcohol-related crime happens, and the cultural context of alcohol-related antisocial behavior.[74]

One study found that adolescents with no history of conduct problems who drank alcohol early in their teen years were more likely to become substance dependent, contract herpes, have early pregnancies, and be convicted of criminal offenses as adults.[75] Alcohol is also deeply connected to aggressive antisocial behavior. Crime suspects are more likely than crime victims to be intoxicated, and

▼ Alcohol is deeply connected to aggressive antisocial behavior.

emergency room studies show that patients with violence-related injuries are two to five times more likely to be drunk at the time than people who sustained injuries unrelated to violence.[76] So, although alcohol is not considered to cause crime, it certainly is related to the behaviors most likely to lead to arrest. Why?

- Alcohol is disinhibiting. Its effects on the brain lead to reduced anxiety about the consequences of aggressive behavior while increasing physical reaction to mental perceptions, which thus raises the intensity and level of aggression. Alcohol also affects the balance of serotonin and dopamine in the brain, which reduces impulse control.[77]

- Alcohol reduces sensitivity to pain, which further lessens individual concern about the consequences of aggressive actions.

- Alcohol impairs physical functioning, which increases the likelihood of a drunk individual invading others' physical space.[78]

- The impairment of mental functioning also affects the ability to create non-aggressive solutions to problems, to focus attention, and to restrain emotions. At the same time, inebriation also generates a form of short-sightedness in which minor incidents are blown out of proportion, which increases the scale of emotional response.[79]

These effects depend not only individual characteristics, but also on cultural and situational contexts. Inebriation presumably has the same disinhibiting effects on everyone, but only some break the law or engage in violence; however, a disproportionate percentage of those people are affected by alcohol. Criminologists are still trying to clarify this issue.

## Drugs

In the U.S. government's war on drugs, the criminal justice system has defined a category of criminal offense related to the trafficking and possession of non-pharmaceutical and pharmaceutical drugs, although it is not against the law to be addicted to anything. Because this complex topic merits its own text, we will not discuss the war on drugs but will focus instead on the relationship between drugs and antisocial behavior.

Criminologists agree there is a definite empirical relationship between offending and drug use as there is with offending and alcohol. What is unknown is the exact nature of that relationship, and there is no agreement that drug use causes crime.[80] Sociologist Erich Goode outlines three models of the drugs–crime connection.

- *The enslavement model.* Drug addicts and abusers are enslaved by drugs and must commit economic offenses to get the money to support that addiction. Legitimate jobs do not pay enough to support the addiction and/or do not allow the user to take drugs at will. If drug users were not enslaved by drugs, they would not break the law to any

great degree. Drug legalization would curtail much drug-related crime because it would allow users to better manage their addictions. Two major assumptions of the enslavement model are that drug users continue their usage to avoid withdrawal symptoms and would be satisfied to maintain their addictions without increasing their usage.

- *The predisposition model.* It is not drug users who turn to crime but criminal offenders who turn to drugs. Drug users were offenders and delinquents first because they are the type of person who is always seeking novel, risky experiences. Drug addiction is merely part of a criminal lifestyle that many habitual drug users prefer, and they would continue to break the law with or without drugs. Legalization would have no effect on their criminal activities in general.

- *The intensification model.* This model combines the other two. Drug usage does not cause crime but intensifies it. It is indeed part of a criminal lifestyle that already exists, but it drives addicts and abusers to break the law even more than they normally would. Drug legalization would not end their criminal careers but would reduce their offending.[81]

Researchers explore elements of these perspectives when probing the relationship between drugs and crime. For example, the amount of offending may be related to the type of drug. Cocaine and heroin are the two most closely related to crime when volume of consumption is considered.[82] However, a 2005 study still found no direct, causal relationship between heroin and crack cocaine use and theft-related offenses, including shoplifting and street robbery. Such offenses tended to be desperate acts that were sometimes committed only once.[83]

Related to the predisposition model, a 2001 study found the order in which offenders' drug dependence and criminal career began was important to the type of offending. Those who began offending after becoming drug dependent were much less likely to commit predatory offenses such as robbery and theft and instead committed victimless offenses such as prostitution. However, those who offended prior to drug dependence were more likely to commit predatory offenses; they also began both criminal careers and drug dependence at earlier ages than people who were drug dependent first.[84] Risky, sensation-seeking behavior is an element: In nearly every study ever conducted, people who frequently broke the law were more likely to use illegal drugs, drink alcohol, and smoke cigarettes than those who did not.[85]

## Critiques

Biological theories of criminology are not popular in mainstream criminology for three principal reasons.

- Not only were early theories classist, racist, and sexist, but the search for a way to cure society of crime led to some heinous public policies directed at people who did not fit within a narrow ideal. Realization of these abuses, along with advances in sociological theory, gave mainstream criminology reason enough to abandon biological theories in the latter half of the 20th century. Modern critics of biocriminology worry that renewed interest in biological theories will lead to a 21st-century version of eugenics.

- Biocriminological research lacks focus and considers an overly broad range of factors. One criminologist stated that even if antisocial behavior does have biological factors, they are so slight that social institutions are better off concentrating on the factors that most certainly contribute to crime, such as social inequality and poverty.[86]

- Biocriminological research translates poorly to the criminal justice and legal systems. Although it may shed some light on the biological sources of some antisocial behavior, its conclusions are not strong enough to support public policy, law, or court decisions. In the case of brain imaging, for instance, researchers have warned that jurors are not qualified to accurately assess the significance of brain scans, which often appear more objective than they really are. Other scholars point out that the legal system asks pointed, direct questions about specific individuals, whereas biological research seeks generalizations about groups that share characteristics.[87]

## Policy Implications

Despite the misgivings of some mainstream criminologists, biological research is making inroads into public policy. Technological advances mean that conclusions about behavior are a far cry from the early days of biological theorizing. For instance, as we saw earlier, brain-imaging evidence stating that adolescents may be unable to exercise mature impulse and emotional control and may tend to underestimate risks was influential in *Roper v. Simmons* (2005).[88] As far as the determination of individual culpability is concerned, brain imaging is considered to show the most promise so far. One researcher lists the following issues brain imaging might help resolve:

- Does the defendant have neurological damage?
- Do the brain abnormalities, if any, fit the nature of the offense?
- Is the defendant faking a mental illness or insanity?
- Is the defendant lying?
- If the defendant is guilty, what is the likelihood of recidivism?[89]

Some criminologists suggest that a better understanding of what makes antisocial behavior tick, even if biological influences are slight or are complicated by environment, will lead to more and better rehabilitative treatments of offenders as well as improved public health initiatives.[90] Before we

**Figure 5.1  Biological and Psychological Theories in Relationship to the Human Body**

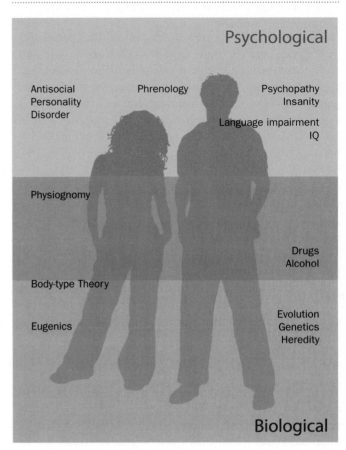

move on, see Figure 5.1 for a look at where the focal points of the biological, psychological, and psychiatric perspectives correspond to the human body.

# Think about it

## Remember

Outline the evidence that contributed to the development of XYY syndrome as an explanation for aggressive behavior.

## Apply

Describe the connection of drugs and alcohol to criminal offending.

## Analyze

How have discoveries about brain chemistry and brain structure contributed to our understanding of crime?

## Create

Formulate reasons based on human evolution to explain why individuals might engage in crime.

# Psychological and Psychiatric Perspectives

Psychological and psychiatric theories consider personality, intelligence, and the mind as factors that can inspire antisocial behavior and criminal offending. The psychological approach focuses on **cognition**—the act of thinking and perceiving—and learned behavior, whereas the psychiatric approach is concerned with neurological processes and illnesses. Throughout this section, you will notice some overlap between the psychological/psychiatric perspectives and the biological perspective. All three share a positivist approach in that they seek the source of antisocial behavior within the brain from either neurological or cognitive standpoints.

**LO3:**

**Trace** the development of psychological and psychiatric theories of criminal behavior.

In this section, we will first take a brief look at the traditional psychiatric perspective on antisocial behavior and crime. We will then turn to current psychological and psychiatric perspectives.

## Traditional Psychoanalytic Theory

Traditional psychoanalytic theory was less concerned with crime than with explaining behavior—including antisocial behavior—in general. The father of psychoanalytic theory is Sigmund Freud (1856–1939), who sought to explain human behavior as the product of internal motives and drives. According to this perspective, human beings are naturally antisocial and selfish. Without the internal control of conscience and the external control of society, they will do anything to get what they want, including steal, lie, and kill.

The main tenet of the psychoanalytic perspective is that the source of human behavior is within the individual unconscious, and the environment has only a limited influence on behavior.[91] Criminality is the result of unconscious conflicts. Two other assumptions place the bulk of socialization firmly in childhood: First, socialization depends on the quality and type of childhood experiences; second, a poor parent-child relationship affects the likelihood of delinquency. Although evidence for the first tenet has been hard to pin down, the last two—that adult behavior is rooted in childhood socialization—are the basis of numerous sociological theories of crime. Traditional psychoanalytical theory has not fallen completely out of favor, but scholars do not use it as a sole explanation for antisocial behavior.[92]

## Modern Psychological and Psychiatric Theory

In this section, we will review a selection of current psychological and psychiatric theories. Although we cannot go

deeply into every theory, these perspectives represent current criminological thinking.

## Behaviorism

A psychological perspective concerned with observable human behavior, **behaviorism** states that environment and learning determine how individuals behave. Psychologist B. F. Skinner, the chief 20th-century proponent of behaviorism, held that behavior is the product of the environment and positive and negative reinforcements. This belief is the basis of **operant conditioning,** a form of learning based on the positive or negative consequences of an action, behavior, or activity. Let's look more closely at Skinner's ideas on reinforcement.

**LO4:**

**Describe** psychological disorders related to crime.

Through **positive reinforcement,** which is the rewarding of a successful action, we engage in behavior designed to gain something we want. Through **negative reinforcement,** which is ending an undesirable consequence as a means of reward, we engage in behavior to avoid something we do not want. An example of positive reinforcement is giving a rat a piece of cheese if it successfully completes a maze. Negative reinforcement is turning off a loud, irritating noise if the rat successfully completes the maze. **Extinction,** according to Skinner, is no reaction to a behavior at all—that is, neither punishment nor reinforcement. Skinner believed punishment to be less effective than extinction because it only temporarily stops a behavior; extinction shows that the behavior brings no reaction. In the case of a misbehaving child, for example, a parent using extinction would not react to the behavior. According to Skinner, the child sees that the behavior brings no reaction and desists.

We can apply Skinner's ideas to operant conditioning and antisocial behavior. According to Skinner, we learn antisocial behavior from the social environment and reinforcements. A financial manager learns from criminal peers that defraud-

---

**behaviorism** A perspective that states that environment and learning determine how individuals behave.

**operant conditioning** A form of learning based on the positive or negative consequences of an action, behavior, or activity.

**positive reinforcement** Rewarding a successful action.

**negative reinforcement** Ending an undesirable consequence as a means of reward.

**extinction** No reaction to a behavior.

**social learning theory** The idea that people learn how to act by watching others and copying the interactions that are rewarded and avoiding those that are punished.

**cognitive psychology** The study of memory, language processing, perception, problem solving, thinking, and other mental processes.

---

**cognition** the act of thinking and perceiving.

ing investors is safe and profitable. The manager's peers have grown wealthy by defrauding investors and have not been caught, so the manager begins her investment scams and becomes wealthy. In this way, the criminal activity is positively reinforced. This, in a nutshell, is Skinner's behavioral theory.

Although Skinner's theory inspired current psychological and sociological criminological theories, such as social learning, most criminologists today find his ideas too simplistic on their own. Skinner believed operant conditioning was the key to all human behavior; he saw little effect from genetics and little value in the study of cognition because we cannot directly observe it.[93]

**Social Learning Theory**    Although considered a behaviorist theory, **social learning theory** is a hybrid of behaviorist and cognitive theories. It holds that people learn how to act by watching others and copying the interactions that are rewarded and avoiding those that are punished. So, like other animals, human beings are subject to reinforcement and punishment and can be conditioned toward certain behaviors. However, we are also complicated, and cognition affects our behavior, too. According to social learning

theory, antisocial behavior is observed and learned from others, then reinforced by criminal activity. Whether an individual continues to break the law, however, depends on what the individual thinks about the activity, which leads us to cognitive theory.

## Cognitive Theory

**Cognitive psychology** is the study of memory, language processing, perception, problem solving, thinking, and other mental processes, in essence, how people think. An area of focus includes the way the mind mediates between an external stimulus and the response to that stimulus. In criminology, we can use cognitive psychology to learn more about the mental processes that precede the decision to break the law. One of the main theories is psychologist Lawrence Kohlberg's stages of moral development, which suggests how we learn to use our minds to negotiate the social world. Let's take a look at this theory and its utility in criminological thought.

**Kohlberg's Stages of Moral Development**    According to Lawrence Kohlberg, children pass through six stages of moral reasoning as they grow up (see Table 5.1).

## Table 5.1    Kohlberg's Six Stages of Moral Development

|  | Style of Reasoning | Ideal Period |
|---|---|---|
| **Level 1** | Pre-conventional level—Moral reasoning is based on obedience and avoiding punishment. | middle childhood |
| **Stage 1** | The rules of others<br>Pursuit of personal interests with the expectation that others will do the same. Exchanges should be equal. | |
| **Stage 2** | Individualism<br>Children obey because they are told to. Moral decisions are based on threat of punishment. | |
| **Level 2** | Conventional level—Moral reasoning is based on the expectations of family and significant others. | late childhood |
| **Stage 3** | Relationships and conformity<br>Moral judgments are based on relationships, trust, and emotions. | |
| **Stage 4** | Law and order<br>Belief in and obedience to the social system. | |
| **Level 3** | Post-conventional level—Moral reasoning extends beyond social conventions. | early adulthood |
| **Stage 5** | The social contract<br>Value of the principles behind the law and some that are beyond the law.<br>Universal ethics | |
| **Stage 6** | Moral reasoning is based on the idea of equal human rights and following one's individual conscience. | |

*Source:* Adapted from Lawrence Kohlberg, "Stage and Sequence: The Cognitive-Developmental Approach to Socialization," in *Handbook of Socialization Theory and Research,* ed. David A. Goslin (Chicago: Rand McNally, 1969).

Kohlberg thought the transition to the post-conventional level of moral development ideally occurred during early adulthood, although some people never move past the early stages, which can lead to delinquency and adult offending. For example, some studies of delinquents found that they exhibit a lower stage of behavior than non-delinquents and function as low as level 2.[94]

Although it makes sense that people who break the law must be morally challenged, some theorists caution that Kohlberg's stages measure moral reasoning, not moral behavior. Therefore, discrepancies often turn up between subjects' answers to questions about which stage of moral development they have achieved and the morality of their actual behavior. A white-collar offender may place himself at stage 5 and agree with the ideas at that stage but exhibit stage 1 behavior.

## Language Impairment and IQ

A psychological perspective related to cognitive theory invokes the roles of IQ and language ability in delinquency and adult crime. Some studies have found low IQ and language impairment, especially in boys, to be solid predictors of later delinquency. Some scholars think the connection is indirect, however, with low intelligence and language ability leading to trouble communicating with others, frustration in school, and eventual withdrawal from pro-social activities. Perspectives on intelligence, IQ, and language are considered developmental because they focus on how the process of cognitive development from child to adult may contribute to antisocial behavior and lawbreaking. Learning to think and communicate are integral to the maturation process, and disruptions can lead to social and psychological isolation, which, according to some researchers, can lead to delinquency and adult offending.

- *Language impairment.* A 1993 study found problems speaking and understanding language at age 3 to be a reliable predictor of adult offending.[95] A later study found that boys who were language impaired at age 5 were far more likely to be delinquent at age 19, with higher rates of arrests and convictions, than boys without language impairment. Language impairment in girls, however, was unrelated to delinquency.[96] A 2008 study found that delinquents in general have trouble both understanding others' language and using language to organize their thoughts and express themselves. As a result, they are more likely to use nonverbal communication such as shoulder shrugging and poor eye contact to cover for their poor language skills. Such body language may be interpreted as insolent, rude, and uncooperative, which, according to the authors, can "incur a significant social penalty."[97]

- *IQ.* **IQ** stands for "intelligence quotient," which is simply a measure of intelligence taken by dividing a person's

mental age by chronological age, then multiplying by 100. The mental age is determined through testing. It is important to understand the difference between IQ and intelligence: IQ is a score on a test, whereas intelligence is represented by a range of mental abilities and is difficult to define. Many psychologists assert that IQ tests are culturally biased because they are encoded with a set of cultural concepts the test-taker must understand to score well. Regardless, IQ and school performance are closely connected: Children who do well on IQ tests do well in school, and good schools have a good effect on IQ. Just as consistent is the relationship between IQ and delinquency. Lower IQs mean a greater likelihood of delinquency; there is a particularly strong relationship between delinquency and low verbal IQ scores, which recalls our previous discussion about the relationship between language impairment and delinquency. These relationships are true not only for delinquents, but also for adult offenders.[98] In the case of delinquency, some researchers look for an indirect effect of IQ. That is, instead of assuming low IQ leads directly to delinquency, they look for other aspects of the juvenile's life that low IQ may be affecting, such as school performance and peer relationships. It is difficult for the juvenile to adopt pro-social attitudes if these elements are dysfunctional.[99]

▼ IQ and school performance have been found to be closely connected: Children who do well on IQ tests do well in school, and good schools have a good effect on IQ.

IQ (intelligence quotient) A measure of intelligence taken by dividing a person's mental age by chronological age, then multiplying by 100.

## Antisocial Personality Disorder, Psychopathy, and Insanity

**Antisocial personality disorder** (APD) is a mental disorder characterized by a pattern of disregard for the rights of others, as well as impulsive, violent, and aggressive behavior without guilt. **Psychopathy,** a mental disorder that involves a severe lack of empathy, is more difficult to define, although it shares symptoms with APD, specifically disregard of other people. Psychopathy and APD share so many characteristics that they are often confused, and some professionals believe they are the same condition.[100] Still others consider APD and psychopathy similar conditions on the same continuum, with psychopathy being the most severe form of APD-type disorders.[101] For now, the two conditions are generally considered distinct. Another controversial condition is insanity, which has different meanings in legal and medical circles and, like APD and psychopathy, is poorly understood.

**Antisocial Personality Disorder**    About 3 percent of males exhibit APD compared to 1 percent of females. To be diagnosed, the individual must be at least 18 years old and have exhibited conduct disorder before age 15. A diagnosis must also include three of the following behaviors:

- failure to conform to social norms or the criminal law; frequent lawbreaking
- irritability and unusual aggression; a tendency to get into fights or commit assaults
- consistent irresponsibility at work and/or with finances
- impulsivity; a failure to make plans
- frequent lying or deceiving others for profit or fun
- disregard for one's own or others' safety
- lack of remorse or guilt for wrongdoing[102]

There are at least two major but not necessarily exclusive perspectives of APD. Both seek to explain why the disorder is so closely associated with offender populations.

- APD commonly occurs within disadvantaged and impoverished populations and is associated with chaotic, dysfunctional households. It is considered to run in families, not because the behavior is biologically inherited, but because children share the same socioeconomic difficulties as their parents.[103]
- Biological in origin, APD is caused by brain abnormalities, possibly dysfunction in the frontal lobe or nervous system. Those with APD display several negative cog-

▲ About 3 percent of males exhibit antisocial personality disorder compared to 1 percent of females. Here, in a homemade video, Eric Harris watches as Dylan Klebold practices shooting a gun. Weeks later the two youths killed 13 people at Columbine High School in Littleton, Colorado.

nitive characteristics, including inflexibility, attention deficits, misunderstanding of contextual cues, and poor behavioral choices.[104]

Although APD is closely associated with crime and antisocial behavior, some scholars and therapists think this association limits the diagnosis to offenders and excludes law-abiding people whose personalities show indications of APD. According to some psychologists, many people with symptoms of APD never enter the criminal justice system and are omitted from the diagnosis because their behavior is largely desirable, such as success in business and politics.[105] This is an intriguing observation, especially given the large number of scandals in business in the late 1990s and early 2000s that bankrupted thousands of people, finished a number of financial institutions, prompted massive government bailouts, and, in 2008, helped bring a recession that some said rivaled the Great Depression.

Recently, the APD diagnosis has fallen out of favor among some criminal justice professionals who believe it has been overused. More than 50 percent of the correctional population—which includes inmates, probationers, and parolees—has been diagnosed with APD, according to one study.[106] The assignment of APD to such a broad swathe of people has been criticized as being of little practical use. A final criticism, also applied to psychopathy, is that the diagnosis is never preemptive and therefore not useful from a criminal justice perspective. Individuals are not tested, found to be symptomatic, then treated so that they will not break the law. Also, APD and psychopathy cannot be predicted to occur like polio or flu, so they cannot be pre-treated much as those diseases are pretreated with vaccination. Diagnoses of APD or psychopathy typically occur only after an individual has become a criminal offender. Conceivably, many people

**antisocial personality disorder**  A mental disorder characterized by a pattern of disregard for the rights of others, as well as impulsive, violent, and aggressive behavior without guilt.

**psychopathy**  A mental disorder that involves a severe lack of empathy.

who do not commit serious offenses also show APD or psychopathy symptoms but are never diagnosed because their behavior does not result in lawbreaking.

**Psychopathy**    We've said APD and psychopathy share many symptoms, including disregard for truth and the feelings of others. Psychologist Robert Hare has compiled several varieties of his primary psychopathy checklist, the Psychopathy Checklist-Revised (PCL-R), which is probably the most used reference for psychopathic characteristics (see Table 5.2). The checklist has been criticized, however. One study concluded it can easily be misused in legal systems and forensic psychiatry and that the characteristics are subjective, judgmental, and not measurable.[107]

Some scholars say psychopaths typically show no signs of mental illness, such as hallucinations, excessive anxiety, severe depression, or obvious delusions. Others dispute this and say that psychopaths who are obviously mentally ill can certainly be found in institutions. Also, not all psychopaths are criminal offenders. Many people who exhibit psychopathic symptoms have broken no laws and probably never will. Hare estimated the rate of psychopaths in the general population to be about 1 percent but about 15 to 25 percent in the adult prison population.[108]

Still, psychopathy has a persistent relationship with crime. Studies have found criminal psychopaths to be especially violent, sadistic, and brutal; they tend to murder and rape for fun. Murders by non-psychopaths are often committed for a reason, however twisted, such as domestic conflict or the heat of argument with a known victim. The murderer will likely feel remorse and never kill again. A criminal psychopath, however, feels nothing for his or her victims. Psychopathic rapists may commit their offenses for non-sexual reasons, such as anger, sadism, malice, or simple opportunity. In all, psychopaths seem to have trouble empathizing with others and comprehending the most basic rules of society because they cannot be aroused to any genuine feelings. Ideally, a child who is corrected for an immoral or improper action feels shame, embarrassment, and the sense that he or she has displeased those who matter the most: parents, siblings, peers, or teachers. The psychopath feels none of this and continues the antisocial behavior because he or she thinks, "Why not?" It is this resistance to remorse or shame that makes psychopaths so difficult to treat or rehabilitate.[109]

**Insanity**    Insanity is a legal term, not a medical term. No physician, psychologist, or psychiatrist uses the term clinically to describe a person's mental state. Under the law, insanity describes an individual's state of mind only at the time he or she committed an offense.[110] Because the term is used to describe a state of mind that is connected with criminal offending, we will review it in this section of the chapter.

▼ The conviction of Andrea Yates, who drowned her five children in the bathtub, was overturned, and she was found insane and confined to an institution.

## Table 5.2    Hare's Psychopathy Checklist-Revised (PCL-R)

Glibness/superficial charm
Grandiose sense of self-worth
Need for stimulation
Pathological lying
Conning/manipulative
Lack of remorse or guilt
Shallow affect
Callous/lack of empathy
Parasitic lifestyle
Poor behavioral controls
Promiscuous sexual behavior
Early behavior problems
Lack of realistic goals
Impulsivity
Irresponsibility
Failure to accept responsibility
Many short-term relationships
Juvenile delinquency
Revocation of conditional release
Criminal versatility

*Source:* Robert D. Hare, *The Hare Psychopathy Checklist—Revised* 2nd ed. (Toronto, ON: Multi-Health Systems, 2003).

## Table **5.3**    Major Standards of Insanity

There are five major standards of insanity. Each state has its own variation of these standards, so these represent what has been used in federal court.

| Standard | |
|---|---|
| M'Naghten rule | In 1843, Daniel M'Naghten tried to kill the British prime minister but mistakenly shot and killed his secretary instead. As a result of this case, a panel of British judges developed what became known as the M'Naghten standard of insanity. The defense must prove the defendant was so delusional, ideally from "disease of the mind," at the time of the offense that he or she did not know right from wrong. This is also called the "right-wrong test."[1] |
| Durham rule | This rule was an attempt to displace the M'Naghten rule. In 1953, 23-year-old Monte Durham, in and out of prison and mental institutions since he was 17, was convicted for housebreaking. The appellate judge stated that M'Naghten was based on an "obsolete and misleading conception" of insanity and set forth that a defendant "is not criminally responsible if his unlawful act was the product of mental disease or mental defect." Federal courts later rejected Durham because almost anyone with an irresistible impulse, including alcoholics and compulsive gamblers, could use the rule to win a case.[2] |
| Brawner rule | In 1972, the American Law Institute developed a new insanity rule based on the decision in the federal appellate case *United States v. Brawner*. In *Brawner,* defendants are considered not responsible for breaking the criminal law if they lack the "substantial capacity" to appreciate the action's criminality or conform their conduct to the law. The *Brawner* rule recognizes partial responsibility as well as irresistible impulses, but it does not allow repeated criminal conduct to be claimed as part of a mental disorder. Repeat offenders, including those diagnosed with APD or psychopathy, cannot claim their behavior is part of a mental disorder.[3] |
| Guilty but Mentally Ill (GBMI) | This standard, created in 1975, represents an alternative to the NGRI defense. It holds an offender responsible for the action but recognizes the presence of a mental disorder. The defendant can be sentenced if convicted, not acquitted as under the NGRI defense, but it also recognized the defendant's need for medical treatment. Unfortunately, research shows that in states that have adopted this standard, the convicted person is no more likely to receive treatment within the prison system than mentally disordered defendants who do not have a GBMI conviction.[4] |
| Comprehensive Crime Control Act of 1984 | The furor after the acquittal of John Hinckley, Jr. (who shot President Ronald Reagan in 1981) inspired the move to abolish the insanity defense. The subsequent Comprehensive Crime Control Act retained it but changed the conditions under which it could be claimed. The new federal insanity defense, considered a return to the M'Naghten standard, requires "clear and convincing evidence" to prove that "at the time of the commission of the acts constituting the offense, the defendant, as a result of a severe mental disease or defect, was unable to appreciate the nature and quality or the wrongfulness of his acts."[5] The new rule changed the *Brawner* rule, which had held sway to this point, in three major ways. (1) The irresistible impulse test was abolished. (2) The act replaced *Brawner*'s "lacks substantial capacity . . . to appreciate" with "unable to appreciate," thus narrowing the cognitive threshold of understanding one's actions. (3) The mental disorder must be severe, and simple personality disorders do not qualify as a defense.[6] |

[1]Mark Tebbit, *Philosophy of Law: An Introduction,* 2nd ed. (New York: Routledge, 2005), 183–87; John P. Martin, "The Insanity Defense: A Closer Look," *Washington Post,* February 27, 1998, http://www.washingtonpost.com/wp-srv/local/longterm/aron/qa227.htm.

[2]Cornell University Law School, Legal Information Institute, "The 'Insanity Defense' and Diminished Capacity," http://www.law.cornell.edu/background/insane/insanity.html.

[3]Curt R. Bartol and Anne M. Bartol, *Criminal Behavior: A Psychosocial Approach* (Upper Saddle River, NJ: Pearson Education, 2008), 245.

[4]Bartol and Bartol, *Criminal Behavior: A Psychosocial Approach,* 248.

[5]Cornell University Law School, Legal Information Institute, "The 'Insanity Defense' and Diminished Capacity."

[6]Bartol and Bartol, *Criminal Behavior: A Psychosocial Approach,* 247.

The insanity defense, **not guilty by reason of insanity** (NGRI), generally means the acquittal of a defendant because he or she is determined to be insane. It has drawn much public criticism and disdain because it appears to give

**not guilty by reason of insanity (NGRI)** Generally, the acquittal of a defendant because he or she is determined to be insane.

"criminals" a chance to escape justice simply by claiming they were crazy at the time of the offense. This is far from the case. The insanity defense is rarely raised and rarely successful. Juries do not like it.[111] Each state has its own form of insanity defense, which makes it difficult to count how often it is used. A 1991 study, however, estimated that only 1 percent of felony cases use the insanity defense.[112]

The purpose of deciding whether an offender is insane is to establish responsibility for an offense. Thus far in U.S. criminal law, an offender deemed insane at the time of the offense is not responsible, whereas a sane offender is responsible. A defendant found both to have committed the offense and to be insane is typically confined to a mental health institution. A defendant not found insane is incarcerated. In both cases, the defendant's freedom is curtailed. Andrea Yates, a Texas woman who drowned her five children in the bathtub, was initially found guilty but not insane and sent to prison. This conviction was later overturned, and she was found insane and confined to an institution.[113] So, contrary to popular belief, defendants ruled not guilty by reason of insanity do not necessarily go free. See Table 5.3 for a look at the current standards of insanity used in U.S. courts.

# Think about it

## Remember
Review the five standards of insanity.

## Understand
Outline the reasons the antisocial personality diagnosis has fallen out of favor with criminal justice professionals.

## Evaluate
Critique the perspective that IQ is related to antisocial behavior.

# Summary

**LO1:** Tell why early biological theories of criminology advance our understanding of criminology.
- The introduction of science revolutionized the development of criminological theory.
- Early biocriminological perspectives sought to measure antisocial behavior and considered it rooted in the physical world.
- Modern biocriminology considers the brain and body as a source of antisocial behavior. Biocriminologists look for behaviors, not crimes. The environment is considered an important factor.
- Early biological theories of criminology were spurred in the 19th century by the work of Italian physician Cesare Lombroso.
- Body-type perspective developed in the first half of the 20th century. Hooton believed the body measurements of lawbreakers were inferior to those of law-abiding citizens. Sheldon developed a system of somatotypes: endomorphs, mesomorphs, and ectomorphs. The Gluecks gathered information about body types in their juvenile delinquency study.
- Heredity and evolutionary theory affected criminological thinking in the early 20th century. Eugenics represented an attempt to breed criminality out of human beings.

**LO2:** Describe how genes, neurotransmitters, hormones, and the brain may interact with the environment to produce antisocial behavior in human beings.
- The suggestion of a direct relationship between genes and behavior is controversial. Raine corrects several misconceptions about the influence of genes on crime: One gene is not responsible for antisocial behavior; genetics cannot explain antisocial behavior in individuals; genetically determined antisocial behavior is not immutable; genetic study reveals information about more than genetic influences; genes may predict a propensity for antisocial behavior.
- Studies of identical twins and adopted individuals are particularly useful for examining the effects of genes and environment on individual behavior.
- According to some perspectives, antisocial behavior influences human evolution.
- Some criminologists and behavioral scholars think neurological conditions affect antisocial behavior.
- Neurotransmitters important to the study of behavior are serotonin, norepinephrine, and dopamine. The hormones thought to influence antisocial behavior are testosterone and cortisol.
- Some researchers think antisocial behavior may be affected by the brain itself, particularly the amygdala and prefrontal cortex. Juvenile brains are func-

tionally different from adult brains because they are still maturing.

- Drugs and alcohol are closely associated with crime, but their role is unclear. Goode outlines three models of the drugs–crime connection: the enslavement model, the predisposition model, and the intensification model.
- Biocriminological theories are unpopular in mainstream criminology for three reasons: Early theories were biased and produced harmful public policy; biocriminological research lacks focus and considers an overly broad range of factors; biocriminological research translates poorly to the criminal justice and legal systems.
- Some criminologists suggest that a better understanding of antisocial behavior, even if biological influences are slight, will lead to better treatments and improved public health initiatives.

## LO3: Trace the development of psychological and psychiatric theories of criminal behavior.

- Psychological and psychiatric theories consider personality, intelligence, and the mind as factors that can inspire antisocial behavior and criminal offending. The psychological approach focuses on cognition and learned behavior. The psychiatric approach is concerned with neurological processes and illnesses.
- Behaviorism states that the environment and learning are behavior's main determinants. Social learning theory holds that people learn behavior from watching others, then develop their own thoughts and attitudes.
- Cognitive psychology is the study of how people think, which can help explain how people decide to break the law.
- According to Kohlberg, children pass through six stages of moral reasoning as they mature. Some people never move past the early stages, which can lead to delinquency and adult crime.

## LO4: Describe psychological disorders related to crime.

- Some studies find low IQ and language impairment predict later delinquency.
- Antisocial personality disorder and psychopathy describes behaviors that include severe, routine disregard for others.
- Insanity is a legal not a medical term. The purpose of deciding whether an offender is insane is to establish his or her responsibility for the offense.

# Questions

1. What is biocriminology?
2. How did Cesare Lombroso attempt to use science to explain antisocial behavior?
3. How did physiognomy and phrenology seek to predict antisocial behavior?
4. What major criminological theorist used the concept of degeneracy to describe how heredity acted to produce offspring inclined to breaking the law?
5. How did some criminologists use XYY syndrome to explain antisocial behavior?
6. How has the study of twins contributed to the development of genetic theories of crime and delinquency?
7. How have brain chemistry and brain structure provided insights into antisocial behavior?
8. What is the relationship between IQ and antisocial behavior?
9. Why is antisocial personality disorder often associated with offender populations?
10. How has the criminal law changed in regard to the psychological concerns of insanity?

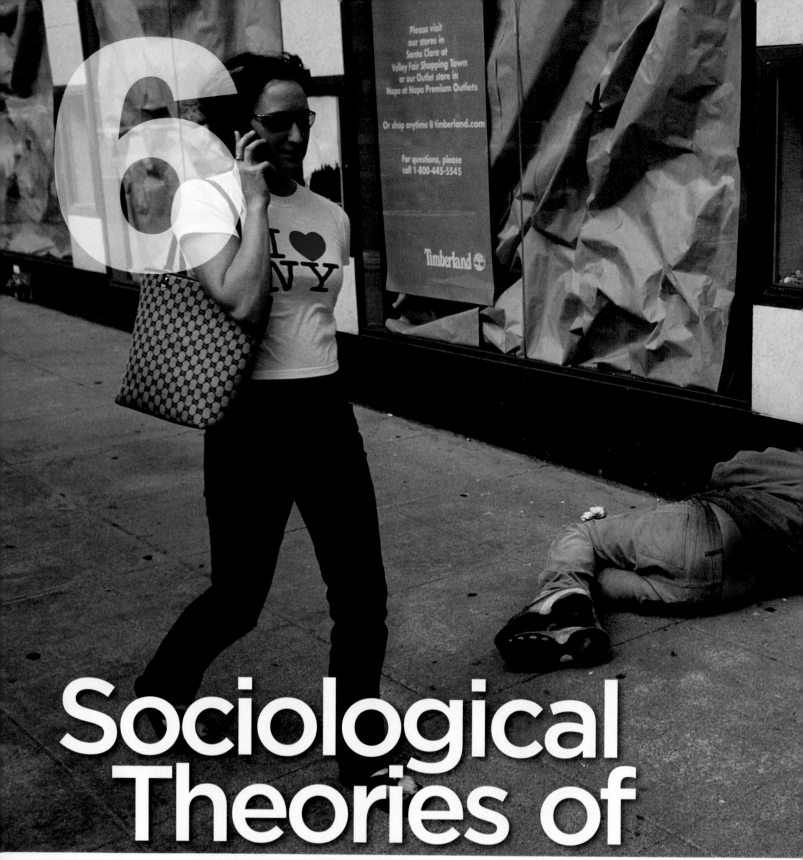

# Sociological Theories of Crime and

# what's inside

# Delinquency

**As you read, keep in mind these learning objectives:**

**LO1:** Discuss how social disorganization theories of crime were developed and demonstrate how they apply to modern urban situations.

**LO2:** Explain why many criminologists contend that antisocial behavior is learned like any other behavior.

**LO3:** Show how strain theories evolved from the concept of anomie.

**LO4:** Discuss how control theories of crime look at the way societies control people and how people control themselves within society.

As social conditions change, criminological theories are being refined and extended, making the sociological perspective a robust and exciting lens from which to view crime. Rather than considering crime a problem of the mind, body, or soul, sociological theories of crime observe society and examine how the interaction between people and their social environment produces antisocial behavior. In this chapter and the next, we will examine the major sociological theories of crime and delinquency. These theories provide an insightful new tool that sociologist C. Wright Mills called the **sociological imagination**—the idea that we must look beyond our personal experiences to the experiences of others in order to evaluate how social location influences how individuals perceive society. This tool allows people to critique how their social location within society influences their opportunities and choices.[1]

Sociological theories provide a basis for formulating policies to address not only crime, but also the societal conditions that are considered to cause or contribute to a range of social problems. For instance, the effects of racism, sexism, and discrimination based on socioeconomic class have been at the heart of civil rights legislation, poverty programs, and anti–sexual harassment legislation.[2] Government and social service agencies have been guided by the ideas of scholars who use a sociological lens to focus on society's problems.[3]

We will review the sociological theories of crime and delinquency in the order in which they were developed. Since the history of social thought is not orderly, we will find that although any particular year is filled with competing theories, long intervals often occur between the introduction of a theory by one scholar and its modification, expansion, or application by another. This quilt-like pattern of sociological and criminological theory makes the study of crime sometimes frustrating but often fascinating. Our study of socio-

logical explanations for crime and delinquency begins with the introduction of sociology in the United States at the University of Chicago in the 1920s and 1930s.

## Social Disorganization Theories of Crime

The study of crime and delinquency in the United States was greatly influenced by the development of sociology, particularly at the University of Chicago. A unique confluence of factors brought reformist scholars together in a city that was undergoing rapid growth and change. In just 20 years, from 1890 to 1910, Chicago's population doubled in size, an explosive expansion that challenged the city's ability to absorb its growing numbers.[4] The city's relatively organized and homogeneous population became disorganized and heterogeneous as culturally, racially, and linguistically diverse people moved in. The crime rate increased, and the wealthy, the impoverished, and the middle class became more stratified even as their members sought to reorganize themselves and their jobs, living situations, and cultural values and norms. Social disorganization theory was developed to explain the social problems facing Chicago in the first part of the 20th century, but it applies to many active urban centers.

**LO1:**

Discuss how social disorganization theories of crime were developed and demonstrate how they apply to modern urban situations.

### Social Disorganization Theory

In addition to delinquency, Chicago's impoverished neighborhoods had high rates of infant mortality, tuberculosis, and dilapidated housing. Some sociologists thought the remedy for crime was not to focus on the individual but rather to organize communities to address the social problems that resulted from a lack of cohesion among neighborhood residents. So, accord-

**sociological imagination** The idea that we must look beyond our personal experiences to the experiences of others in order to evaluate how social location influences how individuals perceive society.

► University of Chicago sociologists asserted that meaningful communities could not be established in unstable neighborhoods.

neighborhoods for higher interest rates for home loans—and dealing with macro-level changes such as the migration of jobs, this theoretical perspective seeks to provide solutions to crime and delinquency.[8]

## Concentric Zones

Sociologists from the University of Chicago saw changes in their city as a natural experiment in the spread of dense urbanization and struggled to explain how the social fabric of the community was being altered. One feature they focused on was the lack of stable neighborhood demographics. As the city grew, it expanded from the downtown core and developed zones that formed concentric circles. The outer zones were populated by middle-class and wealthy homeowners, while inner zones included impoverished families and recent immigrants. Immediately outside the city's core were a factory zone and a transitional zone with high rates of crime, alcoholism, and other social problems.

The transitional zone interested sociologist Ernest Burgess, who saw problems that stemmed from the lack of social organization caused by urban expansion and the economic pressure it exerted on residents who were forced out of their neighborhoods by the unattractive aspects of growth. Boarding houses fell into disrepair; people lived in the neighborhood only as long as it took them to find better places; and the social infrastructure crumbled because of the residents' transitory nature.[9] Burgess, as well as other University of Chicago sociologists, saw this decline as a sign of social disorganization. They hypothesized that meaningful communities could not be established when neighborhoods had no stability and that in order to reform the citizens, society needed to direct urban renewal and social programs at the poor. In many ways, these reformers were victims of their own background. C. Wright Mills contended that the reformers were primarily white, middle-class, Protestant, rural Americans who saw urban dynamics as a symptom of social disorganization that needed to be fixed.[10]

Clifford R. Shaw and Henry D. McKay conducted studies of **concentric zone theory**—the idea that geographical areas radiate out from an expanding urban center and that

ing to **social disorganization theory,** it is not enough to say that impoverished neighborhoods have a culture of crime, but in fact the breakdown of social bonds and the failure of social institutions *cause* crime. Robert J. Sampson and William Julius Wilson extended social disorganization theory to account for the way race and inequality contribute to social disorganization's effect on crime and delinquency. They looked at what they call the "cognitive landscape," which they believed limited the vision of minority people caught in impoverished, transitional neighborhoods. They believed that the residents of some neighborhoods are engulfed in a social isolation that includes going to schools with little socioeconomic diversity, living in segregated housing, and having few experiences outside the neighborhood.[5] Sampson and Wilson then looked at the intersection of race, crime, and urban inequality in an effort to delineate how discrimination and lack of opportunity affect community organization to produce the social isolation of youths that results in delinquency.[6]

This isolation differs greatly from the experiences of affluent children, who receive private lessons and are enrolled in summer camps and sports leagues.[7] Many middle-class parents also provide religious instruction or educational support (or both); act as positive role models; and allow their children to see alternatives to a life of crime, poverty, and conflict. An especially attractive feature of social disorganization theory is that it has public policy implications. Instead of claiming that social isolation is a matter of bad choices or a dysfunctional culture, Sampson and Wilson assert that the social problems of impoverished urban youths are a consequence of persistent racial inequality. By addressing both the policies that allow institutional discrimination—such as banks identifying

**social disorganization theory** The idea that the breakdown of social bonds and the failure of social institutions cause crime.

**concentric zone theory** The idea that geographical areas radiate out from an expanding urban center and that each area has certain, dominant social attitudes.

each area has certain dominant social attitudes—to try to verify that crime would be higher in the transitional zones and lower in those that were more affluent and stable. How did the theory stack up to reality? According to J. Robert Lilly, Frances T. Cullen, and Richard A. Ball, there is substantial support for Shaw and McKay's hypothesis that delinquency flourished in the transition zone and that its prevalence was inversely related to the zone's affluence and distance from the central business district. By studying several decades of Chicago court records, Lilly and his colleagues also showed that crime was highest in impoverished, transitional neighborhoods regardless of which racial or ethnic group resided there, and that as groups moved to other zones, their crime rates decreased.

This observation led the researchers to conclude that the nature of the neighborhood, not the nature of the individuals within the neighborhood, regulated involvement in crime.[11] It also marked a major shift in criminological theory from the micro-perspective, which looks for deficiencies in individuals, to the macro-perspective, which looks at how groups of people demonstrate similar patterns of crime. But what social forces consistently showed that it was the neighborhood and not the individual that was responsible for crime? Shaw and McKay pursued two explanations for these patterns, which we will look at in greater detail later in this chapter. They can be roughly summarized as neighborhood organization and transmission of criminal values.

1. *Neighborhood organization.* Affluent families provide their children with structure and opportunities. Families in transitional neighborhoods lack the financial means to supervise their children through a well-established network of churches, schools, and community recreational facilities. With the pressures of rapid migration, urban growth, and poverty, social disorganization frees children to engage in delinquency.[12]

2. *Transmission of criminal values.* In transitional neighborhoods, children learn negative values from older peers. Even as the racial and ethnic demographics gradually change in the community, life on the street maintains a set of focal concerns that transmits methods of coping with the poverty, lack of legitimate opportunity, and danger that youths must confront. Shaw and McKay developed this perspective from life histories of delinquents based on interviews and autobiographies.[13]

The role of government, as Shaw and McKay saw it, was to provide field workers to act as a catalyst to encourage local democratic participation.[14] In the 1930s, Shaw and McKay, with the help of others, tested their ideas by creating the Chicago Area Project (CAP), which has continued its work for more than 70 years.[15] Shaw's plan was for CAP to discourage community disorganization and encourage social stability through community service, advocacy, and involvement. Programs of the day used punitive methods to discourage crime and delinquency, such as arrest, detention, and incar-

ceration. Shaw, however, directly encouraged gang members to pursue conventional, pro-community lives. CAP developed several strategies, some of which it still uses today.

- *"Curbstone counseling" or "street work."* CAP workers and former gang members frequented youth hangouts and listened to the youths in a non-judgmental fashion.

- *Individual participation.* CAP involved neighborhood residents instead of outside experts and professionals in planning activities and addressing problems.

- *Inclusive involvement.* A strategy that particularly concerned traditional social workers was the involvement of gang members and other offenders directly in neighborhood planning and decision-making. However, Shaw believed it was better to involve them in planning than to avoid them or work against them.

- *Relationships with law enforcement.* Local committees and police officers worked together on delinquency problems. Arresting officers might refer delinquent youths to their local committees, and residents would work with proba-

▼ Shaw and McKay believed government should provide field workers to help citizens participate in their communities. Here, a boy learns emergency procedures at a local police department open house.

tion and parole officers to keep up with delinquents in correctional programs. Parolees often became members of local committees.

See *Doubletake* for a critique of one of CAP's methods.

## Collective Efficacy and Crime

**Collective efficacy** measures the amount of informal social control and social cohesion, or trust, in a community—that is, how much a community's residents trust and depend on one another. A community in which the residents have little trust in one another, rarely communicate, and do not work together to achieve community goals has low collective efficacy.

The social disorganization theories we have examined so far deal with the structure of societies and are based on census and crime-rate data. Although this broad look at communities can yield valuable insights, it cannot tell us about the social dynamics that influence people to break the law. Francis Cullen and Robert Agnew call structural social disorganization theories "static." That is, the community is considered to be a stable condition that people move into or are born into. However, other social disorganization theories consider the community "dynamic," that is, as a condition that can be changed.[16] Collective efficacy theory, as envisioned by Robert Sampson, Stephen Raudenbush, and Felton Earls, is a dynamic social disorganization theory because it considers the community as a collection of individuals who can change their environment.

In a study called the "Project on Human Development in Chicago Neighborhoods," Sampson and colleagues collected data from 8,782 residents in 343 neighborhoods. They measured the "compositional effects" of each neighborhood by assessing which areas had more people prone to lawbreaking. This research allowed them to control for social class, racial diversity, and other variables that might affect crime rates. Then they developed the following two concepts to describe why some areas had higher crime rates than others.

- *Informal social control.* As a measure of informal social control, residents were asked how likely their neighbors would be to intervene if they witnessed a minor criminal offense. This measure demonstrates how socially committed people believe their neighbors are. It also shows how people envision the overall degree of their neighborhood's social responsibility.

- *Social cohesion and trust.* Next, residents answered questions that measured how much they trusted their neighbors and how cohesive they believed the neighborhood to be. By measuring how much neighbors trusted each other, Sampson and his colleagues developed an indication of how socially organized the community appeared to be.[17]

Taken together, these measures of informal social control and social cohesion or trust form what the researchers call "collective efficacy." The study showed that a higher collective efficacy meant a lower crime rate. That is, the more that people were willing to step in and, for instance, stop kids who were writing graffiti on the walls (informal social control), and the more they believed their neighbors would be there to help them (trust and social cohesion), the less crime the neighborhood experienced.

Although the theory of collective efficacy and crime might seem similar to Shaw and McKay's social disorganization theory in that it measures social organization rather than social disorganization, its appeal lies in the potential it sees for a neighborhood's citizens to *do* something about crime and delinquency. Rather than merely being a product of the structural makeup of the community, crime in collective efficacy theory is a variable that community action can address by

# doubletake

### The Chicago Area Project's Detached Worker Program

Critics of the Chicago Area Project (CAP) question how effective it is in reducing gang activity, specifically calling into question its detached worker program. That program, which CAP started in the late 1940s, has community residents work with gang members; advocate for them in court; and help them to find jobs, health care, and educational assistance. The purpose is to transform gangs from antisocial to pro-social groups. Several other programs adopted this approach in the 1960s, including the Group Guidance Program and Ladino Hills Project of Los Angeles. However, the Ladino Hills Project found that instead of decreasing gang activity, the program actually encouraged tighter relationships among gang members and encouraged others to join gangs, which led to even more gang-related crime. As of the 1990s, evaluations of detached worker programs have reported no decrease in gang membership or activity.[1]

[1]Finn-Aage Esbensen, "Preventing Adolescent Gang Involvement," US Department of Justice, Office of Juvenile Justice and Delinquency Prevention, Juvenile Justice Bulletin, September 2000, 6–7, http://www.ncjrs.gov/pdffiles1/ojjdp/182210.pdf.

## THINKING *in* ACTION

Can you think of other ways that gangs might be transformed into pro-social groups?

**collective efficacy** The measure of the amount of informal social control and social cohesion, or trust, in a community.

▲ Some researchers have found that a higher collective efficacy means a lower crime rate.

doing such things as conducting neighborhood watches, letting troublemakers know they will be reported to the police, and alerting local politicians that neighborhood residents expect them to provide adequate police patrols and other social services that affect crime and quality-of-life issues.[18]

Social disorganization theories continue to provide interesting explanations of how a community's social structure can contribute to crime and delinquency. As scholars build on Shaw and McKay's social disorganization ideas, it is becoming clear that a neighborhood's physical, social, and economic conditions affect the residents' behavior.[19] But not all residents of high-crime areas break the law. So we must ask, why do certain individuals adopt antisocial behaviors while others do not? One popular explanation is that crime is learned. Let's turn now to learning theories of crime to develop an appreciation of how social interaction influences the transmission of antisocial behavior.

# Think about it

## Understand

List the reasons why social disorganization theory was developed in Chicago.

## Apply

Demonstrate how collective efficacy theory specifies the way society uses informal social control to control crime.

## Analyze

Examine how the CAP applied social disorganization theory to crime problems.

## Evaluate

Evaluate the concentric zone theory's utility in accounting for urban crime.

# Learning Theories of Crime

**Learning theories of crime** focus on where and how adult offenders and delinquents find the tools, techniques, and expertise to break the law. Many criminologists contend that antisocial behavior is learned from family, peers, and the media, much like any other type of behavior. Children receive messages that it is fun to break the law, which competes with the positive socialization messages that schools, churches, and parents promote. Theorists seek to explain how this learning occurs, while legislators and criminal justice officials try to create public policy that promotes the learning of positive behavior. Learning theories of crime have a good deal of appeal. They seem like a commonsense explanation and appear not only to be testable, but also to suggest policies that can be adopted to reduce crime. The first criminologist to suggest a learning theory of crime was Edwin Sutherland. His differential association theory has stimulated others to look at how the techniques and attitudes required to break the law are transmitted.

**LO2:**

**Explain** why many criminologists contend that antisocial behavior is learned like any other behavior.

## Differential Association

Edwin Sutherland, who taught for five years at the University of Chicago, developed an appreciation for Shaw and McKay's social disorganization ideas. He was interested in the problems of big cities and how crime seemed to be not a function of an individual's pathology, but rather a product of the social organization in which individuals find themselves.[20] Sutherland developed his theory of **differential association**—the idea that offenders learn crime from each other—to account for how criminal offenders and delinquents learn crime (see Figure 6.1). He believed crime is learned through the same mechanisms through which all other learning occurs, and he set out to explain why some people adopt attitudes and behaviors favorable to the violation of the law. Sutherland laid out his theory in nine propositions that attribute the learning of crime to interactions with others, particularly intimate others such as peers and family. Sutherland's nine propositions are:

1. Criminal behavior is learned.
2. Criminal behavior is learned by communication.
3. We learn criminal behavior from those closest to us, such as family and friends.

**learning theories of crime** A perspective that focuses on where and how offenders and delinquents find the tools, techniques, and expertise to break the law.

**differential association** Sutherland's idea that offenders learn crime from each other.

## Figure **6.1**    Differential Association

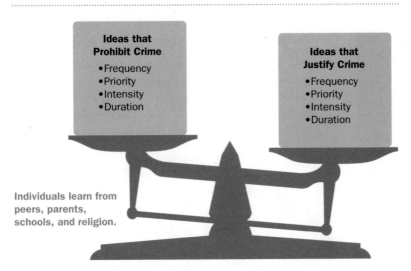

4. Criminal learning includes techniques, motives, rationalizations, and attitudes.

5. We learn our either respectful or disdaining attitudes toward laws from others.

6. Delinquency or criminality occurs when we are exposed to more anti-law attitudes than to attitudes that support the law.

7. The quantity and quality of our social interactions affect our attitudes toward the law. Social interactions vary in frequency, duration, priority, and intensity.

8. We learn antisocial or pro-social attitudes like we learn any other skill.

9. Criminal behavior is an expression of needs and values, but is not explained by those needs and values. For example, the desire to acquire wealth is a normal motive for both working harder at a job and robbing a bank.

One of the attractive features of differential association theory is that it lends itself to empirical observation.[21] Since it contends that lawbreakers have learned more attitudes and techniques favorable to lawbreaking than attitudes and techniques favorable to obeying the law, researchers can readily construct studies that look at this learning process. Sutherland identified four factors for researchers to examine.

■ *Priority.* If a youth is exposed early in life to family members or other children who break the law, then he or she will be more likely to adopt criminal attitudes and learn how to commit crime than someone who is not exposed to such associations until later in life. Young children are more receptive to negative messages because they do not have the experience and knowledge to evaluate antisocial behavior.

■ *Frequency.* According to Sutherland, the more you hear a message, the more you are likely to believe it is true. Youths who are surrounded by others who say that breaking the law is fun, noble, or profitable get the message that crime is normal and desirable. If one associates only with youths who promote these views, then repetition of this message tends to overwhelm the pro-social messages of parents and teachers.

■ *Intensity.* We give some messages more credibility because they have a level of volume, sincerity, or passion that we deem more immediate or important. According to Sutherland, the intensity of a message can influence the recipient to adopt a point of view and, just as important, it is something researchers can measure in their study of the learning of criminal attitudes and techniques.

■ *Duration.* If a person is exposed for a long time to others who advocate violating the law, he or she is more likely to adopt this viewpoint than someone who hears the same message for a short period of time. The longer a youth is a member of a delinquent juvenile gang, the more likely he or she will adopt the gang's viewpoint and behaviors.

Differential association theory has stimulated other scholars to extend and refine the processes under which crime is thought to be learned.[22] Ronald Akers's **social learning theory** of crime, the idea that people learn how to act by watching others and copying the interactions that are rewarded and avoiding those that are punished, retains all Sutherland's ideas but employs the psychological framework of **operant conditioning,** which is a form of learning based on the positive or negative consequences of an action, behavior, or activity. Akers argues that using the concepts of imitation and **differential reinforcement,** or the encouragement of one behavior instead of another, allows social learning theory to explain a greater range of antisocial behavior than differential association. Several studies support social learning theory, and it has become one of the primary theories of why people break the law.[23]

## Techniques of Neutralization

Some learning theories of crime are concerned with offenders' motives, drives, and rationalizations. With their **techniques of neutralization theory,** Gresham Sykes and David

**social learning theory** The idea that people learn how to act by watching others and copying the interactions that are rewarded and avoiding those that are punished.

**operant conditioning** A form of learning based on the positive or negative consequences of an action, behavior, or activity.

**differential reinforcement** The encouragement of one behavior instead of another.

**techniques of neutralization theory** A perspective that refers to the excuses some offenders use to justify breaking the law.

Matza put forth a perspective that refers to the excuses some offenders use to justify breaking the law. They argue that delinquents generally believe in the law and engage in delinquent behavior only after they can rationalize their actions as necessary or unavoidable (see Figure 6.2). Although the theory specifies delinquency, techniques of neutralization can apply to adult offenders as well. Basically, the techniques of neutralization theory tackle the question of how people who commit antisocial behaviors deflect the moral blame from themselves and attempt to excuse their behavior by denying that it is their own fault. Sykes and Matza list five ways that unlawful behavior is excused through techniques of neutralization.[24]

- *Denial of responsibility.* This rationalization allows the offender to blame external forces for inappropriate behavior. According to Sykes and Matza, offenders take the role of a "billiard ball" helplessly propelled into new situations. They blame bad parenting, inadequate schools, deviant peers, or inescapable situations that lead them into trouble. By denying responsibility for their actions, offenders can escape feelings of guilt and, if they are caught, plead that sanctions are unjustified.

- *Denial of injury.* Another method offenders use to escape responsibility is denial of injury. For example, they see writing graffiti on walls or engaging in other vandalism in which there is no immediate personal victim as harmless fun. If the victims have insurance or are wealthy, offenders discount the effects of the damage even more. An offender who is in a fight and does not seriously injure the opponent can neutralize culpability by claiming, "I didn't hurt him, I only smacked him around a bit."

- *Denial of victim.* Offenders may contend that those injured by their actions are not worthy to be considered true victims. In the 1950s, when Sykes and Matza developed this perspective, youths considered attacks on homosexuals, or even on people presumed to be homosexuals, to be morally permissible even though the attacks legally constituted assault. Likewise, attacks on members of minority groups who had "gotten out of hand" were not deemed to be serious transgressions of social norms even though the attacks were illegal. Today, violent juvenile gangs consider it their duty to injure or kill members of other gangs. By defining victims as enemies or undesirables, offenders are able to attack them without feelings of remorse.

- *Condemnation of condemners.* Another way to neutralize blame for antisocial behavior is to question the legitimacy, authority, and motives of those who pass judgment. For example, someone given a ticket for speeding might claim that he or she was caught in a "speed trap," and the police, who just want to fill a "quota" of speeders, are not really concerned with public safety and should be out catching "real criminals."

- *Appeal to higher loyalties.* Often, offenders are not rejecting the norms of the dominant society when they break

## Figure 6.2 Sykes and Matza's Techniques of Neutralization

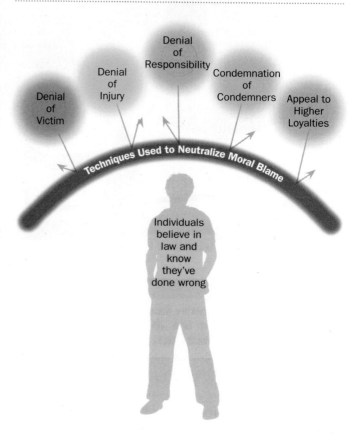

the law. Rather, they are caught on the horns of a dilemma by competing norms they believe they must satisfy. For instance, the demand to be loyal to friends or a gang might cause a youth to jump into a fight he or she has no real interest in. An adult arsonist might claim a particular building was dangerous and he or she had to remove it because no one else would.

Offenders learn these techniques of neutralization at an increasing rate as they delve more deeply into patterns of unlawful behavior. According to Sykes and Matza, this ability to deflect blame is often imperfect, and offenders might feel guilt or shame for some of their actions. However, the more offenders are surrounded by others who share attitudes favoring the violation of the law, the more they internalize and transmit these techniques of neutralization. From a public policy perspective, the way to combat this process of learning and rationalizing crime is to develop programs that allow these offenders, both youth and adult, to interact with others who will provide a different and more positive set of attitudes.[25]

## Miller's Focal Concerns of the Lower Class

Subcultures—which are typically (but not always) based on race, religion, socioeconomic class, or education—form when people are separated from the dominant culture through eco-

▶ **Youths in lower-class neighborhoods crave excitement, risks, and thrills.**

nomics, values, or norms. A subculture has its own values and norms, although it does share some with the dominant culture. According to subcultural theories, adult offenders and delinquents learn the skills, norms, values, and attitudes conducive to lawbreaking from the subcultures in which they live.

Anthropologist Walter B. Miller studied the cultures of lower-class neighborhoods in Boston and concluded that they exhibited value systems different from those of other social classes. Miller's term for "value systems" is **focal concerns**—attitudes that the lower classes perpetuate as a part of the values and norms they believe are necessary for survival in their neighborhoods. He argued that the lower socioeconomic class had focal concerns that encouraged youths to commit delinquent acts.[26] His analysis is limited to this class, and the way he viewed it is important to understanding his theory. Frank Williams and Marilyn McShane describe Miller's view of the lower class:

> The lower class, as an integral part of the larger society, shares many characteristics and concerns with other social classes. At the same time, the lower class also has distinctive features that differ significantly from those of the middle and upper classes. The legal system of the United States and the norms it incorporates conform more closely to the official standards of middle- and upper-class people than those of lower-class people. As a result, certain behaviors, viewed as entirely appropriate by some lower-class subcultures, routinely violate moral or legal codes.[27]

This means that the types of behaviors required to survive on the street in a lower-class neighborhood are considered inappropriate or even unlawful by the greater society. By doing what they need to do in order to participate in their neighborhoods' subcultures, youths often come into conflict with the police. According to Miller, the following are the focal concerns of the lower class.

- *Trouble.* Lower-class youths expect to be in trouble always. Whether in conflict with school authorities, police officers, or parents, lower-class youths believe there is always someone "breathing down their neck" and finding fault with their behavior. Trouble becomes an accepted part of existence, and lower-class youths do not run from it or let it overly concern them. It is just part of life.

- *Toughness.* Lower-class youths place a high priority on being able to physically defend themselves. Toughness means others cannot take advantage. Fighting hard and losing is preferable to backing down from conflict. The youths' self-concept and street credibility are established by toughness.

- *Smartness.* Smartness is street smarts rather than academic success. A youth is considered smart to the extent that he or she can outwit others, cannot be taken advantage of in economic dealings, and can use cunning to deceive others.

- *Excitement.* Youths in lower-class neighborhoods crave excitement. They are willing to take risks, get into dangerous situations, and seek thrills. However, this excitement, a product of present-day orientation, can get a youth into long-term trouble.

- *Fate.* Lower-class youths do not have a great deal of faith in their ability to control their lives. They attribute what happens to them to luck or fate. This allows them to shirk responsibility for their behaviors and justify their negative outcomes as ordained by fate.

- *Autonomy.* Not having to answer to others is a primary goal. Being able to steal what they want and not depend on parents gives the lower-class youth a sense of autonomy. This attitude also prevents them from engaging in many mainstream activities, like joining a sports team, in which rules and coaches' demands can limit their independence.

It is easy to see how these focal concerns can put youths in danger of running afoul of authorities. In many ways, they reflect the behaviors and attitudes common to all teenagers. The primary difference is that Miller envisions lower-class youths to be immersed in these focal concerns because of

**focal concerns** Attitudes that the lower classes perpetuate as a part of the values and norms they believe are necessary for survival in their neighborhoods.

their lower-class culture. Middle-class teenagers have many other opportunities and influences, so these concerns are only minor contributors to their behavior.

## Subculture of Violence

Some groups of people exhibit consistently higher rates of crime and violence than other groups. Shaw and McKay saw this disparity when they observed how particular neighborhoods always seemed to have crime problems although different groups were constantly moving into and out of the area. Marvin Wolfgang and Franco Ferracuti believe something about the particular culture of the groups living in these areas nurtures crime. They argue that some neighborhoods have a subculture composed of teenage and young adult males who consider violence to be the appropriate response to a wide range of situations. This **subculture of violence** is a culture apart from the main social culture that holds violence as part of its values, lifestyle, and socialization. Although it believes in the values of the dominant culture, its members also believe violence is necessary to achieve their goals and desires, as well as to protect their masculinity.[28]

The theory was developed more than 30 years ago, but it is still used to understand crime today, including higher rates of violence in the inner city and higher homicide rates in the southern states.[29] Ethnic enclaves in the nation's large cities insulate many youths from the values of the dominant culture. Often, these youths band together in gangs to protect themselves from others or to provide the strength in numbers to engage in illegal enterprises such as drug sales, home invasions, or gang warfare.[30]

Countering the negative influences of the subculture of violence is easy to suggest but difficult to accomplish. It cannot be done one youth at a time but rather requires the entire subculture to be assimilated into the dominant culture. This entails providing job opportunities, quality schools, and a realistic chance at the "American Dream" for the entire community. When enclaves of immigrants are prevented from assimilating into the dominant culture because of prejudice and discrimination, their subculture might exhibit levels of violence and gang activity that make their communities dangerous for everyone.[31]

## Code of the Street

Sociologist Elijah Anderson extended and updated the subculture of violence thesis with his observations of urban youths in Philadelphia. Anderson contends that urban violence is prompted by a "code of the street" that requires people to quickly resort to violence when they feel they are not getting the proper respect from others.[32] It is difficult to determine where this code originates, but it is a function of several factors, including disadvantaged neighborhoods,

racial and ethnic subcultural influences, peer rivalries, and lack of parental supervision. Anderson distinguishes between "decent families" and "street families." Decent families, according to Anderson, are similar to those found in all neighborhoods in which parents teach their children to respect the law and to work hard. Street families, on the other hand, raise children with the "code of the street" perspective in which violence is considered permissible, desirable, and, in many cases, inevitable in order to preserve one's reputation and dignity. Learning antisocial behavior is potentially a problem for children from both types of families. Children from decent families can be sheltered for only so long before they are exposed to street culture. Children from street families see violence used to settle differences. Anderson provides an excellent view of what it is like to grow up in a family that maintains internal order through violence.

> In these circumstances, a woman—or a man, although men are less consistently present in children's lives—can be quite aggressive with children, yelling at them and striking them for the least infraction of the rules she has set down. Often, little if any serious explanation follows the verbal and physical punishment. This response teaches children a particular lesson. They learn that to solve any kind of interpersonal problem, one must quickly resort to hitting or other violent behavior. Actual peace and quiet, as well as the appearance of calm and respectful children, are often what the young mother most desires, but at times, she'll be very aggressive in trying to achieve these goals. Thus, she may be quick to strike her children, especially if they defy her law, not because she hates them, but because that's the way she knows how to control them. In fact, many street-oriented women love their children dearly.[33]

On the street, this use of violence determines how individuals interact. Children from decent families must quickly decide how they will survive their dealings with street children. Willingness to fight to maintain respect is a pervasive value on the street, and those who are not quick to realize this are likely to become victims of those who are. When street children come home crying after an altercation, their parents tell them to go back out and fight to win. Weak or reluctant children learn to fight back, or they lead a miserable life of being bullied. Being "dissed" or allowing someone to disrespect you is considered a sign of weakness and is cause for personal devaluation not only from opponents, but also from friends. The code of the street requires that youths stand up for themselves even to the point of breaking the law.

Although Anderson studied the code of the street in an urban, black neighborhood, this perspective can be found in varying degrees in many other cultures and is not limited to males. In many circumstances, females must also use verbal and physical violence to maintain their reputations. According to Anderson, the disputes girls engage in are "rooted

**subculture of violence** A culture apart from the main social culture that holds violence as part of its values, lifestyle, and socialization.

in assessment of beauty (which girl is the cutest), competition over boyfriends, and attempts to regulate other people's knowledge of and opinions about a girl's behavior or that of someone close to her, especially her mother."[34] The code of the street is difficult to overcome when poverty and racism are pronounced. Anderson contends that it feeds a vicious cycle whereby hopelessness and alienation fuel violence in young people who are trying to maintain respect when legitimate opportunities are lacking.

# Think about it

## Remember
List Sutherland's nine propositions of differential association.

## Analyze
Categorize Sykes and Matza's techniques of neutralization. Which ones do you use to account for your own behavior?

## Evaluate
Compare and contrast the subcultural theories of Miller, Wolfgang and Ferracuti, and Anderson.

## Strain Theories of Crime

People experience strain when their cultures promote a certain way of life but do not provide the means for everyone to achieve that life. In the United States, the way of life that is culturally promoted as the "American Dream" produces strain because it is not equally available to everyone, although most people reach for it. Although it is certainly desirable for people to strive to be economically independent, the intense focus on this goal changes how Americans think about other desirable goals such as civility, cooperation in the community, and the welfare of others. The principle of ensuring the welfare of others is particularly vulnerable in a society that has the American Dream as its driving force.

**LO3:** Show how strain theories evolved from the concept of anomie.

### Anomie
Strain theories of crime evolved from the sociological concept of **anomie,** the erosion of standards resulting from a lack of social control and values that leads to social insta-

bility. French sociologist Émile Durkheim coined the term "anomie" to refer to a condition known as structural anomie experienced by societies that were undergoing rapid social change. Durkheim observed that when traditional norms were discarded, new norms are slow to emerge. People experience a sense of individual anomie, or normlessness, and are prone to breaking the law because they feel the old rules no longer constrain them to conforming behavior. Individual anomie, a psychological reaction to rapid social change and its consequences that is crucial to the understanding of crime and delinquency, produces a strain that can result in frustration, desperation, violence, and crime.[35]

Criminologists have used both structural and individual anomie to explain why some countries, such as the United States, have high crime rates. Anomie is manifested in a variety of social problems. For our purposes here, crime is of the most concern. The first sociologist to use the concept of anomie in a criminological theory was Robert Merton in classical strain theory.

### Classical Strain Theory
According to strain theorists, Americans strive to achieve economic success. Theorists such as Robert Merton consider this desire to acquire wealth and the status that accompanies financial security a cultural goal. In developing **classical strain theory,** Merton argued that people who experience anger and frustration when they cannot achieve cultural goals through legitimate means try to achieve these goals through illegitimate means. According to Merton, Americans are highly committed to the cultural goal of economic success but are less committed to the culturally approved means of achieving that goal, mainly, working hard, deferring gratification, and investing and saving money.[36]

Not everyone has equal access to the culturally approved goal of wealth. Some people who find access to this goal systematically blocked by poverty, racism, or sexism experience strain and therefore must adapt by adjusting their goals or finding new means for achieving them. Merton identifies five adaptations (see Table 6.1) that individuals use to deal with their inability to achieve their goals through culturally approved means.

Merton's adaptations detail how Americans relate to the cultural goals and institutionalized means of achieving those goals.[37] In Table 6.1, a minus sign (−) indicates rejection of the goals or means and a plus sign (+) indicates acceptance. Following are details of the five types of adaptations.

- *Conformity.* Most people are conformists. This means that we accept the goal of economic success and are willing to use the culturally approved means (working hard at a conventional job) to achieve this goal. According to

**anomie** The erosion of standards resulting from a lack of social control and values that leads to social instability.

**classical strain theory** The idea that people who experience anger and frustration when they cannot achieve cultural goals through legitimate means try to achieve these goals through illegitimate means.

## Table 6.1  Merton's Adaptations

| Adaptation | Culturally Accepted Goals | Culturally Accepted Means |
|---|---|---|
| conformity | + | + |
| innovation | + | − |
| ritualism | − | + |
| retreatism | − | − |
| rebellion | substitution | substitution |

Each combination of goals and means has a related adaptation.

Merton, this orientation is absolutely necessary for meaningful communities to exist. Conformity requires that people accept society's rules and laws and not only follow them, but also encourage sanctions for those who violate them.

- *Innovation.* Those who accept the goal of making a lot of money but are unwilling to work for it in conventional ways might adopt the innovator's adaptation of finding other ways of amassing wealth. For instance, one way of getting money other than working for it is to take it from someone who already has it. Innovators may try to embezzle or steal to meet their goal. Many offenders, in fact, fall into the innovator category.

- *Ritualism.* Ritualists have given up the pursuit of wealth and accomplishment but continue to participate in the culturally approved means because they derive a certain sense of satisfaction and emotional security from simply going through the motions of work. Ritualists have been socialized to believe participating in the proper activities is its own reward, even if there is little hope these activities will ever lead to success and accomplishment. Normally, offenders are not ritualists.

- *Retreatism.* Some individuals are so alienated from conventional society that they simply stop attempting to achieve financial well-being and are not willing to work in a conventional way. In Merton's terms, these individuals reject both the culturally approved goals of society and the culturally approved means of obtaining those goals. Alcoholics and drug addicts, for instance, consider retreating from society preferable to "playing the game" of seeking conventional success. Predictably, retreatists are often in constant contact with police for a variety of petty as well as serious infractions.

- *Rebellion.* Merton's last category of adaptation is rebellion. The rebellionist rejects both the culturally approved

goal of financial success and the means of working hard to achieve that success. Unlike the retreatist, who also rejects goals and means, the rebellionist substitutes new goals and means. Hippies in the counterculture of the 1960s rejected the so-called rat race of the corporate world and instituted a new goal of "authentic" interaction characterized by drug experimentation and opposition to the Vietnam War. Without arguing the merits of this perspective, we can recognize that it represented an entirely new way of dealing with the cultural demands of the United States at a time of rapid social change. Young people challenged the conventional wisdom of their elders and substituted a fresh, if naive, philosophy of sex, drugs, and rock-and-roll. Not surprisingly, they clashed with the authority figures of the time and many ended up arrested and incarcerated.

The strength of Merton's strain theory is that it addresses several types of offenses. Most important, it allows other criminologists to envision how strain might affect offenders' reasons for breaking the law. Now, let's turn to more recent developments in strain theory.

## Strain and Subculture

Merton contends that we all strive for the goal of economic success and that those who break the law are adapting to the blocked means to achieve their goal (see Figure 6.3). Other theorists have modified strain theory and expanded it to explain why people break the law. Albert Cohen, as a student of Merton, was concerned with how individuals immersed in the subculture of juvenile gangs reacted to the strain of blocked goals.

In his book, *Delinquent Boys: The Subculture of the Gang,* Cohen argued that youth caught up in impoverished and

▲ Americans strive to achieve financial success, according to strain theory.

## Figure **6.3**    Merton's Strain Theory

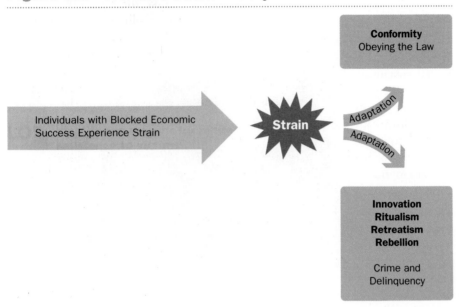

others, and general opposition to conventional standards.[38]

This theory has some limitations that make it of limited use. First, it can explain only a small portion of crime because it is applicable to urban, male delinquents. Second, unlike Merton's strain theory, Cohen's theory posits only one type of adaptation: rebellion that rejects conventional values and substitutes a new one (the gang lifestyle). Finally, as we saw in Matza and Sykes's techniques of neutralization, delinquents might not be as opposed to conventional values as Cohen contends. Remember, the idea behind techniques of neutralization is that they allow delinquents to rationalize why it is permissible for them to violate laws in which they believe.

## Figure **6.4**    **Cloward and Ohlin's Differential Opportunity Theory**

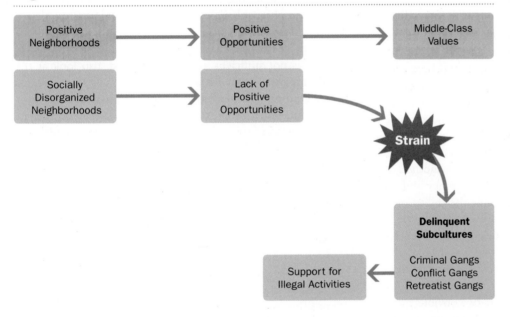

## Delinquency and Opportunity

Strain theory has progressed through several refinements. Richard Cloward and Lloyd Ohlin extend Cohen's idea that the delinquent subculture is an adjustment to the blocked goals of urban youths by specifying three types of delinquent subcultures. These subcultures provide youths with ways of adapting to the lack of legitimate opportunities and with the prospect of developing illegitimate ways of responding to the strain of impoverished and disorganized urban life (see Figure 6.4).[39]

disorganized urban environments are concerned with more than achieving financial success. They also desire middle-class status. The source of strain for these boys is that they do not have a sufficient method for obtaining that status because their means are systematically blocked by poor parenting, bad schools, a juvenile record, and the limitations of growing up in disadvantaged neighborhoods. Although a youth can sell drugs or steal to obtain money, middle-class status cannot be purchased. Therefore, instead of adopting the middle-class value system, delinquent boys reject it and replace it with their own standards of status based on destruction or theft of property, fighting and aggression toward

■ *The criminal subculture.* For delinquents to thrive, they must learn illegitimate ways of adapting to strain. One of these ways is to adopt the criminal lifestyle. This type of subculture can develop only in areas with a concentration of disadvantaged youths who can serve as role models and train younger individuals. There must also be environmental supports for this lifestyle, such as bail bondsmen, fences, and criminal defense lawyers willing to take on petty cases. (Since Cloward and Ohlin developed their theory, the criminal justice and juvenile justice systems have instituted public-defender offices that provide such support.)

- *The conflict subculture.* Many disorganized neighborhoods have a high degree of residential fluctuation. That is, people tend to move in and out a lot. This damages the stability of community relations; cultural conflict arises because individual youths might come from different racial or ethnic backgrounds. Unlike the criminal subculture that provides a support network for the criminal lifestyle, the conflict subculture does not include ways for youths to achieve financial well-being. Consequently, it can address the status concerns of youths only by rejecting the dominant culture and substituting a deviant way of life dependent on fighting and conflict with other groups.

- *The retreatist subculture.* For youths who are unsuccessful in developing a criminal subculture based on delinquency or a conflict subculture based on fighting, Cloward and Ohlin identify a third way of adapting to stress called the retreatist subculture. Much like Merton's strain theory, this perspective accommodates individuals who are not able to function adequately in conventional society and fail at traditional criminal or conflict adaptations. The retreatist subculture involves the abuse of alcohol or drugs as a way of escaping the strains of living in disorganized, impoverished neighborhoods.

Cloward and Ohlin have been criticized for suggesting that youths adopt only one type of lifestyle. Many youths have more than one way to adapt to the strain of not being able to achieve their goals through legitimate means. However, the particular strength of Cloward and Ohlin's theory is the recognition that, in addition to the strain the individual experiences, both legitimate and illegitimate opportunities must be considered. Only by being aware of the opportunities available to the individual can we appreciate why that person would choose one path over another.

Cloward and Ohlin's theory of delinquency and opportunity has policy implications. Reducing the ability and need for youths to develop an antisocial subculture lifestyle might help them fit into conventional society more successfully. This task can be accomplished in two ways. First, the opportunities for engaging in a criminal, conflict, or retreatist subculture must be reduced. Effective law enforcement and limiting the supply of illegal drugs are two obvious methods. Second, the opportunities for conventional success, such as better schools, after-school activities, and job training, must be increased. Youths would presumably feel less stress if they had more viable chances to compete in law-abiding ways.

## Institutional Anomie

Merton's idea that the dominant cultural goal in American society is to acquire wealth as a measure of success might have extensive ramifications for the socialization of young people. Merton believed that having an overarching goal of acquiring wealth in an economic system that does not allow everyone to become equally wealthy results in increased levels of crime as people seek alternative means to get what they are told is desirable. Although this theory seems plau-

▲ Some delinquents adapt to strain by adopting a criminal lifestyle.

sible to many, some theorists contend that it does not go far enough in explaining how strain, which is caused by the values placed on economic success in the United States, plays a role in crime and delinquency. Specifically, Richard Rosenfeld and Steven Messner argue that focusing on the goal of success is not sufficient and that we must also look at the legitimate means that are available.[40]

According to Rosenfeld and Messner, **institutional anomie** occurs when people's commitment to social institutions such as the family, religion, and education becomes subservient to achieving the cultural goal of wealth. This change, in turn, leads to the inability of the neglected institutions to control behavior.[41] Institutional anomie happens for three reasons.

1. *Devaluation of non-economic roles and functions.* When financial success is the primary goal, other institutions such as the family, religion, and education must play a secondary part. For instance, many students think the value of education is limited to getting a good job. Other positive aspects, such as self-awareness, appreciation for great music or literature, or understanding how governments and society work, are relegated to secondary status. For example, evidence of the focus on economic roles can be observed in the high enrollments in business schools and low enrollments in anthropology and philosophy programs. Because the criminal justice system employs so many people, criminology programs enjoy robust enrollments.

**institutional anomie** The condition that occurs when people's commitment to societal institutions becomes subservient to achieving the goal of wealth, which leads to the inability of the neglected institutions to control behavior.

▶ Opportunities for conventional success, such as after-school activities, help children and youths fit into conventional society more successfully.

2. *Accommodation to economic roles.* Some people pursue their careers to the detriment of other institutions. When a father is "married to his job," he might not participate in the Parent Teachers Association or attend school plays or softball games, or he might not be present when his children are ill, injured, or depressed. A working mother climbing the corporate ladder or holding down two jobs to make ends meet might also sacrifice family events for economic gain. Although this reliance on work is necessary for many families, some parents work excessively to acquire new cars, bigger homes, and country club memberships as symbols of financial success at the expense of their families' overall welfare.

3. *Permeation of economic goals.* Economic goals can also become the primary focus of other institutions. When churches and universities operate with the ethics, procedures, and bottom-line mentality of businesses, their manifest goals of education and service to parishioners become secondary. We see this imbalance particularly in the move toward accountability in colleges and universities in which enrollment is the driving force behind funding rather than educational quality.

These conditions foster institutional anomie when the messages sent by society reflect the perspective of economic success. Rosenfeld and Messner argue that Americans' over-reliance on the economic dimension in their value systems devalues other institutional support systems, such as education and family. They suggest we examine how the American Dream undermines our quality of life and the following institutions.

■ *Education.* What is the real value of an education? According to many who pursue the American Dream, a good education is a way to get a high-paying job. Learning for its own sake in order to appreciate art, literature, and history are not highly valued in American society.

■ *Family.* Despite the rhetoric about "family values," we do relatively little compared to other industrialized countries to support families. American families are valued according to how much money their breadwinners provide, and families that deviate from the cultural norm of an intact nu-

clear family get little cultural support. For instance, many families have a difficult time finding affordable daycare, and children in many states are without health insurance. Women, who still do the most extensive work in maintaining the home, find their activities devalued in relationship to the contributions of those who work outside the home. A stay-at-home father is an oddity and is looked upon as not fully enacting his role as the "man of the house."

■ *Politics.* Rosenfeld and Messner point out that politics in the United States is left to the career politicians and that citizens take only a passing interest in participating in the political process. They argue that an "able-bodied" adult who refuses to work is degraded but that those who do not vote (about half of those eligible) are not. Furthermore, the role of government, according to many Americans, is to provide the economic freedom for corporations to thrive and to allow the economy to provide jobs. Other functions of government, such as providing health care, education, and cultural arts, are viewed as discretionary and more properly the purview of the private sector.

When the economic engine drives our cultural values, other aspects of society are left behind or forced to accommodate themselves to the pursuit of financial success. This creates a sense of institutional anomie in a society where, despite the rhetoric that praises a full and rich life, the American Dream is reduced to making money. This cultural goal of economic success is not only limiting in its own right, but it also subverts the ability of other institutions to fulfill their mandates. When a parent sees his or her worth measured by workplace success, the demands of the family, and especially the children, take a back seat. When schools are measured by how successfully they prepare their students for the workplace, important thinkers and artists like Shakespeare, Dante, and Mozart get left out of the curriculum.

According to Messner and Rosenfeld, this perverted view of the American Dream is dysfunctional and produces crime and delinquency. Limited reforms in the criminal justice system are unlikely to have a major effect on crime levels. Social reforms that simply allow more people to participate in the dream of economic independence will not solve the problems of crime and delinquency. Rosenfeld and Messner contend that the cultural goal of the American Dream as defined by money must be recast into one that elevates other social institutions, such as the school and the family, to the same level as the economy.

## General Strain Theory

As we have seen from Messner and Rosenfeld's work, strain theory is more involved and complicated than Merton first envisioned. Criminologist Robert Agnew's **general strain theory,** a revision of classical strain theory, includes three major types and levels of strain, including failure to achieve goals, the loss of positive stimuli, and the gain of negative stimuli. It explains why some strain is more likely to result in crime and delinquency and shows why some people are more likely to cope with strain through crime.[42]

Agnew presents a comprehensive analysis of strains and stressors experienced by those who might respond by breaking the law. He states that not everyone responds to strain in the same way and that much of what stresses individuals might not be actual strain but merely anticipated strain. He further distinguishes between objective strain and subjective strain. *Objective strain* is a problem most people would feel and that we could predict would cause anxiety or pain.[43] For instance, Agnew cites men having their masculinity questioned as an example of objective strain because most males ground their identity in their ideas of manhood.[44] In contrast, Agnew contends that *subjective strains* are a product of personality traits, goals and values, and prior experiences. He provides the example of divorce as evidence that individuals experience stress differently. For one person a divorce is traumatic, whereas for another it is liberating.[45]

According to Agnew, these strains are the most likely to push people into crime:

- parental rejection
- child abuse and neglect
- erratic, excessive, or harsh supervision and discipline
- negative secondary school experiences (low grades, negative relationships with teachers, the experience of school as boring and a waste of time)
- abusive peer relations (insults, threats, physical assaults)
- work in the secondary labor market (low-paying jobs that have few benefits, little opportunity for advancement, and unpleasant working conditions)

**general strain theory** Agnew's revision of classical strain theory identifies three major types of strain: failure to achieve goals, the loss of positive stimuli, and the gain of negative stimuli.

- chronic unemployment
- marital problems
- the failure to achieve selected goals, including thrills/excitement, high levels of autonomy, masculine status, and the desire for much money in a short period of time
- criminal victimization
- residence in economically deprived communities
- homelessness
- discrimination based on characteristics such as race/ethnicity and gender[46]

According to Agnew, some research supports the relationship between these strains and crime.[47] Furthermore, when individuals experience two or more of these conditions, they are even more likely to engage in unlawful behavior. These strains accumulate, so that when someone loses a job, there is an increased likelihood that problems in the family will occur, which can lead to other issues related to delinquency and crime.

General strain theory considers how these strains and stressors lead individuals to develop negative emotions such as frustration, anger, depression, jealousy, and fear. Individuals feel bad and are motivated to take corrective action to obtain revenge, acquire valued property, or elevate their status in their own eyes and in the eyes of the community. These strains also reduce the individual's commitment to conventional society and the socially approved means for obtaining success.[48] (See Table 6.2 for the differences between classical and general strain theory.)

▼ **According to Agnew, bullying by peers is one of the strains most likely to push people.**

**Table 6.2    The Differences Between Classical Strain Theory and General Strain Theory**

|  | Merton (Classical) | Agnew (General) |
|---|---|---|
| **Goals** | Merton assumed that all Americans are influenced primarily by the capitalist dream of achieving financial success. Although this goal is true for many people, it does not affect everyone in the same way. | Agnew recognized Merton's assumption and expanded the idea of striving for cultural goals beyond that of money. |
| **Means** | Merton says crime occurs when means are systematically blocked by such things as poverty and racism. | Agnew argues that the means to achieving cultural goals are also more numerous and varied than Merton suggests and the legitimate and illegitimate means available to potential delinquents more complicated. |
| **Empirical Evidence** | Merton's ideas were purely theoretical, although others have tried to test them. | Agnew's research on strain theory is impressive for its increasing sophistication in both statistical technique and the range of populations. |

# Think about it

## Remember

List the strains that Agnew contends are most likely to lead people to resort to crime.

## Understand

Describe the methods youths use to adapt to their failure to achieve culturally desired goals as described by classical strain theory.

## Evaluate

Critique the ways the American Dream is undermined by institutional practices according to Rosenfeld and Messner.

## Control Theories of Crime

A perplexing aspect of criminological theory is that the assumptions about human nature on which it rests are often left unstated. Criminologists often take human nature as a given, and the goal of a theory is to explain why some people will violate the law. If we assume that well-adjusted people act in conforming ways, all we have to do is specify how non-conforming individuals have not been adequately socialized. However, another way of looking at human nature assumes that antisocial behavior is not an aberration, but rather that it is to be expected.

**Control theories of crime**—a perspective that questions why most people do *not* break the law—have been around

**Discuss** how control theories of crime look at the way societies control people and how people control themselves within society.

for a long time. As we will see with Travis Hirschi's social bond theory, the question of why some people break the law can be reframed to ask why *all* of us do not break the law.[49] This reformulation of the assumptions underlying antisocial behavior requires theorists to consider crime in a different way, one that refocuses our attention on how individuals are connected to society. A look at the development and underlying principles of control theories shows us why this perspective is such a popular way to consider crime and delinquency.

### Containment Theory

Perhaps the best example of the early control theories is Walter Reckless's **containment theory,** the idea that everyone has internal and external structures that hold them within the larger social structure. It distinguishes between internal factors that "push" people into crime and external factors that "pull" them.[50] According to Reckless, all people have an external structure that "contains" (or restricts) their behavior as well as a protective internal structure. Both structures guard against deviance by securing people within the social structure. Loss or corruption of elements of their external structures can "pull" people into lawbreaking activities, while internal issues can "push" them. See Table 6.3 for a look at the elements of containment theory.

Reckless's theory includes many of the ideas covered in social disorganization, differential association, and strain theories. Reckless went one step further, however, and considered the case of the "good boy" in the "bad neighborhood."[51] Why don't all youths exposed to urban problems, negative peer pressure, and economic inequality succumb to delinquency?

**control theories of crime** A perspective that questions why most people do not break the law.

**containment theory** The idea that everyone has internal and external structures that hold them within the larger social structure.

## Table 6.3 Elements of Containment Theory

| Elements of External Structure | Elements of Internal Structure |
| --- | --- |
| Roles that guide individual activities | Positive self-concept |
| Reasonable limits and responsibilities | Self-control |
| Opportunities for status achievement | Strong ego and conscience |
| Cohesion among group members | High tolerance for frustration |
| A sense of belonging and identification with the group | Strong sense of responsibility |
| Identification with others in the group | |
| Alternative ways to achieve satisfaction if some ways are closed | |

▲ According to Reckless, youths with a healthy self-concept are insulated from the negative effects of a bad neighborhood and antisocial peers.

Reckless's answer is that youths with a healthy self-concept are insulated from the negative effects of a bad neighborhood and antisocial peers.[52] This observation has led a number of scholars to explore how youths bond to society so they resist the temptations that lead others to delinquency. The foremost among these theorists is Travis Hirschi.

## Social Bond Theory

Hirschi's **social bond theory** is the idea that there are forces that keep people connected to social norms and values. It has wide appeal because it specifies how youths are connected to the idea that they should not break the law. Rather than looking at delinquents and asking about their motivations to be antisocial, Hirschi looks at all youngsters and asks what keeps them from violating the law. His answer is social con-

**social bond theory** The idea that there are forces that keep people connected to social norms and values.

trol in the form of four elements: attachment, commitment, involvement, and belief. Crime and delinquency occur when these bonds to conventional society are weakened or broken (see Figure 6.5). Let's look at each.

- *Attachment.* We all have emotional attachments to others. We care about others' opinions of us and are worried that we might disappoint or hurt them by our actions. Most youths are strongly attached to their parents and strive to live up to their expectations. When teenagers test their freedom by taking the family car out on a Saturday night, they might be tempted to impress their friends by speeding, drinking, or staying out late. Most curb these impulses because they are emotionally attached to their parents and do not want to violate their trust. This attachment is a form of indirect parental control that acts to keep children out of trouble. The stronger it is, the fewer concrete rules teenagers need. Other teenagers need well-defined rules concerning curfews, where they can go, and whom they should be with. Children who are estranged from their parents may have little consideration for parental approval and feel free to break the law.[53]

- *Commitment.* Youths who are successful in school, in the community, and among their peers are more likely to stay out of trouble because they develop a commitment to the conventional lifestyle. An old saying points out, "If you've got nothing, you've got nothing to lose." Those who have status, responsibility, and the respect of others have a great deal to lose if they are caught breaking the law and therefore are less likely to take chances. From a policy perspective, Hirschi's idea of commitment suggests that parents and communities should find ways to give youths a stake in society, so they feel they can be successful if they commit to law-abiding behavior.[54]

- *Involvement.* If "idle hands are the devil's workshop," then one obvious solution to delinquency is to keep youths busy with conventional activities. If youths are involved in recreational programs, music lessons, or soccer camp, they are

## Figure **6.5**  Hirschi's Social Bond Theory

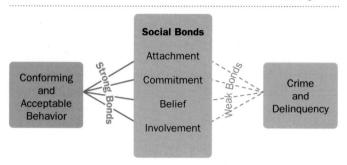

less likely to find the time to get into trouble. As youths move from being adolescents under their parents' supervision to adults who are fully integrated into society, they have a great deal of leisure time to fill. Those who seek involvement in conventional activities are able to develop a set of values that help them resist the lure of delinquency when they have "too much time on their hands."[55]

■ *Belief.* Like other theories such as differential association and techniques of neutralization, Hirschi's social bond theory is concerned with the question of how people who believe in the law can justify breaking it. Most youths obey the law just about all the time. When they do become delinquent, it is because that, for some reason, they are able to convince themselves that their behavior is necessary, inevitable, or out of their control. Although differential association argues that some youths hold definitions that are favorable to the violation of the law, Hirschi's control takes a different tack. Hirschi does not argue that juveniles believe lawbreaking is desirable; he argues only that they do not believe it is bad. This is a fine distinction, but it is an important one because it speaks to the *strength* of youths' beliefs more than to the direction of those beliefs. If the belief that forbids delinquency is weak or absent, then the youth's bond to society is fragile, and the youth will break the law not because it is considered desirable, but simply because his or her belief that crime is bad is not strong enough.[56]

# theory to practice

### Strengthening Social Bonds as Prevention and Treatment for Antisocial Behavior

We can trace most prevention and treatment programs back to sociological criminological theories. The following examples detail how programs have been structured to take advantage of one particular type of theory: Hirschi's social bond perspective. Hirschi identified four ways in which individuals are bonded to conventional society: attachment, commitment, belief, and involvement. Programs that examine the individual's social bonds have met with mixed success in preventing or treating antisocial behavior.

■ In programs run by drug courts, a major goal is to address some of the reasons that youths use drugs. By focusing on a youth's links to conventional society, such as parents, peers, school, and religion, the programs can engage youths in pro-social activities. Results indicate that both positive or negative social bonds play a significant role in youths' success in desisting delinquent behavior and completing the program.[1]

■ Strengthening social bonds can help treat offenders with drug problems. Getting offenders into treatment quickly can prevent the high failure rate observed during the critical first months that offenders are paroled. It is also possible that attending treatment

helps these offenders form stronger social bonds with employers, family, and other conventional institutions.

■ In attempting to keep adolescents from engaging in premarital sex, some programs ask them to pledge abstinence until marriage. This strategy has roots in Hirschi's social bond theory, which encourages attachment to parental values, commitment to good behavior, and belief that doing the right thing pays off in the long run. Unfortunately, the success of abstinence programs is not well established. In one study, 53 percent of youths who took the pledge had sex before marriage. Also, adolescents who pledge abstinence contract sexually transmitted diseases at the same rate as those who do not, and they are less likely to use a condom.[2]

[1]Amna Saddik Gilmore, Nancy Rodriguez, and Vincent J. Webb, "Substance Abuse and Drug Courts: The Role of Social Bonds in Juvenile Drug Courts," *Youth Violence and Juvenile Justice* 3, no. 4 (2005): 287–315; Duren Banks and Denise C. Gottfredson, "The Effects of Drug Treatment and Supervision on Time to Rearrest Among Drug Treatment Court Participants," *Journal of Drug Issues,* (Spring 2003): 385–412.

[2]Sandra G. Boodman, "Virginity Pledges Can't Be Taken on Faith," *Washington Post,* May 16, 2006, F04; Janet E. Rosenbaum, "Reborn a Virgin: Adolescents' Retracting of Virginity Pledges and Sexual Histories," *American Journal of Public Health* 96, no. 6 (June 2006): 1098–1103.

## THINKING *in* ACTION

Develop an idea for a social program that would use Hirschi's social bond perspective.

Hirschi's social bond theory has received considerable attention from researchers and, for the most part, has withstood their scrutiny. Weak bonds to society do appear to increase the likelihood of being involved in crime, although the quality of the evidence depends upon the quality of the research.[57] For a look at how some programs use social bonds to treat drug addiction, rehabilitate offenders and delinquents, and encourage adolescents to conform, see *Theory to Practice*.

## Power-Control Theory

Sociologist John Hagan's **power-control theory of crime** seeks to explain why males commit more offenses and delinquency than females.[58] Hagan considers the family important to the socialization of children. He focuses on the economic inequality that exists between husband and wife and contends that this fosters a condition of patriarchy in which spouses' social roles are determined by gender and are inherently unequal. When this gender inequality is reproduced in the family, the children receive different messages that depend on whether they are male or female. Boys are encouraged to take risks and be independent, while girls are socialized into the values of domesticity and are expected to be socially and economically submissive to males.[59]

This is a highly simplified view of the family; recognizing this, Hagan extends the argument to reflect changing family patterns. He envisions the family on a continuum, ranging from the traditional patriarchal family to the egalitarian family. In the egalitarian family, the wife is likely to have a good job and command a share of the family power. Spouses in the egalitarian family are more equal, which results in a different type of gender socialization of the children. This also means that children whose parents have a relationship characterized by equality in decision-making, salary, job benefits, and status are likely to have children whose own behavior is less gender-biased.[60] Among other things, boys and girls will likely both go to college, have skilled jobs outside the home, and engage in similar patterns of delinquency.

An important part of power-control theory has to do with how youths calculate the benefits of delinquent behavior. Those who are highly tolerant of risk are more likely to break the law than those who are willing to risk less. Furthermore, risk tolerance is different for different types of offending. Hagan contends that power-control theory is better suited to explaining minor offenses such as theft, vandalism, and physical aggression than to explaining more serious offenses such as homicide, where calculation of risk is often absent and anger or fear are the motivating factors.[61]

Hagan's power-control theory is important because it shows how the family environment can produce delinquency.

**power-control theory of crime** A perspective that seeks to explain why males commit more offenses and delinquency than females.

He believes that patriarchal families in which gender roles are distinct produce much higher levels of male delinquency than female delinquency. In egalitarian families, the overall level of delinquency will be lower, and the ratio of the misbehavior of boys and girls will be more equal. This has practical applications for family courts, which can look at the dynamics of the families of children in trouble and prescribe family therapy sessions to reduce the level of patriarchy and encourage greater equality in the treatment of boys and girls.

# Think about it

## Understand

Discuss the attachments to society in Hirschi's social bond theory.

## Analyze

Analyze Hagan's focus on economic inequality within the family as an explanation of why boys break the law more often than girls.

## Evaluate

Explain the fundamentally different approach in Hirschi's social bond theory.

▼ In egalitarian families, the wife may have a good job and a share of the family power, according to Hagan.

# Summary

**LO1:** **Discuss how social disorganization theories of crime were developed and demonstrate how they apply to modern urban situations.**

- The study of crime and delinquency in the United States was influenced by the development of sociology, particularly at the University of Chicago.
- Some sociologists thought the remedy for crime was to address the social problems that result from a lack of cohesion among neighborhood residents, rather than to focus on individuals.

**LO2:** **Explain why many criminologists contend that antisocial behavior is learned like any other behavior.**

- Learning theories focus on where and how offenders find the tools, techniques, and expertise to break the law.
- Sutherland's theory of differential association seeks to account for how offenders learn to break the law.
- Sykes and Matza's techniques of neutralization theory assert that delinquents believe in the law and break it only after they can rationalize their actions as necessary or unavoidable.
- According to subcultural theories, offenders learn the skills, norms, values, and attitudes conducive to lawbreaking from the subcultures in which they live.
- Wolfgang and Ferracuti argue that some neighborhoods have a subculture of violence in which violence is considered to be the appropriate response to many situations and is necessary to achieve goals and desires.
- According to Anderson, urban violence is prompted by a "code of the street" that requires people to quickly resort to violence when they feel others do not respect them.

**LO3:** **Show how strain theories evolved from the concept of anomie.**

- When people experience a sense of normlessness or anomie, they are prone to break the law because they feel the old rules no longer constrain them to conforming behavior.
- People experience strain when their cultures promote a certain way of life but do not provide the means for everyone to achieve that life.
- In classical strain theory, Merton argued that Americans are highly committed to the cultural goal of economic success but less committed to the culturally approved means of achieving that goal.
- Agnew's general strain theory includes several different types and levels of strain, explains why some strain is more likely to result in criminal offending, and shows why some people cope with strain through crime.

**LO4:** **Discuss how control theories of crime look at the way societies control people and how people control themselves within society.**

- One way of looking at human nature assumes that antisocial behavior is not an aberration but is to be expected.
- Reckless's containment theory distinguishes between internal factors that "push" people into crime and external factors that "pull" them.
- Rather than asking why youths break the law, Hirschi's social bond theory asks what keeps youths from violating the law: attachment, commitment, involvement, and belief.
- Hagan's power-control theory seeks to explain why males break the law more often than females.

# Questions

1. What is the "sociological imagination"?
2. What are Shaw and McKay's two ideas for concentric zone theory?
3. How does the theory of collective efficacy and crime differ from Shaw and McKay's social disorganization theory?
4. How does the idea of operant conditioning relate to social learning theory?
5. What are subcultures?
6. Explain Miller's focal concerns of the lower class.
7. What do criminologists use the subculture of violence to explain?
8. What is the code of the street?
9. What is anomie? Why is it important to strain theories?
10. Describe Merton's five adaptations.
11. What does the American Dream have to do with strain?
12. According to Cloward and Ohlin, what do deviant subcultures do?
13. According to Agnew, what's the difference between objective strain and subjective strain?
14. Explain Reckless's containment theory of "pushes" and "pulls."
15. What are Hirschi's four elements of social control?

# 7

# Life-Course
# and Integrated

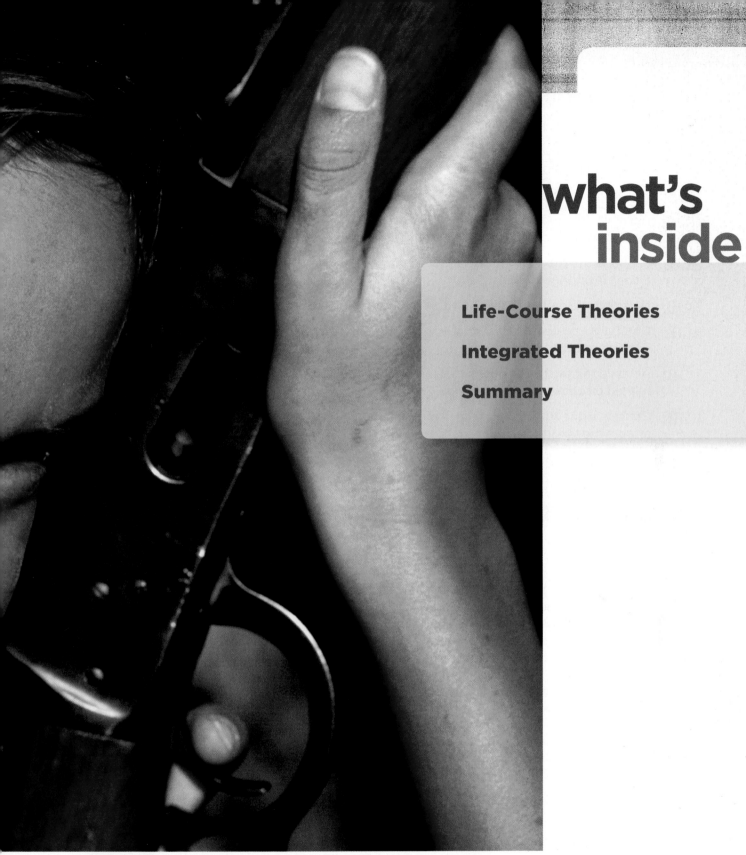

# Theories

**As you read, keep in mind these learning objectives:**

**LO1:** Describe the focus of life-course criminology.

**LO2:** Explain when antisocial behavior begins, according to Patterson's developmental perspective, and how long it continues.

**LO3:** Identify Moffitt's two categories of youthful offenders.

**LO4:** Review Laub and Sampson's focus on the quality of social bonds in persistent offending or desisting from crime.

**LO5:** Examine the theories included in the integrated theoretical perspective of Elliott, Ageton, and Canter.

**LO6:** Describe the emphasis of Thornberry's interactional theory.

**LO7:** Compare and contrast the concepts of control deficit and control surplus in Tittle's control balance theory.

**LO8:** Analyze the ten propositions Cullen uses to explain how social support is related to crime and delinquency.

**LO9:** Critique Agnew's assertion that the interaction between five life domains affects the likelihood of antisocial behavior.

**LO10:** Identify and define the basis of Farrington's integrated cognitive antisocial potential theory.

In preceding chapters we discussed biological, psychological, and sociological theories of crime and delinquency. In this chapter we will consider two types of theories of great concern to contemporary criminologists: life-course theories and integrated theories. Both these theories not only represent a greater sophistication in the level of detail used to explain crime, but they also attempt to expand the range of analysis to include more types of crime.

Life-course and integrated theories build on many of the theories covered in preceding chapters as theorists fine-tune some of the concepts and ideas of other scholars. As new data become available and research techniques more refined, theorists also search for explanations that better reflect the conditions both within society and within individuals that might contribute to crime. Understanding the complexities of life-course and integrated theories is important because, in many ways, contemporary criminological theory increasingly concentrates on these theories. Table 7.1 sets forth the basics of each of the theories discussed in this chapter.

**LO1:**

**Describe** the focus of life-course criminology.

## Life-Course Theories

**Life-course theory** focuses on three issues: the development of antisocial behavior, risk factors at different ages, and the effect of life events on individual development.[1]

Life-course theories are constructed using **longitudinal** data, which means the same individuals are examined at different points in their life course. This dynamic type of theory is significantly different from the static theories that look at the subject at one point in time and do not consider the full context of the person's environment. These "snapshot" theories can neither measure nor account for subsequent changes in behavior.[2] For example, youths account for a large number of arrests. In fact, the Uniform Crime Reports' statistics for arrests by age combine number of arrests by

**>< THINKBACK**

longitudinal (ch. 2)—A type of survey that follows respondents throughout their lives or a significant proportion of their lives.

**life-course theory** A perspective that focuses on the development of antisocial behavior, risk factors at different ages, and the effect of life events on individual development.

## Table 7.1  Life-Course and Integrated Theories

This table presents an overview of the theories presented in this chapter, along with their developing theorists, strengths, and challenges.

| Theory | Theorist | Strengths | Challenges |
|---|---|---|---|
| **Life-Course Theories**<br><br>*Focus on the development of antisocial behavior, risk factors at different ages, and the effect of life events on individual development* | | The behavior of individuals can be examined with respect to aging. | Long periods of study mean that some subjects will be lost.<br><br>There are more subjects early in the research than in later stages. |
| **Developmental perspective on antisocial behavior**<br><br>*Antisocial behavior begins early in life and often continues through adolescence and adulthood.*<br><br>*Advocates early intervention to prevent chronic delinquency.* | Gerald R. Patterson<br><br>Barbara D. DeBaryshe<br><br>Elizabeth Ramsey | Has been tested in the "real world" | Does not address elements that cause some youths to desist from antisocial behavior. |
| **Pathways to crime**<br><br>*Young offenders are adolescent-limited or life-course persistent.*<br><br>*Adolescence-limited offenders break the law during youth.*<br><br>*Life-course-persistent offenders continue antisocial activity into adulthood.* | Terrie Moffitt | Considers biological, psychological, and sociological explanations for delinquency | Divides delinquents into only two groups: adolescent-limited delinquents and life-course-persistent offenders<br><br>Classifies subjects only after adolescence is over |
| **Persistent offending and desistance from crime**<br><br>*Individuals advance into conventional behavior via turning points and personal agency.* | John Laub<br><br>Robert Sampson | Based on strong data (the Gluecks' study)<br><br>Qualitative elements, such as life histories, flesh out the theory | Does not deeply investigate the elements that encourage people to break the law |
| **Integrated Theories**<br><br>*Bring together several theories to explain more types of antisocial behavior* | | Seek to provide more detailed explanations for crime | Can be very complicated<br><br>Currently consider offending at only the individual level |
| **Integrated theoretical perspective on delinquent behavior**<br><br>*Everyone is bound to society.*<br><br>*Strong social bonds produce conventional behavior; weak social bonds produce antisocial behavior.* | Delbert Elliott<br><br>Suzanne Ageton<br><br>Rachelle Canter | Combines strain, self-control, and social learning theories<br><br>Popular among integrated theories | Might try to consider too many variables |

*(continued on next page)*

**Table 7.1    Life-Course and Integrated Theories** *(continued)*

This table presents an overview of the theories presented in this chapter, along with their developing theorists, strengths, and challenges.

| Theory | Theorist | Strengths | Challenges |
|---|---|---|---|
| **Interactional theory of delinquency**<br><br>*Incorporates social learning, social bonds, and life-course theories.*<br><br>*Considers youths' bonds to parents as particularly important.* | Terence Thornberry | Addresses the reciprocity of social learning, social bonds, and life-course perspectives | Links theories in an "end-to-end" approach, which limits the degree of integration |
| **Control balance theory**<br><br>*Individuals exert control over their lives, and society exerts control over individuals.*<br><br>*Imbalance in these factors produces antisocial behavior.* | Charles Tittle | Complex, ambitious; seeks to explain not only whether a person will break the law, but also what kind of offense will be committed | Difficult to test and construct research |
| **Social support and crime**<br><br>*Support from society affects individuals and institutions and the likelihood of crime.* | Francis Cullen | Integrates theories in a unique way; accounts for both micro and macro levels<br><br>"Social support" variable is unique. | Other theories do not employ the concept of social support. |
| **General theory of crime and delinquency**<br><br>*The major causes of crime lie within five life domains.* | Robert Agnew | Links together a broad range of factors that influence crime | It is difficult to test all the variables in such a comprehensive theory. |
| **Integrated cognitive anti-social potential theory**<br><br>*Many factors combine to increase the likelihood of short-term and long-term antisocial behavior.* | David Farrington | Integrates ideas from many classic criminological theories | Focuses on males<br><br>Does not account for race or crime rates<br><br>Does not attempt to explain gangs |

age for ages under 15 years and over 25. For example, there are categories for "under 10," "10–12," "13–14," "25–29," "30–34," and so on until the final category, "65 and over."[3] However, the statistics for number of arrests by age for ages 15 through 24 are separated by each year (see Figure 7.1). As you can see in that figure, the number of arrests rises, peaking at age 19. After that, the number of arrests drops off regularly by age group.

The major advantage of the longitudinal study methodology used in life-course theories is that it can examine the stability or variability of an individual's behavior as the person ages and matures. Longitudinal studies allow researchers to observe behaviors that are part of the normal maturation process and to determine which factors or conditions contribute to antisocial behavior and crime.

The longitudinal approach has its drawbacks, however. The longer the period under consideration, the greater the likelihood of attrition, or loss, of subjects. That is, as the study continues over a period of years, some subjects might decline to continue to participate in the study, the researchers might be unable to find some of the subjects, or some subjects die. Thus, there are many more subjects early in the research than in the later stages. The loss of subjects would not be a big problem if we could assume there was no systematic bias between the groups at various stages of the study. However, it is possible that subjects who cannot be found are incarcerated, were killed while breaking the law, or ultimately abandoned the criminal lifestyle and left the jurisdiction. There is no way to be sure that the remaining group of subjects accurately represents the

## Figure 7.1  Arrests by Age, 2008

**The number of arrests peaks at age 19. In 2008, individuals 18 years of age and over accounted for nearly 85 percent of all individuals arrested.**

Number of Arrests (x 100,000)

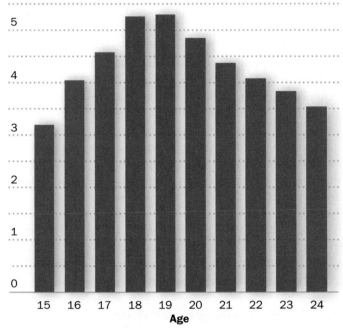

**Age**

*Source:* Federal Bureau of Investigation, *Uniform Crime Reports: Crime in the United States, 2008,* Table 38, http://www.fbi.gov/ucr/cius2008/data/table_38.html.

original group. Nevertheless, the longitudinal data used by life-course theorists are useful in developing a more detailed picture of an individual's commitment to a criminal career or the factors that enable a delinquent to adopt a conventional lifestyle. Many social programs that address child development and delinquency focus on the life course. *Theory to Practice* describes a research center that evaluates these programs.

Child psychologists have long been interested in children's developmental processes and have developed several perspectives that account for a number of variables. We covered some of these perspectives in Chapter 5. Criminologists are now studying developmental processes to see if this perspective better explains antisocial behavior. Let's turn now to three types of developmental theories of crime and examine how they employ the life-course perspective to better explain antisocial behavior.

## Patterson's Developmental Perspective on Antisocial Behavior

According to Gerald R. Patterson, Barbara D. DeBaryshe, and Elizabeth Ramsey, antisocial behavior is a developmental

trait that begins early and often continues through adolescence and adulthood. Patterson and colleagues consider a series of predictable steps that lead to chronic delinquency.[4]

■ *Poor parental discipline and monitoring.* The first step in chronic delinquency is poor parenting. Parents who are inconsistent and harsh in their discipline, provide poor role models, and do not adequately supervise their children's activities are more likely to develop offspring who engage in antisocial behavior. Part of this process can be related to Hirschi's control theory, which states that the bond between parent and child is insufficient to promote strong societal values of conformity at work. In addition, a social-interactional perspective suggests that the child learns ineffective self-control techniques from parents who are inept at controlling their own emotions or teaching their children positive ways of responding to stress.[5]

**LO2:**
**Explain** when antisocial behavior begins, according to Patterson's developmental perspective, and how long it continues.

■ *School failure and social rejection.* The problems of poor parenting and bad conduct in early childhood can lead to more serious concerns in middle childhood. Several

▼ **Poor parenting and bad conduct in early childhood can lead to more serious concerns later on.**

studies have shown that antisocial children perform poorly in school. They spend less time on individual tasks and lack academic survival skills, such as regular attendance and class participation. They might disrupt the classroom and fail to do their homework. Academic failure, as demonstrated by these behaviors, is considered to result directly from antisocial behavior learned in early childhood. Another problem that antisocial children experience is rejection by the normal peer group. Aggressive children are not readily accepted and lack many social-cognitive skills. It can be argued that school failure can cause antisocial behavior as much as antisocial behavior can cause school failure. It is a traditional chicken-and-egg problem. However, Patterson and colleagues argue that a stronger case can be made that children demonstrating early antisocial behavior consistently have problems with academic achievement and making friends.[6]

- *Commitment to antisocial peer groups.* The next step in the developmental process is the formation of an antisocial peer group. Taken from the "birds of a feather flock together" concept, this idea suggests that the developmental process places antisocial youths in groups that reinforce delinquency. The youths provide one another with attitudes and motivations that supply a training ground for antisocial behavior. Because they are placed in the same classrooms, training schools, and treatment programs, they find opportunities to engage in delinquency with one another. Rather than adopting the middle-class values and attitudes of a normal peer group, they continually reinforce and reward their commitment to delinquency and antisocial behavior.[7]

- *Delinquency.* The preceding developmental processes almost inevitably lead to delinquency. Poor parenting results in early childhood conduct problems that lead to school failure and the inability to develop positive social relationships with peers. These problems in turn lead to a commitment to antisocial peer groups that reinforce delinquency. Commitment to an antisocial peer group consequently results in dropping out of school, unemployment, and substance abuse, which are factors that continue the decline toward delinquency.[8]

Contending that early antisocial behavior can lead to more serious consequences, Patterson, DeBaryshe, and Ramsey advocate early intervention to prevent chronic delinquency. Although their theory is more concerned with what leads a child into antisocial behavior than out of it, their developmental perspective has been used in the field to help troubled families (see *Theory to Practice*).

The development of antisocial behavior in children can be prevented if addressed early. Patterson and his colleagues suggest that providing parents with the skills necessary to develop healthy children is more effective than waiting until middle childhood to address delinquency issues. This developmental perspective argues that the factors that cause delinquency are linked in a way that requires early intervention. The suggested intervention would include not only parent training, but also training children in social skills and providing academic remediation so that they can catch up with their peers.[9] According to criminologists Francis Cullen and Robert Agnew, this developmental theory of juvenile delinquency is an important contribution to dealing with troubled children: "It is thus noteworthy that Patterson and his collaborators have achieved a rare feat in criminology: They have designed a theory that not only is well known among academics, but also has achieved real-world success in guiding effective treatment interventions with parents and children mired in troubled families."[10]

## Moffitt's Pathways to Crime

British criminologist Terrie Moffitt offers another influential developmental theory of crime. According to Moffitt, young offenders fall into one of two categories: delinquents who are **adolescent limited**—that is, their antisocial behavior is restricted to the teenage

**LO3:**

Identify Moffitt's two categories of youthful offenders.

▶ Commitment to an antisocial peer group sometimes results in dropping out of school, unemployment, and substance abuse.

# theory to practice

### The Oregon Social Learning Center

Located in Eugene, Oregon, the Oregon Social Learning Center (OSLC) researches social and psychological processes related to healthy family functioning. Clinical psychologist Gerald R. Patterson started the OSLC in 1977 from a research group he developed in the late 1950s that focused on developing the theoretical foundation and techniques for parent-management training. Since the late 1970s, the OSLC has been observing family interactions; interviewing teachers, children, and parents; and collecting school and court records. The center's Multidimensional Treatment Foster Care program, which was originally designed for chronic offending delinquent adolescents, now includes preschool children in the child welfare system. The center's prevention studies also test the effects of parent-management training on various groups, including recently divorced mothers; stepfamilies; the siblings of at-risk youths; parents who are incarcerated, paroled, or on probation; at-risk girls within the child welfare system; and youths at risk for drug and alcohol use. An in-school prevention program called Linking the Interests of Families and Teachers seeks to promote healthy behavior at home, in the classroom, and on the playground.

OSLC's longitudinal Oregon Youth Study, which began in 1983, has been extended to follow its participants' romantic relationships, as well as three generations of their family members. Future research at OSLC will consider biological influences on behavior, examine intervention processes, and develop strategies for implementing evidence-based programs in communities.[1]

[1]Oregon Social Learning Center, http://www.oslc.org/about/overview.html.

▲ Patterson's research focused on developing the theoretical foundation and techniques for parent-management training, such as in-school prevention programs for parents and children. Here, parents learn more about their daughter's educational activities.

## THINKING *in* ACTION

1. In your opinion, how important is good parenting to preventing delinquency?
2. Relate the work of the Oregon Social Learning Center to Patterson's developmental perspective on antisocial behavior

---

years—and **life-course-persistent** offenders, whose antisocial behavior continues throughout adulthood (see Figures 7.2a and 7.2b). The adolescent-limited delinquent breaks the law only during youth. Life-course-persistent offenders are youths who were unable to break the cycle of crime and remain in the lifestyle into adulthood. Life-course-persistent offenders are what we could call "career criminals" and are never fully integrated into conventional society.[11]

Moffitt's theory has strengths and weaknesses. Its primary weakness is that it divides delinquents into only two groups. Certainly, antisocial behavior has more variations, and presumably youths flow from one group to the other. The question is, at what point does a youth move from the adolescent-limited category to the life-course-persistent category? If the only way to answer this question is to study individuals after a life of crime, then the theory has limited policy implications.[12] The theory's strength is that it considers biological, psychological, and sociological explanations

> **adolescent limited**  Moffitt's term to describe antisocial behavior that is restricted to the teenage years.
>
> **life-course-persistent**  Moffitt's term to describe antisocial behavior that continues throughout adulthood.

## Figure **7.2a**   Moffitt's Pathways to Crime: Life-Course-Persistent Theory

**Life-course-persistent offenders are unable to break the cycle of crime and continue to break the law well into adulthood and perhaps for the rest of their lives.**

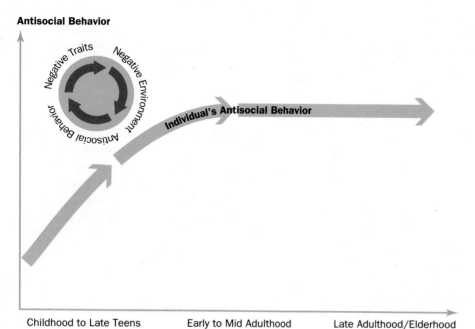

## Figure **7.2b**   Moffitt's Pathways to Crime: Adolescent-Limited Delinquency

**Moffitt states that adolescent-limited delinquents engage in antisocial behavior as they age into adolescence due to social mimicry (that is, their friends break the law, so they do, too) and low maturity. As these delinquents age out of adolescence, they are eventually deterred from antisocial behavior by positive influences.**

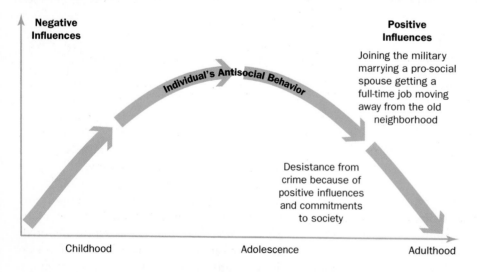

for juvenile delinquency. By looking at how these factors influence youths over their life course, Moffitt brings forth a broad range of explanations that more closely reflect the influences on crime.

## Life-Course-Persistent Offenders

Juvenile delinquents can be responsible for a great deal of crime. Some youths are never fully integrated into conventional society, are always at the margins of social institutions, and eventually land in the juvenile justice system.[13] According to Moffitt, the life-course-persistent offender is constantly breaking the law. Moffitt describes life-course-persistent offenders as

> individuals [who] exhibit changing manifestations of antisocial behavior: biting and hitting at age 4, shoplifting and truancy at age 10, selling drugs and stealing cars at age 16, robbery and rape at age 22, and fraud and child abuse at age 30; the underlying disposition remains the same, but its expression changes form as new social opportunities arise at different points in development. This pattern of continuity across age is matched also by cross-situational consistency: life-course-persistent antisocial persons lie at home, steal from shops, cheat at school, fight in bars, and embezzle at work.[14]

The question of why some people engage in these types of antisocial behaviors has no easy answers. According to Moffitt, the answers lie in a complex set of factors that begins with biological considerations. Among these biological influences Moffitt includes neuropsychological risk factors that contribute to a child's temperament and behavioral problems. Even before a child is born, brain function might be affected by maternal drug abuse, poor prenatal nutrition, or exposure to toxic agents before and after birth.[15] (We should remember that these are merely risk factors and not biological determinants of antisocial behavior.)

Along with biological factors, Moffitt adds psychological deficiencies that have also been linked to juvenile delinquency and antisocial behavior. Children who are reared by parents who provide inconsistent discipline tend to develop behavioral problems and have a difficult time distinguishing between appropriate and inappropriate reactions to negative stimuli. Moffitt argues that the transmission of antisocial behavior from parent to child is as much a psychological as a biological factor.[16]

Finally, sociological variables contribute to delinquents' immersion into a life course of crime. Poor neighborhoods, negative peers, and faulty family structure all contribute to antisocial behavior. This complex of biological, psychological, and sociological factors is persuasive but difficult to measure. Moffitt states that all these factors must be considered when studying the life-course-persistent offender.

The life-course-persistent offender theory might be viewed as a process rather than as a static point. As individuals with negative behavioral traits interact with their negative environment, their negative traits are reinforced, which in turn, leads to antisocial behavior. As Figure 7.2a shows, this process accelerates the youth's immersion into antisocial behavior and a life of crime. A person with a long history of negative behaviors will likely have difficulty breaking the cycle and entering conventional society. Some individuals have very little experience at behaving in socially approved ways and have developed alternative mechanisms such as lying, cheating, and stealing to achieve their goals. Repeated exposure to negative systems exacerbates their antisocial behavior, and the process starts all over again.[17]

Breaking out of this cycle of antisocial behavior becomes more difficult as the delinquents age. There are two reasons for the inability to get off the track of life-course-persistent antisocial behavior. The first is the youths' limited behavioral repertoire. Because of early involvement in the juvenile justice system, they miss out on many opportunities to learn pro-social behaviors. Failure at school, becoming labeled a delinquent, and constantly attempting to solve problems with antisocial behavior combine to produce a cumulative effect that leads to further antisocial behavior. These youths never learn how to act appropriately and successfully engage conventional society. Moffitt contends that "simply put, if social and academic skills are not mastered in childhood, it is very difficult to later recover lost opportunities."[18]

The second reason that life-course-persistent offenders have a hard time reentering conventional society is that they become ensnared by the consequences of their antisocial behavior. The decisions they made as adolescent delinquents create a number of disadvantages later in life. Moffitt contends:

> characteristics such as poor self-control, impulsivity, and inability to delay gratification increase the risk that antisocial youngsters will make irrevocable decisions that close the doors of opportunity. Teenage parenthood, addiction to drugs or alcohol, school dropout, disabling or disfiguring injuries, patchy work histories, and time spent incarcerated are snares that diminish the probabilities of later success by eliminating opportunities for breaking the chain of cumulative continuity.[19]

A number of policy implications can be derived from Moffitt's theory. However, because her theory is so inclusive and complex, these policy implications are complicated, and many of them only indirectly affect antisocial behavior. For instance, children born with neuropsychological problems stemming from poor prenatal nutrition or maternal drug abuse during pregnancy will require extensive attention in order to overcome their difficulties. Similarly, children raised by parents who are poor disciplinarians will require extensive reeducation in order to develop the psychological skills necessary to deal with their impulsivity and low regard for others.

Substandard schools, impoverished neighborhoods, and a national economy suffering from the effects of globalization indirectly affect the ability of life-course-persistent offenders to enter mainstream society. Moffitt's theory is powerful because it includes biological, psychological, and sociological factors, but it is also vulnerable to criticism because transforming policies at all these levels is beyond the capabilities and resources of the juvenile justice system.[20] Furthermore, since life-course-persistent offenders have limited opportunities and few social skills, it is unrealistic to think that they will be able to turn over a new leaf without substantial assistance.

## Adolescent-Limited Delinquents

This second category of juvenile delinquents, according to Moffitt, is much larger than the life-course-persistent group. In fact, according to many self-report studies, most youngsters at one time or another are adolescent-limited delinquents.[21] Young people faced with temptations and opportunities will often engage in antisocial behavior or delinquency to meet specific needs and goals. The most curious aspect of these delinquents is that they will participate in antisocial behavior in some contexts while behaving in pro-social ways in other situations. For example, these youths may fight, shoplift, or periodically use drugs while maintaining good grades in school and obeying their parents. Their periods of sporadic lawbreaking punctuate otherwise conforming lifestyles. In addition, most of the delinquents and offenders in this group eventually desist from crime once they age out of their adolescent years and early 20s (see Figure 7.2b). Moffitt finds that the motivations and rewards for adolescent-limited delinquents differ significantly from those of life-course-persistent offenders.

Like life-course-persistent offenders, adolescent-limited delinquents are affected by biological factors related to puberty. Adolescent males are especially affected. Increases in testosterone compel males to engage in riskier behavior and activities aimed at attracting or impressing the opposite sex.[22] In addition to the biological effects of puberty, teenagers' changing status as they enter high school also affects the development of adolescent-limited delinquency. Moffitt uses the term "social mimicry" to describe young teenagers' attempt to control their environment and make a place for themselves in their social hierarchy by copying the behavior of their supposedly more mature older peers. Moffitt suggests that youngsters envy older peers whom they see as having a more mature status that is associated with power and privilege. By attempting to control their own lives, even though doing so might mean engaging in delinquent behavior, these youths seek to develop an independent self-concept that demonstrates to themselves and the rest of the world that they have the power and resources to do what they want. They seek autonomy and self-reliance through delinquency because other, more conventional adaptations require harder work, demand higher social status, or are nonexistent.

Moffitt contends that a maturity gap is at work in the development of adolescent-limited offenders. As these youngsters enter high school, they find themselves in the grip of a social institution that greatly limits their freedoms and constrains their choices. In our age-graded society, a person can get a driver's license at 16, vote at 18, and buy alcohol at 21. Young people are encouraged to delay marriage until they are financially stable and often do not start careers until they have completed college. Consequently, between the ages of 12 and 22, these youths experience a decade of dependence in which their bodies are mature, but their parents control many of their decisions. Adolescent-limited delinquents often combat this dependence in several ways:

> For teens who become adolescent-limited delinquents, antisocial behavior is an effective means of knifing-off childhood apron strings and of proving that they can act independently to conquer new challenges. Hypothetical reinforcers for delinquency include damaging the quality of intimacy and communication with parents, provoking responses from adults in positions of authority, finding ways to look older (such as by smoking cigarettes, being tattooed, playing the big spender with ill-gotten gains), and tempting fate (risking pregnancy, driving while intoxicated, or shoplifting under the noses of clerks). None of these putative reinforcers may seem very pleasurable to the middle-aged academic, but each of the aforementioned consequences is a precious resource to the teenager and can serve to reinforce delinquency.[23]

The antisocial and delinquency pattern of the adolescent-limited offender peaks during late adolescence. As these youths find more opportunities in society and become more bonded to conventional behavior, they begin to desist from breaking the law. They may give up their antisocial behavior as quickly as they began it. In contrast to life-course-persistent offenders, they are not defined by delinquency and easily cast such behavior aside. Moffitt identifies four changes in the life circumstances of adolescent-limited delinquents that precipitate desistance from crime.

▲ According to Moffitt, youths seek to demonstrate to themselves and the rest of the world that they have the power and resources to do what they want.

■ *Joining the military.* Entering the armed forces is a life-altering event for many young people. Sociologist Erving Goffman likens the military, especially basic training, to a total institution in which rigid rules and regulations, such as dress and communication, are clearly defined and prescribed.[24] Those who join the military quickly learn that there is a very particular way of interacting with superiors that is reinforced with punishment for lapses. For many new recruits, the military lifestyle provides a clearly articulated way of being accepted into a restricted society in which success is achieved by doing what one is told. Basic training can shock young people out of bad habits and into a conventional lifestyle. Stripped of their ability to interact with family and friends, new recruits are provided new goals, new skills for achieving those goals, and rewards and punishments that reinforce the goals. A period of three to four years in the military can shelter young people from the difficulties of life in the unhealthy environment from which they came. Consequently, they return to civilian life with a positive self-concept, an avenue to escape the dysfunctional community they grew up in, and a vision of the middle-class life to which they aspire. These changes, according to Moffitt, enable adolescent-limited delinquents to desist from antisocial behavior.

■ *Marrying a pro-social spouse.* Marriage is another avenue out of crime for adolescent-limited offenders. A spouse with middle-class values who is supportive and demands conforming behavior can compel an adolescent-limited offender to commit to a pro-social lifestyle. A successful marriage can not only alter self-concept, but also provide a reason to give up behaviors that may lead to prison. Becoming a parent provides further incentive to forgo crime and provides an opportunity for becoming a positive role model. Marriage to a pro-social spouse compels the adolescent-limited offender to become more conventional in behavior and establish a longer-term outlook with plans for employment, health care, and pro-social interactions with neighbors and the community.

■ *Getting a full-time job.* Young people who enter the labor market become invested in society. Much like the military, a full-time job requires performance, attendance, and punctuality. Antisocial behavior can jeopardize a person's chances of moving up in the organization or can cause termination. As young people become more invested in their careers, they are more likely to adopt healthier lifestyles in which they are home at a reasonable hour and spend less time in places where antisocial behavior is prevalent. Employment can change the self-concept of marginal youths and give them the confidence to adopt a pro-social lifestyle.

■ *Moving away from the old neighborhood.* The physical and social environment of a disorganized neighborhood is responsible for many of the antisocial motivations of adolescent-limited offenders. Once removed from this neighborhood, they find it possible to adopt a more positive lifestyle. Separating from other marginal youths, whose response to limited resources is breaking the law, enables many youths to make new friends who have more positive views on life. If the neighborhood is economically distressed, moving to a new neighborhood or new city may also provide a broader array of resources and opportunities to change one's behavior.[25]

Each of these factors can have a positive effect on an individual's decision to stop breaking the law. They are not mutually exclusive events, however, as a youth could marry, get a new job, and move to a new city, changes that would produce a cumulative effect. The point is that most adolescent-limited offenders become motivated to engage in more conventional behavior because of these fundamental changes in their lives.

Moffitt's pathways to crime theory provides an interesting and complex look at how antisocial behavior affects the life course. By developing these two categories of offenders, the life-

course-persistent offender and the adolescent-limited delinquent, Moffitt provides an explanation for why some individuals remain mired in crime while others find their way to more socially acceptable lifestyles. She does not neglect the biological and psychological influences that result in crime but rather attempts to integrate them into traditional sociological explanations. Although dividing youthful offenders into only two types is problematic, the categories might be viewed as extreme examples rather than as a comprehensive typology. Often, theoretical explanations must simplify a phenomenon in order to make the theory conceptually manageable.

## Laub and Sampson's Persistent Offending and Desistance from Crime

Sociologists John Laub and Robert Sampson have developed a particularly complex and detailed developmental theory of crime and delinquency.[26] Laub and Sampson were graduate students of Travis Hirschi, and their theory has some elements in common with Hirschi's social control theory, which focuses on why people do not break the law. For Laub and Sampson, the element that keeps people from crime is the quality of their social bonds to pro-social peers, spouses, and parents, as well as jobs and schools.[27] The strength of Laub and Sampson's theory is the data on which it is based. Developmental theories of crime depend upon following at least one group of offenders throughout

## LO4:

**Review** Laub and Sampson's focus on the quality of social bonds in persistent offending or desisting from crime.

their life course. Doing so can be extremely difficult and expensive because researchers typically move on to other subjects or databases or retire from academic life long before

▶ Basic military training can shock young people out of bad habits and into a conventional lifestyle.

# doubletake
doubletake

## The Politics of Theory

Criminological theory is not constructed in a vacuum. It is influenced by the social, economic, and political factors of the times; it is also subject to human factors such as gender, religion, and professional standing. Because criminological theory informs public policy, it is useful to look behind the scenes to see how professional rivalries, research strategies, and even the selection of what to study become important factors in how theories are created, where they are published, and what influence they have on the field.

John Laub and Robert Sampson provide a fascinating analysis of the decade-long debate between Edwin Sutherland, who developed the differential association theory of delinquency, and Sheldon and Eleanor Glueck, who championed the more interdisciplinary and integrated approach that informs life-course criminological theory today. Sutherland was a well-known and highly respected sociologist who contended that the study of delinquency was best left to the field of sociology. The more interdisciplinary Gluecks, on the other hand, published in leading journals in criminology, social work, psychology, sociology, education, law, and psychiatry. Laub and Sampson combed through correspondence between Sutherland and the Gluecks and resurrected the heated debate that influenced the course of criminological theory.

The debate between Sutherland and the Gluecks can be simplified by looking at the theoretical and methodological differences in how they conducted their criminological research. Sutherland embraced analytic induction as a scientific method, which prompted him to reject the multiple-factor approach to the causes of crime. His differential association is essentially a learning theory of crime; consequently, there was little room for the biological, psychological, and multifaceted explanations the Gluecks offered. Sutherland's attack on the Gluecks' work marginalized them even as his own preeminence in the discipline grew.

The Gluecks were at a disadvantage because they did not hold traditional academic posts. Sheldon Glueck, who had a background in the humanities and law, held a position at Harvard Law School. Eleanor Glueck was never able to secure a teaching position at Harvard. She worked as a research assistant and according to Laub and Sampson, was an outcast from mainstream academia at Harvard." Furthermore, the Gluecks did not have the advantage that Sutherland had in training PhD students. Sutherland's students became academic

forces in their own right and were able to advance and popularize his differential association theory.

Sampson and Laub credit the Gluecks with developing the study of crime and delinquency in ways that were ahead of their time. Even though the Gluecks published regularly, their ideas did not fit neatly into mainstream criminology at the time. Laub and Sampson contend, however, that these ideas are central in the development of integrated and life-course theories. They identify four areas in which the Gluecks' work is especially influential.

- *Age and crime.* The relationship between age and crime is now well established. The data collected by the Gluecks more than 40 years ago is being built upon by Laub and Sampson and remains some of the most important evidence for life-course theory.
- *"Career criminals" and longitudinal research.* The Gluecks pioneered the use of longitudinal research to study crime and delinquency. Although some academics dismiss the "career criminal" concept and do not see the utility of longitudinal research, much research being conducted today is based upon the Gluecks' methodological contribution.
- *Stability of crime and deviance.* The Gluecks argued that antisocial behavior and deviance remain remarkably stable across the life course. According to Laub and Sampson, subsequent research has substantiated this idea.
- *Social control, family, and delinquency.* The Gluecks studied the role of the family, schools, and informal sanctions in an effort to determine the cause of delinquency. Today, a number of criminologists who consider how the family and other institutions exert social control on juveniles overwhelmingly agree that these are significant social relationships.

Interactions among criminologists can have a significant effect on how theory is developed. Laub and Sampson construct a convincing argument that the history of criminological theory should include a more sober analysis of the Gluecks' work.[1]

[1]John H. Laub and Robert J. Sampson, "The Sutherland-Glueck Debate: On the Sociology of Criminological Knowledge," *American Journal of Sociology* 96, no. 6 (May 1991): 1402–440.

## THINKING *in* ACTION

How do different academic disciplines provide competing arguments about criminological theory?

life-course offenders progress from juvenile delinquency to adult offending. This logistical problem means that it is almost impossible to keep track of a group of offenders for a period of 40 or more years.[28]

Thanks to some good luck, Laub and Sampson overcame this problem. John Laub was doing research in the archives in the basement of the Harvard University Law School library when he stumbled upon the data from a study published in 1950 by Sheldon and Eleanor Glueck.[29] (See *Doubletake* to learn more about the Gluecks' story.) The Gluecks followed the lives of 500 delinquents plus a control group of 500 non-delinquents in the 1930s and 1940s. They collected data on a vast range of variables. Although they did not focus primarily on life-course theories, the Gluecks did lay the groundwork for Laub and Sampson to contact many of these subjects and update their life histories.[30]

Laub and Sampson published two influential books based upon the Gluecks' data and their investigations of the research subjects: *Crime in the Making: Pathways and Turning Points Through Life* (1993) and *Shared Beginnings, Divergent Lives: Delinquent Boys to Age 70* (2003). In these two books, which followed the Gluecks' subjects as they grew from young men to old, Laub and Sampson examined the arrest records for the entire sample as well as death certificates.[31] They followed the subjects' involvement in crime and ascertained the points at which the men moved toward more conventional behavior. This alone is a significant accomplishment because for the first time we have an indication of a cohort's involvement in crime throughout a complete lifetime. But Laub and Sampson went one step further. They tracked down 52 individuals from the original sample and did extensive life histories on each.

Laub and Sampson added a new feature to the examination of life-course criminology. Most life-course studies are conducted using quantitative data, particularly arrest records, which yield valuable information about the group in question. However, by adding life histories Laub and Sampson provided a qualitative element that gave more detailed information about the subjects' lives. Life histories are conducted as extensive interviews in which the researchers ask the subjects not only what happened in their lives, but also why. Life histories also allow researchers to ask follow-up questions and probe for potentially significant details. The life-history methodology is extremely labor intensive and requires the researchers to develop a rapport with the subjects.

Locating 52 individuals from the original 500 delinquents the Gluecks studied was a remarkable feat considering that it had been more than 35 years since the subjects were first interviewed. Given the state of communication in the 1930s and 1940s, it is a wonder any of the men were found. In an age before private telephones were common and long before the Internet, the types of identifying data that would allow for tracing this cohort were greatly limited. Consequently, the data obtained by the Gluecks and the findings of Laub and Sampson are

extremely valuable contributions to the literature on life-course criminology.

As Moffitt had done, Laub and Sampson found continuities in the life-course behaviors of delinquents. For example, individuals who had difficult childhood and adolescent years were more likely to become involved in crime in their later years. Such individuals are similar to Moffitt's category of life-course-persistent offenders. Laub and Sampson also found changes in the offending patterns of delinquents, and, much like Moffitt's adolescent-limited delinquents, these individuals eventually desisted from breaking the law. But the qualitative nature of Laub and Sampson's theory advanced Moffitt's ideas. An important element in desisting from crime is developing conventional social bonds. As graduate students of Travis Hirschi, Laub and Sampson were especially attuned to the idea that individuals with close ties to families, schools, and communities are invested in good behavior and do not wish to take risks that could put them at a disadvantage in life.[32] Conversely, marginalized individuals have little investment in obeying the law and are much more likely to break it.

These features of social control theory are borne out in the life histories that Laub and Sampson conducted. However, there is more to life-course criminology than a simple updating of control theory. Laub and Sampson "put meat on the bones" of life-course criminology by providing detailed

▼ Conventional social bonds are important in helping youths develop pro-social attitudes.

histories of a set of individuals as they aged. What Sampson and Laub found fits well with what we suspect happens to individuals as they age: They leave antisocial behavior behind and advance into more conventional society. Like Moffitt, Laub and Sampson identified specific events that prompted an individual to desist from crime. These *turning points* include activities such as joining the military, having a family, and securing a good job. A major feature of these turning points, according to Laub and Sampson, is agency. By "agency," Laub and Sampson mean that individuals make a conscious choice to stop breaking the law. Desisting from crime is not just something that happens automatically when a person marries or joins the military. Rather, the individual decides he or she has too much invested in a new lifestyle to risk any more involvement with the criminal justice system. Laub and Sampson provide an example of a man they call Leon, who was arrested several times as a youth for property offenses yet grew into a successful adult who had a long and stable marriage. Describing Leon's change of behavior, Laub and Sampson note:

> Along with the social support and love that came from this successful marriage, additional factors help explain why Leon was able to desist from crime. First, perhaps a response to his wife's investment in him and vice versa, Leon took his marital responsibilities very seriously. He often worked overtime to support his family. Moreover, later in his career, he turned down a promotion because it would have taken more time away from his wife and children. Second, as a direct result of his marriage, Leon was cut off from his former peer group. These peers were replaced by his wife's friends. At his age 25 interview, Leon disclosed that one of his delinquent friends "went away" for murder. Leon continued, "On the very night of the murder, I had a date with my wife and we went to a dance. If it weren't for my wife, I'd probably be up for murder." Third, Leon spent more time with his wife's family that he did with his own. In fact, the couple moved to get away from his family. They relocated to another part of Boston and his in-laws moved in on the first floor of their two-family home. This action solidified his new family bonds, both practically and symbolically.[33]

Criminologist Mark Warr supports the idea of marriage as a turning point, stating that the reason that marriage is associated with desisting from antisocial behavior is that it terminates the antisocial spouse's friendships with antisocial peers.[34] Ronald L. Simons and colleagues add that an antisocial spouse's behavior can be expected to change, however, only if he or she marries a pro-social person. If two antisocial people marry, then both spouses' antisocial behavior can be expected to continue because neither will discourage friendships with antisocial peers.[35]

# Think about it

## Remember

List the steps that can lead to chronic delinquency, according to Gerald Patterson and his colleagues.

## Understand

Review the extraordinary lengths that Laub and Sampson went to in collecting the data that support their life-course theory.

## Analyze

Compare and contrast Moffitt's two categories of young offenders.

## Evaluate

Assess the use of longitudinal data with the use of data that look at individuals at a single point in time.

## Integrated Theories

Throughout this book we have discussed several major theories that attempt to link crime to a variety of causes. Each of these theories has a certain level of relevance to sociological factors associated with deviance, although none of them can completely explain all types of crime. The reason for this is that each of these theories, whether biological, psychological, or sociological, considers the causes of crime to be greatly limited. Few of the theories we have discussed so far try to combine, in an organized way, all the issues that may be responsible for causing people to break the law. We turn now to a discussion of **integrated theories** that attempt to combine several different criminological theories in order to expand the focus on crime.

The life-course theories we have discussed in this chapter are, to a great extent, integrated theories.[36] The limitations of these theories, however, are that they focus primarily on the life-course perspective and do not include several other types of explanations. Integrated theories use several theories to explain more types of antisocial behavior. When considering integrated theories, we must be careful that we do not try to use them to explain too much. A grand theory that attempts to explain everything runs the risk of looking at variables in such a superficial manner that they actually explain very little.[37] The integrated theories that we will examine limit the number of factors or variables they include while trying to take advantage of how each variable can contribute some-

**integrated theories** Perspectives that attempt to combine several different criminological theories in order to expand the focus on crime.

thing to understanding why people break the law. We will consider six integrated theories, the first of which is offered by Delbert S. Elliott and colleagues and focuses primarily on traditional sociological theories of crime.

## Elliott et al.'s Integrated Theoretical Perspective on Delinquent Behavior

Delbert Elliott, Suzanne Ageton, and Rachelle Canter's integrated theoretical perspective on delinquent behavior combines three popular sociological explanations of crime—strain, self-control, and social learning—into an organized theory that specifies how the problems described by these explanations interact to produce crime and delinquency.[38] According to Elliott and colleagues, each of us is exposed to early socialization that binds us to society in a variety of ways. Some individuals are bound to conventional society in ways that others lack. Succeeding at conventional activities, acquiring positive labels, being successfully integrated into conventional society, and developing a personal commitment to good behavior produce strong bonds to society. People with weak social bonds fail in conventional social contexts, acquire negative labels, live in disorganized communities, attend inferior schools, and are not personally committed to good behavior.

**LO5:**

Examine the theories included in the integrated theoretical perspective of Elliott, Ageton, and Canter.

The success or failure of bonding to conventional society leads one to enter peer groups that are either conventional or deviant. Those who are in conventional peer groups and are strongly bonded to society will probably adopt pro-social behavior patterns. Conversely, those who enter antisocial groups and have not successfully bonded to conventional society are more likely to adopt antisocial behavior patterns.

This integrated perspective considers strain theory to be the primary explanation for why both middle-class and lower-class youths sometimes break the law. Middle-class youths experience the same strain as lower-class youths even though their social circumstances are different. Middle-class strain occurs because these youths have high expectations and aspirations for success but find these blocked by factors over which they have no control, such as athletic ability or physical appearance. These youths have internalized the goals of success in conventional society but find that because of some limitations they are unable to achieve success and turn to delinquent behavior. Regardless of the source of strain, youths who experience it are likely to join peer groups that use delinquent behavior as a way of lessening their strain. Youths with low self-control are also more likely to join delinquent peer groups. Elliott and his colleagues have tested their integrated perspective in several studies and are able to specify the relative contribution of each of the three theories to explaining antisocial behavior patterns.[39]

## Thornberry's Interactional Theory of Delinquency

Terence Thornberry's interactional theory of delinquency is similar to the integrated theory of Elliott and colleagues, but it also has some distinct differences. For instance,

**LO6:**

Describe the emphasis of Thornberry's interactional theory.

strain theory is not an important component of Thornberry's interactional theory of delinquency. Thornberry's interactional theory also includes a life-course perspective that allows it to explain individual changes in delinquency and crime over a much longer period of time.[40]

Thornberry considers the social bonds that individuals develop early in life, particularly bonds with parents, as an important influence on delinquency. Youths who bond strongly to parents are less likely to break the law, whereas those with weak bonds are more likely to break the law. Thornberry adds, however, that as individuals progress through their life course, their bonds to parents generally weaken. As youths look to their peers rather than their parents for clues about how to behave, those who become involved with delinquent peers are more likely to break the law.

Thornberry particularly emphasizes the reciprocal effects between delinquent behavior and antisocial peers. Specifically, delinquent youths are more likely to associate with antisocial peers, and those whose friends are antisocial are also more likely to break the law. Thornberry sidesteps the chicken-and-egg question of whether delinquent peers cause delinquency or initial delinquency brings youths into contact with delinquent peers; rather, he focuses on how the two interact to produce an "amplifying causal structure" that leads to increasing involvement in delinquency. The reciprocal effects between peers in delinquency can be difficult to unravel, but it is important to understand how the two are intertwined.[41]

Like life-course theorists Terrie Moffitt, John Laub, and Robert Sampson, Thornberry looks at how some people become committed to conventional society and desist from antisocial behavior. Getting married, securing a good job, or joining the military are ways that individuals become invested in conventional behavior and find breaking the law to no longer be beneficial.

Thornberry's perspective is not limited to the micro level. He also considers structural variables such as gender and class to be important determinants of an individual's initial involvement with delinquency and their ability to control their behavior. According to Thornberry, values and behaviors are often part of the structural conditions in which one grows up, and these are determined to a great extent by one's gender socialization and social class.

In summary, Thornberry's interactional theory of delinquency incorporates three prominent delinquency perspectives: social learning (particularly from delinquent peers),

▲ Thornberry considers how youths bond with parents as an important influence on delinquency.

social bonds (especially as parental bonds weaken), and the life-course perspective. The most important point of Thornberry's theory is the reciprocal nature of these influences, which suggests that once one is on the path to delinquency, the development of delinquent peers is likely to follow, or vice versa.

## Tittle's Control Balance Theory

Charles Tittle developed control balance theory to explain a broad range of antisocial acts. His ambitious theory integrates several perspectives in an effort to provide a comprehensive understanding of why people break the law. This necessarily brief overview of Tittle's complex and complicated theory will demonstrate not only this theory's encompassing range, but also the degree to which it integrates a number of other sociological explanations.

Tittle's theory rests on the concepts of "control deficit" and "control surplus" (see Figure 7.3).[42] Individuals are constantly seeking to control their lives. All persons experience

### LO7:

**Compare and contrast** the concepts of control deficit and control surplus in Tittle's control balance theory.

a control ratio that reflects their status in society, the roles they play, their physical and personal characteristics, their integration with organizations, and the quality of their interpersonal relationships. Tittle's theory states that this control ratio is the starting point for understanding crime and delinquency. Those who have more control exerted on them than they exert are likely to break the law. Those who have a surplus of control are also likely to engage in antisocial behavior. According to Tittle, people who have a balance of control are constrained by external factors but have sufficient freedom to countermand those factors. Thus, those with a balance of control are less likely to engage in unacceptable or unlawful behavior.

According to control balance theory, everyone has a basic impulse to engage in antisocial behavior.[43] This impulse is mediated by control factors outside the individual, such as law enforcement, the rules and regulations of organizations, and lack of opportunity. Individual personality factors, such as a desire for autonomy, motivate people to rebel, but these factors are often checked by external and internal controls. Some factors, such as living in a bad neighborhood or failing in school, encourage antisocial behavior. However, an individual's control surplus or deficit can balance this motivation to break the law. For instance,

## Figure **7.3**   Tittle's Control Balance Theory

People in control deficit (those with more control exerted on them than they exert) and in control surplus (those who exert more control than they experience) are more likely to break the law. Those in control balance are more likely to be law abiding. The arrows pointing toward the figure represent controls exerted on the subject; arrows pointing away from the figures represent the subject's control.

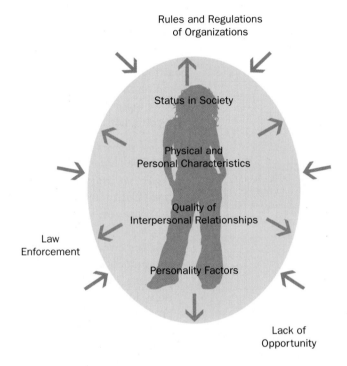

Rules and Regulations
of Organizations

Status in Society

Physical and
Personal Characteristics

Quality of
Interpersonal Relationships

Personality Factors

Law
Enforcement

Lack of
Opportunity

although an impoverished youth with an inferior education is predisposed toward delinquency, holding a job, even a low-paying job, provides some control. This measure of control can counteract the negative forces exerted by the impoverished neighborhood and failure at school. Tittle lists some of the situations that can provoke an individual to engage in antisocial behavior:[44]

- receiving a harsh, commanding order or sharp, hostile reaction from an authority figure
- breaking up with a romantic partner
- falling behind in paying debts and bills
- being questioned about one's authority or rights
- being pushed while waiting in line
- being stopped by the police
- being denied membership in a club
- being hungry, with no money to buy food

Tittle's control balance theory considers how such situational provocations can motivate a person to break the law but can be counterbalanced by external constraints. These constraints can be a situational risk, such as store security cameras or police officers patrolling a neighborhood. An-

other constraint on involvement in delinquency and crime is the seriousness of breaking the law and the punishments associated with it. With this constraint, Tittle integrates the principles of the deterrence perspective into control balance theory.

Finally, the opportunity to break the law and the motivation to take risks are weighed against both external and internal constraints to produce either a control balance surplus or a control balance deficit. Those who have either an extreme surplus or an extreme deficit are much more likely to break the law than those who exhibit a more balanced ratio between the freedom they have to affect their behavior versus the constraints exerted on them by the community, schools, and parents.

The crux of control balance theory is the perception of the amount of control individuals have over their lives. Some people bounce like pinballs from one situational provocation to another and are never able to exert agency or direction on their behaviors. Other people have a surplus of control and see this power as an opportunity to take advantage of situations by engaging in antisocial behavior. Although Tittle's theory is complicated, it is useful in encouraging scholars to think about the connections among many of the traditional psychological and sociological theories of crime and deviance. Tittle's integration of theoretical perspectives is difficult to test because it includes so many factors whose relationships to crime are unclear and also because it is hard to construct research designed to look at how they are related.

▼ According to Tittle's control balance theory, holding even a low-paying job provides youths some control over their lives. Here, a young man receives job training at the Homeboys project in Los Angeles.

## Figure 7.4   Cullen's Social Support Theory

**The quality of social support (represented below by positives and negatives) affects an individual's behavior to become either pro-social or antisocial. Influence from parents, peers, spouses, schools, community programs, and criminal justice systems can be positive or negative.**

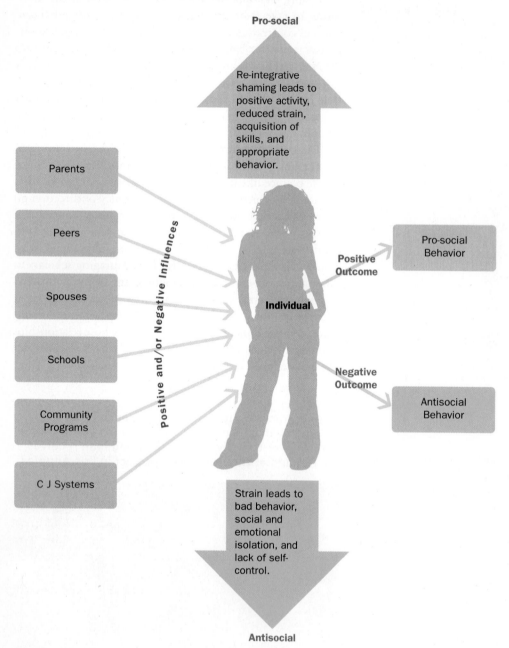

implicit in many of the other theories and uses ten propositions to construct an integrated theory around this theme.[45] This unique way of integrating concepts from other theories develops a convincing case for social support at both micro and macro levels (see Figure 7.4). Social support not only influences individuals' decisions (micro level) but also influences how social institutions (macro level) contribute to the nation's high crime rate. Cullen's concept of social support has four important constructs.[46]

- *Social support is not only an objective factor, but is also subject to individual perception.* Cullen means that the influence of social support might vary according to how it is perceived. Perception of the influence of social support has important implications for how rehabilitation programs might address the psychological barriers that offenders have to bonding with society. For instance, rehabilitation programs can do a better job of explaining to the offender the importance of the social support system, such as parents, school counselors, and clergy.

- *Social support has instrumental and expressive dimensions.* Instrumental support can be conceived of as situations in which offenders receive concrete aid in the form of finding a job, being granted a scholarship, or getting a loan. Instrumental support is necessary at a variety of levels for individuals to advance their social situation and integrate into society. Expressive social support deals with the relationships that offenders have with significant others. In interactions with friends and family, frustrations are vented, needs for love and affection are met, and feelings of companionship and belonging are developed.[47]

- *Social support at the macro level is the influence of social networks and communities that connect individuals to the*

## Cullen's Social Support Theory

Francis Cullen has developed a different sort of integrated theory of crime and delinquency. Rather than selecting components from other theories, as Elliott and Thornberry do, Cullen concentrates on the theme of social support

## LO8:

**Analyze** the ten propositions that Cullen uses to explain how social support is related to crime and delinquency.

*larger society.* Everyone is attached to larger groups in different ways, and the extent of the connections and commitments to these groups directly influences the propensity to engage in antisocial behavior.

■ *Social support encompasses both informal and formal relations with others but distinguishes between them.* Informal relationships include interactions with friends who have no official role in institutions of social control. Formal relations include interactions with authority figures, such as teachers and police officers, whose job is to encourage good behavior and sanction bad behavior.

Within this context of social support, Cullen lays out ten propositions that detail how social support is related to crime and delinquency.

1. *The United States has higher rates of serious crime than other industrialized nations because it is a less supportive society.* Although this proposition may offend some people, Cullen provides an explanation that is difficult to argue with. A core American value is individualism. Americans are encouraged to distinguish themselves by accomplishments and behavior, but such individual acts come at the cost of everyone working for the common good. Individuals in more highly integrated nations, such as Japan, are not only subject to more social control, but are also supported by the culture in social and economic ways. Because of American ideals of individual rights and freedom of action, the United States does not institutionalize social support in the form of health care, welfare, or subsidized schooling to the extent that some other nations, such as Canada and Japan, do. Without this support, Americans all too often decide to turn to crime and delinquency to meet their needs and accomplish their goals. At the informal level, Americans do not feel the social obligation to their fellow citizens found in other nations with higher levels of social support.

2. *The less social support in a community, the higher the crime rate.* Cullen considers a number of ways that social support in the community reduces crime rates. In these communities, welfare and job programs help buffer the effects of poverty. Cullen contends that although some conservative commentators argue that these types of programs make individuals dependent upon government handouts, research demonstrates that this type of social support has a beneficial effect upon crime rates. Lack of social support works in other ways to increase crime rates. Communities with a high degree of family dysfunction, weak friendship networks, and low participation and voluntary organizations have more crime.

3. *The more support a person's family provides, the less likely that person will engage in crime.* Family support lessens the chances that children will break the law. Parents provide *expressive support* by sharing activities, helping with homework, supervising recreational activities with friends, and demonstrating affection. Expressive support is positively related to getting children to conform. Parents provide *instrumental support* by helping adolescents find jobs and ensuring that they are engaged in healthy after-school programs and are not left to fend for themselves on the street or in front of a television. Cullen points out, however, that family support is subject to broad social forces that can undermine parental attention. One prime example is the changing nature of the evening meal. Today, many families do not share any meals in which all family members are present. Parents who are involved with work and children who are caught up in a range of activities often find it hard to find the time to eat together. Fast-food restaurants and long commutes from work have greatly undermined the traditional evening meal in which families reconnect. Poverty, drugs, and alcohol have further weakened family support. According to Cullen, evidence has shown that support given to families in the form of parenting programs, food stamps, and help with daycare can significantly supplement the support children need to avoid delinquency.

4. *The more social support in a person's social network, the less crime will occur.* This proposition draws on strain theory. Social support can help overcome the negative consequences brought on by excessive strain. Adolescents who have friends, family members, and community programs to help them adjust to the challenges and difficulties of their adolescent years are more likely to resist being drawn into delinquency.

5. *Social support lessens the effect of exposure to strains that tend to produce crime.* When individuals are enmeshed in support systems, such as a good marriage, loving family, or satisfying job, they are buffered against the strains of temptation to engage in crime or delinquency. The soothing effect that supportive relationships have on emotional strains allows people to transform their circumstances so they become more integrated into conventional-society and have less time and fewer opportunities for antisocial behavior.

6. *Social support increases the likelihood that offenders will turn away from an antisocial path.* People who have positive social support can find ways to desist from engaging in crime. When people believe that the "deck is stacked against them," they stop looking for ways to enter conventional society and experience a sense of isolation and hopelessness.

7. *Anticipation of a lack of social support increases criminal involvement.* Adolescents who have learned not to expect social support because they have been mistreated, neglected, or abused in the past are more likely to engage in antisocial behavior because they see no reason not to.

8. *Social support lessens involvement in crime.* Social support is a two-way street. Individuals who receive expressive and instrumental support are likely to behave well. The opportunity to provide that support to others increases their sense of self-esteem, being needed, and having a mission or goal in life. By having socially approved and appropriate roles to perform, individuals reduce the strain in their lives and learn the benefits of supporting others. With the reduction of strain and the opportunity to engage in legitimate behavior, people redefine their identities in more positive ways.

9. *Crime is less likely when social support for conformity exceeds social support for crime.* Social support can be destructive when it comes from those who view crime and delinquency as desirable and productive. Social support that is provided by positive peers, law-abiding spouses, or legitimate employment can counteract the support that comes from negative sources. Cullen points out that it is not sufficient to have social support from a spouse if that spouse is also engaged in antisocial activities. The quality of the support is as crucial as the quantity of the support.

10. *Social support is often a precondition for social control.* There are many ways to control antisocial behavior, but several of them can produce negative effects. Cullen cites the work of John Braithwaite on the negative effect of **disintegrative shaming,** or forms of punishment that do not repair the harm done by the offender and offense and exclude the offender from society. In effect, disintegrative shaming permanently stigmatizes offenders. Individuals who are sanctioned in the juvenile or criminal justice systems often come away with the negative labels of "delinquent," "convict," or "criminal." According to **labeling theory**—the idea that society defines an individual, treating him or her differently, and the individual internalizes this definition and acts it out (we will cover this in detail in Chapter 8)—disintegrative shaming can have destructive effects and produce negative self-concepts. Braithwaite, who introduced a more positive way for shaming to be used in social control, uses the term **reintegrative shaming**—or punishment that seeks to repair the harm done by the offender and offense and draw the offender into

society—to describe procedures and ceremonies that allow antisocial individuals to express remorse and seek forgiveness. Reintegrative shaming has two important implications for the relationship between social support and crime. First, it helps individuals take responsibility for their behavior, express their regret, and acknowledge their accountability. Second, reintegrative shaming provides better opportunities for harm to be repaired. Cullen draws on the theoretical principles of peacemaking criminology and restorative justice to suggest that this form of social control can be directly linked to the advantages of providing social support for those engaged in delinquency and crime.

Cullen's social support theory has important implications for criminology. Its focus on the support that individuals give and receive takes advantage of several more traditional criminological theories and places them into a new paradigm. Although Cullen does not specifically borrow the terminology and constructs of many of the theories included in his paradigm, his focus on the theme of social support allows him to link the components of this theory to several other theories. This new paradigm has several advantages.

- *Theoretical integration is achieved.* Cullen draws widely from a number of traditional theories, but he also looks to some emerging perspectives to construct a comprehensive view of delinquency and criminal offending. His social support theory draws upon strain theory, social learning theory, and social control theory, as well as newer and more critical theories, such as feminist theory and peacemaking criminology (see Chapter 8 for more on the last two perspectives). In bringing all the theoretical perspectives together under the theme of social support, Cullen's theory demonstrates how this concept has been hinted at previously but now takes a central role in explaining antisocial behavior.

- *The theory is empirically informed.* Cullen uses empirical studies to construct his theoretical perspective. Social support is based on a number of respected research studies that Cullen places in the context of social support. The use of empirical studies allows others to evaluate Cullen's perspective and design new studies based on his propositions. An important aspect of any theory is its testability, and Cullen has formulated his perspective in ways that encourage future research efforts.

- *The theory has practical implications.* It is not difficult to see how social support theory can inform the practices of the criminal justice system. Cullen is a strong advocate of rehabilitation as criminal justice policy, and his social support theory justifies renewed efforts to provide funding and programs to assist offenders in re-integrating into society.[48] Social support has the potential to not only reduce the amount of harm done by crime, but also to improve the lives of those who have not yet begun to en-

**disintegrative shaming** Braithwaite's term to describe punishment that does not repair the harm done by the offender and offense and excludes the offender from society.

**labeling theory** The idea that society defines an individual, treating him or her differently, and the individual internalizes this definition and acts it out.

**reintegrative shaming** Braithwaite's term to describe punishment that seeks to repair the harm done by the offender and offense and draw the offender into society.

▶ Individuals who receive social support are likely to behave well and find ways to desist from crime.

gage in antisocial behaviors. In many ways, social support theory promises to produce a coherent and effective response to crime.

Cullen's social support theory will no doubt provide opportunities for future scholars to explicate its many implications and ramifications. Most important here, however, is that Cullen shows the advantages of integrating different criminological perspectives into a coherent paradigm that addresses a broad range of crime as well as a number of motivations and policy implications.

## Agnew's General Theory of Crime and Delinquency

Robert Agnew is best known for his general strain theory in which he expanded on Merton's classic strain theory. Recently, however, Agnew has developed a more ambitious integrated theory that includes not only strain, but also a number of other theoretical perspectives. His efforts to develop a general theory of crime and delinquency focus on simple relationships between influences that tend to produce crime.[49]

**LO9:**

**Critique** Agnew's assertion that the interaction between five life domains affects the likelihood of antisocial behavior.

Agnew argues that crime is caused by problems that occur within individuals' five *life domains*: the self, the family, school, peers, and work. Each domain is important on its own, but, according to Agnew, the interaction between them can accelerate and enhance a person's chances of being drawn into antisocial behavior. The important point in Agnew's theory is that these domains do not act alone or independently; rather, they are interdependent, and negative consequences can have a cumulative effect when problems occur in more than one life domain. The following discussion explains how these five life domains are related to crime and delinquency.

■ *The self: irritability/low self-control.* Youths are more likely to engage in delinquent behavior when they get upset and are unable to control their emotions and behaviors. This

behavior is often characterized by intense emotional reactions, blaming others for their problems, impulsivity, chronic anger, lack of motivation, thrill-seeking, and an attitude that favors breaking the law. Although this description may fit almost any teenager, it is the degree to which teenagers possess these attributes that makes them potential delinquents.

■ *The family: poor parenting practices/no marriages or bad marriages.* Youths who do not bond to their parents in positive ways are more likely to engage in antisocial behavior. Delinquency is also more likely when parents do not provide adequate supervision and constructive discipline. Parents who are involved in antisocial activities provide poor role models. Families in which there is conflict and abuse as well as families in which the parents are estranged are also linked to delinquency. Parents who are absent or not involved with their children cannot provide the proper supervision and discipline or bond with them in positive ways.

■ *School: negative school experiences.* Schools can play a large part in the reasons that youngsters break the law. Negative school experiences, such as poor academic performance and spending little or no time on homework, can be linked to delinquent behavior. In troubled schools, teachers do not provide positive role models and often treat students in negative ways. In addition, those who are not intellectually challenged at school are more likely to have limited educational and occupational goals. Those with a limited education find it hard to compete for high-paying jobs and work they find meaningful and fulfilling.

■ *Peers: delinquent friends.* Adolescents with delinquent friends are more likely to become delinquent themselves. Police often interpret peer conflicts, such as fighting, as criminal, and may detain youths involved in such conflicts. Involvement in the juvenile or criminal justice systems exposes youths to others with a history of delinquency. According to **learning theory,** this exposure can draw a youth deeper into delinquency.

>< THINKBACK
learning theory (ch. 6)—A perspective that focuses on how offenders and delinquents find the tools, techniques, and expertise to break the law.

- *Work: unemployment/bad jobs.* Those who are underemployed or employed at low-paying jobs find little self-esteem in the workplace. Such experiences cause individuals to feel alienated not only from a particular job, but also from positive work habits. Estrangement from work and good work habits can make youths cynical about conventional society.

The experiences that individuals have in these five life domains influence whether they choose to conform to conventional society or turn to a delinquent or criminal lifestyle. Good experiences can constrain people against crime by encouraging a high level of self-control and a stake in conformity, as well as by exposing them to interactions with others who share a commitment to law-abiding behavior. Conversely, negative experiences in these five life domains can expose individuals to antisocial role models, strain, a belief that crime is beneficial, and experiences that demonstrate that crime and delinquency can be profitable on a financial or social level. These negative experiences can draw an individual deeper into antisocial behavior.

As noted earlier, Agnew emphasizes the interdependent nature of the five life domains. For instance, a person who is performing poorly in school is likely to seek out peers who share this frustration with the educational system. Those already engaged in delinquency might be labeled by teachers as troublemakers, and such labeling can have a negative effect on their performance in school. Negative experiences in several of these life domains increase the chances of an individual turning to criminal and delinquent activities.

Agnew brings life-course theory into his perspective by pointing out that the influences of each of the five life domains vary as one ages. These influences are stronger for adolescents than they are for adults, and the opportunity for commitment to conventional society increases as the individual ages and has opportunities to get well-paying work or enter a satisfying relationship.

## Farrington's Integrated Cognitive Antisocial Potential Theory

David Farrington's integrated cognitive antisocial potential theory (ICAP) integrates ideas from many classic criminological theories, including strain, control, learning, labeling, routine activities, rational choice, and biological theories. The theory is complicated, but the simplified explanation here provides a general idea of how ICAP works.

According to ICAP, elements from these theories affect what Farrington calls **antisocial potential,** or an individual's likelihood of breaking the law by engaging in antisocial behavior. A person's antisocial potential is unique, like a fingerprint. Imagine the amount of antisocial potential among all individuals in society as running along a continuum from low to high. At the low end of the continuum are some people who are highly unlikely to engage in antisocial behavior; at the high end are some people who are very likely to do so. The antisocial potential of most people lies between the two extremes, with clustering toward the low end of the continuum. Another continuum describing antisocial potential represents age. The prime antisocial years fall between adolescence and young adulthood, with antisocial potential (and behavior) peaking during the late teens. Most people stop antisocial activities not long after this period; however, some people continue until later into adulthood and others continue throughout their lifetimes (see Figure 7.5). After peaking during adolescence, the amount of antisocial potential remains fairly consistent over the life course.

A person's movement from antisocial potential to antisocial behavior is related to cognitive processes, that is, thinking. Short-term antisocial potential is related to concrete motivations and situations, such as inebriation or anger. In adolescents, these motivations include boredom, peer pressure, or frustration. **Routine activities theory** also plays a part. For example, a good opportunity—say, a busy café, combined with an available victim, such as a woman who is not paying attention and leaves her expensive cell phone on the table to go order coffee—may also inspire short-term high antisocial potential. Long-term antisocial potential is more complicated; in this area, other criminological theories come into play. In adolescence, the motivations that move a person from potential to action are the desire for excitement and consumer goods. In adulthood, the motivations are more practical, such as the need for money or drugs. Long-term antisocial potential is related to the following.

>< THINKBACK
routine activities theory (ch. 4)—The concept that three elements are necessary for crime to occur: motivated offenders, attractive targets, and the absence of capable guardians.

- *Strain.* Strain is brought about by the desire for goods, money, status, excitement, or sex. Those who have diffi-

LO10:
**Identify and define** the basis of Farrington's integrated cognitive antisocial potential theory.

**antisocial potential** Farrington's term to describe an individual's likelihood of breaking the law by engaging in antisocial behavior.

## Figure **7.5**   Integrated Cognitive Antisocial Potential Theory

According to Farrington, antisocial potential lies along an age-related continuum. Most people engage in minor antisocial behavior during youth, then
they cease as they age. Delinquents engage in high antisocial behavior during
youth but cease upon adulthood, although a few continue (see arrows). Some
pro-social adults break the law but only under certain conditions, such as inebriation or anger. Career and minor offenders are antisocial their entire lives;
it is just a matter of degree.

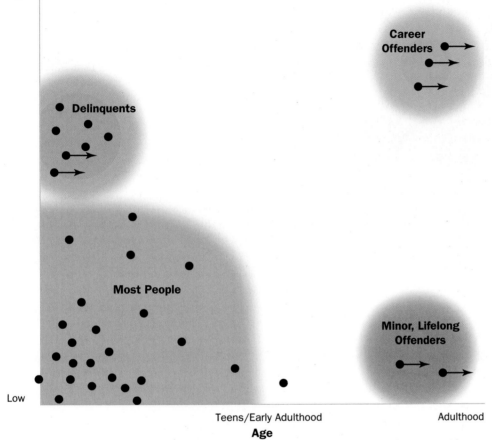

**Antisocial Potential**

High

Delinquents

Career
Offenders

Most People

Minor, Lifelong
Offenders

Low

Teens/Early Adulthood          Adulthood
**Age**

- *Biological factors.* Impulsive
  people have high antisocial
  potential; parents with high
  antisocial potential could transmit that trait to their children. Related biological traits
  include hormonal issues, low
  intelligence (which leads to
  school failure), and low anxiety (which leads to less worry
  about the consequences of
  breaking the law).

- *Rational choice.* A person with
  low antisocial potential will
  not break the law even if it is
  rational to do so (imagine an
  impoverished father stealing
  bread to feed a hungry child).
  A person with high antisocial
  potential may break the law
  even when it is not rational
  to do so (imagine a wealthy
  woman stealing jewelry from
  a department store for excitement). Judgment impairment
  often plays a role in these situations. For example, people
  addicted to alcohol or drugs
  may be motivated to commit
  offenses that they otherwise
  would not.

- *Labeling.* A boy with low antisocial potential might develop
  long-term antisocial potential if he is caught breaking windows in an old house
  and is negatively labeled as
  a vandal for the rest of his
  youth. Likewise, a middle-
  aged man being released from

culty fulfilling these goals, such as the impoverished, the
young, and the disadvantaged, tend to choose antisocial
methods.

- *Modeling and socialization.* Consistent parenting, that is,
  consistent rewards and punishment, leads to low antisocial potential. Inconsistent parenting, such as erratic
  discipline or frequently absent parents, leads to high antisocial potential. Antisocial peers and models also encourage antisocial potential.

- *Life-course events.* Antisocial potential tends to decrease
  after marriage or moving out of disorganized neighborhoods. It increases after separation from a spouse or significant partner.

prison might discover that he cannot find work because
he is a felon. Although his antisocial potential is only
moderate, he returns to breaking the law to survive.

- *Learning.* Peer approval of lawbreaking might increase
  a youth's antisocial potential, as could the disapproval
  of authority figures who have become less important to
  the youth. However, the same parental disapproval of a
  younger child's antisocial activities might decrease that
  child's antisocial potential.

The strength of ICAP is the number of theories it takes
into account. Its disadvantages are that it does not explain
variations in crime rates, and although it includes peer influence, it does not explain the development of gangs. In

▲ The prime antisocial years fall between adolescence and young adulthood, peaking during the late teens, according to Farrington.

addition, ICAP focuses only on male offending and does not account for gender and race differences. For example, although females are assumed to have antisocial potential, they probably have different risk factors than males, which ICAP does not take into account.[50]

# Think about it

## Remember

List the five life domains that Agnew argues are the cause of crime and delinquency.

## Understand

Identify the three types of theories that Elliott and his colleagues combine to form their integrated perspective on delinquent behavior.

## Analyze

Appraise how social support affects the likelihood of crime according to Cullen.

## Evaluate

Evaluate the relative importance of the imbalance between the amount of control a person has over his or her life and the amount of control exerted by society.

# Summary

**LO1:** Describe the focus of life-course criminology.
- Life-course criminology focuses on the development of antisocial behavior, risk factors at different ages, and the effect of life events on individual development.

**LO2:** Explain when antisocial behavior begins, according to Patterson's developmental perspective, and how long it continues.
- According to Patterson, DeBaryshe, and Ramsey's developmental perspective on antisocial behavior, antisocial behavior begins early in life and often continues through adolescence and adulthood. Early antisocial behavior can lead to more serious consequences, and early intervention prevents chronic delinquency.

**LO3:** Identify Moffitt's two categories of youthful offenders.
- In her pathways to crime theory, Moffitt considers young offenders as adolescent-limited or life-course-persistent. The adolescent-limited delinquent breaks the law only during youth. Life-course-persistent offenders continue to break the law and engage in antisocial behavior well into adulthood.

**LO4:** Review Laub and Sampson's focus on the quality of social bonds in persistent offending or desisting from crime.
- Laub and Sampson's theory of persistent offending and desistance from crime, which is based on the Gluecks' data, focuses on what prevents antisocial behavior. For Laub and Sampson, this element is the

what's
inside

of Crime

## As you read, keep in mind these learning objectives:

**LO1:** Define primary deviance and secondary deviance and how these conditions relate to labeling theory.

**LO2:** Understand how conflict theory considers social institutions, especially those rooted in economics and social class, to contribute more to crime than individual antisocial behavior.

**LO3:** Examine how critical theories of criminology not only describe and critique the social structure, but also seek solutions to the problems of crime and criminal justice.

**LO4:** Discuss how feminist criminology deals with issues and problems related to women, crime, and the criminal justice system.

**LO5:** Explain how peacemaking criminology considers not only the offender and victim, but also the social structures that accept, enable, or encourage criminal offending.

**LO6:** Describe the assertion of cultural criminology that culture and the media reflect and produce antisocial behavior.

**LO7:** Demonstrate how postmodern criminology uses language and deconstruction in its critique of society and the criminal justice system.

**LO8:** Assess how critical race theory examines the normality of racism in American culture, the value of story-telling, and the theoretical institution of liberalism.

---

In preceding theory chapters, we studied how criminologists look to biological, psychological, and social factors to account for **antisocial** behavior. Theories that consider offenders to be defective, different, or culpable suggest that the remedy for crime is to punish or treat lawbreakers and to deter potential lawbreakers. However, other ways of considering crime and delinquency shift the focus away from the individual offender and toward the role of social institutions and political dynamics. These theories are known by a number of terms, but the most common are "conflict" and "critical." In this chapter, we will study several types of conflict and critical theories that consider the following:

>**THINKBACK**
antisocial (ch. 1)—
Following standards of behavior intended to harm society and individuals.

- how the government defines acts as criminal
- how personal or group power shapes the criminal law and guides the criminal justice system
- how an economic system, such as capitalism or communism, can determine what is defined as crime and how punishment is determined and meted out

## The Keys to Understanding Conflict Theory and Critical Theory

Conflict and critical theories may seem much like sociological theories at first, but they are quite different. Sociological theories consider crime to originate with the individual, whereas conflict and critical theories consider crime to be rooted in society itself. Before we move on to traditional conflict and critical theories, however, we should review the theory that bridges the gap between sociological theory and conflict and critical theories. **Labeling theory** does this by shifting the focus on the genesis of crime from individuals—those who are labeled—to those who do the labeling: governments and social institutions such as schools and the family.

>**THINKBACK**
labeling theory (ch. 7)—
The idea that society defines an individual, treating him or her differently, and the individual internalizes this definition and acts it out.

# Labeling Theory

Labeling theory became a popular explanation for crime during the 1960s although it was created decades before. In 1938, criminologist Frank Tannenbaum coined the term "tagging" in his book *Crime and Community* for how an individual is labeled in a negative way that identifies him or her as deviant.[1] Labels can be positive (good student, star athlete) or negative (delinquent, ex-convict) and eventually become what sociologist Howard Becker called a **master status**—a social standing that takes precedence over all others.[2] Although individuals have many social statuses, a master status overwhelms them all. A negative master status can have a detrimental effect upon how a person is treated by teachers, parents, society, and the criminal justice system.

**LO1:**

**Define** primary deviance and secondary deviance and how these conditions relate to labeling theory.

Labeling theory is primarily a theory of delinquency, but it can apply to adult offenders. Basically, labeling theory describes two processes that sociologist Edwin Lemert identified as **primary deviance** and **secondary deviance.**[3] Primary deviance occurs when society reacts to an individual's actions, successfully labels that individual, and acts upon that label. This is desirable in many ways. It is useful, for example, to know who the drug addicts, child molesters, and thieves are. However, once this negative label is successfully applied and "sticks," labeled individuals are treated as if the label is the only status that matters, and the label becomes the person's master status. Secondary deviance is complete when labeled individuals internalize the label and see themselves as devalued members of society. If you tell a child often enough that he or she is stupid, this label becomes self-fulfilling when the child no longer attempts to excel at school. Once someone starts to live up to a negative label, it becomes part of his or her self-concept, and rehabilitation becomes much more difficult.

## Critiques

Labeling theory has several limitations. The first is that it does not adequately explain the original deviance. It is reasonable to ask where negative labels originated. For example, why did a child labeled as a delinquent first get involved in burglary, drugs, or gang activity? Primary deviance only explains how society treats an individual once the person has been successfully labeled.

Another limitation involves secondary deviance. White-collar or corporate offenders do not appear to suffer as much from negative labels as street-crime offenders and do not appear to internalize those labels, instead seeing themselves as shrewd businesspeople. In addition, many violent offenders, such as those who commit spouse abuse or acquaintance rape, have not been previously involved with the criminal justice system and have not suffered primary deviance. Nevertheless, criminologists continue to employ labeling theory to explain repeat offending.

## Policy and Practice

First-offender programs in which individuals are diverted from the juvenile or criminal justice systems to rehabilitative programs and/or probation are a good example of the use of labeling theory in criminal justice policy. Many such programs offer to drop the charges—along with the application of a negative label—in exchange for successful completion of the program. The idea is that by limiting an offender's exposure to the criminal justice system and avoiding the labels of "delinquent" or "criminal," society will not treat the individual according to the negative master status, and the individual will not act it out.

Now that we understand how labeling theory locates the origins of crime within social institutions and their definitions of offenders and offenses rather than within offenders' reactions to society (as do sociological theories) or within the offenders themselves (as do biological/psychological and classical theories), we are ready to delve into conflict and critical theory. Conflict and critical theories consider crime to originate within the inequities they consider to be inherent in social institutions.

## Social Location

Before we get into individual theories, you should become familiar with several terms related to **social location,** or the position of an individual within society according to race, sex, class, gender, geography, and, to a lesser extent, age. Sometimes people are identified with antisocial behavior, even if they have broken no laws, because of social location. Social location influences status, opportunities, and obligations. Only by understanding our social location can we appreciate how broad social forces, primarily through social institutions, influence our lives.

Historically, those who were white, male, and economically secure occupied social locations that enabled them to go to the best universities, receive excellent health care, and be welcomed into family businesses. By contrast, people whose social locations were female, impoverished, or within

---

**master status** A social standing that takes precedence over all others.

**primary deviance** Occurs when society reacts to an individual's actions, successfully labels that individual, and acts upon that label.

**secondary deviance** Occurs when labeled individuals internalize the label and see themselves as devalued members of society.

**social location** The position of an individual within a society according to race, sex, class, geography, and age.

▶ One of the major factors of social location is race. Typically, people whose social locations were within minority groups have had a much more difficult time in daily life.

minority groups have had a much more difficult time. Social location is concerned more with who you are than what you do. The major factors of social location include the following.

- **Class.** Class refers to a group defined by a particular social, economic, and educational status. Class is not only an organizing factor of society, but also a basis for discrimination. Social class can reflect how power is wielded in society, and some scholars consider the development of the criminal law and the actions of the criminal justice system to be an example of how stronger social classes seek power over weaker ones.

- **Race.** Race is the use of certain biological characteristics, such as skin color, to classify human beings into categories. Many criminologists believe race is a significant factor in how the criminal justice system creates and applies the law.

- **Gender.** Gender is the social concept of how males and females should behave. The criminal justice system's differential treatment of males and females is based on **sex,** the biological characteristics that distinguish organisms on the basis of their reproductive ability.

- **Age.** Many rights and responsibilities are allocated according to age. For example, U.S. citizens cannot vote until age 18. Many states have mandatory school-attendance policies based on age. People cannot collect social security until age 62. Very young lawbreakers are processed by the

juvenile justice system, although some legal rules specify the waiver of some juvenile delinquents to adult courts.

A final key to understanding critical and conflict theories is the proper definition of the word **political.** Although we most often use "political" in relation to government, it also refers to the relationships of people in groups and their activities. The definition and prosecution of crime has political dimensions. That is, people working in groups decide what constitutes crime and how society deals with offenses and offenders. The social identity of these groups affects their decisions about crime. Groups typically tasked with defining crime and how it is dealt with are often wealthy, male, white, and well into adulthood. According to critical and conflict theorists, the political identity of this group affects what it decides to do about crime and who it classifies as criminals.

There is considerable overlap among the types of theories and heated discussion among criminologists about how they should be categorized.[4] Chronologically, conflict theory came first, and critical theory grew out of conflict theory. However, critical theory is now the larger body of theory and has subsumed conflict theory (see Figure 8.1). Most of the

**class** A group defined by a particular social, economic, and educational status.

**race** The use of certain biological characteristics, such as skin color, to classify human beings into categories.

**gender** The social concept of how males and females should behave.

**sex** The biological characteristics that distinguish organisms on the basis of their reproductive ability.

**political** Refers to the relationships of people in groups and their activities.

## Figure **8.1**    Critical Theories

Conflict theory spawned critical theory, which eventually became the larger body of theories. Conflict theory is now a part of critical theory, along with several other theories of crime. Note that each theory has a specific means by which it performs its critique. Labeling theory uses social expectations, peacemaking criminology uses social justice, and so on around the circle.

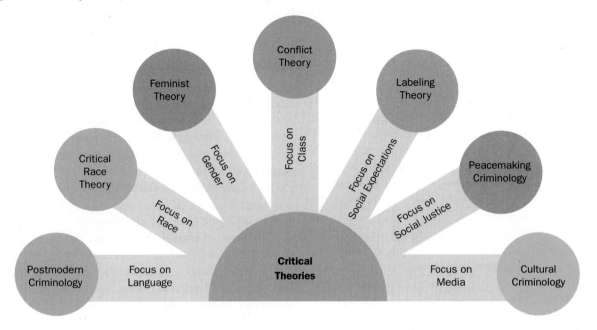

theories in this chapter are critical theories. For the sake of clarity, we will use the following typology of theory which, although not universally accepted, will allow us to differentiate between types of theories.

- **Conflict theory** is a set of criminological theories based on the philosophy of Karl Marx that holds that antisocial behavior stems from class conflict and social and economic inequality. It considers social class to primarily determine both the type and quality of justice an individual receives and how entangled he or she becomes in the criminal justice system.

- **Critical theory** is a set of criminological theories that describe and critique the social structure and seek solutions to the problems of crime and criminal justice. It uses conflict theory to extend its critiques beyond class to other social locations. Labeling theory focuses on social expectations; feminist criminology focuses on gender; peacemaking criminology focuses on social justice; cultural criminology focuses on media; postmodern criminology focuses on language; and critical race theory focuses on race.

> **conflict theory** A set of criminological theories based on the philosophy of Karl Marx that holds that antisocial behavior stems from class conflict and social and economic inequality.

> **critical theory** Criminological perspectives that describe and critique the social structure and seek solutions to the problems of crime and criminal justice.

Because conflict theory came first and its ideas are important to understanding critical theory, we will begin there.

# Think about it

## Remember
Discuss the policy implications of labeling theory.

## Understand
Describe how conflict and critical theories are different from traditional sociological theories.

## Analyze
Compare and contrast primary deviance and secondary deviance.

## Evaluate
Evaluate how conflict and critical theories account for social location.

## Conflict Theory

Conflict theory considers social institutions, specifically those that are concerned with money and social class, to contribute more to crime than does individual antisocial behavior (see Figure 8.2). A strength of conflict theory is that it highlights social and political dynamics that are often taken for granted. Conflict theory explores the idea that crime stems from competition among interest groups, for example rich versus poor,

## LO2:

**Understand** how conflict theory considers social institutions, especially those rooted in economics and social class, to contribute more to crime than individual antisocial behavior.

upper class versus lower class, whites versus nonwhites, men versus women, and so on. These power struggles for economic and political dominance affect the definition of crime and enforcement of the law as dominant interest groups impose their values and judgments through their power to write the criminal law. The uneven distribution of wealth, property, and power leads to want and resentment of the wealthy, which ultimately leads to crime as those without the resources necessary for survival try to acquire them.

A good example is the offense of driving under the influence of drugs or alcohol. A wealthy or even middle-class person arrested for this offense can pay the bail amount and get out of jail before going to court. An impoverished person who cannot pay bail will sit in jail until the court date. The wealthy person can hire the best legal representation, which may seriously affect the sentence. The impoverished person will have to make do with the attorney the state provides, who might not be the best available. According to the Texas Defender Service, death row inmates—who tend to impoverishment and low social class—have a one-in-three chance of being executed without having claims of innocence or un-

fairness heard and without a competent attorney investigating their cases.[5]

Social institutions and the resources and ideas for solving problems are largely handed down from the past, especially in the case of criminal justice and criminological theory. To understand our laws and methods of criminal justice and its theoretical critiques, we must first understand where they came from and how they have changed.[6]

## Marx and Communism

The idea of economics as a primary factor in antisocial behavior can be traced to Karl Marx (1818–1883), a 19th-century German social theorist, philosopher, and economist. Marx did not say much about crime specifically, but his ideas have led other theorists to contemplate the relationship between economic conditions and crime.[7]

Popularly known as the "father of communism," Marx is a major intellectual figure and is considered to have provided the foundation for an alternative economic system to capitalism. Although Marx's theories inspired modern communism in China, the former Soviet Union, Vietnam, North Korea, and Cuba, the communism practiced in these nations is not really what Marx envisioned. In order to appreciate his ideas, we must understand the time and context in which he wrote.

In the late 19th century, Europe underwent a radical transformation from an agrarian, rural population to one that is now heavily industrial and urban. As people moved

▼ The ideas of Karl Marx have led other theorists to contemplate the relationship between economic conditions and crime.

## Figure **8.2**   Conflict Theory

**Social institutions, especially those concerned with money and social class, contribute more to crime than does individual antisocial behavior.**

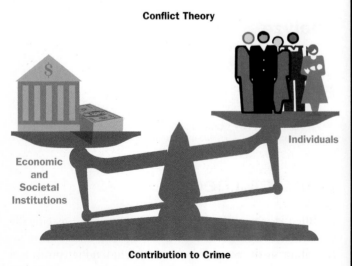

to the city for jobs, they found themselves working hard for low wages. Typically, companies had extensive financial and social relationships with the government that allowed the companies to maximize the value of the workers' labor for a very low cost.

Marx was appalled by the effects of this unbridled capitalism on the working class. The owners of the means of production, whom Marx called the **bourgeoisie** (pronounced *boor-zhwah-ZEE*), paid extremely low wages, maximizing their profits at the workers' expense. Workers were forced to labor in unsafe conditions without any form of safety net for their health or lives. A worker hurt or maimed on the job was out of a job if he or she was unable to continue to work. Companies owed nothing to these workers or to their families, even if company negligence was to blame if the worker was killed. Job security, bonuses, raises, vacations, or clean and safe working conditions were unheard of. Children had to work as hard as adults. Marx believed that a livable wage and decent working conditions were necessary for the **proletariat,** the social class of people who worked for wages. According to Marx, the proletariat's lack of power caused them to sink into despair, withdraw from society, and depend upon fellow workers or turn to crime. Marx called this type of citizen the **lumpen-proletariat,** the lowest social class, which was characterized by its lack of skill, disorganization, and impoverishment. Marx's critiques were a wake-up call for industrialized countries as workers around the world began to organize and demand better conditions and wages.

Many of Marx's ideas have been incorporated into modern societies, including the United States. The provision of Social Security, welfare, aid to families and other safety-net programs can be partly attributed to Marx's concern for the working class. Still, most in the working class in the United States today, although they can pay their bills, cannot achieve financial independence. Marx's ideas about property and wealth advocate a more even distribution of these privileges throughout society. Some nations provide much more subsidized education, health care, housing, and child care, which reduces the need for individuals to have a lot of personal income or inherited wealth. Conceivably, nations with this type of socialist system would have less crime because people would not live in such dire need. Friedrich Engels, a 19th-century social philosopher and one of the founders of communism and socialism, speculated on such a society being crime-free. According to Engels, "Crimes against property cease of their own accord where everyone receives what he needs to satisfy his natural and spiritual urges, where social gradations and distinctions cease to exist."[8]

Many people often have a hard time appreciating Marx's ideas. They believe his ideas are economically naive and that those who espouse Marxism, socialism, or communism are unpatriotic. However, even the U.S. economic system is not purely capitalist. Legislation controls how companies conduct business and pursue profit, and regulatory agencies enforce workplace laws. Regardless, conflict theorists still believe that workers are exploited, a condition they assert leads to crime.

How much government should regulate the marketplace is often a point of contention, but we need only look at the United States in the late 19th and early 20th centuries, as well as Russia during the 1990s after the Soviet Union disintegrated, to understand how the market can be manipulated. For example, in the United States, "robber barons" such as John Jacob Astor, Cornelius Vanderbilt, and John D. Rockefeller took advantage of political corruption, the Industrial Revolution, and nearly nonexistent corporate controls to monopolize industries and throttle competition.

- Astor monopolized the fur trade and used his political connections to call in the U.S. military against American Indians who complained of being defrauded by Astor's American Fur Company. Astor then speculated in New York City real estate where his tenement housing made him one of the city's foremost slumlords.

- Cornelius Vanderbilt used his influence as a shipbuilder to convince Nicaragua to give his Accessory Transit Company sole access to a passage connecting the Pacific and Atlantic oceans. Vanderbilt invaded Nicaragua with mercenaries when the deal soured and later persuaded the U.S. government to send in the Marines.

- John D. Rockefeller's Standard Oil Company monopolized the U.S. oil industry by controlling the railroads and charging competitors exorbitant rates to transport their oil. With the help of corrupt officials, Rockefeller controlled 90 percent of U.S. petroleum production by 1890.[9]

Much the same thing is happening in Russia today. Unbridled capitalism has allowed former Communist Party members to amass monopolies on key industries and products. The Soviet Union's relatively stable albeit somewhat impoverished economic system has given way to incredible inflation, shortages of goods and services, and a dangerous economic system in which power politics and physical force allow some in business to become billionaires while many people starve.

It is probably not fair to compare the emerging Russian economy during the 1990s to other forms of capitalism because it was a time of rapid and overwhelming social change.

**bourgeoisie** In Marxism, the owners of the means of production.

**proletariat** A social class composed of people who work for wages.

**lumpen-proletariat** In Marxism, the lowest social class, which was characterized by lack of skill, disorganization, and impoverishment.

◀ During the Industrial Revolution, children often had to work as hard as adults.

striking, and from a Weberian point of view, this gulf is at the root of both nations' crime rates.[12]

### Ralf Dahrendorf

German sociologist Ralf Dahrendorf (1929–2009) considered social class to be defined by power rather than property.[13] Dahrendorf saw groups desiring domination opposing groups attempting to avoid subjugation, and he considered the interactions of these groups to be the source of constant social conflict.[14] As each group seeks to legitimize its power over other groups, the political process causes infighting, political maneuvering, and coercion. A contemporary example of these ideas is the controversy over drug laws. Some groups are comfortable with the "war on drugs," whereas others see this policy as contributing more problems than it solves. For example, some organizations attempt to influence public policy through legitimate ways to decriminalize marijuana, while other groups press hard to not only keep marijuana illegal, but also to maintain severe punishments for users and dealers.

What we present here simply shows that those who advocate unbridled capitalism might find that its actual practice is devastating in terms of social equality. As Russia reforms its economic system and China enters the world market, both nations have had to adopt some capitalist ideas, thus merging aspects of capitalism and communism.[10] The ultimate effect these nations' new policies will have on their crime rates remains to be seen.

## Other Conflict Thinkers

Although Marx is the best-known conflict thinker, other theorists have significantly contributed to this line of criminological reasoning. This brief review of these scholars' ideas will demonstrate how the conflict perspective is grounded in social structure and economic conditions.

### Max Weber

Max Weber (1864–1930) was a German sociologist who laid the groundwork for analyzing conflict according to three measures of inequality: power, wealth, and prestige. According to Weber, conflict is most likely to occur when an individual or a group possesses all three measures. When this happens, others, who have less or none, feel tension and resentment and are likely to conflict with the privileged.[11] Although Weber did not specifically address crime, his ideas of conflict are used to explain why economic inequality and imbalances in social power influence individuals and groups to break the law. For example, crime rates are high in Brazil and South Africa, both of which have large impoverished and wealthy populations, deep racial divides, and a relatively small middle class. The gulf between the powerful, prestigious "haves" and powerless, disrespected "have nots" is

### Austin Turk

Sociologist Austin Turk made a major contribution to conflict theory with his ideas about the interaction of dominant groups and subordinate groups.[15] Turk identified norms of domination and deference whereby the values, standards, and laws of powerful groups must be recognized and respected by subordinate groups. If this does not happen, then the subordinate groups' behaviors and values will be criminalized. Even when subordinate groups adopt the dominant group's worldview, the behaviors of some individuals in the subordinate group will be considered deviant. Because of the dynamic nature of societies, some groups or individuals will not always be fully invested in the dominant value system and will therefore be considered deviant. Over time, some of this deviance may become normalized. For instance, tattoos were once considered a mark of deviance and rebellion for middle-class people. Today, tattoos have become fashion statements, and the negative social and political consequences of such body art are no longer as extreme as they once were.

Conflict theory has spurred many criminal justice system reforms since the 1960s. However, some scholars resist

▲ The crime rate is high in Brazil, which has large impoverished and wealthy populations and deep racial divides. Here, an impoverished area, called a "favela," is located next to a wealthy, modern area of São Paulo.

conflict theory because it approaches the problems of crime and delinquency in such a different manner. Let's now take a look at some of the critiques of conflict theory.

## Critiques

Some critics of conflict theory consider it to be anti-government because it critiques those who enforce the law.[16] Recall that rather than assuming that offenders are inherently antisocial or that they learn to break the law, conflict criminology examines how societies control their citizens and how this control can sometimes lead to crime. This idea can be uncomfortable for some who want to justify how the criminal justice system operates. Here are some of the critiques of conflict criminology.

- *It is more political than scientific.* **Positivist** criminologists emphasize observable facts. They try to use the **scientific method** to show a relationship between offenses and offenders. Conflict theory, however, does not try to be objective; rather, it advocates its position. According to

> ✕ **THINKBACK**
> scientific method (ch. 4)—
> A process of investigation in which phenomena are observed, ideas are tested, and conclusions are drawn.

| **positivist** Describing the emphasis on observable facts.

conflict theory, there is no such thing as value-free science, and even the selection of a research topic shows political influence. Conflict theorists believe that explicitly stating a position is desirable; many mainstream criminologists contend that conflict theory studies are unreliable because of political bias.[17]

- *It is not measurable.* Research in conflict theory is often not subject to measurement. However, conflict theory is largely still in the theoretical stage and not yet ready to be measured. This does not mean that studies have not looked at the conflict perspective; indeed, many have. However, conflict theory has not advanced as far as differential association theory or strain theory, both of which have been the subjects of numerous sophisticated studies. Therefore, conflict theory is not as theoretically developed as some other criminological theories.

- *It critiques the status quo.* Conflict theory requires close observation of how capitalism distributes and maintains wealth. By considering disparities in wealth and income between those who control the means of production and those who do the work, the conflict perspective may be considered to intrude into the affairs of government and business.[18]

- *Solutions are financially and politically expensive.* Critique of the capitalist system is inherent in conflict theory. This is less of an issue in socialist nations where governments provide such basic needs as food, housing, and health care. Although it can be argued that the United States is becoming more socialist, this journey is incomplete. True socialism would require expensive and politically difficult changes. The United States is deeply committed to capitalism and the idea of the free market. Although communism was popular among some American intellectuals in the 1930s, and some aspects of socialism were introduced during President Franklin D. Roosevelt's administration, both quickly and drastically fell out of favor after World War II. Much of the American public remains deeply skeptical of any movement toward socialist policies.

■ *Solutions are culturally unattractive.* American culture values creativity and risk-taking, and our capitalist economic system presumably rewards the industrious and visionary. Some critics of conflict theory believe that a socialist economic system discourages people from working hard and creating new services and products. Because the value of products or services does not go directly to the individual but rather to society, it is thought people will do as little as possible and simply collect their government checks.[19]

The solutions that conflict criminology suggests are so sweeping and fundamental that it is unlikely they will be uniformly adopted in the United States in the near future. Still, conflict theory has much to contribute to the examination of crime. The economic gulf between the wealthiest Americans and the most impoverished is so great, many scholars continue to question the legitimacy of the capitalist system when viewed in the light of social justice.[20]

# Think about it

## Understand

Describe how the robber barons of the late 19th and 20th centuries manipulated the capitalist system to monopolize industries and throttle competition.

## Analyze

Summarize Karl Marx's view of the power relationship in 19th-century Europe.

## Evaluate

Critique the argument that conflict theory relies more upon political argument than upon the scientific method.

# Critical Theory

According to critical theory, the definitions of crime and justice are located within a social system that is based on and perpetuates social inequality. Although based on conflict theory, critical theories not only describe and critique the social structure, but they also actively seek solutions to the problems of crime and criminal justice.

A historical example of what critical theory would critique is the practice of slavery in the United States prior to the 20th century and the legal apparatus surrounding it. Slave owners were often wealthy and powerful, and, as a result, were often considered to be the backbones of their communities. Today, it is easy to see the paradox of law-abiding, often religious, people perpetuating a deep moral wrong. But prior to the U.S. Civil War, many people considered slavery to be normal and just. To perpetuate this social order, slave laws defined the rights of the owners and the role of the enslaved, and those who broke these laws often faced criminal penalties. These laws were written by the powerful—the wealthy slave owners—to benefit themselves and control the powerless slaves. If a slave broke a law, the problem was considered to be not with the law, but with the slave. Thus, society's idea of justice was deeply rooted in social inequality.

Although laws are generally regarded as desirable and necessary for a working society, slave laws existed to uphold an unjust order that benefited a wealthy few. Slavery was so entrenched in the United States that it was dislodged only by civil war. This is evidence of how difficult it is to alter social paradigms and change citizens' cherished beliefs about their societies. The critical theories we will consider in the rest of this chapter seek to change social paradigms they consider to contribute to social injustice and crime.

## Feminist Criminology

Crime has traditionally been the province of men.[21] Males are arrested more often than females (see Figure 8.3a), and more of them are incarcerated. Most crime victims are male (see Figure 8.3b), and most criminal justice system workers, especially those in prisons, are male. In a society that is **patriarchal**—that is, a social system controlled by males—crime is one of the most patriarchal institutions.

Because of the strides that feminism has made in gender equality, women can now be found at virtually every level of

**patriarchal** A social system that is controlled by males

**feminist criminology** A set of theories that hold that gender inequality is at the root of offenses in which women are the victims or offenders.

## Figure **8.3**    Males and Crime

Crime is traditionally dominated by males. Figure 8.3a shows that more males are arrested, and Figure 8.3b shows that males are most often victimized.

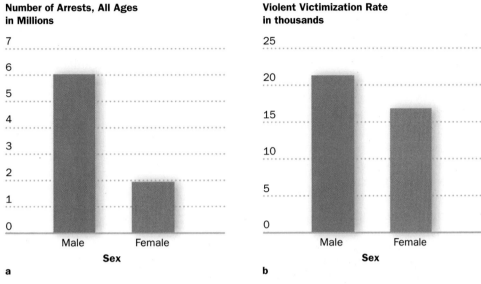

**Number of Arrests, All Ages in Millions**

**Violent Victimization Rate in thousands**

a

b

*Sources:* Figure A: Federal Bureau of Investigation, *Uniform Crime Reports: Crime in the United States, 2008,* "Ten-Year Arrest Trends by Sex, 1999–2008," http://www.fbi.gov/ucr/cius2008/data/table_33.html. Figure B: Michael R. Rand, *Criminal Victimization, 2008* (Washington, DC: Bureau of Justice Statistics, 2009), 4, http://bjs.ojp.usdoj.gov/content/pub/pdf/cv08.pdf.

the criminal justice system, from judges to offenders. **Feminist criminology** is a set of theories that hold that gender inequality is at the root of offenses in which women are the victims or offenders. It deals with the many issues and problems related to women, crime, and the criminal justice system, including incarcerated females, women in the criminal justice workplace, and gender aspects of victimization.

A substantial body of literature applies the feminist perspective to issues of crime and justice.[22] Feminist criminology not only critiques male-centric theories, but also creates hypotheses about crime and gender. For example, in the 1970s, Freda Adler and Rita Simons proposed the "liberation hypothesis," which states that the social equalization of females and males means that females will begin committing the same

types and numbers of offenses as males. More recent theories also consider the ways in which the criminal justice system manages females. The "evil woman" hypothesis, for example, proposes that the criminal justice system treats women who do not meet gender expectations (for example, females who do not act "feminine") differently than it does women who do.

Feminist criminology is also useful for critiquing other theories. Almost all criminological theories have been fashioned to describe and explain the activities of males in the male-dominated world of crime and criminal justice, which, in turn, exists within a male-dominated society. The activities of females as delinquents, offenders, victims, or criminal justice workers were explained by applying male-centric theories to females and not by doing any in-depth research on females. Feminist theory effectively ended this practice by pointing out that females are different from males. Not only are females different biologically and psychologically, but they live their lives differently and have different reasons for the things they do because they occupy a different place in society. Feminist theory states that females require their own

▶ The first wave of American feminism occurred during the late 19th and early 20th centuries as women lobbied for the right to vote.

criminological research and theories to accurately explain their roles in crime and the criminal justice system.

In this section, we will review the feminist perspective and consider some of the theories that seek to explain the importance of gender in crime and the criminal justice system. We will also assess the effect of those theories on how crime is addressed, and we will look at their critiques.

In order to understand the effect of feminism on the criminal justice system, we must briefly review the women's movement. The 1960s saw the beginning of a major feminist initiative in the United States, preceded by a first wave of feminism that came during the late 19th and early 20th centuries as women lobbied for the right to vote.[23] At that time, it was thought (mostly by men) that women were not capable of appreciating the political process and would simply vote as their husbands told them to. Women rejected this perspective and advocated reforms that would allow women to become fully participating citizens. Feminists also fought restrictions that prevented women from owning property in their own name, retaining custody of children after a divorce, and working in many occupations.[24] Although the feminist revolution is largely complete today, women are still treated differently from men in many areas, two of which are crime and criminal justice. Feminist scholars consider women's participation in crime and the criminal justice system in many ways.

- *As offenders.* Males and females break the law in different patterns and at different rates. Although women do break the law on their own, they are often ancillaries to male offending. Women are also significantly less violent than men. Feminist scholars consider the experience of women as convicted offenders by comparing their sentencing, rehabilitation, treatment, and incarceration to that of male offenders. Women's issues as inmates include health care (gynecological issues, pregnancy), children, and sexual harassment by other inmates and correctional officers.[25]

- *As crime victims.* Feminist scholars have made great advances in identifying the special circumstances of female victims. In the case of domestic assault, they have found that the criminal justice system has failed to protect women from violent husbands and boyfriends.[26] In the case of rape, the feminist perspective has helped change some social attitudes, and it is now understood that a rape victim can be further victimized by the criminal justice system's bureaucratic processes.[27]

- *As workers.* Although more women are working within the criminal justice system than ever, many issues remain, most of which are within law enforcement and corrections. The criticism of women as police officers mirrors that of women serving in the military as soldiers: Women cannot do the job because they are not physically strong enough and are too emotional. In corrections, the issues are more focused on females working in all-male environments, especially environments filled with antisocial lawbreakers, many of whom are in prison for violence against women. In this case, federal law that ensures the rights of women to be considered for jobs regardless of their sex runs up against legitimate concerns for their safety in prison environments and for the rights of male inmates, attenuated as they are, to be dealt with in sensitive procedures (like strip searches) by members of their own sex. Some states still restrict the duties of female correctional officers in situations involving personal searches and the transportation of male inmates.[28] Regardless of these concerns, women are serving successfully as correctional officers and as police officers.

According to feminist theory, the criminal justice system's treatment of females mirrors that of the rest of society.[29] Basically, the feminist perspective advocates equal treatment of women and, at its most extreme, advocates a complete reorientation of the power structure of American society.

## Critiques

Feminist theories of crime and delinquency offer an alternative look at how women are motivated to break the law and how the criminal justice system responds to them differently from men. However, they risk minimizing other important factors. For instance, in the victimization of impoverished women, race and social class can be just as important as sex. Although feminist theory may do a good job of explaining female antisocial behavior and victimization, it cannot speak to the antisocial behavior and victimization of men. This is an important point because males commit the most crime, and most crime victims are male.

Feminist theories also tend to consider females who break the law as victims of a patriarchal system and do not give credit to the choices women make. For example, some women who engage in prostitution might not do so because they are oppressed and have few legitimate opportunities, but rather because they enjoy the power it gives them over men, prefer the lifestyle, or want the chance to make a great deal of money quickly. From the **classical criminology** standpoint (see Chapter 4), women who break the law make a rational choice that is not necessarily dictated by economic circumstances or male oppression.

> **>< THINKBACK**
> classical criminology (ch. 4)—Shortened form of "classical school of criminology." A set of ideas that focuses on deterrence and considers crime to be the result of offenders' free will.

## Policy and Practice

At its broadest level, full implementation of feminist theory would require fundamental changes in the allocation of power and privilege in a patriarchal society. It would require that women receive broader educational opportunities, better enforcement of child-support laws, improved support for child care and dealing with workplace sexual harassment, and stronger measures to alleviate the violence against women that appears to be inherent in patriarchal cultures. As men and women become more aware of the role of gender in culture and crime, improvements will likely be made in the socialization of males and females and in the ways institutions deal with gender-based prejudice, discrimination, and violence.

## Peacemaking Criminology

**Peacemaking criminology** considers the social and personal effects of crime as a whole, accounting not only for the offender and victim, but also for the social structures that accept, enable, and encourage crime. Criminologist John Randolph Fuller argues that peacemaking criminology should be considered a perspective because it does not yet rise to the level of specificity that theory requires.[30] However, the peacemaking perspective can be applied to problems of crime at the personal, interpersonal, institutional/societal, and global levels (see Figure 8.4).

> ## LO5:
> **Explain** how peacemaking criminology considers not only the offender and victim, but also the social structures that accept, enable, or encourage criminal offending.

- *The personal level.* At the personal level, peacemaking criminology suggests that each of us be gentler on ourselves. Henry David Thoreau wrote in *Walden,* "The mass of men lead lives of quiet desperation." With this in mind, peacemaking criminology advocates the solving of personal, individual problems before developing external solutions to crime. Only when individuals are aware of their own motivations can they effectively deal with their relationships with others.

- *The interpersonal level.* At the interpersonal level, peacemaking criminology recognizes that manners, politeness, and civility should be used to accomplish goals rather than force, intimidation, and power. Peacemaking criminology guides behavior not only for individuals working within, or caught up in the workings of, the criminal justice system, but also for those who wish for a guide to managing their affairs in all aspects of life, such as education, family life, and the environment, as well as criminal justice. You might think that the peacemaking perspective risks being so broad that

it does not speak specifically to a single issue; however, this would be inaccurate. Peacemaking provides an outline for the conduct of human affairs, and this generalizability makes it an attractive and potentially powerful perspective.[31]

- *The institutional/societal level.* Peacemaking criminology looks at how the institutions that people develop shape their interactions. For instance, structural obstacles within the criminal justice system contribute to crime and delinquency. Consider, for example, gun control laws. If the legal system interpreted the Second Amendment differently and more tightly restricted the sale and possession of firearms, the United States might have a lower homicide rate.[32] Another example of the implementation of peacemaking at the institutional level concerns capital punishment. Peacemaking criminology advocates the elimination of the death penalty because it models the very behavior it is supposed to deter.

- *The global level.* The peacemaking perspective would deal with transnational offenses such as human trafficking, international drug smuggling, and terrorism by trying to solve these problems without violence and in a way that ensures social justice. For example, when dealing with human trafficking, especially trafficking of young women

## Figure 8.4 Peacemaking Criminology

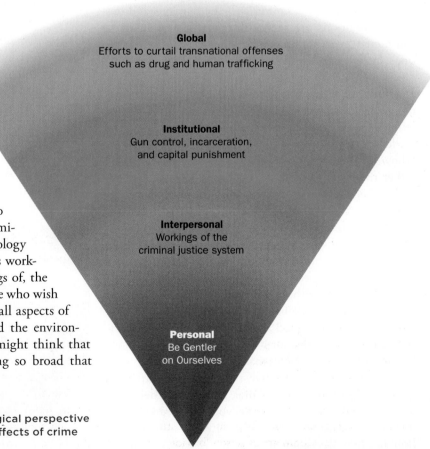

**Global**
Efforts to curtail transnational offenses such as drug and human trafficking

**Institutional**
Gun control, incarceration, and capital punishment

**Interpersonal**
Workings of the criminal justice system

**Personal**
Be Gentler on Ourselves

**peacemaking criminology** A criminological perspective that considers the social and personal effects of crime as a whole.

▶ Peacemaking criminology considers the social and personal effects of crime as a whole.

and children for sexual purposes, peacemaking criminology would not be content to simply catch the smugglers and throw them in prison. Peacemaking criminology would look at the broader social conditions that enable or encourage the practice of human smuggling and advocate improving the economies of developing countries so that selling people for sexual purposes is unnecessary.[33]

Although peacemaking criminology has been around for years, it was not until 1991 when Harold Pepinsky and Richard Quinney published *Criminology as Peacemaking* that the perspective's foundations were defined.[34] Peacemaking criminology derives its ideas and philosophy from the religious and humanist, feminist, and critical traditions. Let's discuss each briefly.

- *Religious and humanist traditions.* The religious and humanist traditions are responsible for much of what is considered peacemaking criminology. Religious traditions include the world's major religions, such as Buddhism, Christianity, Confucianism, Hinduism, Islam, and Judaism.[35] Each tradition has elements that promote the idea of peace. Although it can be said that religious wars have been responsible for much of the world's sorrow, it can also be contended that sincerely following these religions would lead to a peaceful life rather than one filled with conflict.[36] Several scholars, such as criminologist Michael C. Braswell, have expanded on the idea of religion as a peaceful influence in society, identifying how religion can be applied to the criminal justice system in beneficial ways.[37] Like the religious tradition, the humanist tradition specifies peaceful ways for people to live but asserts that it is possible to be moral without adhering to a specific religion or belief in a supreme being. Humanism contends that people are basically good and will strive toward responsible and ethical behavior if the systems they live in allow it.[38] Religious and humanist traditions, then, give the peacemaking perspective substance and direction in promoting responsible, moral, and healthy behavior. Pepinsky and Quinney do not advocate any specific tradition, but rather they assert that any can contribute to human moral development.

- *Feminist traditions.* As explained in the earlier section on feminist criminology, feminism advocates gender equality and the dismantling of patriarchal systems. Gender inequality within the criminal justice system and within crime itself reflects the gender inequality in society.[39] Feminist theorists believe that reforming the criminal justice system will demonstrate how to deal with people who lack power in society and help them to become functioning members of society.[40]

- *Critical traditions.* The critical traditions include conflict theory, especially a Marxian analysis of the relationship between social structure and crime, as well as some of the newer critical ideas such as postmodern criminology and cultural criminology. All are covered in detail later in this chapter.

▼ Reforming gender inequality in the criminal justice system will, according to feminist theorists, help those who lack power become functioning members of society.

# theory to practice

## Peacemaking and Uncommon Sense

One of the most consistent complaints about the peacemaking perspective is that it is unrealistic and soft on crime. But what does "soft on crime" mean? Those who believe in being "tough on crime" use deterrence theory as one of their underlying theoretical perspectives. Briefly, **deterrence** theory holds that if penalties are certain, swift, and severe, potential lawbreakers will choose not to break the law. The perspective of peacemaking criminology, however, is that deterrence is a fundamentally flawed concept.

> **><THINKBACK**
> deterrence (ch. 3)—The idea that punishment for an offense will prevent that offender and others from further breaking the law.

Deterrence theory assumes individuals will weigh the cost of breaking the law against the likelihood of getting caught and punished. However, most people who break the law do not believe they will be caught. Often, they plan the offense and take precautions to escape detection. Even if penalties are substantially increased, potential lawbreakers might not be deterred because they sincerely believe they will not be caught and punished. Deterrence theory also assumes that lawbreakers can accurately weigh the risk of getting caught against the benefits of succeeding. If this were the case, we would not see so many serious offenses that offer such little reward, such as using a gun to rob a convenience store, which often has little cash. In this scenario, the offender risks an armed-robbery conviction, which carries a hefty penalty that dwarfs the reward for robbing the store and getting away with it. This is especially true if the store clerk is killed, and capital punishment becomes a possibility.

Rather than attempting to force the offender into lawful behavior, peacemaking criminology attempts to prevent crime by ensuring social justice and providing treatment options for offenders so they can learn the skills to achieve their needs without breaking the law. Peacemaking would address the robber's impoverished neighborhood, disintegrated family, and lack of adequate employment. Sociologist Robert Agnew suggests how we can correct the causes of crime:

> [W]e now have a reasonably good idea of the causes of delinquency. Such causes include traits like impulsivity and low verbal IQ, child abuse, family conflict, poor parenting practices, poor school performance, low commitment to school, association with delinquent peers and gang members, and growing up in poor, disorganized communities. A number of prevention and treatment programs have been developed to address these causes, like pre- and postnatal health care programs, preschool enrichment programs, parent-training programs, and a variety of school-based interventions.[1]

Instead of relying on deterrence to convince potential lawbreakers to obey the law, peacemaking criminology seeks to protect the community by solving the root problems that give rise to antisocial behavior.

[1]Robert Agnew, "Society Needs to Get Tough on Causes of Crime, Says Agnew," *Emory Report* 50, no. 28 (April 13, 1998), http://www.emory.edu/EMORY_REPORT/erarchive/1998/April/erapril.13/4_13_98FirstPerson.html.

## THINKING *in* ACTION

Consider the crime problems in your neighborhood and think of a peacemaking program that might address them.

## Critiques

A major criticism of peacemaking criminology is that it is naive and utopian. Critics contend that peacemaking does not adequately appreciate the danger in the world and takes a simplistic view of human nature. Another criticism is that much of what peacemaking advocates is already part of the criminal justice system and society. For instance, programs for rehabilitating offenders, although limited, have been around for several decades. Finally, peacemaking criminology would require fundamental changes in the way people relate to each other that are beyond the ability of the criminal justice system to effect.

## Policy and Practice

Peacemaking criminology has policy implications for all four levels of analysis. For example, nonviolence can be applied in several ways to reduce crime. At the personal level, many religions and schools of spiritual thought require their adherents to shun violence. At the interpersonal level, methods of conflict resolution are taught in some schools so children learn how to settle disputes without verbal or physical violence. At the institutional/societal level, the death penalty could be eliminated and the availability of guns greatly curtailed. At the global level, the work of the United Nations in providing a forum for countries to work out their differences without resorting to war is a particularly useful example of the broader implications of peacemaking criminology.

## Cultural Criminology

**Cultural criminology** examines how social ideas, values, and media reflect and produce antisocial behavior. Some of the concerns of cultural criminology are the modeling of police agencies after the military, such as the use of uniforms and ranks, and depictions of crime on television and in film. The images and symbols used by graffiti writers, gang members, and the tattoo and body modification industry are all concerns of the cultural criminologist.[41]

**LO6:**

> **Describe** the assertion of cultural criminology that culture and the media reflect and produce antisocial behavior.

Cultural criminology borrows much from media studies and cultural sociology. These disciplines look at how individuals, small groups, and deviant subcultures construct meaning and transmit it to a wider audience (see *So What's New?*).[42] Cultural criminology adopts this perspective to better comprehend how crime is either culturally supported or culturally discouraged by everyday social structures. Here are a few examples.

- *Gang apparel and gang signs.* Like sports teams, gang members must identify themselves to each other and to rivals, typically with distinctive clothing, special hand gestures, and graffiti.[43] Cultural criminologists consider how these markers symbolize authenticity and power. By understanding how these symbolic behaviors define what is important to gang members, cultural criminologists can better explain why gang conflicts are often more about identity, status, and respect than about disputes over territory or illegal markets. To the broader society, gang activity looks negative, nonutilitarian, and wasteful. However, gang members understand their behavior to be rational and protective of the symbolic meaning of being in a specific gang.

- *Media representation of the war on drugs.* Cultural criminologists consider how the war on drugs attempts to change not only behavior, but also opinions about certain drugs. In an attempt to decrease the demand for drugs, the government has used the media to demonize some drugs and marginalize those who sell and buy them. Cultural criminologists study how the government and other social institutions wage this war, as well as how drug sellers and users respond to media influence.[44] The media's role in the war on

drugs is important because it has set the political agenda so that politicians cannot afford to be seen as soft on drugs and crime. Therefore, despite conflicting information about the actual harm some drugs cause, illegal drugs such as marijuana are represented as uniformly bad. Nicotine is a good example of the media manipulation of the public perception of drugs. Until the 1970s, the media portrayed the smoking of cigarettes and cigars as sexy and sophisticated. Now that tobacco smoking is considered to be harmful to the health of smokers and those around them, only the "bad guys" smoke in movies and on television.

- *Cultural space and crime control.* Cultural criminologists study how subcultures and the authorities contest public space. An obvious example of this is how homeless people are treated throughout the United States. Although homeless people present a significant social problem, in many places they are treated as a public nuisance and embarrassment. Prior to the 1996 Olympics in Atlanta, authorities made a concerted effort to encourage homeless people to leave the city.[45] Similarly, skateboarders are problematic for municipal authorities. Although skateboarding is not illegal, some people consider skateboarders who gather in parking garages, public parks, and malls to be a nuisance.[46] Cultural criminologists look at how authorities attempt to discourage the congregation of skateboarders, as well as how they define their behavior, communicate their culture, and resist social control.

- *Images of authorities.* Criminal justice system administrators work hard to manage the impression they give to politicians and the public. One interesting example is the Special Weapons and Tactics (SWAT) teams that have become a fixture in large police agencies. These teams' duties often put them in dangerous situations, and they have structured their image to resemble that of the military. According to criminologist Peter Kraska, SWAT teams' special para-

**cultural criminology** Examines how social ideas, values, and media reflect and produce antisocial behavior.

▶ Gang members typically identify themselves with distinctive clothing, hand gestures, and graffiti.

# sowhat'snew?

### Video Games: How Bad Can They Be?

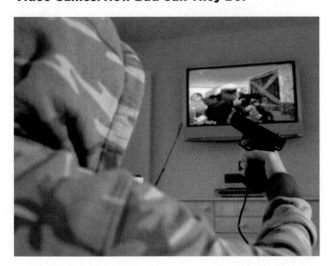

▲ Parents and psychologists are concerned with the mixed messages that realistic, violent video games give to children and youths.

Cultural criminologists consider how popular culture affects the collective behavior of a society. One current controversy is violent video games. Video games are becoming more realistic and popular, and the violent content that games such as Grand Theft Auto contain is alleged to encourage and even cause crime. Parents and psychologists are concerned with the mixed messages such games provide to young people. As of April 2010, the U.S. Supreme Court began considering the constitutionality of California's law banning the sale of violent games to children under the age of 18.[1]

In a video game called NARC, for example, players who take the role of police narcotics officers may confiscate a drug for personal use. The drugs give the users heightened powers for a short time, although the users are eventually burdened with addiction. Psychologists are concerned with how this video game allows players to virtually experiment with drugs and experience through the game the harm drugs do. The problem here is that drug addiction can be cured by clicking the game controller. Although NARC and Grand Theft Auto are only video games, cultural criminologists are concerned with their values and attitudes and the messages impressionable teenagers who play these games for hours at a time might derive from them.[2] For instance, in reviewing the research evidence on video games, psychologist Craig Anderson concludes:

> Immediately after exposure to media violence, there is an increase in aggressive behavior tendencies because of several factors. 1. Aggressive thoughts increase, which in turn increase the likelihood that a mild or ambiguous provocation will be interpreted in a hostile fashion. 2. Aggressive affect increases. 3. General arousal (e.g., heart rate) increases, which tends to increase the dominant behavioral tendency. 4. Direct imitation of recently observed aggressive behaviors sometimes occurs.[3]

The effect that media and culture has on the problems of crime and delinquency in the United States is still not completely known. However, many criminologists are trying to understand this relationship. Cultural criminology has a role to play in testing whether individuals are influenced by what they see on television, motion pictures, and video games.

[1]Ben Fritz and David G. Savage, "Supreme Court to Hear Case on Violent Video Games," *Los Angeles Times,* April 27, 2010, http://articles.latimes.com/2010/apr/27/business/la-fi-court-videos-20100427-39.

[2]Wendy Koch, "Video Game's Release Under Fire," *USA Today,* April 25, 2008, 1A.

[3] Craig A. Anderson, "Violent Video Games: Myths, Facts, and Unanswered Questions," *Psychological Science Agenda* 16, no. 5 (October 2003), http://www.apa.org/science/psa/sb-anderson.html.

## THINKING *in* ACTION

1. In your opinion, do violent video games cause violent behavior? Explain why or why not.
2. What kind of video games do you play? Do you believe they affect your behavior?
3. Has the media ever affected your behavior? Why or why not?

military weapons and clothing have earned a unique and highly valued identity within the police organization.[47] The mere presence of SWAT teams can sometimes be enough to resolve a potentially violent situation. However, SWAT weapons and clothing can also be problematic as citizens sometimes think they are under attack. Sometimes SWAT teams make a mistake by entering the wrong residence and frightening and assaulting innocent citizens.[48]

One aspect of cultural criminology that is particularly ripe for research is how some television news programs focus on one case and burn it deeply into the public consciousness. Often, these cases involve celebrities or individuals that evoke some type of public sympathy or scorn. For example, although it occurred in the mid-1990s, the O. J. Simpson murder trial is a landmark case because it set a new standard for crime as cultural spectacle. The case had a celebrity football star and television personality accused of slaying his attractive white, blonde wife, as well her handsome, young male visitor; an automobile chase; and a televised public trial. The case, however, provided a distorted image of how the criminal justice system operates.[49] Very few people can afford Simpson's legal representation or the constant media coverage and speculation that provided a level of examination virtually no other case has received since.[50] Cultural criminologists point out that people who are less interesting to the media because of their minority status or physical appearance are murdered all the time with little coverage of their cases. Still, the effect of such intense media attention is that criminal justice administrators might feel pressured to allocate more resources to a case at the expense of others.

Cultural criminology makes an important contribution to the study of crime and delinquency because it reminds us that we do not know everything about crime and antisocial behavior or about how images of lawbreaking are produced and transmitted to the public. By understanding how the criminal justice system, victims, and offenders attempt to manage their images in the media, cultural criminology reveals that the quality of justice often reflects social standing.[51]

## Critiques

Cultural criminology considers issues far beyond the criminal justice system as it attempts to explain why people break the law and how society reacts. For instance, the use of symbols by street gangs may be interesting to scholars and useful to police, but little can be done to suppress this behavior without violating gang members' rights of free speech. Similarly, although gang graffiti is a problem, law enforcement does not typically handle clearing it from public spaces. Although graffiti may have implications for criminology, it is the responsibility of other social institutions to deal with it. In another example, although cultural criminology considers the linkage between video games and crime, the criminal justice system can do little to respond to such speculation. Therefore, many of the concerns of cultural criminology, although theoretically interesting, are beyond the purview of the criminal justice system.

## Policy and Practice

The policy implications of cultural criminology include evaluating and examining how the news media report and often sensationalize crime. Cultural criminology examines the role of violence in the media and how it affects its most avid consumers, children and teenagers, as well as society as a whole. Responsible coverage is encouraged rather than the sensationalizing of cases with particularly sexual or emotional aspects. Cultural criminology also proposes finding more positive outlets for the energies and creativity of young people by, for example, supporting sports or music programs in urban areas that have few opportunities for positive or legitimate expression.

## Postmodern Criminology

Like cultural criminology, **postmodern criminology** focuses on how language and traditional ideas affect how we define and perceive crime, the law, and society. It offers a unique way of looking at the problems of negotiating the legal world and the criminal justice system. To understand postmodern criminology, we must first briefly explain postmodern thought.

**LO7:**

Demonstrate how postmodern criminology uses language and deconstruction in its critique of society and the criminal justice system.

Postmodernism explores how language affects the way we construct our perceptions about the world. Language communicates ideas in many ways, not only by words with meanings, but by context, syntax, and even grammar. Language can be used to include group members and alienate outsiders, or it can be used to explain difficult concepts simply. Depending on context, one word can have many different meanings, and the correct use of that word in the correct context can mean inclusion or exclusion from a group. In environments such as a prison or a gang, correct language can mean life or death.

Take, for example, the word "punk." A century ago, you might use a punk, which was another word for kindling, to start a fire. Later, a bum, low-level offender, or even a lazy person might be described as a punk. In the late 1970s, a social movement that was related to a form of popular music came to be called punk rock. Today, punk is no longer necessarily a pejorative term but can be a compliment describing a willingness to be different. However, in prison, a punk is a male inmate who has sex with, and even acts as spouse to, another male inmate. So four contexts involving a simple word emerge: (1) asking someone to start a fire with a punk will probably get you a funny look; (2) calling an elderly person a punk may result in a lecture about respect; (3) calling a youth with a purple mohawk hairstyle a punk will earn you a satisfied sneer; and (4) if you are a prison inmate who is not careful, calling another inmate a punk may get you killed. Of these four contexts, one, the prison, involves a strict and guarded terminology that excludes outsiders and draws insiders closer together by helping them define and understand their context. This, in a nutshell, is the concern of postmodernism: the role of language and ideas in constructing reality.

Postmodern criminology goes beyond that basic example to consider how language and ideas in all aspects of crime and the criminal justice system include and exclude groups of people and how they define the realities of those groups. Postmodern criminology is a critical theory because it examines the status quo and finds it wanting on a number of

**postmodern criminology** A perspective that focuses on how language and traditional ideas affect how we define and perceive crime, the law, and society.

fronts. Criminologist Bruce Arrigo identifies three areas of focus in postmodern criminology.[52]

- *Language in the criminal justice system.* Individuals must negotiate multiple language environments in the criminal justice system, which is crucial to understanding what is happening. Prison can be especially scary for those who are uninitiated and unaware of prison terminology, and the workings of a courtroom often seem foreign to a defendant with little education or experience. When attorneys speak in "legalese," the unsophisticated defendant often cannot understand what is happening and how these proceedings will affect his or her freedom.[53] The legal terminology includes courtroom insiders and excludes just about everyone else, including two of the most important participants: the offender and the victim.

- *Partial knowledge.* The postmodern perspective calls our attention to the fact that in many encounters between police and citizens, each party is acting on partial knowledge. In this case, misunderstandings can have tragic effects on the police, suspects, and victims. When the police stop a person, they require a certain etiquette that shows the detained person is not violent. When a detained person violates this expected behavior and appears defiant or agitated, the officer might interpret this behavior as aggressive and use inappropriate force.[54] The suspect may have a different idea of what the encounter is about—for example, if the detained person is a victim—and challenge the officer's authority. According to postmodernism, this difference in defining the situation causes many detained people to find themselves subdued, arrested, and hauled before a judge.

- *Deconstruction.* Deconstruction is the examination of rules and regulations by questioning traditional assumptions about certainty, meaning, and truth. Arrigo uses the example of mental treatment for those facing execution.[55] The law states that people who are mentally ill cannot be executed, but it stipulates that once they successfully receive treatment and are healthy, they can be put to death. At issue is the word "treatment" because the term, according to Arrigo, connotes the conferring of a gift or a reward. Postmodernists contend that such terminology does not accurately reflect the situation. In another example, it is the job of medical and legal officials to ascertain whether formerly violent mental patients and inmates can be released. Consequently, many subjects have learned to provide the expected answers to questions and to modify their behavior within the institution. Once released, however, successful institutional adaptation does not necessarily ensure the subject will successfully adjust to free society. Learning to follow institutional rules does not guarantee that an inmate or patient has been successfully rehabilitated. Life inside and outside the institution is very different, and forcing individuals to adhere to a strict routine, although useful for maintaining control in an institution, leaves them unprepared for life on the outside where temptations are many, and the punishments for not following the rules are extreme.

Through its examination of language, postmodern criminology forces observers to step outside the conventional wisdom and generally accepted assumptions about crime and justice and consider how power is exercised at the expense of marginal groups of people. For critical criminologists, postmodern criminology represents a fresh way of understanding the workings of the criminal justice system and an opportunity to ensure that justice is fully examined for its unintended consequences.[56]

## Critiques

Postmodern criminology suffers from several limitations that have restricted its popularity. The first is language. Critics of postmodern criminology point to the jargon or parlance of those who engage in postmodern critique and suggest that rather than making things more clear, postmodernists further muddy the waters by providing analyses that are as difficult to understand as the system they critique. Another criticism is the use of models from other disciplines. The models postmodern theorists use, especially the chaos theorists, tend to require a high level of knowledge of fields far removed from criminology, such as physics and mathematics.

## Policy and Practice

Although the use of sophisticated language and complicated models are considered by some to be severe limitations of postmodern criminology, they can also be guides for developing policy. By appreciating how language is used to privilege the wealthy and educated or confuse those who lack the vocabulary and knowledge of legal procedures, the postmodern critique can show how the criminal justice system can be unfair to those who are at the greatest social disadvantage.

Postmodern critique can illustrate how the knowledge of experts may be used to deny victims and offenders full access to the criminal justice system. For instance, in plea bargaining, the prosecutor must move cases through the system and does not always fully explain to victims why pleas are negotiated. Like many of the critical theories we have discussed in this chapter, postmodern criminology speaks only indirectly to the problems of crime. It is more broadly aimed at cultural influences rather than directly at criminology or the criminal justice system. Nevertheless, it provides a fresh look at how issues of crime and delinquency are resolved in the United States.

## Critical Race Theory

The development of a theoretical perspective of race is not as advanced as those of class and gender. However, significant scholarship outside criminology details how race is related

## LO8:

**Assess** how critical race theory examines the normality of racism in American culture, the value of story-telling, and the theoretical institution of liberalism.

to many important issues in health care, education, crime, and the criminal justice system. However, critical race theory is the most extensive theoretical development of race as a social category that influences power.[57] **Critical race theory** is a set of legalistic theories that hold that racial inequity is so ingrained in society it is propagated through legal and social discourse. Critical race theory has three basic principles.

- *The normality of racism in American culture.* The purpose of critical race theory is to eliminate racism by revealing how deeply ingrained it is within American culture.[58]

- *The value of story-telling.* Critical race theory uses personal narrative or story-telling to allow oppressed groups to speak from their own experiences and describe their realities.[59]

- *The critique of liberalism.* Traditional liberal perspectives in terms of historical and current racial reforms are not radical enough to bring about the fundamental changes necessary for equality and justice.[60]

Critical race theory presents important alternative perspectives for looking at how laws are written. Institutional racism has afflicted the United States throughout its history. Even after slavery was abolished, racial minorities were still at a disadvantage because of laws that supported the dominant white majority and prohibited minorities from participating in much of society.[61] In the second half of the 20th century, the civil rights movement challenged the status quo and successfully eliminated overt institutional discrimination in state and federal law.[62]

Despite the successes in challenging institutional discrimination, critical race theorists still see disadvantages for people of color. The disadvantages are not as overt as they were in the past, but they can be significant in the lives and careers of those who are subject to even indirect racial discrimination. For example, although affirmative action policies have brought opportunity and hope to many people of color, critical race theorists have criticized them as limiting rather than emancipating. Sometimes, people attribute the success of a person of color to affirmative action rather than to personal ability. Critical race theorists assert that governments have singled out race as an identifying factor in dispensing justice. Examples of how race has been a deciding factor in the dispensation of justice include the resettlement of U.S. citizens of Japanese descent in the United States during World War II, the Jim Crow laws of the South in the early 20th century, and the treatment of American Indians by the U.S. government.[63]

Critical race theorists also call attention to subtle uses of race to assert control. One example is that the media tends to more extensively cover criminal offenses that affect white people than it covers offenses that affect people of color. (See *Doubletake* for a discussion of what has been called "missing white woman syndrome.") Another example, according to

law professor Dorothy E. Roberts, is that some drug laws are aimed primarily at people of color and used to influence reproductive rights. She cites the example of how the state of Florida used a mother's drug addiction as a way to discourage impoverished, black female addicts from caring for their babies. In the case, the two babies of a woman who admitted she had smoked crack cocaine shortly before the delivery of both tested positive for traces of cocaine. In Florida, mothers cannot be charged with passing substances to their children while in the womb. So, the prosecutor argued that the mother passed the drug to her children after they were born but before they were detached from the umbilical cord. The mother was then found guilty of giving her children cocaine.[64] Because the effect of this legal precedent fell most heavily on blacks, critical race theorists argue that it is race-based.[65]

**Racial profiling,** the disproportionate selection by law enforcement of minority suspects, has also come under the scrutiny of the critical race theorists. It has long been suspected by critics of the criminal justice system that people of color are incarcerated at a greater rate because of racism. Studies have shown that when a white person and a person of color are engaged in the same type of behavior, the police are more likely to confront the person of color. Law enforcement officials contend that race is not at issue but rather the perceptions of experienced police officers that certain people in certain circumstances are more likely to break the law than others.

Another concern of critical race theorists is the disparity in sentencing for possessing crack cocaine as opposed to powder cocaine.[66] The differences between these substances is how they are prepared and consumed: Crack cocaine is smoked, whereas powder cocaine is inhaled. These differences led to the creation of the 100-to-1 sentencing disparity for possession of crack versus powder cocaine, which meant that possessing five grams of crack cocaine triggered a minimum sentence of five years, although it took 500 grams of powder cocaine to warrant the same sentence. Until 2007, when the sentencing structure was changed to reduce the sentences for crack cocaine possession, blacks went to prison for very low-level drug dealing while white drug users escaped incarceration.[67] In 2010, the U.S. House and Senate approved a measure under the Fair Sentencing Act that reduces the disparity in penalties between the use of crack cocaine and powder cocaine from 100-to-1 to 18-1. The new law drops the five-year minimum sentence for both first-time offenders and repeat offenders who possess less than 28 grams of crack.[68]

## Critiques

A major criticism of critical race theory is that by looking at crime and delinquency through the prism of race, the contributions of other social institutions, such as family, schools, and the media, might be devalued. Sexism, ageism, and social-class bias, in addition to race, provide a more holistic view of

**critical race theory** A set of legalistic perspectives that hold that racial inequity is so ingrained in society it is propagated through legal and social discourse.

**racial profiling** The disproportionate selection by law enforcement of minority suspects.

inequality. By privileging race as an explanatory factor, critical race theory might discount other equally important factors.

Further, the reliance on personal narrative, while purposefully getting away from the scientific method, might disregard other important empirical evidence. Social scientists who depend on sophisticated measuring techniques and statistics are especially suspicious of the narrative form because it is difficult to independently verify.

## Policy and Practice

Critical race theory has some policy implications in the criminal justice system. The first important area to consider is how laws are made. When people are systematically excluded from the lawmaking process, it is almost certain their concerns will be excluded, too. Groups who are able to put their members in positions of power are best able to ensure their value system is encoded into the law. In addition,

# doubletake
doubletake

### Missing: White Woman

"Missing white woman syndrome" is a slang term for what appears to be a media bias toward the coverage of the disappearances and murders of white females.[1] This phenomenon can be successfully examined through critical race theory.

Media experts point out that the U.S. news media has typically given more attention to offenses affecting whites than offenses affecting people of color. For example, in 1993 in St. Louis, Missouri, Kimbre Young, a 9-year-old black girl, and Cassidy Senter, a 10-year-old white girl, disappeared within months of each other. The *St. Louis Post-Dispatch* ran two stories on Young and at least 23 stories on Senter.[2] A landmark early case was the 1969 Tate–LaBianca murders in which followers of Charles Manson murdered seven people. To this day, the iconic victim is Sharon Tate, an attractive, young, blonde, white woman. The other victims, two women and four men, were either male or middle-aged or both. Another notable case is the 1994 O. J. Simpson murder case. Simpson's wife, Nicole, a young, blonde, white woman, was found murdered at her home, along with a young white man, Ronald Goldman.

Since the Simpson case, the news media has provided deep coverage of several murder cases involving young, white females, including JonBenet Ramsey, Natalee Holloway, Laci Peterson, Chandra Levy, Polly Klaas, and Caylee Anthony. This coverage, now commonly called "missing white woman syndrome" (although the subjects are often children), has angered many people because similar cases involving women of color have gone unnoticed. For example, few people have heard of LaToyia Figueroa, Stepha Henry, or Tamika Huston.

1. Figueroa, a 24-year-old black and Hispanic Pennsylvania woman who was five months pregnant, went missing in 2005 around the time Natalee Holloway disappeared. After public criticism that her disappearance deserved as much attention as Holloway's, the case got some national coverage. Figueroa's body was found about a month after her disappearance, and the father of her unborn child was charged with her murder.[3]

2. Stepha Henry, 23, a black woman from Brooklyn, New York, disappeared in 2007 while vacationing in Florida. The media was criticized for directing most of its coverage at this time to the jail sentence of hotel heiress Paris Hilton.[4] Although Henry's body has not been found, a male acquaintance was charged with her murder in 2008.[5]

3. In 2004, Tamika Huston, a young black woman, disappeared in Spartanburg, North Carolina. Huston's aunt, a public relations professional, tried to get the national media interested in the case for weeks with little result.[6] Huston's remains were found about a year after her disappearance, and a male acquaintance was convicted of her murder.[7]

[1]See Urban Dictionary at http://www.urbandictionary.com/define.php?term=Missing%20white%20woman%20syndrome&defid=2667082.

[2]Peter Downs, "Paying More Attention to White Crime Victims," *American Journalism Review,* December 1995, http://www.ajr.org/Article.asp?id=2016.

[3]Mark Memmott, "Missing Pregnant Woman Found Dead," *USA Today,* August 22, 2005, 3A.

[4]Stephen J. Lee, "Investigator Who Led Search for Dru Sjodin Urges Larger Focus on Victims," *Grand Forks Herald,* June 13, 2007.

[5]Christine Hauser et al., "Suspect Charged in Death of a Woman Who Vanished in Florida," *New York Times,* January 16, 2008, late edition, sec. B.

[6]Mark Memmott, "Spotlight Skips Cases of Missing Minorities," *USA Today,* June 16, 2005, final edition, 6A.

[7]America's Most Wanted, http://www.amw.com/missing_persons/case.cfm?id=27632.

# THINKING
## *in* ACTION

1. Is the media really biased toward "missing white women"? Give examples of why or why not.

2. Had you ever heard of the Tate–LaBianca murders? Do some brief research on the other victims of the Manson family. Why, in your opinion, did Sharon Tate become the "face" of the murders?

▲ Critical race theorists advocate examining the underlying assumptions behind laws such as those that mandate sentencing disparities between possession of powder cocaine and crack cocaine.

those with a great deal of money can hire lobbyists and develop educational materials to ensure their viewpoints are considered in the making of laws.

The challenge, then, is for minorities to see that their values are encoded in the law. This is not as simple as it seems.[69] Take, for instance, the earlier example of crack cocaine. People of color are no more likely than whites to advocate the legalization of crack cocaine. However, they are concerned about the severity of the sentences allocated to crack users and sellers when compared to other substances, especially powder cocaine. When such disparities exist, critical race theorists argue that the law is aimed not at public safety but rather at the social control of marginal groups. Therefore, critical race theorists advocate examining the underlying assumptions behind the law to determine whether a race-related agenda is being implemented throughout the criminal justice system.

Critical race theory recognizes that gains have been made in the legal system regarding racism, but it still considers the task to be incomplete. Structural and sometimes subtle disadvantages based on race are encoded in the law and must be closely examined to see how the criminal justice system can operate more fairly. At one level, this means including minority groups in the criminal justice system at all levels. More important, it means bringing a new awareness to the role race has always played in the criminal justice system.[70]

# Think about it

## Understand
Discuss the limitations and policy implications of peacemaking criminology.

## Apply
Illustrate how feminist criminology approaches women's participation in crime as offenders, victims, and criminal justice practitioners.

## Analyze
Examine how postmodern criminology uses language to critique how individuals are defined as antisocial.

## Evaluate
Critique the assertion of critical race theory that the criminal justice system and the media are more concerned with offenses against white individuals than those against individuals of color.

## Create
Propose a program consistent with cultural criminology that would enable the media to have a greater effect on reducing crime.

# Summary

**LO1:** Define primary deviance and secondary deviance and how these conditions relate to labeling theory.
- Labeling theory is the idea that individuals structure their behavior according to social expectations.
- Primary deviance occurs when society reacts to an individual's actions, successfully labels that individual, and acts upon that label. Secondary deviance occurs when labeled individuals internalize the label and see themselves as devalued members of society. A negative label can become quickly attached to a person's self-concept, making rehabilitation more difficult.
- Labels can become a master status that overwhelms all others. A negative master status can have a detrimental effect upon how a person is treated by teachers, parents, society, and the criminal justice system.

**LO2:** Understand how conflict theory considers social institutions, especially those rooted in economics and social class, to contribute more to crime than individual antisocial behavior.
- The idea that economics is a primary determining factor in individual antisocial behavior can be traced to the ideas of Karl Marx, which spurred later theo-

rists to contemplate the relationship between economic conditions and crime.

- Rather than assuming that offenders are inherently antisocial or that they learn to break the law, conflict theory examines how societies control their members and how this may lead to crime.

- Conflict theory highlights social and political dynamics that are taken for granted. Critiques are that it is more political than scientific; it is not measurable; it critiques the status quo; solutions are too expensive both financially and politically; and solutions are culturally unattractive.

**LO3:** Examine how critical theories of criminology not only describe and critique the social structure, but also seek solutions to the problems of crime and criminal justice.

- Critical theories consider crime to be rooted within social inequality. The definitions of crime and justice are located within a system that is based on and perpetuates social inequality.

**LO4:** Discuss how feminist criminology deals with issues and problems related to women, crime, and the criminal justice system.

- Feminist theory deals with incarcerated females, women in the criminal justice workplace, and gender dimensions of victimization.

- Feminist theory asserts that the criminal justice system's treatment of females mirrors that of the rest of society.

- Almost all criminological theories describe and explain the activities of males in the male-dominated world of crime and criminal justice. Feminist theory points out that females are different from males, critiques male-centric theories, and creates hypotheses about crime and gender.

**LO5:** Explain how peacemaking criminology considers not only the offender and victim, but also the social structures that accept, enable, or encourage criminal offending.

- Peacemaking criminology operates at four levels: the personal, the interpersonal, the institutional/societal, and the global.

- Peacemaking criminology derives its ideas and philosophy from religious and humanist traditions, feminist traditions, and the critical tradition.

**LO6:** Describe the assertion of cultural criminology that culture and the media reflect and produce antisocial behavior.

- Cultural criminology borrows from disciplines that look at how individuals, small groups, and deviant subcultures construct meaning and transmit it to a wider audience in order to better comprehend how crime is either culturally supported or culturally discouraged by everyday social structures.

**LO7:** Demonstrate how postmodern criminology uses language and deconstruction in its critique of society and the criminal justice system.

- Postmodern criminology considers how language and ideas in all aspects of crime and the criminal justice system include and exclude groups of people and how they define the realities of those groups.

- Arrigo identifies three areas of focus in postmodern criminology: language in the criminal justice system, partial knowledge, and deconstruction (the examination of rules and regulations by questioning traditional assumptions about certainty, meaning, and truth).

- By examining language, postmodern criminology forces observers to step outside the generally accepted assumptions about crime and justice and consider how power is exercised at the expense of marginal groups of people.

**LO8:** Assess how critical race theory examines the normality of racism in American culture, the value of story-telling, and the theoretical institution of liberalism.

- The three basic principles of critical race theory are the normality of racism in American culture, the value of story-telling, and the critique of liberalism.

- Critical race theory presents important alternative perspectives for understanding how laws are crafted, stating that the law reflects the concerns and desires of those who make them. Groups who have no hand in making laws will not see their concerns reflected.

# Questions

1. What is the significance of master status to labeling theory?
2. Why is social location important to the perception, legislation, and control of crime?
3. What does conflict theory consider to contribute more to crime than individual antisocial behavior?
4. How is critical theory related to conflict theory? How does it differ?
5. How did Karl Marx contribute to conflict theory?
6. Describe feminist criminology's critique of other criminological theories.
7. What are the four levels to which the peacemaking perspective applies? What traditions does peacemaking draw from?
8. What aspects of culture and the media does cultural criminology critique?
9. How does postmodern criminology critique the use of language in the criminal justice system? How can deconstruction be used to do this?
10. How does critical race theory critique the war on drugs?

# 9

# Property
# Offenses

# what's inside

**As you read, keep in mind these learning objectives:**

**LO1:** Recognize that burglary requires both the entering of a structure and the offender's intent to commit a felony or theft.

**LO2:** Understand how larceny is different from burglary and robbery.

**LO3:** Describe how check fraud and credit card theft are forms of theft.

**LO4:** Evaluate why motor vehicle theft continues to be a significant problem.

**LO5:** Assess why arson is an exception to the FBI's hierarchy rule.

Individuals value their private property and go to great lengths to protect it. The major distinction between property offenses and personal violent offenses is the elements of fear and danger. Property offenders typically do not use intimidation or physical violence as part of their method of breaking the law but, instead, are more concerned with avoiding detection and recognition. Most criminal offenses in the United States are **property offenses,** that is, an offense that is perpetrated without personal violence and is focused on the entering, taking, or destruction of structures, motor vehicles, or goods. In 2008, more than 9 million property offenses were reported to law enforcement.[1] Although this number seems high, it actually represents a reduction in property offenses over each of the four previous years (see Figure 9.1). Nevertheless, property offenses are frequent enough to be expensive, costing the public an estimated $17.2 billion in lost property in 2008.[2]

In many ways, the amount of property that Americans possess reflects their social status and power. Although many desire financial security, this goal runs a distant second place to what sociologist Thorstein Veblen called "conspicuous consumption."[3] Although comfort and convenience are a couple of reasons that Americans have so much stuff, a more interesting explanation is that the display of property helps to establish social standing in the community. We need only look at the vast quantities of designer jeans, brand-name running shoes, luxury cars, smartphones, and a host of other articles and gadgets that people buy not for their utility but, rather, for their display value. It should not surprise us, then, that what people value is coveted by others. When items are conspicuously displayed to establish social standing and identity, those articles become desired by others. Both expensive and even inexpensive items are the targets of those who would rather steal than expend their own financial re-

**property offense** A criminal offense perpetrated without personal violence and focused on the entering, taking, or destruction of structures, motor vehicles, or goods.

### Figure 9.1 Property Offenses, 2004–2008

**Property offenses steadily declined from 2004 to 2008.**

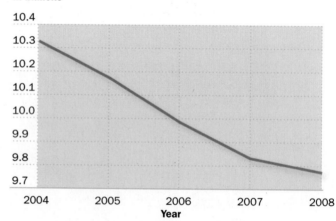

**Estimated Number of Offenses, in Millions**

*Source:* Federal Bureau of Investigation, *Uniform Crime Reports: Crime in the United States, 2008,* "Property Crime," http://www.fbi.gov/ucr/cius2008/offenses/property_crime/index.html.

sources or by those who do not have the financial resources to buy what they want. At least three types of criminological theory can explain why people commit property offenses (see Table 9.1).

Attitudes toward property are culturally and individually variable. Some people prefer to have few personal possessions. Instead of acquiring items intended to display wealth or status, they use their discretionary money to invest, travel, or purchase perishable items such as food and wine. Personal property is not as highly valued in some societies as it is in others. For instance, Paris has a vast network of public bicycles that riders can rent cheaply and simply leave in bike racks scattered throughout the city when they are finished.[4] It would be relatively easy to steal one of these bicycles, but

## Table **9.1**    Criminological Theory and Property Crime

| Classical strain theory | The category of *innovator* in Merton's strain theory captures the motivation of those who have accepted the goal of the American dream of financial gain but have rejected the culturally approved means of hard work. The burglar or the thief aspires to have material goods and money but is not willing to work for either. Therefore, taking the property of others is an alternative means of achieving financial gain. |
|---|---|
| Critical theory | A number of critical theories can be used to explain property offending. Traditional Marxist theory states that those who control the means of production manipulate the system to increase and extend their wealth. Theft and burglary are two ways that those who do not have power can achieve the means of survival. The theory of left realism explains that impoverished people victimize other impoverished people. Left realism advocates economic policies that alleviate poverty and allow everyone the opportunity to make a legitimate living. |
| Psychological theory | For some offenders the risk of taking other people's property presents opportunities for thrills. These thrills range from the joyriding of teenagers who steal cars to the deep psychological needs present in kleptomaniacs who steal without understanding exactly why. Many kleptomaniacs take things they do not need despite having enough money to pay for them, risking their reputation and standing in society. |

because they are readily accessible, people get the benefits of riding a bike without having to own or steal one.[5] Not every large city has such a thriving culture of sharing.

## Burglary

The Federal Bureau of Investigation (FBI) defines **burglary** as the unlawful entry of a structure with the intent to commit a felony or theft. For purposes of reporting, the Uniform Crime Reports (UCR) has three subcategories of burglary: forcible entry, unlawful entry in which no force is used, and attempted forcible entry (see Figure 9.2 for these subcategories by percentage). Note that the offense of burglary includes not only the unlawful entry of a structure, but also the offender's *intent* to commit a felony or theft.

**LO1:**

Recognize that burglary requires both the entering of a structure and the offender's intent to commit a felony or theft.

Recall that because of the FBI's **hierarchy rule,** the most serious offense in a set of offenses is the one measured and reported in the UCR. So, if a burglar breaks into a dwelling and commits a rape, the rape is recorded but not the burglary. If a burglary includes a theft, which is lower on the hierarchy, then the burglary is reported. Therefore, the burglaries reported in the UCR represent theft rather than murder, rape, robbery, or aggravated as-

><THINKBACK

hierarchy rule (ch. 2)—The practice of the FBI of recording in the UCR only the most serious offense in a set of offenses.

**burglary** The unlawful entry of a structure with the intent to commit a felony or theft.

## Figure **9.2**    Types of Burglaries and Attempts by Percentage, 2008

**The Uniform Crime Reporting program has three burglary categories: forcible entry, unlawful entry in which no force is used, and attempted forcible entry. The UCR defines a structure as not only homes, but also apartments, barns, house trailers, houseboats when used as a permanent dwelling, offices, railroad cars, stables, and water-going vessels.**

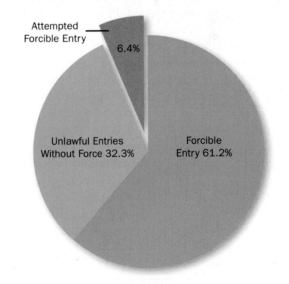

Attempted Forcible Entry — 6.4%

Unlawful Entries Without Force 32.3%

Forcible Entry 61.2%

*Source:* Federal Bureau of Investigation, *Uniform Crime Reports: Crime in the United States, 2008,* "Burglary," http://www.fbi.gov/ucr/cius2008/offenses/property_crime/burglary.html.

sault. Many of the more serious violent offenses recorded in the UCR also include burglary, but those burglaries were not reported because they are the less serious offense.

Burglary is an offense most individuals fear because it often happens when they are away from their property. To have someone break into your home while you are at work or on vacation is frightening. However, it is even more terrifying if someone breaks into your home at night when you are there asleep. Burglary, therefore, includes three violations of an individual's comfort zone. The first is having someone enter your property without your permission, perhaps by using force to break a window, kick in a door, or destroy a lock. The second violation, if the burglar's intent is theft, is the taking of personal possessions. The taking of an expensive television, jewelry, or intimate personal items is not only an economic loss, but it can also be personally devastating. Finally, if the burglary happens while the resident is home, the potential for other victimizations such as assault or rape makes it even more serious. Therefore, the analysis of burglary requires us also to consider its emotional and psychological effect on victims.[6]

It should not be surprising that most dwellings are burglarized when the occupants are away. More than half of all residential burglaries for which the time of offense is known, about 51 percent, happen during the day. When we consider the type of building, it is clear that the absence of occupants is even more important. Of non-residential burglaries in which the time of the offense is known, most occurred at night.[7] Therefore, it is clear that burglars are, for the most part, careful to break into buildings when they are reasonably confident that guardians are not present.

As devastating as a burglary can be, it lacks much of the danger and fear that accompany violent personal offenses. The burglar-thief is interested in avoiding confrontation with the victim and will carefully select targets and strike when it appears no one is around. Burglars also do not often carry weapons, which makes the offense somewhat less problematic for the offender, victim, and criminal justice system than many types of violent personal offenses.[8]

The number of burglaries in the United States is staggering. In 2008, more than 2 million burglaries were reported. The estimated amount of loss was $4.6 billion, which averages $2,079 per offense.[9] Burglaries are not evenly distributed, however; they are more likely to happen in large metropolitan areas than in rural or small towns. These distribution patterns can be explained in several ways. First, the anonymity afforded in major metropolitan areas allows burglars not only to find targets of opportunity because of the dense population, but also to escape detection because the large number of people in metropolitan areas makes it easier for burglars to escape recognition. In addition, since people can be relatively anonymous in metropolitan areas, the burglar is less likely to have to account for ill-gotten gains to neighbors or police. In small towns, where people live in more intimate settings, a burglar might have a more difficult time explaining away or selling stolen property.[10]

Burglars commit their offenses for a number of reasons. It is important to understand these motivations because burglaries are usually not the result of impulse and opportunity. They are not crimes of passion in which the motivation is spontaneous, based on arguments or on opportunities in which someone has left their property unguarded. Rather, burglaries are usually the result of premeditation and planning. Often, a great deal of effort goes into the selection of targets, including place and time of day, based on the potential for stealing valuable items and the lack of close monitoring in terms of owners being present, security cameras, or police patrols. Malcolm X, the political activist and civil rights leader who led an antisocial lifestyle until his incarceration in 1946 for robbery, provides an interesting look at burglars' attitudes and approaches to their craft in the mid-20th century:

> I had learned from some of the pros, and from my own experience, how important it was to be careful and plan. Burglary, properly executed, though it had its dangers, offered the maximum chances of success with the minimum risk. If you did your job so that you never met any of your victims, it first lessened your chances of having to attack or perhaps kill someone. And if through some slip-up you were caught, later, by the police, there was never a positive eye-witness. It is also important to select an area of burglary and stick to that. There are specific specialities [sic] among burglars. Some work apartments only, others houses only, others stores only, or warehouses; still others will go after only safes or strongboxes. Within the residence burglary category, there are further specialty distinctions. There are the day burglars, the dinner- and theater-time burglars, the night burglars. I think that any city's police will tell you that very rarely do they find one type who will work at another time. For instance Jumpsteady, in Harlem, was a nighttime apartment specialist. It would have been hard to persuade Jumpsteady to work in the daytime if a millionaire had gone out for lunch and left his front door wide open.[11]

Although this passage describes incidents that occurred more than 60 years ago, little about successful burglary methods has changed. Sloppy burglars who leave evidence behind or who do not adequately research security systems are soon arrested. However, careful, attentive burglars can ply their trade for years and, if incarcerated, often continue once released from prison.

For instance, Blane Nordahl, who began serving an eight-year sentence in 2004, burglarized wealthy neighborhoods around the Northeast for several years, stealing only sterling silver flatware, tea services, and dishes. According to an investigator who worked on Nordahl's case, silver was a particularly good item to steal because it is typically antique and extremely valuable; sturdy; relatively easy to carry (as opposed to televisions and other electronics); and it is typically stored in dining rooms, kitchens, and pantries, far from homeowners' bedrooms.

Nordahl would scout wealthy targets through publications like *Architectural Digest* and the *Robb Report* and by call-

▶ Burglar Blane Nordahl chose his targets carefully. Nordahl would steal the silverware from mansions such as Wilderstein, which had been the home of a relative of Franklin D. Roosevelt.

ing real estate agents pretending to be a client looking for a home in an old, wealthy neighborhood. He would then drive around during the day and note houses set away from the street. After midnight, he would return to the area, parking in an ordinary location that was sometimes several miles from his target homes.

He would walk to his chosen neighborhood and watch several houses before picking one to burglarize. Then, equipped with a bag of tools, an empty bag for the silver, and cotton gardening gloves to avoid leaving fingerprints, he would find a way into the house. This usually meant getting through an alarm-protected door, sometimes by removing glass panes or by cutting through it. The work also required patience: To steal an ornate tea service and flatware set for 110 people, Nordahl once spent two hours cutting through a door. When he had collected the silver and left the house, he threw away anything not worth stealing and hid the bags near a road. Then he walked back to his car and drove by to get them. If he was within driving distance of New York, he would deliver the silver to his **fence**—a person who sells goods that he or she knows to be stolen; the term also refers to the act of selling goods that are known to be stolen. If he could not drive to New York, he would send the goods by UPS.

Blane Nordahl has given many explanations for why he continued to engage in burglary even after being captured several times. He has told police, interviewers, girlfriends, and even his mother that he did it for the excitement, because he had a difficult childhood, and because he felt it was justifiable to steal from the wealthy. He has promised to reform several times, but after each release from incarceration, he would go back to burglarizing homes.[12] His explanations are reflected in the following reasons burglars commit their offense.

- *Financial reward.* Burglars break into places mainly to steal money, tools, and other types of valuable property. They may keep the items for themselves, give them to friends and family, or attempt to sell them through a fence. Those who make their living as burglars often have a plan for disposing of the goods in ways that convert them to cash.

**fence** Refers to both the act of selling goods that are known to be stolen, as well as the person who sells goods that he or she knows to be stolen.

- *Lack of legitimate opportunities.* Some burglars steal to supplement their income because they have low-paying jobs or are unemployed. Some would not engage in this activity if they could meet their needs in more legitimate ways. They see burglary as a part-time and episodic activity that allows them to obtain discretionary funds for parties, buying gifts for family or girlfriends, and securing items that would normally be outside their purchasing range, such as large-screen televisions or expensive jewelry.

- *Thrill-seeking.* Monetary gain is not the primary motivation for some burglars. Instead, some break into buildings because they can. They get a certain pride of craftsmanship and thrill from overcoming security devices, locks, and other target-hardening efforts. Individuals who identify themselves as professional burglars often see challenges in taking down what guardians consider to be secure buildings. The prospect of getting caught in the act of burglarizing is more of an inducement than a deterrent to thrill-seeking burglars. Sometimes these burglars will not steal anything but will instead leave evidence such as graffiti to show they have been successful in breaking into the building. Thrill-seeking burglars are few, but they can demonstrate an impressive level of skill. In his research on property-crime offenders, Kenneth Tunnell identifies one motive as "crime is sport." The burglar motivated by this idea considers a successful break-in a form of winning. According to Tunnell, "Successfully completing a crime provided them with a sense of accomplishment and purpose, and reinforced their belief that they had 'won the game.'" Furthermore, "Whenever they were arrested and convicted, they simply admitted to having lost the game, but only temporarily."[13]

- *Sexual deviance.* This type of burglar has a fetish for certain objects and breaks in to dwellings to steal them. Such burglars are rare, but their motivations make them particularly interesting to the press. The most notable fetish burglars are men who break into women's homes and steal articles of clothing, particularly underwear or shoes, that they keep as part of a trophy collection that constitutes a sexual stimulus.[14]

- *Lifestyle.* For some burglars, the decision to break the law is part of their street-culture lifestyle. Although they engage in a variety of other offenses, such as larceny and drug dealing, these offenders use burglary as a preferred method of "keeping up appearances" before their peer group. They are heavily active in partying, drug use, alcohol, and sexual exploits. According to researchers Richard Wright and Scott Decker, such burglars treat every night as a Saturday night in which the pursuit of pleasure is paramount. Burglary simply gives them the means to engage in their hedonistic pursuits and provides them with the "street cred" their peer group values. Wright and Decker found that even though the proceeds from burglary were often used for paying bills, they were as likely spent on status symbols such as clothes, cars, and especially drugs. Finally, the influence of peer pressure in a juvenile gang also fits under the lifestyle motivation for committing burglary. Some gangs work as a group in burglarizing homes and businesses, and it is difficult if not impossible for a gang member to opt out.[15]

- *Revenge.* In a study by researchers Paul Cromwell and James N. Olson, about 30 percent of the burglars interviewed reported committing their offenses for revenge. These burglars were usually under age 25 and came from dysfunctional homes. Instead of taking the victim's possessions, they vandalized the victim's home to avenge real or imagined slights based on racial discrimination or because someone had "snitched."[16]

Not all buildings have an equal chance of being burglarized. A great deal of consideration goes into deciding which buildings, either residential or business, are the best candidates for a burglary. The selection of the target is a good example of the classical school of criminology's focus on **deterrence.** Burglars weigh the risk of getting caught against the potential reward for successfully completing the offense. Therefore, in order to fully understand why burglars select one building over another, we must consider the calculus they use to evaluate potential targets.

> ><**THINKBACK**
> deterrence (ch. 3)—The idea that punishment for an offense will prevent that offender and others from further breaking the law.

Researchers have interviewed professional burglars to determine how they decide which dwellings to burglarize. According to Wright and Decker, burglars consider five characteristics of potential targets.

1. *Occupancy.* Burglars will determine whether anyone is in the building at the time they wish to break in. As we have learned, most residential burglaries occur in the daytime when no one is home, and most business burglaries occur at night when businesses are closed. One of the hallmarks of a successful burglary is stealth, and the risk of getting caught because someone is present is usually considered too great. Therefore, burglars ascertain that a dwelling is unoccupied before attempting the offense.

2. *A location not easily observed.* Dwellings that are well off the street or surrounded by trees and bushes are more likely to be broken into than those that are easily seen from the street or neighboring houses. Crime prevention specialists advise homeowners to trim bushes and install motion-detecting lights to deter potential burglars.

3. *Location in a neighborhood where the burglar will not stand out.* Burglars will bypass neighborhoods where they will stand out because of their race, attire, or car. Police officers look for individuals who do not fit the profile of neighborhood residents. This is especially true in upscale neighborhoods or gated communities where potential burglars would have a hard time explaining their presence.

4. *Accessibility.* Burglars will evaluate a home or business to determine how easy it would be to break into. Key considerations are the type of locks on the doors and windows, the presence or absence of security systems, and other considerations such as a barking dog in the yard. Burglars will bypass these types of targets in favor of those that appear more accessible.

5. *Presence of items worth stealing.* The home or business must show the potential to contain items that can be converted into cash. Homes in more prosperous neighborhoods are more attractive targets than run-down homes in disadvantaged areas of the city. Cash, jewelry, electronic items, expensive tools, and silverware are attractive targets for burglars and are more likely to be found in upscale homes. However, there is a delicate balance between the attractiveness of a target and the security with which it is surrounded. Dwellings with items worth stealing are often the least accessible.[17]

Even though this list of target characteristics makes it appear that burglars act rationally and logically, this is not always the case. Often, they spontaneously select homes or businesses for burglary based on a number of factors. A burglar may make a quick decision to burglarize a dwelling because it is unlocked and unoccupied. With virtually no forethought, the offender may see this target of opportunity and strike quickly.[18] Another reason to break into a dwelling without a plan is that the burglars are under the influence of drugs or alcohol and are incapable of doing the careful calculations they would undertake if they were sober.[19] Sometimes they get lucky and are successful in completing the burglary, but sometimes they are so clumsy and careless they get caught in the act, leave abundant clues that can lead to their detection, or even fall asleep in the middle of the offense.

Criminologists look at a number of issues when researching burglary in order to detect patterns and develop plans for prevention. One criterion of recent interest to researchers is the distance between a burglar's home and the target. By looking at the distance a burglar travels, the mode of transportation, and the social similarities and differences between the burglar's and victim's neighborhoods, criminologists aim to develop a better understanding of where and how burglaries are committed.

Researchers Wim Bernasco and Richard Block have looked at where offenders choose to commit their offenses, and they have found some intriguing patterns. In one study dealing with robbery, they studied the racial and ethnic dissimilarity between offenders and their targets, gang territoriality, annual prostitution arrests, and the presence of high schools in the target area.[20] Although these criteria do not specifically apply to burglaries, they do show how various neighborhood characteristics can attract crime. In the case of burglary, some of these factors are the number of retail stores in the area, accessibility by public transportation, and similarities in racial and ethnic makeup between neighborhood residents and potential offenders. Burglary can be a very simple offense with clear evidence about why it is committed. We can also see it in a much more sophisticated manner that reveals the motivational and logistical factors that make it such a popular offense.[21]

# Think about it

## Remember

List the three subcategories of burglary.

## Evaluate

Compare the various motivations of burglars for committing their offenses.

## Create

Propose a better alternative to the FBI's practice of using the hierarchy rule—that is, using only the most serious offense when reporting offenses that occur in a single incident.

## Larceny and Fraud

**Larceny** is the legal term for theft, which is the unlawful taking of property from another person. The UCR, which refers to the offense as "larceny-theft,"

**LO2:**

**Understand** how larceny is different from burglary and robbery.

defines it as, "The unlawful taking, carrying, leading, or riding away of property from the possession or constructive possession of another."[22] Examples are thefts of bicycles, motor vehicle parts, and accessories; shoplifting; pocket-picking; and the stealing of any property or article such as money or jewelry that is not taken by force or fraud. Robbery differs from theft in that it requires the use of or threat of violence. Burglary requires only that a structure be entered with the intent to commit an offense. As we discuss larceny, we will begin to appreciate the many different ways in which people steal and the vast quantities of property they take.

Of all reported offenses, larceny is the most common. About 6.6 million larcenies were reported in the United States during 2008.[23] Although this statistic is distressing, it is important to realize that there are other offenses much more harmful than larceny. Robbery, rape, and murder are relatively rare compared to larceny and cause injury, death, and fear. This is not to diminish larceny, but only to put it into perspective.

The criminal code recognizes two types of larceny. The first, petit (pronounced *petty*) larceny, usually includes the theft of items worth $50 or less. The second, grand larceny, has an almost unlimited price tag.[24] There are also two types of thieves: **opportunistic thieves** and **professional thieves.** The opportunistic thief will pick up something that is temporarily left unguarded. Typically, these thieves do not consider themselves as lawbreakers but as simply taking advantage of a situation. Opportunistic thieves tend to take expensive property and often know the people they steal from. A professional thief is a more serious offender. This person attempts to make a living from larceny and may specialize in a particular form, such as pocket-picking, shoplifting, or breaking into automobiles. The professional thief has honed his or her skills enough to steal on a regular basis without being detected or causing physical harm. Professionals may steal so much merchandise that they must work with another professional in order to fence the goods. Although relatively few in number, professional thieves account for a great deal of the property stolen each year in the United States.

Most people are not victims of professional thieves. Instead, their property is taken by the opportunistic thief.[25] Often these thieves are juveniles who steal for excitement, to obtain status symbols, or to impress others. They have not entered an antisocial lifestyle but rather are experimenting with deviance, and many quickly outgrow the behavior. There is also a range of vocational offenders that includes adults who shoplift, cheat on their taxes, or steal from their places of employment but do not consider themselves "criminals." These adults have conventional jobs and steal only on an infrequent basis and without a great deal of planning.[26]

On the other hand, professional thieves identify themselves as thieves and attempt to make a living from taking others' property. They have honed their skills to the extent

**opportunistic thief** Offenders who only steal items that are temporarily left unguarded and who do not consider themselves as lawbreakers.

**professional thief** Offenders who attempt to make a living from theft and may specialize in a particular form.

**larceny** The unlawful taking of property from another person.

◄ An opportunistic thief will pick up something that is temporarily left unguarded, such as an unlocked bicycle.

international value; art can be exchanged in any nation for any currency or item that the seller requires, often with no questions asked. This is especially useful for terrorists and gangs. For example, a stolen Picasso worth millions of dollars can be traded for several thousand dollars' worth of automatic weapons. Although the painting is worth more than the weapons, both the buyer and seller are happy with the deal. It was much easier for the seller to steal the Picasso than to come up with cash for the weapons, and the buyer got a Picasso—

that they can steal on a regular basis without being detected and without causing physical harm. The goal of the professional thief is to work without being noticed.

The world of the professional thief is difficult to penetrate. Professionals do not advertise their expertise. Often, they appear to be ordinary or even upstanding citizens and depend upon wit and guile to commit theft. The goal is to get in and get out without being discovered and without having to confront victims. The most extensive, although now dated, picture of this type of offender is in Edwin Sutherland's 1937 book, *The Professional Thief.* The offenders Sutherland studied engaged in a limited number of offenses and specialized in such activities as stealing jewelry, shoplifting, picking pockets, stealing from offices, and perpetrating confidence games. Sutherland's typology of the professional thief included such terms as "booster" (a shoplifter), "heel" (a thief who steals from stores, banks, and offices), "pennyweighter" (a jewel thief who substitutes fake jewelry for real jewelry), and "cannon" (a pickpocket). The professional thieves of the 1930s took great pride in developing the skill of taking other people's property without attracting attention.[27] They looked down upon those who were clumsy and inarticulate and who did not abide by the code of honor that often characterized their attitude toward their illegal activities. In the past, these professional thieves were looked up to in prison culture and even considered to be role models.[28]

Many modern thieves share the attitudes of those in the early 20th century. However, the romantic view of them as professionals who abide by a code of honor is no longer prevalent perhaps because thievery has become more widespread since then. In fact, one type of thievery, art theft, has become a mainstay for organized crime. Art theft is reported to be the world's third most profitable criminal enterprise, trailing behind only the drugs and weapons trades. Moving money through banking systems or even physically moving cash across borders is often difficult, so art has become useful as a medium of exchange or as a way to launder money. It also has

although one that can never be publicly displayed or sold—for a bargain.[29]

Most common thievery occurs at a lower level, however, such as the taking of a wallet or purse from a desk drawer or the theft of a child's bicycle from a yard. Anyone over the age of 60 will tell you about the "good old days" when neighbors could be trusted and fear of crime was not an everyday concern. This trust has evaporated for a number of reasons.

▼ Art theft is reported to be the world's third most profitable criminal enterprise because art is often a more convenient means of international exchange than cash.

- *Mobility.* Cars and mass transit give thieves more targets of opportunity. Not only can better transportation help thieves get to distant targets, it can also help them get away quickly and with more loot. Suburban neighborhoods and shopping malls attract shoplifters and pickpockets who come from outside the communities.[30]

- *Increasingly impersonal interactions.* Because Americans commute longer distances to work and change residences more often than ever, our interactions with both strangers and acquaintances are more frequent but less personal. These interactions are also often characterized by acquisition and exchange, rather than trust or a sense of community.

- *Lack of supervision.* The social bonds that once held communities together have been strained. Some parents, for various reasons, cannot or do not keep tabs on their children's whereabouts; law enforcement officers no longer walk beats and get to know local residents, and shop proprietors who once knew their customers have given way to suburban shopping malls where there is little relationship between buyer and seller. Consequently, thieves have greater opportunities to ply their trade with anonymity.[31]

Now let's take a look at some of the techniques professional thieves use.

## Pocket-Picking

The professional pickpocket considers himself or herself an artist. Good pickpockets must practice regularly, be proficient at spotting targets that are both potentially lucrative and accessible, and have a cover story or exit strategy that can explain their behavior if they are detected. Some pickpockets work alone, and some work in teams. Teams have highly choreographed strategies in which one pickpocket will distract the victim, while another picks the pocket and passes the booty to a third confederate, who walks away. Even if the victims discover they have had their pocket picked or purse lifted, they have a difficult time ascertaining who did it and even more trouble finding exactly who has their property. It all happens in a matter of seconds, and the victim has little chance of detecting and apprehending the thieves.

The best method for dealing with pickpockets is target-hardening, or making it more difficult for anyone to lift property from your purse or pocket. But even buttons and zippers on pockets and bags may not be enough to deter the professional pickpocket. Professional pickpockets prefer to work in large crowds where there is a lot of jostling and bumping. They may use razor blades to cut through pockets or purses and lift property without exerting any noticeable pressure. The skill they value most highly is called "the light touch," which refers to lifting someone's property without the victim even being aware the thief is near. An accomplished thief can even cut the straps of a purse and steal the whole thing without the victim knowing. Another technique is for the thief to firmly touch the victim on the shoulder with one hand while lifting the wallet from the victim's back pocket with the other.

▲ The best method for dealing with pickpockets is making it difficult to take property from your purse or pocket.

Picking pockets for a living is risky. It takes a great deal of training and skill to avoid detection, but the thief cannot compensate for all risks. The pickpocket must identify a good target—that is, one who is both vulnerable and likely to have a lot of money—and also be sure the offense is committed in a place that allows a quick escape. Many things could go wrong. The thief might select someone who is keenly aware of his or her surroundings and alert to the possibility of pickpockets lurking about. For instance, a plainclothes police officer may look like a likely target, but it would be a big mistake to attempt to pick the officer's pocket.

Another inherent risk is the possibility of being caught on a security camera. Even though the thief may be successful on one day, returning to the same shopping center or sporting arena can be extremely risky if security personnel are on the lookout for the pickpocket and his or her crew. Video evidence is extremely hard to explain away in a court of law, and the professional pickpocket can become a marked individual.[32]

## Employee Theft

Sometimes those in the best position to commit larceny are those who are the most trusted. One of the biggest problems retailers face is theft by their employees. According to the National Retail Security Survey, employee theft represents the largest category of retail losses. Employees stole $15.9 billion worth of merchandise in 2008, which represented 44 percent of the losses by retail stores that year. (By comparison, shoplifting by customers accounted for $12.7 billion.) [33] This is a staggering amount of money to lose to individuals who are being paid to look out for the retailers' best interests. Let's look at why and how a retail clerk would steal from his or her employer.

- *Large and impersonal stores.* Large chain or "big box" stores have become a dominant form of retail enterprise in the United States. Stores such as Best Buy, Walmart, and Target are national brands with thousands of retail outlets across the country. They provide low-cost merchandise to customers but at the same time often pay low wages. Many have policies designed to keep their labor costs down, such as limiting employees' work hours so they do not qualify for health insurance. Although these savings are passed on to customers, employees often find it difficult to make a living wage. High levels of employee theft under these circumstances are hardly surprising.

- *Rapid turnover of supervisors and employees.* Retail clerks do not enjoy large salaries and extensive benefit packages, so they are constantly on the lookout for new and better employment. It is difficult to develop a culture of trust and responsibility when there is a high rate of turnover of supervisors and employees. Under-qualified employees may be promoted to supervisor positions simply because they have longevity and know the store's policies and products. Supervisors are often conspirators or participants in the largest employee thefts.

- *Ineffective inventory control procedures.* Retail stores consistently struggle to control their inventory. The use of sensors to stop shoplifters is not effective in deterring employee theft. Employees are not only aware of the various security devices, but they are also often responsible for implementing these safeguards. Therefore, they are in an ideal position to steal from a store because they represent "the fox inside the chicken coop." Although large retail stores go to great lengths to prevent employee theft, they have yet to find effective ways of protecting their inventory from those responsible for pricing, stocking, and selling.

- *Organized crime.* Various criminal organizations target retail establishments. These range from highly sophisticated crime syndicates that go after numerous retail outlets to small, localized groups that affect only one store. By placing several confederates in a large retail store, organized crime can arrange to have a tractor trailer truck backed up to the loading dock ready to drive away with thousands of dollars worth of merchandise. A good deal of planning goes into such heists, and by forging documents, using the company's own trucks, and altering the video cameras and tape, thieves are able to accomplish their goals leaving little or no evidence. Some use bribery and corruption to compromise those who should be overseeing the inventory.

- *Organized employee theft.* There are also less sophisticated forms of organized employee theft. A teenager who works in a store may steal merchandise to sell to friends below

cost. By switching price tags and scanning the wrong bar codes, a determined employee can move a great deal of merchandise without being detected. Similarly, a security guard can allow friends to walk out of the store carrying large amounts of merchandise they can later resell.[34]

Retail stores use several strategies to control employee theft. Video technology is particularly popular.[35] Some convenience stores allow managers to keep track of several locations at once via the Internet, either by watching in real time or by checking on previously recorded events, as well as by verifying receipts against stock.[36] Many companies use polygraph (lie detector) examinations, drug testing, and background checks, including researching applicants on the Internet, to attempt to ensure they are hiring honest employees.[37] Most large retail chains have security staff members who specialize in detecting employee theft and shoplifting.[38]

## Shoplifting

Shoplifters take millions of dollars worth of products from stores every year. They range from children experimenting with risky behavior to sophisticated gangs of professional thieves who make their living stealing goods to sell at a discount to their clients. According to the National Association of Shoplifting Prevention (NASP), the primary reason for shoplifting is to "get something for nothing." However, it is not always that simple. Some individuals use shoplifting as a response to other problems. According to NASP, shoplifting is a "substitute for loss" for some who perceive they were unfairly deprived in some way, such as by divorce, serious illness, death of a loved one, loss of income from a job or investments, or an unexpected expense that makes them feel needy. Stealing a bottle of shampoo, for example, can temporarily help the shoplifter relieve anxiety about his or her financial situation and provide a feeling of control. For other offenders, shoplifting is "justified payback" for all they feel they give to others and for which they receive little in return. For still others, it is a "relief mechanism" for anxiety, frustration, boredom, or depression.[39]

When considered this way, shoplifting becomes a much more complicated and puzzling activity. Because it is such a widespread and expensive offense, it bears scrutiny from a critical perspective so we can understand not only how it happens, but also how to better prevent it.

NASP is made up of representatives from retail stores who collect information about the frequency and techniques of shoplifting. According to NASP, shoplifting is an expensive concern for the retail industry.[40] About $13 billion worth of goods—roughly $35 million per day—is stolen from retailers each year.[41] Here are some facts from NASP about shoplifting in the United States.

- Shoplifting does more than harm the offender's record and reputation. It overburdens the police and the courts, adds to stores' security costs, raises the price of goods, and deprives local communities of thousands in sales tax dollars that could be put to work on behalf of the public.

▶ Shoplifters range from children experimenting with risky behavior to professional gangs who steal goods to sell at a discount. In this photo, a law enforcement officer shows goods recovered from a shoplifting ring.

■ Shoplifting is often not premeditated, and there is no typical shoplifter. Men and women shoplift about equally as often. Habitual shoplifters steal nearly twice per week. Many shoplifters buy and steal merchandise in the same visit.

■ Approximately 25 percent of shoplifters are youths, and 75 percent are adults. Fifty-five percent of adult shoplifters say they started in their teens.

■ Shoplifters commonly steal from $2 to $200 per incident depending upon the type of store and item(s) chosen.

■ Shoplifters say they are caught an average of only once every 48 times they steal. They are turned over to the police 50 percent of the time.

■ Approximately 3 percent of shoplifters are professionals who steal for resale or profit as a business. They include drug addicts who steal to feed their habit, hardened professionals who steal as a lifestyle, and international shoplifting gangs who steal for profit.

■ Most shoplifters are non-professionals who steal as a response to social and personal pressures and not with criminal intent or out of financial need or greed.

■ "Getting away with it" produces a chemical reaction shoplifters describe as a "rush" or "high." Many seek this high as their reward, rather than the merchandise itself. Some drug users say shoplifting is as addicting as drugs. More than half of adults and 33 percent of juveniles say it is hard for them to stop shoplifting, even after getting caught.

■ Most non-professional shoplifters do not commit other types of offenses. For example, they would not steal a mobile phone from an acquaintance's house and would return a $20 bill a stranger dropped. Their lawbreaking is restricted to shoplifting, so any rehabilitation program should be specific to the offense.[42]

As this list shows, shoplifting is not just about getting something for nothing. For many, it is a means of working out deep or **antisocial** tendencies. Shoplifting addicts can be categorized as *kleptomaniacs,* who cannot control their urge to

><**THINKBACK**
antisocial (ch. 1)—
Following standards of behavior intended to harm society and individuals.

steal. They are driven to shoplift by unconscious psychological pressures, and some suffer the same types of conditions as people with severe depression and eating disorders. Their theft is not purpose-driven as it is for normal shoplifters. The Mayo Clinic provides the following information about kleptomania.

> Most people with kleptomania steal from public places, such as stores and supermarkets. Some may steal from friends or acquaintances, such as at a party. Often, the stolen items have no value to the person with kleptomania. The stolen items are usually stashed away, never to be used. Items may also be donated, given away to family or friends, or even secretly returned to the place from which they were stolen. In rarer cases, people with kleptomania may repeatedly pilfer the same kinds of items, such as undergarments. In these cases, the kleptomania may include an element of fetishism.[43]

Kleptomania is a medical problem, but there is no standard treatment. Those suffering from kleptomania may attend psychotherapy, be prescribed a variety of drugs including antidepressants and mood stabilizers, or meet with self-help groups.

For juveniles, shoplifting presents a different set of circumstances. Rather than being a way of acquiring material objects or a result of mental illness, juveniles often shoplift because of peer pressure. Groups of young people will dare each other to take the risk of getting caught as a method of establishing status and respect. Young shoplifters will often take things they do not need simply to fit into the group or gang. Juvenile shoplifters who are not involved in a group have a different sort of motivation. These lone shoplifters may engage in risky behavior due to a need to feel empowered or to strike back at society. Like other types of shoplifters, they may steal things of little value as a symbolic way of showing the world, their peers, or their parents that they have some sort of power or autonomy. This is especially true when they feel angry, depressed, unattractive, or unworthy.[44]

Although shoplifting has always been a problem, stores have developed ways to protect themselves. One major retailer, Target, has its own crime laboratory complete with fingerprint, computer forensic, and video analysis labs to deal with organized-crime-related thefts.[45] A number of electronic and other technological devices have been designed to deter or catch shoplifters. However, the loss this illegal activity incurs is still in the billions of dollars a year. Despite efforts by retail associations and organizations such as the NASP, it is difficult to determine what has been lost to shoplifters and what has been lost to employees who steal. Merchandise has simply disappeared, and it is often preferable to think it was lost to shoplifters rather than dishonest employees.

## Fraud

**Fraud** is a known misrepresentation or concealment in a transaction made with the intent to deceive another. Two types of fraud related to larceny are credit card theft and check fraud. Although the UCR neither typifies these types of fraud as property offenses nor collects statistics on them, we cover them here because they involve the taking of money with less trickery than other fraud schemes.[46]

> ## LO3:
> **Describe** how check fraud and credit card theft are forms of theft.

### Credit Card Theft

Credit and debit cards allow their users to make purchases without having to carry much cash. They also enable purchasers to keep records of their financial transactions and purchase items and services and defer payment for months or years. Although many credit card holders abuse their cards and find themselves deep in debt, for the most part, this form of retail payment is a substantial convenience. Debit cards are very similar to credit cards, except they do not allow users to amass debt. They work much like checks in that the bank accounts they are attached to must be funded enough to cover the purchases immediately. A retailer will not honor a debit card without sufficient funds. Credit and debit cards have become increasingly popular and in 2004 began to outnumber the number of check payments for retail goods and services.[47] Both forms of payment are subject to theft and fraud.

Credit card theft is a billion-dollar industry.[48] Cards and the information on them can be stolen in two primary ways. First, the physical card can be stolen and used. This is perhaps the most clumsy method because once the card owner realizes the card is stolen, he or she can phone the credit card company

and have the card discontinued. The second type of offense is to steal the information on the card and not the card itself. This is a much more subtle way to accomplish credit card theft because it might be days or even weeks before the card owner realizes the card number is being used by someone else. Credit card information can be stolen via the Internet—for example, when a card owner enters the card's information to make a purchase from a retail site—or via a method called "skimming." Skimming relies on a device much like the legitimate swipe devices retailers use to read the card's information. The thief's skimmer, however, has a small memory device that records the card's information for later use. These devices are portable and can be worn by the thief—for example, a restaurant worker who accepts a patron's credit card can surreptitiously swipe the card through a skimmer attached to his or her belt before running it through the restaurant's legitimate device—or the device can be attached to ATM machines and disguised as legitimate equipment.[49]

The ability of thieves to commit both low-tech and high-tech larceny makes credit card theft a complicated phenomenon. It is a flourishing industry for reasons that have much to do with the credit card companies' desire to make their products easily accessible to users. Credit card companies do not use some security measures that would make credit card transactions absolutely safe because they deem them too cumbersome and inconvenient for the public. Therefore, the card companies are willing to accept a certain amount of fraud as a business expense in order to offer their customers more convenience. Unfortunately, those who are victimized by credit card thieves have their financial lives severely disrupted. A thief can wreck an individual's credit score, and it can take months or even years for the victim to re-establish good credit. Although credit card companies typically do not hold card users responsible for illegitimate charges, the hassles users experience in dealing with the theft may still be significant.

▼ **Some credit card skimming devices are portable and can be carried or worn by thieves.**

**fraud** A known misrepresentation or concealment in a transaction made with the intent to deceive another.

# theory to practice

### Responding to Check Fraud

Although financial transactions are becoming increasingly electronic and performed with credit and debit cards, many individuals and businesses still rely on checks to move money between accounts, make purchases, and pay employees. Therefore, individuals and institutions must take a number of precautions to limit their exposure to check fraud.

1. Make sure your bank provides you with the latest tamperproof checks. They will have watermarks, holograms, or other features that make them difficult to copy. Although sophisticated offenders always look for ways to overcome advances in security, the types of checks available from most banks today can frustrate occasional and opportunistic offenders.

2. Keep your checks secure. At the office, lock them in a drawer. Do not leave your checkbook in your car. A significant period of time can pass before you discover a check has been stolen from the middle of your checkbook.

3. Be very careful about whom you give your checking account numbers to. E-mail or telephone scams may be difficult to detect. Be careful not to broadcast your account numbers by cell phone because most wireless devices do not provide the level of security necessary to protect financial dealings.

4. Do not mail your bills from your personal mailbox. Take them to the post office and personally place them into the secure mailbox. Thieves sometimes cruise around neighborhoods looking in mailboxes for checks they can alter.

## THINKING *in* ACTION

Do you take any other types of precautions when writing checks? If so, what are they?

## Check Fraud

Another type of offense related to theft is check forgery and the cashing of bad checks. Cashing bad checks is often known as "bouncing a check," "check kiting," or "writing a check with insufficient funds" (see *Theory to Practice* for a closer look at the different types of check fraud). Let's look at some of the more popular variations.

- *Forgery.* Criminals who steal wallets and checkbooks will attempt to match the owner's signature in order to write checks out of the account. Vigilant banks and retail outlets try to prevent this type of fraud by insisting that those trying to cash checks provide photo identification. However, sophisticated offenders alter photo identifications by putting their own picture in. It is almost impossible to stop the sophisticated forger at the retail level.

- *Counterfeiting and alteration.* Making counterfeit checks has become relatively easy to do with computers, scanners, and color copiers. Counterfeiters have access to the same typefaces and fonts that check printers use, so they can produce realistic-looking checks. They can also alter checks that have already been issued by using chemicals to change the payee's name or the amount. This procedure is called "spot alteration" or "check washing" and is relatively easy for the determined forger to accomplish.

- *Paperhanging.* Paperhanging is the writing of checks on closed accounts. By the time the check makes it to the bank, and it is discovered that the account is closed, the paperhanger is long gone.

- *Check kiting.* Check kiting involves opening accounts at more than one bank and writing checks that float between them. Because it takes some time for a check to clear from one bank to another, offenders can obtain money before it is discovered that there are insufficient funds in the account upon which the check was written.

These techniques have been used for a long time and are becoming more complicated as banks' technological sophistication grows. Although the instantaneous electronic transfer of funds may make it more difficult for offenders to pass bad checks, some offenders are still quite bold. In January 2010, a Tennessee man pleaded guilty to cashing an altered $1.8 million check drawn on a Canadian company's account. The check had originally been made out to IBM, but the payee's name was altered to allow the offender to cash the check.[50]

Both criminal and civil penalties are attached to writing bad checks. Each state has its own laws, but all require the offender to repay the initial amount plus fines and court costs. For instance, the criminal penalty for writing bad checks in the state of Florida can draw up to five years in prison or a $5,000 fine for a felony, or up to $1,000 or one year in jail for a misdemeanor.[51] Still, many states offer a grace period of up to 30 days to allow unintentional bad-check writers to address mistakes and oversights. Many people keep small balances in their checking accounts and inadvertently bounce checks because of math errors. However, many people purposefully attempt fraud by writing checks on accounts with insufficient funds or false accounts.

In a classic study, Edwin Lemert identified two types of check forgers. The most common is the naive check forger who does not believe his or her actions will hurt anyone. Because retail establishments want to make transactions simple and friendly, the naive check forger seizes the opportunity to obtain quick money with little risk. The problems come later when the police put together the patterns of naive check forgers and make an arrest.

The second type of check forger Lemert identified is the systematic forger who makes a living passing bad checks. The systematic forger has several techniques such as making counterfeits, altering legitimate checks by changing the amount or the name of the payee, writing checks on closed accounts hoping the time required for processing will allow him or her to collect the money before the check can be canceled, and using someone else's identity to invade their checking account.[52] It is difficult to separate the system-

# doubletake

## So Bad He's Good

Sometimes a case so captivates the public's imagination that a former offender becomes a celebrity. Such is the case of Frank Abagnale (pronounced *ah-bahg-NALL-ee*), a check forger who passed $2.5 million in forged checks throughout the United States and 26 other countries. Abagnale's story is unique because he also assumed false identities that enabled him to work as a lawyer, a medical doctor, and an airline pilot.

Abagnale's story captured the public imagination for many reasons. Steven Spielberg's film about Abagnale's life as a check forger, *Catch Me If You Can,* portrayed him as a likable guy who never physically harmed anyone. Moreover, he used his wit and guile not only to forge checks, but also to talk his way out of tight spots. However, Abagnale's post-conviction history is as fascinating as his criminal history. He was so good at forging

▲ Frank Abagnale passed $2.5 million in forged checks throughout the United States and 26 other countries.

checks that the FBI hired him to help catch check forgers. Because of his expertise, imagination, and diligent hard work, he has been successful in catching numerous check forgers and con artists and in keeping the FBI abreast of new ways to forge checks.

Recognized as one of the foremost experts on check fraud, Abagnale speaks to law enforcement agencies, financial institutions, and the general public around the world about his life as a criminal offender who has redeemed himself. According to Abagnale, the way to deal with bad checks is not through law enforcement because convictions are so rare, but rather through prevention. To this end, he has developed several solutions to bad checks, including his Super-BusinessCheck which contains 15 safety features, including special watermarks, inks, numbers, fibers, and other markings.

Although some people may find it disturbing that a former offender can achieve celebrity status, Abagnale's case is so unique that it deserves some understanding. As Steven Spielberg said, "I did not make this film about Frank Abagnale because of what he did . . . but because of what he has done with his life the past 30 years."[1]

[1]Luke Mullins, "How Frank Abagnale Would Swindle You," *US News & World Report,* May 19, 2008, http://www.usnews.com/blogs/the-collar/2008/5/19/how-frank-abagnale-would-swindle-you.html; Abagnale & Associates, http://www.abagnale.com/index2.asp.

## THINKING *in* ACTION

Do you agree with Abagnale that the best way to deal with check fraud is through prevention rather than law enforcement? Could this philosophy be successfully extended to other forms of financial fraud, such as debit card fraud? Why or why not?

atic forger from the naive forger. The successful systematic forger can pass many checks without being noticed. If apprehended, he or she can appear to be a sloppy and neglectful naive forger, and a pattern of massive check fraud can remain undiscovered. (See *Doubletake* for the story of perhaps the most successful check forger ever.)

The problem of bad checks may one day become a thing of the past as people stop writing as many checks as they used to. Credit and debit cards and online banking are becoming the new media of financial transactions. This, of course, has led to abuses in these new forms of commerce even as the writing of bad checks decreases.

# Think about it

## Remember

Recall the various ways that check fraud is perpetrated.

## Understand

Identify the reasons and techniques that are involved when a retail clerk steals from his or her employer.

Describe the differences between opportunistic thieves and professional thieves.

## Evaluate

Determine the best method for dealing with pickpockets.

## Motor Vehicle Theft

Motor vehicle theft is the stealing or unauthorized taking of a motor vehicle, an automobile, truck, motorcycle, or any other motorized vehicle allowed on public roads and highways. Since 1993, the rate of motor vehicle thefts has been declining (the data collected by the FBI includes attempted thefts).[53] However, motor vehicle theft continues to

**LO4:**

**Evaluate** why motor vehicle theft continues to be a significant problem.

be a significant problem that inconveniences thousands of automobile owners each year. The Insurance Information Institute reports that:

- A motor vehicle is stolen in the United States every 28.8 seconds. The odds of a vehicle being stolen were 1 in 210 in 2006 (the latest year for which data are available, based on Insurance Information Institute calculations), with the odds for theft being highest in urban areas.[54]

- According to the FBI, U.S. motor vehicle thefts fell 13.4 percent between 2007 and 2008. (See Figure 9.3.)

**Figure 9.3   Vehicle Theft Rate by Region, 2007 and 2008**

Nationwide, the rate for motor vehicle theft fell 13.4 percent between 2007 and 2008, with slight drops in each region.

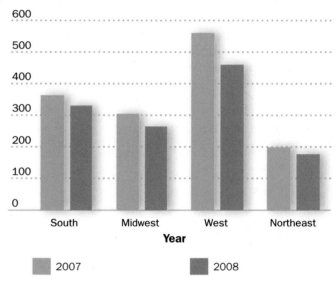

Rate of Theft per 100,000

*Source:* Federal Bureau of Investigation, *Uniform Crime Reports: Crime in the United States, 2008,* "Table 4: Crime in the United States by Region, Geographic Division, and State, 2007–2008," http://www.fbi.gov/ucr/cius2008/data/table_04.html.

In the Old West, horse thieves were hanged. The punishment was harsh for two reasons. First, horses were a major investment, usually a person's most expensive possession. Often, having a horse was necessary for a person to work, whether that meant traveling to a job or running a farm. The second reason was that having a horse often meant the difference between life and death. A settler deprived of his horse out on the prairie or in the mountains would find it hard to survive. The horse was absolutely essential to settlers' ability to negotiate the physical environment.

Although we do not execute car thieves, motor vehicle theft is still considered a serious offense for many of the same reasons horse theft was. Cars and trucks represent a significant financial investment for individuals, perhaps the largest they make aside from the purchase of a home or a college education. Public transportation is not as well developed in the United States as in other industrialized nations, making the automobile an often essential mode of transportation. People depend on their cars to get to work, to help them do their work, and to perform necessary housekeeping duties, such as driving children to school and shopping for groceries. Much as the horse was indispensable in the Old West, the automobile is essential to the American lifestyle.

When a person's car is stolen, there is an additional injury to those individuals who have an affinity for their automobile that makes it a very personal piece of property. Some people go to great lengths to customize their cars and have an intense relationship that they do not feel toward other items they own. Therefore, a stolen car can cause intense feelings of loss. Certainly not all cars elicit the same response. Most car insurance companies cover theft, and some people welcome the opportunity to buy a new car. Professional automobile thieves are very selective about which cars they steal. Often they choose cars based on the market value of their parts. Some garages, called "chop shops," use parts from stolen vehicles so they do not have to buy new parts. According to the National Insurance Crime Bureau, the ten most often stolen passenger vehicles in 2008 were:

1. 1994 Honda Accord
2. 1995 Honda Civic
3. 1989 Toyota Camry
4. 1997 Ford F-150 Pickup
5. 2004 Dodge Ram Pickup
6. 2000 Dodge Caravan
7. 1996 Jeep Cherokee/Grand Cherokee
8. 1994 Acura Integra
9. 1999 Ford Taurus
10. 2002 Ford Explorer[55]

All these cars are several years old, but they are attractive to thieves because they are best-selling models, and many of their parts are interchangeable. It is simply a matter of volume rather than desirability. However, a chopped car or a car sold as stolen goods may bring only a few thousand dollars. A recent tactic of professional thieves that allows them to get almost the full price for the car is "car-cloning." Thieves will steal a desirable, nearly new car and take it across the state line. Then, at a large car dealership, they will find a car identical to the stolen car and copy down the vehicle identification number (VIN). The thieves make a replica of the VIN tag and exchange it for the one in the stolen car. After

▼ Motor vehicle theft is considered a serious offense, and automakers often build security devices into their products.

forging some documents to acquire ownership papers, the thieves can now sell the practically untraceable car to an unsuspecting buyer. This is all possible because states cannot access each other's motor vehicle databases.[56] In 2007, the FBI broke up an international car-cloning ring operating out of Tampa, Florida, that had sold vehicles in 20 states and several other countries.[57]

Amateur thieves go about stealing cars in a different way. Rather than looking for automobiles that can be sold as parts or going to the trouble of "cloning" a car, the amateur thief chooses targets based upon status and personal taste. Sexy sports cars and luxury cars are the most likely targets. Or the amateur might be simply looking for a joyride. Many cars are taken and driven extremely fast around the neighborhood then dumped before the perpetrators can be discovered. Sports cars and luxury cars are also the target of professional thieves who steal to order. Sometimes, these cars are taken to other nations and sold, a type of theft glamorized in the movie *Gone in 60 Seconds*. Tractors and heavy construction equipment are also targets of this kind of theft because they are so expensive. Because motor vehicles are such expensive items, manufacturers and law enforcement officials go to great lengths to safeguard their property.

The prevention of motor vehicle theft relies on a number of strategies. A combination of new technologies, better-informed law enforcement agencies, and common sense on the part of motorists has reduced the number of stolen cars. Technological efforts to prevent motor vehicle theft include the following.

- *Locking devices.* The best-known locking device is The Club, a steel bar that clamps onto the steering wheel and makes the car impossible to steer. It is a visual deterrent to automobile thieves because disabling the device requires cutting through steel or picking a secure lock. Either way, this requires more time and effort than thieves are usually willing to devote to the task. They are more likely to move on to another automobile that is not so well protected. Another type of locking device is a hood restraint, which keeps the hood from being opened and prevents "hot wiring" of the car. A third type of device is a steering column collar that protects the ignition from being compromised. Tire and wheel locks wrap around the tire or wheel and immobilize the car. Finally, gearshift locks prevent the transmission from being shifted into gear.

- *Cut-off devices.* Cut-off devices are switches that either disable the ignition or halt the flow of fuel to the engine. An ingenious protection from all but the most sophisticated thief, they are spliced into the ignition wires or fuel system and are not visible.

- *Alarms.* Alarms are designed to make a lot of noise so a potential thief will leave without breaking into the vehicle. Designs include sensors that are connected to the door, windshield, windows, and trunk. Should any of these be disturbed without the alarm being turned off, a loud, irritating noise will be emitted. At a more sophisticated level, alarms that sense motion, vibration, and ultrasonic fields operate in much the same way. One problem with these types of alarm systems is that they often sound when people innocently pass by without intending to disturb the automobile. False alarms are so numerous that they might be more irritating to the car owner's neighbors than useful in preventing motor vehicle thefts.

- *Tracking devices.* The homing signal emitted by a tracking device allows the car to be located after it is reported stolen. Tracking devices are sold by private companies that coordinate with law enforcement agencies so cars can be recovered. The best-known device is the LoJack, which notifies the monitoring center if the car is started by means other than the use of the ignition key. Some of the more sophisticated tracking devices have the ability to disable the automobile via satellite if it is reported stolen. This could be very inconvenient for a thief who is attempting to elude law enforcement agencies and finds that the car suddenly stops.

# Think about it

## Understand

Identify the two most common reasons that motor vehicles are stolen.

## Create

Formulate a list of techniques for preventing motor vehicle theft.

## Arson

**Arson** is the deliberate setting of fires. Fewer arsons are committed than other types of property offenses, but arson is still a serious problem. According to the FBI, 62,807 arsons were reported in 2008. The average dollar loss per arson was $16,015, but this can be misleading. For instance, for industrial and manufacturing buildings, the average dollar loss was much higher at $212,388.[58] The deliberate setting of fires may result not only in financial loss, but also in loss of life. Because arson is such a serious property offense, it is an exception to the FBI's hierarchy rule. If an arson is committed in a set of offenses, both the arson and the most serious offense in that set of offenses (such as murder) are reported.[59] However, the difficulty of distinguishing between arson and accidental fire-setting makes the determination of homicide by arson difficult to pin down.[60]

The problem of fire-setting stretches across time and cultures. Some of the oldest English common laws define arson

## LO5:

Assess why arson is an exception to the FBI's hierarchy rule.

as the offense of burning another person's dwelling. In 11th-century England, untended fires became such a problem, William the Conqueror banned evening cooking fires with the law of *couvre feu* (cover the fire), which evolved into the modern "curfew," or the banning of any activity after a specified hour.[61]

People deliberately set fires for a number of reasons, and it is worth exploring these motivations in order to suggest ways that arson can be prevented. Motivations for arson include but are not limited to the following.

- *Insurance claims.* Many, if not most, structures are insured. In order to get a mortgage for a home, the owners must prove they have insurance that protects against damage, including fire. When individuals get behind on their mortgage payments and are in danger of losing their home, they may be tempted to burn it down in order to recover, through insurance, whatever equity they have in it. In some areas, the home's value may have fallen well below the insurance coverage, and it makes more financial sense to burn the home down than attempt to sell it. The burning of structures for insurance claims has evolved into such a profitable activity that organized crime has become active in it. Banks are motivated to be complicit in these types of arsons because, like the homeowner, they profit from collecting on inflated insurance coverage of structures that have lost much of their value. The trick to recovering on such claims is to make the fire look accidental. To this end, a person who is a "professional torch" is hired to make the fire look like an accident. It takes an experienced arson investigator to distinguish between accidental fires and arson. One of the primary questions asked is, "Who benefits from this fire?"[62]

- *Profit.* Fighting fires, and recovering and rebuilding afterward, can provide opportunities for individuals to make money. Those who supply bulldozers, mobile food canteens, and other support mechanisms for firefighters have a vested interest in arson. This is especially true in rural areas with national forests and few employment opportunities. In some areas, volunteer firefighters are paid extra to fight fires and thus are tempted to start them. The millions of dollars brought into an area for fighting large fires can offset much of the financial damage done by fires once insurance claims are paid out.[63] Thus, arson investigators will consider the possibility of arson for profit.

- *Thrill-seeking.* Some fires are set for entertainment. Fires can be fascinating to watch as they consume buildings, and some people experience a hypnotic thrill not only from the fire itself, but from the response of fire departments. Sirens and flashing red lights can be stimulating, almost in a sexual way, to some arsonists. To experience this thrill, it is necessary to be in the right place at the right time as fires occur. The only way to achieve this consistently is to set the fires.

- *Hate crimes.* Some fires are set for revenge or intimidation. Individuals in socially marginal groups, such as minorities or those who engage in alternative lifestyles,

**arson** The deliberate setting of fires.

have been targeted by bigots in a number of ways. One of the more extreme messages socially intolerant people send to those who move into a neighborhood is arson. Although victims may be outraged at the injustice, the need to protect their families can be a powerful motivator to move. In terms of revenge, few activities send a stronger message than burning down the business that laid you off or the apartment building you were evicted from. Such arsons not only do financial damage, but they also put lives at risk.[64]

This list of motivations for arson is not exhaustive. There are many other reasons someone might set a fire to achieve financial or emotional rewards. However, one category of arson deserves greater scrutiny here because it is so different and so prevalent: that of juvenile fire-starters.

A 2009 incident in Waterville, Maine, in which nine youths and young adults ranging in age from 14 to 20 threw Molotov cocktails (bottles filled with gasoline) inside an old building is an interesting example of the juvenile fire-starter phenomenon. The youths in this case were so proud of the damage they caused they videotaped the incident, set it to heavy metal music, and posted it on the Internet, complete with a list of credits.[65] Although posting the video on the Internet gives this story an interesting twist—apparently the youths were unconcerned that any authority figures or law enforcement would be able to find the video—this style of offense is not uncommon for juveniles. In fact, juvenile fire-starters can be divided into four types.

1. *Those who play with matches.* These children do not necessarily commit arson, but the results can still be disastrous. Children can be warned against playing with matches and learn to use them responsibly. However, many are tempted by the excitement of fire and either intentionally or accidentally set fires that get out of control. One study found that elementary children through fourth grade who play with matches are more likely to have divorced parents and come from disrupted family backgrounds. For the most part, these are normal children who could be referred to counseling or fire-safety instruction. Without such proper supervision and education, they often become victims of the fires they start.

2. *Cry-for-help fire-setters.* This type of fire-setter deliberately engages in arson. He or she gets personal satisfaction and pleasure from arson and is more likely to **recidivate.** Often a precipitating event can be identified, such as losing a pet, changing a school or residence, or not being allowed to attend a social function. Fire-setting is a way to deal with the frustration and stress. Cry-for-help fire-setters are also sometimes reacting to physical, psychological, or sexual abuse. The child usually acts alone, setting fire to his or her bed, the parents' clothes, or something else that symbolizes the child's anger. There is also a relationship

> **✕ THINKBACK**
>
> recidivism (ch. 1)—Repeat offending. *Also* recidivate.

between this type of fire-setter and bedwetting (enuresis). These children are psychologically more troubled than those in the playing-with-matches category and require an appreciation for their distress, as well as counseling.

3. *Delinquent fire-setters.* Delinquent fire-setters are often engaging in malicious mischief. Because they deliberately set fires, recidivism is higher than in other categories of juvenile arson. Motivations include the desire to commit acts of vandalism, the need to cover other offenses for which the evidence is being destroyed, and a search for excitement. Peer influence often contributes to this type of arson. Although younger children in this category set small fires, teenagers can go to great lengths to set larger fires that do a great deal more damage. One primary target of delinquent fire-setters is school buildings. Such fires are usually set on weekends by students who have had negative experiences in the school or by other juveniles who have a grudge against someone who attends the school.

4. *Severely disturbed fire-setters.* The severely disturbed fire-setter has deep emotional problems and views fire as a way of rebelling against authority or expressing unresolved psychological issues. There are two types of severely disturbed fire-setters. The first is the impulsive neurotic, who is impatient and reckless and tends to destroy his or her own possessions. The second type is the borderline psychotic, who experiences extreme mood swings, uncontrolled anger, violence, and numerous phobias. This type of fire-setter may also have severe family problems such as parents who use drugs, or other psychological issues such as sleep disorders or severe headaches. The severely disturbed fire-setter is more likely to engage in numerous other forms of delinquency than youths in the other

▼ Arson, an exception to the FBI's hierarchy rule, is a serious problem because it may result in both financial loss and loss of life.

three categories. Treatment can include extensive therapy and sometimes placement in a secure institution. In older teenagers, involvement with the juvenile justice system is seen as necessary to control this type of destructive behavior.[66]

Although this typology of juvenile fire-setters is not exhaustive, it illustrates important differences in the motivations, behavior patterns, and treatment of juveniles who commit arson. It is important to note that without proper treatment many will graduate into adult fire-setting patterns that can become much more problematic as they become more proficient and aggressive.

# Think about it

## Apply

Illustrate the connection between arson and curfew laws.

## Evaluate

Justify why juvenile fire-starters deserve special scrutiny when motivations for arson are considered.

## Create

Formulate methods to control arson based on arsonists' motivations.

# Summary

**LO1:** **Recognize that burglary requires both the entering of a structure and the offender's intent to commit a felony or theft.**
- Because of the FBI's hierarchy rule, a burglary may or may not be recorded in the UCR depending on the offense that is committed along with it.
- Burglaries tend to lack much of the danger and fear that accompany violent personal offenses. Most burglars want to avoid confrontation with the victim and will strike when it appears no one is around.

**LO2:** **Understand how larceny is different from burglary and robbery.**
- Larceny is the legal term for theft. It is different from robbery in that it requires the use of or threat of violence. Burglary requires only that a structure be entered with the intent to commit an offense.
- Thieves come in two varieties. The opportunistic thief will pick up something when it is temporarily left unguarded. A professional thief attempts to make a living from larceny.

**LO3:** **Describe how check fraud and credit card theft are forms of theft.**
- Common strategies of professional thieves are pocket-picking, employee theft, shoplifting, writing bad checks, and credit card theft.

- Fraud is a known misrepresentation or concealment in a transaction made with the intent to deceive another.
- Credit card fraud and check fraud involve the taking of money with less trickery than other fraud schemes.

**LO4:** **Evaluate why motor vehicle theft continues to be a significant problem.**
- Motor vehicle theft is the stealing or unauthorized taking of a motor vehicle, an automobile, truck, motorcycle, or any other motorized vehicle legally allowed on public roads and highways.
- Public transportation is not well developed in the United States, so cars and trucks are a significant financial investment for individuals. Most auto thefts are of common cars that are stolen for their parts.

**LO5:** **Assess why arson is an exception to the FBI's hierarchy rule.**
- Arson is the deliberate setting of fires. Because arson is such a serious property offense, it is an exception to the FBI's hierarchy rule in that it is reported separately from the most serious offense in the hierarchy.
- There are four types of juvenile fire-starters: those who play with matches, cry-for-help fire-setters, delinquent fire-setters, and severely disturbed fire-setters.

# Questions

1. What is the most frequent criminal offense?
2. What is the major distinction between property offenses and personal violent offenses?
3. What is it about the American attitude toward property that contributes to property offending?
4. Think of three offenses that could be committed during a burglary. How would the FBI's hierarchy rule apply to each?
5. How does larceny differ from burglary or robbery?
6. Name three types of common larcenies.
7. Why is motor vehicle theft considered such a serious offense?
8. Discuss the exception of arson to the FBI's hierarchy rule.

# 10

# Criminal Offenses Against

# what's inside

People

**As you read, keep in mind these learning objectives:**

**LO1:** Compare and contrast the common sources of violence.

**LO2:** Discuss three common sources of violent crime that stem from the human body and mind.

**LO3:** Evaluate common social and cultural sources of violent crime.

**LO4:** Define violent crime.

**LO5:** Explain the difference between homicide and murder.

**LO6:** Assess some of the problems with the definition of rape as it applies to males and females.

**LO7:** Consider the primary difference between robbery and other offenses involving theft.

**LO8:** Identify the difference between assault and battery.

**A**ggression is the basic ingredient in violent crime. Why are humans sometimes aggressive? Some scholars believe human **aggression,** an offensive action that is a psychological or physical encroachment without the consent of the other party, is learned. Others believe it is genetic and that human beings, as well as many other types of animals, have evolved to be aggressive in order to survive. From this viewpoint, aggression is not a pathological but a normal, often necessary, response to the world.[1]

▼ Some scholars believe aggression is genetic and that human beings, as well as many other types of animals, use aggression to survive.

Scholars recognize two broad types of aggression: active and passive. *Passive aggression* manifests itself in the form of refusals: refusal to speak, refusal to move, refusal to perform a task. The passive-aggressive person takes offensive action by not acting. **Violence** is *active aggression,* that is, physical force with intent to cause fear or to injure, harm, or kill. Psychologist Seymour Feshbach distinguished between two types of aggression: hostile/expressive aggression and instrumental aggression. The purpose of *hostile/expressive aggression* is to draw attention to oneself or to something else or to make victims suffer for the sake of suffering. Much violent crime stems from hostile/expressive aggression. The purpose of *instrumental aggression* is to attain status or resources that belong to others.[2] The criminal offense of robbery is a kind of instrumental aggression, as is war. As an alternative to Feshbach's dichotomy, psychologists Brad J. Bushman and Craig A. Anderson suggest a continuum of aggression since criminal offenses can have multiple motives. Such a continuum is shown in Figure 10.1.[3]

Aggression, then, is the source of violence, but not all aggression is violence. We can see this difference in the distinction between **burglary** and robbery. Burglary is the illegal entry of a structure with intent

><THINKBACK
burglary (ch. 3)—The unlawful entry of a structure with the intent to commit a felony or theft.

**aggression** An offensive action; psychological or physical encroachment without the consent of the other party.

**violence** Aggressive physical force with intent to cause fear or to injure, harm, or kill.

## Figure **10.1**   The Continuum of Aggression

Hostile/expressive aggression draws attention or makes victims suffer for the sake of suffering. Instrumental aggression seeks to attain status or resources that belong to others. An offense—robbery or murder, for example—may fall anywhere along the continuum.

**Hostile/Expressive Aggression**
To Make Others Suffer

**Aggression**

**Instrumental Aggression**
To Take What Belongs to Others

Terrorism

Robbery

to commit a felony or theft. Robbery is forcibly taking an item from another person. Burglary, although aggressive, is not violent. Robbery is both aggressive and violent.

This chapter will focus on criminal offenses that involve violence: **murder, forcible rape, robbery,** and aggravated **assault.** The perpetrators of these offenses are both aggressive and violent. Although not all aggression is antisocial—imagine an especially exciting football game—acts of violence, except in the case of self-defense and police actions, certainly are.

## Sources of Violent Crime

Common sources of violence include psychological abnormality, substance abuse, evolutionary factors, and socialization and cultural values. Some violent crime involves instrumental aggression. A burglar who enters a dwelling intending only to steal a television set might find himself in a fight with the resident who surprises him. In this situation, both combatants are fighting for a reason: The burglar is fighting to get away or to disable the resident in order to steal the television set, and the resident is fighting to disable or frighten away the burglar. Some violent crime, however, includes what we often call "senseless" violence—for ex-

**><THINKBACK**

**murder (ch. 3)**—Willful homicide.

**forcible rape (ch. 3)**—Sexual intercourse performed without the victim's consent through force, threat of violence, or intimidation.

**robbery (ch. 3)**—The taking or attempting to take anything from another person or persons by violence or the threat of violence.

**assault (ch. 3)**—The criminal offense of attempting to inflict immediate bodily harm or making another person fear that such harm is imminent.

ample, when a store clerk, a homeowner, or a person walking down the street is attacked or killed for no apparent reason. Is such violence instrumental or hostile/expressive? The shooting with no apparent motive of a young man on a street corner seems hostile/expressive to those who learn about it on the nightly newscast. But it makes perfect instrumental sense to the gang member who shot the man to gain status in his gang.

Violent crime has many causes, all of which are located somewhere on the continuum from hostile/expressive to instrumental. See Table 10.1 for a look at three types of criminological theories that address violent crime: subculture of violence theory, feminist theory, and evolutionary theories. Each set of theories contains ideas about the reasons for violent crime that range along the continuum of aggression. For example, some aspects of the subculture of violence theory

## LO1:

**Compare** and contrast the common sources of violence.

▼ Some violent crime includes "senseless violence"— when a crime is committed for no apparent reason.

## Table **10.1**  Criminological Theory and Offenses Against People

| | |
|---|---|
| These three sets of theories are examples of how criminological theory can explain violent offending. Other theories discussed in this text may be used the same way, but, for the sake of brevity, these three are discussed here. | |
| **Subculture of violence (sociological theory)** | Violence is instrumental to achieving status and protecting oneself in a subculture that is not bound by the dominant culture's rules. Subcultures in which violence is common are often rooted in poverty. With an absence of legitimate ways to achieve success and status, violence against other people is highly valued. In addition, the willingness to use violence for self-protection against predators is essential. |
| **Feminist theory (critical theory)** | Feminist theories of criminology consider how the patriarchal nature of society encourages men to use violence against women. By having rigid social roles that are determined by gender, the status of women is one of reduced opportunity and service toward men. As women seek greater freedom and control of their own lives, husbands, boyfriends, and fathers often do not easily give up what they believe is their cultural heritage of dominance. The resulting physical, psychological, and sexual abuse that women experience has been a focus of feminist theories of violence. In addition, new research on the concept of masculinity sheds light on how men are systematically taught and encouraged to use violence not only in relationship to the women in their lives, but also as a means of establishing their identities with peers. |
| **Evolutionary theories of violence (biological theory)** | Violence is so pervasive in human societies that some criminologists attribute it to heredity. Instead of being maladaptive violence, for example, forced sexual behavior may be conducive to spreading genes. Violence is a reproductive advantage that has allowed aggressive individuals to produce more offspring than those who are less aggressive. These evolutionary theories of crime suggest that violence is deeply embedded in human nature. Critics of evolutionary theories contend that they give too much credit to nature (biological genes) and not enough credit to nurture (social environment). |

lie more toward the hostile/expressive end of the continuum (making others suffer to draw attention to oneself), whereas others lie more toward the instrumental end (using violence to achieve status and success).

Please keep in mind that the following typologies are broad and are not meant to explain every possible source of violent crime. The best predictor of whether a person will commit a violent or non-violent criminal offense is past behavior, regardless of mental or biological state.[4] The more frequently and regularly a person acts violently, the more predictable his or her violent behavior will be.[5]

## Physical Sources of Violent Crime

Physical sources of violent crime can be traced to human biological/psychological processes and events. Three common sources of violent crime that stem from the human body and mind are mental disorder, substance abuse, and evolutionary factors. Let's examine each of these in detail.

**LO2:**

Discuss three common sources of violent crime that stem from the human body and mind.

### Mental Disorder

**Mental disorder** is a broad term used for a variety of psychological diseases and abnormalities. It is also called mental illness. People with mental disorders have problems coping with daily life and making simple, rational decisions. There are many types and degrees of mental disorder, and some mentally disordered people are more affected by their condition than others. Research has found that individuals within the offender population are three times more likely to have a mental disorder than individuals within the general population, although many experts believe this statistic is a better indicator of the poor state of the nation's mental health system, which we will discuss later, than it is of the likelihood of the mentally disordered to break the law.[6] Although having a mental disorder is not generally an indicator of violent criminality—that is, mentally disordered people as a group are no more likely to commit violent offenses than those with no mental disorder—people suffering certain severe disorders *are* more likely to become violent.[7]

The four types of mental disorders most likely to be associated with violent crime are schizophrenic disorders, paranoid disorders, mood disorders, and antisocial personality disorder.[8] Although each is briefly described here, it is important to understand that these disorders are complicated, often difficult to diagnose, and still not completely understood.

**mental disorder** Term used for a variety of psychological diseases and abnormalities. Mental illness.

▲ There are many types and degrees of mental disorder. It is difficult in the cases of some offenders—such as Theodore Kaczynski, popularly known as the Unabomber—to determine whether an offender is truly mentally disordered.

■ *Schizophrenic disorders.* According to the *Diagnostic and Statistical Manual of Mental Disorders (DSM IV),* a diagnosis of **schizophrenia** includes delusions, hallucinations, disorganized speech, grossly disorganized behavior, and inappropriate affect (facial expressions and behavior). To be diagnosed with schizophrenia, the subject must experience a decline in his or her social and daily living abilities before the onset of the condition (for instance, a tidy person becomes very slovenly and disorganized). The disorder must also be continuously present for six months. According to mental health scholars, schizophrenic people are at an increased risk to commit violent offenses, especially homicide.[9]

■ *Paranoid disorders.* The major symptom of paranoid disorders is realistic delusions, or delusions that are physically possible but unlikely. Someone may be convinced that a foreign government is listening to his or her telephone calls, for instance. Although this is possible, it is unlikely. (An *unrealistic* delusion, the type associated with schizo-

**schizophrenia** A mental disorder that includes delusions, hallucinations, disorganized speech, grossly disorganized behavior, and inappropriate affect.

phrenia, might be that the government of Mars is listening to the telephone calls.)

■ *Mood disorders.* These are also called affective disorder, bipolar depressive disorder, and major depressive disorder. Symptoms include an extremely depressed mood indicated by sluggish mental and physical activity, deep despair, and sometimes thoughts of suicide that persist for at least two weeks.

■ *Antisocial personality disorder.* **Antisocial personality disorder,** according to psychologist Robert Hare, is revealed by a person's lack of respect for others, impulsivity, lack of remorse, irresponsibility, disrespect for social norms and the law, irritability, extreme aggression, and inability to hold a job or maintain a relationship. This diagnosis is reserved for adults; children exhibiting these symptoms are considered to have *conduct disorder.* More males than females are diagnosed with this disorder.[10]

>< THINKBACK
antisocial personality disorder (ch. 5)—A mental disorder characterized by a pattern of disregard for the rights of others, as well as impulsive, violent, and aggressive behavior without guilt.

Most mentally disordered offenders are incarcerated for minor and non-violent offenses, and many professionals in both criminal justice and psychology have criticized the use of the criminal justice system as a "dumping ground" for mentally disordered people who would be better served by treatment than incarceration. In many major cities, more mentally disordered people can be found in jail than in mental hospitals.[11] Some critics point to cuts in public funding for mental treatment and increases in funding for prisons and jails as part of the reason. Many mentally disordered people who cannot afford treatment thus go without it until they break the law and wind up within the criminal justice system.[12]

## Substance Abuse

The relationship between substance abuse and violent crime is complex. Offenders who use illegal drugs commit robbery and assault more frequently than offenders who do not use illegal drugs, although no known substance directly causes people to become violent or break the law.[13]

However, there is a relationship between substance abuse and criminal offending. A 2002 federal study found that more than two-thirds of jail inmates were dependent on or abusers of alcohol or drugs.[14] The substances most associated with crime include marijuana, heroin, cocaine, PCP (phencyclidine), amphetamines, methamphetamine, ecstasy (MDMA), rohypnol, alcohol, inhalants (typically glue and paint solvents), and some pharmaceuticals. Most of these items are illegal (marijuana, heroin, and cocaine); however, some have legitimate uses (inhalants, pharmaceuticals, and some of the ingredients in methamphetamine). The

## Figure **10.2**    Alcohol or Drug Use at Time of Offense Among Convicted Jail Inmates, by Type of Offense, 2002

Alcohol use is a more common element in violent offending (with the exception of robbery), whereas drug use is more closely related to property offending.

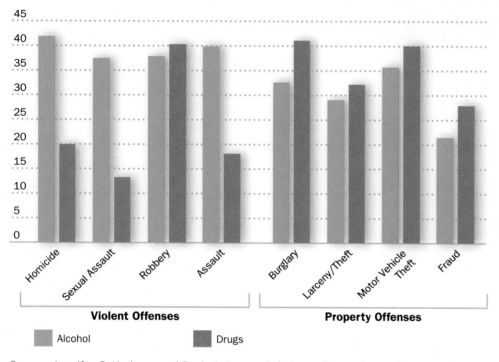

**Percentage of Use at Time of Offense**

Violent Offenses · Property Offenses

■ Alcohol          ■ Drugs

*Source:* Jennifer C. Karberg and Doris J. James, *Substance Dependence, Abuse, and Treatment of Jail Inmates, 2002* (Washington, DC: U.S. Department of Justice Bureau of Justice Statistics, 2005), 1, http://bjs.ojp.usdoj.gov/content/pub/pdf/sdatji02.pdf.

only listed substance that is legal to buy for the purpose of becoming inebriated is also the one most closely associated with violent crime: alcohol.

Some studies suggest that a reduction in the availability or consumption of alcohol would actually reduce violent crime.[15] Alcohol has been found to be more closely related to violent crime than drug use (see Figure 10.2).[16] A 1998 federal study found that "nearly 4 in 10 violent victimizations involve use of alcohol . . . and about 4 in 10 offenders, regardless of whether they are on probation, in local jail, or in state prison, self-report that they were using alcohol at the time of the offense."[17] In a sample studied by the Panel on the Understanding and Control of Violent Behavior, "alcohol drinking—by the perpetrator of a crime, the victim, or both—has immediately preceded at least half of all violent events, including murders."[18] The reason for these relationships is unclear. Is alcohol more likely to cause its users to become violent? Are violent people more attracted to alcohol? Or is alcohol simply the easiest substance to procure and therefore more common?

Alcohol appears to interfere with the brain functions responsible for self-control, although inebriation alone is not

responsible for violence.[19] Usually some other cognitive or situational factor is present—for example, a location where violence is more likely such as a bar or large party, or the inebriated person's belief that alcohol will make her violent so she becomes violent when drunk.[20] In fact, National Incident-Based Reporting System (NIBRS) data show that about 70 percent of alcohol-related violent incidents occurred at a residence, usually after 11 PM.[21]

Two factors related to the substance use/violent crime complex are sex and mental disorder. Not only is alcohol inebriation more likely to be associated with violent crime than drug inebriation, this is especially true among female offenders. Women are less likely than men to commit violent offenses but five times more likely to be drunk when they do.[22] Substance abuse is responsible for more violent crime than mental disorder.[23] However, diagnoses of substance abuse often co-occur with diagnoses of mental disorder in offenders. A study conducted in the San Francisco County jails found that 78 percent of the homeless inmates with a severe mental disorder also had substance-abuse problems. These inmates were also held in jail longer than inmates who had been charged with similar offenses.[24] So, although substance abuse is not a cause of violent crime, it is often one factor among many responsible for violent offending.

### Evolutionary Factors

The study of the effect of evolutionary factors on behavior and societies is a relatively new discipline called **sociobiology.** Its premise is that human social behavior, including antisocial tendencies, evolved for specific reasons much as the human body has. According to psychologists Joshua Duntley and Todd Shackelford, "Just as [natural] selection shaped physiological adaptations with specific problem-solving functions, it also shaped the structure of thoughts, preferences, desires, attitudes, and emotions to guide behav-

**sociobiology** The study of evolutionary factors on behavior and societies.

iors toward solving historically recurrent problems that affected reproductive fitness."[25] Generally, the sociobiological approach to explaining crime is that antisocial behavior is not pathological; it exists because humans evolved antisocial tendencies for specific reasons. Exactly what these reasons are—as well as the relationship between the brain, society, behavior, and crime—is currently under research. Here we look at some of the current scholarly approaches to the relationship between human evolution and violent crime.

As an exercise, let's take a sociobiological view of Terrie Moffitt's theory of life-course-persistent and adolescent-limited offenders from Chapter 7. From an evolutionary standpoint, neither type of offending is pathological, but rather each has a biological purpose. Adolescent-limited delinquent males engage in antisocial behavior as a response to competitive mating disadvantages. Their behavior is not genetic but social. For some reason, these young males are having trouble attracting mates, and they engage in antisocial behavior as a way to compete with more successful males. The behavior of life-course-persistent male offenders, however, might have a genetic basis. The strategy is the same, to compete for mates, but the life-course-persistent male offender is genetically obligated to compete for mates in this fashion. The idea is that a society composed primarily of prosocial individuals leaves a niche for the antisocial individual who propagates his genes in an exploitative, non-reciprocating fashion.[26] This very brief, simplified example offers an idea of how sociobiology seeks to explain violent crime.

Duntley and Shackelford summarize some sociobiological explanations for violent crime.[27]

- *Violence and murder.* Violence and murder are ways to take resources or social status from rivals or eliminate rivals altogether. A fit competitor who inflicts more damage on rivals than he or she sustains is considered by others to be difficult to exploit and therefore has better access to resources and mates. The murder of rivals has an evolutionary purpose beyond disposing of them for resources: It eliminates the possibility of the victim's further reproduction, thus preventing the further spread of his or her genes; it hurts the victim's existing offspring by depriving them of the parent's protection and aid; and it hurts the victim's other close kin by marking them as easy to exploit and depriving them of the victim's social status and aid in group survival. For example, the murder of a kin group's primary hunter would deprive that group of the hunter's food contributions.

- *Intimate partner violence.* Both women and men use aggression and sometimes violence to maintain their reproductive relationships. Men tend to hide their partners and use threats and violence against romantic rivals. Women tend to enhance their appearance to demonstrate to their partners their desirability to other men. Although these strategies often resolve conflicts between men and women so they can successfully reproduce, both men and women may use aggression in a bid to defend their relationships when these strategies fail.

- *Rape.* The idea that rape is an evolutionary reproductive strategy is controversial. The hypothesis is that males use rape to spread their genes frequently and successfully by forcing their offspring upon women of their choosing. This strategy, however, has social and individual costs. It not only damages the women physically and psychologically, but it also prevents them from choosing the mates they believe are most reproductively fit.

Perhaps the most obvious critique of the sociobiological explanation of crime is that it does not explain why, if being antisocial is evolutionarily valuable, humans classify so many antisocial behaviors as criminal offenses. Across generations, nations, and cultures, the same set of violent behaviors—murder, assault, rape, robbery—tend to be classified as crime and bring harsh sanctions. Although these behaviors may benefit individuals from a natural selection standpoint, human societies loathe them if they are unchecked by laws. One reason may be that violent antisocial behavior tends to benefit individuals while harming society. The murder of a good hunter in a small hunter/gatherer tribe may allow the killer to claim the hunter's social and material resources, but the whole tribe is worse off for the loss of a productive member. On the other hand, if the entire tribe is composed of antisocial individuals who cannot cooperate because they are so busy taking advantage of one another, the tribe will be unable to exist for very long, and none of its members' genes will survive. Antisocial individuals, then, occupy a survival niche. Like parasites, their success depends on their peers' pro-social abilities. A group can sustain some antisocial behavior from some members, but when the behavior occurs too often (repeated assaults) or is too severe (murder), the group defines the behavior as "crime" and seeks to deal with the offender.

## Social and Cultural Sources of Violent Crime

Common social and cultural sources of violent crime include family dysfunction, social disorganization, and some subcultural values. Like biological sources of violent crime, social and cultural sources are contributing factors and are rarely, if ever, the sole sources of violent crime.

**LO3:**

Evaluate common social and cultural sources of violent crime.

### Family Dysfunction

Although families are considered the bedrock of American society, sometimes they simply do not work. Dysfunction in families can occur for several reasons—poverty, parental abuse, juvenile delinquency, substance abuse, or disagreements among family members—all of which, in some cases,

▶ One common source of violent crime is family dysfunction.

can lead to violence. Although violence within families used to be considered a "family problem" and the business of the family patriarch, it is now usually treated as a public safety issue and falls within the purview of the criminal justice system. Violence that stems from families can strike at two classes of victim: those within the family and those outside it. This type of violence can occur solely against each victim class, which is relatively rare, or, most commonly, against both classes.

- *Family victimization only.* Family members are victimized by one or more family members. This violence does not extend outside the family. For instance, one spouse beats the other and/or the children. However, neither the victimized spouse nor the children victimize strangers.

# doubletake

### The Bloody Benders

The Bender family allegedly murdered between 8 and 12 people at their inn on the Osage Trail near what is now Cherryvale, Kansas, in the early 1870s. Not much is known about the family, which is thought to have immigrated from Germany. The family, John Bender Sr., his wife Kate, their son John Bender Jr., and their daughter, also named Kate, appeared to have set up their inn and grocery store to attract wealthy travelers, whom they would kill, rob, and then bury in their orchard.[1]

In early 1873, local residents noticed that the Benders' inn seemed to be abandoned. By this time at least 11 people had disappeared. Upon searching the inn and grounds and discovering dead and emaciated livestock and signs of a hurried departure, the townspeople assumed the Benders were victims of the unknown killers thought to be stalking the area. However, a more thorough search revealed not only the bodies buried in the orchard, but also a trapdoor in the house that led to a cellar covered in dried blood.

The Benders' technique was fairly straightforward. The front room—said to be where daughter Kate held séances—was divided by a curtain. The victim would be enticed to sit with his or her back to the curtain and would then be distracted, probably by Kate. One of the men hidden on the other side of the curtain would hit the victim on the head with a hammer and drop the body through the trapdoor to the cellar, where his or her throat would be slit to ensure death.

At least two vigilante groups searched for the family, and the governor of Kansas offered a $2,000 reward. Although sightings of the family were reported for several decades, they were never found.[2]

[1] A. N. Glennon, "When the West Was Really Wild," *U.S. Stamp News* 7, no. 2 (March 2001): 30; R. H. Adleman, *The Bloody Benders* (New York: Stein & Day, 1970).

[2] Kansas State Historical Society, "Cool Things, Bender Knife," http://www.kshs.org/cool2/benderknife.htm.

## THINKING *in* ACTION

Families who work together as serial killers are extremely rare. Think of reasons why this is so.

- *Family victimization leading to extra-family victimization.* Family members are victimized by one or more family members. These family members in turn victimize strangers or may become victimized by strangers. For instance, an abused child beats up other children at school or becomes the victim of bullying.[28]

- *Extra-family victimization only.* Family members are not violent with one another but violently victimize strangers. These cases are rare but have been documented (see *Doubletake* for the story of a murderous Kansas family). However, chances are, those who are violent outside their families are also violent or have experienced violence within their families.

## Social Disorganization

According to **social disorganization theory,** disorganized areas, such as impoverished neighborhoods, lack the social controls that prevent violence. These controls include both formal and informal institutions and range from the local government, police, and community organizations, to businesses, schools, and churches, to families, informal clubs, and neighborhood groups. The weaker these institutions are, the more disorganized the area. According to some theorists, it is this social disorganization that leads to crime.

Generally, theories of social disorganization and crime state that such attributes as income inequality, trust and involvement among neighbors, and social stability all affect an area's general level of crime as well as its level of violent crime. Social disorganization can affect all types of violence, including stranger violence and acquaintance violence, both hostile/expressive and instrumental. One study even found that any form of social instability in neighborhoods becoming more wealthy as well as those becoming impoverished led to more violent crime simply because of the lack of social stability.[29] Yet another study connected violence to personal income inequality: People who believed they were not making enough money felt shamed and disrespected and denied access to the traditional means of status and respect.[30]

## Subcultural Values

We find a final major source of violent crime in some of the values held by subcultures. Subcultures can hold the values of the dominant culture as well as some of their own values that defy those of the dominant culture and that the dominant culture would define as negative. In 1958, criminologist Walter Miller suggested a set of traits he called **focal concerns** that he

**>< THINKBACK**
social disorganization theory (ch. 6)—The idea that the breakdown of social bonds and the failure of social institutions cause crime.

**>< THINKBACK**
focal concerns (ch. 6)—Attitudes that the lower classes perpetuate as a part of the values and norms they believe are necessary for survival in their neighborhoods.

believed some subcultures perpetuate as a part of their values and norms. These traits include trouble (the ability to get into and out of trouble), toughness, smartness, excitement, fate, and autonomy (independence from authority). Although these are not necessarily violence-prone traits, they are not crime or violence averse. The ability to handle trouble is often the ability to handle breaking the law. Being tough, while also pursuing excitement and thumbing a nose at authority, can lead a person into crime or at least into interpersonal violence.

In some subcultures, the desire to maintain personal honor can also lead to violent crime. Avoiding a physical fight after an insult or a slur may incur unacceptable damage to a person's honor. One study found that, contrary to social disorganization theory, social organization in some cultures, specifically in the South and West, can actually lead to more violence if that social organization is particularly concerned with personal honor. If the culture does not consider violence a deviant response in some situations, then more violence will occur.[31]

## Think about it

### Remember
List three physical sources of violent crime.

### Understand
Why may a dysfunctional family life lead an individual to violent behavior?

### Analyze
Summarize the argument that sources of violent crime are embedded in lower-class subcultures.

### Evaluate
Critique the proposal that violent crime may be an evolutionary adaptation.

## Types of Violent Crime

The Uniform Crime Reporting (UCR) program of the Federal Bureau of Investigation (FBI) defines violent crime as offenses that include the use of force or threat of force. The FBI recognizes four violent criminal offenses: murder and non-negligent manslaughter, forcible rape, robbery, and aggravated assault. The FBI estimated that nearly 1.4 million violent offenses occurred in 2008, or about 455 violent offenses per 100,000 people. Most were aggravated assault (see Figure 10.3 for a comparison of the

**LO4:**
**Define** violent crime.

## Figure **10.3**   Comparison of Violent Offenses, 2008

According to the FBI, of the total number of violent offenses reported in 2008, aggravated assault accounted for 60.4 percent; robbery, 32 percent; forcible rape, 6.4 percent; and murder 1.2 percent.

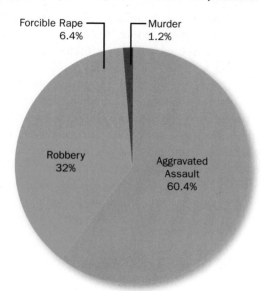

*Source:* Federal Bureau of Investigation, *Uniform Crime Reports: Crime in the United States, 2008,* "Violent Crime," http://www.fbi.gov/ucr/cius2008/offenses/violent_crime/index.html.

number of offenses).[32] The violent crime rate varies by region (see Figure 10.4); it is highest in the South and lowest in the Northeast.

## Murder

The FBI defines **murder** and non-negligent manslaughter as the willful killing of one human being by another (for the sake of brevity, we will refer to murder/non-negligent manslaughter as murder). The FBI's classification of an offense as murder for the UCR is based on police investigation only and not on the determination of courts or medical officials. *Justifiable homicide*—the killing of a felon by a peace officer in the line of duty or the killing of a felon during the commission of a felony by a private citizen— is not counted in these statistics. Therefore, from a statistical standpoint, the number of murders in the United States is determined by the police.

> **>< THINKBACK**
> murder (ch. 3)—Willful homicide.

> **LO5:**
> **Explain** the difference between homicide and murder.

What distinguishes murder from homicide and manslaughter? **Homicide** is simply the killing of one human

**homicide** The killing of one human being by another.

## Figure **10.4**   U.S. Regional Crime Map of Violent and Property Offenses per 100,000 Inhabitants

Both the violent and property offense rates are highest in the South and lowest in the Northeast.

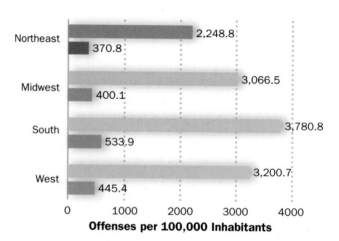

Violent Offenses       Property Offenses

*Source:* Federal Bureau of Investigation, *Crime in the United States: 2008,* "Region," http://www.fbi.gov/ucr/cius2008/offenses/standard_links/regional_estimates.html.

being by another, regardless of intent.[33] A person can kill another person without meaning to, as in an automobile accident. Therefore, all murders and manslaughters are homicides, but not all homicides are murders or manslaughter. Some homicides are legal, as in the cases of self-defense, war, and execution. Manslaughter is a bit more complicated, and the definition varies from state to state. Generally, **manslaughter** is the unlawful killing of another human being

**manslaughter** The unlawful killing of another human being without criminal intent.

without criminal intent, as in the heat of passion (such as in a bar fight); during the commission of a felony; or by omission of action, such as failing to follow proper safety rules. *Vehicular manslaughter* falls into this last category. *Negligent manslaughter* (which the FBI considers as serious as murder) typically involves willful negligence of a duty. For example, a surgeon who performs an operation while inebriated and kills the patient might be charged with negligent manslaughter.

## Murder and the Law

Although the broad definition of murder applies to all states and the federal government, some specific laws differ among the states and federal government. The federal government recognizes two degrees of murder: first and second. Some states recognize a third degree and/or offense called "felony murder."

- *First-degree murder* is typically deliberate and premeditated murder planned and carried out in conjunction with felonies such as rape, burglary, or arson. Killing certain people such as children, police officers, and correctional staff can also bring an automatic first-degree murder charge. The specific criteria for first-degree murder differ slightly by state, and the federal government has its own definition. See Figure 10.5 for the federal definitions of first-degree and second-degree murder, as well as sentencing. State laws are usually some variation on this definition.

- *Second-degree murder* is usually an action in which the victim's death is neither intended nor planned but is a probable result. Imagine, for instance, a bar fight in which

▶ First-degree murder is typically deliberate and premeditated. Here, law enforcement officials remove a victim from a house.

### Figure **10.5**   U.S. Criminal Code: Murder

**OFFENSE**

Murder is the unlawful killing of a human being with malice aforethought. Every murder perpetrated by poison, lying in wait, or any other kind of willful, deliberate, malicious, and premeditated killing; or committed in the perpetration of, or attempt to perpetrate, any arson, escape, murder, kidnapping, treason, espionage, sabotage, aggravated sexual abuse or sexual abuse, child abuse, burglary, or robbery; or perpetrated as part of a pattern or practice of assault or torture against a child or children; or perpetrated from a premeditated design unlawfully and maliciously to effect the death of any human being other than him who is killed, is murder in the first degree.

Any other murder is murder in the second degree.

**SENTENCING**

Whoever is guilty of murder in the first degree shall be punished by death or by imprisonment for life;

Whoever is guilty of murder in the second degree shall be imprisoned for any term of years or for life.

one person breaks a beer bottle over another's head, killing the victim. The assailant did not mean to kill the victim but did so in the heat of the moment. State laws vary on the definition of second-degree murder.

- *Felony murder and third-degree murder.* Some states have special felony murder laws to prosecute murders that happen during the course of a felony, for instance, if a

robber accidentally shoots and kills a convenience store clerk. Some states recognize some manslaughter offenses as third-degree murder or may even combine the felony murder and third-degree murder offenses under one definition. The definition of these types of murder, or even their classification as types of murder, varies by state.

Murder sentencing in the states varies greatly depending on the circumstances of the murder and state law. The sentence for first-degree murder in most states and the federal government is often life in prison or the death penalty. Second-degree murder and some types of manslaughter charges usually bring sentences of many years. According to some research, the offender's sex and race can affect sentencing, as can jurors' sex, race, age, and religion.[34] The victim's sex may also affect sentencing. A 2004 study found a "white, female victim effect" in which defendants in **capital murder** cases—those in which the murder offense, sometimes called a capital offense, is punishable by death—were more likely to receive a death sentence.[35]

Typically, the severity of sentencing is linked to offender actions that aggravated the murder. Aggravating factors like rape, the victim's status (such as a child or police officer),

the use of firearms, and the involvement of illegal substances can push the sentencing from a number of years to the death penalty. A follow-up study to the 2004 research discussed above found that female-victim murder cases may be more frequently selected for capital prosecution because female victims are more likely to be considered vulnerable and also seen as not contributing to their murders. Such cases are also more likely to have severe aggravating factors, especially rape.[36] Other factors that bring the death penalty into the picture include multiple victims, presenting a serious risk to others, murder committed during another serious offense, violence in the offender's history, murder committed for the sake of money, and the use of torture.[37]

Some factors can mitigate the offense. One study found that jurors in a capital murder case were less likely to sentence an offender to death in the case of:

- unmedicated schizophrenia in which the defendant suffers severe delusions and hallucinations
- drug addiction and inebriation at the time of the offense
- a childhood diagnosis of borderline intellectual disability
- severe parental physical and verbal abuse during childhood[38]

## Figure 10.6    Murder Offenders by Race and Age, 2008

**Although more blacks are arrested for murder up to age 29, more whites are arrested for murder after age 29. Also note that the arrests drop for both categories with the increase in age.**

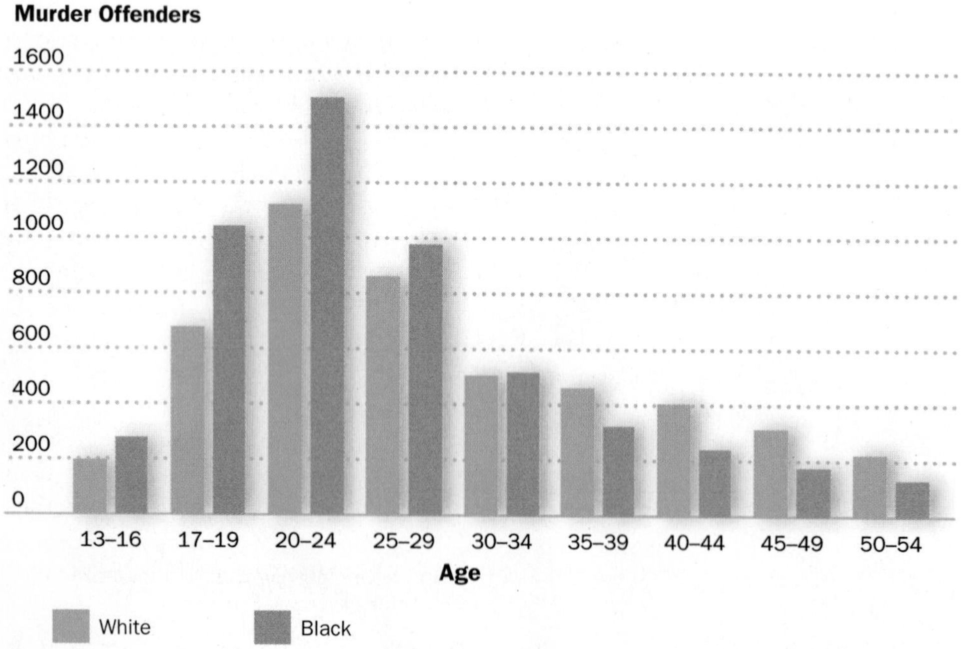

**Murder Offenders**

Source: Federal Bureau of Investigation, *Uniform Crime Reports: Crime in the United States, 2008*, "Expanded Homicide Data Table 3: Murder Offenders by Age, Sex, and Race, 2008," http://www.fbi.gov/ucr/cius2008/offenses/expanded_information/data/shrtable_03.html.

Although these mitigating factors were discussed in a single study, they are a good example of the factors the court may consider in a murder case, especially one involving the death penalty.

## Offender Characteristics

According to the FBI, those most often arrested for murder are blacks between the ages of 9 and 29. After the age of 29, it is whites who are most often arrested for murder (see Figure 10.6). Most suspects are also male. As you will recall, the police determine these statistics, which represent arrests and not convictions. It is possible that clearances by arrest (clearance occurs when a suspect is arrested, charged, and turned over to the court for prosecution) are significantly affected by police discretion and victim characteristics, that is, the more sympathetic the victim, the harder police work to clear the

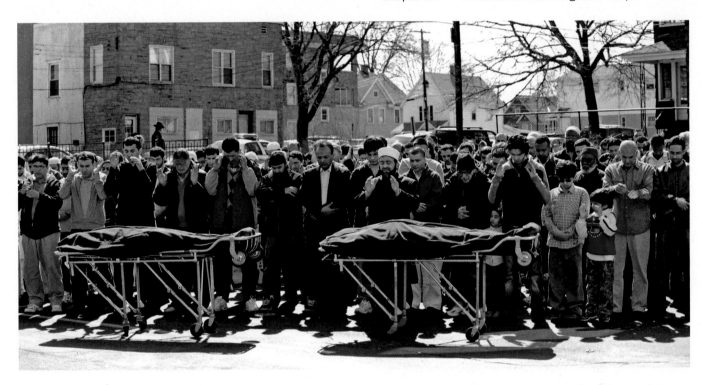

▲ Mass murder is the killing of three or more people in a single incident. Here, friends and family pray over the bodies of Layla Khalil and Parveen Ali, both victims of the April 2009 shooting at the American Civic Association building in Binghamton, NY, where 11 other people were shot dead by a gunman who later killed himself.

case.[39] One analysis found that murder cases with female or young victims were more likely to be cleared, as well as those including drug- or gang-related activities. However, research has found that the presence and type of physical evidence and witnesses are more important than victim characteristics. Incident characteristics such as inebriated offenders, acquaintance between victims and offenders, weapons, and the number of recent or simultaneous serious violent offenses significantly increased the odds of clearance.[40]

We know most serious violent offenses are committed by young males, but could violent offenders have a different way of thinking than non-violent offenders or law-abiding people? Some researchers have reported cognitive differences in extremely violent and murder offenders. They find some similarity between these offenders and people with damage in the orbitofrontal region of the brain, which is responsible for memory, reward-pursuit, and decision-making.[41] Still, this area of brain study is only just beginning, and researchers are careful about connecting brain activity to antisocial behavior (see *Theory to Practice*).

## Mass and Serial Murder

The most common definition of **mass murder** is the killing of three or more people in a single incident. Some criminologists recognize a subcategory of mass murder called *spree murder,* in which a killer takes the lives of several victims at successive locations within a longer period of time than a mass

murder—for example, over a period of a few days or weeks—but a shorter period of time than serial murder. **Serial murder** is the killing of a sequence of victims committed in three or more separate events over an extended period of time. Serial murderers can kill several victims over a very long time, decades even, with relatively long periods between each killing. See Table 10.2 for examples of each type of murderer.

Although mass, spree, and serial murderers have long caught the public's imagination and have sold countless novels, films, and other media since the 19th century, such offenders are relatively rare.[42] (However, at least one study says the annual number of serial murders is underestimated because some missing people are never reported as such.)[43] Their rarity is one reason these types of offenses get so much media attention and remain in the public memory long after the killers are locked away or executed. Although the offenders are often romanticized—while in prison, serial killer Ted Bundy received bags of mail from female fans—their activities may be what the public finds most intriguing.

**capital murder**  A murder offense that is punishable by death. Sometimes called a "capital offense."

**mass murder**  The killing of three or more people in a single incident.

**serial murder**  The killing of a sequence of victims committed in three or more separate events over an extended period of time.

# theory
## to **practice**

### Skeletons in the Closet

> Lizzie Borden took an axe
> and gave her mother forty whacks.
> When she saw what she had done,
> she gave her father forty-one.

One August day in 1892 in Fall River, Massachusetts, Lizzie Borden called out for help to the family maid, who ran downstairs to discover Lizzie with the body of her father, Andrew, who had been "hacked almost beyond recognition." After the town had been alerted, a neighbor who arrived to comfort Lizzie found the body of her stepmother, Abby Borden, who had also been hacked to death. Lizzie, 33, was tried and acquitted, but not only does she remain the most likely suspect, she was also convicted in the popular imagination.[1] Lizzie's case is not helped by the fact that she was but one descendant in a long line of alleged murderers, including Thomas Cornell who was hanged for the 1673 murder of his mother, Rebecca, an ancestor of Cornell University founder, Ezra Cornell.[2]

It is tempting to consider such anecdotes as proof that violent behavior is hereditary. However, if violent behavior were found to originate from the body, it is possible that violent tendencies could be inherited much like eye color. As discussed in Chapter 5, researchers think the functioning of the prefrontal cortex and the amygdala may be connected to violent behavior. Other researchers are looking at genetics, especially the gene responsible for the enzyme MAOA. As you will recall, variants of this gene have been found to be connected to antisocial behavior, depending on environment (see discussion of neurotransmitters in Chapter 5).

Was the family that produced Lizzie Borden and Thomas Cornell itself the victim of a wayward gene or dysfunctional brain structures? What about other members of this family? Were they violent, too, committing deeds that history failed to record?

Enter the Fallon family. A few years ago, the mother of University of California neuroscientist Jim Fallon told him about the possibility of murderous relatives—she had heard some stories about the Fallon side of the family—and asked her son to look into it. After all, Fallon's specialty is the biological basis of antisocial behavior. Was it true that the Fallon branch of the family harbored a lineage of murderers?

When Jim Fallon discovered his family's direct relation to Lizzie Borden, Thomas Cornell, and at least five other alleged murderers, he decided to look a little deeper. Using brain scans and blood samples from himself, his wife, their three children, and his three brothers, Fallon looked for signs of psychopathy and behavioral problems: low activity in the prefrontal cortex and the high-aggression MAOA gene. Everyone's brain scan showed normal activity, and all carried the low-aggression MAOA gene. All, that is, except for one person: Fallon himself. His brain scan not only showed abnormally low cortex activity, he also carries the high-aggression MAOA gene. Fallon told National Public Radio, "If you look at the [brain] scan, I look just like one of those killers."[3]

In the case of biological research into antisocial behavior, a large gulf remains between theory and practice. The research into the effects of brain functioning on antisocial behavior is promising, but much remains to be understood about how nature and nurture interact. Fallon admits that his biological signposts point to a violent, antisocial person. Although Fallon is known in his family for somewhat impulsive, risk-taking behavior—for example, when in Kenya, he took his teenage son fishing in a lion-infested area—he is neither antisocial nor violent. For this, Fallon credits his nurturing: "I had a charmed childhood," he says. "If I'd been mistreated as a child, who knows what might have happened?"[4]

It is possible, then, that Fallon's "Cousin Lizzie," as he calls her, got a bum rap. After her trial, Borden and her sister bought a fine home in Fall River, where Lizzie lived until her death at age 67 in 1927, never harming a soul.[5]

[1]Doug Linder, "Famous Trials: The Trial of Lizzie Borden," 2004, http://www.law.umkc.edu/faculty/projects/ftrials/LizzieBorden/bordenaccount.html.

[2]Cornell University Press, *Killed Strangely: The Death of Rebecca Cornell*, http://www.cornellpress.cornell.edu/cup_detail.taf?ti_id=3824.

[3]Barbara Bradley Hagerty, "A Neuroscientist Uncovers a Dark Secret," National Public Radio (NPR), June 29, 2010, http://www.npr.org/templates/story/story.php?storyId=127888976.

[4]Gautam Naik, "What's on Jim Fallon's Mind? A Family Secret that Has Been Murder to Figure Out," *Wall Street Journal,* November 30, 2009, http://online.wsj.com/article/SB125745788725531839.html.

[5]Linder, "Famous Trials: The Trial of Lizzie Borden."

## THINKING
## *in* ACTION

If Dr. Fallon's brain and DNA are similar to that of other murderers, why does he lead a pro-social life? Discuss the reasoning behind your answer.

## Table **10.2**    Types of Murderer

| | Murderer | Year(s) Active | Incident | Outcome |
|---|---|---|---|---|
| **Mass Murderers** | Charles Whitman | 1966 | Shot and killed his mother, his wife, and 14 people at the University of Texas | Suicide at the scene |
| | James Huberty | 1984 | Shot and killed 21 people at a McDonald's in San Ysidro, CA | Shot and killed at the scene by a SWAT team sniper |
| | Timothy McVeigh | 1995 | Bombed the Murrah Federal Building in Oklahoma City, OK, killing 168 people | Execution by lethal injection in 2001 |
| | Seung-Hui Cho | 2007 | Shot and killed 32 at Virginia Tech | Suicide at the scene |
| **Spree Murderers** | Charles Starkweather and Carol Fugate | 1958 | Killed 11 people, including Fugate's parents and 2-year-old sister, in Nebraska and Wyoming | Starkweather was executed in Nebraska in 1959; Fugate was sentenced to life in prison but paroled in 1976 |
| | Andrew Cunanan | 1997 | Killed five people with a variety of weapons as he fled across the country | Suicide in Miami, FL, as police closed in |
| | John Allen Muhammad and Lee Boyd Malvo | 2002 | Shot and killed 14 people in several states | Muhammad was executed 2009; Malvo was sentenced to life in prison without parole |
| **Serial Murderers** | John Gacy | 1972–1978 | Killed 33 men and boys | Executed in 1994 |
| | Ted Bundy | 1974–1978 | Confessed to 30 murders; possibly committed 34 murders | Executed in 1989 |
| | Dennis Rader | 1974–1991 | Plead guilty to 10 murders | Received 10 consecutive life sentences without parole |
| | Karla Homolka and Paul Bernardo | 1990–1993 | Raped and killed three teenage girls, including Homolka's 15-year-old sister | Homolka plead guilty to manslaughter in exchange for testimony against Bernardo and was released in 2005; Bernardo was sentenced to life without parole for 25 years |
| | Dr. Harold Shipman | 1974–1998 | Convicted of killing 15 of his patients; probably killed at least 215 patients | Sentenced to life in prison in 2002; committed suicide in prison in 2004 |

The identity of Jack the Ripper, probably the most famous murderer in the Western world, has never been discovered even as his offenses have been repeatedly dissected for clues throughout the decades.

If caught, serial, spree, and mass murderers typically receive either death sentences or life sentences with no chance of parole. A notable exception is Karla Homolka, who claimed she was abused by her husband and testified against him in exchange for a guilty plea of manslaughter in the killings of three women, including her sister. Her case was particularly controversial because videotapes that portrayed her as having an active and willing role in the killings were not discovered until after she had made her plea deal.[44] Homolka was released from prison in July 2005.[45]

Numerous theories seek to explain, or at least shed some light on, why mass murderers, spree murderers, and especially serial murderers do what they do. Many serial murder theories focus on psychological motivations connected to childhood experiences, particularly animal cruelty, firesetting, and parental abuse.[46] However, according to a multidisciplinary symposium hosted by the FBI, no single factor causes a person to become a serial killer. It is interesting that the FBI's assembly of academics and criminal justice professionals prefer this classical explanation for serial murder: "The most significant factor [in the development of the serial killer] is the serial killer's personal decision in choosing to pursue their crimes."[47] Theories about mass murder and spree murder often consider mental illness and mental stress as causes, although most mass and spree murderers are not believed to be insane, that is, they know what they are doing. Perhaps the most common example of this is the recently fired, disgruntled office worker walking into the workplace and shooting several co-workers.

## Forcible Rape

Unlike statutory rape—in which the subject, although willing, is considered due to age or mental state to be unable to give valid consent—**forcible rape** is a violent offense. (For the sake of brevity, we will shorten the term "forcible rape" to "rape" in this chapter.) A controversial topic, rape's definition as a violent offense against the person is relatively recent. Rape was once considered an offense involving sex and property and not violence or human rights. In early times it was an offense against men because it diminished the value of the women who were their property, especially daughters, who could not then be married off.[48] An offender had to make reparations to the primary male relative of the victim and not to the victim herself.

>**THINKBACK**
forcible rape (ch. 3)—
Sexual intercourse performed without the victim's consent through force, threat of violence, or intimidation.

## LO6:

Assess some of the problems with the definition of rape as it applies to males and females.

The FBI's definition of forcible rape, "the carnal knowledge of a female forcibly and against her will," reflects these old norms as it does not include males. A misconception was that it was not possible for males to be raped; they could only be assaulted. Advances in criminology and gender studies have helped correct these misconceptions to some extent, but rape remains a difficult topic and often turns on the issue of consent. Also, although rape has long been a tactic in war, the strategy of raping and sexually assaulting not only women and children, but also men has become more common.

**Incidence of Rape**    Rape happens disproportionately to females. Although rape is a vastly under-reported offense, it is estimated that one of every two females will be raped at least once during her life.[49] As of 2006, about 18 million women and 3 million men in the United States had been raped, and more than 300,000 women and almost 93,000 men are estimated to suffer rape annually.[50] A federal study found that more than half the female victims questioned and nearly three-quarters of the male victims had been raped before turning 18. Women who reported being raped when they were juveniles were twice as likely to report being raped as adults. It is estimated that only one in five adult women report the incident to the police.[51]

## Rape and the Law

Human beings are not the only animals that have nonconsensual copulation. It has been observed among primates and other species including dolphins, ducks, insects, crabs, seals, and orangutans.[52] However, rape is possible only among human beings because, like other offenses, it is socially defined.

**Rape Throughout History**    Although rape has always been considered a violation of both the social order and the individual, the nature of that violation has changed throughout the millennia. The Code of Hammurabi, the earliest known recorded legal code, dealt with several types of rape. The rapist of a betrothed virgin was to be killed, but the girl was considered to be without guilt. A father who raped his daughter was thrown out of the city. However, a married woman who was raped was to be thrown in the river along with the rapist because the rape was considered to be adultery and both parties at fault. The woman's husband could rescue her if he saw fit, and the king could pardon the rapist. The same was true under early Hebrew law, except that both woman and attacker were stoned to death as adulterers rather than drowned, and neither could be saved by either husband or king.[53]

Gradually, rape became a survivable ordeal for women (that is, if they survived the rape), although it remained a property dispute in many cultures. In early England, men who raped wealthy virgins were killed and dismembered. The female connection to property—females were allowed to inherit their father's property but could not marry without their lords' permission—gave rise to the practice of "heiress theft" in which a knight or other ambitious individual could gain property by stealing and marrying the heiress who owned it.

The treatment of rape as a public safety issue and an affront to the individual rights of women in U.S. law emerged from England's 13th-century Statutes of Westminster. Under these laws, there was no difference between the rape of virgins and that of married women, and children could not give consent at all (which later provided the basis for U.S. statutory rape laws). For the first time, the state took an active role in rape prosecution on the behalf of victims. If the woman or her family failed to institute a civil suit within 40 days, the right to prosecute passed to the state.[54] Although legal action by women was possible in early England, and later in the North American colonies, it was difficult to pursue. The victims, who had to prove their cases to all-male courts, were often intimidated by the family of the accused as well as by the social stigma of the proceedings. For these reasons, rape trials were relatively rare.[55]

A glaring omission from these historical legal treatments of rape is the rape of males by other males. "Male rape," as it is commonly known, is as old as the rape of females but occupies a different place in ancient cultures. It was generally not considered an act of sex and adultery but of violence and the assertion of power. In many cultures, including Greek and Roman cultures—both of which hold many myths of the rape of men and boys by male gods—defeated soldiers were raped. A raped male soldier was no longer considered able to lead or fight. There appears to be little or no ancient law addressing male rape, possibly because it was carried out as a matter of war and punishment. Although male rape has continued throughout the centuries, the Western view of homosexuality has changed the nature of the stigma somewhat, even as male rape continued to be ignored by the law until very recently. We will further explore the modern treatment of male rape victims later in this chapter.[56]

**Modern Law and the Prosecution of Rape**   As mentioned earlier, the FBI's definition of rape specifies females, as do other definitions of rape. The English common law definition of rape was "carnal knowledge of a woman forcibly and against her will."[57] Although many states and jurisdictions have dropped the sex/gender requirement from their definition of rape, the three general elements of the definition are sexual intercourse, force, and, most important, the victim's lack of consent. (Modern law recognizes the rape of males, but it is often termed "sexual assault" rather than "rape." The FBI's UCR states that "Sexual attacks on males are counted as aggravated assaults or sex offenses, depending on the circumstances and the extent of any injuries."[58]) Traditionally, the most prominent element has been force. The attacker had to physically force the victim to perform intercourse for a rape to be defined as such. Not many decades ago, a woman who took her alleged attacker to court had to prove she had put up an adequate fight.[59] Also, "intercourse" was narrowly defined as penetration of the vagina by the penis. Any other kind of contact was not considered

rape. Today, the basic element in the definition of rape is the victim's lack of consent, regardless of the nature of the victim/attacker relationship.[60]

Although rape laws seem fairly straightforward, prosecution often is not because of the stigma rape carries. It is rare for anyone to think ill of murder or robbery victims, but rape victims are often considered responsible for their victimization, and this presents a problem in the criminal justice system. Rape is the only violent offense whose prosecution depends on proving the lack of something: the victim's consent.[61] A rape trial is sometimes called "the second rape" of the victim because the victim must not only recount the incident, but also prove the case before a jury.

The type of rape and the type of rapist affect the prosecution of the offense. There are two broad categories of rape: stranger rape and acquaintance rape. *Stranger rape* has much in common with other street offenses, such as mugging, in that the victim and attacker do not know each other and the victim was presumably minding his or her own business at the time of the attack. Still, many jurors and even some criminal justice professionals may assume a female victim was "asking for it" by behavior or style of dress, or that a male victim is homosexual and the victimization is simply part of such behavior. Such misconceptions complicate the prosecution of even what appears to be clear-cut stranger victimizations.

*Acquaintance rape* cases are even more difficult to prosecute. If the victim was drugged or inebriated, he or she might be unsure of the circumstances of the rape. If the victim and offender are friends, lovers, or even married, the victim might not know whether the law would even consider the victimization to be rape. Sex workers who are victimized by clients tend to receive even less sympathy. After all, the thinking goes, the sex worker willingly entered the situation, so isn't he or she responsible if things go wrong?[62] Fortunately, these popular attitudes have subsided over the past few decades, and it is now somewhat easier for victims who know their attackers to seek legal redress. Rape shield laws disallow information about an accuser's prior sexual activity from the court case; however, some states' exceptions to these laws allow such information to be heard if it could exonerate a defendant.[63] Until the 1970s, a husband could not be prosecuted for raping his wife because such an offense did not legally exist.[64]

Years of work by feminist activists and criminal justice professionals eventually led to an overhaul of the legal definition of rape. These changes improved the chances for some types of rape victims of finding justice, although rape prosecutions remain difficult, and rape remains the least-reported violent offense.[65] In 1975, Michigan led the states in rewriting rape laws to include a range of circumstances, as well as male victimization; by 1992 all the states had recast their rape laws to some degree.[66] The most common changes were the following:

- replacing the rape offense with a set of gender-neutral offenses specified by any aggravating circumstances such as weapon usage, victim injury, or commission of another felony

- eliminating requirements that the victim physically resist the attacker and corroboration of victim testimony
- introducing rape shield laws[67]

**Rape Combined with Other Offenses** Since the reform of rape laws, most jurisdictions have recognized a continuum of rape violence. What is often called "simple rape" constitutes a single incident of rape. Additional violence or felonies committed along with the rape increase the seriousness along increasing degrees of aggravated rape. Co-occurrence of other felonies as well as use of a weapon increase the chances of a rape being reported to police.[68] However, according to the National Crime Victimization Survey and the NIBRS, most rapes do not co-occur with other felonies. Those offenses that do co-occur with rapes are typically kidnapping, burglary, and robbery.[69]

## Offender Characteristics

The vast majority of rapists are male.[70] Typologies of rapists place rapists into categories of behavior. One of the first rapist typologies was published in 1979 by psychologist A. Nicholas Groth.[71] Since then, other researchers have offered their own typologies or built on Groth's typology. Robert Knight and Raymond Prentky have since come up with a generally accepted four-category typology of rapists that aims to explain what rapists do and why.

- *The anger rapist.* This rapist uses extreme physical violence—so much, in fact, that the rape is nearly secondary. The anger rapist uses one of two methods to approach his victim: the "blitz style," which, as you can imagine, is an overwhelming attack and flurry of violence, or the "confidence style" in which the rapist talks his way into the victim's trust and then commits the rape. The motive appears to be a need to express extreme rage, and the offender gets little sexual pleasure from the rape. It is merely one in a set of the worst things that can be done to debase another person.

- *The power rapist.* The power rapist seeks to control his victims through sexual conquest and be considered by them (and himself) as superior. The power rapist even tends to contact his victims later to ask about them or tell them how much he enjoyed the rape. Power rapists often do not consider their victims as such and even convince themselves that their victims wanted to have sex with them.

- *The sadistic rapist.* The sadistic rapist is much like the anger rapist in that the motive is to debase the victim in an extreme manner. However, unlike the anger rapist for whom rape is merely a part of the degrading violence, the sadistic rapist is preoccupied with sex that is degrading. The anger rapist uses sex to degrade, whereas the sadistic rapist uses degradation to have sex. The victim's "dread, dependency, and degradation" produces pleasure for the rapist. Pre- and post-rape fantasy is integral to this rapist's motivation.

- *The opportunistic rapist.* The opportunistic rapist rapes if and when he has a chance, but he does not fantasize about or plan the act. These rapists typically use only as much force as necessary to complete the rape, but otherwise they do not beat or further degrade the victims.[72]

## Causes of Rape

There is probably no single reason for rape; if there were and it could be isolated and addressed, rape would stop. A biological interpretation of rape is that it is a result of natural selection because it assists male reproduction. This is supported somewhat by the existence of nonconsensual copulation among animals. Because it does not involve courtship, rape is an efficient way for males to spread their genetic material and have as many offspring as possible. A social interpretation is that rape is part of general criminality: The rape offense is concentrated among young males, which is the group who commits the most other offenses, and the rate of rape rises and falls with the general crime rate as well as population density. Where there is crime, there will also be rape.[73] These classes of theories seek to explain rape at a group level. Many specific theories and hypotheses address why individual rapists rape. Although we cannot cover all of them here, a couple of ideas address the behavior of individual rapists.

- *Immaturity.* Behavioral scientist Michael J. Goldstein proposed that in many ways, rapists never grow up. Their attitudes toward sex and females remain mired in adolescent or preadolescent viewpoints. During adulthood, rapists rely more often on masturbation and erotic media than nonrapist males. However, all types of sex offenders actually had less contact with erotic media during childhood and adolescence than non–sex offender males, something that often co-occurs with punitive parental attitudes toward sex and sexual issues.[74]

- *Attitudes about women and an inability to read negative cues.* Some research has found that the beliefs and attitudes of some men about rape contribute largely to the frequency of the offense. Rapists not only believe that men should strive to be controlling and powerful and women should be submissive and compliant, but they also have difficulty reading women's negative behavioral cues. Rapists in general were significantly less accurate in reading women's negative cues than a control group of nonrapists; among rapists, the ability to read negative cues was less accurate among the more violent rapists than the less violent.[75]

## Rape Myths

Although rape is still perpetrated as a way to establish dominance and power and is still used as a weapon in war and as a means of punishment, the feminist, human rights, and anti-prison rape movements have educated the public to some degree about the horrors of rape and its impropriety in all situations. Officially, rape is no longer considered as merely a more forceful means of having sex. The problem of rape in prisons and its prevalence in war is getting some attention, and sexual violence against two groups who were once considered rape-immune, men and wives, is being acknowledged. Myths and misconceptions about rape still abound, however. One consistent finding is that males accept rape myths more readily than females, which affects how the offense is reported, prosecuted, and punished.[76] Here are the categories of the most common rape myths.[77]

- *Victim desire.* Victim desire is the myth that victims were "asking for it" by acting in a promiscuous manner or dressing in provocative clothing. Women who have many sexual partners are so often considered to have precipitated their rapes by being "promiscuous" that rape shield laws now prevent courts from exploring victims' sexual relationships during rape trials. The desire myth also perpetuates the idea of "good girls" and "bad girls." "Bad girls" are in danger of being raped, whereas "good girls" never have to worry.[78]

- *Fabrication.* Victim fabrication is the myth that victims invent or exaggerate their victmization, often because they feel guilty about having sex. Related myths are that the victim is trying to "get back" at the offender for some slight or wrong because he turned down her advances, to deflect blame because she became pregnant during the encounter, or because she is mentally ill.[79]

- *Victim masochism.* Victim masochism refers to the myth that victims want to be raped. In the masochism myth, women want to be raped so they can avoid feelings of guilt or need men to act aggressively because they are passive and will be considered deviant if they act like they want to have sex.[80]

- *Marital rape.* The myth that rape cannot occur within marriage is dying hard. About 10 to 14 percent of married women are raped by their husbands. It was not until 2006, when the Violence Against Women Act became law, that state laws changed to treat spousal rape as having the same degree of seriousness as stranger rape.[81] Recent research has found that when test subjects are presented with two scenarios, one depicting stranger rape and the other depicting spousal rape, the subjects are less likely to label spousal rape as rape.[82] Marital rape victims are also more likely to be blamed than victims of stranger rape.[83]

- *Male rape.* The myths about male rape are similar to the myths about female rape, and, because of under-reporting and relatively low awareness, they are probably even more prevalent. Common myths are: (1) Only gay men are sexually assaulted; (2) Men cannot have sex unless they are sexually aroused; (3) Men are always ready to have sex; (4) "Real" men can defend themselves against sexual assault.[84] As is the case for female rape myths, more men than women believe these fallacies.[85]

## Rape Within Organizations

The frequency of rape and the situational factors differ from culture to culture, but, as stated earlier, there is no "rape-free society." One hallmark of rape is its association with male fraternal groups such as military units; college fraternities; gangs; sports teams; tribal hunter groups; and other small, closely knit male organizations.[86] The common characteristics of these groups include group loyalty; secrecy; competition among group members; and an emphasis on male superiority, commonly accepted notions of masculinity, and hostility toward women. The question is whether these groups foster the characteristics in their members, or whether young men join these groups because they already have the characteristics individually and seek reinforcement from similar males.[87] We do not yet have the answer.

Although the connection between male groups, antagonism toward females, and rape is obvious by now, the prevalence of the rape of males by male groups, specifically of enemy soldiers and prison inmates, emphasizes the importance of dominance, power, control, and social status rather than sex in the rape offense. Let's consider three predominantly male group contexts in which rape is commonly reported: the military, college fraternities, and prisons.

**The Military**    Rape has always existed in war: Opposing sides rape each other's civilian women and children and captured soldiers as a way to demoralize the enemy and assert power and control. However, what is not expected is the rape of soldiers by fellow soldiers, or what the U.S. Veterans Administration calls "military sexual trauma." Although military sexual trauma has increased as more women have joined the armed forces, male soldiers have reported rape as well.[88] A study by the Veteran Affairs Medical Center revealed that a third of former military women reported rape or attempted rape; 79 percent reported sexual harassment; 14 percent reported being gang-raped by fellow soldiers.[89] A 2003 Veterans Administration report revealed that 60 percent of women and 27 percent of men in the reserves had been raped or sexually assaulted. Between 2002 and 2007, the Pentagon reported nearly 600 sexual assault cases in the U.S. military administrative territory of Afghanistan and Iraq. In the military, rape is possibly even more under-reported than in the civilian world because reporting can end a career.[90] According to the Veteran Affairs Medical Center study, one-fourth of rape victims did not report the rape because the rapist was their ranking officer, and one-third did not report because the rapist was the ranking officer's friend.[91]

What is behind the phenomenon of military rape? The Veteran Affairs Medical Center study found that rape was more likely when a supervisor allowed sexual harassment or had a permissive attitude toward behaviors associated with rape.[92] Another possible explanation is that military bases are a microcosm of American society with all the problems that occur in any town or small city concentrated within the base. One former Air Force psychologist explained that a military base is much like a college campus with similar factors of physical proximity, youth, and alcohol consumption, and that rape is more likely to occur in this type of setting.[93] In fact, most reported rapes occurred on base and during off-duty periods; sleeping quarters are particularly high-risk locations.[94] Consistent with other research on rape, alcohol use is a particularly common factor; drinking by offenders or victims occurs in about one-third to two-thirds of military rape offenses.[95]

More women than ever are serving in the U.S. military, which has increased attention to the problem of military sexual trauma. In 2005, the Department of Defense (DOD) established the Sexual Assault Prevention and Response Office as the "single point of accountability" for the military's sexual assault policy and began issuing annual reports.[96] According to the 2009 Annual Report on Sexual Assault in the Military, 2,670 reports of sexual assault involved soldiers as victims. The report details the military's response to alleged sexual assaults; each military branch has its own program for dealing with reports and offenses.[97] However, considering that the Government Accountability Office (GAO) estimates that rape and sexual assault in the military are underreported by as much as half, this makes the DOD's statistics much more sobering. According to the GAO report: "factors that discourage service members from reporting a sexual assault include the belief that nothing would be done; fear of ostracism, harassment, or ridicule; and concern that peers would gossip." The GAO is also critical of the DOD's sexual assault prevention efforts, stating that although the DOD succeeds in reporting the number of alleged sexual assaults, there are few or no criteria for measuring its progress in dealing with the problem.[98]

Finally, rape is not confined to the U.S. military. The Israeli military, which, like the United States, allows women in combat, also reports problems with sexual harassment and rape. In 2004, female Israeli soldiers filed 500 sexual harassment and rape-related complaints. Speculation is that the figure could be higher, but, as in the U.S. military, many female soldiers did not file complaints. Convicted harassers may be suspended from the Israeli army and relieved of their military degrees; however, according to a report, senior officers accused of harassment are rarely punished, especially if they are highly accomplished.[99]

**College Fraternities** Unfortunately, the college fraternity environment sports almost all the hallmarks of the organizational rape offense: youth, male groups who are antagonistic toward women, alcohol, and proximity. Although fraternities are not the only contexts in which rape occurs at colleges and universities—a 2005 UCLA study reported that almost 20 percent of males in college admitted they would

▲ Rape of both female and male soldiers remains a problem in the military, as well as in military contractor organizations. Here, Jamie Leigh Jones discusses her case in which she says seven of her co-workers at defense contractor KBR drugged and raped her at Camp Hope, Baghdad, Iraq.

rape if they knew they would not be caught—the fraternity is a common college organization in which rape is known to occur with some regularity.[100]

Like rape in the military, as well as rape in general, rape in fraternities is motivated by males' need to prove their power and secure their status within an all-male group. It often occurs during parties, on dates, and in groups. Author Peggy Reeves Sanday describes one such scenario in *Fraternity Gang Rape: Sex, Brotherhood, and Privilege on Campus,* in which a young woman at the University of Pennsylvania became inebriated on LSD and beer and went to a college fraternity party where at least five fraternity brothers took advantage of her disoriented condition to rape her.

Research has shown that membership in college fraternities and college sports teams is associated with attitudes related to sexual aggression. In fact, men in these groups score higher on measures of attitudes favorable to sexual aggression than men who are not members.[101] Another study came up with similar results for fraternities and concluded that those who join are more likely to receive different information about women and sexuality, which tends to encourage and promote the degradation of women, than men who do not join fraternities.[102]

Considering that most males in college are fairly young, typically in their teens and just out of high school, joining a fraternity occurs at a crucial juncture in their development. Status and pecking order are particularly important in teams and fraternities, and members of these groups are under tremendous pressure to fit in. As in the military, if the leadership of the group condones antagonistic and degrading attitudes toward women, that will be the prevailing attitude of the group and the males trying to achieve status in it.

Colleges and universities, as well as student groups, have devoted more attention to the problem of rape by campus groups. For example, the national organization One in Four (the name comes from the statistic that one in four college women has survived rape or attempted rape) seeks to educate college students, particularly male social groups, about rape myths and realities.[103]

**Prisons**   Rape in prison is a particularly controversial topic, mainly because there is a general attitude that those who are in prison are there to be punished and not protected.[104] Although prisons in recent decades have become more oriented toward punishment than rehabilitation, the government still has a responsibility to see that prison inmates are serving the sentences the state has prescribed and are not being victimized by more aggressive inmates. Unfortunately, preventing such victimization is very difficult to do, even in the most secure institutions. In some cases, the prison staff members even allow inmates to be victimized because they feel this is a just punishment.

Rape occurs in any combination across the institutional spectrum. Corrections officers have raped inmates, and inmates have raped corrections officers. But the most common offense is inmates raping other inmates. Inmate/inmate rape does occur in female institutions, but the most common form is male-on-male inmate rape because the vast majority of prison inmates in this country are male. As troubling as it is to contemplate, inmate/inmate rape serves a purpose in prison society: to establish social status and control among inmates. However, attempts are being made to prevent the problem. The Prison Rape Elimination Act of 2003 has the following provisions:

- to establish a zero-tolerance standard for the incidence of prison rape in prisons in the United States
- to make the prevention of prison rape a top priority in each prison system
- to develop and implement national standards for the detection, prevention, reduction, and punishment of prison rape
- to increase the available data and information on the incidence of prison rape
- to increase the accountability of prison officials who fail to detect, prevent, reduce, and punish prison rape
- to protect the Eighth Amendment rights of federal, state, and local inmates[105]

Although the Prison Rape Elimination Act is a step in the right direction, it came only after decades of rape occurring as a sort of secondary punishment in prisons. One particularly disturbing story is that of Stephen Donaldson, who became known as "Donny the Punk."[106] In 1973, Donaldson, then a Quaker activist, was arrested at a White House protest. As part of the protest, he refused to post his $10 bail. He was held in a cell with other minor offenders, including convicted Watergate offender G. Gordon Liddy (who was waiting for sentencing) until a rumor arose that Donaldson was an undercover reporter trying to get a story on Liddy.[107] Donaldson was then transferred to a cellblock with the jail's most dangerous offenders, where he was raped continuously for two nights by at least 45 inmates. A fellow

▼ One reason that prison inmates rape other inmates is to establish social status and control.

protester posted Donaldson's bond a couple of days later and sought medical treatment for him. Donaldson's continued activism, combined with the effects of the intense emotional and physical trauma associated with his first rape, landed him in prison four more times.

The prevalence of rape in the nation's prisons and jails is unclear, and attempts at accurate record-keeping of incidents have only begun. A 2006 federal survey estimated more than 6,000 allegations of sexual violence, with most incidents being reported in state prisons.[108] However, we must take into account the general under-reporting of rape combined with the restrictive and fearful nature of prison life. Doubtless, far more sexual violence is occurring in U.S. prisons and jails than is being reported.[109]

## Robbery

The FBI defines **robbery** as the taking or attempting to take anything of value from the care, custody, or control of a person or persons by force or threat of force or violence and/or by putting the victim in fear.

>**THINKBACK**
robbery (ch. 3)—The taking or attempting to take anything from another person or persons by violence or the threat of violence.

The primary difference between robbery and other offenses in which the object is to obtain money or goods is that robbery includes physical contact (or extreme proximity) with the victim and the use of fear and physical intimidation. There were about 441,855 robberies in 2008, and firearms were used in nearly half the offenses.[110]

## LO7:

**Consider** the primary difference between robbery and other offenses involving theft.

### Robbery and the Law

Robbery is an old offense. The early English courts defined robbery even before defining **larceny.**[111] Some states use the simple, common law definition of robbery, which is basically forcible theft, whereas others define degrees of robbery. Each state treats robbery slightly differently, especially if it is combined with other offenses. For example, the state of New Jersey defines robbery as a second-degree offense unless the suspect attempts to kill another person, combines the robbery with assault or battery, or uses a deadly weapon, in which case the robbery is classified as a first-degree offense. The legal codes of some states, such as Georgia, even provide for capital punishment for offenders convicted of certain types of robbery.

>**THINKBACK**
larceny (ch. 3)—The unlawful taking of money or property from another person. Also called larceny-theft.

### Types of Robbery

Most reported robberies took place on streets or highways (see Figure 10.7). Other locations classified by the FBI are

## Figure **10.7** Percentages of Robberies by Location, 2008

**Although robbery is typically associated with banks and convenience stores, most take place on streets or highways.**

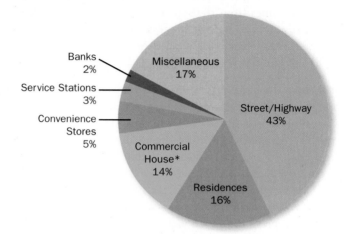

*A "commercial house" is any business that is not a bank, service station, or convenience store.

*Source:* U.S. Department of Justice, Federal Bureau of Investigation, *Uniform Crime Reports: Crime in the United States, 2008,* "Table 7, Offense Analysis, United States, 2004–2008," http://www.fbi.gov/ucr/cius2008/data/table_07.html.

service stations, convenience stores, residences, banks, and miscellaneous. As you can see in Figure 10.7, banks and convenience stores, locations most typically associated with robbery, actually represent a relatively small proportion of robbery locations. Most robberies occur in urban, street locations. According to one study, street robbers tend to work socially disorganized neighborhoods close to their residences or places they frequent.[112] Let's take a look at a few of the most common and persistent types of robbery.

- *Street robbery.* Street robbers are difficult to stop. They are willing to risk committing the offense for the immediate acquisition of small amounts of money or goods; they have a lot of targets; and their offenses do not require much skill or planning.[113] Much of street robbery occurs close to crack cocaine markets since the offense is a quick way for drug buyers to get cash without a lot of preparation.[114] In *Armed Robbers in Action,* authors Wright and Decker suggest that reforming street robbers is difficult because a lifetime of being able to acquire money quickly with little skill or labor, often to support a drug or alcohol habit, is poor preparation for a 9-to-5 job. This is doubtless one reason that street robbery is such a persistent offense.[115]

- *Convenience stores.* Although convenience stores are not robbed as often as many other locations, convenience store robberies are persistent, and the stores themselves are particularly vulnerable to repeated robberies.[116] Convenience store employees are subject to frequent workplace homicide, second only to taxicab drivers.[117]

▲ Most robberies occur in urban locations, especially in disorganized neighborhoods close to where the robbers live.

Police classify convenience store robberies according to how the robber operates: A "straight robbery" occurs when the offender demands money immediately upon entering the store; in a "customer robbery" the offender spends some time in the store pretending to shop; the least common, "merchandise robbery," includes the taking of goods.[118] Robbers generally commit their offenses at night because they are less likely to be seen.[119] This coincides with the fact that the typically late hours convenience stores are open is the strongest factor contributing to robbery.[120] Stores located in high-density commercial settings, such as strip malls, were found to be less likely to be robbed, whereas stores in disorganized neighborhoods or less-dense commercial areas were more likely to be robbed.[121] The profile of convenience store robbers matches that of robbers in general: male, usually under age 25, impulsive, opportunistic, and wanting quick cash.[122] Robbers tend to hit stores in or near their own neighborhoods.[123]

- *Bank robbery.* Like convenience stores, banks are one of the first locations people associate with robbery. In fact, only about 2 percent of robberies are of banks.[124] Most bank robberies occur in urban areas and are reported quickly. The likelihood of catching a bank robber at or near the crime scene is higher than for other offenses because most robberies are perpetrated during the day and have several witnesses. Most bank robbers commit their offenses alone, unarmed, and undisguised. The clearance rate for bank robbery is very high, nearly 60 percent.[125] Although bank robberies are dangerous for bank personnel and bank customers, the person most often killed in a bank robbery is the robber.[126] Most bank robberies are federal offenses, and suspects are tried in federal courts.[127]

Unlike the motivations for some offenses, especially rape, the motivations for robbery are not particularly deep or mysterious. Robbers rob because they need cash now. The robber lifestyle tends to be carefree, unconventional, and deeply tied to street culture in which image, power, control, a willingness to fight, and a desire for excitement and respect are paramount. Armed robbery provides the cash, excitement, and "street cred" to achieve these goals. Armed robbers, who seem to have little or no future orientation, typically spend their take on clothes, jewelry, gambling, or other superfluous goods and services. This pattern is consistent with the young age of most arrested robbers, whose criminal activity typically peaks at 18 and recedes later into adulthood.[128]

## Assault

**Assault** is the criminal offense of attempting to inflict immediate bodily harm or making another person fear that such harm is imminent. Assault is different from **battery** in that battery is physical contact with the intent to do harm. Assault is the intent and attempt to do another person physical harm; battery is a successful assault. This is why "assault and battery" are often treated as one offense. An assault can exist without a battery, but a battery cannot exist without an assault.[129]

**><THINKBACK**
assault (ch. 3)—The criminal offense of attempting to inflict immediate bodily harm or making another person fear that such harm is imminent.

**LO8:**

**Identify** the difference between assault and battery.

Assault is a challenging topic to define because "assault" is largely a legal term that describes the intent to do harm and not the harm itself. From a theoretical perspective, criminologists deal with the more general issue of violence, of which assault is only one aspect. From a criminal justice standpoint, assault is often charged along with other violent offenses, including battery, robbery, stalking, domestic violence, and child abuse. Any violent offense includes assault, from barroom altercations to murder to the most heinous incidences of terrorism. Of the four categories of violent crime covered by the UCR, the first three—murder, forcible rape, and robbery—necessarily involve the fourth category, aggravated assault. Therefore, it is difficult to discuss assault as separate from other criminal offenses or even as separate from violence in general.

The FBI records statistics on both *simple* and *aggravated assault* in the UCR. It keeps more detailed numbers on aggravated assault, which it defines as an "unlawful attack by one person upon another for the purpose of inflicting severe or aggravated bodily injury . . . usually accompanied by the use of a weapon or by other means likely to produce death or great bodily harm." (By comparison, a simple assault does not involve a dangerous weapon, and the victim does not sustain serious or aggravated injuries.)[130] The FBI estimates about 834,885 aggravated assaults occurred during 2008, with nearly 1.3 million arrests for simple assaults.[131] As with other violent offenses, the aggravated assault rate is highest in the South and in metropolitan areas.[132]

### Assault and the Law

Assault is a criminal offense in all states. Most states make simple assault a misdemeanor and aggravated assault a felony. Some states, however, classify a simple assault carried out against a police officer or firefighter as a felony.

In many jurisdictions, one of the elements of aggravated assault is the use of a deadly weapon. Exactly what constitutes a "deadly weapon" and its use often turns on the context of the individual case. Common weapons used in aggravated assaults are blunt instruments, such as clubs, sticks, and other blunt objects. That blunt objects, guns, and knives are usually considered deadly weapons is no surprise. In some cases, however, hands, feet, and shoes have all been considered deadly weapons because of the way they were used to harm another person. The FBI, in fact, collects statistics on the use of "personal weapons"—that is, hands, feet, and fists—as deadly weapons in aggravated assaults.[133] In a 1982 case, *State v. Zangrilli,* the defendant broke his ex-wife's jaw, strangled her, dragged her through the house, and punched her repeatedly in the face and neck before finally shoving her into a bathtub. The courts found that, in this case, the defendant's hands were deadly weapons.[134]

### Types of Assault

All violent crime begins with some form of assault. For example, according to the FBI, robbery is assault plus larceny-theft.[135] However, many assaults (or assaults and batteries) are committed solely for the sake of harming another or making that person afraid. Three broad, important categories of such assaults are stranger assault, intimate-partner violence, and child abuse. Recall the discussion at the beginning of the chapter about Feshbach's differentiation between hostile/expressive aggression and instrumental aggression. Stranger assaults and domestic violence often involve intense emotions as well as the desire for power and control. It is possible, then, that these criminal offenses fall into both of Feshbach's categories: the hostile/expressive, the desire to make the victim suffer for the sake of suffering, as well as the instrumental, the desire to assert personal power and control. In this case, it is probably wiser to plot each case of assault individually along Bushman and Anderson's continuum of aggression.

**Stranger Assault**    Assault by a stranger is the basis for much fear of crime. According to the National Crime Victimization Survey, slightly more aggravated assaults are committed by attackers who are strangers to their victims. In the case of simple assault, however, more offenses are committed by attackers who know their victims at least casually.[136]

The risk of robbery, aggravated assault, and simple assault has declined substantially since the early 1970s.[137] Although the police tend to under-report stranger homicides to statistical agencies such as the FBI's UCR program because of the difficulty of finding the offenders, stranger-committed violence, such as rape, robbery, and assault, is reported more frequently than acquaintance offenses.[138]

**Intimate-Partner Violence**    Much of the violence between people who know one another occurs between intimate partners, including spouses, ex-spouses, and dating partners.[139] Risk factors for intimate-partner violence include the use of drugs or alcohol, the witnessing or experi-

| **battery** Physical contact with the intent to do harm.

▲ Women are much more likely than men to be abused by their intimate partners.

ence of violence during childhood, and unemployment.[140] Most incidences of intimate-partner violence are classified as simple assault; the rest are aggravated assaults and sexual assaults.[141] Although men are affected by intimate-partner violence, women are much more likely to be abused by their intimate partners than men.[142] Annually, women experience about 4.8 million physical assaults and rapes at the hands of intimate partners, whereas about 2.9 million intimate-partner physical assaults affect men. Although these numbers seem high, both non-fatal violence and homicides among intimate partners have declined since 1993. This is probably due in part to both government and private outreach programs: Between 1994 and 2005, both men and women increased reporting of intimate-partner victimization to the police.[143]

In simple assault, one study has found that the police are less likely to make an arrest when the suspect is the victim's intimate partner than when the suspect is a stranger to the victim. Two reasons are that assaults of intimate-partner suspects are less likely to be witnessed by anyone other than the victim, and that such victims are often reluctant to file complaints against their attackers. Men are less likely than women to sign complaints.[144]

**Child Abuse**    Child abuse is harming a child or failing to prevent harm. Child abuse, which can be physical, sexual, or emotional, includes neglect, which is not providing for a child's needs. According to the American Academy of Pediatrics, about 3 million cases of child abuse and neglect are reported annually.[145]

Although most children are abused by someone they know, physical and sexual child abuse still constitutes assault and battery. Unlike other assault offenders, however, most perpetrators of child abuse are women. As in intimate-partner violence, the reporting of child abuse is often problematic because children who are being abused either cannot or will not tell anyone about it, particularly if the perpetrator is a parent or other beloved relative. Infants are also particularly vulnerable to child abuse. An FBI study showed that the most common offense perpetrated against infants (babies under 1 year of age) was simple assault, followed by aggravated assault.[146]

The prosecution of both intimate-partner violence and child abuse is a relatively new phenomenon in the United States. Until recent decades, family violence was considered a private matter: Parents had the right to treat their children any way they wished, and husbands were considered to have the right to beat both their wives and children. Although the criminal justice treatment of family violence has advanced in that the family is no longer treated as a haven for almost any kind of violence that adults wish to perpetrate, vestiges of this attitude can be observed in the fact that, as we have discussed, stranger assaults are more likely to generate arrests than those committed by intimate partners.

# Think about it

## Remember
Recall the definition of murder.

## Apply
Interpret the reasons the offense of rape is rife with so many misconceptions.

## Analyze
Distinguish between the different types of homicide.

## Evaluate
Differentiate robbery from larceny.

# Summary

**LO1:** **Compare and contrast the common sources of violence.**

- Aggression is basic to violent crime. Violence is aggressive physical force with intent to cause fear or to injure, harm, or kill.
- Feshbach distinguished between hostile/expressive and instrumental aggression. Bushman and Anderson suggest a continuum of aggression, rather than a dichotomy.
- Common sources of violence include psychological abnormality, substance abuse, evolutionary factors, and socialization and cultural values.

**LO2:** **Discuss three common sources of violent crime that stem from the human body and mind.**

- Biological sources of violent crime include mental disorder, substance abuse, and evolutionary factors.
- Four types of mental disorders associated with violent crime are schizophrenic disorders, paranoid disorders, mood disorders, and antisocial personality disorder.
- Although drugs and alcohol are associated with violent crime, no known substance directly causes people to become violent or break the law.
- The sociobiological approach to explaining crime is that humans evolved antisocial tendencies for specific reasons.

**LO3:** **Evaluate common social and cultural sources of violent crime.**

- Social and cultural sources of violent crime include family dysfunction, social disorganization, and some subcultural values.
- Family violence is usually treated as a public safety issue rather than a private family problem. Violence that stems from families can strike at victims within the family and victims outside the family.
- Social disorganization theory asserts that disorganized areas, such as impoverished neighborhoods, lack the social controls that prevent violence.
- Some values held by subcultures are a major source of violent crime.

**LO4:** **Define violent crime.**

- The FBI defines violent crime as offenses that include the use of force or threat of force.
- The FBI recognizes four violent criminal offenses: murder and non-negligent manslaughter, forcible rape, robbery, and aggravated assault.

**LO5:** **Explain the difference between homicide and murder.**

- The FBI defines murder and non-negligent manslaughter as the willful killing of one human being by another. Homicide is the killing of one human being by another, regardless of criminal intent.
- The federal government recognizes first and second degrees of murder. Some states recognize a third degree and/or offense called "felony murder."
- According to the FBI, those who are most often arrested for murder are black males between the ages of 9 and 29. After age 29, it is white males who are most often arrested for murder.
- Mass murder is typically the killing of three or more people in a single incident. Serial murder is the killing of several victims over a very long time.

**LO6:** **Assess some of the problems with the definition of rape as it applies to males and females.**

- Rape exists in all societies in some form. All rape is associated with control through violence.
- Forcible rape, according to the FBI, is "the carnal knowledge of a female forcibly and against her will." Although men experience rape, it happens disproportionately to females.
- Most states have rewritten their rape laws to include male rape, to eliminate requirements that the victim physically resist the attacker, and to include rape shield laws.
- Knight and Prentky's four-category typology of rapists includes the anger rapist, the power rapist, the sadistic rapist, and the opportunistic rapist.

**LO7:** **Consider the primary difference between robbery and other offenses involving theft.**

- The difference between robbery and other offenses in which the object is to obtain money or goods is physical contact (or proximity) with the victim and the use of fear and physical intimidation.
- Some states use the common law definition of robbery, whereas others define degrees of robbery.

**LO8:** **Identify the difference between assault and battery.**

- Assault is the intent to do harm, not the harm itself. Battery is the illegal use of force against another person.
- Three general types of assault include stranger assault, intimate-partner violence, and child abuse.

# Questions

1. Why is aggression basic to violent crime?
2. What is violence?
3. What is hostile/expressive aggression? What is instrumental aggression?
4. Why might a continuum of violence be more useful in characterizing violent crime than a dichotomy of violence?
5. What are common sources of violence?
6. What are the four violent criminal offenses recorded by the FBI?
7. How does murder differ from homicide?
8. Is rape always a case of males victimizing females?
9. What is the difference between robbery and other types of larceny-theft?
10. What is assault? How does it differ from battery?

# 11

# Organized and
# White-Collar

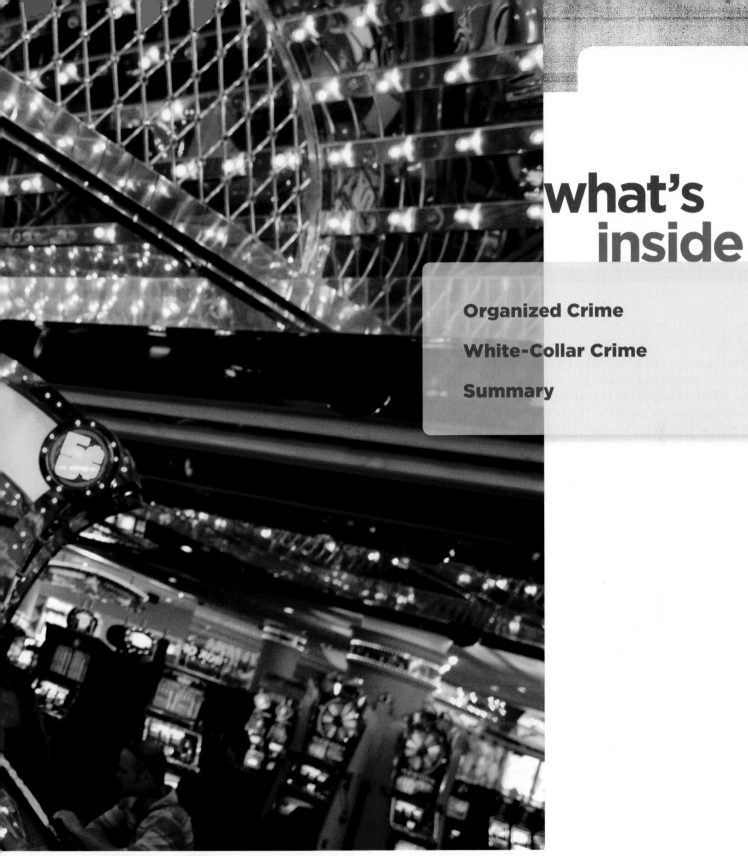

# what's inside

# Crime

**As you read, keep in mind these learning objectives:**

**LO1:** Define and understand the nature of organized crime.

**LO2:** Summarize the types of offenses that criminal organizations typically commit.

**LO3:** Understand the context within which white-collar offenses are committed.

**LO4:** Explain why corporate crime is often difficult to detect.

Organized and white-collar crime are criminal offenses typically perpetrated within the context of organizations. The offenses discussed in this chapter are motivated primarily by the desire to amass wealth, political or social power, or to prevent their loss. These offenses often involve a violation of trust.[1] Although many types of street crime also have a profit or power motive, many of the offenses discussed in this chapter are distinguished by the level of organization, scope, and, in some cases, the otherwise law-abiding nature of those who break the law.[2] The exception to this is white-collar offenses, which are often committed by individuals acting on their own and sometimes acting impulsively. The motivation in these cases is often revenge for real or imagined wrongs to the offender, as well as a desire for money or power.

The three types of criminal offending discussed here overlap to a degree, but we will examine each type separately in order to understand the motives, methods, and harm caused by each. The three types of crime we will discuss are organized crime, white-collar crime, and corporate crime.

1. *Organized crime.* **Organized crime** is a type of business enterprise involving highly structured or organized groups that engage in criminal activities and often use violence to achieve goals. Organized crime has traditionally been involved in vice offenses such as gambling, prostitution, and the smuggling of drugs or alcohol. But it also may use the financial proceeds of crime to invest in legitimate enterprises, such as businesses, and financial instruments, such as stocks and bonds. Criminal organizations have since expanded the scope of their activities to include trafficking in weapons as well as illegal immigrants. These organizations are often referred to as "families" because their participants are often drawn from one ethnic or racial group. Sometimes, the members are actu-

ally related to one another. In the popular imagination, the typical organized crime participant is a member of the Italian Mafia (which we will discuss in greater detail later). As we shall see, this stereotype no longer captures the variety and scope of activities now facing law enforcement officers.[3] Many street gangs that were at one time disorganized bands of juveniles have "grown up" to become effective crime organizations. The Federal Bureau of Investigation (FBI) and state law enforcement agencies are the main investigators of organized crime activities.

2. *White-collar crime.* Although this type of crime takes place within a business or corporate environment, **white-collar crime** refers to the actions of individual employees. A typical white-collar offender might be the bank employee who takes money, the shopkeeper who fails to report income to the Internal Revenue Service (IRS), or the department store clerk who steals merchandise. White-collar crime is perpetrated within the framework of an individual's normal duties and can be very difficult to detect.[4] The FBI and state law enforcement agencies are the main investigators into white-collar offenses.

> **><THINKBACK**
> white-collar crime (ch. 1)—
> A criminal offense committed by an individual employee of a business during the course of legitimate business for the benefit of the employee that takes advantage of the business or its customers.

3. *Corporate crime.* **Corporate crime** consists of offenses committed in the name of a business in the pursuit of money or to prevent losing money. It involves legitimate businesses that engage in unfair business practices, bribe regulators, misrepresent financial assets, or knowingly produce unsafe products or harm the environment. Corporate crime is significantly different from organized

---

**organized crime** A criminal organization that breaks the law for money and often uses violence to achieve its goals.

**corporate crime** Offenses committed in the name of a business for monetary profit or to prevent monetary loss.

crime. The primary purpose of corporations is to make legitimate products, and their criminal offenses are often the result of using shortcuts, taking unfair advantage of other businesses, or negligence and poor oversight. Whereas the organized crime network is fundamentally criminal in nature, corporations exist without a criminal intent. Often, the shareholders, board members, and employees have no idea the executives are engaging in illegal practices. Corporations might drift into and out of illegal activities, while always depending on their legitimate concerns to make money for the company.[5] Depending on the size and nature of the offense, several federal and state agencies, including the FBI, the IRS, and the Department of Justice, might have a hand in investigating and prosecuting corporate crime.

Organized, white-collar, and corporate crime are becoming a major focus within criminology. The dawn of the 21st century has seen a rash of corporate criminal activity and wrongdoing that has not been witnessed for a century. The concern about organized crime, which has always operated along the underbelly of American life, has deepened with the discovery of sophisticated criminal organizations moving illegal drugs across the nation's southern borders. As we progress through this chapter, the distinctions between these types of offenses will become clearer. We note also that these types of offenses require special skill-sets of law enforcement officers. For instance, to follow the paper trail of corporate, white-collar, and some organized crime offenders, an investigator needs expertise in financial accounting. Similarly, the law enforcement officer dealing with a toxic waste polluter needs to know something about chemistry and biology.[6]

# Organized Crime

Organized crime is a global problem that takes a variety of forms around the world. It can be contained within one country, or it can be **transnational** and affect several nations.[7] This variety of forms and geographic dispersal makes defining organized crime problematic. Criminologist Howard Abadinsky states that there is no generally accepted definition of organized crime because those who attempt to define the term have occupational or agency agendas that influence their viewpoints. For instance, police officers in a particular city who are responsible for maintaining the peace and arresting offenders see organized crime in a different way than do scholars at the United Nations who must account for a wide variety of criminal enterprises in different cultures. Instead of defining organized crime, Abadinsky offers a number of

>**THINKBACK**

transnational crime (ch. 3)—Criminal offenses that originate in one nation, cross one or several national borders, and find victims in other nations.

**LO1:**

**Define and understand** the nature of organized crime.

attributes that criminal organizations tend to have.[8] These attributes allow us to consider how criminal organizations differ from other types of conventional offenders and terrorist groups.

- *No political goals.* Unlike a terrorist organization, modern criminal organizations are not trying to advance a political agenda. Although the Ku Klux Klan might share some attributes with organized crime, it has an identifiable political purpose of preserving and enhancing white power. Some criminal organizations might attempt to influence the political environment in order to make money, but such attempts are generally aimed at gaining protection or immunity for the organization's criminal activities rather than promoting a political cause.[9]

- *Hierarchical organization.* Criminal organizations have a definite chain of command. More extensive than "a leader and followers," this chain of command contains three or more levels of direct authority and, often, staff positions such as a legal counselor. Most important, these levels of command do not depend on the personality of any particular individual but are consistent features of the organization, thus making personnel replaceable.[10]

- *Limited or exclusive membership.* Not just anyone can join a criminal organization. Some are limited to persons from particular ethnic backgrounds or with specific criminal experiences. Willingness to put the criminal organization as a first priority is paramount, and often an aspiring member must be sponsored by a current member.[11]

- *Constitutes a unique subculture.* The members of crime organizations see themselves as distinct from mainstream society. They view the laws and rules of society as meaningless to how they construct their own "underworld" in which honor, loyalty, and secrecy are vital.[12]

- *Self-perpetuating.* A criminal organization has a lifespan greater than that of its individual members. Recruitment and succession of power are important features in maintaining the criminal network over a long period of time.[13]

- *Violence and bribery.* These are the primary tools of criminal organizations, which they use to gain a competitive edge and protect their interests. **Bribery** involves influencing public officials or employees of businesses with offers of money or valuables. Alternatively, the use of extreme violence can frighten competitors, customers, and even law enforcement officers and government officials into cooperating.[14]

- *Specialization or division of labor.* Depending on the size of the organization, individuals might be assigned specific tasks and responsibilities. Some might physically enforce the group's goals, while others might be responsible for laundering money and investing it in legitimate assets.[15]

**bribery** The offense of giving money or valuables to influence public officials or employees of business competitors.

- *Monopolistic.* Criminal organizations are not free-market traders. They are concerned with establishing exclusive control over a geographic area or a particular type of business. Much of the violence surrounding organized crime stems from "turf" battles in which one group attempts to encroach on another's business. These disputes can sometimes be negotiated, but more often than not, they are settled by the faction that can muster the most violence.[16]

- *Governed by rules or regulations.* Order within the criminal organization is maintained by rules that demand that participants respect one another's dignity, business, and family. Violation of the rules will result not in a lawsuit, but in violence.

Criminal organizations possess these attributes to varying degrees. Although they provide guidelines for recognizing organized crime, the types of structures that engage in organized crime vary greatly. Examination of some specific examples of organized crime will help our understanding of this type of unlawful activity.

## The Beginning of Organized Crime in the United States

Organized crime in the United States can be traced back to political machines of large cities in the early 20th century. European immigrants supplied the labor for the emerging industrial growth of the United States. With the immigrants came not only opportunities for their exploitation, but also their own attempts at gaining economic and political power to protect themselves.[17]

The Irish were the first immigrant group to arrive in the United States in large numbers since the original influx of Anglo-Saxon Protestants in the 17th and 18th centuries. Fleeing a country ravaged by famine and the exploitive and unfair economic practices of England, the Irish arrived with a political culture that encouraged secrecy, unity, and upward mobility through politics. Irish immigrants settled in the large eastern cities of the United States where they sought to dominate local politics. They found themselves restricted in

educational, economic, and social spheres by the ruling establishment who looked down on the newcomers as a foreign influence that diminished the cultural heritage of the existing social order.[18]

The political power amassed by the Irish can be attributed to two social institutions: the Catholic Church and the local saloon. Both the Church and the saloon gave the Irish opportunities to build community and establish ethnic identity. The saloon of the late 19th and early 20th centuries was a very different social institution from the bars of the 21st century. Saloons provided the main social base for political activity, neighborhood gossip, and a wide array of services for community social life, including rooms for weddings and union meetings. In cities where power was dispersed to the neighborhoods, saloon keepers were central figures in local political machines. Their ability to deliver votes on election day allowed saloon keepers to influence politics in ways that made them not only politically powerful, but also economically successful.[19]

The degree of organization that evolved from city political machines ensured that certain groups of individuals, often ethnic Irish, Italians, or Germans, had enormous influence on the workings of city government. This influence included many illegal activities that usually involved vices such as gambling, the sale of illicit alcohol, and prostitution. The power of the political machine was all-encompassing. In addition to being able to deliver the vote, the machine could also discourage rivals by denying them parade permits, getting friends and relatives hired and enemies fired from government jobs, and providing the muscle to intimidate those who challenged their power. As city governments and local police departments evolved into less violent forms of graft and political influence, these activities increasingly became the province of a criminal underworld.[20]

▶ Organized crime in the United States can be traced to late 19th-century and early 20th-century urban political machines. Tammany Hall was a powerful political machine in New York City in the 1860s and early 1870s. This 1871 political cartoon was a comment on the machine's downfall.

SOMETHING THAT DID BLOW OVER—NOVEMBER 7, 1871

## The Rise of the Underworld

Powerful political machines and the influential economic leaders of the cities developed a relationship that benefited both parties. The political machine oversaw not only the legitimate businesses run by law-abiding citizens, but also the illegitimate vice activities often used by those same citizens. In order to meet the demand for gambling and other vice activities, political machines allowed an underworld of criminal activity to exist that helped keep the machine in power and enriched its leaders. Although periodically engaging in the arrest and conviction of underworld figures, the political machine also profited by accepting bribes and services from those same figures.[21] For instance, in 1890, New York state senator "Big Tim" Sullivan, who was part of the Tammany Hall political machine, was made responsible for Italian and Jewish immigrants to New York City. That is, it was his job to ensure that they voted for Tammany Hall–approved politicians and that those who regularly committed criminal offenses were punctual with their bribes. In return, Sullivan allowed a certain amount of vice in the city.[22]

The best example of how city political machines and the underworld worked in harmony to increase the power and wealth of each is Prohibition, the national ban on the manufacture, transportation, and sale of alcoholic beverages enacted by the Eighteenth Amendment to the Constitution that went into effect in 1920. Congress had already passed the Volstead Act in 1919, which created the Prohibition Bureau in the Treasury Department and charged it with the primary responsibility for enforcing Prohibition. However, this bureau turned out to be ineffective and often counterproductive. For instance:

> In addition to being inept and corrupt, Prohibition Bureau agents were a public menace: they ran up a record of being killed (by 1923, 30 had been murdered) and for killing hundreds of civilians, often innocent women and children. The bureau was viewed as a training school for bootleggers, because agents frequently left the service to join their wealthy adversaries.[23]

Local law enforcement agencies often worked in conjunction with bootleggers, speakeasies, and politicians to reap profits from facilitating alcohol sales. Prohibition greatly weakened citizens' trust in law enforcement and contributed to the rise of organized crime. There was simply too much money at stake, and the public's demand for alcohol was so great that the legal institutions of law enforcement, the courts, and city governments were propelled into acquiescence, corruption, and neglect. Prohibition ended in 1933, when ratification of the Twenty-first Amendment to the Constitution repealed the Eighteenth Amendment and nullified the Volstead Act.

The most significant byproduct of Prohibition was the shift of power from city bosses to private individuals engaged in organized crime. Rather than being errand boys and thugs at the service of politicians, criminal organiza-

▲ This Prohibition-era postcard was produced in 1910 by the National Woman's Christian Temperance Union. The "Vote No" refers to political campaigns to deny the renewals of alcohol licenses for local taverns.

tions became powerful in their own right. They continued to bribe the city officials who were susceptible, and they intimidated those who were hesitant to be bribed. They turned the immense profits of vice crime to their own ends, thus consolidating their power and wealth. The shift of power to organized crime happened in different ways in different cities. In order to understand the rise of organized crime in the United States, we turn now to an examination of how the insularity and unity of ethnic groups facilitated the consolidation of specific vice markets in the United States.

## The American Mafia

When Americans think about organized crime, the first picture that often pops into mind is the Mafia don of Italian descent. The *Godfather* movies, as well as the popular television series *The Sopranos,* provide an entertaining, if somewhat distorted, portrayal of organized crime (see *Doubletake* on page 242). Yet, there is some truth to this view, and a look at the history of the Mafia in the United States shows how Italians in large cities, particularly New York and Chicago, used violence and intimidation to control their criminal empires.[24]

Italians who emigrated to the United States in large numbers between 1890 and 1920 faced economic and social hardships. They found a society in which Protestant Anglo-Americans dominated the private business sector and a powerful Irish-American group that had taken over many of the jobs in municipal government. Several factors facilitated the Italian immigrants' entry into organized crime. The Italian

# doubletake

### Creating the Mafia

Organized crime is a popular subject in entertainment media, and the most popular organized-crime subject is the Mafia. Several Mafia families have reigned since their arrival in the United States in the late 19th century. Today, federal law enforcement efforts have greatly reduced the activities of the New York–based Mafia.[1]

Movies and television, however, have provided us with many more Mafia families: the Corleones of the *Godfather* films, the Sopranos of *The Sopranos,* and the Vittis from *Analyze This,* just to name a few. In one of the most realistic films, *Goodfellas,* which is based on actual Mafia activities, the mobsters engaged in criminal offenses both large and very small, as they "stole $6 million from Lufthansa Airlines and sold unstamped cigarettes from the trunk of a car."[2]

Much of what the media present as Mafia reality is not. Like the situations in all fictional media entertainment, some aspects are glorified and dramatized to make the film, novel, or television show more interesting. According to one film critic, this "indulgent, even romantic mythology is a sign that organized crime has never posed a serious threat to the American social order, providing instead a rich trove of tabloid headlines and hard-boiled metaphors."[3] As violent as the Mafia is, few fictional treatments portray mobsters as actually detrimental to the whole of American society. They are portrayed as misunderstood heroes, regular people who just happen to work for the Mafia, or men of honor who live by a code that the outside world just cannot understand.

Other societies have not been so lucky. An Italian film, *Excellent Cadavers* (1999), portrays the Mafia in a far less forgiving light as it tells the true story of the fight against a Mafia-infiltrated government in Sicily. The two Sicilian prosecutors who risked their lives trying to shut down, or at least diminish, Mafia activities were killed by car bombs in 1992, but not before they secured the convictions of hundreds of Mafia soldiers. In the film, the Mafia, which has severely crippled Sicilian civic life, is portrayed not as "the colorful, violent flowering of ancient Mediterranean peasant customs," but as "a thoroughly vicious organization bent on the subversion of democratic norms and the brutal elimination of anyone who dares to oppose its ambitions."[4]

[1]"Will the Real Mob Please Stand Up," *New York Times,* March 5, 2006, late edition, East Coast, 4–5; "End of the Gambinos?" *Economist* 386, no. 8567 (February 16, 2008): 41.

[2]Ibid.

[3]Ibid.

[4]A. O. Scott, "A Hard, Unromantic Look at the Mafia's Sicilian Reign," *New York Times,* July 12, 2006, late edition, E1.

▲ Organized crime has been a feature of the American crime landscape since the 19th century. Here, law enforcement officials announce the indictment of 14 alleged members of the Gambino organized crime family. The chart shows members of the family who are deceased, convicted or indicted since November 1991.

## THINKING
### *in* ACTION

1. Why has the media fixated on Italian-Americans as representative of organized crime?
2. What societal factors might lead the American media to portray mafia leaders as heroes, while an Italian film portrays them as vicious criminals?

immigrants included a sizable number of Sicilians and Nea-politans (immigrants from Naples) who brought with them an organizational model of loosely connected, independent families. The term *families* requires further explanation. Al-though actual family relationships were the basis for this type of organizational structure, these business enterprises were composed of groups of families who had some intimate connections and provided a sense of security and protec-tion for one another.[25] In short, there was no ancient, fully formed, tightly organized Mafia that arrived in the United States from Sicily. The modern Mafia, in fact, more closely resembles gangs from 17th-century Naples than the Sicilian bandits, who probably originated as antagonists against the region's Spanish government and later against its Italian gov-ernment. The Sicilian word *mafioso* described an attitude, ba-sically to be a brave man. The designation "Mafia"—which even in Italy is a blanket term for criminal groups—probably derives from this word.[26]

The range of offenses that involve Italian organized-crime families is long and varied. The following criminal ac-tivities have been linked to organized crime.

- *Racketeering.* Although criminal organizations are in-volved in many legitimate industries, they engage in **rack-eteering,** which is the use of **extortion**—using threats or intimidation to obtain money, property, or information—and force to engage in illegal business activities. Organized crime has been linked to organized labor unions and, through them, to the vending machine, liquor, movie, trucking, and garbage industries.[27] A particularly suc-cessful law enforcement tool against organized crime has been the 1970 Racketeering Influenced and Corrupt Or-ganizations (RICO) Act (see *Theory to Practice*).[28]

- *Prostitution and pornography.* Criminal organizations have long been involved in the prostitution trade. Some-times, involvement has been at the street-level pimping of prostitutes, but more often criminal organizations provide protection to brothel owners. The distribution of pornographic materials is another area in which orga-nized crime has traditionally been powerful. Criminal organizations owned or controlled theaters that showed X-rated movies and owned or protected stores that sold "adult" books, magazines, or videos. However, the Inter-net has made the distribution of pornographic materials more difficult for organized crime to control.[29]

- *Fraud.* Criminal organizations have found many activi-ties profitable. Credit card **fraud** is a common offense. Often, criminal organizations run up huge amounts of purchases that victims discover only when they receive

---

**racketeering** The use of extortion and force to engage in illegal business activities.

**extortion** The offense of obtaining money, property, or information by threats, intimidation, or false claim to a position of authority.

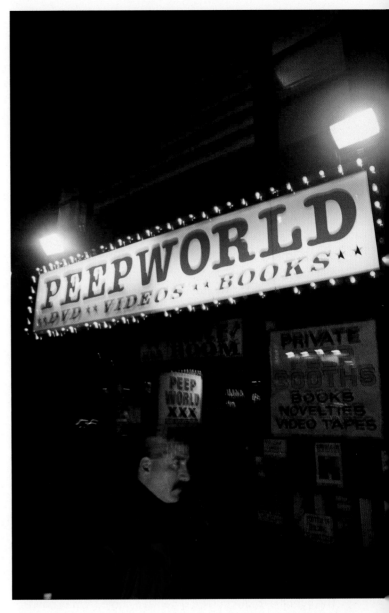

▲ Criminal organizations have long been involved in prostitution. This street scene in New York City is part of a thriving sex trade.

their credit card statements. Organized crime has also targeted the government in fraudulent endeavors. For example, prior to the 1980s, the method of collecting gas-oline taxes was extremely in-efficient in several states, and gas stations owned by crimi-nal organizations would avoid paying taxes. When finally required to pay, the organizations would simply close the station for a few months, then reopen under a new owner. Local, state, and federal governments could not keep track of who the actual owners were because the busi-nesses were often registered to overseas corporations.[30]

>**THINKBACK**
fraud (ch. 9)—A known misrepresentation or concealment in a transaction, made with the intent to deceive another.

# theory
## to **practice**

### Racketeering Influenced and Corrupt Organizations (RICO)

The **Racketeering Influenced and Corrupt Organizations (RICO) Act** is a federal statute enacted in 1970 to control organized crime. The purpose of RICO is "the elimination of the infiltration of organized crime and racketeering into legitimate organizations operating in interstate commerce."[1] RICO allows prosecutors to seize criminally gained assets and provide long prison sentences, typically 20 years to life. In the early 1990s, RICO was expanded to target nontraditional crime groups, such as gangs. For example, in April 2009, five members of the Crips in Wichita, Kansas, were found guilty on conspiracy to engage in racketeering and other charges. In that case, murder, drive-by shootings, and robbery were tools for doing business trafficking illegal drugs.[2]

The RICO statutes are based on **rational choice theory** (see Chapter 4). Criminal organizations are motivated by a business ethic aimed at creating a profit. They have lawyers and accountants to help them determine the potential profit and legal risks for their activities. RICO statutes make offenses that happen across two or more states subject to federal penalties.

>**THINKBACK**
>
> rational choice theory (ch. 1)—The concept that offenders calculate the advantages and disadvantages not only of breaking the law, but of what type of offense to commit.

The intent is to discourage organized crime from expanding its enterprises by increasing the chances that illegal activities will be discovered and to provide severe penalties at the federal level.

The government must prove four conditions to establish violations of the RICO Act.

1. The prosecution must demonstrate that the defendants were associated with an enterprise as defined in the RICO statute. "Enterprise" includes any group of individuals whose association provides for the commission of two or more *predicate crimes,* or offenses that are included in charging another offense and must be committed in order for the other offenses to be charged (see below for a list of predicate crimes). An enterprise must be organized in a way that allows for hierarchic or consensual decision-making (one of the hallmarks of an organization).

2. The government must prove the enterprise engages in, or its activities affect, interstate commerce. An example of interstate commerce would be the use of interstate facilities such as banks, telephones, and wire transfers for drug trafficking.

3. The government must prove that each defendant agreed to participate in the enterprise through a "pattern of racketeering." The "pattern" means the activity requires two or more predicate acts within a decade that must be connected to achieve an illegal end.

4. The government must prove that each defendant agreed to participate in the enterprise's affairs by committing or agreeing to commit at least two predicate offenses.[3]

Predicate crimes include but are not limited to:

- counterfeiting
- money laundering
- murder for hire
- drug trafficking
- prostitution
- sexual exploitation of children
- murder
- kidnapping
- gambling
- arson
- robbery
- bribery
- extortion[4]

[1]The United States Attorneys, "Organized Crime and Racketeering," in *Criminal Resource Manual,* http://www.usdoj.gov/usao/eousa/foia_reading_room/usam/title9/110mcrm.htm.

[2]The United States Department of Justice, "Five Wichita Men Found Guilty on a Federal Racketeering Charge," April 15, 2009, http://www.usdoj.gov/usao/ks/press/April2009/April15a.html; The United States Department of Justice, "Federal Racketeering Charges Filed Against Crips Gang Members in Wichita," Sept. 28, 2007, http://www.usdoj.gov/usao/ks/press/Sept07/09_28a.html.

[3]Jane Morse, USINFO.STATE.GOV, US Department of State, "What Is RICO?" http://usinfo.state.gov/eap/Archive_Index/rico.html. Other information provided by the United States Attorney's Office, Organized Crime Strike Force, Las Vegas, Nevada.

[4]Federal Bureau of Investigation, "Organized Crime," http://www.fbi.gov/hq/cid/orgcrime/glossary.htm.

## THINKING
### *in* ACTION

1. Think of a case that could be prosecuted under RICO.
2. Why did the government deem the RICO statutes necessary?

**Racketeering Influenced and Corrupt Organizations (RICO) Act**  A federal statute enacted in 1970 to control organized crime.

■ *Securities fraud.* **Securities fraud** describes attempts to manipulate the investment market, usually by encouraging investors to purchase securities based on false statements. Organized crime has profited by purchasing securities at low prices, artificially running up the value, and then selling before the deception is detected. As in their other business enterprises, criminal organizations use threats and intimidation to raise the price of their securities. They force brokers to convince their clients to buy an overvalued stock, then liquidate their own holdings, leaving the client with an investment that quickly loses its value.[31] A typical corporate securities offense is the running of "boiler rooms." These operations, which are usually telemarketing outfits, push nearly worthless, obscure, or fraudulent stocks using dishonest sales tactics.

■ *Black-market goods.* A number of legitimate and illegitimate products are sold outside the bounds of conventional commerce. This means that products sold on the street, in flea markets, to businesses through the back door, or over the Internet are not subjected to taxes. In addition, stolen goods are peddled on the black market, as are prohibited items such as weapons, drugs, and alcohol. Engaging in this type of enterprise is risky, and it is fertile ground for the involvement of criminal organizations because they are able to protect themselves, provide protection to those they deal with, and ensure that prices stay high by threatening to harm any competition.

## Ethnically Based Organized Crime in the United States

Not all criminal organizations in the United States are set up like the Mafia. Many criminal organizations more closely resemble loose networks. Criminologist Jay Albanese cautions against falling into the "ethnicity trap" of assuming that people who share an ethnicity, culture, and language coalesce around a specific criminal element, protect them, and supply them with members.

Some criminal organizations operate as fluid networks in which individuals have indirect connections and take on partners only as needed for criminal activity. These networks are not centralized or dominated by a few leaders. Unlike many Mafia groups, no hierarchy exists independent of the criminal offense. One such fluid, organized crime network is that of Russian émigrés in the Brighton Beach area of Brooklyn in New York City.[32] These groups typically have transient members who may be organized around a specific offense, such as the extortion of money from local merchants. There is little or no personal loyalty, and individual group members, even those from common ethnic or cultural backgrounds, typically distrust each other. After the group's criminal objective is attained, say, a successful

drug sale, the group may split up or may go on to another criminal enterprise.

Asian gangs exhibit a similar structure. Larger organizations are split into small cells or even partnerships to pursue a single criminal goal, such as the extortion of a particular target. When that goal is complete, the cell or partnership dissolves. Individual members can conduct several criminal enterprises with different groups simultaneously, regardless of ethnic identity.[33] Both the Russian and Asian gangs are only two examples of the wide variety of ethnic gangs in the United States. Other common gang ethnicities include Dominican, Filipino, Jamaican, Mexican, and Salvadoran.

The network model of organized crime is problematic for both citizens and the criminal justice system. These organizations often do not have a moral code, and the participants have no loyalty either to their ethnic group or to their partners in crime. Criminal groups are loosely organized based upon the specific offenses to be committed and are quickly disbanded and reorganized in different ways for future criminal activities. Albanese suggests that instead of thinking of organized crime in ethnic terms, as does the President's Commission on Organized Crime, it is more useful to think of it in terms of the types of illicit activities that each group engages in.[34]

### Gangs

Some crime organizations started out as street gangs. The difference between crime organizations and street gangs boils down to organization and coherence. For example, when Sicilian bandits began arriving in the United States in the late 19th century, they found street gangs and semi-organized crime groups already operating in cities such as New York, Chicago, and New Orleans. The difference between the Italian bandits and the American gangs was organization. If the head of an American gang was killed or arrested, the gang usually dissipated. Gangs also tended to split into factions. The family structure that the Italian groups brought with them, however, had been forged during hundreds of years of poverty, racism, violence, and political repression. This translated well into the corporate structure later developed by the American Mafia and honed during Prohibition.[35] Some contemporary gangs have adopted this structure. According to scholars Dennis Kenney and James Finckenauer, six other attributes have been cited as differences and similarities between criminal organizations and gangs.

■ *Corruption.* Crime organizations typically make systematic efforts to corrupt public officials, including law enforcement, with large payoffs. Most gangs do not have the relationships with law enforcement and government to do this.

■ *Violence.* Crime organizations and gangs have in common the use or threat of violence to achieve their goals.

■ *Continuity.* Crime organizations are continuous and persist over years or decades. A few gangs have achieved this as well, but most have not.

**securities fraud** An offense in which an individual or entity attempts to manipulate the investment market, usually by encouraging investors to purchase securities based on false statements.

- *Multiple enterprises.* Systematic, continuous engagement in multiple profitable enterprises is a hallmark of criminal organizations. The primary profitable enterprise of gangs is selling drugs.

- *Legitimate businesses.* Regular businesses, such as restaurants, bars, and retail establishments, are just as attractive to criminal organizations as illegitimate businesses. Gangs usually do not operate legitimate businesses.

- *Sophistication, discipline, and bonding.* "Sophistication" refers to the efforts criminal organizations use to hide and advance their businesses, such as the use of paper trails, codes, dummy corporations, lawyers, accountants, and so on. Individual organization members must be disciplined in that they act in the organization's interests rather than their own. Finally, criminal organizations often use some type of entry ritual to promote bonding among members, much as sports teams or fraternities do. Gangs typically only participate in the latter two of these activities.[36]

According to Kenney and Finckenauer, most gangs do not meet all these requirements for criminal organizations. This is not to say that some gangs will never rise to this level of sophistication. After all, many crime organizations started out decades ago as gangs. However, as of today, street gangs simply do not meet all the criteria to be criminal organizations.

## Theories of Organized Crime

Two criminological theories are particularly suited to describing the motivations of individuals within criminal organizations: **differential association theory** and **strain theory.** According to differential association theory, criminal organization members learn crime from each other. This is especially relevant because criminal organizations are often composed of individuals with social commonalities. In the case of the crime family, some organization members may be related or may be members of several families from the same neighborhood. In the case of ethnically based organizations, the members may be of the same nationality or ethnicity. In each case, it is likely the members have known each other since childhood and know each other's families. It is especially easy, in this case, to pass on attitudes and techniques for breaking the law. Older members may start their children's criminal education early, for instance, by having them run errands for the organization. The children are further indoctrinated into the organization's goals and methods as they mature.

The second theory that can be applied to criminal organizations is strain theory. Immigration plays an important

> **>◁THINKBACK**
>
> differential association theory (ch. 6)—Sutherland's idea that offenders learn crime from each other.
>
> strain theory (ch. 6)—The idea that people who experience anger and frustration when they cannot achieve cultural goals through legitimate means try to achieve these goals through illegitimate means.

role in organized crime. It is difficult to start life over in a new country, and culture and language barriers can be quite difficult. Finding employment, housing, and a welcoming neighborhood to live in can be major challenges. Therefore, some immigrants who find the goals of American life attractive can be discouraged by the socially accepted means to attain them. A few members of immigrant communities may innovate by using the proceeds of crime to attain these goals. Belonging to a criminal organization of family, friends, and ethnically similar members makes the innovation that much easier. This innovative attitude can even be passed down through the generations, so that although the members of the criminal organization have assimilated into American culture, they continue within the organization because it provides the best means of attaining goals they know of.

## Organized Crime Offenses

In the following sections, we discuss some of the types of activities criminal organizations engage in. Although these organizations might provide services to people of their own ethnicity, their range of activities, customers, and geographic marketplace often extends a great deal further.

**LO2:**

**Summarize** the types of offenses that criminal organizations typically commit.

### Illegal Drug Trafficking

Organized crime is involved in the manufacturing and distribution of illegal drugs, but no single criminal organization controls the drug trade. The drug trade is a highly fragmented activity that grows or changes depending upon the drug demand, and the degree of organization within criminal organizations varies depending upon the type of drug.[37] At one end of the organizational spectrum are the Colombian drug cartels, which operate as corporations that smuggle cocaine, launder money, and engage in extortion.[38] The cartels can tightly control their business enterprises because the Colombian government is weak. The cartels engage in what is often called "narco-terrorism" in which they assassinate politicians, intimidate those who might testify against them, and bribe those who can assist them.[39] The cartels have a sophisticated division of labor and maintain rigid control of members. At the other end of the organizational spectrum are local drug dealers. Membership in the community of local drug dealers is often temporary, and loyalty to other dealers is nonexistent. Yet there is a level of organization that allows for the flow of drugs into the community and the flow of profits out of it.

Jamaican gangs called *posses* are fluid gangs that engage primarily in the rock cocaine trade. Posse members' only link is their Jamaican heritage. Because of the large profits available in the rock cocaine business, the Jamaican posses have used extreme forms of violence to protect themselves and their illegal drug enterprises.[40]

◄ A weak national government is a factor in the success of Colombian drug cartels, which produce, transport, and sell large amounts of cocaine. Here, Colombian law enforcement officials test a sample from a large cocaine seizure near Bogotá.

As mentioned earlier, Asian gangs tend to have loose organizational structures. The traditional **triads** —a common term for Chinese criminal organizations—have devolved from highly centralized and coordinated organizations to ones that are much smaller, less tightly organized, and more international.[41] International Asian criminal organizations work with many U.S.-based Asian gangs in distributing drugs—primarily marijuana and MDMA (commonly called ecstasy)—in cities and suburban areas. Hong Kong criminal organizations, for instance, maintain strong connections to American-Asian gangs such as the Wah Ching, Black Dragons, Tiny Rascal Gangsters, and Black Star, which operate in Detroit, Los Angeles, New York, San Francisco, and Seattle.[42]

To escape police detection, some criminal gangs decentralize their organizations and divide the gang into subgroups, each of which deals with only one aspect of drug trafficking, such as manufacturing, transportation, smuggling, or distribution. This fragmentation results in "marriages of convenience" in which groups share the risks and rewards of drug trafficking.

### Prostitution and Human Trafficking

Prostitution has long been a primary source of income for criminal organizations. Although some prostitutes work only for themselves, others are connected with criminal organizations. Some organizations engage in the transnational smuggling of women and children to be used as sex slaves.[43] These women and children are smuggled from impoverished nations into tourist areas, large cities, and other places where prostitution flourishes and are psychologically, physically, and economically dominated by criminal networks.[44] Unlike the entrepreneurial prostitute who controls his or her

working conditions, many of those caught up in international smuggling rings have little or no control of their lives.

A related form of human trafficking involves the trade in human organs. Because human organs are so scarce and the process for getting them is determined by the medical establishment, there is a thriving black market for hearts, livers, and kidneys.[45] At present, this is not a very large market primarily because it takes a skilled surgeon to extract the organs and keep them healthy and because the system linking buyers and sellers is inefficient. However, as wealthy Americans and Europeans age and Internet commerce matures, the demand for organs will likely increase, and the prices for them will rise exponentially (see *So What's New?*). This combination of large demand and little supply can produce the types of profits that encourage organized crime.

### Gambling

Criminal organizations are attracted to illegal gambling because the operations require a high degree of cooperation. As legalized gambling has proliferated around the United States in the form of casinos, horse racing, dog racing, and state lotteries, organized crime has lost many of its customers to government-run enterprises.[46] Nevertheless, gamblers have plenty of opportunities to engage in illegal gambling in neighborhood lotteries, poker games, and betting on college and professional sports. The activities are popular with some gamblers because they are often able to bet on credit, they find the odds more favorable, and they enjoy the risk of doing something illegal.

The extent to which organized crime is involved in these activities varies by the amount of profit, the nature of the regulatory agency, and the clientele's sophistication. For instance, before celebrities such as professional football star Michael Vick got involved, dog-fighting was a low-profile activity with a wide-ranging, loosely connected organization. However, because the dogs are transported across state lines to fight, the level of organization and communication that must exist to promote this activity exceeds that of a local or regional network.[47]

A great concern is that organized crime will infiltrate legal gambling activities. The legacy of organized crime in Las

**triad** A common term for Chinese criminal organizations.

# so what's new?

### The Organ Trade

Long derided as only a rumor, trafficking in human organs in developing nations has proven to be real. In 2008, Indian police arrested Dr. Amit Kumar, who led a team of doctors in a profitable illegal kidney operation. The group would send out "kidney scouts" to lure day laborers to their clinic with promises of work or by offering desperately impoverished people money for their kidneys. Several smaller kidney rings had been discovered, but authorities say Kumar's was especially sophisticated. Often, the kidneys were removed at gunpoint, and sometimes those who had been promised thousands of dollars for their kidneys were never paid.[1]

According to Nancy Scheper-Hughes, director of Organs Watch, a research project at the University of California, Berkeley, transplant surgeons are collaborating with organ trafficking networks to acquire organs from impoverished people.[2] Kumar, for example, is said to have conducted more than 500 transplants to patients from Britain, the United States, Turkey, Nepal, Dubai, Syria, and Saudi Arabia. The troubling part, experts say, is that Kumar could not have conducted the transplants in isolation. He needed medical professionals to handle the donors, receivers, and organs, as well as surgeons in wealthy nations to direct patients to him, and street thugs to get the victims whose organs were to be used.

In 2007, the World Health Organization estimated that 10 percent of all transplant surgeries involved patients from developed nations traveling to impoverished nations to purchase organs. Authorities estimate at least 15,000 kidneys are transplanted this way each year.[3] Scheper-Hughes says most kidney-trafficking victims are "coerced by need, not by physical force" and that trafficking can be both intranational and transnational.[4]

A twist on the human organ trafficking debate has been the proliferation of "body shows," typically museum exhibits that display preserved human corpses in dynamic poses that show muscles, bones, and tendons. Many of the cadavers come from China, which now has a small industry devoted to preserving cadavers. As of 2008, at least ten body factories were operating in China to satisfy the demand for museum-quality cadavers. Cheap and plentiful labor from medical schools, lax government regulation, and a steady stream of corpses with weak or nonexistent provenances had allowed the industry to flourish.[5]

[1]Amelia Gentleman and Hari Kumar, "Kidney Theft Ring Preys on India's Poorest Laborers," *New York Times,* January 30, 2008, late edition, A3.

[2]Organs Watch, http://sunsite.berkeley.edu/biotech/organswatch/.

[3]Sandhya Srinivasan, "'Dr Kidney' Arrest Exposes Indian Organ Traffic," *Asia Times,* http://www.atimes.com/atimes/South_Asia/JB22Df03.html.

[4]Associated Press, "Transplant Docs Accused of Organ Trafficking," *MSNBC,* February 14, 2008, http://www.msnbc.msn.com/id/23171562/ns/health-health_care/.

[5]David Barboza, "China Turns Out Mummified Bodies for Displays," *New York Times,* August 8, 2006, late edition, 1A.

## THINKING *in* ACTION

What steps should hospitals, doctors' organizations, and governments take to reform the trade in human organs?

---

Vegas, Nevada, has given the public the impression that all modern casino gambling is completely under the control of criminal organizations. This is no longer true. Major casinos are typically run by large conglomerates or American Indian tribes. There is a fear that as American Indian reservations and states continue to develop their gambling enterprises, organized crime will once again move into the gambling business unless these operations are closely controlled.[48] However, there is also speculation that the immense profits available in gambling have made this enterprise so attractive that criminal organizations may be out-competed by noncriminal enterprises.

Gambling has become an acceptable way of raising revenue for the state and one that is politically popular with some segments of the population. Although some people oppose gambling on moral grounds, others consider it an acceptable alternative to raising taxes to fund local government activities. Because of the inherent advantage that is enjoyed by the state, as well as the long odds, state-sponsored gambling has been called "a tax on stupidity." Threats to legalized gambling from organized crime include the prospect of some organized criminal group rigging a state lottery.[49]

### Stolen Property

The market for stolen goods has grown substantially with the increasing globalization of national economies. No longer must goods be fenced locally; now they can be sold to people half a world away. This is especially true of large-ticket items such as automobiles, farm equipment, and jewelry. The cost of stealing and shipping these items to South America, Asia, Africa, Europe, and the Middle East is more than compensated by the prices they fetch at the new destination. The global

▲ Globalization has expanded the market for luxury stolen goods. In a press conference, New York law enforcement displays vehicles recovered in a raid on an international theft-ring that stole hundreds of cars throughout New Jersey, New York, and Connecticut.

market for stolen goods has become much more lucrative and demands a greater degree of communication and organization than in the past. Criminal organizations, therefore, find the transnational trafficking and sale of goods to be profitable.[50]

There are other, more sinister possibilities of property being stolen not from private individuals, but from governments. For instance, with the dissolution of the Soviet Union, there is a great fear that nuclear weapons or the materials to make them will fall into the hands of terrorists. One of the reasons that nuclear nonproliferation is such a big concern for the United Nations is not only because of worry about a nation developing nuclear weapons, but also that nonstate actors, such as terrorists, will be able to buy the materials necessary to make a nuclear weapon and launch their own nuclear war.[51]

Globalization has also affected intellectual property. Commodities ranging from motion-picture DVDs to books, music, and licensed apparel have been smuggled, pirated, or counterfeited. The United States has worked with other nations to attempt to enforce intellectual-property laws, but this is difficult in impoverished nations because the profit for such items is so immense that sellers are willing to risk capture and prosecution. Also, some nations are very lax about enforcing copyright laws. China, for example, has a thriving market in pirated films, music, and licensed goods from the West, much of which is sold openly in street markets.[52]

## The Globalization of Organized Crime

Whereas organized crime was once limited to ethnic groups within a country, the new reality is that crime has gone global, and the old constraints of ethnic loyalties are no longer sufficient to limit or contain organized criminal activity. Woven into the social networks of temporary and decentralized criminal groups are many legitimate businesspeople who are largely indistinguishable from those engaging in organized crime.[53]

This new face of organized crime is one reason a critical-thinking perspective is necessary. Older conceptions of organized crime based upon the Italian Mafia model are no longer adequate to deal with the problem because the range of activities has expanded greatly, as have the geographic and cultural areas in which organized crime has gained a foothold. To successfully deal with organized crime, nations must cooperate in efforts to identify and prosecute those who engage in transnational crime. Such cooperation is sometimes difficult to achieve because the politicians and bureaucrats in some nations have close ties to organized crime themselves and are unwilling to address the concerns of foreign victims. Another reason that some nations are reluctant to prosecute organized crime too vigorously is that the money brought in by these activities can represent a significant portion of those nations' gross national product.

Although globalization might be one facilitator of transnational crime, it might also be the solution. As disadvantaged nations become more involved in world trade, they have a greater incentive to ensure that such commerce is done fairly. Criminal organizations will always seek to exploit the marketplace, but perhaps exploitation can be kept to a minimum if people in disadvantaged nations are provided with opportunities to make a livable wage.[54]

# Think about it

## Remember
Which ethnic groups have been traditionally associated with organized crime?

## Understand
In what ways did the prohibition of alcohol in the United States contribute to the rise of organized crime?

## Apply
Explain how the Racketeering Influenced and Corrupt Organizations (RICO) Act allows prosecutors to target organized crime.

## Analyze
How has the media distorted our understanding of organized crime?

## Evaluate
How serious is organized crime in terms of financial losses for the nation and personal violence between offenders and victims?

## Create
What types of actions can the government take to control organized crime?

# White-Collar Crime

White-collar crime consists of offenses committed by individual employees for their own benefit during the course of legitimate business. Unlike executives who engage in corporate crime, these employees do not seek to lead the company into illegal activities or cover up illegal activities to preserve profit, but merely to enrich themselves. White-collar offenders, who can be difficult to catch, often feel perfectly justified in stealing from a big, bureaucratic company either because they believe that company "owes them" or because the company is so large and complicated that no one will notice the missing funds or items.

**LO3:**

Understand the context within which white-collar offenses are committed.

## Theories of White-Collar Crime

From a theoretical perspective, white-collar crime does not differ substantially from other types of crime, and it can be addressed by at least three criminological theories. The first is Sutherland's differential association theory, which envisions crime as learned. White-collar offenders learn attitudes and techniques from peers and co-workers. If some office workers routinely help themselves to notepads, pens, paper, and the like, then it is more likely that newly hired workers will adopt the same attitudes and learn the techniques for taking the materials out of the office unnoticed.

Another applicable theory is **conflict theory.** Using conflict theory, we can understand how white-collar offenders determine that the corporations and managers exploit workers, and thus try to even the score. White-collar crime is a way of ensuring that wealth is spread to the employee. Conflict theory might require the utilization of another theory, **techniques of neutralization.** Here, the employee rationalizes that the corporation will not miss the money (denial of injury), that the corporation is overcharging customers and underpaying employees (condemnation of condemners), and that the employee needs the money to provide for his or her family (appeal to higher loyalty). Conflict theory would also apply to corporate crime, which we will discuss later. In this case, corporate officers take advantage of their powerful position to use the corporation to exploit employees, consumers, and even the environment to attain more wealth or power, typically both. See Table 11.1

>**THINKBACK**
conflict theory (ch. 8)—A set of criminological theories based on the philosophy of Karl Marx that hold that antisocial behavior stems from class conflict and social and economic inequality.

>**THINKBACK**
techniques of neutralization (ch. 6)—A perspective that refers to the excuses that some offenders use to justify breaking the law.

## Table 11.1 Theories of Organized, White-Collar, and Corporate Crime

| Type of Crime | Theory |
|---|---|
| Organized Crime | **Differential association**<br>Many criminal organizations are set up along family or ethnic lines. Young members learn the attitudes and techniques of organized crime from relatives and peers.<br><br>**Strain theory**<br>Unable to reach social goals by approved means, members of criminal organizations seek out illegal means. |
| White-Collar Crime | **Strain theory**<br>Rather than trying to attain success through the accepted means of working hard, some employees attempt to reach the goal of financial security by taking advantage of their position of trust within the organization.<br><br>**Differential association**<br>Employees learn attitudes and techniques for white-collar crime from peers and co-workers.<br><br>**Conflict theory**<br>Employees determine that corporations and managers exploit workers, and they try to even the score. |
| Corporate Crime | **Conflict theory**<br>Corporations (the bourgeoisie) attempt to increase their money and power through illegal activities at the expense of workers, consumers (the proletariat), or the environment. |

for a brief description of how criminological theory can be applied to organized, white-collar, and corporate crime.

A third applicable theory is Merton's strain theory. Rather than strive for socially accepted goals by socially accepted means, the white-collar offender accepts the goals but has given up on the means to attain them by being a hard-working, honest employee. Instead, the employee "innovates" (see Chapter 6) and seeks the goals through using his or her position as an employee to commit offenses that will provide financial or material reward.

## White-Collar Offenses by Employees

The difference between street crime and white-collar crime is not so much the offenders' motivations, but rather, the techniques. Specifically, white-collar crime does not use violence or the threat of violence and is usually perpetrated with subterfuge. The victims are consumers, clients, the public, or offenders' employers. For example, an employee may defraud the company by charging the customer extra money for a service or product, which the employee then pockets. This sometimes occurs at drive-through fast-food outlets when the employee slightly overcharges the customer for food and keeps the difference. This type of white-collar offense is extremely difficult to detect and does not inflict great economic hardship on the company or the customer. However, when done hundreds of times, such scams can be a significant source of extra revenue for the employee. Common offenses include the following forms of fraud and theft.

- *Securities fraud.* We discussed securities fraud earlier in the section on corporate crime, but securities fraud can also be committed by individual employees on their own without the employer's knowledge. Typical offenses include churning, insider trading, and stock manipulation. Churning occurs when brokers who earn commissions by buying and selling stocks trade shares frequently to inflate commissions. Insider trading is the use of financial information unavailable to the public to gain an advantage in trading securities. In stock manipulation, or "pump and dump" schemes, a securities professional who owns a particular stock urges clients to purchase it. The stock's price rises as individuals buy in, allowing the securities professional to sell his or her shares at an artificially high price.

- *Fraud against the government.* A common form of fraud against the government is tax fraud in which individual taxpayers either do not pay their taxes or try to find illegal ways to avoid paying the taxes they owe. Other examples are government contractors who deceive the government about the cost of goods and services.

- *Bankruptcy fraud.* In this type of fraud an individual will purposefully overspend on goods and services, then declare bankruptcy to get out of paying bills and/or taxes. Sometimes small businesses engage in this type of fraud when they open a line of credit, order goods they quickly resell on the black market, then close and declare bankruptcy, thus erasing all their debts while keeping the proceeds from the illicit sale of the goods.

- *Embezzlement.* **Embezzlement** is a form of theft in which an employee trusted with funds or goods diverts them to personal use. For example, in 2009, a union pension manager for the International Association of Machinists and Aerospace Workers prepared fake invoices to cover the more than $50,000 he took from the union's pension and health and welfare funds.[55]

- *Consumer fraud.* This entails some form of theft or deception in the delivery of goods or services to a consumer. The earlier example of fast-food workers overcharging customers for purchases is an example of this sort of fraud.

- *Bribery and kickbacks.* One common scheme is for an employee to ask for bribes or kickbacks from their company's clients. In the 1990s, MCI Communications executives were involved in a scam that netted more than $6 million in illicit funds. The scheme allowed some MCI customers who were delinquent on their bills to remain as customers if they agreed to pay the executives a personal fee, which the executives then directed to offshore bank accounts. The executives who committed this offense were not impoverished. At least one, Walt Pavlo, earned a six-figure income. Pavlo ended up serving two years in federal prison and says he will be paying off his $5 million restitution for the next 21 years.[56]

- *Pilfering.* **Pilfering** occurs when employees steal money or goods from the employer. Pilfering is typically a low-level activity, such as the occasional theft of office supplies. However, it can be a major source of revenue loss when systematically practiced by many employees.

## Think about it

### Apply
Explain how conflict theory can be used to explain white-collar crime.

### Analyze
What are the major differences between white-collar offenses committed by employees and those committed by company executives?

### Create
Devise a plan to prevent employees from stealing from a company.

**embezzlement** A form of theft in which an employee trusted with funds or goods diverts them to personal use.

**pilfering** Occurs when employees steal small amounts of money or inexpensive goods from an employer.

## Corporate Crime

Like organized crime, corporate crime is not committed by isolated individuals. Rather, it occurs within the normal scope of business when corporate executives step over the boundary between aggressive, but legal, business practices and outright cheating.[57]

Corporate crime is distinguished from white-collar crime committed by individuals in that corporate officers seek to further their interests by furthering the interests of the company. Through stock options, bonuses, raises, promotions, and other inducements, corporate officers reap the benefits of a successful company. To ensure the company's success, corporate officers will sometimes break the law in the company's name.

> **LO4:**
> **Explain** why corporate crime is often difficult to detect.

Corporate crime is often difficult to detect because the offenders are the chief officers of the corporation (see Table 11.2). In their usual occupational duties, these people are considered model citizens who are engaged in a wide variety of social and civic activities. Law enforcement officers are unlikely to suspect someone who is a major fundraiser for the ballet, on the local university's board of directors, and a leader in his or her church. Corporate crime can go undetected for long periods of time because the profits from the illegal enterprises are not always distinguishable from the legitimate profits.[58]

Another reason that corporate crime does not have the visibility of other types of crime is that its victims are often not easy to identify. When a company is involved in a price-fixing scheme, the harm is diffused over a large number of victims, all of whom are injured in relatively minor ways. However, when the harm done to all the victims is totaled, it is clear that corporate crime has a more devastating effect than street crime.[59]

A final reason that corporate crime has such low visibility is that its perpetrators often do not feel the full brunt of the criminal law. Individuals convicted of corporate offenses are often dealt with more leniently, such as being put on probation or being sent to a minimum security prison because they are not violent and do not represent an immediate threat to society. Sometimes, corporations break obscure business laws and the harm is unclear, or the activity is legal in one nation but illegal in another.

For example, bribery is an accepted way of doing business in many nations. In some nations, it may not even be considered a criminal offense. It is, however, in the United States. Companies that must abide by U.S. business law may have problems competing effectively in nations where bribery is an accepted practice. Nevertheless, the old adage "when in Rome do as the Romans do" is not accepted as a rationalization for bribery.

It is difficult, if not impossible, to measure the amount of corporate bribery in the world, but one example is the case of the German company Siemens, which confessed to breaking the U.S. Foreign Corrupt Practices Act. Siemens was accused of paying bribes throughout the world since the mid-1990s to obtain various contracts. Although accused of bribery, Siemens' avoidance of an actual bribery conviction—by paying $800 million in fines to the U.S. government and $528 million in fines to the German government—allowed the company to retain its "responsible contractor" status, which allows it to continue to bid on public contracts in the United States.[60] As of late 2008, more than ten nations were investigating corruption charges against the company.[61] Siemens' global reach and systematic bribery suggested to investigators that bribery has become part of the overall corporate culture in many nations and that enforcement efforts need to be stepped up by making corporations accountable.

As we have seen, corporations that are convicted of offenses or cheat the public of millions of dollars are often punished by fines rather than incarceration of their executives.[62] One explanation for the types of punishments imposed lies in the distinction between the concepts of **vicarious liability,** which assigns responsibility to those who control the company, and **corporate personhood,** which treats the company as a person.

### Who Broke the Law?

Part of the challenge of bringing a case against a corporation is deciding who to prosecute. As is often the case in corporate crime, the actual offense is perpetrated by a relatively small group of executives at the head of the company, possibly with the collusion of some lower-level employees. However, every secretary, driver, janitor, intern, middle manager, and part-timer is not guilty of any criminal offense; many likely did not even notice that the company was involved in illegal dealings. So who gets prosecuted? Two schools of thought attempt to answer this question.

- *Corporate personhood.* This concept of corporate personhood defines a corporation as an artificial person—although without a mind, body, or soul—who, nevertheless, has a person's rights and responsibilities. Lawyers represent this person in court, and the court treats the corporation as a singular entity.

- *Vicarious liability.* The idea of vicarious liability retains some aspects of corporate personhood in that it still considers the corporation as a legal entity. Although this entity has broken the law, the corporation is not considered responsible. The responsible party consists of those who control the corporation's actions. A good analogy is a small child who breaks a vase in a store. The child has

**vicarious liability** Occurs when a person or group of people is considered legally responsible for the actions of another person, group of people, or corporation.

**corporate personhood** The legal treatment of a corporation as a person.

## Table 11.2   Executive Players in Corporate Scandals

The WorldCom, Tyco, and Enron cases are three infamous corporate scandals. Several more executives than those listed were convicted, but these represent the main players in each scandal and are typical of how the government dealt with them.

In 2002, WorldCom disclosed that it inflated profits by improperly accounting for more than $3.9 billion, making earnings seem larger than they actually were. Stock shares plummeted, and the company filed for bankruptcy.[1]

| | |
|---|---|
| **Bernie Ebbers, former CEO** | Convicted of one count of conspiracy, one count of securities fraud, and seven counts of filing false statements with securities regulators. Sentenced to 25 years in prison.[2] |
| **David Myers, former controller** | Pleaded guilty to conspiracy, securities fraud, and false regulatory filings. Helped the government build its case against Ebbers, which the judge factored into Myers's year-and-a-day sentence. |
| **Scott Sullivan, former CFO** | Pleaded guilty to conspiracy, securities fraud, and false financial filings. Like Myers, he cooperated with prosecutors. Sentenced to five years.[3] |

In 2002, Tyco filed an SEC (Securities and Exchange Commission) document stating its former management engaged in improper and illegal activities, including nearly $100 million in unauthorized payments to employees. Former company executives Dennis Kozlowski and Mark Swartz were convicted of taking more than $600 million in corporate bonuses and loans.[4]

| | |
|---|---|
| **Dennis Kozlowski and Mark Swartz, former CEO and former CFO, respectively** | Convicted of 22 counts each of grand larceny and conspiracy and falsifying business records. Also convicted of defrauding shareholders of more than $400 million. Sentenced to a maximum of 25 years in prison. Ordered to pay $134 million in restitution, with $70 million in fines for Kozlowski and $35 million for Swartz.[5] |

In 2001, after restating third-quarter earnings and disclosing that it was trying to restructure a $690 million obligation, Enron filed for Chapter 11 bankruptcy protection and laid off more than 4,000 employees. Auditor Arthur Andersen was indicted for destroying documents as the SEC began investigating Enron's finances. By 2006, 34 Enron executives were convicted on a variety of financial offenses.[6]

| | |
|---|---|
| **Jeff Skilling, former CEO** | Found guilty in May 2006 of 28 counts of insider trading, securities fraud, and conspiracy-related charges. Sentenced to prison for 24 years and 4 months.[7] |
| **Ken Lay, former CEO** | Found guilty in May 2006 of six counts of Enron-related fraud and fraud related to his personal bank accounts. Lay died in Colorado six weeks after his conviction, which was vacated.[8] |
| **Andrew Fastow, former CFO** | Pleaded guilty to conspiracy to commit wire fraud and conspiracy to commit wire and securities fraud. Helped the government build cases against Lay and Skilling. Sentenced to six years in prison in 2004.[9] |
| **Lea Fastow, assistant treasurer** | Wife of Andrew Fastow. Pleaded guilty to one misdemeanor for not reporting personal income to the IRS. Sentenced to year in prison and one year of post-release supervision. Began sentence in July 2004. Released in June 2005.[10] |

[1] CBC News Online, "The WorldCom Story," September 26, 2006, http://www.cbc.ca/news/background/worldcom/.

[2] Associated Press, "Ebbers Sentenced to 25 Years in Prison," MSNBC, July 13, 2005, http://www.msnbc.msn.com/id/8474930.

[3] Reuters and Associated Press, "Ex-WorldCom CFO Scott Sullivan Gets 5 Years," Fox News, August 11, 2005, http://www.foxnews.com/story/0,2933,165409,00.html.

[4] MSNBC, "Timeline: The Tyco Scandal," http://www.msnbc.msn.com/id/8258997/.

[5] Associated Press, "Ex-Tyco Executives Get Up to 25 Years in Prison," September 20, 2005, MSNBC, http://www.msnbc.msn.com/id/9399803/.

[6] "The Fall of Enron," *Houston Chronicle,* http://www.chron.com/news/specials/enron/.

[7] MSNBC, "Timeline."

[8] Ibid.

[9] Ibid.

[10] Ibid.

broken the vase, but the parent is considered responsible for the child's actions and must pay the damages.

Currently, the legal system prosecutes corporate offenses using vicarious liability. For example, in the Enron case in which the company executives were convicted of a range of financial offenses—including the creation of earnings and cash flow and the concealment of debt—the government prosecuted 34 executives, more than 20 of whom went to prison, including former chief financial officer Andrew Fastow and former chief executive officer Jeffrey Skilling.[63] A brief examination of corporate offenses and their effect on society and the criminal justice system will help distinguish corporate crime from organized crime and white-collar crime, as well as show the range of harm.

## Offenses Against Consumers

A number of schemes, scams, and dishonest activities, including unsafe products, unsafe food, and fraud, are aimed at consumers. These schemes are cloaked in the guise of legitimate business practices and often offer consumers unbelievable deals in conducting business with a company. Often, these schemes prey upon consumers' naiveté and gullibility or the greed of those who want something for nothing.

**Schemes and Scams**    A number of investigations have been conducted into auto-repair scams. These shops will overestimate the cost of repairs, claim to install new parts, and sometimes even sabotage the car to pad the estimates and make the consumer spend more money. Sometimes, it is hard to tell where incompetence stops and criminal activity begins in some of these auto-repair shops. This is one reason why auto insurance companies usually require three estimates for damages. Some auto-repair scams are perpetrated against elderly persons or women because they are assumed to know little about cars.

Some dishonest schemes involve the sale of products that do not work. In 2007, a jury found the owner of a company called Berkeley Premium Nutraceuticals, which sold "Enzyte," an herbal "male enhancement" tablet, guilty of conspiracy to commit mail fraud, bank fraud, and money laundering. The company cheated its customers out of $100 million through deceptive advertising, manipulating credit card transactions, and refusing to accept returns or cancel orders. The company was also accused of creating fictitious doctors to endorse Enzyte, fabricating customer-satisfaction surveys, and making up statistics that supported claims about the supplement's effectiveness.[64]

Consumers are often victimized by false advertising. Grandiose claims are made for a product that promises to produce results that seem incredulous to any rational person but believable to the gullible and desperate. For instance, the Psychic Readers Network collected more than $1 billion from consumers who called the company's television spokesperson, Miss Cleo, a purported psychic, to get advice about their personal lives. As it turned out, Miss Cleo was not a Jamaican fortune-teller as she claimed, but rather an American actress who affected a Jamaican accent. Eventually, the Federal Trade Commission charged two corporations, Access Resource Services and Psychic Readers Network, with deceptive advertising, billing, and collection practices after the "free calls" promised by Miss Cleo actually resulted in hundreds of dollars in charges for those who called.[65] These types of telephone scams harm consumers in two ways. First, they are often conducted by companies or individuals who are offshore and collect exorbitant long-distance telephone fees that become apparent only after the victims receive their phone bills. Second, these scams hurt consumers by giving ridiculous and counterproductive advice to people seeking real answers to real problems in their lives.[66]

**Unsafe Products**    Sometimes a company manufactures a product that proves unsafe, but it does not quickly remove that product from circulation. Companies have a profit motive, and history has shown that many companies are often cavalier about the safety and health of consumers. Nowhere has the disregard for consumers been more apparent than in the tobacco industry. Knowing full well that their product was addictive and contributed to health problems such as cancer, the tobacco industry worked extremely hard to sup-

▼ The Psychic Readers Network collected more than $1 billion from consumers who called its hotlines for "psychic" advice. In 2002, Bob Butterworth—then attorney general of Florida, one of the states that brought a civil suit against the company—holds up a playing card while pretending to talk on the phone to make a point during a news conference.

press, distort, and explain away tobacco's harmful effects.[67] Until 1997, the U.S. tobacco industry won every lawsuit brought against it. Finally, as part of a lawsuit brought in the 1990s, prosecutors found evidence that cigarette companies knew as early as 1970 that smoking causes lung cancer. In 1998, the industry agreed to pay $368 billion in damages.[68]

Many products are unsafe because of faulty design. Manufacturers have found ways to make their products safer, but the cost of doing so is expensive. Automobile manufacturers must make countless decisions about what design elements to put in their vehicles in light of the additional cost. An infamous example of these calculations is the Ford Pinto. During the 1970s, it was discovered that after relatively minor rear-end collisions the car's fuel system ruptured and burst into flames. Ford calculated that it could save more than $87 million by continuing to make the unsafe Pinto even though it was estimated that 180 people would die in rear-end collisions in these cars. Once several cases involving injuries and fatalities hit the courts, Ford found that its calculations were wrong as a jury awarded more than $120 million to a California teenager who was badly burned in a Pinto that burst into flames after it was hit by a car going only 35 miles per hour.[69]

During the 2007 Christmas season, retailers' toy sales declined sharply because many toys were found to contain lead paint. Most of these toys were manufactured in China where safety regulations are relaxed. Although products imported into the United States are supposed to meet minimum standards, the manufacturers of these toys did not sufficiently supervise their Chinese factories to ensure that these standards were being met. Consequently, many toys were recalled as buyers frantically attempted to determine whether the toys on store shelves were made in China, were coated with lead paint, or both. Although globalization has provided inexpensive goods for the U.S. market, the trade-off between inexpensive products and consumer safety has become a continuing problem.[70]

**Unsafe Food**   The Food and Drug Administration has established standards for the safety of the nation's food supply, and ensuring that food meets these standards requires inspectors to be on-site in food-processing plants. Unlike the toy industry, in which the components of a toy determined to be safe stay that way, fresh food that is safe at one time can go bad quickly. Therefore, the food's environment—not only the manufacturing and preparation environment, but also storage and transportation environment—must be considered before food is deemed safe for consumption.[71] Human beings can be healthy only within a narrow range of environmental parameters, and this includes what is consumed.

Globalization has made ensuring the safety of the nation's food supply a difficult task. Ingredients come from all over the world, and it is almost impossible to ensure that each product is safe. In 2007, it was discovered that some popular brands of pet food imported into the United States from China contained the industrial chemical melamine.

The dangers of the tainted pet food were not immediately apparent because the melamine slowly damaged the kidneys of dogs and cats, resulting in thousands of pet deaths.[72] The use of melamine, which was added to wheat gluten to make the pet food appear to have a higher level of protein, gave rise to concerns about the tainting of processed food for humans, which can also contain wheat gluten. In 2009, federal authorities obtained guilty pleas from a U.S. company for importing the tainted ingredients, but they could not pursue the two Chinese companies that exported the ingredients.[73]

There are two basic problems with unadulterated food. One problem is intentional cheating by manufacturers who cut costs by using substandard ingredients, fail to use proper storage and refrigeration equipment, and insert unsafe items into the food. An early example of this type of unsafe practice was detailed in Upton Sinclair's 1906 novel *The Jungle*. In the book, Sinclair described workers falling into the vats of lard and being turned into food sold to consumers. Sinclair's book was influential in the passage of the Pure Food and Drug and the Meat Inspection Acts of 1906.[74]

The second type of problem stems from the attempts of food companies to spend less money producing food. The food industry engages in many practices that are designed to increase profits but have the potential to make people extremely sick or even kill them. For example, the poultry industry uses a technique called forced molting. This practice involves starving hens for a week or more until they begin to lose body weight, stop laying, and lose their feathers. Then when their feed is returned, the chickens begin laying again and produce more eggs. One report claims that "these molted chickens are 5,000 times more susceptible to salmonella than normally fed birds."[75] In February 2007, the U.S. Department of Agriculture (USDA) ordered the largest beef recall in U.S. history after the Humane Society of the United States released video showing workers at a California slaughterhouse shoving sick or crippled cows with forklifts to get them to stand, and dragging sick cows with chains, shocking them with electric prods, and shooting streams of water in their noses and faces. The lawsuit filed by the Humane Society claimed that the workers were trying to get the animals to stand so they could be considered acceptable for human consumption. Fifty million pounds of meat from that slaughterhouse were sent to school lunch programs nationwide.[76]

Although food recalls are cause for concern, in many ways it is encouraging to see the inspection system at work to protect the nation's food supply. It is difficult to estimate how much adulterated food slips past inspectors, but whether or not that amount is substantial, we can reasonably expect the USDA's aggressive inspection system to not only catch a good deal of tainted food, but also to prevent food contamination in the first place.[77] In 2009, federal authorities confirmed that a peanut-processing plant in Georgia was the source of a salmonella outbreak that sickened hundreds of people across the United States, possibly killing eight. The plant produced peanut butter and peanut paste that were used in a host of other processed foods. One Texas company connected to the outbreak was fined $14.6 million by the state's health agency. As of 2009, the federal investigation was ongoing.[78]

**Fraud**    Unsafe products, such as poorly designed automobiles or tainted meat, can kill, so there is an overwhelming positive value to well-designed automobiles and safe meat. There is, however, another type of corporate crime that does not have such a direct effect. Fraud, which involves intentional deception, might not kill, but it can fundamentally damage the economy, a delicate institution that operates smoothly only when people trust it. Corporations and white-collar offenders violate this trust when they commit fraud. Three types of trust violations that are considered fraud are securities fraud, corporate fraud, and fiduciary fraud.[79]

- *Securities fraud.* The rules of financial markets are designed to level the playing field so that everyone has an equal opportunity to use their knowledge and judgment to invest wisely and make money. Some people, however, cheat by providing misleading information about their financial products, colluding with others to artificially drive up stock prices, and using insider information in their business dealings.[80]

- *Corporate fraud.* Corporations are covered by a well-regulated system of accounting practices that are designed to ensure transparency and honesty. However, occasionally some corporations "fiddle with the books" to mask losses or to inflate their earnings or profits. Sometimes, these attempts to manipulate corporation holdings become so convoluted it is difficult for regulators to ascertain the organization's true value.[81]

- *Fiduciary fraud.* Fiduciary fraud occurs when individuals and corporations entrust their money and many of their financial dealings to banks, insurance companies, and investment companies, and the companies violate that trust. These institutions, which assure people that their money is safe, sometimes fall victim to unscrupulous employees. Although embezzlement is a potential problem whenever money is controlled by those who do not own it, a new level of fraud has emerged in recent years in which it is not the lowly bank clerk, but rather the bank president who violates trust. There are three types of this form of fraud. The first type is the outright theft of monies from customers' accounts. Bank officials divert money to their own accounts through elaborate schemes designed to launder and hide assets in offshore banks. This form of corporate crime has much in common with white-collar crime because the motivation for it is greed on the part of the bank administration. In the second type of fraud, officials will use funds from one account to cover shortfalls in other accounts. They usually intend to pay back the accounts from which they "borrowed" funds, often by investing in extremely volatile and risky products. The motivation for this type of fraud has to do with bank officials' desire to keep their jobs when economic forces make the markets

more risky. At some point, this shell game falls apart, the perpetrators are exposed, and investors lose their money. In the end, because the government guarantees deposits through the Federal Deposit Insurance Corporation (FDIC), it is the taxpayers who are stuck with the tab.[82] This type of fiduciary fraud can be so widespread that it affects not only individual investors and depositors, but also the entire banking system. Federal bailouts of financial institutions can be done only a few times before they become problematic. This is one reason that the government pursues corporate crime so thoroughly. It is almost impossible for individuals to conduct business without entrusting money to banks and other financial institutions. Financial institutions are almost always trustworthy, and banking regulations make their business affairs open and transparent. However, when the officials of these institutions get greedy or careless, they have the opportunity to divert large sums of money and cover up their misdeeds by "cooking the books."[83] A third form of fiduciary fraud involves company officials stealing from employee pension funds. In this type of fraud, money set aside for employee retirements is managed and invested by experts to ensure that the pension fund's assets are adequate to pay the promised pensions to employees. From time to time, those entrusted with these pension funds divert the money to their own purposes. Sometimes, they make bad investments with the funds and scramble to recover by making even riskier investments that ultimately fail.[84] The result is that many people who counted on investment managers to make reasonable and safe investments cannot retire because the pension fund no longer has ad-

▼ **Officials from financial services firms AIG and Goldman Sachs testify during a hearing before the Financial Crisis Inquiry Commission. The federal commission was tasked with investigating the crisis that has affected the economy in recent years.**

▶ Environmental crime is pervasive in many regions of the United States. Even federally protected areas are at risk.

equate resources. Individual investors cannot foresee these types of fraud because they do not have the opportunity to review the pension fund's financial records. Those covered by the fund rely on laws and honest fund managers to ensure that their investments are properly handled. Greed mixed with bad luck and incompetence has led some pension-fund managers to overstep the law.

## Offenses Against the Environment

**Environmental crime**—offenses that manipulate the surroundings to the extent that human beings, animals, or plants that live within it are harmed or unable to survive—can be committed by the government, multinational corporations, small businesses, and individuals. In this section, we will discuss environmental crime as a subset of corporate crime because corporations have committed some of the largest and most visible environmental offenses. Much, if not most, U.S. environmental legislation has been passed to control the environmentally harmful activities of corporate entities rather than those of individuals, although these laws may be applied to individuals in some cases. For example, one of the goals of the 1970 Clean Air Act was for the states to set pollutant standards for "appropriate industrial sources" within each state.[85] As with corporate and white-collar crime, a major motivation for environmental crime is money, typically not to make it, but to save it. Following environmental laws, treating hazardous waste, recycling some materials and properly disposing of others, and training workers and designing plants and industrial processes to be environmentally safe can be costly. Unfortunately, many corporations consider these as costs that can be saved.

The damages caused by environmental crime are tricky to assess because they are so long-term and wide in scope. In comparison, the damages caused by a single street crime play out over a relatively short period of time and affect only one or a few people, even in the case of murder. This is not to trivialize the effects of serious street crime, only to point out that the effects are relatively narrow. The effects of a major environmental crime, however, can last for generations and directly affect hundreds or even thousands of people. Tainted water, soil, and air can not only be individually fatal, but also cause serious health issues for survivors and birth defects in their children. In developing nations, massive trash dumps can swallow whole villages, destroy forests and wetlands, and leave no room to grow food or raise farm animals.

Environmental legislation and law enforcement are still relatively weak, not necessarily because lawmakers and citizens do not care about the environment, but because pollution often goes hand-in-hand with economic development. Corporations that pollute the environment through manufacturing processes, the transportation of toxic products, and the manufacture of products that contain toxic materials also happen to be large employers that bring money into their home communities.

Another issue is modern society's limited ability to do without some of these products, such as plastic, computers, and automobiles. The modern Western lifestyle depends on the use of products that are toxic in their manufacture, use, and, often, their disposal. Consequently, the legal system must be careful in its pursuit of corporate polluters. A large fine levied against a polluting corporation might cause the business to raise prices or leave the community and move to a nation where environmental laws are more lenient or nonexistent. In the United States, the Environmental Protection Agency (EPA) helps enforce environmental laws by doing research and investigating "negligent, knowing or willful violations of federal environmental law."[86] Environmental offenses are not always massive, headline-grabbing disasters. Here are two examples of typical environmental offenses that the EPA would be responsible for.

- A manager at a metal-finishing company tells employees not to use the company's wastewater treatment unit

> **environmental crime** An offense that manipulates the surroundings such that human beings, animals, or plants that live within the area are harmed or unable to survive.

because the chemicals needed for the unit are expensive. Instead, the company sends untreated wastewater to the sewer system, violating local environmental regulations. In this instance, the plant manager is guilty of a criminal violation of the Clean Water Act.

■ To avoid the proper, but expensive, treatment of its hazardous waste, the owner of a cleaning-solvents manufacturer sends dozens of buckets of highly flammable, caustic waste to a local, municipal landfill that is not authorized to receive hazardous waste. In this case, the company owner is guilty of a criminal violation of the Resource Conservation and Recovery Act.[87]

**Environmental Criminology**   Environmental criminology is an emerging field as scholars and activists recognize and evaluate the types of harm done by careless or intentional damage to the environment. Environmental criminology, sometimes called "green" criminology, covers a range of activities and behaviors that have not been within the traditional scope of criminology.[88] The forms of environmental crime are numerous, and their financial costs can be staggering. Environmental offenses range from the everyday to the exceptional, and their legal and political consequences can drag on for decades (see *Doubletake*).

The issues that environmental criminology cover include, but are not limited to, the following concerns as suggested by social scientists Piers Beirne and Nigel South:

■ the abuse and exploitation of ecological systems, including animal life

■ corporate disregard for damage to land, air, and water quality

■ profiteering from practices that destroy lives and leave a legacy of damage for subsequent generations

■ military actions that adversely affect the environment, humans, and animals

■ new challenges to international treaties and to the emerging field of bioethics (the philosophical study of moral values and controversies in biology and medicine)

■ illicit markets in nuclear materials

■ legal monopolization of natural resources (e.g., privatization of water, patenting of natural products, etc.) leading to divisions between the resource-rich and the resource-impoverished

■ individual acts of cruelty to animals

■ institutional, socially acceptable human domination of animals in agribusiness, such as in slaughterhouses[89]

Beirne and South demonstrate how a critical-thinking perspective is useful by looking at areas that had previously been governed and controlled by regulatory agencies that defined these behaviors as regulatory violations rather than as criminal offenses. Although extreme cases of these behaviors have resulted in offenses in the past, there is now a new and more aggressive focus on protecting the environment and ex-

tending protections to animals. Because of the harms done by those who damage the environment, the field of criminology must expand its scope to ensure that it fully considers the direct and indirect harms of environmental crime to the environment, animals, and human beings. A few specific examples illustrate the range of environmental criminology and its potential to reformulate its mandate as a discipline concerned with the protection of the various types of victims affected by this type of offense.

**Animal Rights**   The problem of animal exploitation is becoming a concern for criminology. Humans' concern for animal rights exists on a continuum. At one end of the extreme are those who would knowingly harm no animal, even refusing to use them for food. At the other end are those who believe animals are to be used not only for food, but also for labor, apparel, and sport. They also support the use of animals in medical experimentation to ensure that drugs, surgeries, and other procedures are safe.[90]

Animal rights issues present a "slippery slope" for an ecological debate. One important consideration is that the relationship between humans and animals is culturally and historically bound. For instance, in the move to protect whales from being exterminated by large whaling organizations, allowances have been made for indigenous peoples who have historically hunted whales for subsistence. This tension was also apparent in the fox hunts of Great Britain. These hunts, traditionally the purview of aristocrats, were opposed by those who considered the practice immoral. Some people would attempt to sabotage the hunts by laying down artificial scents for the hounds to follow, blowing horns to confuse the hunters, and attempting to physically block access to hunting areas. Fox hunting was banned in England and Wales in 2005.[91]

**Nuclear Energy**   As oil prices rise, a number of individuals and corporations have become vocal proponents of revitalizing the nuclear energy business. Environmentalists who claim that nuclear energy is not safe oppose their efforts. The catastrophic damage that can result when a nuclear power plant malfunctions serves as a persuasive argument to be cautious about adopting this source of energy. Although the safety record of nuclear power plants is actually quite good, these plants present another problem. Nuclear energy produces waste that is not only toxic, but also difficult to dispose of safely. Thousands of tons of nuclear waste have been produced, and, for the most part, it has been stored on the sites of the nuclear energy facilities.

One federal proposal is to move all this nuclear waste to Nevada to a storage facility at Yucca Mountain.[92] Advocates for this proposal claim that the deep underground storage facility is a safe and viable option for the handling of nuclear waste. However, many people are concerned about nuclear waste seeping into the environment, as well as the problems of safely transporting this waste across the nation. Environmental criminologists question the adequacy of

# doubletake

## The Bhopal Disaster

Early one morning near the town of Bhopal, India, in 1984, a valve at a Union Carbide pesticide plant burst, releasing a large amount of deadly gas. The town's 900,000 residents panicked as they tried to escape.[1] In the days following the world's worst industrial accident, 8,000 people died, and 50,000 people were treated for illness and injury.[2] Over the years, 20,000 people have died from the long-term effects of the gas.[3] A 1999 study concluded that Bhopal's groundwater was still toxic.

The Indian government, which considers the disaster a criminal offense, asserted that U.S.-owned Union Carbide was at fault. CEO Warren Anderson was arrested when he arrived to deal with the disaster but fled the country when released on bail. In 1989, Union Carbide paid the Indian government $470 million to settle a civil suit, but accident victims protested that the settlement was far less than what they were owed.[4] In 1991, the Indian government reinstated criminal charges against Union Carbide and Anderson, declared both as fugitives, and requested their extradition by the U.S. government.[5] In 2010, an Indian court convicted eight Indian plant employees—one of whom had since died—of "death by negligence."[6] Union Carbide was later sold to Dow Chemical and no longer does business in India, but the Indian government still holds the company criminally responsible. Anderson, although retired, still faces charges.[7]

The disaster has affected U.S. law. In 1990, as a direct result of the Bhopal disaster, the U.S. Clean Air Act was changed to require refineries and chemical plants to ensure against releases of toxic gas. The first criminal prosecution of that requirement came after a 2005 explosion at a British Petroleum (BP) Texas refinery killed 15 workers, injured more than 170 others, and released poisonous gas. BP admitted failing to maintain the equipment and pleaded guilty to environmental criminal offenses, including a $50 million felony violation of the Clean Air Act. The company agreed to pay $373 million in fines and restitution, serve three years probation, spend $161 million to reduce the refinery's pollution, pay $12 million in penalties, and provide $6 million for a community air-cleaning initiative.[8]

As for the Bhopal disaster, U.S. courts still do not recognize any criminal wrongdoing by Union Carbide, although recent documents suggest that the company cut corners on the plant's design and maintenance to save money.[9] Every year in Bhopal on the anniversary of the disaster, Anderson is burned in effigy in the streets.[10]

[1]BBC, 1984: "Hundreds Die in Bhopal Chemical Accident," http://news.bbc.co.uk/onthisday/hi/dates/stories/december/3/newsid_2698000/2698709.stm.

[2]BBC, "Bhopal Case Still Open for Ex-Chief Warren Anderson," June 8, 2010, http://news.bbc.co.uk/2/hi/world/south_asia/10267196.stm.

[3]Debora MacKenzie, "Fresh Evidence on Bhopal Disaster," *NewScientist* 176, no. 2372 (December 7, 2002): 6.

[4]Devin Leonard, "Bhopal Ghosts (Still) Haunt Union Carbide One CEO's Nightmare," *Fortune,* April 3, 2000, http://money.cnn.com/magazines/fortune/fortune_archive/2000/04/03/277059/index.htm.

[5]Mark Hertsgaard, "Bhopal's Legacy," *Nation* 278, no. 20 (May 24, 2004): 6–7.

[6]BBC, "Bhopal Trial: Eight Convicted over India Gas Disaster," June 7, 2010, http://news.bbc.co.uk/2/hi/south_asia/8725140.stm.

[7]BBC, "Bhopal Case Still Open."

[8]"Explosion Victims Want BP to Pay Bigger Fine," *Wall Street Journal,* November 21, 2007, eastern edition; Peter Haldis, "Victims of BP Texas City Incident Want Plea Bargain Thrown Out," *World Refining & Fuels Today* 2, no. 227 (November 26, 2007): 7; Matthew Tresaugue, "BRIEF: BP to Pay Almost $180 Million to Settle Pollution Case," *Houston Chronicle,* February 19, 2009; Environmental Protection Agency, "BP to Pay Largest Criminal Fine Ever for Air Violations," October 25, 2007, http://yosemite.epa.gov/opa/admpress.nsf/d0cf6618525a9efb85257359003fb69d/ca0637fa729266968525737f0060bc4b.

[9]MacKenzie, "Fresh Evidence."

[10]Hertsgaard, "Bhopal's Legacy."

▲ Environmental disaster can strike at any time. Here, fire-boat crews battle the blaze on British Petroleum's offshore oil rig Deepwater Horizon in April 2010. The disaster killed 11 workers and sank the rig into the Gulf of Mexico, causing the largest offshore oil spill in U.S. history.

## THINKING *in* ACTION

1. Do you agree with India in treating the Bhopal disaster as a criminal offense?
2. Should Union Carbide's CEO have been held accountable in the United States for the disaster?
3. Some victims of the 2005 BP explosion believe the company was not sufficiently punished. Do you agree or disagree?

reports on nuclear safety and argue that the construction of nuclear plants will expose large numbers of people to potential harm.[93]

**Unsafe Materials**  Environmental criminologists are concerned about the harmful ingredients contained in many everyday products. One such product is lead paint, which can affect brain function in children and adults, causing aggressive or violent behavior.[94] Although lead paint is now prohibited in the United States, the 2007 scare over lead paint on toys imported from China demonstrates that the problem of eliminating this unsafe product is still an important consideration.

An interesting aspect of the issue of unsafe materials is that of their disposal. Although consumers have long used toxic materials, such as lead paint and home pesticides, the use of unsafe materials is reaching record levels because of their ubiquity in consumer electronics. Computers, cell phones, video games, personal digital assistants, GPS units, and nearly any other type of consumer electronic contain poisonous substances such as lead, mercury, cadmium, chromium, and materials containing PCBs (polychlorinated biphenyls). These materials, sometimes called "e-waste," are difficult to recycle and tend to pile up in landfills where they might leach toxins and poison the water and soil. Because it is so poisonous, e-waste is often shipped off to developing nations for disposal.

Recyclers and waste contractors in developed nations take the trash with the promise that it will be either thoroughly destroyed or recycled. Unfortunately, this is often not the case. Unscrupulous companies, for example, will label broken computers as "donations" and ship them to nations like Ghana under the guise of charity. When the computers are discovered to be broken, they end up at dump sites like Agbogbloshie, a dumping ground next to a polluted, dead lagoon, that is a common final resting place for tons of the world's e-waste. Ghanaians who live among the electronic trash pick through it looking for salvageable items, such as working hard drives, that they can sell. Nonworking items are usually burned (releasing even more toxins) to release precious metals such as gold and copper.

Environmental watchdog groups estimate that 50 to 80 percent of e-waste collected for recycling is instead shipped to China, India, Africa, and Pakistan. An international treaty, the 1989 Basel Convention, bans the export of e-waste to less-developed nations; however, the United States has not ratified the treaty. The only e-waste exports regulated by the EPA are cathode-ray tubes, which are used in television sets and computer monitors.[95]

**Eco-Bio-Genocide**  Targeting the environment as a military strategy has long-lasting ramifications. For instance, during the Vietnam War, the United States used an herbicide called Agent Orange to defoliate the country-

▲ The use of nuclear energy and what to do with the waste it produces is an important issue as the need for alternative sources of energy grows. Environmental criminologists worry that criminal negligence in the operation of nuclear power plants could have tragic results. Here, protesters rally against using Yucca Mountain, Nevada, as a nuclear waste depository.

side and deny the enemy a place to hide. U.S. veterans of the war as well as the people of Vietnam have felt the repercussions of this policy as Agent Orange has caused early deaths from cancer and birth defects. At present, the United States has practiced the same type of defoliation policy (albeit with different herbicides) in South American nations in an effort to eradicate coca crops, the source of most cocaine in the United States.[96] The long-term effects of this chemical eradication policy on the environment and the people in the affected countries will not be known for many years.[97]

# Think about it

**Remember**

What three types of trust violations are considered fraud?

**Understand**

Why is the problem of unsafe food considered corporate crime?

**Evaluate**

How are the terms "corporate personhood" and "vicarious liability" important in the prosecution of corporate crime?

# Summary

**LO1:** **Define and understand the nature of organized crime.**

- Organized and white-collar crime are criminal offenses perpetrated in order to amass financial assets or to save them.
- It is inaccurate to assume that people who share an ethnicity, culture, and language coalesce around a specific criminal element.

**LO2:** **Summarize the types of offenses that criminal organizations typically commit.**

- Criminal organizations typically engage in illegal drug trafficking, prostitution and human trafficking, gambling, and stolen property.
- Abadinsky offers a number of attributes characteristic of criminal organizations: no political goals, hierarchical organization, limited or exclusive membership, a unique subculture, self-perpetuating, violence and bribery, specialization or division of labor, monopolistic, and governed by rules or regulations.

**LO3:** **Understand the context within which white-collar offenses are committed.**

- White-collar crime takes place within a business or corporate environment, but it refers to the actions of individual employees.
- Offenses include fraud, deception, and theft. Victims of white-collar crime include consumers, clients, the public, or the offenders' employers.

**LO4:** **Explain why corporate crime is often difficult to detect.**

- Corporate crime involves legitimate businesses that engage in unfair business practices, bribe regulators, misrepresent financial assets, or knowingly produce faulty or unsafe products.
- Corporate crime is often difficult to detect because those who engage in it are often the chief executives of major corporations. The profits from the illegal enterprises are not always distinguishable from the legitimate profits. Also, the victims of corporate crime are often not easy to identify.
- Two schools of thought about prosecuting corporate crime are corporate personhood and vicarious liability.
- As suggested by Beirne and South, environmental offenses include the abuse of ecological systems; corporate disregard for damage to land, air, and water quality; profiteering from practices that leave a legacy of damage for subsequent generations; military actions that adversely affect the environment, humans, and animals; bioethics; illicit markets in nuclear materials; legal monopolization of natural resources; and cruelty to animals, including individual acts and those involving agriculture and meat-processing.

# Questions

1. How do criminal organizations differ from conventional offenders and terrorist groups?
2. Trace the development of organized crime in the United States.
3. What are typical organized crime activities?
4. How does corporate crime differ from white-collar crime?
5. In what ways can environmental offenses be committed within corporate, white-collar, or organized crime contexts?
6. What is corporate personhood? Vicarious liability? What is unusual about these ideas?
7. Give examples of corporate crime and white-collar crime.
8. What are the financial and emotional effects of offenses against consumers?
9. What is the typical financial motivation behind environmental crime?
10. Discuss why environmental legislation and law enforcement are still relatively weak.

# 12

# Public-Order
# Offenses and

## what's inside

# Values

**As you read, keep in mind these learning objectives:**

**LO1:** Give an example of a public-order offense.

**LO2:** Discuss why the use and abuse of drugs are important to the study of criminology.

**LO3:** Understand the basis of laws prohibiting prostitution, pornography, and sodomy.

**LO4:** Compare and contrast the concept of gambling as an effective way to raise public revenue with the concept of gambling as a harmful activity that must be controlled by law.

**LO5:** Explain why the work of the criminal justice system would be more efficient if it could focus only on violent and property offenses.

Many behaviors that offend our sense of right or wrong, morality, or public safety have been made criminal offenses by governing bodies. Other people, who do not consider these behaviors to be wrong or dangerous, attempt to change these laws or violate them on a regular basis without feeling a sense of guilt. These crimes of values, or **public-order offenses,** present the criminal justice system with perplexing dilemmas in arresting, prosecuting, punishing, and rehabilitating offenders who do not believe they are harming society. For criminologists, public-order offenses are fascinating examples of how behaviors become defined as crime and how society responds. In many ways, public-order offenses show us how the line between crime and acceptable behavior is constantly in political and social flux and how the criminal justice system adapts to the changing demands of citizens whose values change with the times.[1]

Ideally the criminal law reflects the values of the population to which it is applied. Citizens elect representatives to fashion laws that reinforce their sense of fairness, justice, and morality. However, there is always a certain tension between laws and the people for two reasons. The first is that those who make the laws do not always act in everyone's best interests. In a country where the majority rules, it is inevitable that some people will believe that the law is unfavorable to their concerns. For instance, although slavery was the law of the land for more than a century in the South, it had disastrous consequences for those subjected to its racial discrimination. The second reason for the tension between the law and citizens is that the values of individuals and communi-

ties are a moving target. As social and economic conditions change, so do values.

Public-order offenses are often called victimless crimes.[2] A **victimless crime** offends the values of a segment of society and is against the law but has the willing participation of all parties to the activity and causes no obvious harm to anyone involved. Nevertheless, participants in the activity seek to keep it from becoming known to police. For example, transactions involving drug sales or prostitution include a buyer and a seller; as long as each party is satisfied with the exchange, there is no victim. If the deal goes bad and someone gets hurt or killed, then the offense is assault or homicide. However, when the transaction goes smoothly, both the customer and the seller are satisfied. Those who use illegal drugs do not believe that they are crime victims. They have freely chosen to consume these substances.[3] Those who participate in illegal gambling have a similar attitude. They choose to gamble and prefer that the government stay out of that particular area of their lives. Still, society condemns victimless crimes, and the criminal justice system pursues the "offenders" and "victims" who take part.

## General and Indirect Victims

The class of public-order offenses has been created to protect individuals who do not freely engage in these behaviors but might be general or indirect victims. Some people

---

**public-order offense** An activity that is against the law and offends the values, norms, and/or morals of a dominant sector of society.

**victimless crime** An activity that offends the values of a segment of society and is against the law but has the willing participation of all parties and causes no obvious harm. Those involved in the activity seek to keep it from becoming known to police.

believe that public-order offenses, even when committed by consenting adults in private, affect society in general or family members, neighbors, or the community. Let's briefly consider how three categories of public-order offenses influence the lives of others.

**LO1:**

**Give** an example of a public-order offense.

- *Substance abuse.* The use of and trafficking in illegal drugs affect a variety of people in a number of ways. The drug user might think that no one else is harmed, but drug use can be expensive and addicting. A drug user might use money for rent and food to buy drugs, thus victimizing his or her family by depriving them of a decent standard of living. The effects of drugs can make the user unable to hold down a job, and the drug user must then get money another way, often by stealing or robbery. The danger posed to society can be substantial if violence is used to get or sell the drugs. Drug dealers might use violence to protect their markets, and drug users might use violence to procure the drugs.[4] Finally, those who drive under the influence of illegal drugs can be as dangerous and problematic as those who drive under the influence of alcohol.

- *Prostitution.* Prostitution affects more than the individuals involved, according to those who believe it should be illegal. Indirect victims of prostitution include loved ones whose trust and commitment are violated, lost tax revenue from the underground-economy transaction, and the social dangers of sexually transmitted disease. In addition, some people believe prostitution threatens the institution of marriage and cheapens the concept of love.[5]

- *Gambling.* Many states have legalized some form of gambling, but there is a vast underground network of gambling that affects those who do not gamble. Governments might lose tax revenue to illegal gambling, and sometimes those who cannot pay their gambling debts are beaten or killed. Gambling addicts who lose all their assets can become a financial burden on society and on their families.[6] The get-rich-quick lure of gambling is also believed to affect the working habits of children and young adults. Dreaming of cashing in big on a horse race or poker game is not a reasonable substitute for getting an education or learning a marketable skill.

The victimless nature of public-order offenses is a debatable idea that we will return to often in this chapter. The immediate issue, however, is that many people believe these behaviors are detrimental to society. Therefore, through the democratic process, these behaviors have been deemed to be criminal offenses, and the power of the criminal justice system is brought to bear on those who commit them. The interesting questions that criminologists consider are why certain behaviors are considered public-order offenses and where society draws the line between legal and illegal behavior when morals and values are what is being regulated.[7]

## Morality and Crime

Morality is concerned with values. In Western societies with diverse populations, some people must compromise their values in order to function in the public space. For instance, Americans from certain fundamentally religious backgrounds might find it offensive for females to participate in occupations of responsibility and power such as judge, professor, or police officer.[8] Nonreligious Americans might be offended by public displays of religious belief, such as Bible readings or prayer circles. Other Americans might find dancing, alcohol use, and homosexuality offensive and advocate changes in laws to reflect these values. However, personal values are not encoded into law. Therefore, although certain behaviors might offend some people, there is little likelihood the law will be changed to accommodate their values. If all the behaviors that some groups find objectionable were made illegal, the country would be a very different place than it is now.

The values of some groups, however, are implemented into criminal law through the political process. Political participation allows some groups to have their values supported

▼ In the United States, personal values are not encoded into law. For example, some businesses may be closed for religious observances while others remain open.

by legislators who sponsor bills that outlaw or require certain behaviors. The process of making laws is of great interest to criminologists because it is a function of political compromise and a reflection of social attitudes and religious beliefs. In theocratic countries such as Iran, the values of religious leaders are reflected in the law.[9] In the United States, the law is derived from the will of the people, but the people's will often reflects a variety of historical and religious traditions. Consequently, the law is a tool of the collective morality of some social groups.

## Morality and Social Harm

The stated purpose of laws that prohibit public-order offenses is to protect people and society. Actually, when the patterns of laws are examined, it is obvious that some of the most harmful behaviors are legal, while other behaviors that seem to have little potential for significant damage are illegal. For instance, consider the laws concerning drug use in the United States. Tobacco and alcohol are not only legal, but they also constitute billion-dollar industries, while marijuana, which has some purported medical uses, remains illegal. Similarly, in some states, having a small-stakes poker game in your home can get you arrested, but large-scale gambling is permissible at race tracks, in casinos, and through state lotteries. Social harm, then, is only one imperfect measure of what is judged to be a public-order offense. The other factor that bears consideration is social sensibility. Although some behaviors might not be particularly harmful, they offend some people's sense of decency, morality, and religious sensibilities.[10]

There is a long history of people who have sought to make the world a better place by imposing their moral standards on society. These moral crusaders include those who considered alcohol to be evil and tried to close down saloons in the 19th century and got Prohibition enacted in the 20th century.[11] Today, some jurisdictions still have "blue laws" that restrict the sale of alcohol. For instance, some rural Georgia counties and towns prohibit the sale of all wine and beer on Sundays. However, in urban Atlanta, wine and beer by the drink can be purchased in restaurants and bars at any hour on any day. Why are these laws so different? Part of the answer lies in population size and homogeneity. In less populous jurisdictions, the citizens may share similar sets of values, morals, and norms. If one person thinks that alcohol should not be sold on certain days or at certain times, many others in that jurisdiction—often a majority of others—will likely share that idea. Through the political process, this majority gets its preferences on how, when, and where alcohol should be sold encoded into law, and the businesses of that jurisdiction must follow that law.[12] We will explore these questions in greater detail as we tackle three particularly legally contested areas of public-order offenses: substance abuse, sex offenses, and gambling.

# Substance Abuse and the Law

The use and abuse of drugs are important to the study of criminology for three reasons.

1. *Drugs and alcohol influence behavior.* Although this statement might seem obvious, it lies at the heart of the philosophy behind regulating controlled substances. There is little controversy over the fact that alcohol and drugs impede the judgment and motor functions of those under their influence.[13] From a strict public-safety perspective, many people accept the government's right and obligation to control the sale and consumption of drugs and alcohol. The public generally accepts that those who are under the influence of drugs or alcohol should not be driving. Likewise, it would be difficult to find someone who would defend the right to sell heroin or methamphetamines to 12-year-old children.

   **LO2:**

   Discuss why the use and abuse of drugs are important to the study of criminology.

2. *Substance abuse is related to other types of crime.* The use and sale of alcohol and drugs are not the only ways in which these substances affect the criminal justice system. The illegal drug industry spawns more traditional offenses. For instance, those who have $100-a-day drug habits usually quickly exhaust their discretionary funds and must find money elsewhere if they are to continue the habit. Consequently, those who suffer from drug addiction and lack of financial resources often turn to theft or robbery to obtain the money to buy drugs. As each day demands even more money to finance the habit, the individual gets more desperate and adventurous in victimizing others.[14] Although it can be claimed that drug use itself is a consensual victimless crime, maintaining the drug habit often results in harm to others' lives through property and personal violent offenses. Criminologists must consider substance abuse as a causative or contributing factor when studying a broad range of of-

▲ The vast sums of money generated by the illegal drug trade make the work of law enforcement difficult and dangerous. Here, masked law enforcement officers in Mexico check vehicles in Juarez, one of the nation's most violent cities. The masks help protect the officers' identities.

fenses from domestic assault and child abuse, to robbery, rape, and burglary.

3. *The war on drugs is difficult, dangerous, and costly.* Immense resources are required to combat the illegal sale and use of illegal drugs and underage drinking. Furthermore, the money involved in these illegal activities makes the work of police officers difficult.[15] Those making large sums from the sale of drugs are difficult to deter, are likely to go to great lengths to maintain their cash flow, and are willing to harm others in order to escape detection and punishment. As drug dealers battle over supplies, territory, and customers, they injure or kill not only each other, but also sometimes innocent bystanders who are caught in the crossfire. The war on drugs affects not only those actively involved, but also the entire community because in the course of making legitimate arrests, police officers sometimes make terrible mistakes by entering the wrong house.[16]

Drug use and the war on drugs have dominated the activities of the criminal justice system for several decades as society has struggled to deal with the social problem and public-health issues of drug abuse. Criminologists are concerned about these issues, and we will consider them.

## A Brief Legal History of Alcohol and Drugs in the United States

The process of restricting drugs and alcohol came about slowly and in a patchwork fashion. After the American Revolution, the new government had no laws that restricted the sale or use of drugs or alcohol. Like many areas of commerce at the time, it was believed that alcohol and drug sales were not the government's business and that individuals should be free to pursue their own recreations as long as they did not adversely affect others. In the nation's early years, alcohol was not considered the social problem that it is today. In fact, alcohol was an integral part of the lives of many people.[17] Many of them drank alcohol almost exclusively because it was dangerous to drink the water. We take clean water for granted today, but for much of the country's history, water had to be boiled first to ensure its safety for drinking. Distilled liquor, such as whiskey, provided a safer beverage.[18]

The first U.S. laws restricting the sale of alcohol or drugs were economic and not social. The government did not try to protect people from harmful substances, but rather it wanted to collect the revenue generated from the sale of alcohol. In

1791, Congress passed an excise tax on whiskey. Farmers who made whiskey refused to pay the tax and battled federal tax collectors in states such as Kentucky and Tennessee where much of the whiskey was made. Tax collectors were tarred and feathered, and the new president, George Washington, had to call in the militia to quell the violence.[19] The Whiskey Rebellion was the first test of the federal government's authority to tax citizens. Had Washington been unsuccessful in putting down the rebellion and compelling the farmers to pay the tax, the failure would have established a precedent that would have greatly limited the federal government's power and authority. Legally, the United States would be a substantially different place today. However, the social harm produced by the consumption of drugs and alcohol was not lost on the early Americans. Many recognized the harmful effects that intoxication had on individuals and the economy, but nearly a century passed before social welfare was considered so urgent that the freedom to consume drugs and alcohol had to be curtailed.

Comprehensive drug policy is a recent phenomenon and is still highly contested. The history of restricting drugs and alcohol includes the following motivations and attempts at regulation.

## Opium and the Chinese

After the Civil War, the country turned its attention to opening up the West, and the expansion of the railroad system brought many Chinese laborers to the United States. These laborers brought opium with them from China. Smoking opium helped the Chinese laborers deal with the physical rigors of railroad work, and railroad administrators found that opium helped keep the laborers docile. Opium use quickly spread from railroad workers to the Chinese populations in large cities like San Francisco and then to the rest of society. As the opium habit bubbled up through the socioeconomic classes, and opium-smoking became a trendy recreational pursuit, many people were determined to restrict opium use. San Francisco passed the first law outlawing opium smoking in 1875, followed by New York City in 1882. In 1890, the federal government restricted opium smoking and banned opium imports completely.[20]

## Morphine

As opium became expensive, difficult to find, and risky to use, it was replaced by morphine. American soldiers started to use morphine during the Civil War to relieve the pain of wounds and surgery and to alleviate the symptoms of dysentery. Morphine addiction became known as the "soldiers' disease" because so many became addicted. Many doctors became concerned about the addictive effects of morphine and pushed for its control.[21] In fact, an early treatment for morphine addiction was cocaine because its stimulant nature was thought to counteract the depressant morphine.[22]

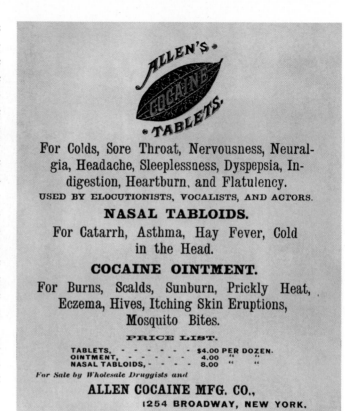

▲ Patent medicines contained ingredients that could be harmful, addictive, or, at best, completely ineffective. This 1885 ad for Allen's Cocaine Tablets offers the main ingredient in tablet, ointment, or "nasal tabloid" form.

## Patent Medicines

In the late 19th and early 20th centuries, patent medicines were popular concoctions of ingredients that were, in turn, medically benign, useless, harmful, and addictive. Typical ingredients included alcohol, morphine, opium, and cocaine. People would buy something like Dr. Mortimer's Magic Cure-All, which would give its users an immediate feeling of well-being and pain relief. The syrup of the soft drink Coca-Cola, which contained a trace of cocaine until 1929, was first marketed as a patent medicine in 1886.[23] Unfortunately, many people became addicted to these so-called medicines. By 1904, patent medicines had grown into a $74 million industry and had harmed many people. Unlike the use of alcohol, which was becoming a social stigma, patent medicines could be camouflaged as something beneficial that could be used without guilt or social disapproval, especially since the ingredients were not listed on the labels. Women who would not be found in a local tavern could get quietly drunk at home, and children with a painful toothache could be given a strong dose of heroin or alcohol that had the immediate effect of quelling their pain and discomfort.

## 1906 Pure Food and Drugs Act

Society eventually responded to the problems brought about by the use of unregulated drugs. Spurred in part by Upton Sinclair's *The Jungle,* a book that graphically detailed the unsafe and unsanitary conditions in the nation's meatpacking plants, the government passed the 1906 Pure Food and Drugs Act.[24] The law did not prohibit the use of drugs in patent medicines but only required that the amount of each ingredient be specified on the label.[25] The idea was that consumers could make their own judgments about what to consume as long as they had accurate information. The government's goal was to protect people from unscrupulous merchants without restricting their personal freedoms. People were permitted to ingest anything they cared to as far as the law was concerned.

## Harrison Act of 1914

The next major impetus toward regulating alcohol and drug use was the Harrison Act of 1914, which was essentially tax legislation. It required those who produced, dispensed, imported, or gave away specified drugs to register with the government and pay a special tax. The goal was not to prevent drug use but to regulate the sale of drugs so the government would get its cut. In many ways, the Harrison Act did what the Whiskey Act had done many years earlier. Penalties for violating this law were not severe, and those who used drugs not prescribed by licensed dealers were not arrested. Part of the motivation behind the Harrison Act was fear and racism. Psychologists Oakley Ray and Charles Ksir, authors of *Drugs, Society and Human Behavior,* described the tactics used by Dr. Hamilton Wright, one of the primary sponsors of the legislation:

> Dr. Wright had written and lectured extensively, waging an effective, emotional, and in some instances outright racist public campaign for additional controls over these drugs. For example, his claims about the practice of "stuffing" cocaine into the nose, which he said was popular among Southern blacks, caused a great deal of concern and fear. Dr. Wright testified before Congress that this practice led to the raping of white women.[26]

The Harrison Act had another profound influence on the legal treatment of drugs in the United States. Although the medical establishment defined drug addiction as a disease and considered the prescription of drugs to alleviate withdrawal distress as ethical, the act made it illegal for doctors to prescribe narcotics for addicts to maintain their habit and keep them comfortable. The U.S. Supreme Court ruled in two cases in favor of the act, which stood for more than 80 years.[27] It was not until 2000 that the Drug Addiction Treatment Act allowed doctors to prescribe certain narcotics to help addicts wean themselves or to maintain their habits.[28]

## Marijuana Tax Act

Marijuana use has an interesting history in the United States. For decades it had a low profile use among jazz entertainers in New Orleans and Mexican laborers in Texas and the Southwest.[29] With the end of Prohibition in 1933, the Treasury Department, which had regulated alcohol, suddenly found itself with a bloated workforce and a limited mandate. According to some scholars, marijuana was not made illegal because it was a dangerous drug but because it provided the Treasury Department with a new villain. The effect of the Marijuana Tax Act was to make marijuana 10 to 12 times more expensive and to criminalize its use.[30] Following the law's passage, considerable research on the drug questioned the scientific evidence on which the law relied. Nevertheless, marijuana use continues to be illegal and its effect on the criminal justice system considerable.

## Comprehensive Drug Abuse Prevention and Control Act of 1970

This act made some sweeping changes in the drug laws. First, the law divided responsibilities over drugs between the Department of Justice, which was to enforce drug laws, and the Department of Health and Human Services, which was to evaluate the scientific evidence and make recommendations about which drugs should be controlled. Second, the law established a hierarchy of controlled substances by creating a five-level schedule that classified the drugs according to how dangerous they are, their potential for abuse and addiction, and whether they possess legitimate medical value (see Table 12.1). Although some people might debate the wisdom of scheduling particular drugs, the schedule's purpose is to make the most harmful drugs the most difficult to obtain. Third, the law set penalties for the use and sale of these illegal drugs. The level of penalties was adjusted and made more complicated in 1988 when mandatory minimum sentences were added.

## Omnibus Drug Act

In 1988, the Omnibus Drug Act made several important changes to the drug laws. The new legislation included proscriptions on money laundering, the use of airplanes in drug activities, and the sale of firearms to felons. It also restricted certain chemicals used to make some illegal drugs and authorized the death penalty for anyone who kills or orders the killing of another while committing a drug-related felony. The act also provides for the prevention and treatment of drug abuse.[31] The most interesting part of the law is the way it expands the control of drugs from law enforcement to other areas of government. For example, someone convicted of a drug offense can receive a civil fine, have their car or boat confiscated if it was used in the commission of the offense, and lose all federal benefits, including student loans. These additional provisions are meant to deter beyond what

## Table 12.1    Federal Drug Schedules

| Schedule I | |
|---|---|
| High potential for abuse. <br><br> No currently accepted medical use in treatment in the U.S. <br><br> A lack of accepted safety for use of the drug or other substance under medical supervision. | heroin, mescaline, psilocybin, psilocin, LSD, marijuana, hashish, peyote, ecstasy, Quaalude, synthetic heroin |

| Schedule II | |
|---|---|
| High potential for abuse. <br><br> Currently accepted medical use in treatment in the United States or a currently accepted medical use with severe restrictions. <br><br> Abuse may lead to severe psychological or physical dependence. | methadone, morphine, cocaine, amphetamine, methamphetamine, PCP, opium, Ritalin, oxycodone, pentobarbital |

| Schedule III | |
|---|---|
| Potential for abuse less than the drugs or other substances in schedules I and II. <br><br> Currently accepted medical use in treatment in the United States. <br><br> Abuse may lead to moderate or low physical dependence or high psychological dependence. | codeine, anabolic steroids, barbiturates, synthetic THC (Marinol), Vicodin, ketamine, pentothal |

| Schedule IV | |
|---|---|
| Low potential for abuse relative to the drugs or other substances in schedule III. <br><br> Currently accepted medical use in treatment in the United States. <br><br> Abuse may lead to limited physical dependence or psychological dependence relative to the drugs or other substances in schedule III. | Xanax, Valium, Darvon, Rohypnol, Halcion, Ativan, Ambien |

| Schedule V | |
|---|---|
| Low potential for abuse relative to the drugs or other substances in schedule IV. <br><br> Currently accepted medical use in treatment in the United States. <br><br> Abuse may lead to limited physical dependence or psychological dependence relative to the drugs or other substances in schedule IV. | cough syrups, preparations with opium or codeine |

*Sources:* National Criminal Justice Reference Service, "In the Spotlight," http://www.ncjrs.gov/spotlight/club_drugs/legislation.html. US Drug Enforcement Administration, "Drug Scheduling," http://www.dea.gov/pubs/scheduling.html.

the criminal justice system can do. Because prisons and jails are so crowded, individuals may escape incarceration. But by instituting a financial penalty, the law can punish much more efficiently, which will presumably prevent would-be drug sellers and users from risking capture.

This brief history of drug regulation in the United States leaves out the thousands of state and local laws that have been passed over the decades. Most of this legislation is built upon prior legislation. There was never a time when an informed panel of experts got together to decide which drugs should be controlled. The rationales for the early drug laws were primarily financial. The government was not looking to

control drug and alcohol use out of concern for public health or safety but simply wanted to generate revenue by taxing its commerce.

## Substance Abuse Today

Substance abuse of legal and illegal substances is common in the United States today despite the war on drugs. The most common abused substance is alcohol, but this probably has much to do with its legality and availability. Pharmaceuticals such as OxyContin and other pain-relief medications are also problematic, but these are legal, although controlled. Common illegal substances include marijuana, cocaine (crack and powder), heroin, methamphetamine, and hallucinogens. Inhalants is a class of drugs that includes many substances not intended for use as drugs, such as glue, spray paint, and compressed air in cans. Use of such inhalants has become such a problem among youths that some retailers now require proof of age to purchase them.[32]

The National Survey on Drug Use and Health (NSDUH) is the main source of information on the nonmedical use of illicit drugs, alcohol, and tobacco in the United States by the civilian, noninstitutionalized population age 12 or older. The survey interviews about 67,500 respondents annually about their substance usage in the past month. According to the 2008 survey, more than 20 million Americans age 12 or older (representing about 8.0 percent of the U.S. population age 12 and older) reported using illegal drugs in the past month.[33]

Marijuana, the most commonly used drug with 15.2 million users, was used by 75.7 percent of illicit drug users and for more than half of them was the only drug they used. About 1.9 million people reported using cocaine. More than 300,000 respondents reported using methamphetamine in the past month in 2008, which was down from 731,000 in 2006. Also in 2008, 114,000 people age 12 or older reported using heroin for the first time within the past 12 months; the average age of first use was 23. Finally, more than a million people reported using hallucinogens. (See Figure 12.1 for a visual comparison of the frequency of usage of types of drugs.) Illegal drug usage tended to drop in later adult years, with adults age 26 or older less likely to be current drug users than people age 12 to 25. However, the rate of illicit drug use among 12- to 17-year-olds did decrease from 11.6 percent in 2002 to 9.3 percent in 2008.[34]

Theories that explain continued drug usage typically concern biological addiction and psychological dependence. Both types of theory focus on a need to have more of a substance that one has already used for reasons ranging from the desire to be more comfortable socially, the desire or need to be more energetic or creative, or the need to control physical signs of withdrawal. The reasons that people begin using substances are more complicated, but one factor likely involves the young ages at which substance use begins, typically after puberty. This is why the NSDUH begins its study at age 12 and why so much anti-drug literature focuses on youths.

According to the NSDUH, the median age at which initial illicit drug use begins is 15 with PCP (phencyclidine, an anesthetic available as tablets, capsules, or powders) and inhalants and continues throughout a variety of drugs until age 24, when initial use of tranquilizers begins (see Figure 12.2). Theories explaining the young age at which substance usage begins may best be drawn from theories of delinquency (see Chapter 6), which focus on dysfunctional families and antisocial peers. Psychological theories may include the adolescent need to experiment with behaviors, develop individual identity, and integrate socially with peers. Biological theories would point to chemical imbalances in the

## Figure 12.1  Illicit Drug Use, Users Age 12 or Older, 2008

The National Survey on Drug Use and Health interviews substance users about the type and amount of their drug usage in the past month. The figure compares the frequency of the types of drugs used. Psychotherapeutics include prescription pain relievers, tranquilizers, stimulants, or sedatives. Hallucinogens include LSD and ecstasy. Inhalants include substances such as nitrous oxide, amyl nitrite, cleaning fluids, gasoline, spray paint, certain aerosol sprays, and glue.

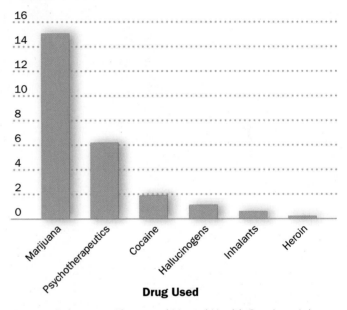

*Source:* Substance Abuse and Mental Health Services Administration, *Results from the 2008 National Survey on Drug Use and Health: National Findings* (Rockville, MD: Office of Applied Studies, 2009), 16, http://oas.samhsa.gov/nsduh/2k8nsduh/2k8Results.pdf.

brain or body that may lead to a need to try to correct the imbalance with substances. Drug use may turn into abuse when people become addicted or psychologically dependent (see Table 12.2).

## Legalization and Decriminalization

If we were to start all over, it is possible that we would construct our drug laws differently. In terms of harm, it is clear that tobacco has killed more people than all the illegal drugs put together. Alcohol continues to be a social problem, yet the government makes it easy to obtain and collects substantial amounts of money from liquor taxes. Some people advocate a return to the days when all the government required of drug manufacturers was disclosure of their products' contents.

Before we consider the consequences of substance legalization and decriminalization, we must first differentiate

## Figure 12.2    Mean Age at First Use for Specific Illegal Drugs, 2008

Drug users tend to begin with PCP and inhalants at age 15. Heroin and tranquilizers tend to be among the last illegal drugs tried, at age 24. Drug usage in this context is nonmedical, so the recreational usage of legal substances such as pain relievers, some stimulants and sedatives, and tranquilizers is considered illegal.

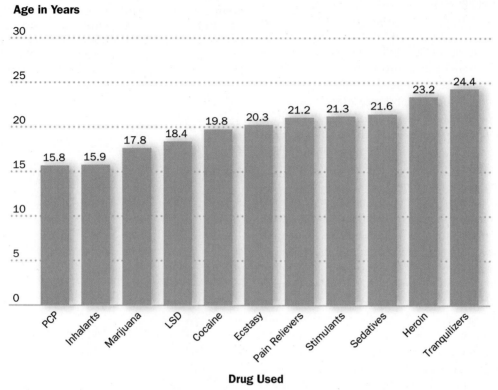

*Source:* Substance Abuse and Mental Health Services Administration, *Results from the 2008 National Survey on Drug Use and Health: National Findings* (Rockville, MD: Office of Applied Studies, 2009), Figure 5.3, 54, http://oas.samhsa.gov/nsduh/2k8nsduh/2k8Results.pdf.

## Table 12.2    Theoretical Explanations of Substance Abuse

| Theory | Explanation |
|--------|-------------|
| Biological addiction | Many illegal drugs are highly addictive. Physical addiction results in symptoms of withdrawal when the body does not get enough of a drug it has become accustomed to. These withdrawal symptoms can make the individual extremely uncomfortable and sick and cause such a craving for the drug that he or she will break the law to get it. |
| Psychological dependence | Individuals may become psychologically dependent on drugs or alcohol. Although the body does not physically crave the substance, the person might use it as a crutch. Psychological dependence is often as difficult to overcome as physical addiction. |

between the terms **legalization** and **decriminalization.** Legalization means a given substance is completely legal to consume, just like soft drinks and chocolate. Cigarettes and alcohol are also considered to be legalized, although there are restrictions on sales to and consumption by minors.

**legalization** The complete removal of legal proscriptions on acts that were previously illegal.

**decriminalization** The lessening or removal of penalties for acts previously subject to criminal prosecution, arrest, and incarceration.

▶ Legalization means a given substance is legal to consume. Here, young men smoke a marijuana cigarette during a "smoke out" gathering at the University of Colorado in Boulder.

Decriminalization is more of a gray area. Under decriminalization, the substance is not completely legal, but neither is it the subject of a full-scale prohibitive criminal justice effort. For instance, in decriminalizing marijuana, the government might change the offense from a felony to a misdemeanor, thus reducing the drug's stigma. Persons caught with small amounts of a decriminalized substance would be subject to few or no sanctions, while substance abusers would be referred to health or rehabilitative agencies rather than incarcerated or otherwise criminally sanctioned.

Drug legalization probably would not legalize all drugs for everyone.[35] Many proposals to legalize or at least decriminalize drugs stop short of such an extreme scenario. Many of those who wish to legalize drugs believe that even though there may be some increase in the use of drugs, society would be safer.[36] If drugs were to be treated as a medical problem rather than a criminal justice problem, some surmise that much of the violence associated with acquiring money to maintain a drug habit would disappear. Drug dealers would not battle one another over customers and territory, and drug commerce would be governed like the commerce in alcohol and tobacco. Finally, drug users could be confident they would be getting unadulterated drugs and would be better able to gauge their potency and prevent the overdoses that are common with illegal drugs.

The legalization or decriminalization of some drugs would carry some risks. Although illegal drugs are easy for many people to obtain now, legalizing them would certainly increase the numbers of people who would be getting intoxicated.[37] Many would-be drug users today desist from drug use because they do not want to get caught breaking the law. Without the legal sanctions, many would be free to use drugs with impunity; such drug use could affect their productivity and safety at work, their motivation to keep steady employment, and their ability to raise children with the necessary values to be good citizens. We have had enough experience with alcohol abuse to know that there are consequences to people being under the influence of behavior-altering substances.[38]

The question of whether to legalize or decriminalize drugs is difficult to answer. People still use illegal drugs,

and the war on drugs has its own consequences in terms of making drug use more dangerous, violent, and expensive. Opinions on what to do about illegal drug use vary widely, ranging from the complete legalization of all drugs to a prohibition on everything, including alcohol. Some people contend that a middle position of decriminalizing some drugs can minimize the harm done by drug use and minimize the war on drugs.[39] Regardless, given the violence currently associated with drug use, the immense resources used by the criminal justice system to stem trafficking, and the high numbers of people in prison for drug-related offenses, it is clear that our present drug policies deserve to be revisited. Other nations have been more successful in limiting the violence associated with drug use without spending billions of dollars on incarceration.[40] One approach to preventing drug abuse is harm reduction (see *Theory to Practice*).

## Think about it

### Remember
List the reasons substance abuse is important to the study of criminology.

### Analyze
Summarize the history of legal efforts in the United States to control the use and abuse of drugs.

### Create
Formulate a plan to legalize certain drugs that will have a good chance of keeping them away from juveniles.

# theory
## to **practice**

### Harm Reduction as a Drug Strategy

Criminological theory informs efforts to deal with crime and is especially relevant in the area of drug use and abuse. Because the war on drugs has been unsuccessful in halting the flow of drugs and limiting their harm, criminologists have developed other approaches based on harm reduction. These approaches also seek to address several unintended consequences of the war on drugs.

- As the price of illegal drugs rises, addicts sometimes break the law to get the money to pay for their habits, committing violent or property offenses.
- Drug users are often at the mercy of sellers who give them adulterated drugs that could be fatal.
- The resources that law enforcement authorities use to fight the war on drugs might be better used in dealing with other types of crime.
- Drug users often do not seek treatment because they are afraid their drug habits will become known to the police and their employers, and they will be arrested or lose their jobs.

Health authorities face the challenge of helping people who are dependent on illegal drugs and who want to be helped without exposing them to the criminal justice system. Rather than treating the drug use as a criminal offense, harm reduction treats it as a medical problem of addiction. Perhaps the best known of the harm-reduction strategies is methadone maintenance.

Methadone is a drug that prevents the withdrawal symptoms experienced by addicts who stop using heroin. The goal of the methadone program is to wean the addict off all drugs. Methadone is taken orally and its effects last longer than those of heroin, but it is also addictive. Many critics believe methadone maintenance is not useful because the addict is simply trading one addiction for another. Proponents of methadone maintenance point to favorable outcomes in a number of areas. Those using methadone are reported to reduce their offending, become employed, and generally improve their psychological and social functioning.

Hundreds of programs prescribe methadone or other drugs as substitutes for illegal substances. Methadone maintenance is now so routine that many insurance

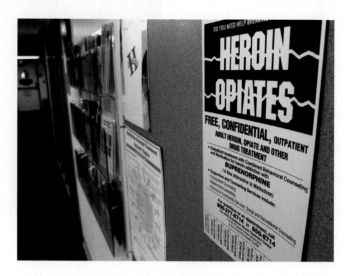

▲ Many programs substitute legal alternatives to help addicts stop using illegal substances such as heroin. This clinic provides buprenorphine, an alternative to methadone, to ease the short-term effects of heroin withdrawal.

plans cover treatment. Patients are also protected by the Americans with Disabilities Act as long as they are taking methadone legally and not abusing other drugs.

This harm-reduction strategy shows how criminologists use theory to develop alternative policies to control crime. It is a good example of how the pendulum swings from punishment to rehabilitation and back again as we seek theoretically informed solutions to social problems.

*Sources:*
Donna Boundy, "Profile: Methadone Maintenance: The 'Invisible' Success Story," Moyers on Addiction, Public Broadcasting Service, 1998, http://www.pbs.org/wnet/closetohome/treatment/html/methprofile.html.

Harm Reduction Coalition, http://www.harmreduction.org/.

Methadone Today, http://www.methadonetoday.org/.

Medical Assisted Treatment of America, Inc., http://www.medicalassistedtreatment.com/.

National Drug Strategy Network, http://www.ndsn.org/.

## THINKING
### *in* ACTION

Apply harm-reduction strategies to the problem of alcoholism.

# Sex Offenses

Another class of public-order offense that garners a great deal of attention from criminologists and criminal justice officials is concerned with sexuality, especially prostitution

## LO3:

**Understand** the basis of laws prohibiting prostitution, pornography, and sodomy.

and pornography. A third public-order offense is that of consensual **sodomy**—oral or anal sexual intercourse—which has only recently been legalized. Although both heterosexual and homosexual activities were written into the states' anti-sodomy laws, these laws were targeted mainly at homosexual activity, making them especially controversial.[41]

Laws proscribing certain forms of sexual activity are common throughout history and throughout the world, and the United States is no exception. In the United States, public-order laws dealing with sex largely emerged from a Christian religious philosophy that held that procreation was the only justification for sex. Sex without intention or desire to procreate (adultery and fornication can be assumed here), or any non-procreative form of sex (such as masturbation or sodomy), was considered immoral.[42] Therefore, states inserted laws proscribing such activities into their legal codes early on, and many states never removed them even as times changed. Today, several states still have laws against adultery (sex with someone other than one's spouse) and fornication (sex without marriage). These laws are rarely, if ever, enforced, although prosecutions sometimes occur. The three activities we will consider in detail, prostitution, pornography, and sodomy, were originally proscribed by law because they flouted the prohibition on non-procreative sex. Although Americans' general opinion on the morality of non-procreative sex has long since changed, prostitution remains a criminal offense in 49 states; which types of pornography are illegal is still being debated, and anti-sodomy laws were struck down only recently. Let's take a look at each of these three activities to get an idea of their nature and extent.

## Prostitution

People have varying attitudes about the place of sexual behavior in society. Some people consider the purchase of sex to be an issue of personal freedom, while others consider it to be immoral, destructive behavior. These differences of opinion can be observed in the terminology used to refer to the sale and purchase of sexual activity. Those who support it and think it should be legalized and regulated refer to the transaction as "sex work." Those who believe it should remain illegal and that it constitutes immoral activity call it **prostitution,** and define it as the unlawful promotion of or participation in sexual activities for profit, including attempts to solicit customers; assisting in or promoting the exchange of sexual activities for money; or owning, managing, or operating an establishment for the purpose of providing

a place where sex is exchanged for money. Because the sale and purchase of sex are illegal in every state except Nevada (which we will discuss later), criminal justice agencies refer to the offense as prostitution rather than sex work.

The government's role in regulating sexual behavior between consenting adults is a central issue in prostitution. Some argue that the government has no place in citizens' bedrooms and that prostitution should be regulated by health agencies.[43] However, a brief history of what has been called "the world's oldest profession" reveals why some people have deemed prostitution to be anything but a victimless crime.[44]

It is difficult to estimate how much prostitution exists in the United States because the seller and the customer are usually consenting parties who are satisfied with the transaction and have no motive to report it to the police.[45] Consequently, most prostitution goes unreported. A United Nations report estimated half a million females in the United States earn all or most of their income from prostitution. More than 100,000 of these are children, many of whom were brought to the United States as part of the international sex trade.[46] It is difficult to define exactly what constitutes an act of prostitution because prostitutes perform some activities that do not involve sexual intercourse. Sociologist Charles H. McCaghy and his fellow researchers describe prostitution as having the following elements.

- *Activity that has sexual significance for the purchaser.* This includes a range of behavior from sexual intercourse to cases in which the seller simply (and literally) walks all over the purchaser.

- *Economic transaction.* Whether the sellers earn part or all of their livelihood from prostitution is inconsequential. Something of economic value, which might or might not be currency, is exchanged for the activity, usually just prior to service.

- *Emotional indifference.* The behavior is limited to an exchange of service for economic consideration. The participants might or might not be strangers (some prostitutes have repeat customers), but their interaction has nothing to do with the seller's affection for the buyer (although the buyer might be attempting to purchase affection).[47]

## Male Prostitution

Although most people would probably identify prostitutes as female, there is research today on the prevalence of male prostitution. According to sociologist Robert McNamara, male prostitution has a long history but was relatively understudied in comparison with female prostitution until AIDS (acquired immune deficiency syndrome) and HIV (human immunodeficiency virus), the virus that causes AIDS,

**sodomy** Oral or anal sexual intercourse.

**prostitution** The unlawful promotion of or participation in sexual activities for profit.

**Table 12.3    Theoretical Explanations of Prostitution**

| Theory | Explanation |
|---|---|
| Psychological<br>Freudian | Young woman suffers from Electra Complex, always trying to win love of her father. She uses men to achieve affection. |
| Sociological<br>Critical feminist | Selling her body gives a woman control of her sexuality. |
| Sociological<br>Differential association | Young girl hangs out with older peers who teach her that prostitution is fun, lucrative, and empowering. |

became significant social problems in the 1980s. In his work detailing the lives of male hustlers in New York City's Times Square, McNamara contends that male prostitution shares many of the concerns of female prostitution for those who engage in it at the street level.[48]

McNamara's research on male prostitutes in Times Square focused on the community that these men and boys developed within the hustling marketplace and the problems they had with HIV/AIDS. Perhaps the most significant observation from his research is the fact that many of these male prostitutes did not consider themselves to be homosexual. Some were married, many had girlfriends, and they considered hustling an occupation and not a defining parameter of their identity. Because these male prostitutes had unprotected sex with their male customers, unprotected sex with their wives and girlfriends, and tended to be intravenous drug users, they were susceptible to acquiring and transmitting HIV.

## Female Prostitution

Female prostitution exists in a variety of forms. The market can be highly regulated, with women working for a female madam or a male pimp.[49] These women consider prostitution an occupation and may live an antisocial lifestyle in which others help them in dealing with police officers, bailing them out of jail, or providing them a place to live and help with their medical care. (Several theoretical perspectives can address why women become prostitutes; for an example, see Table 12.3.) Other prostitutes may have lawful occupations and engage in paid sex only sporadically or may be housewives seeking excitement or relief from monogamy.[50] (For more facts about female prostitution, see *Doubletake.*)

The following typology of female prostitutes covers the most prominent forms of prostitution. Although this typology is neither exhaustive (there might be other forms of prostitution) nor exclusive (women might fall into two or more of these categories), it describes the most common forms of this profession.

- *Call girls.* This type of prostitute occupies the highest rung in the hierarchy of prostitution. Some call girls also act as legitimate escorts in perfectly legal encounters. When a businessman needs a companion for a party or simply a date when out of town, escort and dating services will

# doubletake
doubletake

**Some Facts About Prostitution**

Street prostitution accounts for probably only 10 to 20 percent of all prostitution in the United States. Unlike other forms of prostitution, however, it is the most visible type in the communities in which it takes place.[1] Prostitution is not a significant vector of HIV transmission in the United States because much prostitution is heterosexual, and HIV transmission is more difficult from female to male. Also, most street-prostitution sex acts are oral rather than vaginal, and HIV is less likely to be transmitted orally. Most street prostitutes insist that clients use condoms, although this is less true of drug-dependent prostitutes, who are more likely to contract HIV from sharing needles with other drug users than from sex with clients.[2]

[1]Michael S. Scott and Kelly Dedel, *Street Prostitution*, 2nd ed. (Washington, DC: U.S. Department of Justice Office of Community Oriented Policing Services, 2006), 2, http://www.cops.usdoj.gov/pdf/pop/e10062633.pdf.

[2]Ronald Weitzer, ed., *Sex for Sale: Prostitution, Pornography, and the Sex Industry* (New York: Routledge, 2000).

## THINKING *in* ACTION

If street prostitution is not responsible for the majority of HIV cases, why, in your opinion, is there such a negative public stereotype of prostitutes?

provide a woman who can act in a respectable and appropriate manner and provide the customer with pleasant conversation. The line between legitimate escort services and prostitution is indistinct, and many of the women are willing to do whatever the customer desires. Escort services can be very expensive and cater to people in politics, the movie industry, and big business. A scandal may occur in which notable figures are linked to call-girl services. These escort services can also be highly organized. For example, one San Francisco ring had 35 phone lines and four people answering the phones, dispatching more than 200 call girls. Clients were accepted on a referral basis from trusted customers. The prostitutes in this ring made up to $160 for a one-hour hotel visit. Some call girls, however, can make substantially more money.[51]

- *Bar girls.* Many prostitutes practice their craft in bars, particularly hotel bars where they are likely to meet out-of-town businessmen. Bar girls will accompany the client back to his room or to a nearby apartment. Some bars employ exotic dancers to attract male customers. These dancers are encouraged to get the men to buy them drinks and will order nonalcoholic or extremely expensive drinks to get the customers to run up an expensive bar tab. Some dancers will perform private special shows that include lap-dances and more explicit sexual contact. Many bars actively discourage prostitution and report bar girls to the police, but often these women will take the risk in order to meet potential customers who are willing to pay for sex.[52]

- *Massage parlors and brothels.* Although many businesses provide only clinical massages and legitimate spa services, so-called massage parlors are actually fronts for prostitution. Some openly advertise "body rub" or "body shampoo," but the real service offered is sex for a price. These massage parlors are like brothels where prostitutes sell sex in an establishment run by a madam and pay the establishment part of their earnings. The advantage of brothels (which are legal in Nevada) is that the prostitute does not need to generate customers herself but simply services those who are delivered to her by the madam. The girls have little authority to decide whom they have sex with and must pay a substantial percentage to the house.[53]

- *Streetwalkers.* Streetwalking can be very dangerous work for very low pay. Streetwalkers will perform a variety of sex acts at whatever price they can negotiate. The streetwalker will often claim a territory on a corner, outside a bar or hotel, or on the sidewalks of a busy street. Customers approach the streetwalking prostitute either on foot or in a car and negotiate a price for a particular service. Because the streetwalker must always be concerned that the potential customer is a police officer, she must quickly evaluate his appearance and be careful with what she says. An elaborate linguistic battle can take place in which the streetwalker tries to avoid being the first one to mention the specific activity or the price. She will often use ambiguous phases such as, "Do you want a date?" so she can later claim she was not hustling in case the client turns out to be an undercover police officer. Streetwalkers live a precarious existence because they are susceptible to being attacked by clients. It is hard for them to control their working environment, and many of them have to work under the protection of pimps to be safe from violent customers or other prostitutes who might dispute the use of a particular corner to ply their trade. Pimps are a separate danger to the streetwalker because they are both their protectors and their exploiters.[54]

- *Crack prostitutes.* A new form of prostitution arose with the prevalence of crack cocaine in which prostitutes sell sex for a hit of the drug. When under the influence of crack, they can be indiscriminate in the selection and number of their sex partners and sloppy in the practice of safe sex. These women can also easily become victims of sexual assault or rape.[55]

As this typology indicates, prostitution can take a number of forms. Thus, discussing public policies that deal with prostitution is difficult because some types of prostitution may be less objectionable than others. For example, expensive call girls provide services to customers who can afford to pay for sex, and the transactions are done in private to the satisfaction of both parties. In contrast, streetwalkers, who are often controlled by pimps, may be the victims of beatings, drug addiction, and sexually transmitted disease. Other concerns about the practice of selling sex stem from the public-safety and public-health perspectives. According to the Department of Justice Office of Community Oriented

▼ Some massage parlors are actually fronts for prostitution. This Las Vegas, Nevada, massage parlor was closed down in 2008 after three prostitution arrests.

Policing Services, street prostitution causes a variety of concerns in the community.

- Prostitution is a nuisance to passersby and local residents. Legitimate businesses might lose customers who avoid the area.
- Prostitution offends the moral standards of some people, as well as offending uninterested people when prostitutes solicit them.
- Used condoms, syringes, and other items left in public view are unsightly and potentially hazardous.
- Prostitutes without access to proper facilities might urinate, defecate, or bathe in public.
- Clients might harm prostitutes.
- Clients or prostitutes might be defrauded, robbed, or assaulted.
- Pimps financially and physically exploit prostitutes.
- Street prostitution and street drug markets are often linked.
- Prostitutes create traffic problems where they congregate.[56]

Regardless of the morality issues, the government is obligated to protect all citizens—prostitutes, customers, and the community—from harmful behaviors. One proposal that seeks to ensure such protection is to legalize prostitution.

## Legalized Prostitution

The prospect of legalizing prostitution meets with the same reaction as proposals for legalizing drugs. Many people believe that prostitution and illegal drug use violate community values and are not only socially harmful, but also immoral. Many critics also believe legalization would send the wrong message to young people. Some individuals, however, contend there are good reasons to consider such a policy. Their arguments include the following.

- *Legalization of prostitution would make it safer.* Currently, much prostitution takes place under dangerous conditions. Drugs and violence are often common in areas where prostitution flourishes. Legalizing prostitution would allow people to engage in this behavior in safer places. There would be no need for pimps, and prostitutes who are assaulted or hassled by customers could turn to the police for help.
- *Legalization of prostitution would make it healthier and more fair.* At present, prostitutes must hide their activities. Legalizing the practice would subject it to regulation by public health agencies. Prostitutes could get regular checkups and be certified disease-free. They could be educated to use safe-sex techniques and insist to their customers that the government requires condom use. Group health insurance could help improve medical care for prostitutes, and they could also have their interests openly advocated with insurance companies, the community, and in state legislatures.

- *Legalizing prostitution would allow the government to tax it.* Prostitution occurs in an underground economy in which prostitutes do not pay taxes on their earnings and those who run prostitution businesses do not pay taxes on their businesses. Taxation could create new revenue streams for city, county, and state governments, as well as pay for the bureaucracy required for licensing, inspection, and other regulatory controls.[57]

Despite the potential improvements in the public health of the community and the personal health of prostitutes and their customers, many groups and individuals are opposed to legalizing prostitution. They believe it is better to keep this activity against the law and to fine, jail, and otherwise punish both sellers and buyers of sexual services. There is a tension, then, between the freedom of individuals to purchase sex and the community standards of morality. There are three primary reasons for keeping prostitution illegal.

- *Some religious morals assert that sex between two people is a sacred relationship that should not be bartered or sold.* Legal prostitution would cheapen this relationship in society by reducing it to simply another product that can be bought and sold.
- *Prostitution threatens the bonds of marriage.* The easy and legal availability of prostitutes may tempt spouses to break their marriage vows.
- *Prostitution is responsible for the spread of sexually transmitted diseases.* Legalized prostitution would increase the spread of venereal disease because prostitutes would be much easier to access and diseases more easily transmitted.

## Child Prostitution

The debate on whether to legalize the sale of sex sometimes loses sight of the problem of the exploitation of children. Although prostitution is not a victimless crime when children are involved, child prostitution is still an aspect of the public-order offense category of prostitution. We cover it here not to trivialize the exploitation of children, but simply to put child prostitution in context to show how public-order offenses can include behaviors that harm vulnerable individuals.

The problems of child prostitution are ones of abuse, violence, and exploitation. Children do not have the developmental maturity to enter into such agreements. Even if a child were to say that he or she wants to be a prostitute, adults and the law generally recognize that children have neither the intellectual nor the emotional capacity to make such a decision. Youth prostitution differs from other types of child sexual exploitation such as incest (sex between blood-related family members) and statutory rape because payment is involved. The payment might be in the form of money, drugs, clothing, jewelry, or other items. The incidence of youth prostitution is staggering. Estimates of the number of adolescent and child prostitutes range from 500,000 to 3 million. Some youth prostitutes are as young as five years old. There are two common scenarios in which these problems of child prostitution may occur.

▶ The sexual exploitation of children, adolescents, and very young adults in other nations is a tense political issue. This young woman waits for customers outside a bar in Sungai Kolok, Thailand.

- *Runaway kids.* A common scenario involves runaway children who are befriended by pimps who offer them food and shelter in a strange new city. These pimps, called "chicken hawks," frequent bus stations where runaways often first enter a new city. The pimps quickly entangle the runaways in a lifestyle of parties, drugs, and sex. Soon the pimps demand that the youths contribute financially and coerce them into prostitution. Getting out of the pimp's grasp is difficult, and some child prostitutes grow into adulthood without acquiring any useful skills or education. The result is a life of violence, poverty, and drug use. Clearly, these youths are victims of exploitation by the pimps and by customers.[58] The reasons children end up in this type of situation are sadly consistent. Often, they are running away from both physical and sexual domestic abuse and consider prostitution the only alternative to an intolerable home environment.

- *International sex trade.* The sexual exploitation of children in other countries is becoming a high-profile political issue. A sex tourism industry has developed in several Asian and eastern European nations where people from wealthier nations take holidays for the purpose of having inexpensive sex with children. Airlines, hotels, and, in some cases, local governments facilitate sex tourism because it brings millions of dollars. The negative effects of sex tourism, in addition to the exploitation of children, include the spread of HIV and the undermining of the economy (instead of developing legitimate industries, some nations exploit their young people rather than educating and investing in them for the long-term good) with the easy money based on the selling of children.[59] Clearly this type of prostitution is not a victimless crime; we mention it here simply because it is such an integral aspect of worldwide prostitution.

There is considerable debate about the wisdom of making laws that restrict choice in consensual sexual behavior. Much like the debate on drug use, this issue can be considered from two perspectives: the goal of preserving individual choice and the goal of protecting society from those who make poor choices. A third concern of those who question the necessity of outlawing consensual behaviors is pornography, an industry that pits freedom of speech and the press against those concerned with public morality.

## Pornography

There is little consensus in the United States on what forms of entertainment should be allowed in the public sphere. The advertising and entertainment industries have long used sex, erotica, and nudity to attract attention and sell their products. Various forms of censorship have been tried over the decades, but there's always a tension between local community standards and the public's desire to be entertained. Pornography is difficult to define. When discussing "hardcore pornography" in *Jacobellis v. Ohio* (1964), U.S. Supreme Court Justice Potter Stewart stated, "I know it when I see it."[60] Although everyone "knows" pornography when they see it, putting that knowledge into a legal definition has been difficult. Basically, **pornography** refers to "representations designed to arouse, and give sexual pleasure to those who read, see, hear, or handle them."[61] However, this definition is a moving target because the standards of pornography vary across jurisdictions and over time. The general liberalizing of pornography standards has allowed Hollywood to present movie scenes that would have been censored a few decades ago.

Deciding what is pornographic is a personal judgment. Everyone has different standards. Pornography publisher Al Goldstein said, "Eroticism is what turns me on; pornography is what turns you on."[62] Such definitions are not very useful guides because we can apply the definition only after experiencing the pornographic material, not before. We have to see

**pornography** Images, sounds, writing, or other communication designed to give sexual pleasure.

the pornographic material first to "know it when we see it." The motion picture and television industries have been legislated to adopt labeling systems that warn potential viewers about the sexual content of their products, but comedy clubs, magazines, and the Internet are virtually unregulated and contain something to offend everyone. Discussions of the purported harm of pornography must consider two issues.

- *Morality and values.* The morality of pornography is a contested and changing issue in American society. Some people believe that pornography weakens moral character. Many who oppose pornography believe that allowing the media to sell material of explicit sexual content makes the general public less respectful of what these opponents consider "decent" behavior. Young people today appear in public wearing clothes that would have raised eyebrows or gotten them arrested in past decades. Many parents and elders are shocked by the permissive nature of today's fashions and blame such styles for corrupting youth. The availability of sexually explicit material on the Internet has prompted many people to urge that the Internet should be subject to the same decency standards required of other media.[63] Yet no matter what laws might be implemented, there will always be those who argue that the laws do not go far enough.

- *Pornography and violence.* Many feminists and others concerned with women's rights contend that pornographic material dehumanizes females and promotes violence against them. They argue that female pornography treats women's bodies only as objects of sexual desire and portrays women in a submissive and inferior way. Sexist, racist, or homophobic pornography caters to those who are stimulated by subjugation. These aspects of pornography raise questions about the role of pornography in rape, sexual abuse, and domestic violence. Many feminists claim that female pornography is a way for men to maintain power over women and use that power in sexualized ways that demean not only women, but also, through its distorted portrayal of sex, all people.[64]

At present, pornography is legal in the United States unless it meets the three-part *Miller* test of obscenity, which was developed in the Supreme Court ruling in *Miller v. California* (1973). According to the *Miller* test, material is obscene if it meets the following three standards.

- An average person, applying contemporary community standards, must find that the work, taken as a whole, appeals to the prurient interest.

- The work must depict or describe, in a patently offensive way, sexual conduct or excretory functions specifically defined by applicable state law.

- The work, taken as a whole, must lack serious literary and/or artistic, political, or scientific value.[65]

Often, the issue is not whether a work is obscene by *Miller*'s standards, but the definition of the standards within the

▲ Pornography is legal in the United States unless it is obscene, a standard that is still being debated. In New York City, people walk past a three-story billboard featuring porn actor Jenna Jameson.

test. Who is an "average person"? What are "contemporary community standards"? Who decides what is "patently offensive"? Who determines whether material has "serious literary and/or artistic, political, or scientific value"?

The courts are still debating these definitions and, so far, have taken a fairly hands-off approach to the control of questionable material. In prior decades, the debate over what is obscene occurred over print material, including novels and magazines, and broadcast material, including film and television. Currently, the contested medium is the Internet. The Supreme Court held that the Communications Decency Act of 1996, which criminalized "certain Internet speech," was unconstitutional because, in part, less restrictive alternatives were available to protect juveniles from questionable Internet content. In *Ashcroft v. American Civil Liberties Union* (2004), a lower court concluded that the Child Online Protection Act (COPA), a federal law enacted to protect juveniles from "exposure to sexually explicit materials on the Internet," was not the least restrictive means required to protect juveniles. The Supreme Court later agreed because COPA "likely" violated the First Amendment.[66]

## Sodomy

Until recently, consensual sodomy was illegal in the United States and is still proscribed by the Uniform Code of Military Justice. Unlike forcible sodomy—a form of forcible rape, a violent criminal offense—consensual sodomy was a public-order offense. Until 1960, all states had anti-sodomy laws which were used mainly to prosecute homosexual sexual activity and, in rare cases, heterosexual activity. Until the U.S. Supreme Court in *Lawrence v. Texas* (2003) struck down a Texas law prohibiting consensual sex between same-sex adults, the states of Kansas, Missouri, Oklahoma, and Texas prohibited sodomy between same-sex couples, and Alabama, Florida, Idaho, Louisiana, Mississippi, North Carolina, South Carolina, Utah, and Virginia prohibited sodomy for all adults. Regardless, consensual sodomy is estimated to be committed rather often, with estimates of about 90 percent of American heterosexual couples regularly engaging in it.[67]

The history of U.S. anti-sodomy laws is often misunderstood. In *Lawrence,* the Supreme Court noted that homosexual sexual activities originally were not criminalized in the United States. The Court stated that early sodomy laws were meant to prevent non-procreative sex and were not "enforced against consenting adults acting in private," but instead against predatory individuals, such as those committing forcible or statutory rape or those engaging in sex with animals. Laws specifically targeting homosexuality did not develop until the mid-20th century.[68]

In *Robinson v. California* (1962), the Supreme Court held that a person could not be prosecuted for having a status or condition, such as homosexuality or drug addiction. But, like drug users, homosexuals were often presumed to be criminal because of the illegality of the private activities in which they were assumed to participate. However, states could prosecute individuals caught in the act of sodomy, just as they could prosecute individuals caught in the act of possessing or using drugs. The *Lawrence* decision lifted this presumption of criminality by decriminalizing an act that became commonly associated with homosexuality.[69]

As of mid-2010, sodomy remained an offense within the military as defined by Article 125 of the Uniform Code of Military Justice. Although the article applies to both homosexuals and heterosexuals, like the old state anti-sodomy laws, it is considered to criminalize homosexual behavior and is used to exclude homosexuals from military service. In March 2010, the military confirmed that a nine-month study on homosexuals in the military would probably include a review of Article 125.[70]

Recall that **criminology** is the study of the making of laws, the breaking of laws, and society's reaction to the breaking of laws. In the case of sodomy, the relationship between the breaking of the law and society's reaction to the offense is interesting. Legal authorities admit that the breaking of sodomy laws—even between homosexuals—was rarely prosecuted; even when it was, the punishments were light. The lower court fined the two plaintiffs in *Lawrence v. Texas* $200 each for breaking Texas' anti-sodomy law. Justice Kennedy noted this in giving the Supreme Court's opinion in the case, stating, "[T]here is a pattern of non-enforcement with respect to consenting adults acting in private. The state of Texas admitted in 1994 that as of that date it had not prosecuted anyone under these circumstances."[71] This was echoed in a 2009 review of the Uniform Code of Military Justice, which stated that "most acts of consensual sodomy committed by consenting military personnel are not prosecuted, creating a perception that prosecution of this sexual behavior is arbitrary."[72] In discussing the issue, review committee chairman Walter Cox stated that such arbitrariness creates a general disrespect for the law.[73] From a social perspective, lack of enforcement could be interpreted that society is perhaps ready for such laws to be changed or removed to reflect new attitudes.

>< THINKBACK

criminology (ch. 1)—The study of the making of laws, the breaking of laws, and the social reaction to the breaking of laws.

# Think about it

## Remember

Outline the arguments that pornography is harmful to society.

## Apply

Show how sodomy laws have changed to reflect society's evolving view of government control of sexual behaviors.

## Analyze

Distinguish between male and female prostitution in terms of the dangers facing its practitioners.

## Evaluate

Compare the different forms of prostitution in terms of their perceived harms to society.

# Gambling

The United States has an ambivalent attitude toward gambling. Throughout the nation's history, gambling has been criminalized, tolerated, and embraced, often all at the same time. Many states that outlawed gambling in the past now use it as a major source of revenue. People who do not approve of casino gambling or going to a horse track might bet on a college basketball tournament in an office pool. There are so many legal and illegal opportunities to gamble in the United States that it can be considered a major form of entertainment, a rich source of government revenue, and a significant law enforcement and social problem.[74] For a look at the theoretical explanations of why people gamble, see Table 12.4.

Gambling includes more than the element of chance as all forms of human behavior include uncertainty. For example, many consider marriage to be the biggest gamble of

## LO4:

**Compare** and contrast the concept of gambling as an effective way to raise public revenue with the concept of gambling as a harmful activity that must be controlled by law.

## Table 12.4    Gambling and Criminological Theory

| Theory | Explanation |
| --- | --- |
| Psychological<br>Operant conditioning | Gambling works on the behavior principle of intermittent reinforcement. It only pays off some of the time, which makes it exciting, and, to some individuals, addicting. Treatment requires the gambler to understand the psychological principles behind the behavior. |
| Sociological<br>Strain theory | Merton's strain theory would contend that gamblers are utilizing the adaptation of innovation. They embrace the cultural goal of amassing economic wealth but are unable or unwilling to employ the cultural means of hard work, thrift, and deferred gratification. |
| Sociological<br>Subcultural theory | Gambling is a cultural norm in various subcultures. Animal fighting is shunned by the dominant culture but is an integral part of some subcultures. Just as gambling on a golf game is considered a way to make the sport more exciting in upper-class subcultures, raising and fighting pit bulls is attractive to others. |

a lifetime. Everyone goes to the altar with a feeling that success is a sure thing, but evidence shows us that more than half of marriages end in divorce. Psychologist Nancy Petry defines gambling as:

> placing something of value on an event that has a possibility of resulting in a larger, more beneficial outcome. Inherent in gambling is risk. Another defining feature of gambling is that chance influences results.[75]

Some games are strictly based on chance. Playing a state lottery gives one very little opportunity to affect the outcome. Aside from buying multiple lottery tickets, any person has as good of a chance as anyone else (very little in fact) of becoming a millionaire based on a dollar bet. Other games have an element of skill associated with them. One can improve the chances of winning at casino blackjack by being aware of the rules of probability. However, casinos attempt to keep too much skill out of the game and do not allow gamblers to count cards to improve their odds of winning. So why are games of chance frowned upon by society and made illegal in many jurisdictions? There are several reasons for this attitude.

- *Gambling can divert people from productive work.* When people think they can get rich easily by betting on games of chance, they are less likely to work hard at getting an education, finding gainful employment, and saving for the future.
- *Gambling has often been thought to weaken moral character.* Those who gamble are thought to lack the moral fortitude to engage in family, religious, and social affairs in which concern for others and responsibility are important.
- *Gambling can divert money from worthy endeavors.* Whether it is a mother spending the grocery money at the dog track or a local government giving large tax breaks to

attract a major casino, money associated with gambling produces little in terms of family security, community infrastructure, or a stable economy. Gambling sells an elusive hope of material gain for little effort and is thought to weaken, not strengthen, the financial conditions of those involved. An economic development consultant who assessed the economic effect of casinos on the local economies of cities involved in gambling development concluded, "[W]e're just rearranging dollars. . . . And the people who usually win, quite frankly, are the casino operations. The people who lose are the cultural activities in the city, the eating and drinking establishments in other parts of the city. . . . There's absolutely no net gain in terms of the economic impact from gamblers who are located within the immediate trade area of fifty miles."[76]

- *Gambling can become addictive.* The lure of quick, easy money can cause some people to bet compulsively with money they cannot afford to lose. Problem gamblers can become involved in illegal enterprises to attempt to compensate for their losses.
- *Gambling brings unsavory people into the community.* The argument can be made that crime follows gambling. Those who exploit gamblers, such as prostitutes, thieves, robbers, and loan sharks, start to appear in communities where there is gambling. The history of illegal gambling in the United States is replete with evidence of the influence of organized crime.[77]

Gambling proponents agree that these concerns are valid when taken to the extreme, but they argue that, for the most part, these claims are exaggerated. For every mother betting with the family's grocery money, there are many more who bet responsibly and for whom gambling is a form of entertainment and relaxation, much like going on a cruise or a vacation at the beach. Furthermore, gambling proponents claim that the jobs and businesses that gambling brings into a community, such as restaurants, gas stations, hotels, and banks, stimulate local economies. Although organized crime was a feature of illegal gambling in the past, organized crime was involved precisely because the activity was illegal. Legalized gambling is a legitimate business and attracts those who employ honest and ethical business practices.

The moral and financial issues of gambling are subject to debate; however, illegal gambling has historically been considered a public-order offense and has been the focus of considerable attention by the criminal justice system. In order to understand why, we must look at the history of gambling in the United States.

## A Brief History of Gambling

Moral objections to gambling are as old as the United States. England has a considerable history of gambling, and many colonists brought the practice with them. However, life in the colonies was precarious and harsh, and it demanded that all colonists carry their weight in being productive workers. In its first year of existence, Massachusetts Bay Colony outlawed dice, cards, and other games thought to produce idleness. According to scholars Edward A. Morse and Ernest P. Goss:

> Though such provisions now seem quite odd in a society where leisure is an important value— perhaps even rising to the level of a human right— the struggles of the time might have demanded it. Difficult winters, diseases, and other travails presented a battle for survival. Those who failed to engage in productive activities drained the resources of the larger group, which had little margin to maintain a safety net for those who could work but chose not to work.[78]

Other colonies had more liberal attitudes. The Dutch who settled New York saw gambling as commonplace. Gambling was also common in the southern colonies, where newly landed aristocrats owned large plantations worked by slaves. After the American Revolution, the new United States became more hostile toward gambling. In its 1885 ruling in *Irwin v. Williar,* the U.S. Supreme Court declared that debts incurred as part of gambling losses were void because the activity was il-

legal.[79] This meant that the courts would not enforce gambling laws, and winners had to use threats and violence to get their money. In some states, laws against gambling focused primarily on gambling operations and less heavily on individual gamblers. In other states, an individual gambler might lose the right to hold public office for five years.

Governments did not treat all forms of gambling in the same way. Betting on horse racing was viewed more favorably because the sport had implications for animal husbandry. Gambling encouraged horse breeders to improve equine genetics, which was considered to be beneficial to the horse industry.[80] Gambling gained its strongest toehold in Nevada, where it was legalized in 1869. Gambling licenses were expensive, and regulations prohibited gambling by minors and relegated games to back rooms out of public view. Although Nevada outlawed gambling from 1909 to 1931, it was the only state to allow casinos until New Jersey opened its first casinos in 1976.

## Legal Gambling

Today, gambling is a common feature of the economy in many states. Every state except Utah and Hawaii has some form of legal gambling. Why are these two states the exception? First, Utah has a large religious demographic. The Mormons who initially settled in the state are still the state's most populous and powerful group and have banned gambling for religious reasons. Until recently, Hawaii had a different reason for not engaging in legal gambling. Many states have instituted lotteries to generate revenue. However, Hawaii's chief form of revenue was tourism. Because Hawaii is such a desirable vacation destination, it has not needed gambling to make money. However, as of 2010, state lawmakers were debating the legalization of casino gambling to boost flagging tourism during the recession.[81] Other states that once proscribed legalized gambling, such as Mississippi and Georgia,

▶ Nevada was the only state to allow casinos until 1976. Here, monitors at the Bellagio Hotel's race and sports book display a horse race and the betting odds.

# sowhat'snew?

### Dogfighting, Gambling, and Crime

Gambling on animals is a centuries-old form of entertainment. Some of these sports, such as racing, have become mainstream and have regulatory bodies that ensure the animals' health and safety. Other forms, such as dogfighting, continue in the shadows of society.

According to The Humane Society of the United States, dogfighting is a competition in which dogs are bred, conditioned, and trained to fight each other. Two dogs are placed in a small, enclosed area called a "pit," where they fight each other until one can no longer continue. Fights usually last about an hour but can last as long as two hours. To get the dogs to fight, a weak "prey" animal, such as a cat, rabbit, or injured dog, is thrown between the two dogs. Spectators typically place bets on which dog will win. Dogs that win three times are "champions" and might be retired to stud, while losing dogs are often left to die.[1]

Dogfighting, which has been popular in the rural South for decades, has recently increased in popularity throughout the United States, especially in North Carolina and Virginia.[2] The betting pool at some fights can grow to $10,000 or more. A Baltimore animal rescue expert calls dogfighting "big sport, big-money betting."[3] Ohio Attorney General Marc Dann, who observed a southwest Ohio raid, said the warehouse that housed the activity resembled a casino.[4]

Aside from animal cruelty, a major reason that dogfights concern law enforcement is that they attract a criminal subculture that also tends to be involved in drug-dealing, illegal gun sales, and illegal gambling. A 2001–2004 Chicago Police Department study found that in 382 dogfighting cases, 59 percent of the owners were gang members, and 86 percent had been arrested at least twice. A local police official in Ohio—who said that in all his department's dogfighting search warrants, drugs were found in every case but one—explained that dogfighting is an expensive activity that requires the kind of disposable income that drug-selling provides.[5]

Currently, dogfighting is a felony in every state. The Animal Fighting Prohibition Enforcement Act of 2007 amended existing federal law to impose a fine and/or prison sentence of up to three years for "(1) sponsoring or exhibiting an animal in an animal fighting venture; (2) buying, selling, transporting, delivering, or receiving for purposes of transportation, in interstate or foreign commerce, any dog or other animal for participation in

▲ Although dogfighting is a felony in every state, people continue to raise animals specifically for fighting.

an animal fighting venture; and (3) using the mails or other instrumentality of interstate commerce to promote or further an animal fighting venture."

[1] Childs Walker, "Dogfight 'Culture' Reaches to Baltimore," *Baltimore Sun,* June 1, 2007, 1A.

[2] Bill Burke, "Once Limited to the Rural South, Dogfighting Sees a Cultural Shift," *Virginian-Pilot,* June 17, 2007.

[3] Walker, "Dogfight 'Culture' Reaches to Baltimore," 1A.

[4] James Hannah, "Dogfighting Bust Shows How Crime Is Becoming More of a Focus," Associated Press, April 4, 2007.

[5] John Futty, "Dogfight Raids Not Just About Animals: Crackdown Turns Up Many Other Crimes," *Columbus Dispatch,* April 2, 2007.

## THINKING
### *in* ACTION

Discuss the reasons why dogfighting is a felony in all states. What is your opinion of the criminalization of dogfighting?

now allow casinos or state lotteries to raise money that may be used for infrastructure and education.

State lotteries are one of the most popular legal forms of gambling. States have relaxed their attitude toward gambling as a revenue source but have kept tight control on who runs the programs. Unlike other forms of gambling in which private businesses can get into the game, state lotteries restrict this benefit to state government. This restriction allows for better regulation and control of legalized gambling and ensures that the state gets its cut because the state government does the actual accounting. State lotteries generate a lot of money. In 2004, lotteries in 41 states and the District of Columbia took in more than $48 billion. Per capita spending ranged from $9.27 in North Dakota to $1,370.95 in Rhode Island, which allows video lottery terminals. Although this is a great deal of money for states to take in, only $13.9 billion of this $48 billion actually went to the states. The rest went to the cost of running the lotteries and as payouts to the winners.[82]

Criminologists are interested in legalized gambling because it demonstrates how public-order offenses reflect individual and community values; the ways that these values change over time; and the economic, social, and political pressures they incur. Legal gambling takes regulation out of the hands of law enforcement and gives that responsibility to administrative agencies. However, in cases of fraud or political corruption connected with legal gambling, law enforcement may once again become involved.[83]

### Illegal Gambling

Despite the availability of so much legal gambling, people still risk their money and the possibility of getting arrested by gambling illegally. The reason for this risk has to do primarily with the patchwork availability of legal gambling, which many gamblers find insufficient to meet their desires. A state lottery might be fine for someone who wants a bit of entertainment, but it is purely a game of chance. There is no way for someone to excel at playing the lottery. You pay your money and take your chances. Some gamblers find casinos and traditional games dull and want to wager on something that involves not only chance, but also violence and extreme cruelty. For this reason, dogfighting and cockfighting have seen a resurgence in popularity (see *So What's New?*).

Poker games, played for money, are illegal in many states. The game pits players against one another, and those with card skills and the ability to judge others can win. Hence, many people regard poker as more of a skill-based competition than a game of chance. Cable television stations regularly broadcast poker tournaments as if they are sporting events, making the game attractive to consumers without nearby access to casinos. This problem has been compounded by Internet poker in which the players are essentially anonymous and are spread across many states and sometimes the world. Internet poker is difficult to regulate, and minors can play undetected.[84]

The online environment also allows for betting on sporting events. For many people, pro and collegiate baseball, football, and basketball are attractive not so much for the excitement of the game, but for the excitement of betting on it. Major league sports have long had a delicate relationship with gambling. In the 1970s, national sport shows routinely provided viewers with the betting odds on major games. Today, there is still a relationship between these sports and the betting world. For instance, teams are required to report players' injuries or list them as probable starters so that no inside information can be traded that would give some bettors an advantage.

The number and variety of illegal gambling opportunities are endless. From country club members betting on a golf game to little old ladies betting on their bridge game to sophisticated urban numbers games (a form of informal neighborhood lottery), illegal gambling is a persistent feature of American society. As law enforcement authorities attempt to police gambling offenses, they encounter an ambivalent attitude from citizens, a lack of resources from the government, and a growing problem with corruption and graft. As a result, law enforcement no longer tries to eliminate illegal gambling, but simply seeks to keep it under some control so that it takes place out of public view and, to the extent possible, is unavailable to minors.

## Think about it

### Remember

Why have some societies tried to discourage gambling?

### Apply

Demonstrate how technology has altered both the forms of gambling and the ability of the law to control gambling.

### Evaluate

Justify the reasoning that all but two states have employed to legalize some form of gambling.

## The Public Order, Victims, and Values

The work of the criminal justice system would be much easier if it did not have the mandate to enforce public-order laws. If the criminal justice system could concentrate on offenses that have a firm

### LO5:

**Explain** why the work of the criminal justice system would be more efficient if it could focus only on violent and property offenses.

majority consensus, such as homicide, larceny, and embezzlement, it could focus its resources more efficiently, enlist the support of citizens more effectively, and limit the numbers of incarcerated people. Some believe that other government agencies or the private sector could better deal with the issues that arise out of the activities of consenting citizens. It is possible the existence of criminal sanctions for drug use, prostitution, and other public-order offenses does not reduce the amount and severity of these behaviors. In fact, in some ways, criminal sanctions promote the illegal underground economy that arises to supply the demand for these services.

Public-order offenses certainly affect society, but some people wonder if the problems that arise from these offenses are made worse or better by using the criminal justice system to control them. The work of criminologists is important in examining the problems and issues of dealing with offenses against the public order.

# Think about it

## Evaluate

Does the existence of criminal sanctions for drug use, prostitution, and other public-order offenses reduce the amount and severity of these behaviors? Why or why not?

# Summary

**LO1: Give an example of a public-order offense.**
- Public-order offenses are often called victimless crimes because all who participate in them are typically willing parties.
- Morality is concerned with values. The process of creating laws is a function of political compromise and a reflection of social attitudes and religious beliefs.
- Some harmful behaviors are legal, whereas other behaviors that seem to do little significant damage are illegal.
- Three general categories of public-order offenses are substance abuse, sex offenses, and gambling.

**LO2: Discuss why the use and abuse of drugs are important to the study of criminology.**
- The use and abuse of drugs are important to the study of criminology for three reasons: drugs and alcohol influence behavior; substance abuse is related to other types of crime; and the war on drugs is difficult, dangerous, and costly.
- The early United States had no laws that restricted the sale or use of drugs or alcohol. The first laws restricting the sale of alcohol or drugs were economic, not social.

**LO3: Understand the basis of laws prohibiting prostitution, pornography, and sodomy.**
- Some people consider the purchase of sex to be an issue of personal freedom, whereas others consider it to be immoral.

- Currently, pornography is legal in the United States unless it meets the *Miller* test of obscenity.
- Sodomy was illegal in the United States until recently. Early sodomy laws were meant to prevent non-procreative sex and target predatory individuals.

**LO4: Compare and contrast the concept of gambling as an effective way to raise public revenue with the concept of gambling as a harmful activity that must be controlled by law.**
- In the United States, gambling, whether legal or illegal, is a major form of entertainment, a source of government revenue, and a significant law enforcement and social problem.

**LO5: Explain why the work of the criminal justice system would be more efficient if it could focus only on violent and property offenses.**
- Limiting criminal justice attention to offenses with a firm majority consensus, such as homicide, larceny, and embezzlement, would allow it to focus resources more efficiently, enlist the support of citizens more effectively, and limit the numbers of incarcerated people.

# Questions

1. Why are public-order offenses often called victimless crimes?
2. How can public-order offenses affect the lives of individuals not involved in these offenses?
3. Why is substance use and abuse important to the study of criminology?
4. Discuss the history of restricting drugs and alcohol in the United States.
5. What is the difference between substance legalization and decriminalization?
6. In the past, how did states criminalize homosexuality?
7. Why do some segments of society question the morality of gambling?
8. Why are some forms of gambling legal, whereas others are not?

# 13

# Terrorism

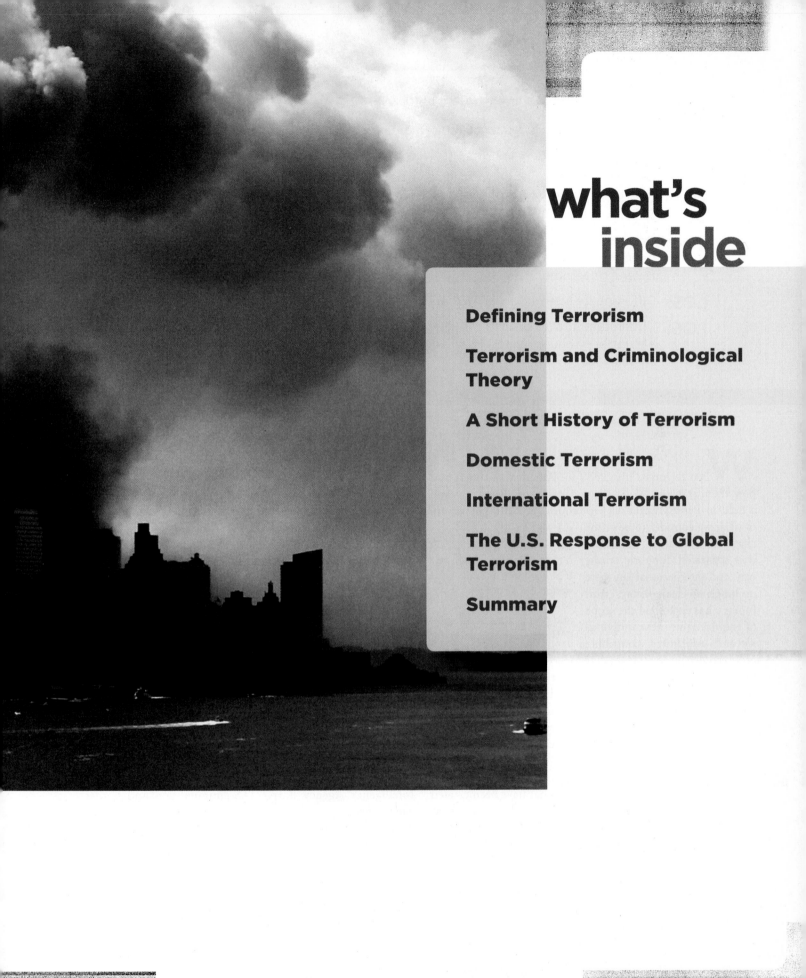

# what's inside

**As you read, keep in mind these learning objectives:**

**LO1:**  Explain why terrorism is so difficult to define.

**LO2:**  Discuss how the classical and positivist schools of criminological thought consider terrorism.

**LO3:**  Give some examples of how groups throughout history have used terrorism to achieve their political goals.

**LO4:**  Describe incidents of domestic terrorism in the United States that have been motivated by racism, fundamentalist religious beliefs, hatred of the federal government, and ecological concerns.

**LO5:**  Differentiate international terrorism from domestic terrorism.

**LO6:**  Understand that in dealing with terrorism, the United States must consider a number of issues related to civil rights, the Constitution, privacy, and surveillance.

When terrorists hijacked four American airliners and flew them into the World Trade Center, the Pentagon, and a field in Pennsylvania on September 11, 2001, the nature of what we consider to be crime changed radically.[1] The lines that separated domestic crime, war, and international law were no longer so clear. Today, criminology has expanded the scope of inquiry from how individuals and institutions contribute and respond to antisocial behavior to broader subjects such as war, international crime, **transnational crime,** and **terrorism,** which is politically motivated violence against civilians by political groups for the purpose of drawing attention to their cause. Terrorism and globalization have shrunk the world, so to speak, so that all antisocial behavior is now of concern to the field of criminology.

>< THINKBACK

transnational crime (ch. 3)—Criminal offenses that originate in one nation, cross one or several national borders, and find victims in other nations.

We will study how Americans have adjusted to this new threat and examine the new agencies that have been created and the new laws that have been enacted to deal with terrorism. The events of September 11, 2001, and the subsequent wars in Iraq and Afghanistan have changed the nature of the U.S. military mandate and domestic law enforcement's mission. For example, the Federal Bureau of Investigation (FBI), which once specialized in bank robberies and other types of interstate domestic crime, now plays a major role in dealing with terrorism. This change in mandate has been controver-

**terrorism** Violence perpetrated against civilians by political groups for the purpose of drawing attention to their cause.

sial. Some people believe that terrorism has become more of a media-created crisis and that the government response to terrorism presents the greater threat to individual rights and freedoms. Consequently, we must now view criminology in an entirely different way in order to accommodate this radical shift in the way public order is preserved.[2]

Crime control in the United States is a work in progress and will require constantly revisiting how crime is addressed, how the criminal justice system is structured, and how responsibility is allocated. This is an exciting time to be a criminology student because many of the traditional responses to crime are being modified to address both foreign and domestic terrorism.[3]

Terrorism has expanded the range of issues that concern scholars of crime. The rise in global terrorism means that those who study crime will need to be better versed in international relations and foreign languages and cultures. Law enforcement officers at every level must be able to coordinate with intelligence agencies such as the FBI and the Central Intelligence Agency (CIA). U.S. immigration and border patrol agencies must take terrorism into account when performing their duties. In short, terrorism has changed the nature of the response to crime in the United States, causing some unanticipated consequences. Primary among these problems is the tension between protecting the homeland and preserving the civil rights and privacy of citizens.

Crime control in the United States is historically based, meaning that the structures and agencies that deal with crime have a history and mission that cannot easily be discarded or altered. The attempt to find the most rational and effective way to respond to crime while preserving individual liberties requires negotiation between various agencies and

◀ Government response to the September 11 attacks in New York City, as well as attacks in Europe, have made some impositions on freedoms and liberties, such as the tightening of security for air travelers.

violence perpetrated against non-combatant targets by subnational groups or clandestine agents."[6] However, the axiom "One person's terrorist is another person's freedom fighter" makes it clear that terrorism is relative. Terrorism is a political tool, and people can have legitimate differences of opinion about what defines terrorism and what defines self-defense. For instance, the Iraqi insurgents might regard the U.S. soldiers with their jet planes, tanks, and other high-technology weapons as terrorists yet view themselves with their low-tech methods and weapons as freedom fighters battling a superpower. In contrast, U.S. soldiers may believe they are fighting a conventional war against a dishonorable enemy who uses terror as a weapon. Both sides believe they are fighting for values and ideas that are morally correct.[7]

The ambiguity in determining exactly what terrorism means resides in the fact that terrorism is a unique problem because it uses violence or the threat of violence in a quest to establish control over the lives of others. Depending upon one's position and viewpoint, it is possible for reasonable individuals to observe the same behavior and evaluate it differently. Many people and organizations have developed definitions of terrorism, but in our examination of terrorism, we will use the one created by political scientist Cindy C. Combs because it acknowledges that terrorism must attract attention to be effective. According to Combs, terrorism is "a synthesis of war and theater, a dramatization of the most proscribed kind of violence—that which is perpetrated on innocent victims—played before an audience in the hope of creating a mood of fear, for political purposes."[8] Combs's definition has four components.

branches of government. Working out compromises and accommodations is no easy task because many vested interests are involved in the criminal justice system, and any change in crime control policy and strategy requires not only retraining personnel, but also that agencies and individuals give up some of their rights and power.[4]

For instance, local law enforcement agencies traditionally distrust federal agencies such as the FBI, but the global threat of terrorism has made inter-agency cooperation absolutely crucial. Thus, ways must be found to encourage local and federal agencies to work together and share information. The anti-terrorism laws passed by Congress and its allocation of funds to control terrorism encourage local, state, and federal agencies to develop a coordinated response. As the process continues to take shape in the next decade, the types of threats that terrorism poses will change, and the response of the criminal justice system will change as well.[5]

Because neither the United Nations nor any other international organization can referee the situation between the United States and the deposed governments in Iraq and Afghanistan, those who win the wars will get to establish the government and laws of these nations. As a result, criminology must adjust to reflect how this new state of international order affects the study of crime and the response of the criminal justice system. A first step is agreeing on a definition of terrorism.

## Defining Terrorism

Defining terrorism is difficult because the definition varies depending upon who is defining the term. The U.S. government defines terrorism as "premeditated, politically motivated

**LO1:**

Explain why terrorism is so difficult to define.

■ *The use of violence or the threat of violence.* Terrorist activities can range from assassination and bombings to other forms of violence that strike at the state. Once a credible possibility of terrorism has been established, the mere threat of it is enough to frighten people and cause them to change their behavior. Although airplane hijackings are infrequent, nations around the world have instituted elaborate and expensive precautions that inconvenience airline employees and passengers.[9]

■ *A political dimension.* Terrorism can be distinguished from many types of crime because it has a goal of changing

◄ A favorite tactic of terrorists is to strike at civilian rather than military targets. Timothy McVeigh, who was responsible for the deaths of 168 people in the 1995 Oklahoma City bombing, referred to the children killed in the blast as "collateral damage."

Combs's definition allows us to consider a wide range of behaviors and to distinguish terrorism from other crime. However, we must always be aware that the term *terrorism* is pejorative. This means that it is loaded with negative and derogatory meanings and that we distinguish between similar behaviors committed by individuals who have different motivations, grievances, or social standing.

For example, a government can mistakenly kill people and excuse it as a mistake, whereas the same type of behavior committed by a politically motivated individual would be called terrorism. The 1983 bombing of the U.S. Marine Corps barracks in Beirut, Lebanon, was defined as a terrorist act. In this incident, an Islamist suicide bomber drove a truck loaded with a bomb into a building housing Marines and other military personnel, killing 241 people. (A U.S. judge later declared Iran liable for the attack.)[12] In contrast, in 1999, the United States mistakenly bombed the Chinese Embassy in Belgrade, Yugoslavia, killing three people. Although the results of these two incidents were similar, the motivations were different. The Marine barracks bombing was intentional. The embassy bombing was not, and the United States apologized and agreed to pay China $4.5 million for its mistake.[13] The term *terrorism* describes the Marine barracks bombing and is distinguished from the Chinese Embassy tragedy, which is not considered a terrorist act because it was unintentional.

Terrorist acts have become an important factor in how governments structure their criminal justice and national defense systems. Although they are relatively infrequent, terrorist acts have come to the forefront in criminology and consume a great deal of governments' attention and resources.[14]

the policies of formal social institutions, such as corporations and governments, as well as informal institutions, such as cultures and norms. The political aims of terrorists who have a religious motivation can range from trying to bring down a government to attempting to enforce specific dress codes, dietary habits, and access to places of worship.[10]

■ *The killing of innocent people.* Terrorists often strike at entire populations rather than just government leaders. People who have little control over the issues that terrorists are concerned with, or even little knowledge of the terrorists' grievances, are targets. For instance, many of the victims of the 1993 bombing of the World Trade Center were completely unaware of the Middle East terrorists' concerns. When Timothy McVeigh set off a truck bomb outside the Murrah Federal Building in Oklahoma City that killed 168 people, including many children in a daycare center located in the building, he referred to the casualties as "collateral damage."[11]

■ *Symbolic meaning.* The targets of the September 11 attacks were selected because of their symbolic meaning. The World Trade Center represented the global economy, and the Pentagon was a symbol of U.S. military power. The fourth airplane that crashed in a field in Pennsylvania is suspected to have been targeted at either the White House or the U.S. Capitol. Such targets are now protected by multiple layers of security, forcing terrorists to either step up their techniques in delivering their acts of violence or choose other targets that are less guarded.

# Think about it

## Understand

List the four components that underlie our definition of terrorism.

## Evaluate

Critique the axiom "one person's terrorist is another person's freedom fighter."

## Terrorism and Criminological Theory

Because the terrorist threat to the United States is fairly new and is so recently of concern to the criminal justice system, no traditional criminological theories *directly* address terrorist activities. However, some may indirectly address the reason for terrorist activities. Two prevailing schools of criminological thought that may be used to this end are the classical school and the positivist school.

**LO2:**

**Discuss** how the classical and positivist schools of criminological thought consider terrorism.

The classical school states that lawbreaking is the result of a rational choice that offenders make. According to the classical school, then, terrorists make a rational choice to break the law to further awareness of themselves and their political causes. Instead of choosing peaceful forms of protest and discourse, they choose violence. Terrorists whose offenses were successful, such as Timothy McVeigh and Osama bin Laden, planned their actions carefully, financed their work, recruited others, and had a logical reasoning for their actions.

The positivist school looks for causes external to the offender to explain crime, such as urban decay, impoverishment, failure within society's institutions, poor nutrition, and disease. According to the positivist school, terrorists would not pursue violence if not for the social disorder and desperate poverty in which many of them live. Western powers have intervened in the Middle East for decades, setting up arbitrary borders that create new countries such as Iraq while ignoring established tribal territories. Many terrorists start out as youths who have nothing but fundamentalist religion to give them hope.

## Think about it

### Analyze

Compare and contrast how the classical school of criminology and the positivist school of criminology consider terrorism.

### Create

Propose how some traditional criminological theories might indirectly address terrorism.

## A Short History of Terrorism

Terrorism is an old political weapon that has been used by both the powerful and the powerless throughout history. At any point in human history, groups have carried out terrorist attacks to frighten others from continuing to pursue their political goals. Historian Michael Burleigh points out that incidents of terrorism are recounted in the Bible and that acts of terrorism have been perpetrated just as effectively by governments as by the stateless. The European crusaders and the Spanish Inquisitors acted as extensions of the governments they served as they sowed their share of terror in those whose minds they wanted to change.[15]

**LO3:**

**Give** some examples of how groups throughout history have used terrorism to achieve their political goals.

In the American Revolution, the British considered the colonial soldiers and militia to be terrorists because they did not abide by the established European standards of warfare. The colonial soldiers were considered cowards because they did not stand in straight rows and trade volleys with the British. Instead, they hid behind trees and rocks and fought only when they had the advantage. To the British, one particularly egregious violation of the rules of war was the colonists' intentional killing of British officers. Today, killing an army's officers might be considered a tactical advantage because doing so would deprive the enemy of leadership and cause confusion. During the American Revolution, however, killing officers was considered a violation of the rules of war.[16]

### The Modern Concept of Terrorism

Although acts of terrorism have been committed throughout history, the word *terrorism,* as well as our modern concept of it, entered the Western mindset at the end of the 18th century with the French Revolution, according to political scientist David C. Rapoport.[17] During the upheaval, revolutionary leaders were responsible for a "reign of terror" in which thousands of "enemies of the revolution" were beheaded. Rapoport divides modern terrorism into four waves.

■ *The first wave.* This wave began in 19th-century Russia and ended with the 1914 assassination of Austrian archduke Franz Ferdinand that led to World War I. Terrorism in this era was largely concerned with political reform. In Russia, the terrorist rebel group *Narodnaya Volya,* or The People's Will, which chose victims for their symbolic importance, assassinated Tsar Alexander II in 1881. The late 19th century saw a number of other assassinations, with kings, presidents, and prime ministers being killed, many by anarchists, terrorists of the period who had no trouble finding their targets in the low-surveillance 19th-century world. U.S. Presidents Abraham Lincoln, James Garfield, and William McKinley were all assassinated during this period. In 1901, U.S. President Theodore Roosevelt called for an international movement against the anarchists, saying, "Anarchy is a crime against the whole human race. . . ."[18] In Western Europe, groups such as the Fenians, who supported the cause of Irish nationalism, demonstrated their resentment of British rule in Ireland with several bombing campaigns that claimed dozens of lives.

- *The second wave.* According to Rapoport, this wave, which extended from the 1920s to the early 1960s, was brought on by desires for "national self-determination" and the fading of colonial power. Attacking symbolic political figures was not as important, and some terrorist groups even gave advance warnings to minimize harm to civilians. Instead, terrorist groups targeted what they considered to be the "eyes and ears" of their governments, the police forces. A major development of this era was the terrorist "cell," isolated groups whose members knew little or nothing about other organizational members or leadership. Also, in September 1920, the world was introduced to the vehicular bomb when an Italian anarchist drove a horse and cart packed with a hundred pounds of dynamite down Wall Street in New York City, killing at least 30 people.[19]

- *The third wave.* In the 1960s, the success of Vietcong guerrillas against the formal military powers of France and the United States inspired the third wave of terrorism as groups saw that with the right tactics and discipline they could defeat powerful technology, big budgets, and large standing armies. Several terrorist groups sprang up in the United States as well, including the Weather Underground and the Symbionese Liberation Army. In 1967, the Palestine Liberation Organization continued to fight after Israel's victory in the 1967 Six-Day War. Airline hijacking also became a favorite tactic during this period, with more than 100 carried out annually throughout the 1970s.

- *The fourth wave.* This wave, according to Rapoport, was fueled by Iran's 1979 Islamic revolution and the Soviet defeat in Afghanistan in 1989, which was assisted by the United States. In this wave, which continues to this day, politics has taken a backseat to religious fundamentalism as a motivating force. The 1991 dissolution of the Soviet Union, a political giant that kept the lid on centuries of political and religious ill will throughout its 15 separate republics, set free a torrent of pent-up unrest.[20]

### Terrorism and Guerrilla Warfare

As the rules of war have changed over the years, so too has the concept of terrorism. This is an especially important distinction because there is a long history of attempting to limit wars to the combat of soldiers, thus sparing civilian populations. However, as mentioned previously, throughout history those who lacked the advantage in weapons or numbers of soldiers have sought ways to equalize their tactical positions. **Guerrilla warfare** is military or paramilitary operations

**guerrilla warfare** Military or paramilitary operations conducted within hostile territory by irregular forces.

conducted within hostile territory by irregular forces. The term was coined to describe how those who lacked powerful weapons used deceit, diversion, and misdirection to fool or trick their enemies into making poor tactical decisions. Guerrilla fighters strike when least expected, attack government infrastructure, and hide among the people. Once considered to be terrorism, guerrilla warfare is now deemed a legitimate way to fight. Although guerrilla warfare has some aspects in common with terrorism, it also differs from terrorism in significant ways. Perhaps the most important difference is that guerrilla warfare is used by groups who wish to establish their own legitimate governments. In contrast, groups who use terrorism do not have the goal of constructing a legitimate government but rather seek to destroy property, bring down social institutions, and spread fear to further a goal that is sometimes known only to the terrorists.[21]

For example, the United States used its military force to depose the existing government in Iraq. Iraq's formal military resistance was considered legitimate warfare. However, the violence that followed the fall of Iraq's government is considered terrorism because those who perpetrate this violence are not connected to any legitimate government. They target civilian populations as well as soldiers, and they fight all aspects of the governments that have been put in place by the United States. The various religious and ethnic factions within Iraq also use terrorism to fight one another.[22]

To understand the scope and level of terrorism in the 21st century, we must distinguish between terrorism committed by U.S. citizens and terrorism committed by citizens from other nations, either within the United States or elsewhere. This distinction is required to understand terrorist motivations and tactics and to differentiate between terrorism as a form of war and terrorism as a form of social protest. We will look first at domestic terrorism in the United States as a violent method of protest.

## Think about it

### Understand

Describe why in colonial times the British considered American colonists terrorists.

### Analyze

Discriminate between terrorism and guerrilla warfare.

## Domestic Terrorism

As previously stated, terrorism is a tactic, not a cause. Therefore, it is important to recognize that terrorism is not something imported from overseas and committed against Americans, but rather, something that is also homegrown. U.S.

◀ The violence that followed the fall of Iraq's government in 2003 is considered terrorism. Here, a man grieves beside the body of his brother who was killed in a suicide-bomb attack outside a Baghdad hospital.

citizens have committed acts of terrorism since the birth of the nation, and the focus on international terrorism should not blind us to the recognition of terrorist acts committed by U.S. citizens within the nation's borders. Incidents of domestic terrorism in the United States have been motivated by racism, fundamentalist religious beliefs, hatred of the federal government, and ecological concerns.

## LO4:

**Describe** incidents of domestic terrorism in the United States that have been motivated by racism, fundamentalist religious beliefs, hatred of the federal government, and ecological concerns.

The Ku Klux Klan, which emerged shortly after the Civil War, is one example of an early American terrorist group.[23] Southern whites upset by the freeing of the slaves sought to maintain their social, economic, and political superiority by intimidating black Southerners. The Ku Klux Klan burned homes and churches, committed murder, and conducted numerous highly visible lynchings in an attempt to maintain the social hierarchy in the South. This terrorism was not committed by a few disgruntled people, but rather by some of the most important people within the society, such as bankers, merchants, and law enforcement officials. Concealing their identity by wearing robes and hoods, Ku Klux Klan members could engage in terrorist actions without being held personally accountable. In many ways, this was a form of state-sponsored terrorism because the victims were not able to turn to the criminal justice system for relief.[24]

The Ku Klux Klan is still active but no longer advocates violence and has officially moderated its message and tactics to be more socially acceptable. Its members still argue that whites are genetically superior and protest government policies such as affirmative action. However, other extremist white-power groups have arisen to replace the Ku Klux Klan that do engage in terrorist behaviors and sincerely believe that God intended whites to rule over other races.

According to criminologist Adam Silverman, modern extremist white-power terrorists can be traced to the reactionary Christian Identity movement.[25] This movement advocates the separation of races and inserts its own theology into the ideological underpinnings of the government. Members contend that minorities and liberals have subverted the true intentions of the founders of the United States and that only by revamping the nation's political ideology so that it is based on white supremacy can God's true will be accomplished. According to Silverman, the white identity movement makes a number of extreme claims, including:

> the belief that only whites—the descendents of the Anglo-Saxons and other northern Europeans—are really human. The reason for this is that the Hebrew word Adam, the first man, means "red man". Christian Identity teaches that if you smack a white person's face, the blood rushes to it in a blush. Identity members believe that since it is not possible to see nonwhites blush, they are not humans. If you cannot see the blood in the face, then the person is obviously not human. This understanding of who is a human (whites) and who is not—Jews, Africans, Asians, Hispanics, indigenous peoples, and people of mixed ethnicity ("mud people")—provides a theological set of definitions favorable for Christian Identity–based violence. If members of these groups are not really human, then sanctions against killing them do not apply. This definition neutralizes the normal prohibitions against homicide.[26]

One of the best-known branches of the Christian Identity movement is the Aryan Nation. One of its adherents,

Robert Matthews, was involved in several violent incidents, including the 1984 assassination of Denver talk-show host Alan Berg. In August 1992, another Aryan Nation adherent, Randy Weaver of Ruby Ridge, Idaho, engaged in a two-week standoff with FBI agents over a weapons charge that resulted in the deaths of three people, including Weaver's wife and young son. This incident fueled the ire of right-wing fundamentalists: Although Weaver was acquitted of murder and conspiracy charges, no federal charges were filed against the FBI agents. (State involuntary manslaughter charges were later filed then dismissed against FBI sharpshooter Lon Horiuchi, who killed Weaver's wife.)[27] Several high-level FBI agents were disciplined, and the federal government made a $3.1 million settlement with the Weaver family.[28] However, the incident at Ruby Ridge remains a symbol of the religious right's distrust of the federal government.[29]

Another well-known terrorist connected to the Christian Identity movement is Eric Rudolph, better known as the Centennial Olympic Park bomber. Rudolph was convicted of bombing a gay nightclub in Atlanta, a women's health clinic in Birmingham, Alabama, and Centennial Park during the 1996 Olympics in Atlanta. Rudolph's religious beliefs allowed him to target gay people, abortion clinics, and representatives of the "New World Order" (the Olympics). He hid in the North Carolina mountains until he was captured in 2003 behind a grocery store. Rudolph, who pleaded guilty to the attacks, said the violence was to protest the legalization of abortion and "aberrant sexual behavior."[30] His sister told the Southern Poverty Law Center (see *Theory to Practice*) that Rudolph believed white people were becoming an endangered minority, that he found out his brother was gay, and that he was angry at the government because he had failed to be admitted into the Army Special Forces.[31]

The Army of God is another religion-based terrorist organization in the United States. This group, sometimes called True Believers or God's Patriots, advocates the violent overthrow of the government because members believe that the principles upon which the nation was founded have been subverted by outside groups.[32] According to criminologist Chester Quarles:

> In this perspective, America's Army of God shares the destructive attributes of the anarchist and the nihilist, who seek to destroy society as we know it. The soldier in the Army of God believes that he or she has the right to destroy America because America—with its topless clubs, nude beaches, child pornography, adult bookshops, abortion-on-request, capitalistic usury, and the U.S. government's 'Satan tithe,' (the individual income tax of every wage earner)—no longer deserves the right to exist. We no longer hold 'in God we trust' as any reasonable value except for religious hyperbole embossed on our coins.[33]

These religious-based terrorist organizations reject the idea that all people deserve human and civil rights. They are opposed to the government because they believe their religious ideals have been betrayed by a democracy that values everyone. In their opinion, the United States is influenced by those who defy what these organizations believe is God's plan, and they believe the United States has been hijacked by secular groups who allow evil influences.[34] In their quest to return the government to what they see as its rightful Christian foundations, they adopt a warlike attitude that they believe is guided by divine will. They contend that the laws of God supersede the laws of man and that terrorist actions, including murder, are justified.

The best-known example of domestic terrorism by right-wing extremists fueled by their hatred of the federal government is the 1995 bombing of the Murrah Federal Building in Oklahoma City by Timothy McVeigh. McVeigh—whose motivation was not religious, but political—used the bombing to express his dissatisfaction with a number of government policies. Specifically, McVeigh was upset with how federal authorities handled the Ruby Ridge and Waco, Texas, incidents and considered his violent act as both payback and a warning. (In 1993, federal authorities raided the Branch Davidian compound in Waco in connection with an illegal firearms investigation. A shootout ensued leading to a 51-day standoff, which ended when federal agents overran the compound using tear gas. Seventy-six Branch Davidians died in the resulting conflict.) McVeigh, a veteran of the first Gulf War, used his knowledge of explosives to construct a fertilizer bomb that he delivered in a rented truck. The bomb destroyed the building, killing 168 people, including many children who attended a daycare facility located on the first floor. McVeigh was executed in 2001. His co-defendant, Terry Nichols, who helped construct the bomb, received a life sentence in prison.[35]

One tradition of domestic terrorism is based on the belief that the government and industry are violating the laws of nature and destroying the planet. These terrorists are bent on protecting animals and the natural environment through the use of violent tactics that range from intimidation and harassment to assault, vandalism, and homicide.[36] For example, the Animal Liberation Front (ALF) considers the use of animals to serve human needs of any kind as morally wrong. The group opposes using animals for food, clothing, entertainment, or in the production of medicine. In 2001, the ALF claimed responsibility for firebombing a medical research center in New Mexico. According to Kelly Stoner and Gary Perlstein:

> The methods and targets of the ALF are primarily dictated by the loosely knit outfit's stated core goals—liberate animals, inflict economic damage to targets connected with animal use, and educate the public about animal harm. ALF adherents have until recently restricted their criminal activities to the theft and destruction of public, private, and corporately owned property. These actions, although certainly meant to terrorize individuals connected

# theory to practice

### The Southern Poverty Law Center

Domestic terrorism is often associated with criminal offenses against minorities, women, and homosexuals. It is primarily the purview of white men who see the shift of power in democratic societies moving toward all people and their own influence being diminished. When minorities and women take advantage of laws that provide equal opportunities, and supervisory positions and leadership are allocated based on competence rather than tradition, some neo-Nazi and white supremacist groups resort to domestic terrorism to attempt to keep women and minorities in a subservient status. Consequently, many state legislatures have passed laws with additional penalties for offenses based on racial or gender status. These "hate crime laws" have been instrumental in targeting domestic terrorists.

A number of organizations attempt to raise the visibility of hate groups that engage in or seek to engage in domestic terrorism. The idea is that by raising awareness of these groups' activities, purposes, and motivations, the less effective their activities will be. The most successful of these groups is the Southern Poverty Law Center (SPLC) based in Montgomery, Alabama. The center's website not only alerts the public to the existence of hate groups, but also promotes a progressive agenda for social justice in the United States. The SPLC, which maintains a database of hate groups and their prevalence in the United States, counted 932 active hate groups in the United States in 2009. According to the center, "All hate groups have beliefs or practices that attack or malign an entire class of people, typically for their immutable characteristics."[1] These groups include neo-Nazi groups, racist skinheads, the Ku Klux Klan, and black separatist groups. By tracking the activities of hate groups, the SPLC can gather evidence to sue them for any violent acts committed by their members.

[1]Southern Poverty Law Center, "Hate Map," http://www.splcenter.org/get-informed/hate-map.

▲ The National Socialist Movement, based in Detroit, Michigan, is one of the largest neo-Nazi groups in the United States. Here, members salute during an anti–illegal immigration rally.

## THINKING
### *in* ACTION

In your opinion, do hate crime laws help control the number of hate crime offenses that are committed? Why or why not?

---

with animal use, have not yet resulted in physical harm. However, other clandestine militant animal rights radicals have taken direct aim at people. This willingness to cause physical harm for the animal-rights cause signals the possible adoption of more violent tactics within the broader movement.[37]

In addition to protecting animals, environmental terrorist groups seek to protect the planet. A prominent example is the Earth Liberation Front (ELF), a worldwide organization that aims primarily to cause property damage and make it unprofitable for companies to operate. One of the ELF's primary targets is the logging industry, which the ELF holds responsible for not only destroying trees, but also for ruining the natural habitat of animals and the quality of water resources. According to Stoner and Perlstein:

ELF arson attacks cause much greater damage than the other tactics used by the group's operatives, which include the traditional methods of monkey wrenching—such as pouring sugar in gas tanks, gluing door locks, and cutting brake lines. Perpetrators of ELF-claimed crimes often use multiple timed incendiary devices and accelerants to ensure as much destruction to their targets as possible. Acts of vandalism, such as smashing windows and thrashing equipment, also occur, both in conjunction with arsons and individually. Crop

◄ Terrorists typically consider their violent acts to be legitimate social protest. In 1998, the radical group Earth Liberation Front claimed responsibility for fires that caused $12 million in damages to a Vail, Colorado, restaurant.

that it is within their civil rights to criticize the government and resort to extreme measures when they believe that their messages are not being seriously considered. The law recognizes citizens' rights to protest or demonstrate but draws a line at violence.

crushing—the destruction of genetically modified food crops—is another tactic of the ELF. Graffiti, including the group's initials and slogans denouncing the offending activity, is often, although not always, left at the crime site.[38]

Although the ELF aims its destruction at property, it also threatens the safety and security of people who work in government agencies or corporations. The motivation behind this type of terrorist activity, often called **ecoterrorism**—terrorist acts committed for the purpose of bringing attention to what the perpetrators believe are offenses against the natural environment or animals—is based on the belief that change cannot be accomplished through normal democratic channels and that ELF members are engaging in "self-defense" of the planet. Ultimately, the group's goal is to overthrow the government and capitalist corporations. What would replace the status quo is questionable, but leftist activists believe the alternative would be more environmentally friendly.

When discussing domestic terrorism, it is important to remember that many actions the government defines as criminal offenses are considered by terrorists to be acts of legitimate social protest. Americans have a long history of opposition to the government that is deemed not only appropriate but desirable in a democracy. However, when social protest becomes violent, it is considered criminal activity. There is a fuzzy line between appropriate social protest and crime, and those who demonstrate against the authorities often cross this line without believing that what they are doing is wrong. Many people who engage in social protest believe

**ecoterrorism** Terrorist acts committed for the purpose of bringing attention to what the perpetrators believe are offenses against the natural environment or animals.

## Think about it

### Understand
Enumerate the reasons why the Ku Klux Klan has been considered a terrorist organization.

### Apply
Show the similarities of three domestic religious-based terrorist organizations.

### Evaluate
Critique the idea that ecoterrorism is a different type of problem than other forms of domestic terrorism.

## International Terrorism

International terrorist attacks involve a national or a group of nationals from one nation crossing international borders and attacking targets in another nation.[39] One challenge of international terrorism is that the governments of the affected nations are limited in what they can do to investigate, arrest, and try terrorist suspects.

**LO5:**
Differentiate international terrorism from domestic terrorism.

For instance, for attacks in the United States, the government must cooperate with the governments of other nations, including their criminal justice systems, to track down terrorist suspects. Sometimes, the U.S. criminal justice system cannot deal with those who attack U.S. citizens or U.S. assets outside the country. For example, 179 Americans died in the 1988 terrorist bombing of Pan Am Flight 103 over Lockerbie, Scotland. However, the trial was held in the Netherlands, and Abdelbaset al-Megrahi, the Libyan man convicted of the bombing, served time in a Scottish prison and was released in 2009 because he was terminally ill with cancer.[40] Because international terrorism can involve several countries, international cooperation is crucial to the control of global terrorism.

The distinction between domestic terrorism and international terrorism is somewhat arbitrary. However, it allows us to consider not only the tactics of terrorism, but also understand how terrorists' motivations differ. In examining international terrorism, it is useful to consider the religious and economic motivations that underlie how and why these offenses are committed. Rather than viewing international terrorism as a single entity, we will discuss it in relation to the part of the world or the particular country in which it occurs. The following nations and regions we will discuss are not the only places where international terrorism occurs.

Nearly every region in the world has some degree of international terrorism (see Figure 13.1). However, the terrorism in these regions is at its most active.

## Spain

The sporadic terrorist activity in Spain is an example of nationalistic terrorism. In the Pyrenees Mountains between Spain and France lies the Basque Country (see Figure 13.2), or as it is called in the Basque language, *Euskal Herria*. Many Basques living in the Spanish Basque region want to separate from Spain because they have their own language and culture and believe that the Spanish have not allowed them to establish their own identity. Both Spain and France have engaged in periodic attempts to stamp out the Basque culture and language.

A terrorist group called "Basque Homeland and Freedom," or *Euskadi Ta Askatasuna* (ETA), began in 1959 as a student movement opposed to the oppressive Spanish dictator Francisco Franco.[41] The ETA, which began to push for full Basque independence in 1975 when Franco died, has killed 850 people over the last 30 years. This terrorism, which is aimed at the tourist industry, has been conducted primarily through assassinations and bombings. The ETA, however, has not been particularly persuasive to many of the Basque people. Its members are not full-time terrorists, and most hold regular jobs while infrequently committing terrorist acts. Observers speculate that the ETA has as few as 30 full-time members.[42]

Although the ETA is not very large or very destructive compared to other terrorist groups, it is interesting because of the way it has been co-opted by the Spanish government. The ETA cannot be said to represent the Basque people when the government allows the Basques control over their own schools, local parliament, and other government institutions. Furthermore, since the Spanish government is no longer attempting to suppress the Basque language or culture, the government has deprived the ETA of an enemy. Thus, the ETA finds it increasingly difficult to recruit members and get them

## Figure 13.1    International Terrorism Fatalities and Incidents by Region, 2008

**Most attacks and fatalities occurred in the Near East and South Asia, with more fatalities occurring in South Asian nations for the first time since the start of National Counterterrorism Center data collection. Compared to 2007, attacks decreased by 18 percent and deaths decreased by 30 percent. Attacks in Iraq have declined since 2007, but attacks in Pakistan more than doubled in 2008. Also in 2008, the number of reported attacks in the Western Hemisphere fell by about 25 percent.**

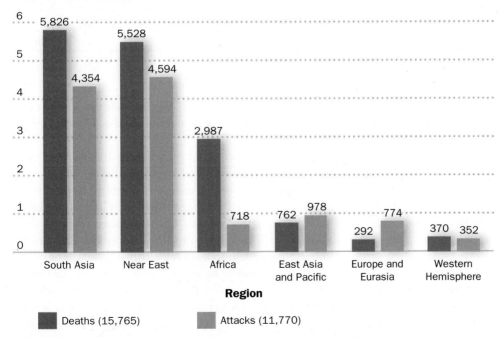

*Source:* National Counterterrorism Center, *2008 Report on Terrorism*, April 30, 2009, 10, http://wits-classic.nctc.gov/ReportPDF.do?f=crt2008nctcannexfinal.pdf.

## Figure 13.2    Spain

The Basque Country is located within both Spain and France.

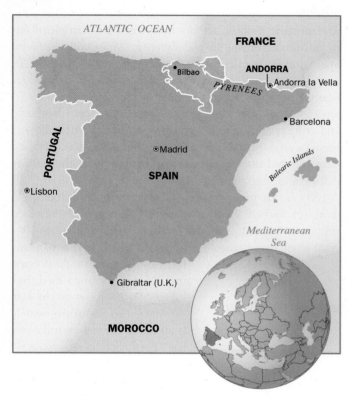

## Figure 13.3    The United Kingdom of Great Britain and Northern Ireland

Southern Ireland is an independent nation, while the six northern counties are part of the United Kingdom.

to engage in violence since legitimate opportunities are available. Although terrorist activities in Spain are infrequent, a new generation of disaffected young people may take up the call to terrorism. However, the success in integrating the Basque people into the Spanish culture without destroying their ethnic identity serves as an example to other nations that have experienced terrorism motivated by nationalistic ideals.[43]

## Northern Ireland

Ireland has a long history of terrorist activities. For hundreds of years, Ireland was a colony ruled by Great Britain (see Figure 13.3 for a map). Subjugated by the British, the Irish worked on large tracts of land owned by British royal families. Over the years, Irish peasants protested the poverty in which they were forced to live and their exploitation by the British. A political settlement in 1921 split the country, allowing the larger southern part to become an independent nation (the Irish Free State, later the Republic of Ireland), while the six northern counties remained part of the British Empire. However, a large contingent of Catholics in the northern counties wanted Ireland to be a single, intact, independent country. Therefore, after 1921, while the newly independent Republic of Ireland experi-

enced peace and prosperity, Northern Ireland experienced a continuing wave of terrorist activities and occupation by the British military.[44]

The causes for terrorism in Northern Ireland were both religious and economic. The large shipbuilding industry and other manufacturing concerns are controlled primarily by the British and the Protestant Irish. The Catholic majority, who lived in dire economic circumstances, resented their perceived exploitation by the British and the Protestants. Although many Catholics were satisfied with the way the country was divided, hard-line loyalists formed an underground military organization called the Irish Republican Army (IRA). The IRA engaged in numerous terrorist actions throughout the 20th century and provoked the British government into sending occupying troops.[45] Conflict between the Irish and English lasted more than a hundred years and

## Figure **13.4**   Turkey

**Geographically, Turkey connects Asia, Europe, and the Middle East.**

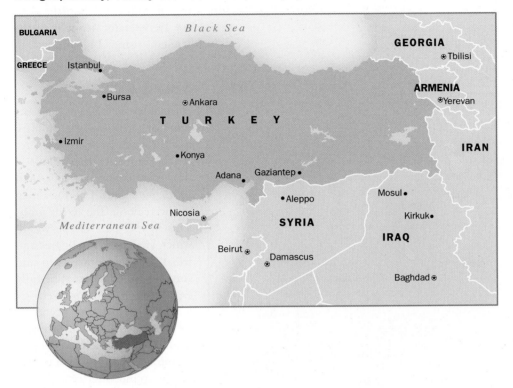

tries they occupy, but an independent Kurdistan cannot be accomplished without taking land and resources from Iran, Iraq, and Turkey. Turkey and Iran are unsympathetic to the idea of an independent Kurdistan, but because of the political uncertainty in Iraq, the Kurds have been emboldened for the first time in many decades.[47]

The most militant Kurds are in Turkey where they have developed a political organization known as Kongra-Gel, formerly the Kurdistan Workers' Party (PKK). Kongra-Gel was formed as a Marxist-Leninist group and has utilized traditional terrorist tactics, such as bombing tourist sites and hotels and kidnapping foreign tourists. Its members have been trained in other nations, such as Syria, and maintain links with other international terrorist groups; however, the group primarily operates in Turkey, Europe, the Middle East, and Asia. Although Kongra-Gel declared in 2006 that it would target only Turkish soldiers and security forces, affiliated groups have continued to kidnap tourists.[48]

continued even after Ireland was divided. Only relatively recently has a political solution been crafted that seems to have resolved the problem.[46] The Good Friday Agreement (or Belfast Agreement), a major step in the peace process, was signed in April 1998, marking the end of violence and instituting a set of political changes and human rights legislation that has held up for more than a decade.

## Turkey

Turkey, a fascinating nation with a long history of terrorism, is a secular democracy with one foot in Asia and the other in Europe (see Figure 13.4 for a map). With a population that is 99 percent Muslim, Turkey has maintained separation of church and state since 1923, despite calls for an Islamic-based government.

The political situation in Turkey has been affected by the U.S. war in Iraq. After the first Persian Gulf War in 1990–1991, northern Iraq was designated a no-fly zone, and the people living there, the Kurds, were able to develop a stable and relatively prosperous government because of the protection they enjoyed from Saddam Hussein. However, the success of the Kurds in northern Iraq greatly concerns the Turkish government because they occupy a territory that includes not only northern Iraq, but also eastern Turkey and western Iran. The Kurds wish to develop a Kurdish state—a new country called Kurdistan—in the areas of the three coun-

## Africa

Decades of civil war, poverty, and unrest have made many African nations vulnerable to domestic and international terrorism and allowed them to serve as places where terrorists from other parts of the world can hide and train. A particularly vulnerable nation is Somalia with its fragile government; violent instability; long and exposed coastline; ill-guarded borders; and proximity to the Arabian Peninsula, which includes the nations of Bahrain, Kuwait, Oman, Qatar, the United Arab Emirates, Yemen, and Saudi Arabia.[49] (See Figure 13.5 for a map.)

According to the U.S. State Department, Al Qaeda operatives and the Islamic militant group Al-Shabaab pose the most serious threats to U.S. and allied interests. Reported to be affiliated with Al Qaeda, Al-Shabaab currently controls much of southern Somalia. However, many Somalis continue to protest the group's presence because of its harsh, violent tactics and its adherence to strict Wahhabi Islam rather than the Sufi Islam practiced by many Somalis.[50] Al Qaeda operates in western regions as well, carrying out terrorist attacks in Mauritania and Mali by targeting tourist areas, such as nightclubs, taking foreign hostages, and kidnapping and

## Figure **13.5**  Africa

Somalia on Africa's east coast has a long and exposed coastline near the Arabian Peninsula. Terrorist attacks have also occurred in Mauritania and Mali on the continent's west coast.

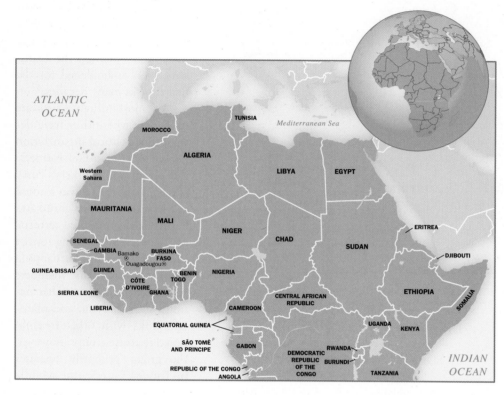

▼ Reported to be affiliated with Al Qaeda, Al-Shabaab controls much of southern Somalia. Here, the group parades its weapons in Mogadishu, the nation's capital.

killing security forces.[51] Generally, violence against civilians in Africa was particularly related to instability in Somalia and the Democratic Republic of the Congo, rising 140 percent in 2008 to about 2,200 fatalities.[52]

## South Asia

Although all of Asia has its share of terrorism, the problem is most acute in South Asia (refer to Figure 13.1), particularly in Afghanistan, Pakistan, and India (see Figure 13.6 for a map of the region). The terror problems in this part of the world, which are based in religious and tribal differences, are deep and complicated and cannot be fully explicated here. However, by touching on the most recent terrorist incidents and surface reasons for the turmoil, we seek to encourage a basic understanding of why so much terror occurs in these nations and emerges from them.

As in Africa, several nations in this region are vulnerable because of weak governments and poor security. The Taliban remains strong in Afghanistan where it has success in recruiting from rural Pashtun tribes. Because of the relative political and social chaos that has reigned in Afghanistan for so long, the nation is an excellent harbor for terror groups, primarily the Taliban, to thrive and train members. Although a more stable nation, Pakistan also presents a safe haven for terrorist organizations, which is especially problematic because it borders Afghanistan.[53] Although U.S. troops are currently fighting the Taliban in Afghanistan, a war based on the events of September 11, the United States has diplomatic relations with Pakistan and cannot cross its borders without creating an international incident. Terrorists

## Figure **13.6**   South Asia

**Afghanistan, Pakistan, and India are particularly vulnerable to terrorism. Terrorist groups with safe havens in Pakistan often cross the borders to carry out attacks in Afghanistan and India.**

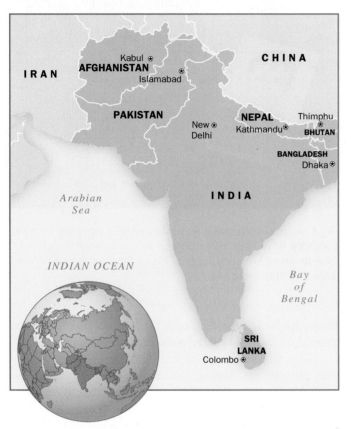

the British government estimates that most of the terror plots it discovered in the past decade took root in Pakistan. A probable reason for this state of affairs is that Pakistan was founded as an ideological Islamic country that sought to use terror against its rival, India. Today, the Pakistani military is said to relentlessly pursue domestic terrorists that target Pakistan's government for its cooperation with the United States but ignore groups that target Afghans, Westerners, and Indians.[54]

India, which is friendly to U.S. interests and is a U.S. trade partner, is plagued by both international and domestic terrorism. The most devastating recent attack was a coordinated operation in Mumbai in November 2008 in which gunmen used automatic weapons and grenades to blast their way through hotels, an airport, a railway station, the police headquarters in south Mumbai, and a café as they targeted British and U.S. tourists as well as wealthy Indians.[55] They also planted bombs in two taxicabs that exploded in different locations in Mumbai. At least 183 people were killed, including 6 Americans and 14 members of police and security forces. More than 300 were injured.[56] India blames Pakistan-based militant group Lashkar-e-Taiba for the attacks and in 2010 convicted the only surviving gunman. The goal of Lashkar-e-Taiba is to unite Kashmir (the region is currently divided between India, Pakistan, and China) under Pakistani jurisdiction.

## Chechnya

The Russian republic of Chechnya in the Caucasus region of Asia has been in constant conflict with the governments of Imperial Russia, the Soviet Union, and modern Russia (see

are believed to be using this to their advantage by carrying out operations in Afghanistan then retreating across the border to Pakistan.

Pakistan also has pervasive problems with domestic terrorism. The nation is in a precarious position because it accepts large amounts of U.S. military and economic assistance to fight terrorism, and the nation's government appears to cooperate with U.S interests. However, the nation is also reputed to be a haven for several terrorist groups, including those targeting the United States and India. Pakistan has a dual identity, then, as a citizen of the world and a sponsor of terror. Although Pakistan is active in the United Nations,

▼ **A fire burns at Taj Mahal Palace and Tower Hotel following the 2008 armed siege that killed at least 183 people in Mumbai, India.**

Figure 13.7 for a map). Although the conflict is based upon nationalism, much like the issues in Turkey, it also has religious overtones. The people of Chechnya are Muslim and have received a lot of attention and support from other Islamic countries that consider the Chechnya-Russian conflict a losing campaign for Russia, much as Afghanistan was for the Soviet Union in the 1980s. To understand the current Chechnya conflict, we must look at what happened when the Soviet Union disintegrated in 1991 and many of its territories declared independence. Russia rejected the claim of Chechnyan independence, touching off a conflict that continues today and that has evolved from guerrilla warfare to terrorism as Chechnyan rebels contest Russian domination.[57]

One aspect of this conflict that is reminiscent of September 11 is the way in which the terrorists have taken the violence to the Russian homeland. Two shocking incidents captured the world's attention and cast Russia as the victim of ruthless terrorists. The first was the 2002 Nord-Ost theater siege in which Chechen rebels took over a Moscow theater. More than 100 hostages died, most from the gas that Russian soldiers released into the theater to end the siege.[58] Two years later, Chechen terrorists besieged a school in Beslan, Russia, taking more than 1,200 people hostage, many of

▲ A woman cries as she walks with a portrait of her relative who was killed in the 2004 school siege in the town of Beslan, Russia. Over 300 hostages were killed in the incident.

## Figure **13.7**   Chechnya

**The Russian republic of Chechnya is located in the Caucasus region of Asia between Russia and Georgia.**

them children. A fire-fight with Russian troops left 330 hostages dead, as well as 26 terrorists and 10 Russian soldiers.[59]

Terrorism in Chechnya is difficult to eradicate because the nationalistic, historic, economic, and religious grievances that provoke the violence must be addressed on several levels. First, Chechnya is rich in oil, a valuable commodity necessary to help stabilize Russia's economy.[60] Second, Russia's desire to control the states on its borders to act as a buffer against religious extremism means Chechnya will not be allowed independence without guarantees of security for economic cooperation with Russia.[61]

## Israel and the Palestinians

Some of the most intractable terrorist problems are occurring in the disputed territories of Israel and what was once Palestine (see Figure 13.8). After World War II, the Allied victors carved up the map of the world and created a number of new political configurations. In addition to giving France its historic colony in Vietnam, the new political arrangements included granting independence to a number of African countries and, in 1946, providing the Jewish people with a homeland in the Middle East. This homeland, Israel, was forged from the existing country of Palestine and given to the Jewish people who came from Europe and Russia. From its inception, Israel has experienced conflict, war, and terrorism.[62]

The Arab nations surrounding Israel did not recognize the political legitimacy of Israel and sought to drive out the Jewish settlers and reclaim the land for the Palestinian

## Figure **13.8**    Israel and Surrounding Regions

**The Palestinian people are confined to the West Bank, in the center of Israel bordering Jordan, and the Gaza Strip, which borders Egypt and the Mediterranean.**

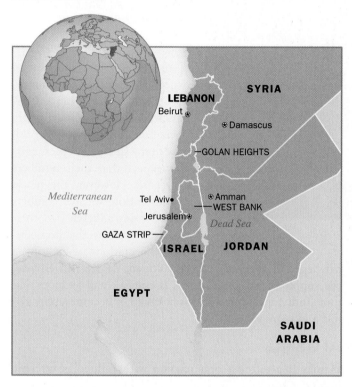

parts cannot accept. As Palestinian terrorism becomes more frequent, the Israelis counter with overwhelming military force that often includes the killing of civilians caught in the crossfire. This endless cycle of violence has resulted in suspicion, mistrust, and hate that has touched every family in the region and prompted politicians to take an extremely hard line in dealing with the other side.[64]

Volatile conditions in neighboring nations add to the difficulties. For instance, the nation of Lebanon, which lies immediately north of Israel, has experienced a crippling civil war and has become a haven for foreign terrorists, particularly the Hezbollah. Hezbollah is an Iranian-backed terrorist group that is attempting to gain political legitimacy. Israel does not recognize Hezbollah because the group advocates the destruction of the Jewish state. Periodically, Israel invades southern Lebanon, targeting terrorist training camps and military fortifications that launch missiles at Israel. The struggles between Hezbollah and Israel have destabilized Lebanon to such an extent that much of the control of that nation has been taken over by Syria.[65]

Further complicating the quest for peace in the region has been the Palestinians' inability to develop a stable leadership. In part, this is caused by Israel, which keeps assassinating emerging leaders in the Palestinian organizations. The Gaza Strip is also the site of a civil war between the Palestine Liberation Organization (PLO) and Hamas, two terrorist organizations that are vying for control. In order to attract followers, each of these organizations attempts to appear tougher on Israel than the other. Any Palestinian leader from one of these organizations who seems likely to engage in peace talks with Israel is assassinated by the other terrorist group, thus making it difficult for the Israelis to find legitimate leaders with whom to negotiate.

The terrorist tactics used by Palestinian groups such as Hamas include suicide bombings. Outsiders sometimes have difficulty understanding the motivations and reasoning behind this type of activity. Political psychologist Jerrold Post describes the social psychology of suicide bombers, as explained by Israeli terrorism expert Ariel Merari:

> First the volunteer or recruit is identified, usually by friends or relatives in the organization, and commits himself to becoming a *shahid* [martyr]. Then he is publicly identified as a 'living martyr,' a member of the 'walking dead.' This brings great prestige both to the perspective martyr and to his or her family. Finally, just before the mission, he is videotaped reading his last will and testament, in which he explains his motivations and his goals. This cements his commitment, and makes it nearly impossible for him to back out, for it would bring unbearable shame and humiliation. These videos then are disseminated on Hamas websites, where they glorify the martyrs and contribute to further recruitment.[66]

people. A number of wars were fought in which the Israelis successfully defended their homeland against neighboring countries, including Syria, Jordan, and Egypt. In 1978, U.S. President Jimmy Carter helped negotiate a peace between Israel and Egypt that became known as the Camp David Accords.[63]

Israel has been successful in annexing most of Palestine and has confined the Palestinian peoples within two areas: the West Bank and the Gaza Strip. The West Bank, a large patch of land on the western side of the Jordan River, is home to numerous Palestinian villages. The Gaza Strip is a small piece of land on the banks of the Mediterranean Sea that borders Egypt. These two Palestinian territories are separated by Israel, which greatly restricts the flow of goods and people between the two areas. This causes a number of hardships for the Palestinians. The Israelis, fearing terrorist activities, have established a number of military checkpoints to control the Palestinians.

The Palestinians and the Israelis do not recognize each other's political legitimacy. Negotiations are difficult when each party denies the other the basic right to live and prosper. Furthermore, both the Israelis and the Palestinians have established preconditions for negotiations that their counter-

◄ Suicide bombers often do not fit the profile of a terrorist. These four young men, rounded up during a security sweep in the northern Iraq city of Mosul, were suspected of being trained by Al Qaeda to carry out suicide bombings.

Becoming a martyr for one's cause is a somewhat alien concept in American culture. Even in war, Americans are not encouraged to sacrifice their lives in suicide missions. Although there are certainly times when individuals make this choice, it is neither encouraged nor demanded. In the United States, someone who is martyred is usually the victim of an assassin, not a suicide. In other societies, however, suicide committed while killing enemies is valued and promoted.

In the Middle East, voluntary martyrdom, or sacrificing oneself for one's cause, is deeply bound up with Islam. Although the Koran does not permit suicide in principle, it does encourage individuals to fight for Islam, so there is cultural support for martyrdom. The decision to become a martyr is an individual choice made by the suicide bombers. However, because many of them are young and impressionable, it is reasonable to suspect that they are heavily indoctrinated by their elders and see martyrdom as a heroic act that will benefit them in the afterlife.[67]

Suicide attacks are very difficult to combat. Suicide bombers are recruited in part because they do not fit the profile of a terrorist. Suicide bombers are often young teenagers, sometimes female, who are able to approach targets without raising much suspicion. If they are challenged before they reach their target, they will often blow themselves up in places like military checkpoints, killing soldiers. If they go unchallenged, they enter marketplaces, employment offices, or retail stores where they inflict maximum damage to innocent civilians. Suicide bombers often use automobiles or trucks to deliver larger explosive packages to their targets and kill even more people. Because suicide bombers strike in public places frequented by large numbers of people going about their routine daily business, it is extremely difficult to prevent them from succeeding in their mission.[68]

It would seem reasonable to expect that the suicide bombings would decrease since individuals can kill themselves only once. One might reasonably ask how many suicide bombers exist and expect that their numbers are finite. However, the praise and attention suicide bombers receive from adherents to their cause as well as the bombers' own expectations of entering a privileged afterlife serve as recruitment devices. In essence, the supply of suicide bombers is endless, and as more and more individuals commit this behavior, it becomes more visible and more valued.[69]

## Al Qaeda

Hamas is a terrorist organization with limited geographic influence because it is confined to the Gaza Strip and parts of the West Bank. It has virtually no international presence, and its targets are primarily Israelis. Thus, it differs substantially from Al Qaeda, a generously funded international terrorist organization. Al Qaeda, under the direction of Osama bin Laden, was responsible for the September 11, 2001, terrorist attacks on the United States. Al Qaeda also orchestrated bombings in Tanzania and Kenya in 1998 and the attack in Yemen on the U.S. Navy destroyer USS *Cole* in 2000. Presently, Al Qaeda is the most influential terrorist organization in the world, with a global reach from the Middle East to Indonesia. Its organizational structure, lines of communication, and actual number of members are unknown.[70]

Al Qaeda differs from Hamas in several significant ways. For example, the suicide terrorists who participated in the September 11 attacks were older than the typical Hamas suicide bombers. The September 11 terrorists were in their late 20s and early 30s; their leader, Mohamed Atta, was 33. They came primarily from comfortable middle-class families in Saudi Arabia and Egypt, and, as adults, they were considered "true believers." A brief analysis of Al Qaeda's leader, Osama bin Laden, will help us appreciate the scope and effects of this organization.[71]

Osama bin Laden is a multimillionaire whose family made its fortune, estimated to be between $2 and $3 billion, in the Saudi Arabian construction industry. He is the 17th son of a man who has fathered at least 52 children. Bin Laden's mother was one of his father's several wives and, reportedly, one of the least favorite. As the only child of this union, bin Laden had few allies within the family. Nevertheless, at age 16, bin Laden inherited approximately $57 million from his father's estate. Bin Laden was educated at a university in Jeddah, Saudi Arabia, where he came under the influence of a radical Islamic professor named Abdullah Azzam. Azzam convinced bin Laden to go to Afghanistan in the 1980s and fight the Soviets. The goal was to unite the Islamic warlords against the Soviets and drive them from the country. With the help of money and arms from the United States, the Islamic warriors succeeded in forcing the Soviet Union to end the expensive and unpopular war in Afghanistan.[72]

During the war in Afghanistan, Osama bin Laden became a leader of deeply religious Islamic peoples bent on restoring the supremacy of religious fundamentalism in the region. Even though he was a very rich man, he lived an ascetic life, often in caves, and gave much of his fortune to the cause. Emboldened by the success in defeating the Soviets, he turned his attention toward what he considered to be other infidels, primarily Israel and the United States. He justified the September 11 attacks on the United States, stating:

> It is very strange for Americans and other educated people to talk about the killing of innocent civilians. I mean, who said our children and civilians are not innocent, and that the shedding of their blood is permissible? Whenever we kill civilians, the whole world yells at us from east to west, and America starts putting pressure on its allies and puppets. Who said that our blood isn't blood and that their blood is blood? What about the people that have been killed in our lands for decades? More than one million children died in Iraq, and they are still dying, so why do we not hear people that cry or protest, or anyone who reassures or anyone who sends condolences?
>
> As for the World Trade Center, the ones who were attacked and who died in it were part of a financial power. It wasn't a children's school! Neither was it a residence. The great consensus is that most of the people who were in the towers were men that backed the biggest financial force in the world, which spreads mischief throughout the world. And those individuals should stand before God, and rethink and redo their calculations. We treat others like they treat us. Those who kill our women and our innocent, we kill their women and innocent, until they stop from doing so.[73]

A particular difficulty in stopping Al Qaeda's terrorist attacks is the fact that the organization has so many targets. In addition to attacking the Soviets in Afghanistan and the United States in Africa and New York City, Al Qaeda targets other nations that have cooperated with the United States or the United Nations in the Persian Gulf War and the wars in Iraq and Afghanistan. Al Qaeda's targets include not only Western countries, but Middle Eastern countries as well. For example, bin Laden considers nations such as Saudi Arabia, where the royal family has benefited from an economic relationship with the West, to have been corrupted by money and Western values. His desire to return Islamic countries to fundamentalist tenets of Islam as he understands them means that terrorist attacks will continue wherever individuals and nations deviate from a very rigid interpretation of the Koran.[74]

Al Qaeda also targets Western countries that have economic or social dealings in the Middle East because they support rulers who do not abide by fundamentalist Islamic values. Therefore, secular governments, such as those in Pakistan and Iraq, are potential targets for Al Qaeda. Combating terrorism in such a wide geographic region and in countries where there is a tension between secular and fundamentalist values practically ensures that terrorism will be a continuing problem.

Osama bin Laden and Al Qaeda have been extremely difficult to deal with because they have taken great precautions against exposing themselves to Western technological warfare. They have gone low-tech in a high-tech world. Despite all the sophistication of the National Security Agency, the FBI, and the CIA, plus countless other federal law enforcement agencies, bin Laden has not been found. When Al Qaeda bombed two U.S. embassies in Africa, the United States first attempted to retaliate by firing long-range missiles at suspected Al Qaeda targets in the Sudan and Afghanistan. Although the missiles caused a good deal of damage, they did not find Osama bin Laden. The fundamental problem in finding bin Laden is that he does not use communication technology that can be traced, and he is surrounded by loyal followers who cannot be bribed. Intelligence agencies suspect that he is hiding in caves somewhere along the Afghanistan-Pakistan border. Because of the fragile and changing nature of the Pakistani government, Western leaders do not have the authority to search for bin Laden within Pakistan.[75]

# Think about it

## Apply

Demonstrate why Al Qaeda is such a difficult international terrorist organization to deal with.

## Analyze

Distinguish how the cultures of individual nations influence international terrorism.

## Create

Develop some plans that will help cooperating nations resist international terrorism.

# The U.S. Response to Global Terrorism

Terrorism, both domestic and international, has fundamentally altered the mandate of the U.S. legal and criminal justice systems. The nation must consider several issues in order to deal with terrorism. Among these concerns are the following.

## LO6:

**Understand** that in dealing with terrorism, the United States must consider a number of issues related to civil rights, the Constitution, privacy, and surveillance.

- *International versus national security.* The lines between security abroad and security at home have been blurred. Threats to U.S. citizens in other countries, as well as to those in the United States, are no longer easily separated. The problems of terrorism require more cooperation and coordination among agencies. For example, traditionally there was a distinction between the mandates of the CIA and the FBI. The CIA was designed to gather information on external threats to the United States and was forbidden to engage in espionage within the nation. Conversely, the FBI was limited to dealing with threats within the country. Now, these lines of authority have been extended for both agencies as they deal with the terrorist threat.[76]

- *The Department of Homeland Security.* After September 11, the federal government implemented a major reorganization in an effort to better address the terrorist threat. Several agencies and parts of other agencies were combined into a new Department of Homeland Security (see Figure 13.9). Included in this new department are the U.S. Customs Service (formerly part of the Treasury Department), the U.S. Citizenship and Immigration Services (formerly the Immigration and Naturalization Service within the Department of Justice), and the Federal Emergency Management Agency (FEMA), which used to be an independent agency. The mission of the Department of Homeland Security is to lead and coordinate the national effort to secure the country; to prevent and deter terrorist attacks; and to prepare for and respond to all hazards, disasters, and threats to the nation. The department is structured to ensure that its component agencies are organized in the most efficient and productive manner. What is especially interesting about the Department of Homeland Security is not the organizations that were included, but those that were not. One of the indictments of the September 11 Commission, which investigated the terrorist acts, was that there was insufficient coordination between agencies such as the CIA and the FBI. Neither of these agencies is included in the De-

partment of Homeland Security even though their major mandates now are to deal with terrorism. Leaving the CIA and the FBI out of the Department of Homeland Security was more of a political decision than a tactical or organizational one. The CIA and the FBI had the political clout to remain independent. The effectiveness of the new Department of Homeland Security has not yet been fully evaluated since it will take some time to integrate its diverse agencies (see *Doubletake*).[77]

- *Expansion of the definition of terrorism.* One of the unanticipated consequences of the war on terror is the way in which traditional criminal offenses are now being defined as terrorism. For instance, there is a relationship between money used in the illegal drug trade and the funding of terrorist activities. For example, the Taliban in Afghanistan funds itself by taxing farmers who raise heroin-producing poppies.[78] Consequently, drug dealers are being subjected to increased scrutiny and penalties designed to combat terrorism. Although no one defends illegal drug trafficking, it appears that the criminal justice agencies and the legal system are unable to distinguish between normal drug crime and crime that provides financial support for terrorist organizations. Also, violent individuals are now being charged with offenses under new laws designed to combat terrorism. In many ways, this overlap has allowed law enforcement agencies to control traditional crime more effectively. However, that is not the original intent of the law, and the result might well be that resources allocated to fight terrorism are being diverted to non-terrorist offenses, making them easier to detect and prosecute.[79]

- *The increase in anti-terrorism resources.* The new national focus on terrorism has resulted in the allocation of substantial resources aimed at preventing, detecting, and prosecuting terrorist activities. In tough economic times, Congress has increased the money available to the broad range of agencies responsible for addressing terrorism. However, the process used to determine who gets the money has not been without controversy. Members of Congress have added provisions that allocate resources to jurisdictions that have little to fear from terrorists. This sort of "pork-barrel spending" has resulted in public dissatisfaction among those who argue that resources have been diverted from important targets. For example, only a very small fraction of the cargo shipped into the United States is ever inspected. If a terrorist wishes to deliver a nuclear weapon to the United States, it would be relatively easy to do so on a container ship in one of the major ports of the east or west coast.[80]

- *The Patriot Act.* The USA PATRIOT Act (H.R. 3162) was passed on October 24, 2001, by the 107th Congress. President George W. Bush signed it into law two days later. The act's official title is *The Uniting and Strength-*

## Figure **13.9** Department of Homeland Security Organizational Chart

The Department of Homeland Security leads and coordinates the national effort to secure the country; prevents and deters terrorist attacks; and prepares for and responds to all national hazards, disasters, and threats.

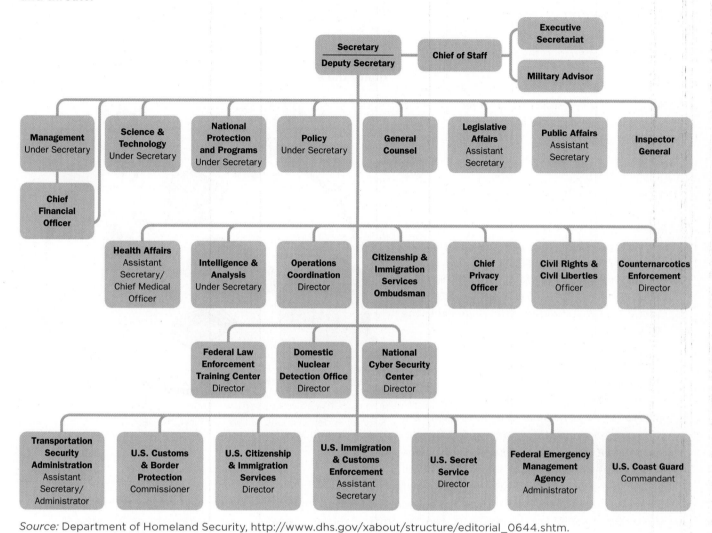

*Source:* Department of Homeland Security, http://www.dhs.gov/xabout/structure/editorial_0644.shtm.

ening *America by Providing Appropriate Tools Required to Intercept and Obstruct Terrorism Act of 2001.* The act was passed very quickly, with little time allowed for public debate and criticism. Few legislators even had time to read the full text of the act before voting on it. Yet, only 66 representatives and 1 senator voted against the act, which modified nearly 20 federal statutes.[81] Much of the act provides funds and staff positions to government agencies for anti-terrorism initiatives.[82] According to some critics, the act is problematic because it violates some constitutional rights, including those governing searches and seizures, due process, freedom of speech, and the protection against cruel and unusual punishment. In 2007, a federal judge ruled that the act violates the Constitution because it allows the government to conduct surveillance

and searches of U.S. citizens without probable cause.[83] In 2005, Congress made permanent 14 of the USA PATRIOT Act's main provisions and enacted four-year sunset requirements for two other provisions.[84] In March 2010, President Barack Obama extended three controversial sections of the act for one year. The first two allow the government to seize suspects' records without their knowledge and conduct surveillance of suspects with no known ties to an organized terrorist group. The third allows roving wiretaps or, rather, wiretaps that follow a suspect rather than a communications device. For instance, if the suspect discards a phone in an effort to shake surveillance, the government does not need to acquire a new surveillance order on the suspect's new phone; investigators simply transition surveillance to the new phone.[85]

# doubletake

## The National Data Exchange

After September 11, 2001, federal agencies were faulted for not sharing the information they had gathered about foreign terrorists and the possibility that they might attack the United States. Before the attacks, distrust and secrecy were the norm among federal law enforcement agencies, state law enforcement agencies, and the military. Each agency or military branch had its own mission, and any intrusion onto another's "turf" was looked upon with suspicion. A congressional report charged that the September 11 attacks might have been prevented had the FBI and CIA shared information about two of the hijackers. The report also found that the National Security Agency, which monitors foreign electronic communications, acquired information in 1999 about the hijackers that it did not share with either the FBI or CIA.[1]

Improvements in information-sharing, which began shortly after September 11 with the formation of the Department of Homeland Security and certain provisions of the USA PATRIOT Act, are still underway.[2] In 2008, the Department of Justice announced the formation of the National Data Exchange, or N-DEx, a search engine for sensitive criminal justice information about anyone in the United States who has encountered the criminal justice system. N-DEx allows law enforcement agencies to "search, link, analyze, and share" information about suspects, arrests, incarcerations, and parole/probation data.

Figure 13.10 shows how N-DEx works. Local, state, tribal, and federal systems supply data, which are then correlated and prepared for access. Law enforcement agencies then query the system.[3] In the case of a wanted suspect, an agency can enter the suspect's name and find out whom he or she has associated with throughout various jurisdictions. Results, according to the *Washington Post*, "will include names of suspects, associates, victims, persons of interest, witnesses and any other person named in an incident, arrest, booking, parole or probation report."[4]

Civil liberties experts are critical of N-DEx because it allows files to be built on just about anyone, including law-abiding people who might be considered troublemakers, such as political dissidents. Thirty years ago, Congress limited the collection of domestic intelligence after it was discovered that the FBI, the U.S. Army, and

## Figure 13.10    N-DEx

**Local, state, tribal, and federal systems submit data, which are prepared for law enforcement agencies that query the system.**

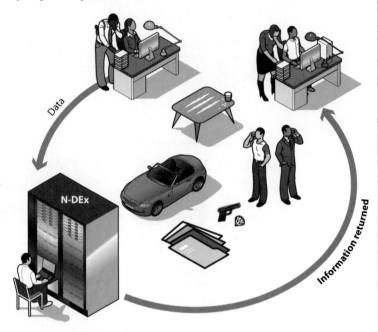

*Source:* Federal Bureau of Investigation, "N-DEx: Concept," http://www.fbi.gov/hq/cjisd/ndex/ndex_concept.htm.

some local police agencies had misused their authority to monitor people involved in legal activities. Those reforms separated day-to-day police inquiries from federal national security intelligence-gathering.[5] However, since September 11, laws have been passed to eliminate that separation and allow databases like N-DEx.

[1]David Johnston, "Sept. 11 Laid in Part to CIA and FBI Lapses," *New York Times/International Herald Tribune,* July 25, 2003, news, 1.

[2]Siddharth Mohandas, "How 9-11 Happened: A New Book Chronicles the Pitfalls of Counterterrorism," *Newsweek,* November 25, 2002, Atlantic edition, 65.

[3]Federal Bureau of Investigation, "N-DEx: Law Enforcement National Data Exchange," http://www.fbi.gov/hq/cjisd/ndex/ndex_home.htm.

[4]Federal Bureau of Investigation. See note 1.

[5]Robert O'Harrow, Jr., and Ellen Nakashima, "National Dragnet Is a Click Away: Authorities to Gain Fast and Expansive Access to Records," *Washington Post,* March 6, 2008, A01, http://www.washingtonpost.com/wp-dyn/content/article/2008/03/05/AR2008030503656_pf.html.

## THINKING *in* ACTION

Will N-DEx lead to privacy abuses by federal agencies such as those discussed in the text? Why or why not?

▲ Some critics of the Patriot Act contend that it violates constitutional rights. Here, four Connecticut librarians discuss their battle against the demands for patrons' library records.

## Controlling Terrorism

Terrorism is difficult to control because it can be extremely hard to identify, locate, and engage the enemy. Dealing with terrorist networks that operate out of several different nations and have a decentralized organizational structure makes the problem of controlling terrorism especially difficult. The most important concern in dealing with these types of terrorist organizations is developing actionable intelligence. How intelligence is gathered and the problems of ensuring privacy rights for all citizens are so complex that we will devote the final chapter of this book to these issues. Here we will take a brief look at intelligence-based strategies.

There is a somewhat artificial distinction between the employment of military forces and the dedication of law enforcement and criminal justice resources to fighting terrorism. For instance, the invasions of Iraq and Afghanistan are military actions that treat terrorism as war rather than as crime. However, the new terrorist threat has deeply altered both the traditional criminal justice response to crime and the military response to war, causing both institutions to adopt some of the other institution's tactics. For example, in Iraq, the U.S. military has had to adopt some of law enforcement's mandate to preserve social order and deal with civilian issues, such as training police officers. In turn, U.S. law enforcement and emergency response agencies have had to deal with some aspects of global terrorism within the United States.

## Dealing with Terrorists

Only since 2001 has the U.S. criminal justice system become involved in the control of terrorism. Before 2001, ter-

rorism in the United States was generally considered to be an international political issue that had more to do with war than with crime. Only in the past few years have criminologists begun to take a more analytical look at terrorism and its relationship to crime. Criminology, as you will recall, is the study of the making of laws, the breaking of laws, and society's reaction to these two events. We will consider terrorism within this framework.

It is the third part of the definition of criminology—society's reaction to the making and breaking of laws—that has made terrorism a complicated criminological issue. Society's reaction to "normal" crime is fairly well established. Citizens try to prevent crime in many ways: being alert in public places, locking doors and cars, installing alarm systems, setting up Neighborhood Watch groups, and the like. The police detain criminal suspects, secure arrestees in jails, and begin the first steps of inserting suspects into the criminal justice system. The courts try criminal defendants, and the corrections system deals with the convicted. What is society's reaction to terrorists? So far, it is fear, suspicion, and the scrambling of federal agencies to try to control the problem. Society's reaction to terrorists is not yet well established within any framework of laws.

Terrorists have broken the laws of numerous nations, and terrorist acts certainly qualify as criminal offenses. Murder, assault, kidnapping, vandalism, destruction of property, theft, and illegal weapons dealings are criminal offenses that occur within the framework of terrorism. However, the definition of terrorists themselves as criminal offenders, rather than as soldiers or political rebels, has proven to be a complicated issue for the world's judicial systems.

Prior to September 11, terrorists who struck within the United States were treated as criminal defendants. The six foreign-born terrorists who carried out the 1993 bombing of the World Trade Center were tried, convicted, and sentenced to prison with the full complement of constitutional rights extended to any criminal defendant.[86] This was also the case with Timothy McVeigh, the bomber of the Murrah Federal building in Oklahoma City, and his co-conspirator, Terry Nichols.

This situation has changed since the events of September 11, however. Terrorists who attack the United States in foreign lands pose another problem. To date, the United States has classified these terrorists as "enemy combatants" rather than as soldiers or criminal suspects and is holding them indefinitely. The most well-known of the detention camps is Camp Delta in Guantanamo Bay, Cuba.[87] There, enemy combatants are treated much like prison inmates. The only difference is that they appear to have no constitutional rights as criminal suspects—such as the right to a trial or to a lawyer—or rights as soldiers under the Geneva Convention, which set the standards of international law for the treatment of prisoners of war. In a legal limbo, these foreign enemy combatants appear to have no rights at all.

In 2002, John Walker Lindh, a U.S. citizen who converted to Islam and was caught in Afghanistan fighting with the Taliban, received a trial and a plea deal and was sentenced to 20 years in a U.S. prison.[88] In contrast, Ali Saleh Kahlah al-Marri, a citizen of Qatar attending college in Illinois, was arrested in December 2001 on suspicion of being an Al Qaeda agent. He was held in civilian custody until 2003 when he was transferred to military custody and held as an enemy combatant within the United States. It took another four years for a federal appeals court to decide that al-Marri could not be detained indefinitely without being charged.[89] Meanwhile, about 300 detainees remain at Camp Delta. In 2008, the U.S. government finally began charging some of the inmates in preparation for legal prosecution.[90] These cases illustrate how the way that the United States deals with terrorism has changed. A U.S. citizen who attacked the United States while in a foreign land was put on trial, convicted, and incarcerated within the United States. A non-citizen living in the United States and suspected of being involved with attacks on the United States has been detained indefinitely without status.

## Safeguarding the Homeland

The United States is vulnerable to attacks by both foreign and domestic terrorists. In a nation as vast as the United States, there is simply no way to protect all potential targets. Even high-profile targets such as the World Trade Center in New York City and the Pentagon in Washington, DC, could not be secured from a determined and inventive attack. The Murrah Federal Building in Oklahoma City was a low-profile federal office building that no one had any reason to suspect would be a terrorist target. In looking around the country, it is easy to see hundreds of potential targets that could be attacked in a variety of ways.

To prevent and deter terrorism, with its great potential for devastating damage and loss of life, the nation must take precautions that can disrupt the everyday life of citizens. The difficulty lies in finding a balance between allowing people freedom and protecting them from harm. This balance requires certain compromises and adjustments that may cause individuals a variety of inconveniences such as the following.

■ *Restrictions on entering buildings.* Citizens must now undergo searches in order to enter many public and private buildings. For the most part, the searches are done electronically and are intended to make sure that people do not bring firearms, weapons, or explosives into courthouses, office buildings, or other public buildings that might serve as terrorist targets. As technology improves, the screening of people entering buildings might even

## Figure **13.11**    Bomb Threat Standoff Distances

This graphic warns that terrorists try to attract bystanders to windows, doorways, and the outside with gunfire, small bombs, or other methods, and then detonate a larger, more destructive device to increase casualties.

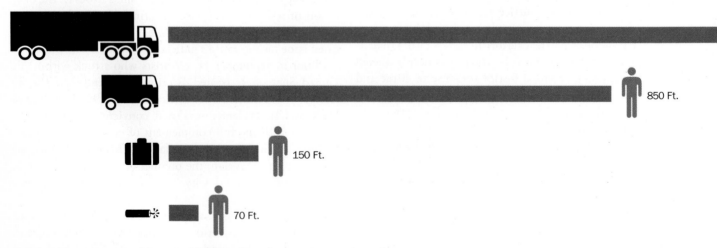

850 Ft.

150 Ft.

70 Ft.

*Source:* National Counterterrorism Center, http://www.nctc.gov/docs/2006_calendar_bomb_stand_chart.pdf.

involve cameras that compare faces to a database of suspected terrorists or other suspects.[91]

- *Physical barriers designed to impede traffic flow.* Architectural designers are incorporating security measures into building design in a number of ways. For example, large concrete and steel barriers are intended to serve as obstructions to prevent someone from driving a vehicle loaded with explosives into a target with large numbers of innocent people. Often, we do not realize that these architectural features are really obstructions designed with security in mind; rather, we see them as simply attractive, if somewhat bulky, components of the building's architecture. In addition, traffic flows in critical areas have been altered so vehicles containing explosives cannot get too close to their targets. Other ways of protecting buildings include reinforcing parking garages with concrete and steel or simply moving parking spaces away from buildings. Another popular innovation is closing streets and the creation of pedestrian walkways to prevent threatening vehicles from getting near important buildings.[92]

- *Designing buildings to minimize the effect of terrorists.* Steps have been taken to make buildings more resistant to terrorist attacks, such as limiting the amount of glass exposed to the street, using blast-resistant safety glass, and employing a setback of 30 to 50 feet so that car bombs cannot be set off nearby. Figure 13.11 lists the government-recommended evacuation distances for various types of bomb threats.

These examples describe the ways in which the physical environment of buildings and streets can be altered to protect buildings and individuals from terrorist attacks. A number of other steps designed to assess the qualifications and motivations of individuals using public facilities are also being implemented. The airline industry, for example, has suffered greatly from the terrorist threat, and a number of measures have been implemented to increase security in airports and on airplanes. For instance, at airports, only those people holding tickets are allowed onto the concourses. Those picking up or dropping off passengers are restricted to the central terminal, and automobiles parked near the terminal may not be left unattended for any period of time. People who work at the airport are required to wear photo ID cards, and background checks are done on all employees who have the opportunity to get close enough to airliners to hijack them.[93]

Increased airport security is not without its critics. Food and souvenir concessions at airports have lost much revenue because only people with tickets can get to many of these outlets. The time and inconvenience of dealing with airport security measures have motivated many travelers to forgo airline travel for other modes of transportation. There is also some concern that security at all airports is not implemented at the same level. For instance, security at the international airport in Athens, Greece, is reported to be lax in comparison to other international airports, making it a likely place for terrorists to enter the aviation system. Travelers who have cleared security at one airport are not subjected to further security checks and can transfer planes at other airports, where they may then initiate terrorist activities. Once an airplane is in the air, a number of other steps have been taken to protect it from terrorist activities.

- *Armed pilots.* U.S. law allows pilots trained in the use of firearms to have pistols in the cockpit. The idea is that pilots will be the last line of defense, and an armed pilot is much more capable than an unarmed pilot in thwarting terrorists. Many pilots have military backgrounds and are experienced with firearms. It is impossible to know how many pilots are actually armed, but it is estimated that up to a third have the proper training.[94]

1,850 Ft.

■ *Federal air marshals.* Air marshals are armed federal agents who were first introduced in 1961 by President John Kennedy in response to a number of skyjackings. According to the Transportation Security Agencies, it is the duty of air marshals "to detect, deter, and defeat hostile acts targeting U.S. air carriers, airports, passengers, and crews."[95] Many people share the same concern with air marshals that they have with armed pilots. Primary among these concerns is the damage that can be done to an airliner should a bullet penetrate the fuselage and destroy the pressurization of the cabin. At 30,000 feet, changes in pressure can cause catastrophic damage to the airliner. Several steps can be taken to limit this danger, such as using soft bullets that can damage human tissue but will not penetrate the airliner. The use of air marshals is controversial even though in a number of instances these agents have been able to subdue unruly passengers.[96]

■ *Reinforced cockpit doors.* Since September 11, airlines have installed more secure doors on the cockpits of their airliners. In addition, when pilots leave the cockpit, the door is quickly shut and locked to prevent unauthorized passengers from gaining access.

Although these security measures might help prevent terrorist attacks on airliners, questions remain about their cost-effectiveness. More important, however, terrorists are aware of the increased security in public spaces and airports. Other targets become more attractive because they are guarded less. Law enforcement officials at every level are constantly trying to anticipate where terrorists might strike next. Of most concern are nuclear power plants, water reservoirs, buildings with symbolic value, such as the White House, and theme parks such as Disney World where the population is dense and the symbolic visibility is high.

# Think about it

## Remember
Recall how the Department of Homeland Security came into being.

## Understand
Identify some of the criticisms that are expressed about the legality of holding suspected terrorists in places such as Guantanamo Bay.

## Apply
Illustrate some of the restrictions and inconveniences Americans are experiencing due to the war on terror.

## Evaluate
Appraise how criminology is changing to better address the issues and concerns raised by terrorism.

# Summary

**LO1:** **Explain why terrorism is so difficult to define.**
- Terrorism is relative. What one person might consider terrorism, another might regard as legitimate rebellion or freedom fighting.
- The U.S. government defines terrorism as "premeditated, politically motivated violence perpetrated against noncombatant targets by subnational groups or clandestine agents."
- The four components of terrorism as defined by Combs are the use of violence or the threat of violence, a political dimension, the killing of innocent people, and symbolic meaning.

**LO2:** **Discuss how the classical and positivist schools of criminological thought consider terrorism.**
- The classical school of criminology holds that individuals choose to perpetrate their actions. According to the positivist school, individuals turn to terrorism in part because of external causes, such as social disorder and desperate poverty.

**LO3:** **Give some examples of how groups throughout history have used terrorism to achieve their political goals.**
- Terrorism is an old political weapon. The word *terrorism* entered the Western mindset in the 18th century with the French Revolution, according to Rapoport.
- American Revolutionaries did not abide by European standards of warfare; the Russian terrorist rebel group Narodnaya Volya chose victims for their symbolic importance; terrorist groups from the 1920s to the 1960s targeted police and security forces; the Vietcong guerrillas of the 1960s used tactics and discipline to defeat more sophisticated standing armies;

many terrorist groups of today are motivated by religious fundamentalism and attack civilian targets.

**LO4:** **Describe incidents of domestic terrorism in the United States that have been motivated by racism, fundamentalist religious beliefs, hatred of the federal government, and ecological concerns.**

- The early Ku Klux Klan burned homes and churches, committed murder, and conducted lynchings.
- The best-known example of domestic terrorism by right-wing extremists fueled by their hatred of the government is the bombing of the Murrah Federal Building in Oklahoma City by Timothy McVeigh.
- Eric Rudolph, connected to the Christian Identity movement, bombed Centennial Olympic Park during the 1996 Olympics in Atlanta.
- Two well-known ecoterrorist groups are the Animal Liberation Front and the Earth Liberation Front.

**LO5:** **Differentiate international terrorism from domestic terrorism.**

- International terrorist attacks involve a national or a group of nationals from one nation crossing international borders and attacking targets in another

nation. Domestic terrorist attacks involve a group attacking targets within its own nation.
- International terrorist groups include the Basque *Euskadi Ta Askatasuna* in Spain; the Irish Republican Army in Northern Ireland; Kongra-Gel in Turkey; Al-Shabaab in Somalia; the Taliban in Afghanistan; Chechen rebels in Russia; various Palestinian groups around Israel, including the Hezbollah and Hamas; and Al Qaeda internationally.

**LO6:** **Understand that in dealing with terrorism, the United States must consider a number of issues related to civil rights, the Constitution, privacy, and surveillance.**

- Two measures the United States has taken to deal with the problem of terrorism are creating the Department of Homeland Security and passing the USA PATRIOT Act.
- The difficulty in controlling terrorism is finding the balance between providing security and protection from harm and allowing individuals their rights and freedom. Some security compromises that Americans have had to make include restrictions on entering government buildings, airports, and airplanes.

# Questions

1. What is terrorism? What are four components of terrorism, according to Cindy Combs's definition of the term?
2. What aspects of terrorism are easily defined as criminal offenses? What aspects of terrorism present problems for the traditional definitions of crime?
3. How has the relationship between federal, state, and local law enforcement agencies changed since September 11, 2001?
4. Political scientist David Rapoport identified four waves of modern terrorism. What are these four waves, and what characterizes each wave?

5. How do traditional criminological theories explain terrorist activities?
6. What have been motivations behind incidents of domestic terrorism in the United States?
7. Identify examples of modern international terrorism. What has motivated the terrorist groups involved in these activities?
8. Which issues must the United States consider in dealing with the problem of terrorism?
9. What measures has the United States implemented to prevent and deter terrorism?

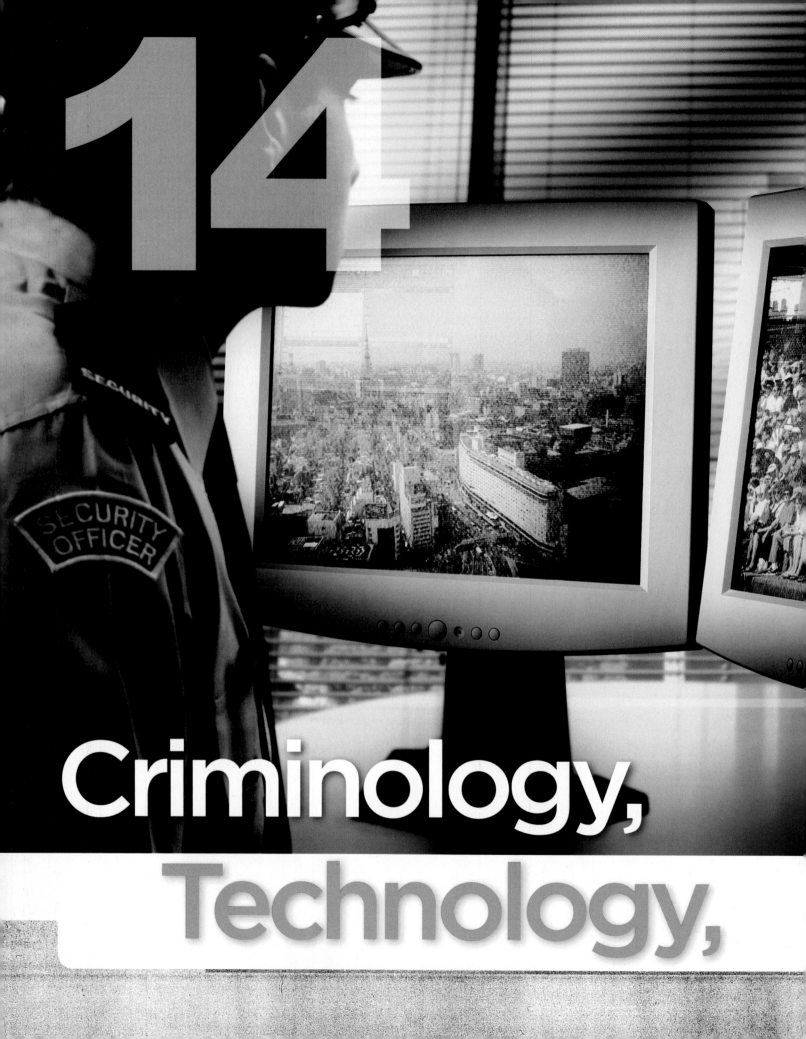

# 14

# Criminology, Technology,

# what's inside

# and Privacy

Technology has always been an issue in crime prevention. However, in the 21st century, technology has taken on a new importance because so much of our personal, economic, public safety, and security information is now stored on computers that sophisticated thieves might access. Today's criminology student must have a greater appreciation of the role of technology in preventing and controlling crime and develop skills that did not even exist a generation ago. This chapter will provide a broad overview of the technological issues of working in the criminal justice system and suggest some emerging concerns.

One theme of this text is that criminology has changed in the 21st century. Changes have occurred for a number of reasons, but perhaps the most important one has to do with the rapid increase in the sophistication of technology. This final chapter will begin with a short history of technology and crime and then concentrate on three effects of technology on the criminal justice system that have made the study of criminology more interesting and more complex.

1. *Technology gives lawbreakers more opportunities.* As society becomes more dependent upon technology, lawbreakers with knowledge of how to use and manipulate sophisticated electronic equipment and systems have more opportunities to engage in illegal activities. Law enforcement officers who have been trained to deal with more traditional types of crime face greater difficulties in discovering and apprehending these offenders. In this section of the chapter, we will look at how some criminals use technology to break the law in ways that were not possible in decades past.

2. *The criminal justice system employs technology to discover, apprehend, process, and incarcerate offenders.* Criminal justice officials employ technology to counter the technological expertise of lawbreakers and make the criminal justice system more efficient and less costly. Here, we will concentrate on how the criminal justice system uses technology to prevent crime and dispense justice.

3. *Technology alters our concepts of privacy.* Technology allows law enforcement officials to keep better track of offenders and protect life and property, and it also allows for the surveillance of ordinary law-abiding citizens in ways that challenge our concepts of privacy. Rights guaranteed by the Constitution are being reinterpreted in the 21st century to deal with terrorism with the unintended consequences of reducing privacy for all citizens. This section of the chapter will examine the delicate balance between individual rights and public security and suggest that this balance will take a long time to achieve because of the rapidly changing nature of technology.

# Criminology and Technology

The use of technology to break the law is not new. The cat-and-mouse game between lawbreakers and those who wish to protect themselves and their property has always existed. Bars on windows, deadbolt locks, safety deposit boxes in banks, and countless other examples of technology are a testament to how lawbreakers have had to overcome artificial obstacles to get what they want (see *Theory to Practice*). In some ways, computers and security technology have greatly increased the level of sophistication required to commit such offenses as larceny, theft, robbery, and most property offenses. However, we should realize that these "technological" offenses are mostly an extension of street crime. The theft of an identity using computers is still theft. The use of a denial-of-service (DoS) attack to disable an Internet server is still vandalism, malicious mischief, or perhaps a prelude to theft. The Internet has simply made it easier to break the law on a large scale as well as in a more comprehensive and nearly anonymous manner.

The use of technology to break the law has caused major concerns among law enforcement agencies and financial institutions, as well as the general public. These concerns have jump-started a computer-security industry that requires workers with a high level of technological expertise, and law enforcement agencies have had to develop new protocols for investigating offenses committed with computers (see Figure 14.1). Criminology students looking for a lucrative and rewarding career in the criminal justice system must now learn electronic and computer skills and develop a level of

# theory to practice

## Because That's Where the Money Is

When asked why he robbed banks, Willie Sutton replied, "Because that's where the money is." Individuals have long sought to protect their money from the likes of Willie Sutton and have gone to great extremes to make it more difficult for bank robbers and thieves to take it. A great lesson in technology can be learned from the efforts at protecting banks, which are attempts at **situational crime prevention,** an extension of **rational choice theory.**

>**THINKBACK**
rational choice theory (ch. 4)—The concept that offenders calculate the advantages and disadvantages not only of breaking the law, but of what type of offense to commit.
situational crime prevention (ch. 4)—An offshoot of rational choice theory that considers direct factors that can be modified to discourage crime.

Author Robert Letkemann traced the evolution of bank security in his book *Crime and Work* in which he interviewed bank robbers and safe crackers to find out how they learned their trade. According to Letkemann, the increasing level of bank security is a result of the success of robbers and safe crackers in penetrating the defenses designed to secure the contents of the bank. These advances include the design of vaults, security cards, cameras, infrared sensors, and a host of other technological mechanisms designed to thwart bank robbers. However, bank robbers have found a way around each of these innovations. For example:

- When bank managers found that thieves were able to penetrate their safes, they designed stronger safes with more sophisticated locks. The response from bank robbers was to remove the safe from the bank to a place where the robbers had the time and tools to successfully crack the safe.
- Bank managers responded by making the safes bigger, heavier, and bolting them to the floor. Robbers began using dynamite to blow the safes open.
- Bank managers used stronger metals that could not be penetrated by dynamite. Bank robbers responded by using nitroglycerin and other more powerful explosives.
- Safe companies designed safes with circular doors so that the nitroglycerin would drain to the bottom of the door, rendering the explosive ineffective. So thieves kidnapped bank managers and forced them to open their safes.

▲ Cameras record the activities of everyone who visits a bank, including ATMs.

- Security companies then developed safes with timers that prevented employees from opening them during nonbanking hours.

You get the idea. The result of trying to make banks a harder target for thieves to penetrate has been that bank officials have essentially given up on many of the target-hardening aspects of situational crime prevention and now instead try to limit their losses. Bank employees are instructed to cooperate with robbers and hand over the cash on demand. However, each teller has a limited amount of cash, and each bank has a limited total amount of cash. Cameras also photograph or record the likenesses and activities of everyone at the bank, both inside and outside at the drive-through windows or ATMs. Because so much banking is now done electronically, physically robbing a bank is no longer considered a big score. Although bank robbers sometimes get away with their offenses, they must rob many banks to make a living, increasing the likelihood of capture.

## THINKING *in* ACTION

How does situational crime prevention describe the efforts to physically secure banks?

## Figure 14.1   Collecting Digital Evidence Flow Chart

**These instructions are for law enforcement first-responders who must secure crime scenes that contain computers or other electronic devices.**

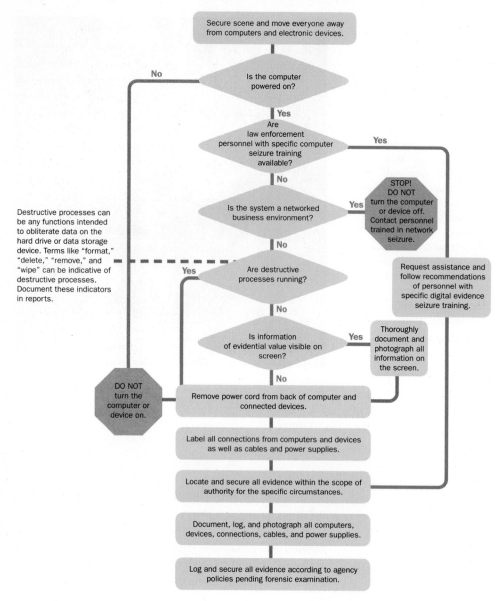

Destructive processes can be any functions intended to obliterate data on the hard drive or data storage device. Terms like "format," "delete," "remove," and "wipe" can be indicative of destructive processes. Document these indicators in reports.

Secure scene and move everyone away from computers and electronic devices.

Is the computer powered on?

Are law enforcement personnel with specific computer seizure training available?

Is the system a networked business environment?

STOP! DO NOT turn the computer or device off. Contact personnel trained in network seizure.

Are destructive processes running?

Request assistance and follow recommendations of personnel with specific digital evidence seizure training.

Is information of evidential value visible on screen?

Thoroughly document and photograph all information on the screen.

DO NOT turn the computer or device on.

Remove power cord from back of computer and connected devices.

Label all connections from computers and devices as well as cables and power supplies.

Locate and secure all evidence within the scope of authority for the specific circumstances.

Document, log, and photograph all computers, devices, connections, cables, and power supplies.

Log and secure all evidence according to agency policies pending forensic examination.

*Source:* U.S. Department of Justice Office of Justice Programs, *Electronic Crime Scene Investigation: A Guide for First Responders,* 2nd ed. (Washington, DC: Government Printing Office, 2008), 29, http://www.ncjrs.gov/pdffiles1/nij/219941.pdf.

will always seek opportunities to break the law, society must set up safeguards to protect property, information, and public safety. For instance, many homes now have private security systems that are integrated with systems that control lighting, heating and air conditioning, home entertainment centers, and other appliances. Without the advances in private security system technology, many of these other systems would not have been developed in such advanced ways. Fear of crime has created a profit motive for manufacturers of these systems not only to develop technology to provide security, but also to tack on other features to make their systems more marketable.

Another area in which crime has advanced technology is that of geographic information systems. One example is the LoJack system, a vehicle recovery system that allows police to track stolen vehicles. Geographic information systems that were designed to locate people or objects precisely are now being used in a variety of contexts. Golfers can carry small devices that will tell them exactly how far they are from a sand trap or a green. Internet users can use satellites paired with interactive maps to get an aerial view of their neighborhoods or any place in the world. Without the geographic information systems that were developed to prevent auto theft, such technological advances would not have occurred so quickly.

technological sophistication that will enable them to step outside the traditional bounds of criminology.

## A Short History of Technology and Crime

There is a case to be made that crime, in many ways, is responsible for the advancement of technology. Although we must be careful not to overstate this point because some people

The popularity of television programs based on crime-scene investigation techniques has inspired new interest in chemistry and biology. Many students are drawn to criminology because they want to become crime-scene technicians or work in crime labs. The attractiveness of crime-scene investigation derives in part from the answers that science can provide to help solve

## LO1:

**Describe** how technology has always been used to break the law.

▲ The popularity of television programs based on crime-scene investigation techniques has inspired many students to pursue chemistry and biology so that they may find jobs in the field.

cases. Even though many television shows present science in an unrealistic and even distorted light, this use of technology has been popularized because of its association with crime.

Finally, crime has pushed technological advances in the area of security of money and identity. The Treasury Department has continuously battled counterfeiters by making money distinctive and difficult to replicate. These efforts have led to advances in special inks, optical effects, and technologies such as holograms to thwart counterfeiters. Security concerns in protecting identity have prompted the development of fingerprint and handprint scanners, voice recognition software, and technology that scans human irises to validate identification.

We must be careful not to overstate that crime is responsible for advances in technology. However, in a capitalist society, the profit motive is crucial to developing practical applications for technological innovations. The disruption that crime causes in society creates markets for technological products that prevent criminal offending or help solve cases.

One of the most momentous technological innovations of the last 50 years is that of **information technology,** a general term used to describe devices and software that transmit, receive, and store data. Information technology includes any device that provides information about another person, including tracking, identification, and surveillance devices, as well as computer databases. Although information technology was not developed primarily in response to crime, one of its uses has been to establish the security of governments, corporations, and individuals through the

movement and restriction of information. Currently, the star application of information technology systems is the Internet, which was, in its early stages, intended to provide secure communications for the U.S. government.

## The Beginnings of the Internet

The Internet grew out of various government projects that began at the end of World War II and the start of the Cold War. The reasons for developing a decentralized national computer network were military and scientific. One of the first projects, Whirlwind at MIT, monitored and coordinated radars that tracked the movement of Russian aircraft. The U.S. government also wanted a system that could provide multiple routes for electronic communication in the aftermath of a nuclear conflict. In the 1960s, the Advanced Research Projects Agency (ARPA) initiated a project that would allow computers at the nation's science labs, government agencies, and universities to communicate with one another.[1] ARPANET officially went online in October 1969 with a test message sent from UCLA to the Stanford Research Institute. In 1987, the National Science Foundation (NSF) took over responsibility for ARPANET'S civilian nodes. Initially called NSFnet, the NSF's system eventually became known as the Internet. ARPANET was discontinued in 1990; in 1991, the NSF lifted the restrictions on the commercial use of its network. (The government had allowed no commercial activity on ARPANET.)[2] From that date, civilian use of the Internet took off, and, presumably, the first laws were broken with its help shortly thereafter.

## The Internet and Crime

Crime is socially defined. In other words, it takes a society, a network of people, to define the rules of behavior, decide how they are applied, determine when they are broken, and assess the consequences of their breakage. Crime cannot exist in a society of one (imagine a person marooned on a deserted island). The formation of a human network of any sort means that rules will be made and broken, and the breakage of some of these rules will be regarded as crime. The Internet is a tool for communication; like any tool, it is not a source of crime, but it does offer unscrupulous people new and creative ways to break the law. The Internet also offers unprecedented anonymity (although probably not as much as some people think). As with any network, the larger and more open to new membership it is, the more crime will occur. Probably little to no crime occurred on ARPANET because it was a tightly controlled network of individuals from the closed communities of science and the military.

Perhaps the most interesting and serious consequence the Internet has had for traditional criminal justice is its effect on **jurisdiction,** or legal authority. In the United States, as

---

**information technology** A general term used to describe devices and software that transmit, receive, and store data.

**jurisdiction** The right and power to interpret and apply the law; legal authority.

## Table 14.1    Federal Computer Crime Investigation Agencies and Divisions

**These agencies investigate offenses that are perpetrated via computer networks.**

| Agency or Division | Task |
| --- | --- |
| National Cyber Security Division Mission | The task of the National Cybersecurity Division is to collaborate with public, private, and international entities to build and maintain an effective national Internet response system and to implement a risk management program to protect critical national infrastructure. |
| US-CERT | The United States Computer Emergency Readiness Team (US-CERT) is a partnership between the Department of Homeland Security and the public and private sectors. Established in 2003 to protect the nation's Internet infrastructure, US-CERT coordinates responses to computer-based attacks in the United States. |
| FBI Cyber Investigations | The mission of the FBI Cyber Investigations unit is to stop those behind the most serious computer intrusions and the spread of malicious code; to identify and thwart sexual predators who use the Internet to meet and exploit children and to produce, possess, or share child pornography; to counteract operations that target U.S. intellectual property; and to dismantle national and transnational organized criminal enterprises that engage in Internet fraud. |
| Internet Crime Complaint Center (IC3) | The Internet Crime Complaint Center (IC3), a partnership between the FBI and the National White Collar Crime Center, receives, tracks, analyzes, and organizes Internet crime complaints and refers the complaints to the appropriate federal, state, local, or international law enforcement agency or regulatory agency for investigation. |
| Department of Justice Computer Crime and Intellectual Property Section | The Computer Crime and Intellectual Property Section implements national strategies in combating computer and intellectual property offenses throughout the world. |

throughout much of the world, legal jurisdiction is one of the cornerstones of criminal justice. Jurisdiction can be established politically (federal, state, and local jurisdictions), geographically, or by the nature of the offense. For example, an offense that takes place within a state is handled by that state's criminal justice agencies depending on the seriousness of the offense. Local law enforcement deals with drunk drivers. A serial murderer who does not cross state lines will be pursued by the state's major law enforcement agency. A serial murderer who does cross state lines involves the Federal Bureau of Investigation (FBI). A person who commits tax fraud is pursued by the Internal Revenue Service (IRS). Someone who commits an offense involving the postal service is investigated by that agency's law enforcement bureau. All these cases flow through the criminal justice system in order of jurisdiction.

This way of allotting criminal justice resources worked just fine until the Internet. Today, a major financial offense that involves both copyright and illegal pornography can be committed by a group of people distributed throughout one country, via servers in a second country, against victims located in yet a third country, for clients in a fourth country. Where is the jurisdiction? Who investigates the case, arrests the suspects, tries the defendants, and punishes the convicted? The Internet has set up these questions, and criminal justice systems across the globe are trying to come up with

an answer. (See Table 14.1 for a list of federal agencies that investigate computer-related crime.) To understand crime on the Internet, we must first understand how it began.

### The Whistler, Cap'n Crunch, and the Evolution of Computer Network Crime

The use of a technological network to break the law did not start with the Internet. Undoubtedly the law had been broken with the use of radios early in the 20th century, but the modern era of **hacking**—the unauthorized use of an information system or network—emerged with Joe Engressia in the 1950s. Also known as "The Whistler," Engressia (who in 1991 changed his name to Joybubbles) was born blind but gifted with excellent hearing and perfect pitch. As a child in the 1950s, Engressia learned to manipulate the telephone system, which, at the time, was based on tones.

While still a toddler, Engressia discovered he could dial a phone by tapping the hookswitch like a telegraph key. At the age of seven, he whistled a sound he heard on a long-distance phone call and discovered that it disconnected the call. Engressia later began to whistle the telephone company's tones to manipulate the phone system and make free

**hacking** The unauthorized use of an information system or network.

▲ Joe Engressia, who changed his name to Joybubbles in 1991, pioneered manipulation of the telephone system.

calls. Years later, the University of South Florida expelled Engressia for making free long-distance phone calls for his friends. In 1971, Engressia was convicted of telephone fraud, but his skills were so rare that by 1975 Mountain Bell had hired him to diagnose its network problems. As the first "phone phreak" (see *Doubletake* for why the term is spelled

that way), Engressia became legendary and developed a following that included such computing pioneers as Steve Jobs and Steve Wozniak of Apple Computer. In one stunt, Engressia whistled his way through telephone systems around the globe so that he could talk into one phone and listen to himself on another.[3]

Computer pioneer John Draper expanded on Engressia's methods by using a toy whistle from a box of Cap'n Crunch cereal to make the same tone. Draper, now known as "Cap'n Crunch," was arrested several times throughout the 1970s for stealing long-distance phone calls (Draper graduated to other methods to make his phone calls when the telephone company dropped the tone system in 1971) and went to prison for telephone fraud even as he was writing ground-breaking software for the fledgling computer industry.[4]

What is interesting to note about this early form of technology-based crime is that its perpetrators, for the most part, broke the law in pursuit of knowledge rather than money. They wanted to learn more about how the telephone system, then the primary communications system in the United States, worked. Also, it was not unusual for phone phreaks and other early hackers to work on both sides of the law. Some began their careers breaking the law to learn more about computer and telephone networks, then were later employed by the very companies they had victimized. Others, like John Draper, continued their unlawful activities while working legitimate jobs in the same industry.

## Computer Network Crime for Profit

Since the early 1980s, more computer and network crime is pursued for profit and has more in common with street crime in terms of the perpetrators' intent. In 1995, Kevin Mitnick was arrested and sentenced to five years in prison for breaking into the systems of Motorola, Novell, Fujitsu, Sun Microsystems, and Nokia to steal software code. Active for 15 years, Mitnick spent 2 years on the run from the FBI; however, he appears never to have used or sold his stolen goods, which consisted of corporate intellectual properties.[5] Today the valuable items are personal information such as names, social security numbers, and credit card numbers. Security experts say a supermarket-like economy has developed, with specialists stealing identifying information and providing it to brokers who offer it on the market.[6] According to the FBI, common frauds are fake e-mails (a popular scam is an e-mail purported to be from the FBI in an effort to gain information from the victim), with perpetrators operating out of the United States, United Kingdom, Nigeria, Canada, Malaysia, and Ghana.[7]

# doubletake
doubletake

### Phun with Fonics

Students of Internet crime will notice that some of the offenses—the ones that begin with an "f" sound—have odd spellings. The reason for this is most likely connected to the word "phone," short for "telephone," which was probably the first public network to be hacked. Early telephone network hackers substituted "ph" for "f" in creating a moniker for themselves: "freaks." Thus, "freaks" became "phreaks," and telephone hackers became known as "phone phreaks" and telephone hacking as "phreaking." Now, nearly anytime the letter "f" appears at the beginning of a word associated with hacking or Internet crime, that "f" is replaced with a "ph." For example, an identity thief's "fishing" for information is often spelled "phishing."

## THINKING *in* ACTION

Subcultures, such as street gangs and hackers, for instance, often use alternative spellings and clever wordplay to describe themselves and their activities. Discuss possible reasons for this.

A particularly odd form of offense involves a combination of computer vandalism and theft. In one case, a New Zealand teenager managed to infect hundreds of personal computers around the world with a form of hidden software that allowed him to control the computers, creating a "robot network" or "botnet." He then rented the botnet to a company in the Netherlands, which wanted to use the network to secretly install its advertising software on other computers.[8]

## Think about it

### Remember

List the federal agencies responsible for investigating computer crime.

### Analyze

Examine how Internet crime creates problems for law enforcement agencies with regard to their issues of jurisdiction.

### Evaluate

Assess how those who engaged in early forms of technology-based crime broke the law in pursuit of knowledge rather than money.

## Types of Computer Network Crime

Today, most people equate the Internet with the World Wide Web, but other basic applications include e-mail, FTP (file transfer protocol), and telnet (a protocol to run a remote computer). All four of these Internet applications can be used in various ways to break the law. Internet crime is actually street and white-collar crime perpetrated with a different sort of human network. Much Internet crime involves fraud, larceny-theft, vandalism, and copyright violation, offenses that existed long before the Internet. In 2006, of all the offenses committed using computers, 42 percent were white-collar offenses, and 31 percent of those were larceny-thefts.[9] Networks on which crime is common share some characteristics.

**LO2:**

**Show** why the Internet provides a nearly ideal network for crime.

- They are large.
- They offer some degree of anonymity.
- They offer something of economic value or access to it.
- They are easy to access and use.
- They are versatile.

We can use these characteristics to trace the development and likelihood of crime on technology-based networks. ARPANET offered none of these characteristics and so was virtually crime-free. (Rules were still broken, however; see The Computer Crime Toolbox section later in this chapter). The U.S. phone system offers some of these characteristics: It is large; it can be anonymous, although less so today than in decades past; it offers economic value (phone service) and access to something of economic value (other people); and it is easy to access and use. Although a great deal of crime occurs over the phone, mainly related to fraud and the 1970s incidences of phone phreaking, phone service does not offer the versatility that the Internet does. Therefore, much more crime occurs on the Internet. If some technological network were to be developed that was better than the Internet on these five characteristics, it is likely even more crime would occur on that network. In fact, a lot of crime is already occurring with the use of other networked devices, such as cell phones and credit-card readers. See Table 14.2 for theories about Internet crime. Keep these in mind as we discuss various types of Internet-based offenses.

The age and sex of those who commit computer network crime tend to reflect the range of "real world" crime. That is, computer crime perpetrators tend to be young and male. According to the Internet Crime Complaint Center, more than 76 percent of computer-crime perpetrators were male in complaints in which perpetrator information was known.[10] Some experts have estimated the ratio of male to female perpetrators to be as high as 99:1. Other researchers have found computer network crime to be almost a juvenile delinquency problem in that teenage males and very young adult males are overwhelmingly represented among computer-crime perpetrators.[11] The term *script kiddies,* referring to typically inexperienced youngsters who seek to commit what are usually minor computer offenses—such as website defacement—using pre-written programs, attests to this characteristic of offenders. They want to impress their friends with their computer skills, although they are not sophisticated enough to write their own programs.

As computer crime becomes more profitable and more international, these statistics might change, especially as computer network crime becomes a significant source of profit for criminal organizations throughout the world. However, at present, young males are responsible for much of the highly technical work of computer crime.

### The Computer Crime Toolbox

The programs and methods used to break the law via computer are a strange array of creatures that include viruses, worms, Trojan horses, spam, and logic bombs. The names of these programs and methods succinctly describe what they do and how they work. Most of the offenses committed using these tools involve theft and vandalism. The list of methods of committing computer network crime presented here is not exhaustive. New and increasingly technical methods

## Table **14.2**    Theories of Internet Crime

| Theory | Explanation |
| --- | --- |
| Space transition theory | People behave differently in different spaces. "Space transition" describes the movement of people from one space to another. Space transition theory holds that people engage in illegal behavior online that they would avoid in physical space. Space transition theory seeks to explain only offenses committed via computer, not those committed in physical space.[1] |
| Neutralization theory | The neutralization techniques that computer network offenders use most often to justify their activities are denial of injury, denial of victim, condemnation of the condemners, appeal to higher loyalties, and self-fulfillment. They rarely use denial of responsibility or the "sad tale."[2] |
| Routine activities theory | For the law to be broken, three things must happen simultaneously: A suitable target must be present; there must be no suitable guardian to prevent the offense; a motivated offender must be present.[3] Deterrence occurs when any one of these elements is shifted. However, such shifting is difficult on the Internet: Suitable guardians are rare, and motivated offenders are present everywhere, as are suitable targets. A motivated offender might be presented with a suitable target at any time. Therefore, the Internet is a more likely place for some laws to be broken than physical space. |
| Opportunity theory | Opportunity must exist for a criminal offense to occur. If an offense cannot be committed in one place, it will be committed in another. The opportunity for crime on the Internet is increased because it is no longer bound by physical place.[4] |

[1]K. Jaishankar, "Space Transition Theory of Cyber Crimes," in *Crimes of the Internet,* ed. Frank Schmalleger and Michael Pittaro (Upper Saddle River, NJ: Pearson Prentice Hall, 2009), 292.

[2]Orly Turgeman-Goldschmidt, "The Rhetoric of Hackers' Neutralizations," in *Crimes of the Internet,* 317–32.

[3]Raymond W. Cox III, Terrance A. Johnson, and George E. Richards, "Routine Activity Theory and Internet Crime," in *Crimes of the Internet,* 302–15.

[4]Ibid., 302–15.

▼ Script kiddies use pre-written programs to commit what are usually minor computer offenses.

are being invented every day. However, most of the common computer network offenses and the tools used to commit these offenses fall within the broad categories discussed here.

### Social Engineering

**Social engineering**—manipulating individuals so they give away information or perform actions—is one of the oldest tools used in breaking into computer networks. However, social engineering takes advantage of the human network rather than a computer network and has much in common with con games. Many of the most infamous network break-ins involved not cracking a system's passwords but merely inventing a story, then asking someone in charge to reveal the passwords. This particular form of social engineering is called "pretexting."

In one example, in 1994, Kevin Mitnick posed as an employee of software maker Novell, Inc., and called the company's systems administrator late at night to request access to Novell's network. Mitnick explained that he was out of town and needed to connect to the network to work

**social engineering** The manipulation of individuals so that they divulge information or perform actions.

on a project. As a security check, the systems administrator called the employee's voice mail to make sure the voice that answered matched the voice that he had heard on the phone. The voices matched, and the systems administrator let Mitnick access the system. However, earlier Mitnick had called another Novell technician and convinced that technician to give him access to the employee's voice mail account. Mitnick recorded a new answering message using his voice, so when the systems administrator called to check if the voices matched, they did. Once inside Novell's systems, Mitnick copied the code for Novell's most important product, NetWare.[12]

Companies are a bit wiser to social engineering attempts now than they were in 1994, but social engineering and pretexting are still regularly attempted. A popular target is financial information. The 1999 Gramm-Leach-Bliley Act specifically prohibits pretexting to obtain consumers' personal financial information, such as bank balances, from financial institutions. Enforced primarily by the Federal Trade Commission (FTC), the law prescribes fines and imprisonment for violators, with enhanced penalties for aggravated cases. The 2006 Telephone Records and Privacy Protection Act makes it a federal offense to use pretexting to obtain telephone records, with penalties of up to ten years in prison.[13]

Other forms of social engineering rely more specifically on the use of computers to acquire information.

- *Phishing.* Phishing involves the use of an e-mail that resembles an important communication from a bank or other trusted institution. The e-mail asks recipients for sensitive account information or refers recipients to a false website that resembles the institution's website in order to trick them into entering their passwords and account numbers. Often, the website will respond with a "bad password" message to get victims to enter their information repeatedly.

- *Trojan horses.* These often arrive in the form of e-mail attachments that appear interesting to recipients, promising exciting pictures, screensavers, music, software, or other goodies. Clicking on the attachment releases a hidden program or "malware" that allows control of the computer by a third party, downloads sensitive information from the computer, destroys data on the computer, or otherwise vandalizes the system. Unlike computer viruses, Trojans do not self-replicate.

- *Road apples.* This is a physical Trojan horse that might be an abandoned CD, diskette, or USB drive. The perpetrator loads the media with malware, places an interesting label on it (such as "financial records" or "music"), and leaves it in a public space. When someone picks up the media and inserts it into their computer to see what it contains, the Trojan horse is released.

## Viruses and Worms

A computer virus is a program that is attached to another file or program. When the file or program is run, the virus runs, too. A virus can copy and attach itself to other programs and files. When these files are sent to another computer, either over a network or by media (such as a floppy disk or USB drive), the virus goes, too, and infects the new system. A worm is much like a virus but is not attached to another file or program. Once resident on a computer, worms scan the network for specific types of security holes that they can move through to infect new machines.[14]

Before computer networks were common, early viruses were transmitted via floppy disks. The virus would save itself to a floppy disk inserted into an infected computer, then install itself on the next computer the disk was inserted into. The first computer virus, called Creeper, appeared in the early 1970s on ARPANET. Computers infected with Creeper would display the message: "I'M THE CREEPER: CATCH ME IF YOU CAN." Shortly after Creeper came the virus Reaper, which apparently had the task of deleting the Creeper virus. The authors of these two viruses are unknown. The first virus to spread among common computer users was Elk Cloner, which was transmitted between Apple II computers via floppy disks in the early to mid-1980s. Like the Creeper and Reaper viruses, Elk Cloner was not written with criminal or destructive intent and only displayed a string of rhyming verses.[15]

Since then, computer viruses have become steadily more destructive and, thanks to the variety of networking tools, more easily spread. Destructive viruses typically damage computers by deleting data and interfering with the computer's operation, such as causing the computer to turn itself off or causing the hard drive to reformat itself, or by using up computer memory and processing speed. One of the most problematic viruses was the Melissa virus of 1999, a Microsoft Word 2000 macro virus that propagated via e-mail attachments. A person would receive an infected Word document via e-mail attachment; opening the attachment would infect the recipient's computer with the virus (which gave the virus much in common with a Trojan horse). The virus corrupted many e-mail servers, and several companies, including Microsoft, had to shut down their e-mail systems until Melissa could be brought under control.[16]

IT WILL GET ON ALL YOUR DISKS
IT WILL INFILTRATE YOUR CHIPS
YES. IT'S CLONER!

IT WILL STICK TO YOU LIKE GLUE
IT WILL MODIFY RAM TOO
SEND IN THE CLONER!

▲ The relatively benign Elk Cloner was the first virus to become common among computer users.

Unlike viruses, worms were first created by professional programmers to work on computer systems. In 1978, Xerox PARC (Palo Alto Research Center) researchers John Shoch and Jon Hupp designed a worm that would find idle computers on the network and put them to work on specific tasks, thus increasing computing efficiency. Although the worm was beneficial and designed to expire after a certain period, it was difficult to control and crashed several computers.[17] Since then, worms have grown increasingly destructive, with the main goal of worm writers apparently being the control of computers and harvesting of data. For example, the Storm Worm, which became active in 2007, added infected computers to a botnet, which was then used to spread spam, steal identities, and shut down computer networks.

Because the Internet has connected so many computers around the world, including critical public systems, virus protection is not only big business, but also a major concern of government authorities. A particularly devious virus or worm could do immense damage to government and military computers, putting public safety and security at risk. Many virus and worm writers have said that the purpose of their activities is to exploit security holes in software and operating systems so that they can be patched. However, in recent years, the profit motive behind these activities has become clear.

Historically, the legal consequences for virus and worm writers have been light. According to computer security experts Thomas M. Chen and Jean-Marc Robert, there are several reasons for this.

- Anonymity is easy for virus and worm writers to maintain, so cases are difficult to prosecute.

- Virus/worm writers are usually teenagers and college students, so long prison sentences have been considered too harsh. Punishments are usually probation, fines, and community service. This treatment recalls the punishment bias against street crime when compared to white-collar and corporate crime. Computer network crime is not considered as damaging as street crime, and computer offenders tend not to be violent, so the sentencing is less likely to include incarceration.

- The virus/worm writer might live in another country that has no statute or weak statutes covering such offenses. For example, Chen Ing-hau of Taiwan was arrested for the 1998 Chernobyl virus but released after no one filed a complaint. Onel de Guzman was arrested in the Philippines for the 2000 LoveLetter virus, which caused $7 billion in damages, but he was released because there were no laws against writing computer viruses.[18]

## Spam

**Spam,** or unsolicited e-mail advertising a product or service that is sent in bulk to large numbers of people, was invented in 1978 by Gary Thuerk of the Digital Equipment Corporation. Thuerk decided to advertise the company's new computer system by sending an e-mail to 600 people on ARPANET. Because ARPANET was not supposed to be used for commercial advertising, Thuerk was reprimanded, and the academic debate about network usage and free speech began.[19]

Unfortunately, spam is now more than a debate topic for university network administrators. Spam clogs servers, overloads individual e-mail accounts, and delivers inappropriate and pornographic messages, as well as viruses, Trojan horses, and worms. Spam is more problematic than unsolicited bulk postal mail because of the low costs associated with sending spam. Bulk mail sent through the postal system incurs printing and postage costs as well as the costs of storing, sorting, and sending the mail. Spam, however, because it is electronic, requires little more than an Internet account and a list of e-mail addresses. Lists of millions of e-mail addresses are typically purchased or compiled automatically from the Internet with the use of software, so the lists are not very expensive. Because of the low overhead costs, enough spam can be sent to overload Internet servers and e-mail accounts, costing individuals and businesses millions in time and money to deal with it. As the spamming business matured in the late 1990s, spam began to contain Trojans, viruses, and other harmful programs, as well as pornography. Much of this spam wound up in individuals' e-mail accounts at work and in children's e-mail.

In an effort to control spam, the U.S. Congress passed the Controlling the Assault of Non-Solicited Pornography and Marketing Act (CAN-SPAM Act) in 2003. The act "establishes requirements for those who send commercial email, spells out penalties for spammers and companies whose products are advertised in spam if they violate the law, and gives consumers the right to ask e-mailers to stop spamming them." The act's provisions include a ban on false or misleading source information; a ban on deceptive subject lines; a requirement that recipients be allowed to decline further e-mails; and a requirement that commercial e-mail be identified as an advertisement and include the sender's valid physical postal address.[20] Violations of the Act are subject to fines of up to $11,000, plus penalties for false or misleading advertising, as well as additional penalties for acts related to the spamming process, such as harvesting e-mail addresses.

The first application of CAN-SPAM occurred in 2007, when two men, Jeffrey A. Kilbride and James R. Schaffer, were sentenced to more than five years in prison for sending pornographic spam. Kilbride and Schaffer were fined $100,000 and ordered to pay $77,500 in restitution to AOL Inc., as well as forfeit more than $1.1 million in profits from their spamming operation.[21]

## Denial-of-Service Attacks and Logic Bombs

DoS attacks and logic bombs are two forms of computer network crime that are often combined with worms, viruses, Trojans, and spam as their "payload." A DoS attack is an

spam Unsolicited e-mail advertising a product or service that is sent in bulk to large numbers of people.

◄ Some destructive computer programs are set up to benefit an individual or group of individuals. In the 1999 film *Office Space*, disgruntled office workers plant a program that will deposit small amounts of money into a personal bank account.

attempt to make a computer or server so busy with meaningless activity that it is unavailable for useful activity. A logic bomb is code contained within a piece of software that will set off a destructive function under certain conditions. For example, a virus's payload may be a logic bomb, or a worm's payload may initiate a DoS attack.

Sometimes, logic bombs are not associated with a virus, worm, or Trojan but are planted independently to benefit a specific individual rather than to do random, anonymous damage.

- In 2006, Roger Duronio, a former UBS Paine Webber systems administrator, was sentenced to more than eight years in federal prison for setting a logic bomb that caused more than $3 million in damage to the company's computer network. Duronio was also ordered to pay $3.1 million in restitution. Duronio's plan was to profit from short sales of UBS stock after the logic bomb went off, wrecking UBS's system and causing the company's stock price to drop.[22]

- In 2008, Yung-Hsun Lin, a systems administrator at Medco Health Solutions, was sentenced to 2½ years in federal prison for a logic bomb designed to delete all the data on the company's servers. If the logic bomb had gone off as planned (it was shut down by another employee), it would have prevented Medco customers from filling their prescriptions, which could have been life-threatening to some people. Lin was apparently worried about being laid off by the company.[23]

The typical target for a DoS attack is a popular website that attracts a lot of traffic and provides a vital service, such as bank or credit card payment sites, or very popular sites, such as gaming servers. A DoS attack makes the servers so busy that they cannot deal with the thousands of legitimate requests from the site's users.

Often, the purpose of such an attack is extortion. The perpetrators contact the site's owners and demand money in exchange for leaving the site alone. If the site owners do not pay, then the site is attacked. In what has been called the "street crime of the Internet," DoS extortionists prefer to target smaller sites, whose owners are turning a profit, but not so much that they can afford to hire the best computer security or lawyers. Other likely targets are site owners who are involved in questionable activities themselves, making them unlikely to go to authorities. Such sites would include gambling and pornography websites. These site owners simply pay off the extortionists in order to stay online and avoid involving the police.[24] These kinds of targets make DoS extortionists very difficult to track down and prosecute.

## The Most Serious Offenses

Every day, hundreds, if not thousands, of serious criminal offenses are perpetrated via the Internet. These include copyright infringement, child pornography, identity theft, and e-mail scams. Although this list does not include every possible form of criminal offense that takes place online, they do represent the most common types of offense. Because the Internet is not limited by geography, investigation and prosecution of nearly all online offenses require cooperation among several jurisdictions and types of law enforcement agency, including those located outside the United States.

### Copyright Infringement

Copyright infringement is the duplication of information without permission from the copyright's owner. Copyright is a legal concept that makes information, such as that in the form of media or ideas, profitable. Only the entity that owns the copyright to a piece of information can reproduce that information, usually for the purpose of sale. Copyrights have economic value and can be bought, sold, or otherwise transferred. Restricting the public's ability to reproduce copyrighted information protects that information's economic value for the copyright owner. For example, a piece of music can legally be reproduced only by the copyright owner, who may then sell those reproductions (as digital or analog files in the form of MP3s, CDs, or vinyl albums). However, if listeners reproduce that music on their own without permission from the copyright holder, theoretically they do not need to purchase that music. The music then loses its economic value for the copyright holder, who has also lost control of the copies because it has become free of charge.

Prior to the Internet, copyright infringement was not a great problem for copyright holders, and few cases were pursued in the courts. Copies made by individuals were of low quality and often required special equipment, so it made more sense for consumers to purchase the item. However, the Internet and digitalization have changed those circumstances for media producers, especially those who specialize in recorded music, film, and software. These items have proven particularly, even disastrously, suitable for digitalization, copying, and transmission over the Internet. For instance, prior to digitalization, a person could make an audio tape of a song from the radio or a vinyl album. However, doing so was not a serious problem for the music companies because the copies were of relatively low quality as compared to the originals. Furthermore, the copies could not be transmitted electronically (at least not easily). Now, dozens of programs and peer-to-peer networks exist to copy and transmit digital media, and the copies are, in the case of music and film, nearly as good as the originals. In the case of software, the copies are an exact match.

Since the early 1990s, when Internet file-trading became popular enough to cause concern in the media and software industries, several legal bouts have taken place between corporate interests and the public. For example, for several years, modified peer-to-peer networks, of which Napster was the most popular, were the target of corporate music interests. These networks, which still exist although their focus has changed somewhat, allowed users to log on to the network, search each other's hard drives for the desired files, and download the files directly from each other. After court rulings made it impossible for these services to continue operating, file-trading moved to a true peer-to-peer model, the most popular of which is BitTorrent. This protocol allows individuals to trade small pieces of files until all users have the whole file. This is a much more difficult protocol for copy-

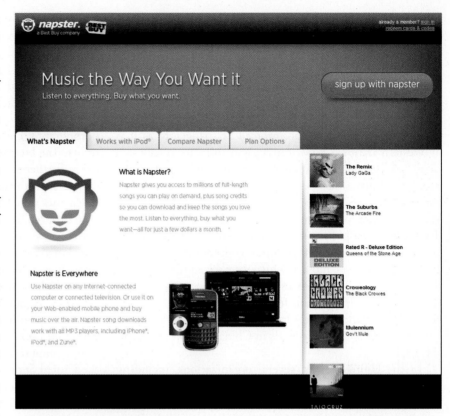

▲ Many programs are available to facilitate the sharing of digital media. Early versions of Napster, created by college student Shawn Fanning in 1999, allowed users to trade any files they wished, regardless of copyright. After the original service was shut down, the brand was later revived as a pay service that adheres to copyright law.

right holders to control than the modified peer-to-peer models because most users have only pieces of files. Presumably, once users collect a whole file, they log off the system. The tug-of-war over copyright infringement is likely to continue for years to come.

A common term for copyright violation is **piracy** in part because copyright infringement is a form of theft. This idea is hotly debated on the Internet because copying a work does not deprive the copyright owner of the original work. However, it does deprive the owner of the economic value of that work as well as control of the copies. In the Supreme Court case *MGM v. Grokster* (2005), Justice Stephen Breyer stated that "Deliberate unlawful copying is no less an unlawful taking of property than garden-variety theft."[25] Another point of contention regarding piracy is its definition. Some definitions state that it involves the reproduction *and* distribution of copyrighted material without the copyright owner's permission. More restrictive definitions state that the material only must be copied to constitute piracy. We

**piracy** In computer usage, the copying and distribution of copyrighted information without the owner's permission.

will use the definition that includes both reproduction and distribution since those functions violate the most critical economic aspects of copyright: the right to reproduce material and the profit that derives from distributing the material to a market.

Although the piracy of intellectual property is common throughout the world, it is especially problematic in Asia where copyright law is not enforced as stringently as it is in Western nations. Film, music, and software piracy is a large-scale, profitable business in several Asian countries; the goods are often sold openly in public markets. For example, in 2008, the Motion Picture Association (MPA), which pursues international film piracy, stated that its "Operation Blackout" investigation in Asia netted the arrest of 675 suspects as well as more than 2.6 million optical discs and 1,200 optical disc burners, most of which were seized in China and the Philippines. The MPA estimates that piracy worldwide cost its studios $6.1 billion in 2005.[26] In 2007, the United States filed World Trade Organization complaints against China, stating that piracy levels in China "remain unacceptably high."[27]

In the United States, several organizations, including federal agencies, strive to uphold copyright law. The Recording Industry Association of America (RIAA), the Motion Picture Association of America (MPAA), and the Business Software Alliance (BSA) are trade groups that pursue copyright infringement for their member companies, occasionally bringing civil cases against suspected copyright violators.

Although copyright infringement is illegal, state, federal, and local agencies usually do not pursue violators unless the case is high-profile and involves a large-scale piracy operation. The reasons for this include the difficulty of proving cases and catching individuals in the act of copyright infringement, as well as allocation of scarce police resources. The police simply cannot afford to pursue every individual who violates copyright law. Instead, the police focus on busting larger, professionalized shops, such as one in Philadelphia in 2007, which was a streamlined copying operation with more than 8,000 CDs and DVDs.[28] However, it is mostly up to the industries to protect their copyrights. Industry organizations, such as the MPAA and RIAA, typically assist police with their investigations, with industry representatives setting up the investigation and the police making arrests when enough evidence has been collected.[29]

## Child Pornography

The Internet has made child pornography easier to distribute and obtain and more difficult to control. In the mid-1980s, before Internet usage became common, law enforcement felt confident that child pornography had almost been stamped out. According to the U.S. Department of Justice, "Child pornographers had become lonely and hunted individuals."[30] Because the child pornography trade involved the use of tangible photographs, magazines, and videotapes, it was fairly easy to trace the source of the pornographic materials, which were expensive to produce and distribute. The Internet made the transmission of electronic material easy, fast, and anonymous, reviving what had been a fading criminal offense.

It is important to note that, like other computer network offenses, the distribution of child pornography is an old offense. Although the Internet augmented the trade in child pornography, child pornography was not invented on the Internet. The Internet is simply a tool that child pornographers use to further their antisocial behavior, much as photography was in the 19th century.[31] More than 200 child pornography magazines were being sold in the United States by 1977.[32]

However, because the idea of children as a protected class with its own rights and justice system is a relatively modern American concept, the offense of exploiting children sexually is also relatively new. Until the 1880s in the United States, girls as young as 10 years old could consent to sexual activity.[33] As late as 1977, only two states specifically banned the use of children in obscene material, and the first federal child pornography law was passed in 1978. Laws specifying computers and child pornography were not passed in the United States until 1988.[34] Because of the international nature of the Internet, the trade in pornographic material crosses jurisdictions as well as international boundaries. It is a problem many nations must deal with. To help define the scope of online child pornography, the Australian government has compiled a useful typology of pornographers.

- *Browser.* This Internet user happens upon pornography accidentally but decides to keep the material.

- *Private fantasy.* A computer user creates pornographic material for private use and stores the material on electronic media but does not distribute the material via a computer network.

- *Trawler.* This person actively seeks child pornography using openly available Web browsers using little to no security.

- *Non-secure collector.* This person actively seeks material through peer-to-peer networks, which are somewhat more secure.

- *Secure collector.* This individual actively seeks material through secure networks only. Some networks require that members submit a certain number of images to join. In this way, all the network's members take responsibility for the network's activities.

- *Groomer.* A groomer pursues online relationships with children with the intent to establish either a virtual or physical sexual relationship.

- *Physical abuser.* This person physically abuses a child, with pornography being used to augment the abuse in some way (possibly by frightening or trying to seduce the child). The abuse might be recorded for the personal use of the abuser.

- *Producer.* A producer physically abuses a child, records the abuse, then distributes the material.

- *Distributor.* This person might be more interested in the business of child pornography rather than the material or actual activity. In that case, the distribution of pornographic material is solely an avenue to make money. However, this does not preclude some distributors from any of the above categories as well.[35]

Most major investigations of Internet child pornography require the cooperation of law enforcement agencies in multiple nations or jurisdictions. In one incident, Christopher Neil, a Canadian man living in South Korea, posted on the Internet photographs of himself sexually abusing several Vietnamese and Cambodian children. Neil had digitally scrambled his face in the photos to hide his identity. German police discovered the photos and unscrambled them to reveal Neil's face. Interpol then issued a bulletin on the Internet asking anyone who knew the man to come forward. According to Interpol, 350 people responded, with five sources from three continents identifying Neil, who was then arrested in Thailand.[36]

As is the case with many types of crime, large law enforcement agencies will have specialized departments, whereas small agencies will not. In small agencies, responsibility for investigating Internet child pornography often falls to officers who do not specialize in this type of crime. However, one study found that more than half of Internet child pornography arrests were made by agencies that did not specialize in such investigations.[37] Although several federal law enforcement and legal agencies prosecute child pornography, the FBI's Innocent Images National Initiative focuses specifically on electronic exploitation through investigation, enforcement of child pornography laws, and the search for and rescue of child victims.[38]

Federal law treats child pornography much more stringently than it does adult pornography. Currently, the following standards apply to all forms of child pornography.

- A child is anyone under the age of 18.
- The definition of child pornography includes any sexually explicit behavior, not just obscene behavior or nudity. In *United States v. Knox* (1993), a man was convicted for possessing images that focused on the clothed genital areas of young girls.[39]
- Possession, production, and distribution of child pornography are criminal offenses. Electronic images have only to be accessed, not necessarily printed, saved to digital media, or otherwise retained to be considered a criminal offense.[40]

The Internet has introduced several new challenges to the control of child pornography. According to the Department of Justice, these include the following.

- The Internet's decentralized structure, which makes it very difficult to track offenders.
- International jurisdictional issues that require cooperation between the criminal justice systems of several countries, as well as some countries' lack of regulation or vastly different legislation. For example, the age of consent in some countries might be far lower than 18 or even nonexistent.
- The advanced computer skills of some offenders, which can make them very difficult to catch and prosecute, as well as the increasing sophistication of Internet applications and security.
- The high volume of Internet traffic, which decreases the chance of any individual offender being caught.[41]

### Identity Theft

**Identity theft,** one of the fastest growing offenses in the United States, occurs when one party steals the information required to legally pose as another party.[42] This information typically includes full names, home addresses, telephone numbers, financial account numbers, and, perhaps most important of all, social security numbers. Like the Internet-based offenses we have discussed, identity theft is an old offense, but the Internet has made it much easier to do (see Figure 14.2 for an FBI warning poster).

Increasingly, social security numbers are required to participate in anything connected to the public network, that is,

▼ A Thai court convicted Canadian school teacher Christopher Neil of child molestation in 2008 and sentenced him to nine years in prison.

**identity theft** The taking of critical personal information that comprises an individual's legal person.

## Figure 14.2    FBI Internet Safety Alert Poster

**This FBI poster warns Internet users about various identity theft scams.**

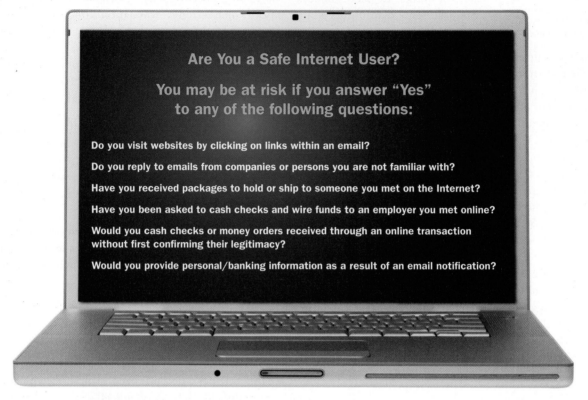

*Source*: Internet Crime Complaint Center, http://www.ic3.gov/media/IC3-Poster.pdf.

to get a job, enroll in college, collect benefits, open bank accounts, get a loan, apply for a credit card, and so on. In some ways, a social security number has become as necessary as a name. Thieves are especially attracted to social security numbers because any institution that deals with money requires them to establish individual identity. With a social security number, a person can set up accounts, move money, receive money, and spend money. Using the Internet, the person can do all of these tasks without leaving home. Using a fairly sketchy set of personal information, a skilled identity thief can steal thousands of dollars before a victim even knows what has happened. Although it can be easy for a thief to steal an identity, it can be very difficult for a victim to get that identity back. According to the FTC, most victims spent about four hours getting the problem straightened out. However, 10 percent of victims spent at least 55 hours, and 5 percent of victims spent at least 130 hours.[43]

A common method of identity theft via the Internet is "phishing," which involves tricking a victim into revealing personal information. On the Internet, phishing is usually carried out by sending out thousands (if not millions) of e-mails that appear to be from banks or other financial institutions. Although only a small percentage of victims will respond to these e-mails (hence, the term *phishing*), enough people usually respond to make the phishing expedition

worthwhile. E-mails will often ask victims to go to a website, which is made up to look like the institution's real website, and enter the information asked for. The identity thieves then collect this information into a database and sell or use it to victimize the person immediately.

The FTC and the FBI typically handle identity theft complaints.[44] Most victims notify the local police, but in 2009 nearly 30 percent did not (see Figure 14.3). The Identity Theft and Assumption Deterrence Act of 1998 makes identity theft a federal crime. Under this law, identity theft takes place when someone "knowingly transfers, possesses or uses, without lawful authority, a means of identification of another person with the intent to commit, or to aid or abet, or in connection with, any unlawful activity that constitutes a violation of federal law, or that constitutes a felony under any applicable state or local law." The 2004 Identity Theft Penalty Enhancement Act established for aggravated identity theft a mandatory two-year minimum sentence to be served in addition to any other sentence.[45]

### E-mail Scams

According to the Internet Crime Complaint Center, e-mail was the Internet application used in 73.6 percent of Internet fraud cases that it referred to other law enforcement agencies.[46] Like street con games, e-mail scams often rely on per-

## Figure 14.3    Consumer Sentinel Network Identity Theft Complaints Law Enforcement Contact, January 1–December 31, 2009

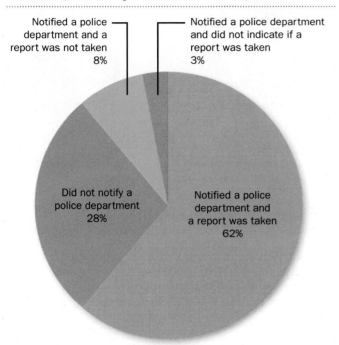

Notified a police department and a report was not taken 8%

Notified a police department and did not indicate if a report was taken 3%

Did not notify a police department 28%

Notified a police department and a report was taken 62%

*Source:* Federal Trade Commission, *Consumer Sentinel Network Databook for January–December 2009* (Washington, DC: Federal Trade Commission, 2010), 12, http://www.ftc.gov/sentinel/reports/sentinel-annual-reports/sentinel-cy2009.pdf.

such as letterhead stationery, and bank names and account numbers.

As the scam progresses, the victim continues to be asked for money, often in increasing amounts, to pay for a variety of expenses. This scam takes advantage of the victims' greed and their feeling that because they have already invested money in the project, they should continue to send money to protect that investment.[48] These scams can be very well planned and intricate, sometimes involving faxes, forged documents, phone calls, even personal visits from foreign "officials." Once the perpetrators believe that they have drained all the money possible from a victim, the communications dry up, and the perpetrators vanish.

As with identity theft, investigations, depending on the exact type of offense, often involve the Internet Crime Complaint Center, Department of Justice, the FBI, the U.S Postal Inspection Service, the U.S Secret Service, the FTC, and state and local agencies. Complaints filed at the Internet Crime Complaint Center website are referred to the appropriate federal, state, local, or international law enforcement or regulatory agencies for investigation.

## Think about it

### Remember

List the characteristics of computer network crime.

### Apply

Demonstrate the methods that computer system administrators use to combat problems caused by spam.

### Analyze

Investigate how social engineering exploits human mistakes.

### Evaluate

Evaluate the effects of computer viruses and worms.

sonal contact with victims to convince them to hand over money or personal information. Like identity theft scams, the perpetrators only have to fool a small percentage of the thousands of people they target with messages.

Many e-mail scams are actually very old street scams. According to the United States Computer Emergency Readiness Team, the most common ones include bogus business opportunities, communications from false IRS and bank officials, health and diet scams, discount software offers, and, perhaps the most infamous, 419 or Nigerian letter scams.[47] Because it is so common, we will take a closer look at the 419 scam.

The Nigerian Letter Scam/419 scam is so called because the e-mails overwhelmingly originate from Nigeria. The designation "419" refers to the violation of Section 419 of the Nigerian Criminal Code. Scammers, who usually purport to be government officials or relatives of government officials, send e-mails stating that they must move a very large amount of money out of Nigeria. The tone of the e-mails is usually very friendly and plaintive, begging the recipient for help. The scam works by offering the victim a share of the money that is to be moved out of Nigeria in exchange for helping with the deal. The target is asked only to pay what often seems like reasonable amounts of money to bribe officials, pay legal fees, and open accounts in foreign banks. Victims are also encouraged to send personal information,

## Information Technology in the Criminal Justice System

Like many other aspects of society, the criminal justice system is saturated with technology. Sophisticated lethal and less-than-lethal weapons, armor, computers, and tracking and communications devices are now used routinely by law enforcement, the courts, and

**LO3:**

**Analyze** how the criminal justice system uses technology.

correctional facilities. The type of technology that arguably has advanced criminal justice work the most—and is also the most controversial in terms of personal privacy—is information technology. Because information technology has such profound implications for the criminal justice system and its relationship with the rest of society, we will concentrate our discussion on this form of technology.

The criminal justice system uses information technology to collect and share information on criminal offenders and thus provide better security for citizens. For instance, the purpose of closed-circuit cameras is to catch lawbreakers in the act with the greater purpose of discouraging people from breaking the law at all, thus making everyone more secure. The same philosophy lies behind other forms of information technology: If people know they are being watched, that their movements are being tracked, and that every transgression of the law will be entered into a "permanent record" of sorts, then they will be less likely to break the law. Of course, this means that a lot of information is being recorded about a lot of citizens, from litterbugs to serial killers, and that many people who have broken no law are being watched without their knowledge or consent.

▲ Electronic monitoring is the surveillance of individuals by electronic means. Store security cameras are a common method of electronic monitoring.

## Technology for Surveillance and Short-Term Tracking

Surveillance technology includes cameras, electronic monitoring via ankle bracelets, radio frequency identification tags, and the relatively low-tech telephone. Cameras and telephones are probably the devices used most often, followed by ankle bracelets. In the future, advances in technology may produce even smaller devices feasible for keeping up with probationers, parolees, and offenders deemed to be more appropriate for house arrest than incarceration.

### Cameras

Cameras were first used as surveillance devices in 1942 when German engineer Walter Bruch designed a system to monitor the launch of missiles.[49] Since then, various types of cameras have been developed to keep an eye on both people and things. The high cost of the technology and the low quality of the images kept the use of surveillance cameras relatively rare—large retailers that could afford the expense used closed-circuit cameras to protect their merchandise from shoplifters—until the 1980s when the price of electronics began to drop and their sophistication began to rise.[50] Surveillance cameras became commonplace in the 1990s to watch not only retail and industrial situations, but also convenience stores, local banks, street corners, school buses, and the traffic whizzing down the highway.[51] By 2000, high-quality security cameras were being trained on anything by just about anybody and the images sent to the Internet.

Although those concerned about privacy and civil liberties continue to question the use of surveillance cameras in public places, the general public seems to have accepted their use and even welcomed it in some situations. Much of the funding for surveillance cameras comes from the Department of Homeland Security for the purpose of spotting potential terrorist activity. For example, in 2008, surveillance cameras were part of a $4.6 million federal grant that went to nine Boston, Massachusetts, communities.[52]

Britain, the country that uses the most surveillance cameras, had more than 4 million surveillance cameras as of 2008, or one camera for every 14 citizens.[53] Cameras continue to be installed with the stated purpose of controlling crime and terrorism, but critics say they simply are not effective. In 2008, a senior London police detective pronounced the use of surveillance cameras to control crime "an utter fiasco," stating that footage had been used to solve only 3 percent of London's street robberies and that the cameras did not scare offenders.[54]

As of 2008, various agencies in New York City, Chicago, and Los Angeles had installed thousands of public surveillance cameras, and Washington, DC, expanded its use of cameras. However, the fact that the cameras typically are not centrally controlled is problematic according to some critics. For example, the city of Los Angeles has networks at Los Angeles International Airport, the port, and city buildings, while the Los Angeles Department of Transportation and the Los Angeles Police Department each operate their own separate networks. Meanwhile, Washington, DC, is working on centralizing its camera system.[55] The debate about whether surveillance cameras reduce crime continues with few conclusions; some police studies report that the cameras reduce crime, other critical studies claim that they do not.[56] However, with terrorism still a national threat and the federal government continuing to provide millions of dollars in funding for surveillance systems, jurisdictions will probably continue to install surveillance camera networks.

## Electronic Monitoring

**Electronic monitoring** refers to the surveillance of individuals by electronic means. The first personal electronic monitoring device was developed in the 1960s by Dr. Ralph Schwitzgebel and other researchers at Harvard's Science Committee on Psychological Experimentation. Offenders, mental patients, and other researchers tested Schwitzgebel's experimental device between 1964 and 1970, which worked by sending signals to "repeater stations" installed throughout the community. Although the device was patented in 1969, the expense of electronic monitoring discouraged its use to track offenders until the 1980s.[57]

Currently, the most commonly used method of electronically monitoring parolees and probationers is by way of an electronic device that is strapped to the ankle. These devices are called "electronic tethers," "electronic monitoring systems," or more typically, "ankle bracelets." Many electronic monitoring systems work by radio frequency, although wireless **global positioning systems** (GPS)—networks of satellites that provide accurate geographic position and time information—are becoming more common. As of 2008, at least one ankle bracelet on the market combined a GPS transmitter, cell phone, computer processing chip, and an alarm in a device that not only monitored the wearer's exact location, but allowed communication between the tracker and the wearer (see Figure 14.4 for a sketch of how these systems work).[58] Ankle bracelets send signals that identify the individual wearer and alert the monitoring center if the device is tampered with or removed. Offenders usually pay the costs of their monitoring, which can be from $5 to $15 a day. The most common use of electronic monitoring is by states for offenders on probation.[59]

## Figure **14.4**  Electronic Monitoring of Offenders Using Global Positioning

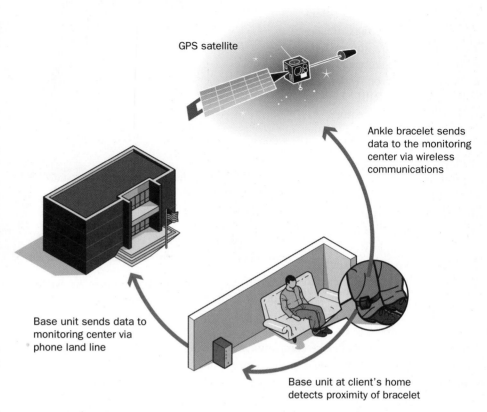

GPS satellite

Ankle bracelet sends data to the monitoring center via wireless communications

Base unit sends data to monitoring center via phone land line

Base unit at client's home detects proximity of bracelet

Although electronic monitoring has its critics, one four-year study of nearly 75,000 offenders on home confinement found that the devices "significantly reduce[d] the likelihood of technical violations, reoffending, and absconding."[60] Critics of electronic monitoring say that it does nothing to rehabilitate offenders, assist their socialization, or facilitate their return to society. However, proponents of electronic monitoring say that its purpose is punitive and designed to be harsher than traditional parole/probation, yet less restrictive than incarceration. The inventor of electronic monitoring, Ralph Schwitzgebel, also criticizes its widespread use for offenders. Schwitzgebel states that the relatively low recidivism rate of those on electronic monitoring can be attributed to the likelihood that offenders deemed safe enough to live outside prison walls are less likely to break the law again. Schwitzgebel and other critics of electronic monitoring also question the devices' effect of **net-widening,** measures that draw more offenders and individuals in the criminal justice system or more deeply involve those within the system, claiming that devices are being used for low-risk offenders who otherwise would have been placed on regular probation.[61]

**electronic monitoring**  The surveillance of individuals via electronic means.

**global positioning system (GPS)**  A network of satellites that provides accurate geographic position and time information.

**net-widening**  Measures that involve more offenders and individuals in the criminal justice system or more deeply involve those already within the system.

## RFID Tags

One of the latest technological additions to the criminal justice system, **radio frequency identification (RFID) tags** are devices that transmit information embedded in the tag via radio to a special receiver or reader. Retailers have used RFID tags for years to monitor inventory. Although RFID tags are a common sight—they are usually found in the form of a thick, plastic tag on a piece of merchandise—many people do not know exactly what they are. RFID tags are also used on "contactless" credit cards, which users simply wave over a card reader to pay for a purchase. RFID chips have been implanted in pets for several years, and it is now possible to implant RFID chips in human beings. In 2007,

▲ RFID tags transmit data via radio frequency and are an especially common sight in clothing stores seeking to protect their wares.

two employees of a surveillance company called CityWatcher .com had RFID chips implanted in their arms. The company stated that the chips restricted the employees' access to sensitive data held at the company.[62]

Prisons throughout the world, including the United States, have been experimenting with RFID tags for inmates and guards. For example, in 2007, the Minnesota Department of Corrections began using a system that detects such activities as when an inmate ventures too close to a fence or two gang leaders get too close to each other. Prison administrators know exactly who is doing what because the tags also transmit the complete histories and identities of the inmates. The guards also have RFID devices that signal their exact location and identities; if trouble breaks out, administrators can locate the guards and direct their activities accordingly.[63]

The tracking of citizens is moving at a quicker pace in other countries, especially China. In 2007, the city of Shenzhen began tracking its 12.4 million residents by issuing RFID cards containing each resident's name, address, work history, education, religion, ethnicity, police record, medical insurance status, landlord's phone number, and reproductive history. The Chinese government plans to issue the cards to all residents of large cities to facilitate police work and better control the expanding population.[64]

## Telephones

Parole and probation officers have been using the telephone for decades to keep up with their clients. In fact, the tele-

phone has been used to keep track of probationers and parolees for so long that it is often overlooked as a significant technological development. Basically, officers will call their clients' homes or workplaces to make sure that they are where they are supposed to be. However, with the advent of cellular telephones and call forwarding, officers can now never be sure if clients are at home or elsewhere. Therefore, the future of parole and probation supervision rests with GPS and electronic monitoring, which can provide information about clients' exact locations at any time.

Some electronic monitoring equipment still depends on the telephone: Radio-frequency ankle bracelets communicate with an electronic base unit that is connected to the wearer's land-line home telephone. For example, the ankle bracelet that socialite Paris Hilton wore when she was on house arrest in 2007 had a range of up to 4,000 square feet and allowed her to spend up to 30 minutes outside her home. Any violation of the bracelet's range would signal its base unit, which would then call the monitoring system.[65] Now being developed are GPS systems that use cell phone technology not only to track the wearer, but also to allow two-way communications so that the parole/probation officer can converse with the client at any time.

## Technology for Identification and Long-Term Tracking

Although some devices described in the preceding section could also be listed here, technology for identification and long-term tracking focuses on identifying people and tracking them throughout their lives rather than just a short period of time, such as a few months or years on parole or probation. Technologies for these purposes include com-

**radio frequency identification (RFID) tags** Devices that transmit information embedded in the tag via radio to a special receiver or reader.

puter databases and biometrics, both of which are used in sectors other than the criminal justice system, such as private security, marketing, and retail. This variety of uses heightens concerns about privacy and information sharing. For example, there are concerns that biometrics information, such as fingerprints taken by private companies for security purposes, could be used by the state in criminal investigations. Because these technologies are so new, there are few or no laws specifying the handling and jurisdiction of this information.

## Databases

A computer **database** is an organized set of information that is kept on computer. The concept of the database is decades old—old library card catalogs are databases, as are telephone books and other organized repositories of information. The advantage of a computer database is the volume of information that it can hold and the ease with which users can search and collate that information. Although we are accustomed to the idea of vast computer databases, it is important to understand implications they have not only for the criminal justice system, but also for individual privacy.

Before computer databases, the ease of organizing and accessing information was linked to its volume. Because information was usually recorded in writing on paper, a small amount of information was easier to access than a large amount. Imagine wading through the New York City telephone book looking for someone named "Smith." Computer databases solved this problem. Typing the name "Smith" into a digitized New York City phonebook, along with a few other details, makes it a lot easier to find the Smith you are looking for. The same goes for criminal offenders, inmates, suspects, and arrestees. Information that is recorded about these individuals is not only far more easily accessed than it was a few decades ago, it is also accessed by more people. As an exercise, find the website for your state's department of corrections. Chances are that website has an "inmate search" or an "inmate locator" that provides personal details about specific prison inmates, their offenses, and often even their photographs. There are also several online databases designed to search only for sex offenders. Before computer databases and the Internet, this information was not easily available to the public. Now, anyone with a computer and an online connection can find it.

Some of the most controversial types of crime-related databases are those that contain samples of human DNA. DNA, the molecule that transmits genetic information, is present in all human tissue, including blood, bone, hair, and saliva. Human beings differ by only one-tenth of a single percent of DNA, so forensic scientists use those specific bits of DNA to create genetic profiles of individuals.[66] DNA databases contain this information and make it easily searchable.

The nation's premier criminal DNA databases are the FBI's CODIS (Combined DNA Index System) and NDIS (National DNA Index System). NDIS is a database of DNA profile records provided by state criminal justice agencies, and CODIS is the information-processing and telecommunication system that supports NDIS.[67] CODIS comprises the entire system of DNA databases: the National DNA Index System, the State DNA Index System, and the Local DNA Index System.[68] As of 2008, NDIS contained more than 6,031,000 offender profiles and 225,400 forensic profiles.[69] The larger CODIS contains DNA profiles of convicted offenders, arrestees, missing persons, unidentified human remains, and biological relatives of missing persons, as well as DNA collected from crime scenes.[70]

DNA databases are controversial because of concerns about accuracy and privacy. Critics of DNA collection fear that the information might eventually be used for something other than its original purpose of identifying criminal offenders or victims. Others fear that the DNA of people who have broken no laws might be collected and permanently retained. Britain has been collecting DNA on its citizens, some of whom have broken no laws, for years. Currently, Great Britain has the world's largest DNA database with 4.5 million genetic profiles.[71]

Another criticism is that DNA profiles are not as accurate as once thought. In 2001, an Arizona state crime laboratory analyst found that the DNA between two unrelated people can be remarkably similar. In one case, the DNA of two unrelated felons was found to match at 9 of 13 locations on the chromosomes, the odds of which the FBI had calculated at 1 in 113 billion. At that time, states compared only nine locations (they now attempt to compare 13 locations); this means that each of those felons could have been convicted of the other's offenses based on DNA evidence.[72]

## Biometrics

**Biometrics** are methods used to verify identity based on physiological or behavioral characteristics, such as iris or retinal scans, facial recognition, hand/finger characteristics, voice identification, or signatures. The National Institute of Justice and Department of Defense began developing biometrics for criminal justice purposes in 2000; however, like other methods of surveillance and identification, biometrics is older than you might think.[73] In 1879, French police inspector Alphonse Bertillon proposed a system of body measurements to identify repeat offenders; by 1896, British scholars began the development of the fingerprint classification system, an early form of biometrics.[74]

Currently, the primary criminal justice use for biometrics is to maintain security in prisons and jails. The use of biometrics identification for criminal justice purposes is still under

---

| **database** An organized set of information.

| **biometrics** The methods used to verify identity based on physiological or behavioral characteristics, such as iris or retinal scans, facial recognition, hand/finger characteristics, voice identification, or signatures.

development. It is likely that biometrics will be combined with other technologies, such as databases and electronic monitoring, to identify and track offenders inside institutions and out. In 2008, the FBI began developing the Next Generation Identification system, a biometric expansion of the Integrated Automated Fingerprint Identification System. Along with fingerprints, the system would also use facial and iris imaging, as well as palm prints, to identify individuals.[75]

# Think about it

## Understand

> Describe how DNA is used in criminal justice databases.

## Analyze

> Examine the arguments that extensive criminal justice databases are a threat to privacy.

## Evaluate

> Assess how effective tracking technology is at reducing or preventing crime.

# Privacy, Security, and the Future

**Surveillance** is systematic, institutionalized encroachment into individual privacy that is often done in secret.[76] The most common form of government surveillance is something that has been called *dataveillance,* or "the systematic use of personal data systems in the investigation or monitoring of the actions or communications of one or more persons."[77] Governments—which have always conducted dataveillance, collecting information on births, deaths, and marriages, as well as data for taxes, voter registration, social services, and education—are increasingly conducting dataveillance via information technology.[78] Although many Americans, maybe even most, expect the government to collect such information, there is concern about the government's ability to keep it safe and private, as well as about how the government will use such information. For example, such data, when combined with other forms of surveillance and dataveillance, such as criminal records, video surveillance, and communications surveillance, could be used to build a comprehensive database on citizens. In some

## LO4:

**Discuss** the reasons for the tension between privacy and security.

**surveillance** Systematic, institutionalized, usually secret encroachment into individual privacy.

cases, however, citizens may not even know the information has been collected.

A current example of this involves the use of wireless devices, specifically cell phones, which may be used to send voice or text messages, or photographs. Cell phones may also be used to establish their users' locations. In an investigation of a 2008 bank robbery, the FBI monitored, without a warrant, the locations of about 180 cell phones. The agency ordered nine telephone companies to provide "all cell site tracking data and cell site locator information for all incoming and outgoing calls to and from the target numbers." Two men were eventually arrested for the robbery, but, as of 2010, the case was at risk of being dismissed because the evidence had been obtained without a warrant. According to the American Civil Liberties Union (ACLU), the FBI's "dragnet" order, in an effort to narrow the search to the suspects, violated the privacy rights of Americans who were not suspected of any criminal offense.[79] According to an ACLU brief, "Cell site location information is protected by the Fourth Amendment because individuals have a reasonable expectation of privacy in their location and movement information, which can reveal intimate details of their lives—not only their presences in protected locations like their home, but their doctors' visits, shopping habits, attendance at church, or association with others."[80]

Despite the concerns about security, however, so-called warrantless wiretapping faces an uphill battle in the courts. In March 2010, a federal judge ruled that the National Security Agency (NSA) in 2004 illegally intercepted the phone calls of an Islamic charity and two of its lawyers. This incident was part of a program—which was secretly authorized by President George W. Bush after the September 11 attacks and not made public until 2005—that allowed the NSA to monitor without a warrant the international e-mails and phone calls of people inside the United States. The Bush administration argued that its wartime powers allowed the president to bypass the 1978 Foreign Intelligence Surveillance Act (FISA), which set down the rules for the surveillance of people in the United States in order to collect intelligence related to foreign powers. The act was rewritten in 2008 to more closely match the Bush administration's secret program. The program has continued under the administration of President Barack Obama, which has claimed that the NSA's lapses in obeying FISA have been corrected.[81]

Governments will continue to use technology to investigate and watch criminal suspects, and, since the law cannot keep up with the capabilities of technology, the way that governments are allowed to use technology to conduct surveillance will continue to be tested in the courts. The important questions are: How much information can the government collect? How can it be legally collected? Whose information can we collect?

These are important questions. Unfortunately, since suspects look a lot like non-suspects, watching suspects means watching everyone else, too. To date, there is no technology that conducts surveillance only on lawbreakers or those who seek to break the law. As we saw in the case of the bank robbers, law enforcement must sift through a lot of data on a given population to collect information on the "bad guys." As technology makes this easier, it is becoming apparent that personal privacy and security are in a delicate balance in which having more of one means having less of the other. It is up to the citizens to decide which they prefer.

The tension between privacy and security has always been with us. It is difficult to predict how the relationship between these two areas will change, but we do know that it will be different than it is now. We must consider this tension between privacy and security, so we must be aware of several key issues.

- *Privacy is not what it used to be.* Americans have voluntarily given up much of what they used to consider private. For the ease of ordering products on the Internet, buying items on eBay, or doing online banking, much information about individual citizens is now stored on databases. Although these databases are supposedly secure, they are shared by many organizations and government agencies. In many ways, we have sacrificed our privacy and financial security to ease commerce.

- *Technology changes everything.* While our concept of privacy was developing over the course of several decades, technology was changing as well. The technology in use today is very different than it was in the past or will be tomorrow. Today's rapidly changing technology forces us to reconsider our laws, habits, and ideas of privacy. Technology has become so sophisticated it has outstripped our ability to control what information about us remains private and secure.

- *Security is now a global concern.* Not only must we be concerned about thieves taking our mail from our mailboxes, we now are faced with the prospect of individuals in distant countries stealing our identities and spending our money without our being able to seek legal recourse in U.S. courts. In addition, governments routinely read our e-mails and use networked databases to monitor our travels, financial dealings, correspondence, and medical records.

- *Things will continue to change.* We cannot predict the future relationship between privacy and security. As governments and corporations develop new ways to track citizens and target consumers, more and more information about each of us will be available to a wider variety of people, agencies, and corporations that we would prefer not know very much about us. The information genie is out of the bottle and will be difficult to put back in.

- *Young people have different ideas about privacy.* Many teenagers and young adults who grew up with the Internet and the World Wide Web are very comfortable with the technology, to the point that they give little thought to how their private information is viewed or by whom. Many young people place their personal information on social networking websites and expect that information to be available only to their friends and families. The problem is that many of the personal items young people post online are likely to remain there practically forever. Even if the social networking website is taken offline, any information that was posted to the site is likely to remain in a database that may be searched and accessed from the Internet, possibly for decades to come. Some of these young people who apply for jobs at age 40 might be surprised to discover that a photograph of them doing a keg-stand (or something more embarrassing) at age 19 might be readily available online.

We must now reconcile the gap between privacy and security so that we can enjoy our freedoms and liberties and still protect ourselves from those who would harm us. This tenuous balancing act can be accomplished only by recognizing that the relationship between individuals, corporations, and governments is changing and by requiring that those who make our laws consider the values and ideals that the United States was founded upon.

# Think about it

## Understand

Express your opinion on how social networking websites may be problematic for personal privacy.

## Analyze

Examine the reasons for the tension between privacy and security.

# Summary

**LO1:** **Describe how technology has always been used to break the law.**

- Technology affects the criminal justice system in three major ways: It gives lawbreakers more opportunities; the criminal justice system uses technology in its processes, and technology alters our concepts of privacy.
- Crime has helped advance technology. Although some offenses now require more technological sophistication to commit, many offenses using technology are an extension of street crime.
- The Internet, which grew out of government projects between the end of World War II and the start of the Cold War, was developed in part to provide secure military and scientific communication for the U.S. government.

**LO2:** **Show why the Internet provides a nearly ideal network for crime.**

- The Internet is not a source of crime, but it provides another type of human network on which crime can occur.
- Because crime can occur on the Internet across several nations, the Internet has made jurisdiction problematic for the world's criminal justice agencies.
- Perpetrators of early forms of technology-based crime, for the most part, broke the law in pursuit of knowledge, such as how computer and telephone networks worked, rather than for profit.
- Much Internet crime involves the sale of information, including identities, software, and other forms

of intellectual property. Serious offenses include copyright infringement, piracy, child pornography, identity theft, and e-mail scams.

- Networks on which crime is common share some characteristics: They are large; they offer some degree of anonymity; they offer something of economic value or access to it; they are easy to access and use; and they are versatile.

**LO3:** **Analyze how the criminal justice system uses technology.**

- The criminal justice system uses information technology for surveillance and the tracking of offenders. These technologies include cameras, electronic monitoring (ankle bracelets), RFID tags, telephones, databases, and biometrics.

**LO4:** **Discuss the reasons for the tension between privacy and security.**

- Surveillance is systematic, institutionalized encroachment into individual privacy that is often done in secret.
- Governments will continue to use technology to investigate and watch criminal suspects.
- Having more personal privacy may mean having less security, and vice versa.
- The law cannot keep up with the capabilities of technology, so the way that governments are allowed to use technology to conduct surveillance will continue to be tested in the courts.

# Questions

1. What effects has technology had on criminology and the criminal justice system?
2. How has crime helped advance technology?
3. What technological networks besides the Internet have been used to break the law?
4. What are the origins of the Internet?
5. What makes crime on the Internet different from street crime?
6. What effect has the Internet had on jurisdiction?
7. What is hacking?
8. What do networks on which crime occurs have in common?
9. What are some of the most serious offenses that occur on the Internet?
10. What types of technologies does the criminal justice system use and for what purposes?
11. What is surveillance?

# Glossary

**adolescent limited** Moffitt's term to describe antisocial behavior that is restricted to the teenage years.

**aggression** An offensive action; psychological or physical encroachment without the consent of the other party.

**anomie** The erosion of standards resulting from a lack of social control and values that leads to social instability.

**antisocial** Following standards of behavior intended to harm society and individuals.

**antisocial personality disorder** A mental disorder characterized by a pattern of disregard for the rights of others, as well as impulsive, violent, and aggressive behavior without guilt.

**antisocial potential** Farrington's term to describe an individual's likelihood of breaking the law by engaging in antisocial behavior.

**arson** The deliberate setting of fires.

**assault** The criminal offense of attempting to inflict immediate bodily harm or making another person fear that such harm is imminent.

**atavism** The idea that some people are born before progressing through all the evolutionary stages to become fully human.

**battery** Physical contact with the intent to do harm.

**behaviorism** A perspective that states that environment and learning determine how individuals behave.

**biocriminology** The search for the causes of antisocial behavior within the brain or body.

**biometrics** The methods used to verify identity based on physiological or behavioral characteristics, such is iris or retinal scans, facial recognition,

hand/finger characteristics, voice identification, or signatures.

**black market** A business that involves the illegal buying and/or selling of goods and/or currency.

**body-type theory** The idea that the shape of the body directly predicts the propensity for criminal offending.

**bourgeoisie** In Marxism, the owners of the means of production.

**bribery** The offense of giving money or valuables to influence public officials or employees of business competitors.

**burglary** The unlawful entry of a structure with the intent to commit a felony or theft.

**capital murder** A murder offense that is punishable by death. Sometimes called a "capital offense."

**civil law** Law that is related to private rights and disputes between citizens.

**class** A group defined by a particular social, economic, and educational status.

**classical school of criminology** A set of ideas that focuses on deterrence and considers crime to be the result of offenders' free will.

**classical strain theory** The idea that people who experience anger and frustration when they cannot achieve cultural goals through legitimate means try to achieve these goals through illegitimate means.

**clearance** The closure of an offense by either arrest or other means.

**cognition** The act of thinking and perceiving.

**cognitive psychology** The study of memory, language processing, perception, problem solving, thinking, and other mental processes.

**cohort** A group of people who share statistical or demographic characteristics.

**collective efficacy** The measure of the amount of informal social control and social cohesion, or trust, in a community.

**concentric zone theory** The idea that geographical areas radiate out from an expanding urban center and that each area has certain, dominant social attitudes.

**conflict theory** A set of criminological theories based on the philosophy of Karl Marx that holds that antisocial behavior stems from class conflict and social and economic inequality.

**containment theory** The idea that everyone has internal and external structures that hold them within the larger social structure.

**control theories of crime** A perspective that questions why most people do not break the law.

**corporate crime** An offense committed in the name of a business for monetary profit or to prevent monetary loss.

**corporate personhood** The legal treatment of a corporation as a person.

**crime rate** The number of offenses divided by the population, usually expressed as a rate of offenses per 100,000 people.

**criminal law** Legal statutes that guide the prosecution and definition of crime.

**criminology** The study of the making of laws, the breaking of laws, and the social reaction to the breaking of laws.

**critical race theory** A set of legalistic perspectives that hold that racial inequity is so ingrained in society it is propagated through legal and social discourse.

**critical theory** Criminological perspectives that describe and critique the social structure and seek solutions to the problems of crime and criminal justice.

**cross-sectional survey** Research in which different individuals are studied during each research period.

**cultural criminology** Examines how social ideas, values, and media reflect and produce antisocial behavior.

**dark figure of crime** A term that describes criminal offenses that are unreported to law enforcement officials and never recorded.

**database** An organized set of information.

**decriminalization** The lessening or removal of penalties for acts previously subject to criminal prosecution, arrest, and incarceration.

**demonology** An ancient perspective of crime that considers antisocial behavior as caused by an evil entity who lives inside an individual and overtakes his or her personality.

**deterrence** The idea that punishment for an offense will prevent that offender and others from further breaking the law.

**deterrence theory** The concept that punishment prevents more crime from occurring.

**differential association theory** Sutherland's idea that offenders learn crime from each other.

**differential reinforcement** The encouragement of one behavior instead of another.

**disintegrative shaming** Braithwaite's term to describe punishment that does not repair the harm done by the offender and offense and excludes the offender from society.

**ecoterrorism** Terrorist acts committed for the purpose of bringing attention to what the perpetrators believe are offenses against the natural environment or animals.

**electronic monitoring** The surveillance of individuals via electronic means.

**embezzlement** A form of theft in which an employee trusted with funds or goods diverts them to personal use.

**Enlightenment, the** A period during the 17th and 18th centuries in Europe in which great strides in philosophy and science were made.

**environmental crime** An offense that manipulates the surroundings such that human beings, animals, or plants that live within the area are harmed or unable to survive.

**eugenics** The concept that human beings can degenerate or improve through breeding.

**extinction** No reaction to a behavior.

**extortion** The offense of obtaining money, property, or information by threats, intimidation, or false claim to a position of authority.

**felony** A serious offense usually punishable by a prison sentence of more than one year or sometimes by life imprisonment or death.

**feminist criminology** A set of theories that hold that gender inequality is at the root of offenses in which women are the victims or offenders.

**fence** Refers to both the act of selling goods that are known to be stolen, as well as the person who sells goods that he or she knows to be stolen.

**focal concerns** Attitudes that the lower classes perpetuate as a part of the values and norms they believe are necessary for survival in their neighborhoods.

**forcible rape** Sexual intercourse performed without the victim's consent through force, threat of violence, or intimidation.

**fraud** A known misrepresentation or concealment in a transaction made with the intent to deceive another.

**gender** The social concept of how males and females should behave.

**general deterrence** The idea that punishing one person for an offense will provide an example to others not to engage in crime.

**general strain theory** Agnew's revision of classical strain theory identifies three major types of strain: failure to achieve goals, the loss of positive stimuli, and the gain of negative stimuli.

**globalism** The act of placing the interests of the world above those of individual nations.

**global positioning system (GPS)** A network of satellites that provides accurate geographic position and time information.

**guerrilla warfare** Military or paramilitary operations conducted within hostile territory by irregular forces.

**hacking** The unauthorized use of an information system or network.

**hedonistic calculus** A method proposed by Jeremy Bentham in which criminal offenders calculate the worth of breaking the law by estimating the positive consequences versus the possible negative consequences.

**heredity** The biological process in which genetic characteristics are inherited by one generation from the last.

**hierarchy rule** The FBI's practice of recording in the Uniform Crime Reports only the most serious offense in a set of offenses.

**homicide** The killing of one human being by another.

**human trafficking** The buying and selling of human beings.

**identity theft** The taking of critical personal information that comprises an individual's legal person.

**impulsivity** Action on a whim without consideration of the consequences.

**information technology** A general term used to describe devices and software that transmit, receive, and store data.

**institutional anomie** The condition that occurs when people's commitment to societal institutions becomes subservient to achieving the goal of wealth, which leads to the inability of the neglected institutions to control behavior.

**integrated theories** Perspectives that attempt to combine several different criminological theories in order to expand the focus on crime.

**intimate-partner violence** Abuse that occurs between two people in a spousal, domestic, or romantic relationship.

**IQ (intelligence quotient)** A measure of intelligence taken by dividing a person's mental age by chronological age, then multiplying by 100.

**jurisdiction** The right and power to interpret and apply the law; legal authority.

**labeling theory** The idea that society defines an individual, treating him or her differently, and the individual internalizes this definition and acts it out.

**larceny** *See* larceny-theft.

**larceny-theft** The unlawful taking of money or property from another person.

**learning theories of crime** A perspective that focuses on where and how offenders and delinquents find the tools, techniques, and expertise to break the law.

**legalization** The complete removal of legal proscriptions on acts that were previously illegal.

**life-course-persistent** Moffitt's term to describe antisocial behavior that continues throughout adulthood.

**life-course theory** A perspective that focuses on the development of antisocial behavior, risk factors at different ages, and the effect of life events on individual development.

**longitudinal** A type of survey that follows respondents throughout their lives or a significant proportion of their lives.

**lumpen-proletariat** In Marxism, the lowest social class, which was characterized by lack of skill, disorganization, and impoverishment.

**macro-victimization** The harm caused to masses of people by large-scale criminal offenses.

**manslaughter** The unlawful killing of another human being without criminal intent.

**mass murder** The killing of three or more people in a single incident.

**master status** A social standing that takes precedence over all others.

**mental disorder** Term used for a variety of psychological diseases and abnormalities. Mental illness.

**methodology** The rules and principles that govern how research is performed.

**micro-victmization** The harm caused to small groups of people or individuals by small-scale criminal offenses.

**murder** Willful homicide.

**National Crime Victimization Survey (NCVS)** A survey of a nationally representative sample of residences that collects information about crime from victims.

**National Incident-based Reporting System (NIBRS)** The Federal Bureau of Investigation's incident-based reporting system in which data are collected on every single offense.

**negative reinforcement** Ending an undesirable consequence as a means of reward.

**neoclassical criminology** A theoretical resurgence in classical criminology that emphasizes free will and deterrence and acknowledges some of the effects of positivism on decision-making.

**net-widening** Measures that involve more offenders and individuals in the criminal justice system or more deeply involve those already within the system.

**not guilty by reason of insanity (NGRI)** Generally, the acquittal of a defendant because he or she is determined to be insane.

**operant conditioning** A form of learning based on the positive or negative consequences of an action, behavior, or activity.

**opportunistic thief** Offenders who only steal items that are temporarily left unguarded and who do not consider themselves as lawbreakers.

**organized crime** A criminal organization that breaks the law for money and often uses violence to achieve its goals.

**pain of incarceration** The personal and social deprivations that are considered to be part of the purpose of incarceration.

**patriarchal** A social system that is controlled by males.

**peacemaking criminology** A criminological perspective that considers the social and personal effects of crime as a whole.

**phrenology** The practice of determining a person's character and mental faculties by measuring bumps and other features of an individual's skull.

**physiognomy** The practice of determining a person's character by facial characteristics.

**pilfering** Occurs when employees steal small amounts of money or inexpensive goods from an employer.

**piracy** In computer usage, the copying and distribution of copyrighted information without the owner's permission.

**political** Refers to the relationships of people in groups and their activities.

**Ponzi scheme** A financial offense in which the offender accepts money for investments from clients but uses it to pay returns to earlier investors instead of investing the money.

**pornography** Images, sounds, writing, or other communication designed to give sexual pleasure.

**positive reinforcement** Rewarding a successful action.

**positivist** The emphasis on observable facts.

**positivist school of criminology** A set of ideas that considers crime to be the result of external, observable forces that can be measured.

**postmodern criminology** A perspective that focuses on how language and traditional ideas affect how we define and perceive crime, the law, and society.

**power-control theory** A perspective that seeks to explain why males commit more offenses and delinquency than females.

**predicate crime** A criminal offense that is included in charging another offense and must be committed in order for the other offenses to be charged.

**premeditation** In reference to crime, the planning of a criminal act.

**primary deviance** Occurs when society reacts to an individual's actions, successfully labels that individual, and acts upon that label.

**professional thief** Offenders who attempt to make a living from theft and may specialize in a particular form.

**proletariat** A social class composed of people who work for wages.

**property offense** A criminal offense perpetrated without personal violence and focused on the entering, taking, or destruction of structures, motor vehicles, or goods.

**proportionality** The idea that the most serious criminal offenses should have the most severe penalties.

**pro-social** Following standards of behavior that are supportive of society and individuals.

**prostitution** The unlawful promotion of or participation in sexual activities for profit.

**psychopathy** A mental disorder that involves a severe lack of empathy.

**public-order offense** An activity that is against the law and offends the values, norms, and/or morals of a dominant sector of society.

**race** The use of certain biological characteristics, such as skin color, to classify human beings into categories.

**racial profiling** The disproportionate selection by law enforcement of minority suspects.

**racketeering** The use of extortion and force to engage in illegal business activities.

**Racketeering Influenced and Corrupt Organizations (RICO) Act** A federal statute enacted in 1970 to control organized crime.

**radio frequency identification (RFID) tags** Devices that transmit information embedded in the tag via radio to a special receiver or reader.

**rational choice theory** The concept that offenders calculate the advantages and disadvantages not only of breaking the law, but also of what type of offense to commit.

**recidivism** Repeat offending. *Also recidivate.*

**reintegrative shaming** Braithwaite's term to describe punishment that seeks to repair the harm done by the offender and offense and draw the offender into society.

**reliability** Refers to how successfully research can be repeated and provide similar results.

**restitution** Money paid to compensate for loss or injury.

**restorative justice** A form of resolving offenses that emphasizes repairing the harm done by crime through cooperation of the victim, offender, and justice system.

**retribution** The idea that any punishment proportional to the offense is just.

**robbery** The taking or attempting to take anything from another person or persons by violence or the threat of violence.

**routine activities theory** The concept that crime occurs when three elements converge: motivated offenders, attractive targets, and the absence of capable guardians.

**schizophrenia** A mental disorder that includes delusions, hallucinations, disorganized speech, grossly disorganized behavior, and inappropriate affect.

**scientific method** A process of investigation in which phenomena are observed, ideas are tested, and conclusions are drawn.

**secondary deviance** Occurs when labeled individuals internalize the label and see themselves as devalued members of society.

**securities fraud** An offense in which an individual or entity attempts to manipulate the investment market, usually by encouraging investors to purchase securities based on false statements.

**self-report study** Research based on data that is offered by respondents about themselves.

**serial murder** The killing of a sequence of victims committed in three or more separate events over an extended period of time.

**sex** The biological characteristics that distinguish organisms on the basis of their reproductive ability.

**situated transaction** The idea that a scenario is the result of agreed-upon norms, interactions, and roles played by those involved.

**situational crime prevention** An extension of rational choice theory that considers situational factors that can be modified to discourage crime.

**social bond theory** The idea that there are forces that keep people connected to social norms and values.

**social contract** The idea that individuals in a society are bound by reciprocal obligations.

**social Darwinism** The idea that public welfare of any sort only helped the unfit survive to weaken society.

**social disorganization theory** The idea that the breakdown of social bonds and the failure of social institutions cause crime.

**social engineering** The manipulation of individuals so that they divulge information or perform actions.

**social learning theory** The idea that people learn how to act by watching others and copying the interactions that are rewarded and avoiding those that are punished.

**social location** The position of an individual within a society according to race, sex, class, geography, and age.

**sociobiology** The study of evolutionary factors on behavior and societies.

**sociological imagination** The idea that we must look beyond our personal experiences to the experiences of others in order to evaluate how social location influences how individuals perceive society.

**sodomy** Oral or anal sexual intercourse.

**soft determinism** The idea that free will is affected by outside influences.

**somatotype** The practice of determining a person's character by the shape of the body.

**spam** Unsolicited e-mail advertising a product or service that is sent in bulk to large numbers of people.

**specific deterrence** The idea that punishing one person for an offense, usually by incarceration or execution, will prevent that person from committing another offense.

**strain theory** The idea that people who experience anger and frustration when they can't achieve cultural goals through legitimate means try to achieve these goals through illegitimate means.

**street crime** Materially destructive or violent criminal offenses that are often interpersonal and represent those for which the police are most often called.

**subculture of violence** A culture apart from the main social culture that holds violence as part of its values, lifestyle, and socialization.

**surveillance** Systematic, institutionalized, usually secret encroachment into individual privacy.

**techniques of neutralization theory** A perspective that refers to the excuses some offenders use to justify breaking the law.

**terrorism** Violence perpetrated against civilians by political groups for the purpose of drawing attention to their cause.

**theory of evolution** The idea that biological forms change over time through genetic inheritance.

**transnational crime** Criminal offenses that originate in one nation, cross one or several national borders, and find victims in other nations.

**triad** A common term for Chinese criminal organizations.

**Uniform Crime Reports** A Federal Bureau of Investigation program that collects law enforcement statistics from voluntarily participating agencies throughout the United States.

**utilitarianism** The idea of seeking the greatest good for the most people.

**validity** A statistical property that describes how well a study is measuring what it is designed to measure.

**vicarious liability** Occurs when a person or group of people is considered legally responsible for the actions of another person, group of people, or corporation.

**victim** In criminology, a person who suffers a criminal offense.

**victim-impact statement (VIS)** A communication to the court by those directly affected by an offense that states the personal effects of the offense.

**victimless crime** An activity that offends the values of a segment of society and is against the law but has the willing participation of all parties, and causes no obvious harm. Those involved in the activity seek to keep it from becoming known to police.

**victimology** The study of the effects of crime on victims.

**victim precipitation** An offense in which the victim plays an active role in initiating or escalating the offense.

**violence** Aggressive physical force with intent to cause fear or to injure, harm, or kill.

**white-collar crime** A criminal offense committed by an individual employee of a business during the course of legitimate business for the benefit of the employee that takes advantage of the business or its customers.

**XYY syndrome** Syndrome that occurs when males receive an extra copy of the Y chromosome.

## Chapter 1

1. *Wichita Eagle,* "A Double Life," http://media.kansas.com/pdfs/btk/022905btkrader_timeline.pdf; CNN, "Rader Details How He Killed 10 People," June 28, 2005, http://www.cnn.com/2005/LAW/06/27/btk/index.html; Biography.com, Dennis Rader Biography, http://www.biography.com/articles/Dennis-Rader-241487.

2. Sam Coates, "Rader Gets 175 Years for BTK Slayings," *Washington Post,* August 19, 2005, A3; "The Otero Family," *Wichita Eagle,* March 12, 2007, http://www.kansas.com/2005/06/28/16542/the-otero-family.html; Mark Hansen, "How the Cops Caught BTK," *ABA Journal* 92, no. 4 (April 2006): 44–48.

3. Edwin H. Sutherland, *Principles of Criminology* (Philadelphia: Lippincott, 1939), 2.

4. CNN, "Japan Executes Serial Killer," June 17, 2008, http://edition.cnn.com/2008/WORLD/asiapcf/06/17/japan.executions/index.html.

5. David E. Kaplan, "More Stressed, but Still Safer," *U.S. News & World Report* 142, no. 11 (March 26, 2007): 66.

6. Josef Stalin is credited with saying this, although Russian historians apparently have no record of it. Julia Solovyova, "Mustering Most Memorable Quips," *Moscow Times,* October 28, 1997.

7. Mark Dolliver, "In Our Minds, at Least, Crime Is Coming Back," *Adweek* 50, no. 38 (October 26, 2009): 17.

8. James D. Unnever and Francis T. Cullen, "The Social Sources of Americans' Punitiveness: A Test of Three Competing Models," *Criminology* 48, no. 1 (February 2010): 99–129; Michael T. Costelloe, Ted Chiricos, and Marc Gertz, "Punitive Attitudes Toward Criminals," *Punishment & Society* 11, no. 1 (January 2009): 25–49; Monica Williams, "Beyond the Punitive Public: Governance and Public Opinion on Penal Policy," Conference Papers—Law & Society (Annual Meeting 2009): 1; Lydia Saad, "Americans Hold Firm to Support for Death Penalty," *Gallup Poll Briefing* (November 17, 2008): 1.

9. Diana C. Mutz and Lilach Nir, "Not Necessarily the News: Does Fictional Television Influence Real-World Policy Preferences?" *Mass Communication & Society* 13, no. 2 (April 2010): 196–217.

10. Dan Mitchell, "Manson's Family Affair Living in Cyberspace," *Wired,* April 16, 1997, http://www.wired.com/culture/lifestyle/news/1997/04/3182; Ted Rowlands, "Charles Manson Spends Most of His Time Alone," CNN, March 20, 2009, http://www.cnn.com/2009/CRIME/03/20/charles.manson.prison/index.html.

11. *New York Times,* "Execution Date Only Hours Off for John Gacy," May 9, 1994, http://www.nytimes.com/1994/05/09/us/execution-date-only-hours-off-for-john-gacy.html?pagewanted=1.

12. Bonnie L. Cook, "Web 'Murderabilia' Sales Spark Outrage," *Philadelphia Inquirer,* June 17, 2009.

13. Brooks Egerton, "Scales of Justice Can Swing Wildly," *Dallas Morning News,* April 23, 2006.

14. Brooks Egerton, "Outrage Leads to a Joyful Reunion," *Dallas Morning News,* March 16, 2007.

15. David F. Musto, interview, "Busted: America's War on Marijuana," http://www.pbs.org/wgbh/pages/frontline/shows/dope/interviews/musto.html.

16. House of Representatives Committee on the Judiciary Subcommittee on Crime, Terrorism, and Homeland Security, *Hearing on Keeping Youth Safe While in Custody: Sexual Assault in Adult and Juvenile Facilities: Testimony of Troy Erik Isaac,* 111th Cong., February 23, 2010, http://judiciary.house.gov/hearings/hear_100223.html; Lynn Neary, "Juvenile Inmates Report Sexual Abuse at Detention Centers," Tell Me More (NPR), January 19, 2010, http://www.npr.org/templates/story/story.php?storyId=122725085; AP/ABC News, "Report: Sex Abuse High at 13 Juvenile Centers," January 7, 2010, http://abcnews.go.com/US/wireStory?id=9502399.

17. John R. Emshwiller, "The Last of the Golden Swindlers," *Wall Street Journal,* March 6, 2010, Eastern edition, W1, http://online.wsj.com/article/SB10001424052748704187204575101863502272290.html.

18. Ibid.

19. Richard Johnson, Corynne Steindler, and Neel Shah, "Madoff Wowed Kid Probers," *New York Post,* August 12, 2009, http://www.nypost.com/p/pagesix/item_AFEekbB6muXtTrhpggY1XO.

20. Evelyn Fox Keller, *A Feeling for the Organism: The Life and Work of Barbara McClintock* (New York: W. H. Freeman, 1983), 174.

## Chapter 2

1. Douglas Clement, "Beware of Data," *Fedgazette* 21, no. 2 (March 2009): 8.

2. Josine Junger-Tas and Ineke Haen, "The Self-Report Methodology in Crime Research," *Crime and Justice* 25 (1999): 291–367.

3. Clayton J. Mosher, Terance D. Miethe, and Dretha M. Phillips, *The Mismeasure of Crime* (Thousand Oaks, CA: Sage Publications, 2002), 173.

4. Stephen Woods, "By the Numbers," *Documents to the People* 34, no. 1 (Spring 2006): 11–14.

5. James P. Lynch and John P. Jarvis, "Missing Data and Imputation in the Uniform Crime Reports and the Effects on National Estimates," *Journal of Contemporary Criminal Justice* 24, no. 1 (2008): 69–85.

6. Mosher, Miethe, and Phillips, *The Mismeasure of Crime,* 60.

7. Ibid., 36.

8. Ibid., 37.

9. Federal Bureau of Investigation, Uniform Crime Reports, *Crime in the United States: Preliminary Annual Uniform Crime Report, 2008,* http://www.fbi.gov/ucr/cius2008/about/about_ucr.html. The Uniform Crime Reports used to break down crime by Part I and Part II offenses. This practice was discontinued in 2004.

10. Lynch and Jarvis, "Missing Data," 69–85.

11. Federal Bureau of Investigation, Uniform Crime Reports, *Crime in the United States, 2008,* "Offenses Cleared," http://www.fbi.gov/ucr/cius2008/offenses/clearances/index.html.

12. Federal Bureau of Investigation, Uniform Crime Reports, *Crime in the United States, 2008,* "Offenses Known to Law Enforcement," http://www.fbi.gov/ucr/cius2008/offenses/index.html.

13. Federal Bureau of Investigation, Uniform Crime Reports, *Crime in the United States, 2008,* "Arrests," http://www.fbi.gov/ucr/cius2008/arrests/index.html.

14. Federal Bureau of Investigation, Uniform Crime Reports, *Crime in the United States, 2008,* "Law Enforcement Officers Killed & Assaulted," http://www.fbi.gov/ucr/killed/2008/index.html.

15. Federal Bureau of Investigation, Uniform Crime Reports, *Crime in the United States, 2008,* "Police Employee Data," http://www.fbi.gov/ucr/cius2008/police/index.html.

16. Federal Bureau of Investigation, Uniform Crime Reports, *Crime in the United States, 2008,* "Arson," http://www.fbi.gov/ucr/cius2008/offenses/property_crime/arson.html.

17. Federal Bureau of Investigation, Uniform Crime Reports, *Crime in the United States, 2008,* "Expanded Offense Data," http://www.fbi.gov/ucr/cius2008/offenses/expanded_information/index.html, and "Murder," http://www.fbi.gov/ucr/cius2008/offenses/violent_crime/murder_homicide.html.

18. Federal Bureau of Investigation, Uniform Crime Reports, *Crime in the United States, 2008,* "Hate Crime Statistics," http://www.fbi.gov/ucr/hc2008/index.html.

19. Federal Bureau of Investigation, Uniform Crime Reports, *Crime in the United States: Preliminary Annual Uniform Crime Report, January to December 2008,* http://www.fbi.gov/ucr/08aprelim/index.html.

20. Zachary Bookman, "Convergences and Omissions in Reporting Corporate and White Collar Crime," *DePaul Business & Commercial Law Journal* 6, no. 3 (Spring 2008): 347–92.

21. Lynch and Jarvis, "Missing Data," 69–85.

22. Federal Bureau of Investigation, Uniform Crime Reports, *Crime in the United States, 2008,* "Directory of State Uniform Crime Reporting Programs," http://www.fbi.gov/ucr/cius2008/about/state_ucr_contacts.html.

23. Lynch and Jarvis, "Missing Data," 69–85.

24. Ibid.

25. Ibid.

26. Ibid.

27. Michael D. Maltz, "Missing UCR Data and Divergence," in *Understanding Crime Statistics,* ed. James P. Lynch and Lynn A. Addington (New York: Cambridge University Press, 2007), 269–94.

28. Lynch and Jarvis, "Missing Data," 69–85.

29. Maltz, "Missing UCR Data," 269–94.

30. Federal Bureau of Investigation, Uniform Crime Reports, *Crime in the United States, 2008,* "About the UCR Program," http://www.fbi.gov/ucr/cius2008/about/about_ucr.html.

31. Mosher, Miethe, and Phillips, *The Mismeasure of Crime,* 72.

32. Ibid., 86.

33. Ibid., 87–92.

34. Michael Rand, "The National Crime Victimization Survey: 34 Years of Measuring Crime in the United States," *Statistical Journal of the UN Economic Commission for Europe* 23, no. 4 (December 2006): 289–301.

35. Janet L. Lauritsen, "Social and Scientific Influences on the Measurement of Criminal Victimization," *Journal of Quantitative Criminology* 21, no. 3 (September 2005): 245–66.

36. Lauritsen, "Measurement of Criminal Victimization," 245–66; Rand, "The National Crime Victimization Survey," 289–301.

37. Rand, "The National Crime Victimization Survey," 289–301.

38. Lauritsen, "Measurement of Criminal Victimization," 245–66.

39. Stephen Woods, "By the Numbers," *Documents to the People* 34, no. 1 (Spring 2006): 11–14.

40. Rand, "The National Crime Victimization Survey," 289–301.

41. Mosher, Miethe, and Phillips, *The Mismeasure of Crime,* 168.

42. Ibid., 163, 168.

43. Michael Planty and Kevin Strom, "Understanding the Role of Repeat Victims in the Production of Annual US Victimization Rates," *Journal of Quantitative Criminology* 23, no. 3 (September 2007): 179–200.

44. Ibid.

45. Maltz, "Missing UCR Data," 269–94.

46. Junger-Tas and Haen, "The Self-Report Methodology," 291–367.

47. James P. Lynch and Lynn A. Addington, eds., *Understanding Crime Statistics* (New York: Cambridge University Press, 2007). See the introduction.

48. Shannan M. Catalano, *The Measurement of Crime* (New York: LFB Scholarly Publishing, 2006). See Chapter 6.

49. Ibid.

50. Ibid.

51. Lynch and Addington, *Understanding Crime Statistics,* 331–32.

52. Todd R. Clear, "Policy and Evidence: The Challenge of the American Society of Criminology: 2009 Presidential Address to the American Society of Criminology," *Criminology* 48, no. 1 (February 2010): 1–25.

53. Ibid. See Chapter 10, Michael D. Maltz, "Missing UCR Data," 269–94, and the conclusion, 297–332.

54. Junger-Tas and Haen, "The Self-Report Methodology," 291–367.

55. Ibid.

56. Ibid.

57. Ibid.

58. Ibid.

59. Ibid.

60. Terence P. Thornberry and Marvin D. Krohn, "The Self-Report Method for Measuring Delinquency and Crime," *Criminal Justice 2000* 4, 33–83, http://

www.ncjrs.gov/criminal_justice2000/vol_4/04b.pdf.

61. Ibid.

62. Ibid.

63. Junger-Tas and Haen, "The Self-Report Methodology," 291–367.

64. Thornberry and Krohn, "The Self-Report Method," 33–83, http://www.ncjrs.gov/criminal_justice2000/vol_4/04b.pdf.

65. Junger-Tas and Haen, "The Self-Report Methodology," 291–367.

66. Ibid.

67. David Huizinga, Scott Menard, and Delbert S. Elliott, "Delinquency and Drug Use: Temporal and Developmental Patterns," *Justice Quarterly* 6 (1989): 419–55; Suzanne S. Ageton, *Sexual Assault Among Adolescents* (Lexington, MA: Lexington Books, 1983); Delbert S. Elliott, David Huizinga, and Suzanne S. Ageton, *Explaining Delinquency and Drug Use* (Beverly Hills, CA: Sage Publications, 1985); Delbert S. Elliott, David Huizinga, and Scott Menard, *Multiple Problem Youth: Delinquency, Drugs and Mental Health Problems* (New York: Springer, 1989).

68. Monitoring the Future: A Continuing Study of American Youth, http://monitoringthefuture.org/purpose.html.

69. Ibid.

70. National Survey on Drug Use and Health, https://nsduhweb.rti.org/. Prior to 2002, this survey was called the National Household Survey on Drug Abuse.

71. Mosher, Miethe, and Phillips, *The Mismeasure of Crime,* 41.

72. William Alex Pridemore, "A Cautionary Note on Using County-Level Crime and Homicide Data," *Homicide Studies* 9, no. 3 (August 2005): 256–68.

73. Vincent J. Webb, Charles M. Katz, and Scott H. Decker, "Assessing the Validity of Self-

Reports by Gang Members: Results from the Arrestee Drug Abuse Monitoring Program," *Crime & Delinquency* 52, no. 2 (April 2006): 232–52.

74. David Kirk, "Examining the Divergence Across Self-Report and Official Data Sources on Inferences About the Adolescent Life-Course of Crime," *Journal of Quantitative Criminology* 22, no. 2 (June 2006): 107–29.

**Chapter 3**

1. William G. Doerner and Steven P. Lab, *Victimology,* 5th ed. (Newark, NJ: Matthew Bender & Company, 2008). See Chapter 1.

2. Andrew Karmen, *Crime Victims: An Introduction to Victimology,* 6th ed (Belmont, CA: Thomson Wadsworth, 2007), 12–13.

3. Ibid., 2.

4. Joel Best, "Victimization and the Victim Industry," *Society* 34, no. 4 (May 1997): 9–17.

5. Michael R. Rand, *Criminal Victimization, 2008* (Washington, DC: U.S. Department of Justice Office of Justice Programs Bureau of Justice Statistics, 2009), 2, http://bjs.ojp.usdoj.gov/content/pub/pdf/cv08.pdf.

6. Ibid., 4.

7. Ibid., 6.

8. Ibid., 5.

9. Ibid., 6.

10. Ibid.

11. Federal Bureau of Investigation, *Crime in the United States, 2008,* "Robbery," http://www.fbi.gov/ucr/cius2008/offenses/violent_crime/robbery.html; ibid., "Larceny-Theft," http://www.fbi.gov/ucr/cius2008/offenses/property_crime/larceny-theft.html.

12. Federal Bureau of Investigation, *Crime in the United States, 2008,* "Burglary," http://www.fbi.gov/ucr/cius2008/offenses/

property_crime/burglary.html; ibid., "Arson," http://www.fbi.gov/ucr/cius2008/offenses/property_crime/arson.html.

13. Federal Trade Commission, "Consumer Fraud and Identity Theft Complaint Data January–December 2007," (Washington, DC: Federal Trade Commission, 2008), 2, http://www.ftc.gov/opa/2008/02/fraud.pdf; National Association of Crime Victim Compensation Boards, "Crime Victim Compensation Helps Victims" (Alexandria, VA: NACVCB, 2008), http://www.nacvcb.org.

14. Centers for Disease Control and Prevention, "National Violent Death Reporting System," http://www.cdc.gov/Violence Prevention/NVDRS/index.html.

15. William Gibson, "Panther Modern's Eyes," October 31, 2004, http://www.williamgibsonbooks.com/blog/2004_10_01_archive.asp.

16. Haya Itzhaky and Rachel Dekel, "Helping Victims of Terrorism: What Makes Social Work Effective?" Social Work 50, no. 4 (October 2005): 335–43.

17. Arnold A. P. van Emmerik et al., "Single Session Debriefing After Psychological Trauma: A Meta-analysis," The Lancet 360, no. 9335 (September 2002): 766–71.

18. U.S. Department of Justice, "Terrorism and International Victims Unit," http://www.ojp.usdoj.gov/ovc/publications/factshts/tivu/welcome.html.

19. Samantha Levine, "The Value of a Lost Life," U.S. News & World Report 131, no. 27 (December 31, 2001): 46.

20. Jill Schachner Chanen and Margaret Graham Tebo, "Accounting for Lives," ABA Journal 93, no. 9 (September 2007): 58–62.

21. National Counterterrorism Center, 2008 Report on Terrorism, April 30, 2009, 12, http://wits-classic.nctc.gov/Reports.do?f=crt2008nctcannexfinal.pdf.

22. Ibid.

23. Jelena Jauković, "The Form of Victimization in the Territory of the Former Yugoslavia," European Journal of Crime, Criminal Law & Criminal Justice 10, no. 2/3 (May 2002): 109–16.

24. OSCE and Office of Democratic Institutions and Human Rights, "High-Level Meeting Victims of Terrorism," background paper, September 13–14, 2007, Vienna, http://www.osce.org/documents/odihr/2007/09/26120_en.pdf.

25. Environmental Protection Agency, "Exxon Valdez," http://www.epa.gov/oem/content/learning/exxon.htm.

26. Brandon Keim, "The Exxon Valdez Spill Is All Around Us," Wired Science, March 25, 2009, http://www.wired.com/wiredscience/2009/03/valdezlegacy/; Tony Long, "March 24, 1989: Valdez Spill Causes Environmental Catastrophe," Wired, March 24, 2009, http://www.wired.com/science/discoveries/news/2009/03/dayintech_0324.

27. Richard S. Gruner, Corporate Criminal Liability and Prevention (New York: Law Journal Seminar Press, 2004).

28. Nina Totenberg, "Supreme Court Weighs Exxon Valdez Damages," National Public Radio, February 27, 2008, http://www.npr.org/templates/story/story.php?storyId=48308288.

29. Brandon Keim, "The Exxon Valdez Spill Is All Around Us."

30. Tony Long, "March 24, 1989: Valdez Spill Causes Environmental Catastrophe."

31. Ted Land, "20 Years Later, Cordova Still Trying to Move Past Spill," KTUU.com, March 22, 2009, http://www.ktuu.com/Global/story.asp?S=10051949.

32. Danny Teigman, "Former Valdez Captain Noncommittal on Court's Ruling on Damages," Newsday, June 26, 2008.

33. Bob Egelko, "Court Cuts Payouts to Victims Again in Exxon Spill Case," San Francisco Chronicle, June 26, 2008, A3.

34. ScienceDaily, "Amazon Rainforest Carbon Sink Threatened by Drought," March 9, 2009, http://www.sciencedaily.com/releases/2009/03/090305141625.htm; Woods Hole Research Center, "The Amazon," http://www.whrc.org/southamerica/index.htm.

35. Jeff Tollefson, "Brazil Goes to War Against Logging," Nature 452, no. 7184 (March 13, 2008): 134–35.

36. "Brazilian Rainforest Destruction on the Rise," Geographical 80, no. 12 (December 2008): 9.

37. Cahal Milmo, "The Human Casualties of Brazil's Rainforest Disaster," The Independent, November 1, 2004, http://www.independent.co.uk/news/world/americas/the-human-casualties-of-brazils-rainforest-disaster-535581.html.

38. Scott Cohn, "Some Enron Victims Still Trying to Recover," MSNBC, May 26, 2006, http://www.msnbc.msn.com/id/12976443/.

39. Ibid.

40. Eric Berger, "Banks to Pay $255 Million to Enron Victim Fund," Houston Chronicle, August 4, 2003.

41. Thom Weidlich and Laurel Brubaker Calkins, "Enron's Skilling Sentenced to 24 Years for Fraud," Bloomberg.com,

October 23, 2006, http://www.bloomberg.com/apps/news?pid=20601087&sid=a_Jbjnng.4u4.

42. Mary Flood, "Judge Sets Skilling's Resentencing for July," *Houston Chronicle,* March 26, 2009, http://www.chron.com/disp/story.mpl/special/enron/6345182.html.

43. Weidlich and Calkins, "Enron's Skilling Sentenced to 24 Years for Fraud."

44. Brenda Sapino Jeffreys, "Former Enron CEO Jeffrey Skilling Sentenced to 24 Years in Prison," Law.com, http://www.law.com/jsp/article.jsp?id=1161606924042.

45. Chad Bray and Amir Efrati, *The Wall Street Journal Asia,* March 18, 2009, M11, Hong Kong edition; AP, "Madoff Sentenced to 150 Years in Prison," Fox News, June 29, 2009, http://www.foxnews.com/story/0,2933,529412,00.html.

46. Kara Scannell, "Madoff Chasers Probed for Years, but to No Avail," *The Wall Street Journal Asia,* January 6, 2009; Larry Neumeister, "Madoff Won't Appeal 150-Year Sentence," *Pittsburgh Post-Gazette,* July 10, 2009.

47. "Bernie Madoff's Foray into Food," *Restaurant Hospitality* 93, no. 4 (April 2009): 20.

48. Martha Graybow, "Hunt for Madoff Money to Drag On for Years," Reuters, http://www.reuters.com/article/reutersEdge/idUSTRE54E5SS20090515.

49. John D. McKinnon and Jane J. Kim, "Ponzi Scheme Victims in U.S. Get Tax Relief," *Wall Street Journal,* March 18, 2009, 10, Europe: Brussels edition.

50. Julie Creswell and Landon Thomas, Jr., "The Talented Mr. Madoff," *New York Times,* January 25, 2009, http://www.nytimes.com/2009/01/25/business/25bernie.html.

51. Allied Control Council, 1945, cited in Daniel Maier-Katkin, Daniel P. Mears, and Thomas J. Bernard, "Towards a Criminology of Crimes Against Humanity," *Theoretical Criminology* 13, no. 2 (May 2009): 227–55.

52. Rome Statute, 2002, cited in "Towards a Criminology of Crimes Against Humanity."

53. Ibid.

54. Donald L. Niewyk and Francis R. Nicosia, *The Columbia Guide to the Holocaust* (New York: Columbia University Press, 2000), 45.

55. Douglas O. Linder, "Famous Trials: Nuremberg Trial, 1945–1949" University of Missouri–Kansas City School of Law, http://www.law.umkc.edu/faculty/projects/ftrials/nuremberg/nuremberg.htm.

56. "Swiss Fund to Disburse Millions to Nazi Victims," *New York Times,* July 08, 1997, 6.

57. Stephen A. Hart, "Liberation of the Concentration Camps," BBC, http://www.bbc.co.uk/history/worldwars/wwtwo/liberation_camps_05.shtml.

58. "Ethnic Cleansing in Bosnia," *CQ Researcher* 14, no. 29 (August 27, 2004): 697–97.

59. Rod Nordland and Zoran Cirjakovic, "The Death of a Monster," *Newsweek,* March 20, 2006, 44.

60. "482 Srebrenica Victims Found in Mass Grave," *Irish Times,* October 17, 2005.

61. "Ethnic Cleansing in Bosnia," *CQ Researcher* 14, no. 29 (August 27, 2004): 697.

62. Nordland and Cirjakovic, "The Death of a Monster."

63. "Slobodan Milosevic," *Economist,* March 18, 2006, 83.

64. Charles Forelle, "War-Crimes Courts Build Reputation for Efficacy," *Wall Street Journal,* July 31, 2008, Eastern edition.

65. Hilmi M. Zawati, "Impunity or Immunity: Wartime Male Rape and Sexual Torture as a Crime Against Humanity," *Torture: Quarterly Journal on Rehabilitation of Torture Victims and Prevention of Torture* 17, no. 1: 27–47.

66. Joanne Barkan, "As Old as War Itself: Rape in Foca," *Dissent* (00123846) 49, no. 1 (Winter 2002): 60.

67. Judith Pintar, "Anticipating Consequences: What Bosnia Taught Us About Healing the Wounds of War," *Human Rights Review* 1, no. 2 (January 2000): 56–66.

68. "Sudan," *New York Times,* March 6, 2009, http://topics.nytimes.com/top/news/international/countriesandterritories/sudan/index.html; BBC, "Q&A: Sudan's Darfur Conflict," March 5, 2009, http://news.bbc.co.uk/1/hi/world/africa/3496731.stm.

69. "A Warrant for Bashir," *Economist,* March 07, 2009, 20.

70. U.S. Department of Justice Office of Community Oriented Policing Services, "Bringing Victims into Community Policing," 2002, http://www.cops.usdoj.gov/files/RIC/Publications/e03021477.pdf.

71. Doerner and Lab, *Victimology,* 321.

72. Federal Bureau of Investigation, *Crime in the United States: 2008,* "Crime in the United States by Volume and Rate per 100,000 Inhabitants, 1989–2008, Table 1," http://www.fbi.gov/ucr/cius2008/data/table_01.html.

73. Federal Bureau of Investigation, *Crime in the United States: 2008,* "Murder Circumstances, 2004–2008, Expanded Homicide Data Table 12," http://www.fbi.gov/ucr/cius2008/offenses/

expanded_information/data/shrtable_12.html; ibid., "Murder Victims by Weapon, 2004–2008, Expanded Homicide Data Table 8," http://www.fbi.gov/ucr/cius2008/offenses/expanded_information/data/shrtable_08.html.

74. Federal Bureau of Investigation, *Crime in the United States: 2008,* "Murder Victims by Race and Sex, 2008, Expanded Homicide Data Table 1," http://www.fbi.gov/ucr/cius2008/offenses/expanded_information/data/shrtable_01.html.

75. Federal Bureau of Investigation, *Crime in the United States: 2008,* "Murder: Race and Sex of Victim by Race and Sex of Offender, 2008, Expanded Homicide Data Table 6," http://www.fbi.gov/ucr/cius2008/offenses/expanded_information/data/shrtable_06.html.

76. Federal Bureau of Investigation, *Crime in the United States: 2008,* "Murder Victims by Race and Sex, 2008, Expanded Homicide Data Table 1," http://www.fbi.gov/ucr/cius2008/offenses/expanded_information/data/shrtable_01.html.

77. Federal Bureau of Investigation, *Crime in the United States: 2008,* "Murder Circumstances by Relationship, 2008, Expanded Homicide Data Table 10," http://www.fbi.gov/ucr/cius2008/offenses/expanded_information/data/shrtable_10.html.

78. Margaret A. Zahn and Patricia L. McCall, "Trends and Patterns of Homicides in the 20th-Century United States," in *Homicide: A Sourcebook of Social Research,* ed. M. Dwayne Smith and Margaret A. Zahn (Thousand Oaks, CA: Sage, 1999), 17; Federal Bureau of Investigation, *Crime in the United States: 2008,* "Murder Circumstances by Relationship, 2008, Expanded Homicide Data Table 10," http://www.fbi.gov/ucr/cius2008/offenses/expanded_information/data/shrtable_10.html.

79. Wendy C. Regoeczi and Terance D. Miethe, "Taking on the Unknown: A Qualitative Comparative Analysis of Unknown Relationship Homicides," *Homicide Studies* 7, no. 3 (2003): 211–34.

80. E. A. Fattah, *Understanding Criminal Victimization: An Introduction to Theoretical Victimology* (Englewood Cliffs, NJ: Prentice Hall, 1991), 291.

81. Lisa R. Muftic, Leana Allen Bouffard, and Jeffrey A. Bouffard, "An Exploratory Analysis of Victim Precipitation Among Men and Women Arrested for Intimate Partner Violence," *Feminist Criminology* 2, no. 4 (October 2007): 327–46.

82. David F. Luckenbill, "Criminal Homicide as a Situated Transaction," *Social Problems* 25, no. 2 (December 1977): 176–86.

83. Doerner and Lab, *Victimology,* 330–31.

84. Rand, *Criminal Victimization, 2008,* Tables 1, 6, 7.

85. Ibid., 13, 29.

86. Susan Brownmiller, *Against Our Will* (New York: Simon and Schuster, 1975), 286.

87. Federal Bureau of Investigation, *Crime in the United States: 2007,* "Forcible Rape," http://www.fbi.gov/ucr/cius2007/offenses/violent_crime/forcible_rape.html.

88. Patricia Tjaden and Nancy Thoennes, *Extent, Nature, and Consequences of Rape Victimization: Findings from the National Violence Against Women Survey,* U.S. Department of Justice Office of Justice Programs National Institute of Justice, 2006, http://www.ncjrs.gov/pdffiles1/nij/210346.pdf.

89. Leslee R. Kassing and Loreto R. Prieto, "The Rape Myth and Blame-Based Beliefs of Counselors-in-Training Toward Male Victims of Rape," *Journal of Counseling & Development* 81 no. 4 (Fall 2003): 455–61; "Police Learn Skills in Dealing with Male Rape Victims," *Nursing Standard* 19, no. 6 (October 20, 2004): 9; Sandesh Sivakumaran, "Male/Male Rape and the 'Taint' of Homosexuality," *Human Rights Quarterly* 27, no. 4 (August 2005): 1274–1306.

90. American Academy of Child & Adolescent Psychiatry, "Child Sexual Abuse," May 2008, http://www.aacap.org/cs/root/facts_for_families/child_sexual_abuse.

91. Howard Snyder and Melissa Sickmund, *Juvenile Offenders and Victims: 2006 National Report* (Washington, DC: U.S. Department of Justice, Office of Justice Programs, Office of Juvenile Justice and Delinquency Prevention, 2006), 31.

92. James M. Donovan, "Combating the Sexual Abuse of Children in France, 1825–1913," *Criminal Justice History* 15 (1994): 59–93.

93. Linda Greenhouse, "Justices Bar Death Penalty for the Rape of a Child," *New York Times,* June 26, 2008, A1, late edition; Warren Richey Staff, "Despite Gaffe, Supreme Court Won't Revisit Landmark Child-Rape Ruling," *Christian Science Monitor,* October 2, 2008, 25.

94. Rand, *Criminal Victimization, 2008,* 4–5.

95. Federal Bureau of Investigation, *Crime in the United States, 2008,* "Table 29: Estimated Number of Arrests United States, 2008," http://www.fbi.gov/ucr/cius2008/data/table_29.html; ibid., "Table 39: Arrests of Males, by Age, 2008," http://www.fbi

.gov/ucr/cius2008/data/ table_39.html.

96. Richard T. Wright and Scott H. Decker, *Armed Robbers in Action: Stickups and Street Culture* (Boston: Northeastern University Press, 1997).

97. Federal Bureau of Investigation, *Crime in the United States: 2008,* "Table 21: Robbery by State, Types of Weapons, 2008," http://www.fbi.gov/ucr/cius2008/data/table_21.html.

98. Curt R. Bartol and Anne M. Bartol, *Criminal Behavior: A Psychosocial Approach,* 8th ed. (Upper Saddle River, NJ: Pearson Education, 2008), 489.

99. Wright and Decker, *Armed Robbers in Action: Stickups and Street Culture.*

100. Department of Justice Office of Justice Programs Bureau of Justice Statistics, "National Crime Victimization Survey, Criminal Victimization in the United States, 2006 Statistical Tables, Table 93," 2008, http://www.ojp.usdoj.gov/bjs/pub/pdf/cvus06.pdf.

101. Rand, *Criminal Victimization, 2008,* 4–5.

102. Ibid., 6.

103. Bartol and Bartol, *Criminal Behavior,* 299.

104. Shannan Catalano, Department of Justice Office of Justice Programs Bureau of Justice Statistics, "Intimate Partner Violence in the United States," http://www.ojp.usdoj.gov/bjs/intimate/ipv.htm.

105. Mary Swanton, "Victims' Rights," *InsideCounsel* 16, no. 178 (September 2006): 2–28.

106. Federal Bureau of Investigation, *Crime in the United States: 2008,* "Property Crime," http://www.fbi.gov/ucr/cius2008/offenses/property_crime/index.html.

107. Federal Bureau of Investigation, *Crime in the United States: 2008,* "Property Crime," http://www.fbi.gov/ucr/cius2008/offenses/property_crime/index.html.

108. Federal Bureau of Investigation, *Crime in the United States: 2008,* "Burglary," http://www.fbi.gov/ucr/cius2008/offenses/property_crime/burglary.html; ibid., "Larceny-Theft," http://www.fbi.gov/ucr/cius2008/offenses/property_crime/larceny-theft.html; ibid., "Motor Vehicle Theft," http://www.fbi.gov/ucr/cius2008/offenses/property_crime/motor_vehicle_theft.html); ibid., "Arson," http://www.fbi.gov/ucr/cius2008/offenses/property_crime/arson.html.

109. Rand, *Criminal Victimization, 2008,* 5.

110. Mark S. Umbreit, Robert B. Coates, and Betty Vos, "Victim-Offender Mediation: Three Decades of Practice and Research," *Conflict Resolution Quarterly* 22, no. 1/2 (Fall/Winter 2004): 279–303.

111. Jo Phoenix, "Sex Traffic: Prostitution, Crime and Exploitation/ Human Traffic and Transnational Crime: Eurasian and American Perspectives," *British Journal of Criminology* 47, no. 3 (May 2007): 515–17.

112. Kevonne Small and Bruce Taylor, "State and Local Law Enforcement Response to Transnational Crime," *Trends in Organized Crime* 10, no. 2 (December 2006): 5–17.

113. Lorraine Elliott, "Transnational Environmental Crime in the Asia Pacific: An 'Un(der)securitized' Security Problem?" *Pacific Review* 20, no. 4 (December 2007): 499–522.

114. R. Barry Ruback and Martie P. Thompson, *Social and Psycho-*

logical Consequences of Violent Victimization (Thousand Oaks, CA: Sage, 2001), vii.

115. U.S. Department of Justice Office of Justice Programs Office for Victims of Crime, *First Response to Victims of Crime, 2008,* 2, http://www.ovc.gov/publications/infores/pdftxt/FirstResponseGuidebook.pdf.

116. Thomas Simon, James Mercy, and Craig Perkins, *Injuries from Violent Crime, 1992–98,* Bureau of Justice Statistics, 2001, 1, http://www.ojp.usdoj.gov/bjs/pub/pdf/ivc98.pdf.

117. U.S. Department of Justice Office of Justice Programs Bureau of Justice Statistics, "National Crime Victimization Survey, Criminal Victimization in the United States, 2007 Statistical Tables, Table 76," March 2010, http://bjs.ojp.usdoj.gov/content/pub/pdf/cvus07.pdf.

118. Ibid., "Table 79."

119. Jongyeon Tark and Gary Kleck, "Resisting Crime: The Effects of Victim Action on the Outcomes of Crimes," *Criminology* 42, no. 4 (November 2004): 861–909.

120. U.S. Department of Justice Office of Justice Programs Bureau of Justice Statistics, "National Crime Victimization Survey, Criminal Victimization in the United States, 2006 Statistical Tables, Table 70," August 2008, http://www.ojp.usdoj.gov/bjs/pub/pdf/cvus06.pdf.

121. Diane L. Green and Naelys Diaz, "Predictors of Emotional Stress in Crime Victims: Implications for Treatment," *Brief Treatment & Crisis Intervention* 7, no. 3 (August 31, 2007): 194.

122. Tracy Sharp et al., "Exploring the Psychological and Somatic Impact of Identity Theft," *Journal of Forensic Sciences* 49, no. 1 (January 2004): 131–36.

123. Laurence Miller, "Family Survivors of Homicide: I. Symptoms, Syndromes, and Reaction Patterns," *The American Journal of Family Therapy* 37 (2009): 67–79.

124. Ibid.

125. Ibid.

126. Gary T. Engel, "Criminal Debt: Court-Ordered Restitution Amounts Far Exceed Likely Collections for the Crime Victims in Selected Financial Fraud Cases: GAO-05-80," *GAO Reports* (January 31, 2005): 1.

127. David Brietkopf, "State of Va. Creates Special Cards for Crime Victims," *American Banker* 168, no. 222 (November 18, 2003): 21A.

128. George Tita, Tricia Petras, and Robert Greenbaum, "Crime and Residential Choice: A Neighborhood Level Analysis of the Impact of Crime on Housing Prices," *Journal of Quantitative Criminology* 22, no. 4 (December 2006): 299–317.

129. Uli Orth, "Secondary Victimization of Crime Victims by Criminal Proceedings," *Social Justice Research* 15, no. 4 (December 2002): 313–25.

130. Sarah Goodrum, "Victims' Rights, Victims' Expectations, and Law Enforcement Workers' Constraints in Cases of Murder," *Law & Social Inquiry* 32, no. 3 (Summer 2007): 725–57.

131. Doerner and Lab, *Victimology,* 62.

132. Ruback and Thompson, *Social and Psychological Consequences of Violent Victimization,* 113.

133. Rand, *Criminal Victimization, 2008,* 1.

134. Doerner and Lab, *Victimology,* 3.

135. M. Regina Asaro, "Working with Adult Homicide Survivors, Part I: Impact and Sequelae of Murder," *Perspectives in Psychiatric Care* 37, no. 3 (July 2001): 95–101.

136. Ross Macmillan, "Violence and the Life Course: The Consequences of Victimization for Personal and Social Development," *Annual Review of Sociology* 27 (2001): 1–22.

137. Ibid.

138. David Finkelhor, Janis Wolak, and Lucy Berliner, "Police Reporting and Professional Help Seeking for Child Crime Victims: A Review," *Child Maltreatment* 6, no. 1 (February 2001): 17.

139. Katherine J. Bennett, "Legal and Social Issues Surrounding Closed-Circuit Television Testimony of Child Victims and Witnesses," *Journal of Aggression, Maltreatment & Trauma* 8, no. 3 (June 2003): 233–71.

140. Ronet Bachman and Michelle L. Meloy, "The Epidemiology of Violence Against the Elderly: Implications for Primary and Secondary Prevention," *Journal of Contemporary Criminal Justice* 24, no. 2 (May 2008): 186–97.

141. Andrew Karmen, *Crime Victims: An Introduction to Victimology,* 6th ed. (Belmont, CA: Thomson Wadsworth, 2007), 236.

142. Donna J. Rabiner, David Brown, and Janet O'Keeffe, "Financial Exploitation of Older Persons: Policy Issues and Recommendations for Addressing Them," *Journal of Elder Abuse & Neglect* 16, no. 1 (January 2004): 65–84.

143. United States Senate Committee on the Judiciary, "Abuse of the Elderly," Congressional Testimony of James Wright, September 23, 2003, http://judiciary .senate.gov/hearings/testimony .cfm?id=935&wit_id=2647.

144. Mara H. Gottfried, "Woman, 27, Charged in Forced Prostitution of Half-Sister: Alleged Victim Is Developmentally Disabled," *Saint Paul Pioneer Press,* May 25, 2006.

145. Joan R. Petersilia, "Crime Victims with Developmental Disabilities: A Review Essay," *Criminal Justice and Behavior* 28, no. 6 (December 2001): 655–94.

146. Ibid.

147. I. Hershkowitz, M. E. Lamb, and D. Horowitz, "Victimization of Children with Disabilities," *The American Journal of Orthopsychiatry* 77, no. 4 (October 2007): 629–35.

148. Richard Lucardie and Dick Sobsey, "Homicides of People with Developmental Disabilities: An Analysis of News Stories," *Developmental Disabilities Bulletin* 33, no. 1 (2005): 71–98.

149. Dean G. Kilpatrick, "Interpersonal Violence and Public Policy: What About the Victims?" *Journal of Law, Medicine & Ethics* 32, no. 1 (Spring 2004): 73–81.

150. Executive Office for United States Attorneys, Office of the Victims' Rights Ombudsman, "The Rights Established Under the Crime Victims' Rights Act of 2004," http://www.usdoj.gov/ usao/eousa/vr/cvra/index.html.

151. Robert C. Davis and Carrie Mulford, "Victim Rights and New Remedies: Finally Getting Victims Their Due," *Journal of Contemporary Criminal Justice* 24, no. 2 (May 2008): 198–208.

152. Ibid.

153. Farai Chideya, "What Rights Do Crime Victims Have?" (National Public Radio), January 16, 2009, http://www.npr.org/templates/ story/story.php?storyID= 99466602.

154. Gerard V. Bradley, "Retribution: The Central Aim of Punishment," *Harvard Journal of Law & Public Policy* 27, no. 1 (Fall 2003): 19–31.

155. Gerry Johnstone, "Review of Repair or Revenge: Victims and Restorative Justice," *International Review of Victimology* 10, no. 2 (2003): 178–80.

156. R. Barry Ruback, "The Imposition of Economic Sanctions in Philadelphia: Costs, Fines, and Restitution," *Federal Probation* 68, no. 1 (June 2004): 21–26.

157. Marilyn Peterson Amour and Mark S. Umbreit, "Exploring 'Closure' and the Ultimate Penal Sanction for Survivors of Homicide Victims," *Federal Sentencing Reporter* 19, no. 2 (December 2006): 105–12.

158. "Really Really Sorry," *Economist* 368, no. 8335 (August 2, 2003): 54.

159. Roman David and Susanne Y. P. Choi, "Getting Even or Getting Equal? Retributive Desires and Transitional Justice," *Political Psychology* 30, no. 2 (April 2009): 161–92.

160. Lawrence W. Sherman et al., "Effects of Face-to-Face Restorative Justice on Victims of Crime in Four Randomized, Controlled Trials," *Journal of Experimental Criminology* 1, no. 3 (September 2005): 367–95.

161. Carrie J. Petrucci, "Apology in the Criminal Justice Setting: Evidence for Including Apology as an Additional Component in the Legal System," *Behavioral Sciences & the Law* 20, no. 4 (July 2002): 337–62; Jaimie P. Beven et al., "Restoration or Renovation? Evaluating Restorative Justice Outcomes," *Psychiatry, Psychology and Law* 12, no. 1 (April 2005): 194–206; Mark S. Umbreit, Robert B. Coates, and Betty Vos, "Victim-Offender Mediation: Three Decades of Practice and Research," *Conflict Resolution Quarterly* 22, no. 1 (September 2004): 279–303.

162. The National Center for Victims of Crime, "Victim Impact Statements," http://www.ncvc .org/ncvc/main.aspx?dbName =DocumentViewer&Document ID=32515.

163. Trina M. Gordon and Stanley L. Brodsky, "The Influence of Victim Impact Statements on Sentencing in Capital Cases," *Journal of Forensic Psychology Practice* 7, no. 2 (April 2007): 45–52.

## Chapter 4

1. Daniel J. Boorstin, *The Seekers: The Story of Man's Continuing Quest to Understand His World* (New York: Vintage Books, 1998).

2. Andrew Marr, "On History: Why Has the Magna Carta Lasted?" *More Intelligent Life,* Spring 2009, http://www.moreintelligentlife .com/story/history-magna-carta- revisited.

3. Bassam Tili, "The Challenge of Fundamentalism," in *The Challenge of Fundamentalism: Political Islam and the New World Disorder* (Berkeley: University of California Press, 1998).

4. Stephen Pfohl, *Images of Deviance and Social Control: A Sociological History,* 2nd ed. (New York: McGraw-Hill, 1994), 3.

5. Jamaal E. O'Neal, "Couple Charged in Death Tried to 'Rid Infant of Demons,'" *Longview News-Journal,* December 4, 2008; Deborah Simmons, "Mom Declines Insanity Defense in Murder Trial," *Washington Times,* February 14, 2009; Paul James, "Ill Mother Who Killed Sons May Face Execution," *JournalLive,* December 8, 2007, http://www.journallive .co.uk/north-east-news/todays- news/2007/12/08/ill-mother- who-killed-sons-may-face- execution-61634-20220951/.

6. Pfohl, *Images of Deviance and Social Control,* 23.

7. Frank J. Lechner and John Boli, eds., *The Globalization Reader,* 3rd ed. (Malden, MA: Blackwell Publishing, 2008). See Part VIII, "Cultural Globalization II: The Role of Religions," 343–98.

8. Michel Foucault, *Discipline and Punish: The Origins of the Prison,* trans. Alan Sheridan (New York: Pantheon, 1978).

9. Pfohl, *Images of Deviance and Social Control,* 29.

10. Graeme Newman, *The Punishment Response* (Philadelphia: Lippincott, 1978), 37.

11. Aaron Fichtelberg, *Crime Without Borders: An Introduction to International Criminal Justice* (Upper Saddle River, NJ: Pearson-Prentice Hall, 2008), 196.

12. William J. Bennett, John J. Dilulio, Jr., and John P. Walters, *Body Count: Moral Poverty and How to Win America's War Against Crime and Drugs* (New York: Simon and Schuster, 1996).

13. Joel Richman, Dave Mercer, and Tom Mason, "The Social Construction of Evil in a Forensic Setting," *Journal of Forensic Psychiatry* 10, no. 2 (September 1999): 300–8.

14. Dan J. Stein, "The Neurobiology of Evil: Psychiatric Perspectives on Perpetrators," *Ethnicity & Health* 5, no. 3/4 (August 2000): 303–15.

15. Bennett, Dilulio, and Walters, *Body Count.*

16. William J. Bennett, John J. Dilulio, Jr., and John P. Walters, "Moral Poverty and Crime," in *Criminological Theory: Past to Present,* 3rd ed., ed. Francis T. Cullen and Robert Agnew (Los Angeles: Roxbury, 2006), 477.

17. Stephen E. Brown and Fin-Aage Esbensen, "Thoughts of Deterrence: Evolution of a Theoretical Perspective," *International Journal of Offender Therapy and Comparative Criminology* 32, no. 3 (December 1988): 219–32.

18. Crane Brinton, ed., *The Portable Age of Reason Reader* (New York: The Viking Press, 1956).

19. Isaiah Berlin, ed., *The Age of Enlightenment: The 18th Century Philosophers* (New York: Meridian, 1984).

20. Stephen E. Brown and Fin-Aage Esbensen, "Thoughts of Deterrence." 219–32.

21. Peter Gay, ed., *The Enlightenment: A Comprehensive Anthology* (New York: Simon and Schuster, 1973), 15–25.

22. Thomas Hobbes, "A Tough-Minded View of Power and Nature," in *The Portable Age of Reason Reader,* ed. Crane Brinton (New York: The Viking Press, 1956), 137–41.

23. Michael E. Tigar, *Thinking About Terrorism: The Threat to Civil Liberties in Times of National Emergency* (Chicago: American Bar Association, 2007), 160–61.

24. John Locke, "Politics and the State," in *The Portable Enlightenment Reader,* ed. Isaac Krammick (New York: Penguin Books, 1985), 395–404.

25. John Locke, "On the Reform of the Poor Laws," in *The Enlightenment: A Comprehensive Anthology,* ed. Peter Gay (New York: Simon and Schuster, 1973), 100.

26. Jean Jacques Rousseau, *The Social Contract,* trans. Charles Frankel (New York: Hafner Publishing, 1947).

27. Karl Marx and Frederick Engels, *The Communist Manifesto* in *Selected Works* (New York: International Publishers, 1968).

28. Pfohl, *Images of Deviance and Social Control,* 71.

29. Cesare Beccaria, *On Crimes and Punishments,* trans. Henry Paolucci (Indianapolis, IN: Bobbs-Merrill, 1764/1963), 99.

30. Pfohl, *Images of Deviance and Social Control,* 71–73.

31. Robert J. Mutchnick, Randy Martin, and W. Timothy Austin, *Criminological Thought: Pioneers Past and Present* (Upper Saddle River, NJ: Prentice Hall, 2009), 1–13.

32. Gilbert Geis, "Jeremy Bentham (1748–1832)," in *Pioneers in Criminology,* ed. Hermann Mannheim (Montclair, NJ: Patterson Smith, 1972), 15–68.

33. Mark M. Lanier and Stuart Henry, *Essential Criminology* (Boulder, CO: Westview Press, 1998), 70–71.

34. Jeremy Bentham, *An Introduction to the Principles of Morals and Legislation* (London: The Athlone Press, 1970).

35. David Cole, *Enemy Aliens: Double Standards and Constitutional Freedoms in the War on Terrorism* (New York: The Press, 2003).

36. Michel Foucault, *Discipline and Punish.*

37. Christian Parenti, *The Soft Cage: Surveillance in America from Slavery to the War on Terror* (New York: Basic Books, 2003).

38. Biographers note one humorous incident in which Darwin was collecting beetles and, having one in each hand, spied a third specimen that he wanted. He popped that beetle into his mouth and was promptly rewarded with a foul taste as the beetle excreted a mild poison designed to ward off predators. Janet Browne, *Charles Darwin: Voyaging* (Princeton, NJ: Princeton University Press, 1995).

39. David Quammen, *The Reluctant Mr. Darwin: An Intimate Portrait of Charles Darwin and the Making of His Theory of Evolution* (New York: W. W. Norton and Company, 2006).

40. Ian Taylor, Paul Wilson, and Jock Young, *The New Criminology: For a Social Theory of Deviance* (New York: Harper and Row, 1973).

41. Ruth Kornhauser, *Social Sources of Delinquency* (Chicago: University of Chicago Press, 1984).

42. Mark M. Lanier and Stuart Henry, *Essential Criminology* (Boulder, CO: Westview Press, 1998), 108.

43. Marilyn Irvin Holt, *The Orphan Trains: Placing Out in America* (Lincoln: University of Nebraska Press, 1992).

44. William Julius Wilson, *When Work Disappears: The World of the New Urban Poor* (New York: Alfred A. Knopf, 1996).

45. Derek B. Cornish and Ronald V. Clarke, *The Reasoning Criminal* (New York: Springer, 1986).

46. James Q. Wilson, *Thinking About Crime* (New York: Vintage, 1975).

47. Gregg Pogarsky, "Identifying 'Deterrable' Offenders: Implications for Research on Deterrence," *Justice Quarterly* 19 (2002): 431–52.

48. Daniel S. Nagin and Raymond Paternoster, "Enduring Individual Differences and Rational Choice Theories of Crime," *Law and Society Review* 27 (1993): 467–96.

49. Richard Moran, *Knowing Right from Wrong: The Insanity Defense of Daniel M. Naughter* (New York: The Free Press, 1981).

50. Marvin E. Wolfgang, Robert Figlio, and Thorsten Sellin, *Delinquency in a Birth Cohort* (Chicago: University of Chicago Press, 1972).

51. Mark C. Stafford and Mark Warr, "A Reconception of General and Specific Deterrence," *Journal of Research in Crime and Delinquency* 30 (1993): 123–35.

52. Alex R. Piquero and Greg Pogarsky, "Beyond Stafford and Warr's Reconceptualization of Deterrence: Personal and Vicarious Experiences, Impulsivity, and Offending Behavior," *Journal of*

*Research in Crime and Delinquency* 39 (2002): 153–86.

53. Kenneth D. Tunnel, *Choosing Crime* (Chicago: Nelson-Hall, 1992).

54. Ronald V. Clarke and Derek B. Cornish, "Rational Choice," in *Explaining Criminals and Crime,* ed. Raymond Paternoster and Rona Bachman (Los Angeles: Roxbury Publishing, 2000), 23–42.

55. Derek B. Cornish and Ronald V. Clarke, *The Reasoning Criminal* (New York: Springer, 1986).

56. Ronald V. Clarke, *Situational Crime Prevention: Successful Case Studies* (Albany, NY: Harrow and Heston, 1997).

57. Bill McCarthy and John Hagan, "Danger and the Decision to Offend," *Social Forces* 83 (2005): 1065–96.

58. Lawrence E. Cahan and Marcus Felson, "Social Change and Crime Rate Trends: A Routine Activities Approach," *American Sociological Review* 44 (1979): 588–607.

59. John E. Eck, "Preventing Crime at Places," in *Evidence-Based Crime Prevention,* ed. Lawrence W. Sherman et al. (London: Routledge, 2002), 241–94.

60. Pamela Wilcox, Kenneth C. Land, and Scott A. Hunt, *Criminal Circumstance: A Dynamic Multicontextual Criminal Opportunity Theory* (New York: Aldine de Gruyter, 2003).

**Chapter 5**

1. The title of the work in English is *Criminal Man.*

2. Nicholas Dobelbower, "The Arts and Science of Criminal Man in Fin-de-Siècle France," *Proceedings of the Western Society for French History* 34 (2006): 205–16.

3. Judith Burns, "Facial Expressions 'Not Global,'" BBC, August 14, 2009, http://news.bbc.co.uk/2/hi/science/nature/8199951.stm.

4. "Musings on Physiognomy," *Britannia Monthly Magazine* 2 (March 1836): 227–30 in *Pioneering Perspectives in Criminology: The Literature of 19th Century Criminological Positivism,* ed. David M. Horton (Incline Village, NV: Copperhouse Publishing Company, 2000), 5–8.

5. Phrenology, http://www.phrenology.org/.

6. "Phrenology Epitomized," *Continental Repository* 2 (August 1841): 156–59 in *Pioneering Perspectives in Criminology,* 17–24.

7. Stephen M. Soreff and Patricia H. Bazemore, "Examining Phrenology," *Behavioral Healthcare,* January 1, 2007, 14–18.

8. Eric Nagourney, "Exercise Link Is Seen Between Crime and Fitness," *New York Times,* June 17, 2008, late edition, F6; Sean Maddan, Jeffery T. Walker, and J. Mitchell Miller, "Does Size Really Matter? A Reexamination of Sheldon's Somatotypes and Criminal Behavior," *Social Science Journal* 45, no. 2 (June 2008): 330–44.

9. Nicole Rafter, *The Criminal Brain* (New York: New York University Press, 2008). See Chapter 7.

10. Earnest Hooton, *Crime and the Man* (Cambridge, MA: Harvard University Press, 1939), 181.

11. Rafter, *The Criminal Brain,* Chapter 7.

12. Ibid.

13. Ibid.

14. Peter Monaghan, "Biocriminology," *Chronicle of Higher Education* 55, no. 32 (April 17, 2009): B4.

15. Rafter, *The Criminal Brain,* 93–94.

16. Ibid., 95.

17. Ibid.

18. Ibid., 98–99.

19. Edwin Black, *War Against the Weak* (New York: Four Walls Eight Windows, 2003), 24.

20. Michael F. Guyer, *Being Well-Born: An Introduction to Eugenics* (Indianapolis, IN: Bobbs-Merrill, 1916).

21. Edwin Hardin Sutherland, *Criminology* (Philadelphia: J.B. Lippincott, 1924), 622.

22. Black, *War Against the Weak,* Chapters 6 and 19.

23. George Hodak, "Eugenics Challenged in *Skinner v. Oklahoma,*" *ABA Journal* 95, no. 6 (June 2009): 72; *Skinner v. State of Okl. Ex Rel. Williamson,* 316 U.S. 535 (1942), 316 U.S. 535; Michael G. Silver, "Eugenics and Compulsory Sterilization Laws: Providing Redress for the Victims of a Shameful Era in United States History," *George Washington Law Review* 72, no. 4 (April, 2004): Geo. Wash. L. Rev. 862.

24. U.S. National Library of Medicine, Genetics Home Reference, "47,XYY Syndrome," http://ghr.nlm.nih.gov/condition=47xyysyndrome.

25. Patricia A. Jacobs et al., "Aggressive Behaviour, Mental Subnormality and the XYY Male," *Nature* 208 (December 25, 1965): 1351-2.

26. Nkanginieme Ike, "Current Thinking on XYY Syndrome," *Psychiatric Annals* 30, no. 2 (February 2000): 91–95.

27. Guang Guo, "The Linking of Sociology and Biology," *Social Forces* 85, no. 1 (September 2006): 145–9.

28. Adrian Raine, *The Psychopathology of Crime: Criminal Behavior as a Clinical Disorder* (San Diego, CA: Elsevier, 1993), 48–53.

29. Guo, "The Linking of Sociology and Biology," 145–9.

30. Richard P. Ebstein and Robert H. Belmaker, "Genetics of Sensation or Novelty Seeking and Criminal

Behavior," in *The Neurobiology of Criminal Behavior,* ed. Joseph Glicksohn (Dordrecht, Netherlands: Kluwer Academic Publishers, 2002), 51–78; L. F. Lowenstein, "The Genetic Aspects of Criminality," *Journal of Human Behavior in the Social Environment* 8, no. 1 (October 2003): 63–78.

31. Harriet A. Ball et al., "Genetic and Environmental Influences on Victims, Bullies and Bully-Victims in Childhood," *Journal of Child Psychology and Psychiatry* 49, no. 1 (January 1, 2008): 104–12.

32. Guang Guo, Michael E. Roettger, and Tianji Cai, "The Integration of Genetic Propensities into Social-Control Models of Delinquency and Violence Among Male Youths," *American Sociological Review* 73, no. 4 (August 2008): 543–69.

33. Ethan Watters, "DNA Is Not Destiny," *Discover* 27, no. 11 (November 2006): 32–75.

34. Ibid.

35. Michael Rutter, Terrie E. Moffitt, and Avshalom Caspi, " Gene–Environment Interplay and Psychopathology: Multiple Varieties but Real Effects," *Journal of Child Psychology and Psychiatry* 47, no. 3/4 (2006): 226–61.

36. Soo Hyun Rhee and Irwin D. Waldman, "Testing Alternative Hypotheses Regarding the Role of Development on Genetic and Environmental Influences Underlying Antisocial Behavior," in *Causes of Conduct Disorder and Juvenile Delinquency,* ed. Benjamin B. Lahey, Terrie E. Moffitt, and Avshalom Caspi (New York: Guilford Press, 2003), 305–18.

37. Catherine Tuvblad, Martin Grann, and Paul Lichtenstein, "Heritability for Adolescent Antisocial Behavior Differs with Socioeconomic Status: Gene–Environment Interaction,"

*Journal of Child Psychology and Psychiatry* 47, no. 7 (July 2006): 734–43.

38. Vernon L. Quinsey et al., *Juvenile Delinquency: Understanding the Origins of Individual Differences* (Washington, DC: American Psychological Association, 2004), 50–51.

39. Randy Thornhill and Craig T. Palmer, *A Natural History of Rape: Biological Bases of Sexual Coercion* (Cambridge, MA: MIT Press, 2000).

40. Elisabeth A. Lloyd, "Violence Against Science: Rape and Evolution," in *Evolution, Gender, and Rape,* ed. Cheryl Brown Travis (Cambridge, MA: MIT Press, 2003), 235–61.

41. Christopher J. Ferguson, "An Evolutionary Approach to Understanding Violent Antisocial Behavior: Diagnostic Implications for a Dual-Process Etiology," *Journal of Forensic Psychology Practice* 8, no. 4 (October 2008): 321–43.

42. Lee Ellis, "Sex, Status, and Criminality: A Theoretical Nexus," *Social Biology* 51, no. 3/4 (Fall–Winter 2004): 144–60; Lee Ellis, "Reducing Crime Evolutionarily," in *Evolutionary Forensic Psychology: Darwinian Foundations of Crime and Law,* ed. Joshua D. Duntley and Todd K. Shackelford (New York: Oxford University Press, 2008), 249–67.

43. Avshalom Caspi et al., "Role of Genotype in the Cycle of Violence in Maltreated Children," *Science* 297, no. 5582 (August 2, 2002): 851; EurekAlert, "Gene May Protect Abused Kids Against Behavior Problems," http://www.eurekalert.org/pub_releases/2002-08/uow-gmp072602.php.

44. Ibid.

45. Ibid.

46. Alan Booth et al., "Testosterone and Social Behavior," *Social Forces* 85, no. 1 (September 2006): 167–91.

47. Andrea L. Glenn, "Neuroendocrine Markers of Psychopathy," in *The Handbook of Neuropsychiatric Biomarkers, Endophenotypes and Genes, Vol. 3: Metabolic and Peripheral Biomarkers* (New York: Springer Science and Business Media, 2009), 59–70.

48. Alan Booth et al., "Testosterone and Social Behavior," 167–91.

49. Alan Booth and D. Wayne Osgood, "The Influence of Testosterone on Deviance in Adulthood: Assessing and Explaining the Relationship," *Criminology* 31, no. 1 (February 1993): 93–117.

50. Lee Ellis, Shyamal Das, and Hasan Buker, "Androgen-Promoted Physiological Traits and Criminality: A Test of the Evolutionary Neuroandrogenic Theory," *Personality & Individual Differences* 44, no. 3 (February 2008): 699–709.

51. Ibid.

52. Ibid.

53. Glenn, "Neuroendocrine Markers of Psychopathy," 61–62.

54. David Terburg, Barak Morgan, and Jack van Honk, "The Testosterone-Cortisol Ratio: A Hormonal Marker for Proneness to Social Aggression," *International Journal of Law and Psychiatry* 32, no. 4 (July 15, 2009): 216–23; Arne Popma et al., "Cortisol Moderates the Relationship Between Testosterone and Aggression in Delinquent Male Adolescents," *Biological Psychiatry* 61, no. 3 (February 2007): 405–11.

55. Timo D. Vloet et al., "Structural and Functional MRI-Findings in Children and Adolescents with Antisocial Behavior," *Behavioral Sciences & the Law* 26, no. 1 (January 2008): 99–111.

56. Shelley Batts, "Brain Lesions and Their Implications in Criminal Responsibility," *Behavioral Sciences & the Law* 27, no. 2 (March 2009): 261–72.

57. Elizabeth A. Shirtcliff et al., "Neurobiology of Empathy and Callousness: Implications for the Development of Antisocial Behavior," *Behavioral Sciences & the Law* 27, no. 2 (March 2009): 137–71.

58. Batts, "Brain Lesions," 261–72; Mike Mayo, "Whitman, Charles," *American Murder* (February 2008): 372–74.

59. J. Bramham et al., "Social and Emotional Functioning Following Bilateral and Unilateral Neurosurgical Prefrontal Cortex Lesions," *Journal of Neuropsychology* 3, no. 1 (March 2009): 125–43; D. C. Krawczyk, "Contributions of the Prefrontal Cortex to the Neural Basis of Human Decision Making," *Neuroscience and Biobehavioral Reviews* 26, no. 6 (2002): 631–64.

60. Batts, "Brain Lesions," 261–72.

61. Ibid.

62. Ibid.

63. Vloet et al., "Structural and Functional MRI-Findings," 99–111.

64. Batts, "Brain Lesions," 261–72.

65. Mary Beckman, "Crime, Culpability, and the Adolescent Brain," *Science* 305, no. 5684 (July 30, 2004): 596–99.

66. Michael Meacher, "Diet Can Make You Nice," *New Statesman,* February 16, 2004, 30.

67. Frank D. Roylance, "Lead Tied to Criminal Behavior: Poisoning Damages Crucial Brain Matter, Studies Find," *Baltimore Sun,* May 28, 2008.

68. Jennifer C. Karberg and Doris J. James, *Substance Dependence, Abuse, and Treatment of Jail Inmates, 2002* (Washington, DC: Bureau of Justice Statistics U.S. Department of Justice Office of Justice Programs, 2005), 3, http://www.ojp.usdoj.gov/bjs/pub/pdf/sdatji02.pdf.

69. Ibid.

70. Gavan Palk, Jeremy Davey, and James Freeman, "Prevalence and Characteristics of Alcohol-Related Incidents Requiring Police Attendance," *Journal of Studies on Alcohol & Drugs* 68, no. 4 (July 2007): 575.

71. Ibid.

72. Lawrence A. Greenfeld, *Alcohol and Crime* (Washington, DC: US Department of Justice Office of Justice Programs, 1998), iii, http://www.ojp.usdoj.gov/bjs/pub/pdf/ac.pdf.

73. Ibid.

74. Susan E. Martin, "The Links Between Alcohol, Crime and the Criminal Justice System: Explanations, Evidence and Interventions," *American Journal on Addictions* 10, no. 2 (April 2001): 136–58.

75. Candice L. Odgers et al. "Is It Important to Prevent Early Exposure to Drugs and Alcohol Among Adolescents?" *Psychological Science* 19, no. 10 (October 2008): 1037–44; World Health Organization, "Children's and Adolescents' Health in Europe," September 8, 2003, http://www.euro.who.int/document/mediacentre/fs0203e.pdf.

76. Gary Michael McClelland and Linda A. Teplin, "Alcohol Intoxication and Violent Crime: Implications for Public Health Policy," *American Journal on Addictions* 10 (January 15, 2001): 70–86; Martin, "Links Between Alcohol, Crime and the Criminal Justice System," 136–58.

77. Martin, "Links Between Alcohol, Crime and the Criminal Justice System," 136–58.

78. Ibid.

79. Ibid.

80. David Farabee, Vandana Joshi, and M. Douglas Anglin, "Addiction Careers and Criminal Specialization," *Crime & Delinquency* 47, no. 2 (April 2001): 196–220.

81. Erich Goode, *Drugs in American Society* (New York: McGraw-Hill, 2007). See Chapter 12.

82. Erich Goode, "Drug Use and Criminal Behavior," in *Out of Control: Assessing the General Theory of Crime,* ed. Erich Goode (Palo Alto, CA: Stanford University Press, 2008), 185–99.

83. Chris Allen, "The Links Between Heroin, Crack Cocaine and Crime: Where Does Street Crime Fit In?" *British Journal of Criminology* 45, no. 3 (May 2005): 355–72.

84. David Farabee, Vandana Joshi, and M. Douglas Anglin, "Addiction Careers and Criminal Specialization," *Crime & Delinquency* 47, no. 2 (April 2001): 196–220.

85. Goode, "Drug Use and Criminal Behavior," 185–99.

86. Peter Monaghan, "Biocriminology," *Chronicle of Higher Education* 55, no. 32 (April 17, 2009): B4.

87. Yaling Yang, Andrea L Glenn, and Adrian Raine, "Brain Abnormalities in Antisocial Individuals: Implications for the Law," *Behavioral Sciences & the Law* 26, no. 1 (2008): 65–83.

88. Ibid.

89. Dean Mobbs et al., "Law, Responsibility, and the Brain," Public Library of Science Biology 5, no. 4, (2007), http://www.plosbiology.org/article/info%3Adoi%2F10.1371%2Fjournal.pbio.0050103.

90. Stephen H. Dinwiddie, "Biological Causes of Criminality and Expert Testimony—Some Cautionary Thoughts," in *The Science, Treatment, and Prevention of Antisocial Behaviors: Application to the Criminal Justice System,*

ed. Diana H. Fishbein (Kingston, NJ: Civic Research Institute, 2000), 24.1–24.10.

91. Curt R. Bartol and Anne M. Bartol, *Criminal Behavior: A Psychosocial Approach* (Upper Saddle River, NJ: Pearson Education, 2008), 9–10.

92. David Putwain and Aidan Sammons, *Psychology and Crime* (New York: Routledge, 2005), 44–45.

93. Bartol and Bartol, *Criminal Behavior: A Psychosocial Approach*, 115–21.

94. Jack Arbuthnot, Donald A. Gordon, and Gregory Jurkovic, *Handbook of Juvenile Delinquency*, ed. Herbert C. Quay (Chichester, UK: Wiley, 1987). See Chapter 6.

95. Håkan Stattin and Ingrid Klackenberg-Larsson, "Early Language and Intelligence Development and Their Relationship to Future Criminal Behavior," *Journal of Abnormal Psychology* 102, no. 3 (August 1993): 369–78.

96. E. B. Brownlie et al. "Early Language Impairment and Young Adult Delinquent and Aggressive Behavior," *Journal of Abnormal Child Psychology* 32, no. 4 (August 2004): 453–467.

97. Pamela C. Snow and Martine B. Powell, "Oral Language Competence, Social Skills and High-Risk Boys: What Are Juvenile Offenders Trying to Tell Us?" *Children & Society* 22, no. 1 (January 1, 2008): 16–28.

98. Bartol and Bartol, *Criminal Behavior: A Psychosocial Approach*, 54–55.

99. Jean Marie McGloin, Travis C. Pratt, and Jeff Maahs, "Rethinking the IQ-Delinquency Relationship: A Longitudinal Analysis of Multiple Theoretical Models," *Justice Quarterly* 21, no. 3 (September 2004): 603–35.

100. Bartol and Bartol, *Criminal Behavior: A Psychosocial Approach*, 237.

101. Frederick Rotgers and Michael Maniacci in *Antisocial Personality Disorder: A Practitioner's Guide to Comparative Treatments*, ed. Frederick Rotgers and Michael Maniacci (New York: Springer, 2006). See Chapter 1, "Antisocial Personality Disorder: An Introduction."

102. Bartol and Bartol, *Criminal Behavior: A Psychosocial Approach*, 235.

103. Ibid., 236.

104. Katherine L. Fitzgerald and George J. Demakis, "The Neuropsychology of Antisocial Personality Disorder," *Disease-A-Month: DM* 53, no. 3 (March 2007): 177–83.

105. Rotgers and Maniacci, *Antisocial Personality Disorder: A Practitioner's Guide*, Chapter 1.

106. Bartol and Bartol, *Criminal Behavior: A Psychosocial Approach*, 236.

107. Willem H. J. Martens, "The Problem with Robert Hare's Psychopathy Checklist: Incorrect Conclusions, High Risk of Misuse, and Lack of Reliability," *Medicine and Law* 27, no. 2 (June 2008): 449–62.

108. Bartol and Bartol, *Criminal Behavior: A Psychosocial Approach*, 195.

109. Ibid., Chapter 6.

110. Ibid., 241.

111. Jennifer Eno Louden and Jennifer L. Skeem, "Constructing Insanity: Jurors' Prototypes, Attitudes, and Legal Decision-Making," *Behavioral Sciences & the Law* 25, no. 4 (July 2007): 449–70.

112. L. A. Callahan et al., "The Volume and Characteristics of Insanity Defense Pleas: An Eight-State Study," *Bulletin of Psychiatry and the Law* 19 (1991): 331–38.

113. Georgia Lee Sims, "The Criminalization of Mental Illness: How Theoretical Failures Create Real Problems in the Criminal Justice System," *Vanderbilt Law Review* 62, no. 3 (April 1, 2009): 1053–83.

## Chapter 6

1. C. Wright Mills, *The Sociological Imagination* (New York: Oxford University Press, 1959).

2. Claire M. Renzetti, Lynne Goodstein, and Susan L. Miller, eds. *Rethinking Gender, Crime, and Justice* (Los Angeles: Roxbury Publishing Company, 2006).

3. Elliot Currie, *Crime and Punishment in America* (New York: Metropolitan Books, 1998).

4. Paul Frederick Cressey, "Population Succession in Chicago: 1898–1930," *The American Journal of Sociology* 44, no. 1 (July 1938): 55–69.

5. Douglas S. Massey and Nancy A. Denton, *American Apartheid: Segregation and the Making of the Underclass* (Cambridge, MA: Harvard University Press, 1993).

6. Robert J. Sampson and William Julius Wilson, "A Theory of Race, Crime, and Urban Inequality," in *Criminological Theory Past to Present*, ed. Francis T. Cullen and Robert Agnew (Los Angeles: Roxbury Publishing, 2006), 102–7.

7. Michael Sokolove, "Constructing a Teen Phenom," *New York Times Magazine* 154, no. 53047 (Nov. 28, 2004): 80–85.

8. Diana M. Pearce, "Black, White, and Many Shades of Gray: Real Estate Brokers and Their Racial Practices" (PhD diss., University of Michigan, 1976).

9. Ernest W. Burgess, "The Growth of the City," in *The City*, ed. R. E. Park, E. W. Burgess, and Roderick D. McKenzie (Chicago:

University of Chicago Press, 1925), 47–62.

10. C. Wright Mills, "The Professional Ideology of Social Pathologists," *American Journal of Sociology* 49 (1943): 165–80.

11. J. Robert Lilly, Francis T. Cullen, and Richard A. Ball, *Criminological Theory: Context and Consequences,* 4th ed. (Thousand Oaks, CA: Sage, 2007), 38.

12. Jon Snodgrass, "Clifford R. Shaw and Henry D. McKay: Chicago Criminologists," *British Journal of Sociology* 16 (1976): 1–19.

13. Clifford R. Shaw, *The Jack-Roller: A Delinquent Boy's Own Story* (Chicago: University of Chicago Press, 1930).

14. Solomon Kobrin, "The Chicago Area Project: A 25-Year Assessment," *Annals of the American Society of Political and Social Science* (March 1959): 19–29.

15. Chicago Area Project Pioneers include Ernest W. Burgess, Tony Sorrentino, Daniel "Moose" Brindisi, Sadie Waterford Jones, Beatrice Caffrey, and E. Toy Fletcher. See Chicago Area Project, http://www.chicagoareaproject.org.

16. Francis T. Cullen and Robert Agnew, eds., *Criminological Theory: Past to Present,* 4th ed. (Los Angeles: Roxbury Publishing, 2007), 92.

17. Robert J. Sampson, Stephen W. Raudenbush, and Felton Sams, "Neighborhoods and Violent Crime: A Multilevel Study of Collective Efficacy," *Science* 227 (Aug. 15, 1997): 918–24.

18. Robert J. Sampson, Stephen W. Raudenbush, and Felton Sams, "Collective Efficacy Theory: Lessons Learned and Directions for Future Inquiry," in *Taking Stock: The Status of Criminological Theory (Advances in Criminological Theory),* ed. Francis T. Cullen, John Paul Wright, and Kristie R. Blevins (New Bruns-

wick, NJ: Transaction, 2006), 149–67.

19. Robert J. Bursik, Jr., and Harald G. Grasmick, *Neighborhoods and Crime: The Dimensions of Effective Community Control* (New York: Lexington, 1993).

20. Gill Geis and Colin Goff, "Edwin H. Sutherland's White-Collar Crime in America: An Essay in Historical Criminology," *Criminal Justice History* 7 (1986): 1–31.

21. Gerben J. N. Bruinsma, "Differential Association Theory Reconsidered: An Extension and Its Empirical Test," *Journal of Quantitative Criminology* 8, no. 1 (March 1992): 29–49.

22. Ronald L. Akers, "Is Differential Association/Social Learning Cultural Deviance Theory?" *Criminology* 34 (1996): 229–47.

23. Gresham M. Sykes and David Matza, "Techniques of Neutralization," *American Sociological Review* 22 (1957): 664–70.

24. Shadd Maruna and Heith Copes, "What Have We Learned from Five Decades of Neutralization Research?" in *Crime and Justice 32: A Review of Research,* ed. Michael Tonry (Chicago: University of Chicago Press, 2005), 221–320.

25. Marvin E. Wolfgang and Franco Ferracuti, *The Subculture of Violence: Towards an Integrated Theory in Criminology* (Beverly Hills, CA: Sage, 1982).

26. Walter Miller, "Lower-Class Culture as a Generating Milieu of Gang Delinquency," *Journal of Social Issues* 14 (1958): 5–19.

27. Frank P. Williams, III and Marilyn M. Shane, *Criminological Theory,* 4th ed. (Upper Saddle River, NJ: Prentice Hall, 2004), 125.

28. Jo Dixon and Alan J. Linzotte, "Gun Ownership and the 'Southern Subculture of Violence,'" *American Journal of Sociology* 93 (1987): 383–405.

29. Karen F. Parker, "A Move Toward Specificity: Examining Urban Disadvantage and Race and Relationship-Specific Homicide Rates," *Journal of Quantitative Criminology* 17 (2001): 89–110.

30. Ramiro Martinez, Jr., and Matthew T. Lee, "Comparing the Context of Immigrant Homicides in Miami: Haitians, Jamaicans, and Mariels," *International Migration Review* 34 (2000): 794–812.

31. Elijah Anderson, *Code of the Street: Decency, Violence, and the Moral Life of the Inner City* (New York: W.W. Norton and Company, 1999).

32. Elijah Anderson, "The Code of the Street," in *Criminological Theory: Past to Present,* ed. Francis T. Cullen and Robert Agnew (Los Angeles: Roxbury Publishing, 2006), 154.

33. Ibid., 159.

34. Anderson, "The Code of the Street," 154.

35. Émile Durkheim, *The Division of Labor in Society,* trans. George Simpson (1893; repr., New York: The Free Press, 1933).

36. Robert K. Merton, "Social Structure and Anomie," *American Sociological Review* 3 (1938): 672–82.

37. Richard Cloward and Lloyd Ohlin, *Delinquency and Opportunity* (Glencoe, IL: Free Press, 1960).

38. Albert K. Cohen, *Delinquent Boys* (Glencoe, IL: Free Press, 1955).

39. Steven F. Messner and Richard Rosenfeld, *Crime and the American Dream,* 3rd ed. (Belmont, CA: Wadsworth, 2000).

40. Robert Agnew, "General Strain Theory: Current Status and Directions for Further Research," in *Taking Stock: The Status of Criminological Theory,* 101–23.

41. Messner and Rosenfeld, *Crime and the American Dream.*

42. Robert Agnew, "Building on the Foundations of General Strain Theory: Specifying the Types of Strain Most Likely to Lead to Crime and Delinquency," *Journal of Research in Crime and Delinquency* 38 (2001): 319–61.

43. Robert Agnew, "Pressured into Crime: General Strain Theory," in *Criminological Theory: Past to Present,* 3rd ed., ed. Francis T. Cullen and Robert Agnew (Los Angeles: Roxbury Publishing, 2006), 202.

44. E. E. Lemasters, *Blue Collar Aristocrats: Lifestyles at a Working Class Tavern* (Madison: University of Wisconsin Press, 1976).

45. Robert Agnew, "Pressured into Crime: General Strain Theory." See note 42, p. 206.

46. Velmer S. Burton, Jr., and Francis T. Cullen, "The Empirical Status of Strain Theory," *Journal of Crime and Justice* 15 (1992): 1–30.

47. Robert Agnew, "The Origin of Delinquent Events: An Examination of Offender Accounts," *Journal of Research in Crime and Delinquency* 27 (1990): 267–94.

48. Travis Hirschi, *Causes of Delinquency* (Berkeley: University of California Press, 1969).

49. Michael R. Gottfredson, "The Empirical Status of Control Theory in Criminology," in *Taking Stock: The Status of Criminological Theory,* 77–100.

50. Walter C. Reckless, Simon Dinity, and Ellen Murray, "The 'Good Boy' in a High Delinquency Area," *Journal of Criminal Law, Criminology, and Police Science* 48 (1957): 18–25.

51. Walter C. Reckless, Simon Dinity, and Ellen Murray, "Self-Concept as an Insulator Against Delinquency," *American Sociological Review* 21 (1956): 744–56.

52. Stephen A. Cernkovich and Peggy Giordano, "Family Relationships and Delinquency," *Criminology* 25 (1987): 295–321.

53. Eric Poole and Robert Regoli, "The Commitment of Delinquents to Their Misdeeds: A Re-Examination," *Journal of Criminal Justice* 6 (1978): 261–68.

54. Allen F. Liska and Mark D. Reed," Ties to Conventional Institutions and Delinquency: Estimating Reciprocal Effects," *American Sociological Review* 50 (1985): 547–60.

55. Travis Hirschi, *Causes of Delinquency.*

56. Josine Junger-Tas, "An Empirical Test of Social Control Theory," *Journal of Quantitative Criminology* 8 (1992): 9–28.

57. Michael R. Gottfredson and Travis Hirschi, *A General Theory of Crime* (Stanford, CA: Stanford University Press, 1990).

58. John Hagan, *Structural Criminology* (New Brunswick, NJ: Rutgers University Press, 1989).

59. Edem F. Avakame, "Modeling the Patriarchal Factor in Juvenile Delinquency: Is There Room for Peers, Church, and Television?" *Criminal Justice and Behavior* 24 (1991): 477–94.

60. Gary F. Jensen and Kevin Thompson, "What's Class Got to Do With It? A Further Examination of Power Control Theory," *American Journal of Sociology* 95 (1990): 1009–23.

61. Hagan, *Structural Criminology.*

## Chapter 7

1. David P. Farrington, "Developmental and Life-Course Criminology: Key Theoretical and Empirical Issues," *Criminology* 41, no. 2 (2003): 221.

2. Michael L. Benson, *Crime and the Life Course: An Introduction* (Los Angeles: Roxbury, 2002).

3. Federal Bureau of Investigation, Uniform Crime Reports, *Crime in the United States, 2007,* Table 38, http://www.fbi.gov/ucr/cius2007/data/table_38.html.

4. Gerald R. Patterson, Barbara D. Baryshe, and Elizabeth Ramsey, "A Developmental Perspective on Antisocial Behavior," in *Criminological Theory: Past to Present,* 3rd ed., ed. Francis T. Cullen and Robert Agnew (New York: Oxford University Press, 2006), 495–521.

5. James D. Unnever, Francis T. Cullen, and Robert Agnew, "Why Is 'Bad Parenting' Criminogenic? Implications from Rival Theories," *Youth Violence and Juvenile Justice* 4, no. 1 (2006): 3–33.

6. Anthony Bryk and Barbara Schneider, *Trust in Schools: A Core Resource for Improvement* (New York: Russell Sage Foundation, 2002).

7. Mark Warr, *Companions in Crime: The Social Aspects of Criminal Conduct* (New York: Cambridge University Press, 2002).

8. Alex R. Piquero, Robert Brame, and Donald L. Lynan, "Studying Criminal Career Length Through Early Adulthood Among Serious Offenders," *Crime and Delinquency* 50, no. 3 (2004): 412–35.

9. Patterson, Baryshe, and Ramsey," A Developmental Perspective on Antisocial Behavior," 495–521.

10. Francis T. Cullen and Robert Agnew, *Criminological Theory: Past to Present* (Los Angeles: Roxbury, 2006), 496.

11. Terrie E. Moffitt, "Adolescence-Limited and Life-Course-Persistent Antisocial Behavior: A Developmental Taxonomy," *Psychological Review* 4 (1993): 674–701.

12. Amy V. D'Unger et al., "How Many Latent Classes of Delinquent/Criminal Careers? Results from Mixed Poisson Regression Analyses," *American*

*Journal of Sociology* 103, no. 6 (May 1998): 1593–1630.

13. Marvin E. Wolfgang, Robert M. Figlio, and Thorsten Sellin, *Delinquency in a Birth Cohort* (Chicago: University of Chicago Press, 1987).

14. Terrie E. Moffitt, "Pathways in the Lifecourse," in *Criminological Theory: Past to Present,* 504.

15. David C. Rowe, *Biology and Crime* (Los Angeles: Roxbury, 2002).

16. David C. Rowe and David P. Farrington, "The Familial Transmission of Criminal Convictions," *Criminology* 35, no. 1 (1997): 174–201.

17. Jay Macleod, *Ain't No Making It: Leveled Aspirations in a Low Income Neighborhood* (Boulder, CO: Westview Press, 1987).

18. Moffitt, "Pathways in the Lifecourse," 502–21.

19. Ibid., 510–11.

20. Gary LaFree, *Losing Legitimacy: Street Crime and the Decline of Social Institutions in America* (Boulder, CO: Westview Press, 1998).

21. Terence Thornberry and Marvin D. Krohn, "The Self-Report Method for Measuring Delinquency and Crime," *Criminal Justice 2000: Measurement and Analysis of Crime and Justice* (Washington, DC: US Department of Justice, 2000), 33–83.

22. Diana Fishbein, *Biobehavioral Perspectives in Criminology* (Belmont, CA: Wadsworth, 2001), 41–45.

23. Moffitt, "Pathways in the Lifecourse," 517.

24. Erving Goffman, *Asylums: Essays on the Social Situation of Mental Patients and Other Inmates* (Garden City, NY: Anchor Books, 1961).

25. William Julius Wilson, *The Truly Disadvantaged: The Inner City, the Underclass, and Public Policy* (Chicago: University of Chicago Press, 1987).

26. Robert J. Sampson and John H. Laub, *Crime in the Making, Pathways and Turning Points Through Life* (Cambridge, MA: Harvard University Press, 1995).

27. Farrington, "Developmental and Life-Course Criminology," 221.

28. Benson, *Crime and the Life Course.*

29. Cullen and Agnew, *Criminological Theory,* 489.

30. Sheldon Glueck and Eleanor Glueck, *Unraveling Juvenile Delinquency* (New York: Commonwealth Fund, 1950).

31. John H. Laub and Robert J. Sampson, *Shared Beginnings, Divergent Lives; Delinquent Boys to Age 70* (Cambridge, MA: Harvard University Press, 2003).

32. Cullen and Agnew, *Criminological Theory,* 490.

33. Sampson and Laub, *Shared Beginnings, Divergent Lives,* 121.

34. Mark Warr, "Life-Course Transitions and Desistance from Crime," *Criminology* 36 (1998): 183–215.

35. Ronald L. Simons et al., "A Test of Life-Course Explanations for Stability and Change in Antisocial Behavior from Adolescence to Young Adulthood," *Criminology* 40, no. 2 (May 2002): 426.

36. David P. Farrington, ed., *Integrated Development and Life Course Theories of Offending: Advances in Criminological Theory* 14 (New Brunswick, NJ: Transaction, 2005).

37. Robert K. Merton, *Social Theory and Social Structure* (Glencoe, IL: Free Press, 1957).

38. Delbert S. Elliott, Suzanne S. Ageton, and Rachelle J. Canter, "An Integrated Theoretical Perspective on Delinquent Behavior," in *Criminological Theory: Past to Present,* 3rd. ed., ed. Francis T. Cullen and Robert Agnew (Beverly Hills, CA: Sage, 2006), 537–50.

39. Travis Hirschi, "Exploring Alternatives to Integrated Theory," in *Theoretical Integration in the Study of Deviance and Crime: Problems and Prospects,* ed. Steven F. Messner, Marvin D. Krohn, and Allen E. Liska (Albany: State University of New York Press, 1989), 37–49.

40. Terence P. Thornberry, "Toward an Interactional Theory of Delinquency," *Criminology* 25, no. 4 (2006): 863–92.

41. Ibid.

42. Charles R. Tittle, *Control Balance: Toward a General Theory of Deviance* (Boulder, CO: Westview, 1995).

43. Ibid.

44. Charles R. Tittle, "Control Balance Theory," in *Criminological Theory: Past to Present,* 563–81.

45. Actually, Cullen lists 13 propositions, but we have selected 10 here for the sake of clarity.

46. Ibid.

47. John Paul Wright and Francis T. Cullen, "Parental Efficacy and Delinquent Behavior: Do Control and Support Matter?" *Criminology* 39, no. 3 (2006): 677–706.

48. Francis T. Cullen, "The Twelve People Who Saved Rehabilitation: How the Science of Criminology Made a Difference—The American Society of Criminology 2004 Presidential Address," *Criminology* 43, no. 1 (March 2005): 1–42.

49. Robert Agnew, *Why Do Criminals Offend? A General Theory of Crime and Delinquency* (Los Angeles: Roxbury, 2005).

50. David P. Farrington, "Developmental and Life-Course Criminology: Key Theoretical and Empirical Issues—The 2002 Sutherland Award Address," *Criminology* 41, no. 2 (May 2003): 221–55.

# Chapter 8

1. Frank Tannenbaum, *Crime and the Community* (New York: Columbia University Press, 1939), 19.

2. Howard S. Becker, *Outsiders: Studies in the Sociology of Deviance* (New York: Macmillan, 1963).

3. Edwin M. Lemert, *Social Pathology: A Systematic Approach to the Theory of Sociopathic Behavior* (New York: McGraw-Hill, 1951), 17.

4. Thomas J. Bernard, "The Distinction Between Conflict and Radical Criminology," *Journal of Criminal Law and Criminology* 72, (1981): 362–79.

5. Texas Defender Service, *Lethal Indifference: The Fatal Combination of Incompetent Attorneys and Unaccountable Courts* (Austin: Texas Defender Service, 2002), x, http://www.texasdefender.org/front.pdf.

6. David F. Greenburg, *Crime and Capitalism: Readings in Marxist Criminology* (Palo Alto, CA: Mayfield Publishing Company, 1981), 19.

7. George B. Vold, Thomas J. Bernard, and Jeffrey B. Snipes, *Theoretical Criminology* (New York: Oxford University Press. 2002), 251–52.

8. Friedrich Engles, "Crime in Communist Society" in *Crime and Capitalism: Readings in Marxist Criminology;* Becker, *Outsiders: Studies in the Sociology of Deviance,* 51.

9. Howard Abadinsky, *Organized Crime,* 8th ed. (Belmont, CA: Thomson 2007), 35–43.

10. In 1997, I participated in a Fulbright program study tour to China. In one interesting and candid conversation with a Chinese scholar, I asked how long the country could remain communist in light of the pressures of capitalism. The professor told me that although he expected China to continue its rapid move toward capitalism, it was unwise to move too quickly lest the entire system disintegrate as it did in the former Soviet Union. He contended that it was only responsible to maintain a stable economic system even as the political system changed.

11. Jonathan H. Turner, *The Structure of Sociological Theory,* 4th ed. (Chicago: Dorsey, 1986).

12. Jack Chang, "Crime Rate Plummets in Brazil's Largest State," Knight Ridder Tribune Washington Bureau (DC), December 26, 2007; "Escalating Crime Rate Strangling the Rainbow Ethos," *The Gold Coast Bulletin,* October 7, 2007.

13. William Grimes, "Ralf Dahrendorf, Sociologist, Dies at 80," *New York Times,* June 22, 2009, http://www.nytimes.com/2009/06/22/world/europe/22dahrendorf.html.

14. Ralf Dahrendorf, *Class and Class Conflict in an Industrial Society* (London: Routledge & Kegan Paul, 1959).

15. Austin T. Turk, *Criminality and the Legal Order* (Chicago: Rand McNally, 1969).

16. David E. Barlow, Melissa H. Barlow, and W. Wesley Johnson, "The Political Economy of Criminal Justice Policy: A Time Series Analysis of Economic Conditions, Crime and Federal Criminal Justice Legislation," *Justice Quarterly* 13 (1996): 223–42.

17. Greenburg, *Crime and Capitalism;* Becker, *Outsiders: Studies in the Sociology of Deviance,* 20.

18. Greenburg, *Crime and Capitalism,* 180.

19. Dragen Milovanovic, "The Political Economy of Liberty and Property Interests," *Legal Studies Forum* 11 (1981): 147–72.

20. Stuart Russell, "The Continuing Relevance of Marxism to Critical Criminology," *Critical Criminology* 11 (2002): 113–35.

21. Mike Callison, "In Search of the High Life: Drugs, Crime, Masculinities and Consumption," *British Journal of Criminology* 36 (1996): 428–44.

22. Jody Miller and Christopher W. Mullins, "The Status of Feminist Theories in Criminology," in *Taking Stock: The Status of Criminological Theory,* ed. Francis T. Cullen, John Paul Wright, and Kristie R. Blevins (New Brunswick, NJ: Transaction Publishers, 2006), 217–49.

23. Betty Friedan, *The Feminine Mystique* (New York: W. W. Norton & Company, 2001).

24. Judith Nies, "Elizabeth Cady Stanton," in *Seven Women: Portraits from the American Radical Tradition* (New York: Penguin Books, 1977), 33–61.

25. Candace Kruttschnitt, Rosemary Gartner, and Amy Miller, "Doing Her Own Time? Women's Responses to Prison in the Context of the Old and the New Penology," *Criminology* 38, no. 1 (2000): 681–717.

26. Daniel W. Webster et al., "Women with Protective Orders Report Failure to Remove Firearms from Their Abusive Partners: Results from an Exploratory Study," *Journal of Women's Health* 19, no. 1 (January 2010): 93–98; Anne O'Dell, "Why Do Police Arrest Victims of Domestic Violence? The Need for Comprehensive Training and Investigative Protocols," *Journal of Aggression, Maltreatment & Trauma* 15, no. 3/4 (December 2007): 53–73; Carolyn M. West, "Sorry, We Have to Take You In: Black Battered Women Arrested

for Intimate Partner Violence," *Journal of Aggression, Maltreatment & Trauma* 15, no. 3/4 (December 2007): 95–121; Murray A. Straus, Richard J. Gelles, and Suzanne Steinmetz, "Behind Closed Doors: Violence in the American Family" (Garden City, NY: Anchor Books, 1980).

27. Rosemarie Skaine, *Power and Gender: Issues in Sexual Dominance and Harassment* (Jefferson, NC: McFarland & Company, 1996), 91–99; Rebecca Campbell et al., "Preventing the Second Rape," *Journal of Interpersonal Violence* 16, no. 12, (2001): 1239–259; Diana Russell, *The Politics of Rape* (New York: Stein and Day, 1975).

28. U.S. Department of Justice, National Institute of Corrections, *Women as Correctional Officers in Men's Maximum Security Facilities: A Survey of the Fifty States,* July 1991, http://www.nicic.org/pubs/1991/009504.pdf.

29. M. Kay Harris, "Moving into the New Millennium: Towards a Feminist Vision of Justice," in *Criminology as Peacemaking,* ed. Harold E. Pepinsky and Richard Quinney (Bloomington, IN: University of Indiana Press, 1991), 83–97.

30. John R. Fuller, *Criminal Justice: A Peacemaking Perspective* (Boston: Allyn & Bacon, 1998).

31. Richard Quinney, *Bearing Witness to Crime and Social Justice* (Albany: State University of New York Press, 2000).

32. U.S. homicide rates are typically higher than those of comparable nations, such as those of western Europe. See "Determining Trends in Global Crime and Justice: An Overview of Results from the United Nations Surveys of Crime Trends and Operations of Criminal Justice Systems," *Forum on Crime and Society* 3, nos. 1–2 (December 2003): 44–45, http://www.unodc.org/pdf/crime/forum/forum3_Art2.pdf.

33. Christopher Williams, "Toward a Transevaluation of Criminal 'Justice': On Vengeance, Peacemaking, and Punishment," *Humanity and Society* 26 (2002): 101–16.

34. Pepinsky and Quinney, *Criminology as Peacemaking.*

35. Michael Braswell, John Fuller, and Bo Lozoff, *Corrections, Peacemaking, and Restorative Justice: Transforming Individuals and Institutions* (Cincinnati, OH: Anderson Publishing, 2001). See especially Chapter 2, "Compassionate Correcting: Contributions of Ancient Wisdom Traditions," 11–27.

36. Kevin Anderson, "Radical Criminology and the Overcoming of Alienation: Perspectives from Marxian and Gandhian Humanism" in *Criminology as Peacemaking,* ed. Pepinsky and Quinney.

37. Bo Lozoff and Michael Braswell, *Inner Corrections* (Cincinnati, OH: Anderson Publishers, 1989).

38. Erich Fromm, ed., *Socialist Humanism* (New York: Doubleday, 1965).

39. Ngaire Naffine, *Feminism and Criminology* (Philadelphia: Temple University Press, 1996).

40. Christy Vicher, "Gender, Police Arrest Decisions, and Notions of Chivalry," *Criminology* 21 (1983): 5–28.

41. Jeff Farrell and Clinton R. Sanders, "Culture, Crime, and Criminology," in *Cultural Criminology,* ed. Jeff Ferrell and Clinton R. Sanders (Boston: Northeastern University Press, 1995), 3–25.

42. Gregg Barak, "Newsmaking Criminology: Reactions on the Media, Intellectuals, and Crime," *Justice Quarterly* 5 (1988): 573.

43. Louis Kontos and David C. Brotherton, *Encyclopedia of Gangs* (Santa Barbara, CA: Greenwood Press, 2007); Jody A. Miller, "Struggles over the Symbolic: Gang Style and the Meanings of Social Control," in *Cultural Criminology,* ed. Ferrell and Sanders, 213–34.

44. Robert Hornik and Lela Jacobsohn, "The Best Laid Plans: Disappointments of the National Youth Anti-Drug Media Campaign," *LDI Issue Brief* 14, no. 2 (December 2008): 1–4; Craig Reinarman and Harry G. Levine, "Crack in Context: Politics and Media in the Making of a Drug Scare," *Contemporary Drug Problems* 16 (1989): 535–78.

45. Ronald Smothers, "As Olympics Approach, Homeless Are Not Feeling at Home in Atlanta," *New York Times,* July 1, 1996, A8.

46. Jessica Kartalija, "Skateboarding Banned in Much of Eastern Shore Town," WJZ, August 15, 2007, http://wjz.com/topstories/skateboard.eastern.shore.2.429331.html.

47. Peter B. Kraska and Victor E. Kappeler, "Militarizing American Police: The Rise and Normalization of Paramilitary Units," *Social Problems* 1 (1997): 1–17.

48. Peter B. Kraska, "Militarization and Policing: Its Relevance to 21st Century Police," *Policing: A Journal of Policy and Practice* 1, no. 4 (2007): 501–13; Doug Guthrie and Valerie Olander, "Family Grieves Death of Girl, 7, in Police Raid," *Detroit News,* May 17, 2010, http://www.detnews.com/article/20100517/METRO01/5170340/Family-grieves-death-of-girl--7--in-police-raid.

49. Bruce Arrigo, "Media Madness as a Crime in the Making: On O. J. Simpson, Cultural Icons, and Hyper-Reality," in *Representing O. J.: Murder, Criminal*

*Justice, and Mass Culture,* ed. Gregg Barak (New York: Harrow and Heston, 1996), 123–36.

50. "Famous American Trials, The O. J. Simpson Trial, 1995," http://www.law.umkc.edu/faculty/projects/ftrials/Simpson/simpson.htm.

51. Ray Surette, *Media, Crime and Criminal Justice: Images, Realities, and Policies* (Belmont, CA: Wadsworth Publishing, 2006).

52. Bruce A. Arrigo, "Postmodern Justice and Critical Criminology: Positional, Relational, and Provisional Science," in *Controversies in Critical Criminology,* ed. Martin D. Schwartz and Suzanne E. Hatty (Cincinnati, OH: Anderson Publishing, 2003), 43–55.

53. Abraham S. Blumberg, "The Practice of Law as a Confidence Game," *Law and Society Review* (June 1, 1967): 15–39.

54. Jerome Skolnick, *Justice Without Trial: Law Enforcement in a Democratic Society,* 3rd ed. (New York: Macmillan, 1994).

55. Bruce Arrigo, *The Contours of Psychiatric Justice: A Postmodern Critique of Mental Illness, Criminal Insanity, and the Law* (New York: Garland, 1996).

56. Martin D. Schwartz and David O. Friedrichs, "Postmodern Thought and Criminological Discontent: New Metaphors for Understanding Violence," *Criminology* 32 (1994): 221–46.

57. Kathryn K. Russell, "Critical Race Theory and Social Justice," in *Social Justice, Criminal Justice,* ed. Bruce Arrigo (Belmont, CA: Wadsworth, 1999), 178–88.

58. Richard Delgado and Jean Stefanic, eds., *Critical Race Theory: The Cutting Edge* (Philadelphia: Temple University Press, 1995), xiv.

59. Gloria Ladson-Billings, "Just What Is Critical Race Theory and What's It Doing in a Nice Field like Education?" *International Journal of Qualitative Studies in Education* 11, (1998): 7–24.

60. Kimberle Williams Crenshaw, "Race, Reform, and Retrenchment: Transformation and Legitimation in Anti-Discrimination Law," *Harvard Law Review* 101, no. 7 (May 1988): 1331–387.

61. Barbara Jeanne Fields, "Slavery, Race, and Ideology in the United States of America," *New Life Review* 181 (1991): 113–14.

62. Delgado and Stefanic, *Critical Race Theory: The Cutting Edge.*

63. Patricia Williams, *The Alchemy of Race and Rights* (Cambridge: Harvard University Press, 1991).

64. Dorothy Roberts, "Making Reproduction a Crime," in *The Reproductive Rights Reader: Law, Medicine, and the Construction of Motherhood,* ed. Nancy Ehrenreich (New York: New York University Press, 2008), 374–75.

65. Dorothy E. Roberts, "Punishing Drug Addicts Who Have Babies: Women of Color, Equality, and the Right of Privacy," in *Critical Race Theory: The Key Writings that Formed the Movement,* ed. Kemberle Crenshaw et al. (New York: The New Press, 1995), 384–85.

66. Donna Leinwand, "Lawmakers Consider Lessening Crack Penalties; Federal Guidelines Require Heavier Sentences than for Powder Cocaine," *USA Today,* March 12, 2007, 4A.

67. Alexandra Marks, "More Equity in Cocaine Sentencing," *Christian Science Monitor,* November 2, 2007, http://www.csmonitor.com/2007/1102/p01s02-usju.html. As of 2010, Congress was considering reducing the sentencing disparity.

68. Terry Frieden, "House Passes Bill to Reduce Disparity in Cocaine Penalties," CNN, July 28, 2010, http://www.cnn.com/2010/POLITICS/07/28/house.drug.penalties/.

69. Neil Gotanda, "A Critique of 'Our Constitution Is Color-Blind,'" in *Critical Race Theory: The Key Writings that Formed the Movement.*

70. Barbara Hudson, "Beyond White Man's Justice: Race, Gender, and Justice in Late Modernity," *Theoretical Criminology* 10, no. 1 (February 1, 2006): 29–47.

## Chapter 9

1. Federal Bureau of Investigation, *Uniform Crime Reports: Crime in the United States, 2008,* "Property Crime," http://www.fbi.gov/ucr/cius2008/offenses/property_crime/index.html.

2. Ibid.

3. Thorstein Veblen, *The Theory of the Leisure Class: An Economic Study of Institutions* (1912; repr., New York: New American Library, 1953).

4. John Ward Anderson, "Paris Embraces Plan to Become City of Bikes, *The Washington Post,* March 23, 2007, A10.

5. Ibid, March 24, 2007, http://www.washingtonpost.com/wp-dyn/content/article/2007/03/23/AR2007032301753.html.

6. William G. Doerner and Steven P. Lab, *Victimology,* 5th ed. (Cincinnati, OH: LexisNexis, 2008). See Chapter 3, "The Costs of Being a Victim."

7. Federal Bureau of Investigation, *Uniform Crime Reports, 2008,* "Table 23: Offense Analysis Number and Percent Change, 2007–2008," http://www.fbi.gov/ucr/cius2008/data/table_23.html.

8. Paul Cromwell and James N. Olson, *Breaking and Entering: Burglars on Burglary* (Belmont, CA: Wadsworth, 2003), 41.

9. Federal Bureau of Investigation, *Uniform Crime Reports, 2008,* "Burglary."

10. Robert J. Bursik, Jr., and Harold G. Grasmick, *Neighborhoods and Crime: The Dimensions of Effective Community Control* (New York: Lexington Books, 1993).

11. Malcolm X, *The Autobiography of Malcolm X: As Told to Alex Haley* (New York: Ballantine), 154.

12. Stephen J. Dubner, "The Silver Thief," *New Yorker* 80, no. 12 (May 17, 2004): 74.

13. Kenneth D. Tunnell, *Choosing Crime: The Criminal Calculus of Property Offenders* (Chicago: Nelson-Hall Publishers, 1992).

14. Eric W. Hickey, ed., *Sex Crimes and Paraphilia* (Upper Saddle River, NJ: Pearson, 2006).

15. Richard T. Wright and Scott Decker, *Burglars on the Job: Streetlife and Residential Break-ins* (Boston: Northeastern University Press, 1994).

16. Cromwell and Olson, *Breaking and Entering: Burglars on Burglary,* 41.

17. Richard T. Wright and Scott Decker, *Burglars on the Job: Streetlife and Residential Break-ins.* See note 39.

18. Paul F. Cromwell, James N. Olson, and D'Aunn W. Avary, *Breaking and Entering: An Ethnographic Analysis of Burglary* (Newbury Park, CA: Sage, 1991).

19. Eric Baumer et al., "The Influence of Crack Cocaine on Robbery, Burglary, and Homicide Rates: A Cross City Longitudinal Analysis," *Journal of Research in Crime and Delinquency* 35, no. 3 (1998): 316–40.

20. Wim Bernasco and Richard Block, "Where Offenders Choose to Attack: A Discrete Choice Model of Robberies in Chicago," *Criminology* 47, no. 1 (2009): 93–130.

21. Andy Hochstetler, "Opportunities and Decisions: Interactional Dynamics in Robbery and Burglary Groups," *Criminology* 37, no. 4 (2001): 737–63.

22. Federal Bureau of Investigations, *Uniform Crime Reports: Crime in the United States, 2008,* "Larceny-theft," http://www.fbi.gov/ucr/cius2008/offenses/property_crime/larceny-theft.html.

23. Ibid.

24. Criminal codes vary across jurisdictions, and the distinction between petit larceny and grand larceny is not as clear-cut as we make it appear here. In fact, the amount of discretion on the part of the prosecutor may have more to do with the charge than the value of the stolen goods.

25. Cromwell and Olson, *Breaking and Entering: Burglars on Burglary,* 41.

26. John Hepburn, "Occasional Criminals," in *Major Forms of Crime,* ed. Robert Meier (Beverly Hills, CA: Sage, 1984), 73–94.

27. Edwin Sutherland, *The Professional Thief: By a Professional Thief* (Chicago: The University of Chicago Press, 1937). This book is the result of collaboration between Sutherland and a professional thief named Chris Cornwell.

28. John Irwin, *The Felon* (Englewood Cliffs, NJ: Prentice Hall, 1970). Irwin argues that the category of thief is "probably the oldest existing criminal system" (8). He adds "a thief, to be considered 'all right' by his peers (something which is extremely important to him), must meet his obligations, pay his debts, keep his appointments, and most importantly, never divulge information to anyone which may lead to the arrest of another person" (8).

29. Frank Browning, "Stolen Fine Art: Organized Crime's New Commodity?" *All Things Considered* (NPR), May 31, 2007, http://www.npr.org/templates/story/story.php?storyId=10588693.

30. Keith R. Ihlanfeldt, "Rail Transit and Neighborhood Crime: The Case of Atlanta, Georgia," *Southern Economic Journal* 70, no. 2 (October 2003): 273–94; Sung-suk Violet Yu, "Bus Stops and Crime: Do Bus Stops Increase Crime Opportunities in Local Neighborhoods?" Dissertation Abstracts International Section A, 2009; Leon E. Pettiway, "Mobility of Robbery and Burglary Offenders: Ghetto and Non-Ghetto Spaces," *Urban Affairs Quarterly* 18 (1982): 255–70.

31. Ronald V. Clarke, ed., *Situational Crime Prevention Successful Case Studies* (Albany, NY: Harrow and Heston, 1997).

32. Howstuffworks, "How Pickpockets Work," http://money.howstuffworks.com/pickpocket.htm. A number of websites give practical advice for avoiding being a victim of pickpockets.

33. National Retail Federation, "Troubled Economy Increases Shoplifting Rates, According to National Retail Security Survey," 2009, http://www.nrf.com/modules.php?name=News&op=viewlive&sp_id=746.

34. "Organized Crime Are Shoplifters," *Souvenirs, Gifts, & Novelties* 46, no. 6 (August 2007): 166–71.

35. "A Dollar Spent Is Money Earned in Loss Prevention," *Security Director's Report* 5, no. 11 (November 2005): 8.

36. Tammy Mastroberte, "An Ounce of Prevention," *Convenience Store News* 42, no. 4 (March 27, 2006): 52–53.

37. Garrett Gleeson, "Keeping an Eye on Shrink," *Dance Retailer*

*News* 7, no. 10 (October 2008): 36–38.

38. Dick Silverman, "With Shoplifting and Employee Theft on the Rise, New Measures Are Being Taken to Stem Losses," *Footwear News,* November 15, 1999.

39. Peter Berlin, "Why Do Shoplifters Steal?" National Association for Shoplifting Prevention, 2006, http://www.shopliftingprevention.org/whatnaspoffers/NRC.htm.

40. National Association for Shoplifting Prevention, "Shoplifting Statistics," http://www.shopliftingprevention.org/whatnaspoffers/NRC/PublicEducStats.htm.

41. Kathy Grannis, "Troubled Economy Increases Shoplifting Rates, According to National Retail Security Survey," National Retail Federation, 2009, http://www.nrf.com/modules.php?name=News&op=viewlive&sp_id=746.

42. National Association for Shoplifting Prevention, "Shoplifting Statistics."

43. The Mayo Clinic, "Kleptomania," October 30, 2009, http://www.mayoclinic.com/health/kleptomania/DS01034/DSECTION=symptoms.

44. Lloyd W. Klemke, *The Sociology of Shoplifting: Boosters and Smiths Today* (Westport, CT: Praeger, 1992).

45. John Colapinto, "STOP, THIEF!" *New Yorker* 84, no. 26 (September 2008): 74–83.

46. Federal Bureau of Investigation, *Crime in the United States: Uniform Crime Reports, 2008,* "Larceny-theft."

47. Federal Reserve Board, "A Summary of the Roundtable Discussion on Retail Payments Fraud," July 2007, 2 (see footnote 1), http://www.federalreserve.gov/paymentsystems/retailpmtfraud/retailpmtfraud.pdf.

48. Colapinto, "STOP, THIEF!" 74–83.

49. Gizmodo, "Attack of the Card Skimmers: It's Happening Right Here, Right Now," April 7, 2009, http://i.gizmodo.com/5202776/attack-of-the-card-skimmers-its-happening-right-here-right-now.

50. Federal Bureau of Investigation, "LaFollette Man Pleads Guilty to $1.8 Million Check Fraud Scheme," January 25, 2010, http://knoxville.fbi.gov/dojpressrel/pressrel10/kx012510.htm; *Henegar v. Agilysys, Inc.,* 2006 U.S. Dist. (E.D. Tenn., Aug. 8, 2006).

51. 2009 Florida Statutes, Chapter 832, "Violations Involving Checks and Drafts," http://www.flsenate.gov/statutes/index.cfm?App_mode= Display_Statute&URL=Ch0832/ch0832.htm.

52. Edwin Lemert, "An Isolation and Closure Theory of Naïve Check Forgery," *Journal of Criminal Law, Criminology, and Police Science* 44 (1953): 297–98.

53. Bureau of Justice Statistics, "Motor Vehicle Theft Rates," http://bjs.ojp.usdoj.gov/content/glance/tables/proptrdtab.cfm.

54. Insurance Information Institute, "Auto Theft," April 2009, http://old.iii.org/media/hottopics/insurance/test4/.

55. National Insurance Crime Bureau and Insurance Information Institute, "Auto Theft," May 2010, http://www.iii.org/media/hottopics/insurance/test4/.

56. Federal Bureau of Investigation, "Car Cloning: A New Twist on an Old Crime," March 27, 2007, http://www.fbi.gov/page2/march07/carcloning032907.htm.

57. Keith Morelli, "FBI: $25 Million International Car-Cloning Theft Ring Broken Up," *Tampa Tribune,* March 24, 2009.

58. Federal Bureau of Investigation, *Uniform Crime Reports: Crime in the United States, 2008,* "Arson," http://www.fbi.gov/ucr/cius2008/offenses/property_crime/arson.html.

59. Federal Bureau of Investigation, *Uniform Crime Reporting Handbook,* 2004, 12, http://www.fbi.gov/ucr/handbook/ucrhandbook04.pdf.

60. Federal Bureau of Investigation, *Uniform Crime Reports: Crime in the United States: 2007,* "Arson," http://www.fbi.gov/ucr/cius2007/offenses/property_crime/arson.html.

61. Technical Working Group on Fire/Arson Scene Investigation, *Fire and Arson Scene Evidence: A Guide for Public Safety Personnel* (Washington, DC: US Department of Justice, 2000), 2, http://www.ncjrs.gov/pdffiles1/nij/181584.pdf.

62. James Brady, "The Social Economy of Arson: Vandals, Gangsters, Bankers, and Officials in the Making of an Urban Problem," in *Crime and Capitalism: Readings in Marxist Criminology,* ed. David Greenberg (Philadelphia: Temple University Press, 1993), 211–57.

63. Richard Cole, "Arsonists Burning U.S. Forests for Profit on Equipment, Timber," AP/*Austin American-Statesman,* September 4, 1995, A17.

64. Sarah A. Soule and Nella Van Dyke, "Black Church Arson in the United States, 1989–1996," *Ethnic and Racial Studies* 22, no. 4 (1999): 724–42.

65. Amy Calder, "More Arrests Likely in YouTube Arson," *Portland Press Herald/Maine Sunday Telegram,* April 3, 2009, http://www.pressherald.com/archive/more-arrests-likely-in-youtube-arson_2009-04-02.html.

104. Cathy Young, "Assault Behind Bars," *Reason,* May 2007, 17–18.

105. Prison Rape Elimination Act of 2003, http://ojjdp.ncjrs.org/about/PubLNo108-79.txt.

106. Donaldson was born Robert Anthony Martin Jr., but later changed his name.

107. G. Gordon Liddy, *Will: The Autobiography of G. Gordon Liddy* (New York: St. Martin's Press, 1980), 318–21.

108. Allen J. Beck, Paige M. Harrison, and Devon B. Adams, *Sexual Violence Reported by Correctional Authorities, 2006* (Washington, DC: US Department of Justice Office of Justice Programs Bureau of Justice Statistics, 2007).

109. "The Silent Horror," *Economist* 376, no. 8438 (August 06, 2005): 25.

110. Federal Bureau of Investigation, *Uniform Crime Reports, Crime in the United States, 2008,* "Robbery," http://www.fbi.gov/ucr/cius2008/offenses/violent_crime/robbery.html.

111. Thomas J. Gardner and Terry M. Anderson, *Criminal Law* (Belmont, CA: Thomson Wadsworth, 2006), 309.

112. William R. Smith, Sharon Glave Frazee, and Elizabeth L. Davison, "Furthering the Integration of Routine Activity and Social Disorganization Theories: Small Units of Analysis and the Study of Street Robbery as a Diffusion Process," *Criminology* 38, no. 2 (2000): 489–523.

113. Richard T. Wright and Scott H. Decker, *Armed Robbers in Action: Stickups and Street Culture* (Boston: Northeastern University Press, 1997).

114. Michael S. Scott, *Robbery at Automated Teller Machines* (Washington, DC: U.S. Department of Justice Office of Community Oriented Policing Services, 2001), http://www.popcenter.org/problems/robbery_atms/.

115. Wright and Decker, *Armed Robbers in Action.* See Chapter 5.

116. Paul Catalano, Bryan Hill, and Brennan Long, "Geographical Analysis and Serial Crime Investigation: A Case Study of Armed Robbery in Phoenix, Arizona," *Security Journal* 14, no. 3 (2001): 27–41.

117. Charles F. Wellford, John M. MacDonald, and Joan C. Weiss, *Multistate Study of Convenience Store Robberies* (Washington, DC: Justice Research and Statistics Association, 1997), http://www.popcenter.org/problems/robbery_convenience/PDFs/Wellford_etal_1997.pdf.

118. Kimberly A. Faulkner, Douglas P. Landsittel, and Scott A. Hendricks, "Robbery Characteristics and Employee Injuries in Convenience Stores," *American Journal of Industrial Medicine* 40, no. 6 (2001): 703–09.

119. Alicia Altizio and Diana York, *Robbery of Convenience Stores, Guide No. 49,* Center for Problem Oriented Policing, 2007, http://www.popcenter.org/problems/robbery_convenience/.

120. Natalie Taylor, "Robbery Against Service Stations and Pharmacies: Recent Trends," *Trends & Issues in Crime and Criminal Justice,* no. 223 (Canberra: Australian Institute of Criminology, 2002).

121. Ronald D. Hunter, "Convenience Store Robbery Revisited: A Review of Prevention Results," *Journal of Security Administration* 22, nos. 1 & 2 (1999): 1–13; Scott A. Hendricks et al., "A Matched Case-Control Study of Convenience Store Robbery Risk Factors," *Journal of Occupational and Environmental Medicine* 41, no. 11 (1999): 995–1004.

122. Research Division Correctional Service of Canada, "A Profile of Robbery Offenders in Canada, 1995," http://www.popcenter.org/problems/robbery_convenience/PDFs/CSC_robbery_1995.pdf; Martha J. Smith and Derek B. Cornish, *Theory for Practice in Situational Crime Prevention,* vol. 16 (Monsey, NY: Criminal Justice Press, 2003).

123. Thomas Gabor and Andre Normandeau, "Preventing Armed Robbery Through Opportunity Reduction: A Critical Analysis," *Journal of Security Administration* 12, no. 1 (1989): 3–19.

124. Federal Bureau of Investigation, *Uniform Crime Reports: Crime in the United States,* 1989–2004.

125. Deborah Lamm Weisel, *The Problem of Bank Robbery, Guide No. 48,* Center for Problem Oriented Policing, 2007, http://www.popcenter.org/problems/robbery_banks.

126. Kathleen Maguire and Ann L. Pastore, *Sourcebook of Criminal Justice Statistics 2003* (Washington, DC: Office of Justice Programs Bureau of Justice Statistics, 2005).

127. Weisel, *The Problem of Bank Robbery,* 123.

128. Bartol and Bartol, *Criminal Behavior,* 493–94.

129. Gardner and Anderson, *Criminal Law,* 274.

130. Federal Bureau of Investigation, *Uniform Crime Reports: Crime in the United States, 2008,* "Aggravated Assault," http://www.fbi.gov/ucr/cius2008/offenses/violent_crime/aggravated_assault.html.

131. Federal Bureau of Investigation, *Uniform Crime Reports: Crime in the United States, 2008,* "Aggravated Assault"; Ibid., Table 29: "Estimated Number of Arrests United States, 2008," http://

www.fbi.gov/ucr/cius2008/data/table_29.html.

132. Federal Bureau of Investigation, *Uniform Crime Reports: Crime in the United States, 2008,* "Table 3: Crime in the United States Offense and Population Percent Distribution by Region, 2008," http://www.fbi.gov/ucr/cius2008/data/table_03.html; Ibid., "Table 2: Crime in the United States by Community Type, 2008," http://www.fbi.gov/ucr/cius2008/data/table_02.html.

133. Federal Bureau of Investigation, *Uniform Crime Reports: Crime in the United States, 2008,* "Aggravated Assault Table: Aggravated Assault, Types of Weapons Used Percent Distribution by Region, 2008," http://www.fbi.gov/ucr/cius2008/offenses/expanded_information/data/agassaulttable.html.

134. Gardner and Anderson, *Criminal Law,* 275.

135. Federal Bureau of Investigation, *Uniform Crime Reports: Crime in the United States, 2008,* "Aggravated Assault."

136. National Crime Victimization Survey, Criminal Victimization in the United States, 2006 Statistical Tables, Table 33 (Washington, DC: U.S. Department of Justice Office of Justice Programs Bureau of Justice Statistics, 2008), http://www.ojp.usdoj.gov/bjs/pub/pdf/cvus06.pdf.

137. Janet L. Lauritsen and Karen Heimer, "The Gender Gap in Violent Victimization, 1973–2004," *Journal of Quantitative Criminology* 24, no. 2 (June 2008): 125–47.

138. Marc Riedel, "Stranger Violence: Perspectives, Issues, and Problems," *Journal of Criminal Law & Criminology* 78, no. 2 (Summer 1987): 223–58.

139. National Crime Victimization Survey, Criminal Victimization in the United States, 2006 Statistical Tables, Table 34.

140. Centers for Disease Control and Prevention, "Understanding Intimate Partner Violence," 2006, http://www.cdc.gov/ncipc/dvp/ipv_factsheet.pdf.

141. Shannan Catalano, Bureau of Justice Statistics, "Intimate Partner Violence in the United States: Circumstances," December 2007, http://bjs.ojp.usdoj.gov/content/pub/pdf/ipvus.pdf.

142. Janet M. Torpy, "Intimate Partner Violence," *The Journal of the American Medical Association* 300, no. 6, (August 13, 2000): 754, http://jama.ama-assn.org/cgi/reprint/300/6/754.pdf.

143. Shannan Catalano, Bureau of Justice Statistics, "Intimate Partner Violence in the United States: Reporting to Police."

144. Richard B. Felson and Jeff Ackerman, "Arrest for Domestic and Other Assaults," *Criminology* 39, no. 3 (August 2001): 655–75.

145. American Academy of Pediatrics, HealthyChildren.org, March 2010, http://www.aap.org/publiced/BK0_ChildAbuse.htm.

146. Federal Bureau of Investigation, *Uniform Crime Reports: Crime in the United States, 2004* (Washington, DC: US Department of Justice, 2005), 360, http://www.fbi.gov/ucr/cius_04/documents/CIUS2004.pdf.

## Chapter 11

1. President's Commission on Law Enforcement and Administration of Justice, Task Force Report: Organized Crime (Washington, DC: US Government Printing Office, 1967).

2. Terry L. Leap, *Dishonest Dollars: The Dynamics of White-Collar Crime* (Ithaca, NY: Cornell University Press, 2007).

3. William Kleinknecht, *The New Ethnic Mobs: The Changing Face of Organized Crime in America* (New York: Free Press, 1996).

4. James W. Coleman, *The Criminal Elite: The Sociology of White Collar Crime* (New York: St. Martin's Press, 1985).

5. Marshall B. Clinard and Peter C. Yeager, *Corporate Crime* (New York: Free Press, 1980).

6. Michael J. Lynch and Paul B. Stretesky, "Conspiracy, Deceit and Misinformation: Standard Operating Procedure in the Chemical Industry," *The Critical Criminologist* 4 (1999): 14–18.

7. Sean Grennan and Marjie T. Britz, *Organized Crime: A Worldwide Perspective* (Upper Saddle River, NJ: Prentice Hall, 2006).

8. Howard Abadinsky, *Organized Crime,* 8th ed. (Belmont, CA: Wadsworth, 2007).

9. Gary Potter, *Criminal Organizations: Vice, Racketeering and Politics in an American City* (Prospect Heights, IL: Waveland, 1994).

10. Joseph F. O'Brien and Andris Kurins, *Boss of Bosses: The FBI and Paul Castellano* (New York: Dell, 1991).

11. Robert M. Lombardo, "The Black Mafia: African American Organized Crime in Chicago, 1890–1960," *Crime, Law, and Social Change* 38 (2002): 33–65.

12. Richard Gambino, *Blood of My Blood: The Dilemmas of the Italian-American* (Garden City, NJ: Doubleday, 1974).

13. Andrew Martin, "Even with Drug Leaders in Jail, Gang's Drug Business Is Flourishing," *Chicago Tribune,* January 29, 1996, 1.

14. Guy Gugliotta and Jeff Leen, *Kings of Cocaine: Inside the Medellin Cartel: An Astonishing Story of Murder, Money, and International Corruption* (New York: Simon & Schuster, 1989).

15. Mark Motivans, *Money-Laundering Offenders, 1994–2001* (Washington, DC: Bureau of Justice Statistics, 2003).
16. Federico Varese, *The Russian Mafia: Private Protection in a New Market Economy* (Oxford: Oxford University Press, 2001).
17. Lincoln Steffens, *The Shame of the Cities* (New York: Hill & Wang, 1957).
18. Lawrence J. McCaffrey, *The Irish Diaspora in America* (Bloomington: Indiana University Press, 1976).
19. Edward M. Levine, *The Irish and Irish Politicians* (Notre Dame, IN: University of Notre Dame Press, 1966).
20. Lyle W. Dorsett, *The Pendergast Machine* (New York: Oxford University Press, 1968).
21. Patrick Downey, *Gangster City: The History of the New York Underworld* (Fort Lee, NJ: Barricade Books, 2004).
22. Thomas Reppetto, *American Mafia: A History of Its Rise to Power* (New York: Henry Holt, 2004), 26–27.
23. Abadinsky, *Organized Crime.*
24. Francis A. Janni, *A Family Business: Kinship and Social Control in Organized Crime* (New York: Russell Sage Foundation, 1972).
25. Gambino, *Blood of My Blood.*
26. Thomas Reppetto, *American Mafia,* 4.
27. Richard L. Bourgeois et al., "Racketeer Influenced and Corrupt Organizations," *American Criminal Law Review* 37 (2000): 879–91.
28. Martin G. Urbina and Sara Kreitzer, "The Practical Utility and Ramifications of RICO: Thirty-Two Years After Its Implementation," *Criminal Justice Policy Review* 15, no. 3 (September 2004): 294–323.
29. Charles Winick and Paul M. Kinsie, *The Lively Commerce* (Chicago: Quadrangle, 1971).
30. Richter H. Moore, Jr., "Motor Fuel Tax Fraud and Organized Crime: The Russian and Italian-American Mafia," in *Contemporary Issues in Organized Crime,* ed. Jay Albanese (Monsey, NY: Willow Tree Press, 1995), 195.
31. John Sullivan and Alex Berenson, "Dozens Named in Stock Fraud Linked to Mob," *New York Times,* June 15, 2000, late edition, C27.
32. Jay S. Albanese, *Organized Crime in Our Times,* 5th ed. (Cincinnati, OH: Anderson Publishing, 2007).
33. Abadinsky, *Organized Crime,* 186–87, 199–200.
34. Ibid., p. 208.
35. Reppetto, *American Mafia.*
36. Dennis J. Kenney and James O. Finckenauer, *Organized Crime in America* (Belmont, CA: Wadsworth, 1995), 286–89.
37. Howard Abadinsky, *Drug Abuse: An Introduction,* 5th ed. (Belmont, CA: Wadsworth, 2004).
38. Ron Chepesiuk, *The Bullet or Bribe: Taking Down Colombia's Cali Drug Cartel* (Westport, CT: Praeger, 2003).
39. Don Barnard, "Narco-Terrorism Realities: The Connection Between Drugs and Terror," *Journal of Counterterrorism and Homeland Security International* 9 (2003): 31–34.
40. Julian Borger, "Bodies Pave Way to Jamaican Polls," *Guardian,* July 12, 2001, 6.
41. Gerald L. Posner, *Warlords of Crime: Chinese Secret Societies, the New Mafia* (New York: McGraw-Hill, 1988).
42. National Drug Intelligence Center Attorney General's Report to Congress on the Growth of Violent Street Gangs in Suburban Areas, "Gang-Drug Trafficking Organization Connections Affecting Suburban Areas," April 2008, http://www.usdoj.gov/ndic/pubs27/27612/gang.htm.
43. Donna M. Hughes and Tatyana Denisova, "The Transnational Political Nexus of Trafficking in Women from Ukraine," *Trends in Organized Crime* 6 (2001): 43–67.
44. Albanese, *Organized Crime in Our Times,* 214.
45. Ibid.
46. Vicki Abt, James F. Smith, and Eugene Martin Christiansen, *The Business of Risk: Commercial Gambling in Mainstream America* (Lawrence: University Press of Kansas, 1985).
47. April Yee, "Organized Dog Fights Emerging in Mass.," *Boston Globe,* August 7, 2007, first edition, metro section, B1.
48. Roger Dunstan, "Gambling in California, XI, Gambling and Crime," California Research Bureau, 1997, http://www.library.ca.gov/crb/97/03/Chapt11.html.
49. Florida Department of Criminal Law Enforcement, *The Questions of Casinos in Florida—Increased Crime: Is It Worth It?* (Tallahassee, FL: FDCLE, 1994).
50. Matti Joutsen, "The Growth of Organized Crime in Central and Eastern Europe," in *Contemporary Issues in Organized Crime,* ed. Jay Albanese (Monsey, NY: Willow Tree Press, 1995).
51. Lyudmila Zaitseva and Kevin Hand, "Nuclear Smuggling Chains: Suppliers, Intermediaries, and End-Users," *American Behavioral Scientist* 46, no. 6 (2003): 822–44.
52. "Chinese Cultural Officials 'Not Optimistic' About Fight Against Piracy," *BBC Monitoring Asia Pacific,* August 18, 2006; Jeff Pao and Bien Perez, "Piracy Crackdown Could Reap Dividends,"

*South China Morning Post,* January 29, 2008, business, 7; Maricel E. Estavillo, "Software Piracy Still a Formidable Problem," *BusinessWorld,* May 24, 2006, S1/1.

53. Jack Seamonds and Scott Minerbrook, "Ethnic Gangs & Organized Crime," *U.S. News & World Report* 104, no. 2 (January 18, 1988): 29–33.

54. Grennan and Britz, *Organized Crime.*

55. Robert Patrick, "Brief: A Union Pension Manager Has Been Indicted on Embezzlement Charges, the U.S. Attorney's Office said Tuesday," *St. Louis Post-Dispatch,* February 10, 2009.

56. Lou Hirsh, "Cal State Students Hear Talk on White-Collar Crime from Someone Once on the Inside," *Press-Enterprise,* January 31, 2008, http://www.pe.com/business/local/stories/PE_Biz_D_pavlo01.343e1f1.html.

57. Gilbert Geis and Joseph Dimento, "Should We Prosecute Corporations and/or Individuals?" in *Corporate Crime: Contemporary Debates,* ed. Frank Pearce and Laureen Snider (Toronto: University of Toronto Press, 1995), 72–86.

58. Russell Mokhiber and Robert Weissman, *Corporate Predators: The Hunt for Mega-Profits and the Attack on Democracy* (Monroe, ME: Common Courage Press, 1999), 8.

59. Jeffrey Reiman, *The Rich Get Richer and the Poor Get Prison: Ideology, Class, and Criminal Justice* (Boston: Allyn & Bacon, 2001).

60. "Siemens Ends Bribery Scandal with €1b Fine," *TCE: The Chemical Engineer* (February 2009): 4.

61. David Crawford and Mike Esterl, "Siemens Pays Record Fine in Probe," *Wall Street Journal,* December 16, 2008, Eastern edition, B2.

62. Robert Trigaux, "$1.4-Billion Settlement Just a Slap on Wall Street's Wrist," *St. Petersburg Times,* May 5, 2003, South Pinellas edition, Business section, 1E.

63. Federal Bureau of Investigation, "Financial Crimes Report to the Public," 7, http://www.fbi.gov/publications/financial/fcs_report2006/publicrpt06.pdf.

64. Associated Press, "This Is Bob. Bob's Not Doing So Well," *Beaumont Enterprise,* February 23, 2008, D1.

65. Federal Trade Commission, "FTC Charges 'Miss Cleo' with Deceptive Advertising, Billing and Collection Practices," February 14, 2002, http://www.ftc.gov/opa/2002/02/accessresource.shtm.

66. Consumeraffairs.com, "Miss Cleo Settles for $500 Million," Nov. 12, 2002, http://www.consumeraffairs.com/news02/cleo_settle.html.

67. Sheryl Stolberg, "Tobacco Exec Lied to Congress About Nicotine, Scientist Charges," *Houston Chronicle,* January 27, 1996, A4.

68. PBS Frontline, "Inside the Tobacco Deal," http://www.pbs.org/wgbh/pages/frontline/shows/settlement/.

69. Francis T. Cullen and William J. Maakestad, *Corporate Crime Under Attack: The Ford Pinto Case and Beyond* (Cincinnati, OH: Anderson, 1987).

70. David Barboza, "Chinese Exporters Face Crisis in Quality Control," *International Herald Tribune,* May 19, 2007, news, 1; David Barboza, "When Fakery Turns Fatal," *New York Times,* June 5, 2007, late edition, C1; Jayne O'Donnell, "Some Skeptical as China Bans Lead Paint in US Toys," *USA Today,* September 12, 2007, money, 1B.

71. Geoffrey Cowley and John McCormick, "How Safe Is Our Food?" *Newsweek* 121 (1993): 7–10.

72. David Barboza and Alexei Barrionuevo, "In China, Additive to Animals' Food Is an Open Secret," *New York Times,* April 30, 2007, section A; Elizabeth Weise, "Lab Says Melamine Not Only Culprit," *USA Today,* May 8, 2007, money, 1B.

73. Tony Rizzo, "2 Plead Guilty in Tainted Pet Food Case," *Kansas City Star,* June 16, 2009.

74. Upton Sinclair, *The Jungle* (New York: Bantam, 1906/1981).

75. Stephen Rostoff, Henry Pontell, and Robert Tillman, *Profit Without Honor: White-Collar Crime and the Looting of America* (Upper Saddle River, NJ: Prentice Hall, 2007), 121.

76. Gillian Flaccus, "USDA Sued Over 'Downer' Cow Rules," Associated Press/*USA Today,* February 27, 2008, http://www.usatoday.com/news/nation/2008-02-27-4234314486_x.htm.

77. Beatrice T. Hunter, "Will Beefed Up Inspection Assure Food Safety?" *Consumer's Research* 76 (1993): 17–21.

78. Jordan Lite, "Salmonella Peanut Company Hit with Huge Fine," *Scientific American,* April 10, 2009, http://www.scientificamerican.com/blog/60-second-science/post.cfm?id=salmonella-peanut-company-hit-with-2009-04-10.

79. Leap, *Dishonest Dollars.*

80. Mark Stevens, *The Insiders: The Truth Behind the Scandal Rocking Wall Street* (New York: G. P. Putnam's Sons, 1987).

81. Brian Cruver, *Anatomy of Greed: Telling the Unshredded Truth from Inside Enron* (New York: Carroll & Graf, 2003).

82. William K. Black, Kitty Calavita, and Henry N. Pontell, "The Savings and Loan Debacle of the 1980s: White Collar Crime or Risky Business?" *Law and Policy* 17 (1995): 23–55.

83. Kathleen Day and Peter Berg, "Enron Directors Backed Moving Debt Off Books," *Washington Post,* January 31, 2002, A1.

84. Michael A. Hiltzik, "SEC Says First Pension Ran Pyramid Scam," *Los Angeles Times,* May 14, 1994, D1.

85. U.S. Environmental Protection Agency, "Summary of the Clean Air Act," http://www.epa.gov/lawsregs/laws/caa.html.

86. Environmental Protection Agency, Criminal Enforcement, "What Is an Environmental Crime?", http://www.epa.gov/compliance/criminal/investigations/environmental crime.html.

87. Ibid.

88. Rob White, "Green Criminology and the Pursuit of Social and Ecological Justice," in *Issues in Green Criminology: Confronting Harms Against Environments, Humanity, and Other Animals,* ed. Piers Beirne and Nigel South (Portland, OR: Willan Publishing, 2007), 32–54.

89. Piers Beirne and Nigel South, eds., *Issues in Green Criminology: Confronting Harms Against Environments, Humanity, and Other Animals* (Portland, OR: Willan Publishing, 2007), xiv.

90. Piers Beirne, "Animal Rights, Animal Abuse, and Green Criminology," in *Issues in Green Criminology,* 55–83.

91. BBC, "2005: Ban on Fox Hunting Comes into Force," http://news.bbc.co.uk/onthisday/hi/dates/stories/february/18/newsid_4930000/4930896.stm.

92. U.S. Department of Energy, "Office of Civilian Radioactive Waste Management," http://www.ocrwm.doe.gov/.

93. Lawrence Becker and James David Ballard, "Federal Programs and Their Potential to Provoke Political Violence: The Transportation Program for Yucca Mountain and Terrorist Adversaries," in *Terrorism: Research, Readings, and Realities,* ed. Lynne L. Snowden and Bradley C. Whitsel (Upper Saddle River, NJ: Prentice Hall, 2005), 63–79.

94. Paul B. Stretesky and Michael J. Lynch, "The Relationship Between Lead and Crime," *Journal of Health and Social Behavior* 45 (2004): 214–29.

95. Frontline, "Ghana: A Digital Dumping Ground," http://www.pbs.org/frontlineworld/stories/ghana804/video/video_index.html.

96. J. P. Messina and P. L. Delamater, "Defoliation and the War on Drugs in Putumayo, Colombia" *International Journal of Remote Sensing* 27, no. 1/2 (January 10, 2006): 121–28.

97. Fred A. Wilcox, *Waiting for an Army to Die: The Tragedy of Agent Orange* (New York: Vintage, 1983).

## Chapter 12

1. Bruce A. Jacobs, *Investigating Deviance: An Anthology* (Los Angeles: Roxbury Publishing, 2002). See Introduction, Part 1, "Constructing Deviance."

2. Robert F. Meier and Gilbert Geis, *Victimless Crime? Prostitution, Drugs, Homosexuality and Abortion* (Los Angeles: Roxbury Publishing, 1977).

3. Ethan A. Nadelmann, "The Case for Legalization," *The Public Interest,* no. 2 (Summer 1988): 3–32.

4. Duane C. McBride and Clyde B. McCoy, "The Drug-Crime Relationship: An Analytical Framework," *The Prison Journal* 73 (1993): 257–78.

5. Marianne Macy, *Working Sex: An Odyssey into Our Cultural Underworld* (New York: Carroll and Graf Publishers, 1996).

6. Nancy M. Petry, *Pathological Gambling: Etiology, Comorbidity, and Treatment* (Washington, DC: American Psychological Association, 2005).

7. D. Kirk Davidson, *Selling Sin: The Marketing of Socially Unacceptable Products* (Westport, CT: Praeger, 2003).

8. Elaine Ganley, "Among Islamic Countries, Women's Roles Vary Greatly," *Washington Times,* April 15, 1998, A13.

9. Najati Sayyid Ahmad Sanad, *The Theory of Crime and Criminal Responsibility in Islamic Law: Shari'a* (Chicago: University of Illinois at Chicago, 1991).

10. James Davidson Hunter, *American Evangelicalism: Conservative Religion and the Quandary of Modernity* (New Brunswick, NJ: Rutgers University Press, 1983).

11. Edward Behr, *Prohibition: Thirteen Years that Changed America* (New York: Arcade Publishing, 1996).

12. Jonathan Finer, "Old Blue Laws Are Hitting Red Lights: Statutes Rolled Back as Anachronisms," *Washington Post,* December 4, 2004, A3.

13. Diana Fishbein, David Lozovsky, and Jerome H. Jaffe, "Impulsivity, Aggression, and Neuroendocrine Responses to Serotonergic Stimulation in Substance Abusers," *Biological Psychiatry* 25, no. 8 (April 15, 1989): 1049–66.

14. Charles E. Faupel and Carl B. Klockars, "Drugs-Crime Connections: Elaborations from the Life Histories of Hard-Core Heroin Addicts," *Social Problems* 34, no. 1 (February 1987): 54–68.

15. Mark H. Moore and Mark A. R. Kleiman, "The Police and Drugs," *Perspectives on Policing* (Washington, DC: National Institute of Justice, Office of Justice Programs, 1989).

16. CNN, "Ex-Atlanta Officers Get Prison Time for Cover-Up in Deadly Raid," February 24, 2009, http://www.cnn.com/2009/CRIME/02/24/atlanta.police/index.html.

17. William L. White, *Slaying the Dragon: The History of Addiction Treatment and Recovery in America* (Bloomington, IN: Chestnut Health Systems, 1998).

18. H. W. Brands, *The First American: The Life and Times of Benjamin Franklin* (New York: Anchor Books, 2000), 70–71.

19. Oakley Ray and Charles Ksir, *Drugs, Society and Human Behavior* (Boston: McGraw-Hill, 2004).

20. D. T. Courtwright, *Dark Paradise: Opiate Addiction in America Before 1940* (Cambridge, MA: Harvard University Press, 1982).

21. Ray and Ksir, *Drugs, Society and Human Behavior.*

22. Howard Wayne Morgan, *Drugs in America: A Social History,* 1800–1980 (Syracuse, NY: Syracuse University Press, 1981).

23. Frederick Allen, *Secret Formula: A History of the Coca-Cola Company* (New York: HarperCollins, 1994); James A. Inciardi, *The War on Drugs III* (Boston: Allyn & Bacon, 2002), 21.

24. Upton Sinclair, *The Jungle* (New York: Bantam, 1906/1981).

25. Morgan, *Drugs in America.*

26. Ray and Ksir, *Drugs, Society and Human Behavior,* 91.

27. *Webb v. United States* 249 U.S. 96 (1919); *United States v. Behrman* 258 U.S. 280, 289 (1922); *Linder v. United States,* 286 U.S. 5 (1925).

28. H. Westley Clark, "Office-Based Practice and Opioid-Use Disorders," *New England Journal of Medicine* 349, no. 10 (September 4, 2003): 928–30.

29. Jerome L. Himmelstein, *The Strange Career of Marijuana: Politics and Ideology of Drug Control in America* (Westport, CT: Greenwood, 1983).

30. Ray and Ksir, *Drugs, Society and Human Behavior,* 458–59.

31. Ibid., 101–2.

32. Steve Daniels, "Teens Inhale Common Office Supply," WTVD, February 23, 2007, http://abclocal.go.com/wtvd/story?section=triangle&id=5063559.

33. Substance Abuse and Mental Health Services Administration, *Results from the 2008 National Survey on Drug Use and Health: National Findings* (Rockville, MD: Office of Applied Studies, 2009), 1, http://oas.samhsa.gov/nsduh/2k8nsduh/2k8Results.pdf.

34. Ibid., 15–16.

35. Bruce K. Alexander, "Alternatives to the War on Drugs," *Journal of Drug Issues* (20): 1–27.

36. Randy E. Barnett, "Curing the Drug-Law Addiction: The Harmful Side Effects of Legal Prohibition," in *Dealing with Drugs: Consequences of Government Control,* ed. Ronald Hamowy (Lexington, MA: D.C. Heath, 1987), 73–162.

37. Presidents' Commission on Organized Crime, *America's Habit: Drug Abuse, Drug Trafficking, and Organized Crime* (Washington, DC: U.S. Government Printing Office, 1986).

38. Rosa Maria Santana, "Drinking Blamed for Teen Death," *Chicago Tribune,* January 3, 1996, metro section.

39. David Corcoran, "Legalizing Drugs: Failures Spur Debate," *New York Times,* November 27, 1989, 9.

40. Herbert P. Barnard, "The Netherlands' Drug Policy: 20 Years of Experience" (Royal Netherlands Embassy, Washington, DC).

41. Robert P. McNamara, *The Times Square Hustler: Male Prostitution in New York City* (Westport, CT: Praeger, 1994).

42. Edward L. Rubin, "Sex, Politics, and Morality," *William & Mary Law Review* 47, no. 1 (October 2005): 1–48.

43. Linda M. Rio, "Psychological and Sociological Research and the Decriminalization and Legalization of Prostitution," *Archives of Sexual Behavior* 20 (1991): 205–18.

44. Susan Brownmiller, *Against Our Will: Men, Women, and Rape* (New York: Simon & Schuster, 1975).

45. Harold R. Holzman and Sharon Pines, "Buying Sex: The Phenomenology of Being a John," *Deviant Behavior* 4 (1982): 111.

46. Charles H. McCaghy et al., *Deviant Behavior: Crime, Conflict, and Interest Groups* (Boston: Allyn & Bacon, 2006), 380.

47. Ibid.

48. McNamara, *The Times Square Hustler.*

49. Julia O'Connell Davidson, *Prostitution, Power, and Freedom* (Ann Arbor: University of Michigan Press, 1998). See 18–21, "Brothels as Business Enterprises."

50. "Police Break Up Prostitution Ring that Employed 200 Housewives, Career Women," *Daily Sentinel-Tribune* (Bowling Green, OH), August 23, 1983, 7.

51. McCaghy et al., *Deviant Behavior,* 382.

52. Carol Rambo Ronai and Carolyn Ellis, "Turn-Ons for Money: Interactional Strategies of the Table Dance," in *Investigating Deviance: An Anthology,* ed. Bruce A. Jacobs (Los Angeles: Roxbury Publishing, 2002), 273–88.

53. Paul K. Rasmussen, "Massage Parlors as a Sex-for-Money Game," in *The Sociology of Deviance,* ed. Jack D. Douglas (Boston: Allyn & Bacon, 194), 199–212.

54. Celia Williamson and Terry Cluse-Tolar, "Pimp-Controlled Prostitution: Still an Integral Part of Street Life," *Violence Against Women* 8, no. 9 (2002): 1074–92.

55. James A. Inciardi et al., "Prostitution, IV Drug Use, and Sex-for-Crack Exchanges Among Serious Delinquents: Risks for HIV Infection," *Criminology* 29 (1991): 221–36.

56. Michael S. Scott and Kelly Dedel, *Street Prostitution,* 2nd ed. (Washington, DC: U.S. Department of Justice Office of Community Oriented Policing Services, 2006), 2, http://www.cops.usdoj.gov/mime/open.pdf.

57. Mary Gibson, "The State and Prostitution: Prohibition, Regulation, or Decriminalization?" in *History and Crime: Implications for Criminal Justice Policy,* ed. James A. Inciardi and Charles E. Faupel (Beverly Hills, CA: Sage Publications, 1980), 193–200.

58. R. Barri Flowers, *Runaway Kids and Teenage Prostitution: America's Lost, Abandoned, and Sexually Exploited Children* (Westport, CT: Praeger, 2001).

59. Nancy A. Wonders and Raymond Michalowski, "Bodies, Borders, and Sex Tourism in a Globalized World: A Tale of Two Cities—Amsterdam and Havana," *Social Problems* 48 (2001): 545–71.

60. *Jacobellis v. Ohio* 378 US 184 (1964).

61. Joseph W. Slade, *Pornography in America: A Reference Handbook* (Santa Barbara, CA: ABC-CLIO, 2000).

62. "Pornography: A Roundtable Discussion," *Harper's* (November 1984): 31–39, 42–45.

63. Ethel Quayle and Max Taylor, "Child Pornography and the Internet: Perpetuating a Cycle of Abuse," *Deviant Behavior* 23 (2002): 331–61.

64. Mimi H. Silbert and Ayala M. Pines, "Pornography and Sexual Abuse of Women," *Sex Roles* 10, nos. 11–12 (June 1984): 857–68.

65. *Miller v. California* 413 U.S. 15 (1973).

66. *Ashcroft v. American Civil Liberties Union* 542 U.S. 656 (2004).

67. Henry F. Fradella, "Legal, Moral, and Social Reasons for Decriminalizing Sodomy," *Journal of Contemporary Justice* 18, no. 3 (August 2002): 284.

68. *Lawrence v. Texas,* 539 U.S. 558 (2003).

69. Joseph J. Wardenski, "A Minor Exception? The Impact of Lawrence v. Texas on LGBT Youth," *Journal of Criminal Law & Criminology* 95, no. 4 (Summer 2005): 1363–1410.

70. CBS/AP, "Military to Review Sodomy Ban," CBSNEWS, March 3, 2010, http://www.cbsnews.com/stories/2010/03/03/politics/main6263819.shtml.

71. *Lawrence v. Texas,* 539 U.S. 558 (2003).

72. National Institute of Military Justice and the Military Justice Committee, Criminal Justice Section of the American Bar Association, *Report on the Commission of Military Justice,* October 2009, 15, http://www.wcl.american.edu/nimj/documents/CoxCommissionFinalReport.pdf.

73. William H. McMichael, "Report: Outdated Sodomy Law Should Be Repealed," *Army Times* 70, no. 18 (November 16, 2009): 12.

74. Vicki Abt, James F. Smith, and Eugene Martin Christiansen, *The Business of Risk: Commercial Gambling in Mainstream America* (Lawrence: University Press of Kansas, 1985).

75. Nancy M. Petry, *Pathological Gambling: Etiology, Comorbidity, and Treatment* (Washington, DC: American Psychological Association, 2005), 4.

76. Robert Goodman, *The Luck Business* (New York: The Free Press, 1995), 32–33.

77. Davidson, *Selling Sin,* 77–83.

78. Edward A. Morse and Ernest P. Goss, *Governing Fortune: Casino Gambling in America* (Ann Arbor: University of Michigan Press, 2007), 3.

79. *Irwin v. Williar,* 110 U.S. 499 510 (1885).

80. Morse and Goss, *Governing Fortune,* 6.

81. Associated Press/MSNBC, "Is Hawaii Gambling with Paradise?" February 18, 2010, http://www.msnbc.msn.com/id/35463885.

82. Ibid., para.10.

83. Charles T. Clotfelter and Phillip J. Cook, *Selling Hope: State Lotteries in America* (Cambridge, MA: Harvard University Press, 1989).

84. Mark Griffiths and Richard T. A. Wood, "Youth and Technology: The Case of Gambling, Video-Game Playing, and the Internet," in *Gambling Problems in Youth: Theoretical and Applied Perspectives,* ed. Jeffrey L. Derevensky and Rina Gupta (New York: Kluwer Academic/Plenum Publishers, 2004), 101–20.

## Chapter 13

1. Strobe Talbott and Nayan Chanda, *The Age of Terror: America and the World After September 11* (New York: Basic Books, 2001).

2. John Mueller, *Overblown: How Politicians and the Terrorism Industry Inflate National Security Threats and Why We Believe Them* (New York: Free Press, 2006).

3. Alan M. Dershowitz, *Why Terrorism Works: Understanding*

the Threat, Responding to the Challenge (New Haven, CT: Yale University Press, 2002).

4. Juliette N. Kayyem and Arnold M. Howitt, *Beyond the Beltway: Focusing on Hometown Security* (Boston: John F. Kennedy School of Government, Harvard University, 2002), http://belfercenter .ksg.harvard.edu/files/beyond_ the_beltway.pdf.

5. James Risen and David Johnston, "FBI Report Found Agency Not Ready to Counter Terror," *New York Times,* June 1, 2002, late edition, A1.

6. CIA, "CIA & the War on Terrorism," November 16, 2007, https:// www.cia.gov/news-information/ cia-the-war-on-terrorism/ terrorism-faqs.html.

7. Larry Diamond, "What Went Wrong in Iraq," *Foreign Affairs* 83 (2004): 34–56.

8. Cindy C. Combs, *Terrorism in the Twenty-First Century,* 4th ed. (Upper Saddle River, NJ: Prentice Hall, 2006), 11.

9. Edgar O'Ballance, *The Language of Violence: The Blood Politics of Terrorism* (San Rafael, CA: Presidio Press, 1979).

10. Mark Juergensmeyer, *Terror in the Mind of Gods: The Global Rise of Religious Violence* (Berkeley: University of California Press, 2000).

11. Morris Dees, *Gathering Storm: America's Militia Threat* (New York: Harper Perennial, 1996).

12. Rick Hampson, "25 Years Later, Bombing in Beirut Still Resonates," *USA Today,* October 18, 2008, http://www.usatoday.com/ news/military/2008-10-15-beirut-barracks_n.htm#.

13. James Harding, "US Pays $4.5m for Embassy Bombing," *Financial Times* (London), July 31, 1999, Europe section, 3.

14. Mark S. Hamm, *Terrorism as Crime: From Oklahoma City to Al-Qaeda and Beyond* (New York: New York University Press, 2007).

15. Michael Burleigh, *Blood and Rage: A Cultural History of Terrorism* (United Kingdom: Harper-Collins, 2008).

16. John Ferling, *Almost a Miracle: The American Victory in the War of Independence* (New York: Oxford University Press, 2007).

17. David C. Rapoport, "The Fourth Wave: September 11 in the History of Terrorism," *Current History* (December 2001): 419–24.

18. Cited in Richard B. Jensen, "The United States, International Policing and the War Against Anarchist Terrorism," *Journal of Terrorism and Political Violence* 13, no. 1 (Spring 2001): 19.

19. Australian Broadcasting Corporation, RadioEye, "A Short History of the Car Bomb," http:// www.abc.net.au/rn/radioeye/ stories/2008/2141652.htm.

20. David C. Rapoport, "The Fourth Wave."

21. Robert B. Asprey, *War in the Shadows: The Guerrilla in History* (Garden City, NY: Doubleday, 1995).

22. Fawaz A. Gerges, *The Far Enemy: Why Jihad Went Global* (New York: Cambridge University Press, 2005).

23. Kenneth S. Stern, *A Force upon the Plain: The American Militia Movement and the Politics of Hate* (New York: Simon & Schuster, 1996).

24. Ty West, "History Prof Says Terrorism Has American Roots Going Back to the Civil War," February 7, 2003, TuscaloosaNews.com, http:// www.datelinealabama.com/ article/2003/02/07/3709_ news_art.php3.

25. Adam L. Silverman, "Zealous Before the Lord: The Construction of Christian Identity Theology," in *Terrorism: Research, Readings, and Realities,* ed. Lynne L. Snowden and Bradley L. Whitsel (Upper Saddle River, NJ: Prentice Hall, 2005), 293–302.

26. Ibid., 297.

27. Paul Leavitt, "No Charges in Mountain Assault," *USA Today,* December 9, 1994, 3A; Gary Fields and Kevin Johnson, "FBI Sharpshooter Charged in Ruby Ridge," *USA Today,* August 22, 1997, 1A; Associated Press, "F.B.I. Agent Cleared in Idaho Siege Shooting," *New York Times,* May 15, 1998, late edition, 14A.

28. George Lardner, Jr., and Pierre Thomas, "U.S. to Pay Family in FBI Idaho Raid," *Washington Post,* August 16, 1995, final edition, A1.

29. Catherine Wessinger, *How the Millennium Comes Violently: From Jonestown to Heaven's Gate* (New York: Seven Bridge Press, 2000).

30. CNN, "Rudolph Reveals Motives," April 19, 2005, http://www.cnn .com/2005/LAW/04/13/eric .rudolph/index.html.

31. Jack Warner, "Rudolph Indicted in Four Bombings," *The Atlanta Journal and Constitution,* November, 16, 2000, 3A.

32. Chester L. Quarles, "Rural Radical Religion: Christian Identity and Covenant Community Militias," in *Terrorism: Research, Readings, and Realities,* 353–65.

33. Ibid., 356.

34. Howard L. Bushart, John R. Craig, and Myra Barnes, *Soldiers of God; White Supremacists and Their Holy War for America* (New York: Kensington Books, 1998).

35. CNN, "Nichols Gets Life for Oklahoma Bombing," June 4, 1998, http://www.cnn.com/ US/9806/04/nichols.update .pm/index.html; Lois Romano, "Nichols Is Spared Death Penalty

*Public Policy* 5, no. 1 (February 1, 2006): 61–91.

61. Ralph Kirkland Gable and Robert S. Gable, "Electronic Monitoring: Positive Intervention Strategies," *Federal Probation* 69, no. 1 (January/December 2005), http://www.uscourts.gov/FederalCourts/ProbationPretrial Services/FederalProbation Journal/FederalProbation Journal.aspx?doc=/uscourts/FederalCourts/PPS/Fedprob/2005-06/index.html. (The authors changed their names from Schwitzgebel.)

62. Todd Lewan, "Microchips in Humans: High-Tech Helpers or Big Brother Surveillance?" MSNBC/AP, July 23, 2007, http://www.msnbc.msn.com/id/19904543/.

63. Marc L. Songini, "Minnesota Turns to RFID to Monitor Inmates," *Computerworld,* June 18, 2007, http://www.computerworld.com/action/article.do?command=viewArticle Basic&articleId=9024960&intsrc=news_ts_head.

64. Keith Bradsher, "China Enacting High-Tech Plan to Track People," *New York Times,* August 12, 2007, late edition, A1.

65. *Popular Mechanics,* "Paris Hilton's Ankle Bracelet," June 27, 2007, http://www.popularmechanics.com/blogs/technology_news/4217756.html.

66. DNA.gov, "About Forensic DNA," http://www.dna.gov/basics/.

67. Federal Bureau of Investigation, "Federal Bureau of Investigation Privacy Impact Assessment: National DNA Index System (DNS)," February 24, 2004, http://foia.fbi.gov/ndispia.htm.

68. The No Suspect Casework DNA Backlog Reduction Program, "Glossary of Terms and Acronyms," http://www.usdoj.gov/oig/reports/OJP/a0502/app2.htm.

69. Federal Bureau of Investigation, "CODIS-NDIS Statistics," http://www.fbi.gov/hq/lab/codis/clickmap.htm.

70. Federal Bureau of Investigation, "CODIS brochure," http://www.fbi.gov/hq/lab/html/codisbrochure_text.htm.

71. Ian Drury, "40,000 Child Innocents on the DNA Log for Life: 'Proof' the Database Is Being Built Up by Stealth," *Daily Mail,* August 16, 2008.

72. Jason Felch and Maura Dolan, "DNA: Genes as Evidence," *Los Angeles Times,* July 20, 2008, A1.

73. Christopher A. Miles and Jeffrey P. Cohn, "Tracking Prisoners in Jail with Biometrics: An Experiment in a Navy Brig," *NIJ Journal* 253, January 2006, http://www.ojp.usdoj.gov/nij/journals/253/tracking.html.

74. Anil K. Jain and Sharath Pankanti, "Beyond Fingerprinting," *Scientific American* 299, no. 3 (September 2008): 78–81.

75. Federal Bureau of Investigation, "FBI Announces Contract Award for Next Generation Identification System," http://www.fbi.gov/pressrel/pressrel08/ngicontract021208.htm.

76. Sun Sun Lim, Hichang Cho, and Milagros Rivera Sanchez, "Online Privacy, Government Surveillance and National ID Cards," *Communications of the ACM* 52, no. 12 (December 2009): 116–20.

77. Roger Clarke, "Information Technology and Dataveillance," *Communications of the ACM* 31, no. 5 (May 1988): 498–512.

78. Lim, Cho, and Sanchez, "Online Privacy, Government Surveillance and National ID Cards," 116–20.

79. Declan McCullagh, "ACLU: FBI Used 'Dragnet'-Style Warrantless Cell Tracking," CNET News, June 22, 2010, http://news.cnet.com/8301-31921_3-20008444-281.html.

80. United States Court District of Connecticut, *United States of America v. Luis Soto,* Memorandum of *Amici Curiae* in Support of Motion to Suppress, June 18, 2010, http://www.aclu.org/files/assets/2010-6-18-USvSoto-AmiciBrief.pdf.

81. Charlie Savage and James Risen, "Federal Judge Finds N.S.A. Wiretaps Were Illegal," *New York Times,* March 31, 2010, http://www.nytimes.com/2010/04/01/us/01nsa.html.

## Chapter 1

p. 4 Edwin H. Sutherland, *Principles of Criminology* (Philadelphia: Lippincott, 1939), 2.

## Chapter 2

p. 22 Source: Federal Bureau of Investigation, Uniform Crime Reports, *Crime in the United States*, 2005–2008, http://www.fbi.gov/ucr/ucr.htm. p. 23 Source: Federal Bureau of Investigation, Uniform Crime Reports, *Crime in the United States*, 2008, http://www.fbi.gov/ucr/cius2008/index.html. p. 24 Source: Federal Bureau of Investigation, Uniform Crime Reports, *Crime in the United States*, 2008, Table 6, www.fbi.gov/ucr/cius2008/data/table_06.html. p. 27 Source: Federal Bureau of Investigation, National Incident-based Reporting System, http://www.fbi.gov/ucr/faqs.htm.

## Chapter 3

p. 44 Source: Michael R. Rand, *Criminal Victimization,* 2008 (Washington, DC: U.S. Department of Justice Office of Justice Programs Bureau of Justice Statistics, 2008), 4. Online at http://bjs.ojp.usdoj.gov/content/pub/pdf/cv08.pdf. p. 46 Source: National Counterterrorism Center, *2008 Report on Terrorism,* April 30, 2009, http://wits-classic.nctc.gov/Reports.do?f=crt2008nctcannexfinal.pdf. p. 51 Fig. 3.3 Source: Federal Bureau of Investigation, *Crime in the United States, 2008,* Expanded Homicide Data Table 12, http://www.fbi.gov/ucr/cius2008/offenses/expanded_information/data/shrtable_12.html. p. 51 Fig. 3.4 Source: Federal Bureau of Investigation, *Crime in the United States, 2008,* Murder Race and Sex of Victim by Race and Sex of Offender, 2008, Expanded Homicide Data Table 6, http://www.fbi.gov/ucr/cius2008/offenses/expanded_information/data/shrtable_06.html. p. 52 Source: Federal Bureau of Investigation, *Crime in the United States, 2007,* Expanded Homicide Data Table 9, http://www.fbi.gov/ucr/cius2007/offenses/expanded_information/data/shrtable_09.html. p. 54 Fig. 3.6 Source: U.S. Department of Justice Office of Justice Programs Bureau of Justice Statistics Bureau of Justice Statistics, *Criminal Victimization in the United States, 2007 Statistical Tables,* February 2010, Table 38: Percent distribution of single-offender victimization, by type of crime and perceived gender of offender; Table 2: Number of victimizations and victimization rates for persons age 12 and over, by type of crime and gender of victims. Online at http://bjs.ojp.usdoj.gov/index.cfm?ty=pbdetail&iid=2173. p. 54 Fig. 3.7 Source: Howard N. Snyder, *Sexual Assault of Young Children as Reported to Law Enforcement: Victim, Incident, and Offender Characteristics* (Washington, DC: Bureau of Justice Statistics, 2000), 2. Online at http://bjs.ojp.usdoj.gov/index.cfm?ty=pbdetail&iid=1147.

## Chapter 4

p. 71 Stein, Dan J., "The Neurobiology of Evil: Psychiatric Perspectives on Perpetrators," *Ethnicity & Health* 5, no. 3/4 (August 2000): 303–315. p. 73 The Declaration of Independence. p. 75 Bentham, Jeremy, *An Introduction to the Principles of Morals and Legislation* (London: The Athlone Press, 1970). p. 89 Bentham, Jeremy, *An Introduction to the Principles of Morals and Legislation* (London: The Athlone Press, 1970).

## Chapter 5

p. 112 Hare, Robert D. "Hare's Psychopathy Checklist-Revised" © 2003 Robert D. Hare. Reprinted with permission of Multi-Health Systems, Inc.

## Chapter 6

p. 128 Source: Merton, Robert K. "Social Structure and Anomie," *American Sociological Review* 3 1938:672-682.

## Chapter 7

p. 142 Source: Federal Bureau of Investigation, Uniform Crime Reports, *Crime in the United States, 2008,* Table 38, http://www.fbi.gov/ucr/cius2008/data/table_38.html.

## Chapter 8

p. 175 Fig. 8.3A Source: Federal Bureau of Investigation, *Uniform Crime Reports: Crime in the United States, 2008,* Ten-Year Arrest Trends by Sex, 1999–2008, http://www.fbi.gov/ucr/cius2008/data/table_33.html. p. 175 Fig 8.3B Source: Michael R. Rand, *Criminal Victimization, 2008* (Washington, DC: Bureau of Justice Statistics, 2009), 4. Online at http://bjs.ojp.usdoj.gov/content/pub/pdf/cv08.pdf.

## Chapter 9

p. 190 Source: Federal Bureau of Investigation, *Uniform Crime Reports: Crime in the United States,* 2008, http://www.fbi.gov/ucr/cius2008/offenses/property_crime/index.html Accessed May 31, 2010. p. 191 Source: Federal Bureau of Investigation, *Uniform Crime Reports: Crime in the United States,* 2008, Burglary, http://www.fbi.gov/ucr/cius2008/offenses/property_crime/burglary.html Accessed May 31, 2010. p. 203 Source: Federal Bureau of Investigation, *Uniform Crime Reports: Crime in the United States,* Table 4: Crime in the United States by Region, Geographic Division, and State, 2007–2008, http://www.fbi.gov/ucr/cius2008/data/table_04.html Accessed May 31, 2010.

## Chapter 10

p. 214 Source: Jennifer C. Karberg and Doris J. James, *Substance Dependence, Abuse, and Treatment of Jail Inmates, 2002* (Washington, DC: U.S. Department of Justice Bureau of Justice Statistics, 2005), 1. Online at bjs.ojp.usdoj.gov/content/pub/pdf/sdatji02.pdf Accessed June 6, 2010. p. 218 Fig. 10.3 Source: Federal Bureau of Investigation, *Uniform Crime Reports: Crime in the United States, 2008,* http://www.fbi.gov/ucr/cius2008/offenses/violent_crime/index.html Accessed June 6, 2010. p. 218 Fig 10.4 Source: Federal Bureau of Investigation, *Crime in the United States, 2008,* http://www.fbi.gov/ucr/cius2008/offenses/standard_links/regional_estimates.html. p. 219 Source: "Murder." Title 18 US Code, Sec. 1111. 29 ed., 310. p. 220 Source: Federal Bureau of Investigation, *Uniform Crime Reports*: *Crime in the United States, 2008,* Expanded Homicide Data Table 3: Murder Offenders by Age, Sex, and Race, 2008, http://www.fbi.gov/ucr/cius2008/offenses/expanded_information/data/shrtable_03.html Accessed June 6, 2010. p. 230 Source: U.S. Department of Justice, Federal Bureau of Investigation, *Uniform Crime Reports: Crime in the United States, 2008,* http:/www.fbi.gov/ucr/cius2008/data/table_07.html.

## Chapter 12

p. 270 Source: National Criminal Justice Reference Service, http://www.ncjrs.gov/spotlight/club_drugs/legislation.html. Accessed June 10, 2010. US Drug Enforcement Administration, http://www.dea.gov/pubs/scheduling.html. Accessed June 10, 2010. p. 271 Source: Substance Abuse and Mental Health Services Administration, *Results from the 2008 National Survey on Drug Use and Health: National Findings* (Rockville, MD: Office of Applied Studies, 2009), 16. Online at http://oas.samhsa.gov/nsduh/2k8nsduh/2k8Results.pdf Accessed June 10, 2010. p. 272 Source: Substance Abuse and Mental Health Services Administration, *Results from the 2008 National Survey on Drug Use and Health: National Finding,* Figure 5.3 (Rockville, MD: Office of Applied Studies, 2009), 54. Online at http://oas.samhsa.gov/nsduh/2k8nsduh/2k8Results.pdf Accessed June 10, 2010.

## Chapter 13

p. 299 Source: National Counterterrorism Center, 2008 Report on Terrorism, April 2009, p. 10, http://wits-classic.nctc.gov/ReportPDF.do?f=crt2008nctcannexfinal.pdf Accessed June 18, 2010. p. 309 Source: Department of Homeland Security, http://www.dhs.gov/xabout/structure/editorial_0644.shtm Accessed June 19, 2010. p. 310 Source: Federal Bureau of Investigation, N-Dex, http://www.fbi.gov/hq/cjisd/ndex/ndex_concept.htm Accessed June 18, 2010. p. 312 Source: National Counterterrorism Center, http://www.nctc.gov/docs/2006_calendarbomb_stand_chart.pdf Accessed June 19, 2010.

## Chapter 14

p. 320 Source: U.S. Department of Justice Office of Justice Programs, *Electronic Crime Scene Investigation: A Guide for First Responders,* 2nd ed. (Washington DC: Government Printing Office, 2008), 29. Online at http://www.ncjrs.gov/pdffiles1/nij/219941.pdf Accessed June 22, 2010. p. 332 Source: Internet Crime Complaint Center, http://www.ic3gov/media/IC3-Poster.pdf Accessed June 22, 2010. p. 333 Source: Federal Trade Commission, *Consumer Sentinel Network Databook* (Federal Trade Commission: Washington, DC, 2010), 12. Online at http://www.ftc.gov/sentinel/reports/sentinel-annual-reports/sentinetl-cy2009.pdf Accessed June 22, 2010.

# Photo Credits

# CHAPTER 6: SOCIOLOGICAL THEORIES OF CRIME AND DELINQUENCY

| THEORY | MAJOR THEORISTS | WHAT THE THEORY EXPLAINS | POLICY IMPLICATIONS | INFLUENTIAL ACTORS |
|---|---|---|---|---|
| **SOCIAL DISORGANIZATION THEORY** | Robert J. Sampson, William Julius Wilson | | Urban renewal, neighborhood programs, planned communities, law-enforcement programs. | legislators, activists, neighborhood organizers, social workers, developers |
| **Concentric zones** | Ernest Burgess, Clifford R. Shaw, Henry D. McKay | Geographical areas radiate from an expanding urban center; each area has specific social attitudes. | | |
| **Collective efficacy** | Robert Sampson, Stephen Raudenbush, Felton Earls | Measures the amount of informal social control and social cohesion in a community. | | |
| **LEARNING THEORIES** | | Focus on where and how offenders and delinquents find the tools, techniques, and expertise to break the law. | Parents and other authority figures should monitor children's friends and ensure they are enrolled in programs that provide pro-social activities and messages. | parents, teachers, coaches, clergy, law enforcement, social workers |
| **Differential association** | Edwin Sutherland | Crime is learned through interactions with antisocial peers. | | |
| **Techniques of neutralization** | Gresham Sykes, David Matza | Delinquents generally believe in the law and break it only after they can rationalize their actions as necessary or unavoidable. | | |
| **Focal concerns of the lower class** | Walter B. Miller | The lower socioeconomic class has focal concerns that encourages youths to break the law. | Parents and other authority figures should monitor children's friends and ensure they are enrolled in programs that provide pro-social activities and messages. | parents, teachers, coaches, clergy, law enforcement, social workers |
| **Subculture of violence** | Marvin Wolfgang, Franco Ferracuti | Describes how cultures apart from the main culture hold violence as part of their values, lifestyle, and socialization. | | |
| **Code of the street** | Elijah Anderson | Requires people to quickly resort to violence when they feel they are not getting proper respect. | | |

| THEORY | MAJOR THEORISTS | WHAT THE THEORY EXPLAINS | POLICY IMPLICATIONS | INFLUENTIAL ACTORS |
|---|---|---|---|---|
| **STRAIN THEORY** | Robert Merton, Robert Agnew | Blocked opportunities cause strain within individuals which propels them toward unlawful behavior. | Increasing opportunities so strain does not build up to the point that individuals select crime as a way to release it; increasing quality of housing, jobs, relationships. | job coaches, employers, employment counselors, developers, clergy |
| Anomie | Émile Durkheim, Albert Cohen | Erosion of standards resulting from a lack of social control and values that leads to social instability. | | |
| Deviant subcultures | Richard Cloward, Lloyd Ohlin | Deviant subcultures allow youths to adapt to the lack of legitimate opportunities to develop illegitimate ways of responding to the strain of impoverished and disorganized urban life. | | |
| Institutional anomie | Richard Rosenfeld, Steven Messner | Institutional anomie occurs when commitment to social institutions such as family, religion, and education becomes subservient to achieving the goal of wealth. | | |
| **CONTROL THEORIES** | | Looks at why people do not break the law rather than why they do. | Develop more programs and support services so they do not resort to crime to fulfill their needs. | parents, teachers, counselors, recreational directors, clergy |
| **CONTAINMENT THEORY** | Walter Reckless | Internal factors "push" people into crime and external factors "pull" them. | | |
| **SOCIAL BOND THEORY** | Travis Hirschi | Asks what factors keep juveniles law-abiding. | | |
| **POWER-CONTROL THEORY** | John Hagan | Seeks to explain why males commit more offenses and delinquency than females; focus on familial patriarchy. | | |

# CHAPTER 7: LIFE-COURSE AND INTEGRATED THEORIES

| THEORY | MAJOR THEORISTS | WHAT THE THEORY EXPLAINS | POLICY IMPLICATIONS | INFLUENTIAL ACTORS |
|---|---|---|---|---|
| **LIFE-COURSE THEORIES** | | Focuses on the development of antisocial behavior, age-related risk factors, and the effect of life events on development. | Early intervention to prevent chronic delinquency; rehabilitation programs, employment, higher education | coaches, teachers, spouses, military, employers, |
| **Developmental perspective on antisocial behavior** | G. R. Patterson, Barbara D. DeBaryshe, Elizabeth Ramsey | Antisocial behavior begins early in life and often continues through adolescence and adulthood. | | |
| **Pathways to crime** | Terrie Moffitt | Adolescent-limited offenders break the law during youth; life-course-persistent offenders continue into adulthood. | | |
| **Persistent offending and desistance from crime** | John Laub, Robert Sampson | Individuals advance into conventional behavior via turning points and personal agency. | | |
| **INTEGRATED THEORIES** | | Combines theories to explain antisocial behavior. | Crime is explained in a more comprehensive manner, so policy implications are numerous. | Integrated theories use some or all of the actors already mentioned. |
| **Integrated theoretical perspective on delinquent behavior** | Delbert Elliott, Susan Ageton, Rachel Canter | Strong social bonds produce conventional behavior; weak social bonds produce antisocial behavior. | | |
| **Interactional theory of delinquency** | Terence Thornberry | Combines social learning, social bonds, and life-course theories; parent-youth bonds are important. | | |
| **Control balance theory** | Charles Tittle | Individuals control their lives and society controls individuals; imbalance produces antisocial behavior. | | |
| **Social support theory** | Francis Cullen | Social society affects individuals and institutions and the likelihood of crime. | | |
| **General theory of crime and delinquency** | Robert Agnew | The major causes of crime lie within five life domains. | | |
| **Integrated cognitive antisocial potential theory** | David Farrington | Factors combine to increase the likelihood of short-term and long-term antisocial behavior. | | |